COMPUTER LITERACY
BASICS

A Comprehensive Guide to IC^3

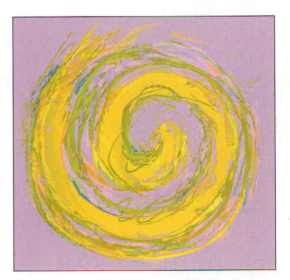

CEP Inc.
Ann Ambrose
Marly Bergerud
Dr. Donald Busche
Connie Morrison
Dolores Wells-Pusins

THOMSON

COURSE TECHNOLOGY ™

Australia • Canada • Mexico • Singapore • Spain • United Kingdom • United States

THOMSON
™
COURSE TECHNOLOGY

Computer Literacy BASICS: A Comprehensive Guide to IC³

By CEP Inc., Ann Ambrose, Marly Bergerud, Dr. Donald Busche, Connie Morrison, and Dolores Wells-Pusins

Vice President, School Publishing and Marketing
Cheryl Costantini

Managing Editor
Alexandra Arnold

Product Manager
David Rivera

Editorial Assistant
Justine Brennan

Director of Production
Patty Stephan

Senior Manufacturing Coordinator
Trevor Kallop

Production Management
Custom Editorial Productions Inc.

Senior Marketing Manager
Kim Ryttel

School Market Specialist
Meagan Putney

Development
Custom Editorial Productions Inc.

Compositor
GEX Publishing Services

Get Back to the Basics...
With these *exciting new products*

Our exciting new Computer Literacy BASICS text is part of a series of concepts and application suite books that provide everything needed to learn computing.

NEW! Computer Literacy BASICS: A Comprehensive Guide to IC[3] by CEP Inc., Ambrose, Bergerud, Busche, Morrison & Wells-Pusins
75+ hours of instruction

0-619-24382-1	Textbook, hardcover
0-619-24383-X	Textbook, softcover
0-619-24384-8	Instructor Resources
0-619-24391-0	Review Pack (Data CD)

Computer Projects BASICS by Korb
35+ hours of instruction for additional projects on all software applications

0-619-05987-7	Textbook, softcover, spiral-bound
0-619-05988-5	Instructor Resource Kit

Internet BASICS by Barksdale, Rutter, & Teeter
35+ hours of instruction for beginning through intermediate features

0-619-05905-2	Textbook, softcover, spiral-bound
0-619-05906-0	Instructor Resource Kit

Web Design BASICS by Stubbs & Barksdale
35+ hours of instruction for beginning through intermediate features

0-619-05964-8	Textbook, softcover, spiral-bound
0-619-05966-4	Instructor Resource Kit
0-619-05977-X	Review Pack (Data CD)

Microsoft Office 2003 BASICS by Pasewark and Pasewark
35+ hours of instruction for beginning through intermediate features

0-619-18335-7	Textbook, hardcover, spiral-bound
0-619-18337-3	Instructor Resources
0-619-18336-5	Activities Workbook
0-619-18338-1	Review Pack (Data CD)

Join Us On the Internet **http://www.course.com**

How to Use This Book

What makes a good computer instructional text? Sound pedagogy and the most current, complete materials. Not only will you find an inviting layout, but also many features to enhance learning.

Objectives— Objectives are listed at the beginning of each lesson, along with a suggested time for completion of the lesson. This allows you to look ahead to what you will be learning and to pace your work.

Step-by-Step Exercises—Preceded by a short topic discussion, these exercises are the "hands-on practice" part of the lesson. Simply follow the steps, either using a data file or creating a file from scratch. Each lesson is a series of these Step-by-Step exercises.

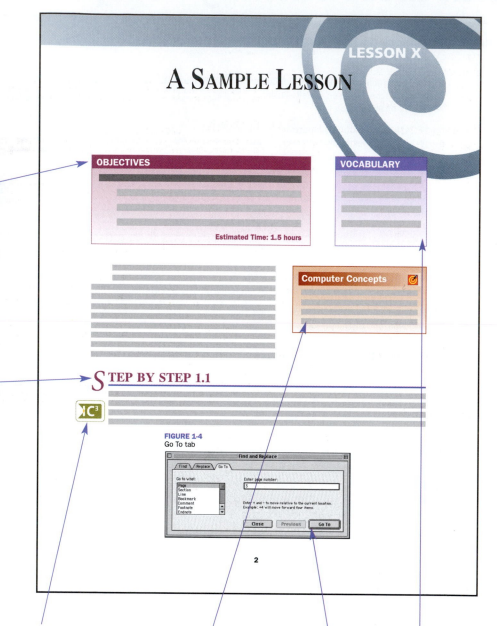

IC³—Internet and Computing Core Certification program skills satisfied by the text or Step-by-Step instruction.

Marginal Boxes— These boxes provide additional information, such as *Computer Concepts*, *Notes*, *Technology Timeline*, *Working in a Connected World*, and *Ethics in Technology*.

Vocabulary—Terms identified in boldface throughout the lesson and summarized at the end.

Enhanced Screen Shots—Screen shots now come to life on each page with color and depth.

How to Use This Book

Summary—At the end of each lesson, you will find a summary to prepare you to complete the end-of-lesson activities.

Vocabulary/Review Questions—Review material at the end of each lesson and each module enables you to prepare for assessment of the content presented.

Lesson Projects—End-of-lesson hands-on application of what has been learned in the lesson allows you to actually apply the techniques covered.

Critical Thinking Activities—Each lesson gives you an opportunity to apply creative analysis and use various resources to solve problems.

End-of-Module Projects—End-of-module hands-on application of concepts learned in the module provides opportunity for a comprehensive review.

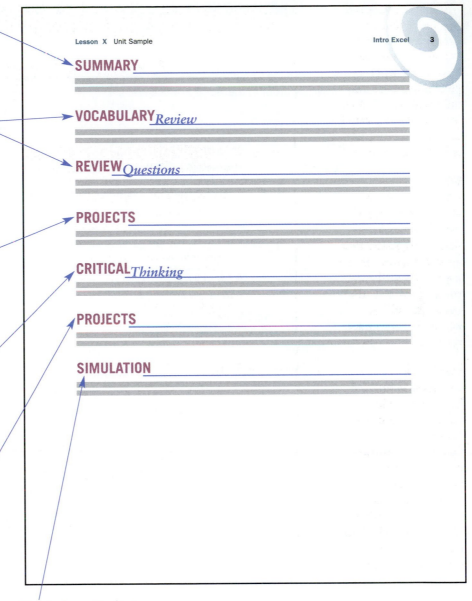

Lesson X   Unit Sample   Intro Excel   **3**

SUMMARY

VOCABULARY *Review*

REVIEW *Questions*

PROJECTS

CRITICAL *Thinking*

PROJECTS

SIMULATION

Simulation—Realistic simulation jobs are provided at the end of each module, reinforcing the material covered in the module.

IC³ INTERNET AND COMPUTING CORE CERTIFICATION

SETTING THE STANDARD

IC³ ... WHAT IS IT?

IC³, or the Internet and Computing Core Certification program, is a global training and certification program providing proof to the world that you are:

- Equipped with the needed computer skills to excel in a digital world.

- Capable of using a broad range of computer technology - from basic hardware and software, to operating systems, applications and the Internet.

- Ready for what the work employers, colleges and universities want to throw your way.

- Positioned to advance your career through additional computer certifications such as CompTIA's A+, and other desktop application exams.

IC³ ... WHY DO YOU NEED IT?

Employers, Colleges and Universities now understand that exposure to computers does not equal understanding computers. So now, more than ever, basic computer and Internet skills are being considered prerequisites for employment and higher education.

THIS IS WHERE IC³ HELPS!

IC³ provides specific guidelines for the knowledge and skills required to be a functional user of computer hardware, software, networks, and the Internet. It does this through three exams:

- **Computing Fundamentals**
- **Key Applications**
- **Living Online**

By passing the three IC³ exams, you have initiated yourself into today's digital world. You have also given yourself a globally accepted and validated credential that provides the proof employers or higher education institutions need.

Earn your IC³ certification today - visit www.certiport.com/ic3 to learn how.

CERTIPORT™
Lifetime advancement through certification.

INTERNET AND
COMPUTING CORE
CERTIFICATION

CERTIFICATION ROADMAP

Whether you are seeking further education, entering the job market, or advancing your skills through higher ICT certification, IC³ gives you the foundation you need to succeed.

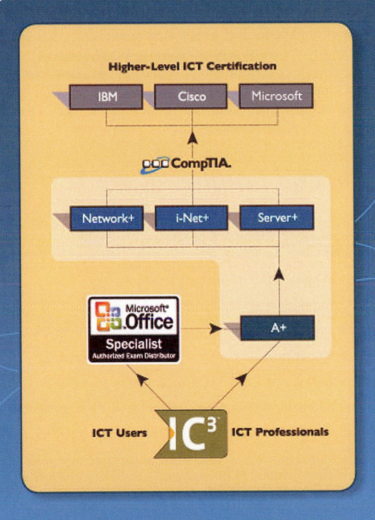

www.certiport.com/ic3

PREFACE

Computer Literacy BASICS: A Comprehensive Guide to IC³ provides complete coverage of topics for the new 2005 Internet and Computing Core Certification (IC³) and is approved by Certiport Inc. IC³ standards and skills are listed and explained in an appendix and on the pages where they are discussed. All objectives from the three modules are presented to provide preparation for the 2005 IC³ exams.

The *Computing Fundamentals* module provides information on computing basics, including computer hardware and components, applications and operating system software, and social issues related to computing and technology.

The *Key Applications* module focuses on software applications that learners use on a regular basis. Instruction is provided on word-processing, spreadsheet, database, and presentations.

The *Living Online* module covers the concepts of computer networking, with comprehensive coverage of the Internet and the various services and resources it offers.

An appendix at the end of the text lists each module's skills and objectives and gives a brief explanation.

Organization and Features of the Text

The text is divided into three modules that correlate to the three IC³ exams. Lessons within each module introduce concepts in a logical progression to build on previously learned concepts and features within the module. Each lesson includes the following features:

- Lesson objectives that specify goals for the learner.

- Estimated time for completion of the lesson.

- Vocabulary list that summarizes the new terms introduced in the lesson.

- Step-by-step exercises that provide guidance for using the features.

- Screen illustrations that provide visual reinforcement of features and concepts.

- Sidebars with notes and computer concepts related to the lesson topics.

- Special features that provide information about careers, computer ethics, and historical concepts.

The end-of-lesson features focus on review and reinforcement of the skills and concepts presented in the lesson. They provide a comprehensive review of the lesson and offer a variety of ways to apply the newly learned skills. The end-of-lesson features include the following:

- Lesson summary.

- A vocabulary review listing the new terms presented in the lesson.

- Review questions to assess the comprehension of material.

- Lesson projects for applying the concepts and features learned.

- Teamwork projects that suggest activities in which learners can work together.

- Critical thinking activities that require learners to analyze and process information or to do research.

  Each module is summarized in a module review designed to assess comprehension. Each module review includes the following:

- Review questions covering material from all lessons in the unit.

- Projects that provide integration of the skills and functions presented within the module.

- Workplace simulations that propose real-world tasks.

Instructor Resource Kit and Review Pack CD-ROMs

All data files necessary for the Step-by-Step exercises, end-of-lesson projects, and end-of-module projects and simulations are located on the *Review Pack* CD-ROM.

The *Instructor Resources* CD-ROM contains a wealth of instructional material you can use to prepare for teaching this course. The CD-ROM stores the following information:

- IC^3 correlation grid that lists and explains IC^3 skills and topics and references where those skills are discussed within the textbook.

- ExamView® tests for each lesson. ExamView is a powerful testing software package that allows instructors to create and administer printed, computer (LAN-based), and Internet exams. ExamView includes hundreds of questions that correspond to the topics covered in this text, enabling learners to generate detailed study guides that include page references for further review. The computer-based and Internet testing components allow learners to take exams at their computers. Instructors can save time since ExamView grades each test automatically.

- Electronic *Instructor Manual* that includes lecture notes for each lesson.

- Answer keys that contain answers to the lesson and module review questions, and suggested/sample solutions for some end-of-lesson activities and projects.

- Copies of the figures that appear in the learner text, which can be used to prepare transparencies.

- Suggested schedules for teaching the lessons in this course.

- Additional instructional information about individual learning strategies, portfolios, and career planning, and a sample Internet contract.

- PowerPoint presentations that illustrate objectives for each lesson in the text.

START-UP CHECKLIST

HARDWARE

- ✓ IBM or IBM-compatible PC
- ✓ 233-MHz or higher Pentium-compatible process (a 600-MHz or faster is preferred)
- ✓ 128 MB of RAM (256 MB of RAM is preferred)
- ✓ One hard disk (2 GB) with at least 650 MB of free hard disk space
- ✓ CD-ROM drive
- ✓ SVGA-capable video adapter and monitor (SVGA resolution of a minimum of 800 × 600 pixels with 256 or more colors)
- ✓ Enhanced keyboard
- ✓ Mouse or pen pointer
- ✓ 14,000 or higher baud modem (56,000 is preferred)
- ✓ Printer

SOFTWARE

- ✓ Windows 2000 with SP3 or later or Windows XP or later operating system
- ✓ Microsoft Office recommended (Microsoft Office XP for *Key Applications* module)
- ✓ Web browser

TABLE OF CONTENTS

MODULE 1 COMPUTING FUNDAMENTALS

MODULE 2 KEY APPLICATIONS

MODULE 3 LIVING ONLINE

Photo Credits

Computing Fundamentals

Lesson 1

Figure 1-3   Courtesy of International Business Machines Corporation. Unauthorized use not permitted.

Figure 1-4   ©PhotoDisc

Figure 1-5   Courtesy of Cray Research, a Silicon Graphics Company

Lesson 2

Figure 2-3   ©PhotoDisc
Figure 2-4   ©PhotoDisc
Figure 2-9   Courtesy of Tejima Lab
Figure 2-10   ©PhotoDisc
Figure 2-12   ©PhotoDisc
Figure 2-13   ©PhotoDisc
Figure 2-15   Courtesy of Xerox
Figure 2-18   Courtesy of Iomega

Lesson 6

Figure 6-1   ©PhotoDisc

Living Online

Lesson 23

Figure 23-4   ©PhotoDisc

Lesson 28

Figure 28-2   ©PhotoDisc

Lesson 29

Figure 29-3   Courtesy of IriScan. IriScan's iris recognition technology identifies people by the patterns in the iris of the eye.

COMPUTING FUNDAMENTALS

Module

Estimated Time for Module: 14 hours

COMPUTING FUNDAMENTALS

Computer Concepts

Lesson 1
Introducing Computers

1-1.1.1	1-1.1.8	1-1.1.11
1-1.1.2	1-1.1.9	1-1.2.2
1-1.1.3	1-1.1.10	1-2.1.1

Lesson 2
Computer Hardware

1-1.1.4	1-1.2.1	1-1.2.5
1-1.1.5	1-1.2.2	1-1.3.2
1-1.1.6	1-1.2.3	1-1.4.2
1-1.1.7	1-1.2.4	1-2.1.1
1-1.1.8		

Lesson 3
Maintaining and Protecting Hardware

1-1.2.2	1-1.3.4	1-1.4.5
1-1.2.6	1-1.4.1	1-1.4.6
1-1.2.7	1-1.4.2	1-1.4.7
1-1.3.1	1-1.4.3	1-1.4.8
1-1.3.2	1-1.4.4	1-3.1.5
1-1.3.3		

Lesson 4
Computer Software

1-1.1.8	1-2.2.3	1-2.2.8
1-2.1.1	1-2.2.4	1-3.1.1
1-2.1.2	1-2.2.5	1-3.1.2
1-2.2.1	1-2.2.6	1-3.1.3
1-2.2.2	1-2.2.7	1-3.1.4

Lesson 5
Essential Computer Skills

1-1.1.8	1-3.2.2	1-3.3.6
1-1.4.2	1-3.2.4	1-3.3.7
1-2.1.3		

Lesson 6
Using Technology to Solve Problems

1-2.1.1	1-2.2.3	1-2.2.7
1-2.2.1	1-2.2.4	1-2.2.8
1-2.2.2	1-2.2.5	

Introduction to Microsoft Windows

Lesson 7
The Windows Operating System

1-2.1.3	1-3.1.5	1-3.2.3
1-3.1.1	1-3.2.1	1-3.2.4
1-3.1.3	1-3.2.2	

Lesson 8
Changing Settings and Customizing the Desktop

1-3.2.4	1-3.3.2	1-3.3.4
1-3.2.5	1-3.3.3	1-3.3.5
1-3.3.1		

Lesson 9
Using Windows Explorer

1-3.2.6

Lesson 10
File Management with Windows Explorer

1-3.2.7	1-3.2.8

INTRODUCING COMPUTERS

OBJECTIVES

Upon completion of this lesson, you should be able to:

- Define a computer.

- Identify how computers are used in our daily lives.

- Compare and classify types of computers.

- List the parts of a computer system.

- Explain how computers are integrated into larger systems through networks.

Estimated Time: 1.5 hours

VOCABULARY

Channel

Computer

Computer system

Data

Data communications

Hardware

Internet

Local area network (LAN)

Mainframe computers

Microcomputer

Microprocessors

Minicomputers

Network

Notebook computer

People

Protocol

Receiver

Sender

Software

Supercomputers

Wide area networks (WANs)

The computer is one of the most important inventions of the past century. The widespread use of computers affects us not only individually, but also as a society as a whole. You can see computers in use almost everywhere!

- In educational institutions, they are used to enhance instruction.

- Game systems can transport you to an imaginary world.

- At banks, computers allow you to withdraw cash from your account without having to talk with a teller.

- Instant messaging and e-mail allow you to communicate with people almost anywhere in the world.

- On television and at the movies, you can see instant replays in sports or amazing special effects that take you to outer space. The list could go on and on.

As technology produces more powerful computers, our society continues to find more ways to use them to enhance our lives (see Figure 1-1).

FIGURE 1-1
One example of the wide variety of ways people use computer systems

What Makes a Computer a Computer

1-1.1.1
1-2.1.1

Just what is a *computer*? What does it really do? It is an electronic device that receives data (input), processes data, stores data, and produces a result (output). Figure 1-2 shows how a computer is used in a video store to track movies rented by customers.

- *Receives data:* Customers' names and the names of the movies rented are entered into the computer.

- *Processes data:* The computer will change the data from what we entered into what we want the result to be.

- *Stores data:* The information is stored in the computer's memory.

- *Produces a result:* We will see a final display of the information we enter.

FIGURE 1-2
The processing cycle of the computer

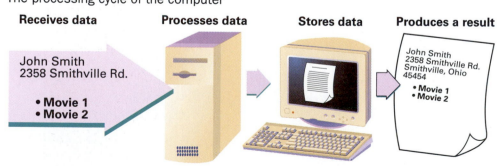

Now you know what a computer is and what it does. Basically, it performs only three operations:

- arithmetic operations (adding, subtracting, multiplying, and dividing)

- logical comparison of values (examples: equal to, greater than)

- storage and retrieval operations

But why have computers become so popular? Some of the reasons computers are so widely used today are that they:

- perform these functions very quickly.

- produce accurate and reliable results.

- store large amounts of data.

- provide versatility in various applications.

- provide cost-effective applications.

- are becoming more powerful and more useful.

How Computers Are Used Today

1-1.1.3
1-1.1.9

Computers in the 1950s, 1960s, and 1970s were large and limited in what they could do (see Figure 1-3). They were temperature sensitive and difficult to repair. Only large companies and government organizations could afford them and only a few visionary people like Steve Jobs and Bill Gates saw a future for small home computers.

Computer Concepts

In 1969, the Neiman Marcus catalog advertised the first home computer, a Honeywell H316 model called the "Kitchen Computer," for $10,600.

FIGURE 1-3
Early generation computers

Small desktop and laptop computers are the most popular type of computer in use today. They are much more powerful and less expensive. These home computers are called personal computers because they were designed to be used by one person at a time. The first affordable personal computers became available to consumers in the late 1970s. Now they are in millions of homes and offices.

Technology for Everyday Life

Computers have vastly impacted our lives. They have changed the way:

- we get news and information.
- we shop for books, music, groceries, and other consumer products.
- we do homework.
- we make reservations for travel.

They are so important in our lives today that without them, businesses, government, news media, transportation systems, and even your home appliances could come to a sudden halt. Computers have become necessary tools in almost every type of activity and in almost every type of business. They are capable of performing many different tasks. Think of the many ways computers affect *you* every day. Any time you go to the movies, shop in a grocery store, send an instant message to a friend, or take a trip on an airplane, you are benefiting from the capabilities of computers.

> **Computer Concepts**
>
> Original music can be created using computers. People do not necessarily need a lot of musical talent or even specific instruments to make music. With a computer, the next top ten hit may be a few clicks away!

Computers at Work

If you are employed at a video store as a sales clerk, you will see the computer used a lot (Figure 1-4). You thought it was just being used as a cash register and to enter customers' information when they rented a DVD. If you were to ask your supervisor how the computer is used in the operation of the store, you would probably be surprised at the answer. You would learn that the computer is used to:

- maintain inventory of all the movie titles.
- maintain records of all the members.
- maintain personnel records.
- maintain the store's budget.
- record sales figures.
- interact with the computers at headquarters.
- order inventory and other items.
- advertise on the Internet.
- communicate with other stores, suppliers, customers, and so on.

FIGURE 1-4
An employee at a video store or supermarket uses a computer to check out items and record inventory. Customers can use a credit or debit machine (also a computer) to pay for their purchases.

Types of Computers

1-1.1.2

The personal computer or microcomputer is only one type of computer. There are other types more suited for various tasks and organizations. Computers are classified by their size, speed, and application.

Classifying Computers

1-1.1.1

Computers have evolved in the past sixty years from room-sized and often project-specific machines to include many types of smaller, multiuse devices. The supercomputers and mainframe computers developed by government agencies and big businesses in the 1940s, 1950s, and 1960s were considered major advances in their days, but in the past decade the boom in smaller computers that can perform many different tasks has changed our lives. Businesses and individuals can chose computers that give them the flexibility and power to perform an endless array of tasks more efficiently.

> **Computer Concepts**
>
> Charles Babbage is the father of computers. He created plans for "Calculating Engines" in the 1850s, which were powerful but flexible calculators that incorporated many features later used in modern computers.

Supercomputers are the largest and fastest computers (Figure 1-5). These computers are used by government agencies and large corporations with tremendous volumes of data to be processed. The processing speed is much faster than any other type of computer, and the cost of a supercomputer can be as much as several million dollars.

FIGURE 1-5
The supercomputer was first developed for high-volume computing tasks such as predicting the weather

Mainframe computers are smaller and less powerful than supercomputers, but they are still large compared to the personal computers we are used to seeing everyday. They perform processing tasks for many users and often cost hundreds of thousands of dollars. Mainframe computers are used for centralized storage, processing, and management of very large amounts of data and are used by large institutions and government installations.

Minicomputers are larger than personal microcomputers and basically have the same capabilities. The cost, however, is much higher. A company would choose to use minicomputers rather than microcomputers if there are many users and large amounts of data. Minicomputers may run Unix, which is a portable operating system—meaning it can run on almost any computer hardware—often preferred by programmers and scientists. Linux and AIX are variations of the Unix operating system.

Microcomputers

The *microcomputer*, also called a personal computer or desktop computer, is the type of computer used at home or at the office by one person (Figure 1-6). Its size and shape allow it to fit on top of or under a desk. Microcomputers are generally classified by the operating system they use, most commonly including PCs (sometimes also referred to as IBM PC compatibles) running a version of Microsoft Windows and Apple Macintosh computers with a version of Mac OS. (Some older PCs might run DOS (Disk Operating System),

> **Note**
>
> The lessons in this book are written for a personal or notebook computer with the Windows XP operating system and Microsoft Office 2003 software, but the concepts and exercises are also applicable for learners on Macintosh computers.

although this is rare today.) Personal computers, both Windows and Mac models, are typically used for writing papers or letters, tracking personal finances, playing games, and connecting to the Internet.

FIGURE 1-6
Two microcomputers, a PC and a Mac

The *notebook computer* or laptop computer has the same capabilities as the desktop computer (Figure 1-7). However, it is much smaller and usually more expensive than a microcomputer. Because of its small size, it is portable and can run on power from an electrical outlet or batteries. Notebook computers are often equipped with wireless connection to the Internet, and businesspeople and students find the notebook computer very convenient to use when they are away from their desks.

Computer Concepts

Supercomputers are often used as testers for medical experiments.

FIGURE 1-7
Notebook computer

Other Computing Devices

1-1.1.3

The personal digital assistant (PDA), also known as a palm-top computer, is even smaller than a notebook computer (Figure 1-8). It has limited capabilities and may lack traditional components such as the keyboard. On such a PDA, a touch-sensitive screen accepts characters drawn with your finger or a special stylus. PDAs often use a specialized operating system such as PalmOS, Windows CE, or PocketPC, but most can connect to desktop computers to exchange and update information. The cost of a PDA is not necessarily lower than a microcomputer, but the price has been reduced in recent years so that PDAs are becoming a common tool for business and professional people as well as students.

FIGURE 1-8
A personal digital assistant, or palm-top computer

Cellular phones now also include many features previously associated with microcomputers, including the ability to connect to the Internet and send and receive e-mail. Some cell phones are even equipped with digital cameras.

Calculators, interactive books, digital cameras, and game systems are all examples of new technology that quickly becomes accepted as they offer new and practical solutions to make everyday tasks easier to accomplish. You may find *microprocessors*, computer chips that perform specific functions, all around your house:

- in the dishwasher and the refrigerator in your kitchen.

- in the CD player/clock radio in your bedroom.

- in the DVD player in your family room.

- in the engine of the automobile in your garage.

Microprocessors in household appliances, automobiles, and industrial equipment allow this machinery to process information and perform more efficiently or effectively.

Computer Systems

1-1.1.8
1-1.1.9
1-1.2.2

What makes it possible for a computer to perform the work it does? It uses a combination of several parts working together called a *computer system* (Figure 1-9). A computer system consists of four parts:

- *Hardware* is the tangible, physical equipment that can be seen and touched. Examples include the keyboard, processor, monitor, and printer.

■ *Software* is the intangible set of instructions that tells the computer what to do. These instructions are called programs or software programs. There are two types of software programs: system software programs and application software programs.

■ *Data* is the new facts entered into the computer to be processed. Data consists of the following:

  ■ text

  ■ numbers

  ■ sounds and images

It is entered into the computer as raw data and the computer manipulates (processes) it into the final form that the user needs. This data can be entered into the computer in several ways including:

  ■ the keyboard

  ■ voice activation

  ■ diskettes

  ■ scanning

Likewise there are various sources from which data can come including:

  ■ handwritten notes

  ■ diskettes

  ■ voice input

  ■ typed reports

  ■ bar codes

■ *People* are the users of the computers who enter the data and use the output.

FIGURE 1-9
The hardware components of a typical microcomputer system

Computer Networks

The earliest computers did not "talk" to each other. There were many reasons for this. One was that they didn't speak the same language. It was as if Computer "A" spoke French and Computer "B" spoke Swedish, so they couldn't understand each other. As technology expanded, standards were developed that enabled computers to communicate by making them speak the same "language," or giving them the ability to "translate" a different computer language into one that could be understood.

Data communications, the technology that enables computers to communicate, is defined as the transmission of text, numeric, voice, or video data from one machine to another. Popular examples are the Internet, electronic messages (e-mail), faxes, and electronic banking. Data communications has changed the way the world does business and the way we live our lives, making it almost effortless to communicate around the globe. Figure 1-10 illustrates the four components of data communications:

- *Sender:* the computer that is sending the message.

- *Receiver:* the computer receiving the message.

- *Channel:* the media that carries or transports the message. This could be telephone wire, coaxial cable, microwave signal, or fiber optic.

- *Protocol:* the rules that govern the orderly transfer of the data sent.

Technology Timeline

COMPUTERS ON THE JOB

In the past few decades, computers have had dramatic effects on how we live, learn, and work. For example, the kinds of jobs available have changed because of computers. Fifty years ago, only a handful of people were computer programmers, and there were no Web designers or "dot.com entrepreneurs." Today few if any prospective employees will find work that does not require some computer skills.

Time-consuming, labor-intensive communications tasks that used to require face-to-face meetings, telephone calls, overnight deliveries, or paging through printed materials are now performed quickly and efficiently using Internet browsers and e-mail. Students can participate in a distance-learning class to take a course of study not available where they live. Even the electric meter reader and delivery person now carry hand-held computers that track a consumer's electric use or the location of a package. Cashiers use computers for retail sales, and computers also update the store's inventory, handle customer calls, and advertise the products. All these advances, now taken for granted by many of us, are very recent innovations.

FIGURE 1-10

Data communications use modems or wireless connections to send and receive information

Networks

One of the most utilized types of data communications in the business world is a *network* connection (Figure 1-11). A network connects one computer to other computers and peripheral devices. This connection enables the computers to share data and resources. If the computers are located in a relatively close location such as in the same building or department, they are part of a *local area network (LAN)*. The data and software for these computers are stored on a central computer called the file server.

FIGURE 1-11

A network system may consist of workstations, servers, and printers

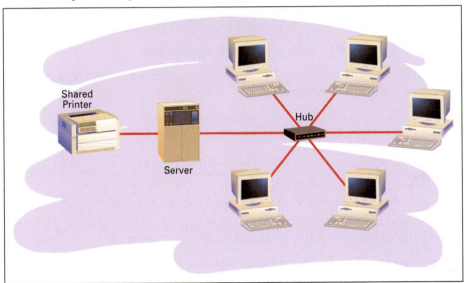

These local area networks can be expanded to include several local area networks within a city, state, region, territory, country, continent, or the world. These are called *wide area networks (WANs)*.

Many companies have implemented networks within their own organizations called intranets. An intranet is used exclusively within an organization and contains only company information. Company manuals, handbooks, forms, and newsletters are just a few of the types of documents distributed via an intranet. The major advantage of using an intranet is reliability and security—possible because the organization can control access.

Extranets are applications that allow outside organizations to access internal information systems. Access is controlled very tightly. These are usually reserved for suppliers or customers.

The Internet

The *Internet* was originally developed for the government to enable researchers around the world to be able to share information. Today it is the largest network in the world. It is used every day by millions of users and has become an invaluable communication tool for businesses, individuals, and governments.

The most commonly used feature on the Internet is electronic mail, better known as e-mail. This is the capability to send a message from one person's computer to another person's computer. E-mail is stored on a server and then downloaded to an individual's computer. E-mail has reduced the number of letters mailed each day and has increased productivity in the workplace.

SUMMARY

In this lesson, you learned:

- A computer is an electronic device that receives data, processes data, and stores data to produce a result.

- Early computers were large, expensive machines used by governments and major corporations.

- Computers can be found in almost every aspect of our lives.

- Computers are classified by size, speed, and application.

- There are different types of computers including supercomputers, mainframe computers, minicomputers, and microcomputers.

- Microcomputers are classified by the type of operating system they use, most commonly Windows on PCs and Mac OS on Macintosh computers.

- Notebook computers are small, portable computers that allow people to work away from their desks.

- Other devices that incorporate computers or task-specific microprocessors include personal digital assistants, cellular phones, digital cameras, interactive books, game systems, home appliances, automobile engines, and industrial equipment.

- A computer system consists of the following components:

  - Hardware: tangible, physical equipment that can be seen and touched.

  - Software: the intangible set of instructions that tell the computer what to do. This set of instructions is called a software program.

  - Data: the information entered into a computer to be processed.

  - People: the users who enter the data and use the output.

- Data communications is the transmission of text, numeric, voice, or video data from one machine to another. The four components of data communications are as follows:

  - Sender: the computer that is sending the message.

  - Receiver: the computer receiving the message.

■   Channel: the media that carries or transports the message. This could be telephone wire, coaxial cable, microwave signal, or fiber optic.

■   Protocol: the rules that govern the orderly transfer of the data sent.

■ A local area network connects multiple computers within a building to share data and resources. A wide area network includes several local area networks within a city, region, country, continent, or the world.

■ The Internet was originally developed so information could be shared by government researchers around the world. E-mail is the most common experience most people have with the Internet, allowing messages to be sent from one computer to another locally and around the world.

VOCABULARY *Review*

Define the following terms:

Channel	Local area network (LAN)	People
Computer	Mainframe computers	Protocol
Computer system	Microcomputer	Receiver
Data	Microprocessors	Sender
Data communications	Minicomputers	Software
Hardware	Network	Supercomputers
Internet	Notebook computer	Wide area networks (WANs)

REVIEW *Questions*

MULTIPLE CHOICE

Circle the best response for each of the following statements.

1. The most popular type of computer in use today is the _____.
   A. personal digital assistant
   B. minicomputer
   C. desktop computer
   D. microprocessor

2. The Internet's most commonly used feature is _____.
   A. e-mail
   B. buying on the Web
   C. viewing videos
   D. creating Web pages

3. A _____ consists of hardware, software, data, and users.
   A. computer
   B. computer system
   C. telecommunications
   D. Web pages

4. The _____ was developed for government researchers.
   A. Internet
   B. mainframe computer
   C. electronic mail
   D. World Wide Web

5. _____ computers share files, data, and software.
   A. Apple
   B. IBM
   C. Networked
   D. Protocol

6. The basic functions of a computer are _____.
   A. receive data, change data, and store data
   B. receive data, process data, and store data to produce a result
   C. send a message through a channel using correct protocol
   D. Windows, DOS, Mac OS, and Unix

7. _____ computers are used for central storage and to process large amounts of data.
   A. Apple
   B. Palm-top
   C. Personal
   D. Mainframe

8. A computer system includes hardware, software, _____, and people.
   A. networks
   B. protocol
   C. data
   D. e-mail

9. Electronic mail messages are stored on a _____ until downloaded by the recipient.
   A. channel
   B. server
   C. diskette
   D. keyboard

10. Connected computers and peripherals within an office building create a(n) _____.
    A. wide area network
    B. software network
    C. extranet
    D. local area network

TRUE/FALSE

Circle T if the statement is true or F if the statement is false.

T　F　**1.** Computers have been a part of society for over 100 years.

T　F　**2.** The Internet was first developed for government use.

T　F　**3.** Computers are classified by size, cost, and Internet abilities.

T　F　**4.** Because notebook computers are much smaller than microcomputers, they are usually less expensive.

T　F　**5.** Software is a set of instructions that tells the computer how to perform certain tasks.

PROJECTS

PROJECT 1-1

Select a career in the field of mathematics such as teacher or statistician. Use the Internet or other resources to research information explaining how computers are being used in a specific mathematics career. Write a two-page report explaining what you learn. If you have access to the Internet for your research, try the keyword *mathematics careers* with one or two search engines (Excite, Mamma, AskJeeves, etc.) to obtain information.

PROJECT 1-2

Use the Internet and other resources to locate information regarding computers in our future. We know that computers are getting more and more powerful every day and are making our lives easier. One example is robotics. These computerized helpers perform many activities that may be dangerous or unpleasant for humans to perform. What are some other capabilities we can anticipate? Write a one- to two-page report describing these capabilities. Use the Ask Jeeves Web site (*www.ask.com*) to ask for information for this report.

PROJECT 1-3

Using the Internet or other resources, see what information you can find on computers that were developed in the early 1950s and 1960s. Write a one- to two-page report on the capabilities of these computers. Also include specific uses of these early computers. Visit *www.looksmart.com* to locate information regarding earlier computers. The Obsolete Computer Museum Web site at *www.obsoletecomputermuseum.org* has photographs and descriptions of many old computers.

TEAMWORK PROJECT

Your supervisor is considering buying a new computer for her office as well as for the office used by the part-time supervisor and other employees. She wants to look into the possibilities of having these two computers networked with the main computer in the store. She knows this is possible, but she is not really sure about what is involved.

She needs to know if there are a minimum number of computers that must be networked. What kind of information and resources can be shared? What special hardware is required? Working with the other part-time sales clerk, research information on local area networks and find answers to your supervisor's questions. You may also include any other information about networks you think will be beneficial. Prepare a written report of your findings. You may find useful information by using the keyword *local area network* with the search engine at *www.ask.com*.

CRITICAL*Thinking*

ACTIVITY 1-1

Computers and microprocessors have greatly influenced the way we communicate today. Use the Internet and other resources to locate information on some of these ways. Write a two-page report on your findings.

COMPUTER HARDWARE

VOCABULARY

American Standard Code for Information Interchange (ASCII)

Bit

Byte

CD-ROM

Central processing unit (CPU)

Controller

DVD

Execution cycle (E-cycle)

Hard disk drive

Impact printers

Input devices

Instruction cycle (I-cycle)

Keyboard

Main memory

Memory

Motherboard

Mouse

Network drive

Nonimpact printers

Optical storage devices

Output devices

Plotter

Pointer

Random access memory (RAM)

Read-only memory (ROM)

Scanner

System clock

In today's technological world, a little knowledge about what's inside a computer can make you a more effective user and help you select the right computer for the job you need it to do. In this lesson you will learn how the CPU processes data and turns it into information. And you will learn about some of the basic components contained on the computer's motherboard. You will also find out more about the processing speed of a computer, how its memory works, and how data is stored. The computer's CPU does the work of processing data, but it needs help. Data must be entered into the computer. Once the data has been entered and processed, it has to be "presented" to the user. Special input and output devices are used for these tasks.

System Components

1-1.1.4
1-1.1.5
1-1.2.2
1-1.3.2

We use computers for all kinds of tasks—to predict weather, to fly airplanes, to control traffic lights, to play games, to access the Internet, to send e-mail, and so on. You might wonder how a machine can do so many things.

19

To understand what a computer really does takes a degree in computer engineering. But most of us don't need that level of understanding. Instead, we need an overview for a basic understanding.

Just about all computers, regardless of size, take raw data and change it into information you can use. The process involves input, process, output, and storage (IPOS). For example,

- You input data with some type of input device.

- The computer processes it to turn it into information.

- You output the information to some type of output device.

- You store it for later retrieval.

Input, output, and processing devices grouped together represent a computer system, as shown in Figure 2-1. First we look at the components that the computer uses to process data. These components are contained within the system case.

FIGURE 2-1
Computer system components

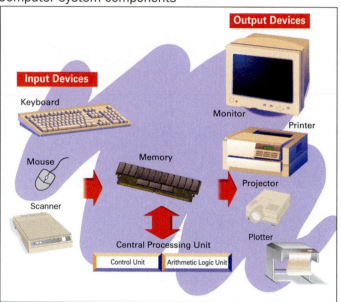

The PC system case is the metal and plastic case that houses the main system components of the computer. Central to all of this is the *motherboard* or system board that mounts into the case. The motherboard (Figure 2-2) is a circuit board that contains many integral components. A circuit board is simply a thin plate or board that contains electronic components. Some of the most important of these components are as follows:

- The central processing unit

- Memory

- Basic controllers

- Expansion ports and expansion slots

FIGURE 2-2
Simplified motherboard

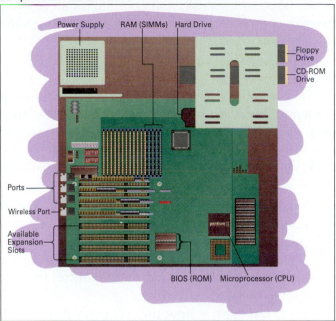

The Central Processing Unit

The *central processing unit (CPU)*, also called the microprocessor, the processor, or central processor, is the brains of the computer. The CPU is housed on a tiny silicon chip. This chip contains millions of switches and pathways that help your computer make important decisions. The switches control the flow of the electricity as it travels across the miles of pathways. The CPU knows which switches to turn on and which to turn off because it receives its instructions from computer programs. Programs are a set of special instructions written by programmers that control the activities of the computer. Programs are also known as software.

The System Clock

The speed of a computer processor is often a key factor in decisions about which computer to purchase. The *system clock* controls the speed of the processor. The system clock is an electronic pulse that is used to synchronize processing, and the rate of pulse is measured in megahertz (MHz), or million cycles per second. For example, a 280 MHz processor has a system clock rate of 280 cycles per second. Early personal computers had much slower processor speeds; for example, the Apple Macintosh II was introduced in 1987 with a processor speed of 16 MHz, and the IBM PC-AT had a processor speed of 6 MHz in 1984. Today's computers have clock speeds of 2.5 GHz to 3.4 GHz or higher, and the higher the number, the faster the computer will process data.

The Arithmetic/Logic Unit

The CPU has two primary sections: the arithmetic/logic unit and the control unit. The arithmetic/ logic unit (ALU) performs arithmetic computations and logical operations. The arithmetic operations include addition, subtraction, multiplication, and division. The logical operations involve comparisons, such as asking the computer to determine if two numbers are equal or if one number is greater than or less than another number. These may seem like simple operations, but by combining these operations, the ALU can execute complex tasks. For example, your video game uses arithmetic operations and comparisons to determine what displays on your screen.

Communicating with the CPU through the Control Unit

The control unit is the boss, so to speak, and coordinates all of the CPU's activities. Using programming instructions, it controls the flow of information through the processor by controlling what happens inside the processor.

We communicate with the computer through programming languages. You may have heard of programming languages called BASIC, COBOL, C++, or Visual Basic. These are just a few of the many languages we can use to give the computer instructions. For example, we may have a programming statement such as Let X = 2 + 8. With this statement, we are using a programming language to ask the computer to add 2 + 8. However, when we input this instruction, something else has to happen. The computer does not understand our language. It only understands machine language, or binary, which is ones and zeros. This is where the control unit takes over.

The control unit reads and interprets the program instruction and changes the instruction into machine language. Recall that earlier we discussed the CPU and pathways and switches. It is through these pathways and by turning switches on and off that the CPU represents the ones and zeros. When electricity is present, it represents a one. The absence of electricity represents a zero. After changing the instructions into machine language, the control unit then sends out the necessary messages to execute the instructions.

You may wonder, though, just exactly how the computer determines what combination of zeros and ones represent the letter A or the number 1. This is accomplished through standardized coding systems. The most popular system is called *ASCII* (pronounced as-kie) and stands for *American Standard Code for Information Interchange*. There are other standard codes, but ASCII is the most widely used. It is used by nearly every type and brand of microcomputer and by many large computers as well.

Each one or zero in the computer's binary language is a *bit*. Eight bits or combinations of ones and zeros represent a letter such as A. Eight bits are called a *byte* or character. Each capital letter, lowercase letter, number, punctuation mark, and various symbols has its own unique combination of ones and zeros.

> **Computer Concepts**
>
> Another type of standard code is called Extended Binary Coded Decimal Interchange Code, or EBCDIC (pronounced EB-si-dik). This code is mostly used in very large computers.

Basic Controllers

The computer motherboard also contains several controllers. A *controller* is a device that controls the transfer of data from the computer to a peripheral device and vice versa. Examples of common peripheral devices are the keyboard, mouse, monitor, and printer. Controllers are generally stored on a single chip. When you purchase a computer, all the necessary controllers for the standard devices are contained on the motherboard.

Peripheral Ports and Expansion Slots

Ports, or specialized plugs connected to the motherboard, are used to connect peripheral devices to the computer. Expansion slots are openings on the motherboard where a circuit board or expansion board can be inserted. For example, if you want to add more memory, it's a relatively simple process. Motherboards contain special expansion slots for additional memory. Expansion boards are also called expansion cards, add-ins, and add-ons. Figure 2-3 shows a typical expansion card.

FIGURE 2-3
Expansion card

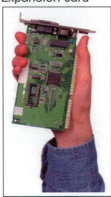

1-1.1.6
1-1.1.7
1-1.1.8

Types of Computer Memory

Memory is also found on the motherboard. Sometimes understanding memory can be confusing because it can mean different things to different people. The easiest way to understand memory is to think of it as "short term" or "long term." Short-term memory is used in the task of processing data; it is the memory required by the processor when you are using the computer. When you want to store a file or information permanently, you use secondary storage devices such as the computer's hard disk drive or a floppy disk or CD-ROM, which provides long-term memory for data storage.

Random Access Memory

You can think about the memory on the motherboard as short term. This type of memory is called *random access memory*, or *RAM*. You may have heard someone ask, "How much memory is in your computer?" Most likely they are asking how much RAM is in your computer. Data, information, and program instructions are stored temporarily on a RAM chip or a set of RAM chips (Figure 2-4).

FIGURE 2-4
RAM chip: memory

When the computer is turned off or if there is a loss of power, whatever is stored in the RAM memory chips disappears. Therefore, it is considered volatile. The computer can read from and write to this type of memory. RAM is also referred to as *main memory* and primary memory.

To better understand how RAM works and how the computer processes data, think about how you would use a word-processing program to create an address list of customers at the video store for a promotional mailing. First, you start your word-processing program. The computer then loads your word-processing program instructions into RAM. You would input the names and addresses of each customer (your data). Your data is also stored in RAM. Next you would give your word-processing program a command to process your data by arranging it in a special format. This command and your processed data, or information, is also now stored in RAM. You would then click the Print button. Instructions to print are transmitted to RAM and your document is sent to your printer. Then, you click the Save button. Instructions to provide you with an opportunity to name and save your file are loaded into RAM. Once you save your file, you exit your word-processing program and turn off the computer. All instructions, data, and information are erased from RAM; the data, however, is stored in another location, such as a hard disk, because you used the Save command to do this. The next time you start your computer, RAM will again be available as the "working" memory the computer uses to process data.

> **Computer Concepts**
>
> Early personal computers often had only 64K (kilobytes) of RAM; today's computers have 264MB, 512MB, or more RAM, which allows the processor to work more quickly, so computer programs operate faster.

This step-by-step process is known as the ***instruction cycle*** or ***I-cycle*** and the ***execution cycle*** or ***E-cycle*** (see Figure 2-5). When the CPU receives an instruction to perform a specified task, the instruction cycle is the amount of time it takes to retrieve the instruction and complete the command. The execution cycle refers to the amount of time it takes the CPU to execute the instruction and store the results in RAM.

FIGURE 2-5
Processing cycle

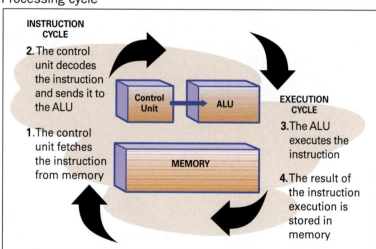

Together, the instruction cycle and one or more execution cycles create a machine cycle, shown in Figure 2-6. Machine cycles are measured in microseconds (millionths of a second), nanoseconds (billionths of a second), and even pico seconds (trillionths of a second) in some of the larger computers. The faster the machine cycle, the faster your computer processes data. As explained earlier, the speed of the processor (the speed of the system clock, the electronic pulse that controls the processing) has a lot to do with the speed of the machine cycle. However, the amount of RAM in your computer also can help increase how fast the computer processes data. The more RAM you have, the faster the computer processes data.

FIGURE 2-6
Machine cycle

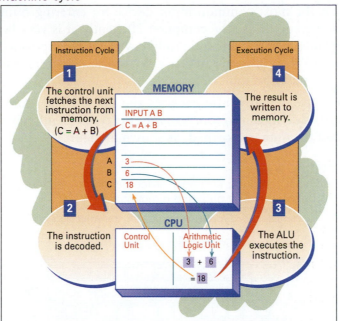

Read-Only Memory

Another type of memory you will find on the motherboard is *ROM*, or *read-only memory*. ROM chips are found throughout a computer system. The computer manufacturer uses this type of chip to store specific instructions that are needed for the computer operations. This type of memory is nonvolatile, which means that these instructions remain on the chip when the power is turned off. The most common of these is the BIOS ROM. The computer uses instructions contained on this chip to boot or start the system when you turn on your computer. A computer can read from a ROM chip, but cannot write or store data on the chip.

> **Computer Concepts**
>
> Another type of memory is called cache memory. This very high-speed RAM is used to increase the speed of the processing cycle by creating a "cache" where instructions or operations used multiple times can be stored and quickly accessed.

1-1.2.1
1-1.2.3
1-2.1.1

Input Devices

When customers come into the video store to rent videos, they leave with the rented videos and a receipt. In order for the receipt to be printed, you enter the customer's information into the computer and the printer produces a receipt. You used the keyboard or a scanner to enter the information or to input the data. The printer produced a copy of the transaction, or the output of the information.

Input devices enable you to input data and commands into the computer and *output devices* enable the computer to give you the results of the processed data.

Some devices perform both input and output functions. The modem is an example. When it is used for transmitting an e-mail message, it is an input device for the sender who inputs the message to be sent to the receiver. The message received is the modem's output.

The type of input device used is determined by the task to be completed. An input device can be as simple as the keyboard or as sophisticated as those used for specialized applications such as voice recognition or remote environmental monitoring.

Keyboard

The *keyboard* is the most common input device for entering numeric and alphabetic data. Therefore, if you are going to use the computer efficiently, it is very important that you learn to keyboard. Keyboarding means being able to key without having to look at the keys. When you enter information into the computer at the video store, it is important to be able to enter the information in a reasonable amount of time.

The keyboard comes in many different sizes and shapes. The standard keyboard, similar to a typewriter keyboard, is divided into four sections: the typewriter keyboard, the function keys, the directional keys, and the numeric keypad, as shown in Figure 2-7.

FIGURE 2-7

A typical computer keyboard divided into four sections: function keys, typewriter keyboard, numeric pad, and directional keys

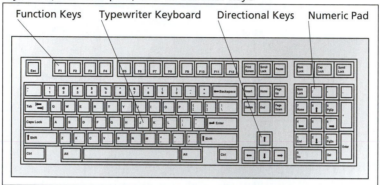

The keyboard of a notebook computer and other specialized computer keyboards may have the numeric keyboard and the function keys set up in a different way; for example, some notebook computers do not have a separate numeric keyboard at all. The tasks you will use a computer for should guide you in deciding whether the keyboard will be efficient for data input.

In addition to the alphabetic and numeric keys, most desktop computer keyboards also include some additional keys to make data input more efficient:

■ *Modifier keys*: These keys are used in conjunction with other keys. They include the Shift, Ctrl (control), and Alt (alternate) keys. A letter or number must be depressed while the modifier key is held.

■ *Function keys*: The keys labeled F1, F2, and so forth are usually located at the top of the keyboard. These keys are used to give the computer commands. The function of each key varies with each software program. For example, F2 in Corel WordPerfect performs a different function than F2 in Microsoft Excel.

■ *Arrow keys*: These keys allow you to move the position of the cursor on the screen.

■ *Special-purpose keys*: There are several other keys on the keyboard that perform a specialized function. The Esc key's function depends on the program being used. Usually it will back you out of a command. The PRINT SCRN sends a copy of whatever is on the screen to the printer. The Scroll Lock key, which does not operate in all programs, usually controls the strolling of the cursor keys. The Num Lock key controls the use of the number keypad. Remember: In order for the keypad to operate as a calculator, the light on Num Lock must be lit. The Caps Lock key controls typing text in all capital letters.

Some keyboards may have additional keys for specialized input data, such as the keyboard on a cash register or a bank teller's workstation. Many keyboards are now ergonomic, which means they have been designed to fit the natural placement of your hands and should reduce your risk of repetitive motion injuries such a carpal tunnel syndrome. Other specialized keyboards have been designed to enable physically challenged workers to input data more easily.

Mouse

The *mouse* is a pointing device that controls the pointer on the screen. The *pointer* is an on-screen arrow-shaped object used to select text and access menus. As you move the mouse, the arrow on the screen also moves and sometimes changes shape to an I-beam, a hand, or another graphic icon, depending on the task being performed.

The mouse fits conveniently in the palm of your hand (Figure 2-8). Originally, a mouse had a ball located on the bottom that rolled around on a flat surface as the mouse was moved. Many of these are still in use, but the optical mouse, which operates with a sens-

> **Computer Concepts**
>
> The mouse was invented in 1963 by Douglas Engelbart of Stanford Research Center, although it did not become a common computer peripheral until graphical user interfaces allowed users to take advantage of the "point-and-click" method of selecting options, text, and other images on the computer screen.

ing device in place of the mechanical ball, is becoming more common. Another innovation is the cordless mouse, which isn't physically connected, but instead uses infrared or radio waves to communicate with the computer. A thumb mouse is a very small device, often with a retractable cord, that is controlled by using your thumb to scroll and click.

FIGURE 2-8
The mouse is used as a pointing device to select an option

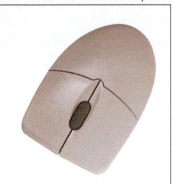

Usually a mouse has two buttons; however, some have three buttons. You usually use the left button for most mouse operations. Once you place the on-screen pointer where you want it, depress a button on the mouse. This will cause some type of action to take place in the computer; the type of action depends on the program being used.

Everything that you do with the mouse will be done by these techniques:

- *Pointing:* placing the on-screen pointer at a designated location.

- *Clicking:* pressing and releasing the mouse button.

- *Dragging:* pressing down the mouse button and dragging the mouse while continuing to hold down the button.

■ *Double-clicking:* pressing and releasing the mouse button twice in rapid succession.

■ *Right-clicking:* pressing the right mouse button.

Voice Recognition Devices

Voice recognition devices are used to "speak" commands into the computer and to enter text. These devices are usually microphones. The computers must have some type of voice recognition software installed on the computer. Voice recognition technology has also enabled disabled persons to command wheelchairs and other objects that will make them more mobile, as shown in Figure 2-9.

Note

The built-in mouse on a notebook often is a sensitive square below or to the side of the keyboard that moves the cursor on the screen when you move your finger over the square, with two buttons below it to right-click or left-click.

FIGURE 2-9
Speech recognition devices can be used by handicapped persons to command computerized wheelchairs

Courtesy of Tejima Lab

Scanners

Scanners are devices that can change images into codes for input to the computer. There are various sizes and types of scanners:

■ *Image scanners* convert images into electronic form that can be stored into a computer's memory. The image can then be manipulated.

■ *Bar code scanners* such as the one shown in Figure 2-10 read bar lines that are printed on products (for example, in a grocery store or department store).

■ *Magnetic scanners* read encoded information on the back of credit cards. The magnetic strip on the back of the cards contains the encoded user's account number.

FIGURE 2-10
An optical character-reading scanner is frequently used in grocery stores to read the price on an item

Image scanners also can be used to read text and convert it to a form the computer can understand, so that a manuscript does not have to be rekeyed. For example, using a scanner and optical character recognition software, you can scan the synopsis of each movie at the video store from the blurb on the back of DVD boxes and create a word-processing file without keyboarding the text. Then you can edit or format the text file for use in an inventory program or an advertisement for the video store, just like data that has been entered with the keyboard. This technology saves time and creates searchable files quickly and easily. Most OCR software is able to recognize a variety of fonts, although handwriting is still a challenge for optical character recognition software because the letter shapes are inconsistent.

 Working in a Connected World

PC SUPPORT SPECIALIST

The PC support specialist provides support for application software and related hardware via telephone, e-mail, and/or site visits to workstation users. As a PC support specialist, you need to be knowledgeable about current software and have good oral communication and organizational skills. You will be required to interface with all departments within the company and work with users with various skill levels ranging from novice to expert. You need to be familiar with other areas of management information systems (MIS) such as networking, printer maintenance, and wireless Internet connections.

A bachelor's degree is preferred for most of these jobs; however, impressive experience is also accepted. Experience performing actual hands-on hardware and software upgrades is important.

Other Input Devices

Figure 2-11 illustrates a few specialized input devices used to enter data quickly and efficiently. Joysticks, trackballs, graphics tablets, touch display screens, digital cameras, and sensor devices have all been developed to accommodate the input of specific kinds of data into computer systems for processing.

FIGURE 2-11
Specialized input devices make it easy to enter many different kinds of data for processing by a computer

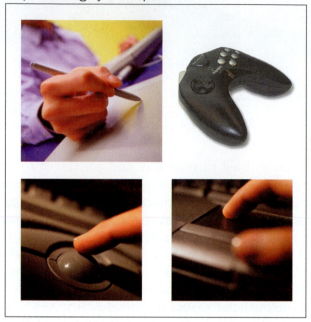

Joystick

The joystick is also a pointing device. It consists of a plastic or metal rod mounted on a base. It can be moved in any direction. Some joysticks have switches or buttons that can input data in an on/off response. Joysticks are most often used for games.

Trackball

The trackball is a pointing device that works like a mouse turned upside down; the ball is on top of the device. You use your thumb and fingers to operate the ball, thus controlling the arrow on the screen.

Graphics Tablet

A graphic tablet, also called a digitizing tablet, is a flat drawing surface on which the user can draw figures or write something freehand. The tablet is connected to the computer. Once the drawing has been inputted to the computer, it can be manipulated like a regular graphic.

Touch Display Screen

The touch display screen has pictures or shapes and you use your fingers to "point" to the desired object to make a selection (Figure 2-12). These screens can be found in many public establishments such as banks, libraries, delivery services, and fast-food restaurants. These are very user-friendly input devices.

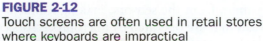

FIGURE 2-12
Touch screens are often used in retail stores where keyboards are impractical

Digital Cameras and Video Input

The pictures taken with a digital camera are stored in the camera's memory and can be transferred to the computer's memory. These pictures can be viewed quickly and you can eliminate any imperfections or add special effects. Images captured with a digital camcorder (Figure 2-13) or from a VCR also can be transferred to a computer, and you can edit the video and view it on screen.

FIGURE 2-13
A digital video camera stores images that can be uploaded to a computer, edited with movie-making software, and then viewed on the monitor

Sensors and Remote Recording Devices

New specialized input devices for computers are being developed all the time. If you have had your temperature or blood pressure measured with a device that provides a quick computer readout of the data, you are familiar with the use of electronic probes. Environmental sensors are used at remote sites to transfer information back to a computer about airplane noise, pollution levels, or temperature fluctuations. The data can be monitored at

Computer Concepts

The Mars Rover allows scientists on Earth to explore the surface of another planet through the use of remote controls that operate the vehicle and sensors that record data and send it back to be analyzed by NASA's computers.

a desk in a laboratory miles from the sensors, making it much simpler to collect scientific statistics. Remote recording devices that are operated by microprocessors can send an intruder alert, collect and transmit counts of visitors or traffic, or monitor seismic activity in a fault far below ground surface.

Output Devices

1-1.2.4
1-2.1.1

Output devices display information. Examples of output are printed text, spoken words, music, pictures, or graphics. The most common output devices are monitors and printers.

Monitors

Monitors are called video display screens because images are displayed on the screen. They can be either monochromatic or color. A monochromatic (monochrome) monitor screen is a one-color display. It could be white, green, or amber. Color monitors display thousands of colors. Most computer monitors today are color.

Factors that influence the quality of a monitor are screen size, resolution, and dot pitch. Screen size is the diagonal measurement in inches from one corner of the screen to the other. Larger monitors make the objects on the screen appear larger or fit more information on the screen. The larger screens are more expensive, however. Most desktop computers are sold with 15- to 17-inch monitors (Figure 2-14). Resolution is the number of pixels or dots that a monitor can display. Most 15-inch monitors have pixel grid settings of 640 × 480, 800 × 600, and 1024 × 768. Dot pitch measures the distance between pixels.

FIGURE 2-14
Many computer monitors today are flat panel screens that free up space on a desktop, or in the case of notebook computers, fold down to create the lid of the unit

Printers

Printers are used to produce a paper or hard copy of the processing results. There are several types of printers with tremendous differences in speed, print quality, price, and special features.

When selecting a printer, consider the following features:

- *Speed:* Printer speed is measured in pages per minute (ppm). The number of pages a printer can print per minute varies for text and for graphics. Graphics print slower than regular text.

■ *Print quality:* Print quality is measured in dots per inch (dpi). This refers to the resolution.

■ *Price:* The price includes the original cost of the printer as well as what it costs to maintain the printer. A good quality printer can be purchased very inexpensively; a high-output system can cost thousands of dollars. The ink cartridges and toners need to be replaced periodically.

The three most popular types of printers are laser, inkjet, and dot matrix. Printers are classified as either impact or nonimpact. *Impact printers* use a mechanism that actually strikes the paper to form images. Dot matrix printers are impact printers. *Nonimpact printers* form characters without striking the paper. Laser printers and inkjet printers are examples of nonimpact printers.

> ### Computer Concepts
>
> Downloading graphic and text files from the Internet is another form of computer input. Once you download a file from the Internet, you can save it on your computer's hard drive or to a floppy disk if there is enough space to hold it.

Laser Printers

Laser printers produce images using the same technology as copier machines. The image is made with a powder substance called toner. A laser printer produces high-quality output. The cost of a laser printer has come down substantially. Color laser printers are much more expensive, sometimes costing thousands of dollars.

Inkjet Printers

The use of inkjet printers is a less expensive way to have color printing available. The color is sprayed onto the paper. Unlike earlier versions of the inkjet printers, newer versions use regular photocopy paper. Inkjet printers are also combined with other technologies to create complete "three-in-one" office machines. These machines combine printer, copier, and fax capabilities into one (Figure 2-15).

FIGURE 2-15
An inkjet printer that also functions as a copier and fax machine

Courtesy of Xerox

Dot Matrix Printers

Impact printers have been around for a long time. They print by transferring ink to the paper by striking a ribbon with pins. The higher the number of pins (dpi), the better the resolution or output. The mechanism that actually does the printing is called a printhead. The speed of the dot matrix printer is measured in characters per second (cps). Impact printers are still used for printing out large quantities of data—you may have seen financial information or your class schedule printed on characteristic paper with holes in a perforated strip on each side, which keeps the paper on a track as it feeds through the printer. You might find that the video store uses a dot matrix printer to print receipts for customers; they are used to print invoices and receipts in many retail settings.

Other Output Devices

People need to use the data processed by computers for many different applications, and specialized output devices such as plotters, projectors, speakers and voice synthesizers, and robotic controls have been developed that allow a computer to create specific kinds of output and to perform many kinds of jobs. Figure 2-16 shows some of the specialized output devices available today.

FIGURE 2-16
There are output devices that can generate processed data for many specialized purposes

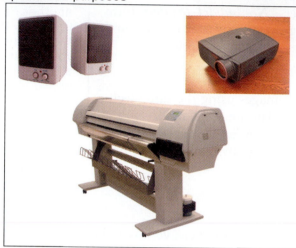

Plotters

A *plotter* is a kind of printer that uses pens to draw lines rather than creating images with a pattern of dots, as conventional printers do. Plotters are used to print maps, charts, engineering and architectural drawings, and diagrams generated by computer-assisted drafting software.

Projectors

A video projector connected to a computer works in a way that is similar to a conventional slide or movie projector. It projects an enlarged image of what is on the computer monitor onto a screen so that a group of people can view the data.

Speakers and Voice Synthesizers

Some computers can use voice recognition to input data for processing. There are also output devices that can create sounds as the result of that processing. The simplest of these devices are speakers, which allow you to hear recorded music or speech from your computer. But if you've ever seen a *Star Trek* episode, you know that the computer actually speaks back to the crew members, giving them data they need. This is not just science fiction—if you call directory assistance or a telephone banking line today, you will hear a voice synthesizer give you the telephone number you need or the balance in your checking account. There are also other output devices for physically challenged people that allow them to "speak" through a voice synthesizer by typing on a keypad.

Robotic Controls

A simple example of a machine operated by robotic control is the plotter. It has pens inserted in mechanical arms that move on rails to draw a chart or map as directed by the computer. More complicated applications for robotic controls are being developed every day: computer-driven robot arms and other computer-controlled mechanical devices are used to assemble cars, adjust thermostats, start, stop, and direct water spray in garden sprinkling systems, and refocus the Hubble telescope.

Storage Devices

1-1.2.5
1-1.4.2

As data is entered into the computer and processed, it is stored in RAM. If you want to keep a permanent copy of the data, you must store it on some type of storage medium such as the following:

- Floppy diskettes
- Hard disk drives
- CDs and DVDs
- Magnetic tape cartridges
- WORM disks (Write once, read many)
- Zip and Jaz diskettes
- Network drives
- Virtual or Internet storage
- Flash memory and memory cards

Storage devices are categorized by the method they use to store data. Magnetic storage devices such as floppy disks and tape cartridges use oxide-coated plastic storage media called Mylar. As the disk rotates in the computer, an electromagnetic read/write head stores or retrieves data in circles called tracks. The number of tracks on a disk varies with the type of diskette. The tracks are numbered from the outside to the inside. As data is stored on the disk, it is stored on a numbered track. Each track is labeled and the location is kept in a special log on the disk called a file allocation table (FAT).

Floppy disks are still used extensively, but many new computers have replaced the floppy disk drive with a CD/DVD drive. Hard drives, Zip drives, and memory cards or virtual storage are all used to store data also.

Floppy Diskettes

Floppy diskettes, usually just called diskettes, are flat circles of iron oxide-coated plastic enclosed in a hard plastic case. Most floppy diskettes are 3½ inches, although you may see other sizes. They have a capacity to hold 1.44MB or more of data. A megabyte (MB) is 1,048,576 bytes or 1,024 kilobytes; these measurements are often rounded off so that a kilobyte (K) is defined as 1,000 bytes and a megabyte as 1,000 kilobytes.

> **Computer Concepts**
>
> In 1956, IBM created the first hard drive, called RAMAC 305, with 50 two-foot diameter platters. The drive had a total capacity of 5MB, or less than what four floppy diskettes can store today.

Hard Disk Drives

Hard disk drives are used to store data inside of the computer (Figure 2-17). They provide two advantages: speed and capacity. Accessing data is faster and the amount of data that can be stored is much larger than what can be stored on a floppy diskette. The size of the hard drive is measured in megabytes or gigabytes. Early personal computer hard drives had a capacity of about 20MB, but now hard drives of 60 gigabytes or more are common. A gigabyte (GB) is 1,024 megabytes (usually rounded to 1,000MB), or approximately a billion bytes.

FIGURE 2-17
How a hard drive works

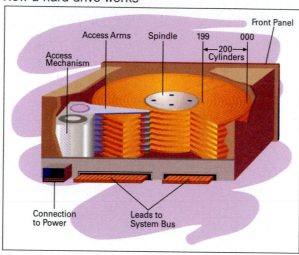

Zip Drives and Jaz Drives

Zip drives and Jaz drives house disks that have many times the storage capacity of floppy disks, even though they are only the size of a 3-inch diskette. The Zip drives are slower than the Jaz drives; they can hold as much as 70 floppy diskettes but are less expensive than the Jaz drive. The Jaz drive is much faster and can store up to a gigabyte of data.

Magnetic Tape Drives

Magnetic tape drives are used for making backup copies of large volumes of data. This is a very slow process and therefore not used for regularly saving data. The tape can be used to replace data that may have been lost on the hard drive, and this storage option is still commonly used by businesses that depend on archived data, although optical storage devices and virtual storage are replacing tape drives in many companies.

Optical Storage Devices

Optical storage devices use laser technology to read and write data on silver platters. These disks can be used to store text, images, sound, and video data.

CD-ROM

The *CD-ROM* (Compact Disk Read-Only Memory) can store up to 680MB. This is the equivalent of about 450 floppy diskettes! You can only read data from the CD; you cannot store data on a CD unless you are using a writable CD with a CD-R drive (sometimes called a CD burner because the drive actually heats sections of the disk, changing the reflectivity of the recording layer as it stores data). Data, music, and even photographs can be stored and uploaded from a CD-ROM.

WORM Disks

WORM (Write Once Read Many) disks are optical disk storage devices that use laser beams and optical technology. They are usually used for permanently storing large volumes of data. The data is stored by making imprints into the surface of the disk that cannot be removed. WORM disks are not as common as the more versatile recordable CD-ROMs that are now available.

CD-R Drives

CD-R (Recordable) drives make it possible for you to create your own CD-ROM disks that can actually be read by any CD-ROM drive. Once information has been written to this type of disk, it cannot be changed.

DVD Media

Full-length movies can be stored on a *DVD* (Digital Versatile Disk). It is the size of a regular CD and can be played in a CD/DVD drive. DVD-R drives are currently available that allow video information to be recorded from a computer to a DVD disk. These are commonly used to make the output of video editing programs such as I-Movie and Windows Movie Maker portable to other DVD devices.

Network Drives

The hard disk drive or floppy drive on your computer is physically a part of your computer system, but it is also possible to store data in a location that is not part of your computer, but that it can access through a cable or wireless connection. A *network drive* is located on another computer or server that provides space you can use for storage. It might appear as the Q:\ or R:\ drive, or use some other designation to differentiate it from the drives that are part of your computer.

Virtual or Internet Storage

Virtual storage available on the Internet is another way to store data that you can access from your computer, but like a network drive, it is not physically a part of your computer system. You use a Web site address to access storage on a distant server to store or retrieve data. There are also forms of data storage that use a computer's hardware and software programming to create more storage than is actually available on your hard disk drive, so it is not "real" storage but "virtual" storage. This is done by using a method that maps virtual addresses to real addresses in the computer's main storage area. This may sound impossible, but remember that many aspects of computer science that seemed more like science fiction a few years ago—such as wireless connections or speech recognition—are now accepted and widely used.

Flash Memory and Memory Cards

Flash memory is a type of memory that is rewritable and nonvolatile (it retains data even when power is turned off). It functions like a combination of RAM and a hard disk. Flash memory sticks or cards are used in portable electronic devices such as digital cameras, cell phones, pagers, and palm-top computers. Figure 2-18 shows a memory stick, which is quite small in comparison to the optical storage disks and high-capacity drive shown with it.

FIGURE 2-18
A memory stick is small compared to disks and removable disk drives, but it can easily store a hundred digital photographs

Zip Drive Courtesy of Iomega

Memory cards can be used for other purposes. For example, a credit-card sized memory card can store monetary value for use in pay phones or retail terminals, or it may contain prerecorded data for an on-board navigation system in an automobile. Such a card may also serve in place of disk storage in a laptop or palm-top computer.

SUMMARY

In this lesson, you learned:

- Just about all computers perform the same general options: input, process, output, and storage.

- Input, output, and processing devices grouped together represent a computer system.

- The motherboard is the center of all processing.

- The motherboard contains the CPU, memory, and basic controllers for the system.

- The motherboard also contains peripheral ports and expansion slots.

- The central processing unit is the brains of the computer.

- The computer is given instructions through computer programs.

- The CPU has two main sections—the arithmetic logic unit and the control unit.

- All calculations and comparisons take place in the ALU.

- The control unit coordinates the CPU activities.

- The ASCII code is a standard code used to represent the alphabet, numbers, symbols, and punctuation marks.

- A controller is used to control the transfer of data between the computer and peripheral devices.

- The motherboard contains different types of memory.

- Random access memory (RAM) is volatile and is used to store instructions, data, and information temporarily.

- The machine cycle is made up of the instruction cycle and the execution cycle.

- Read-only memory (ROM) is nonvolatile and is used to store permanent instructions needed for computer operations.

- Input devices enable you to input data and commands into the computer. The most common input devices are the keyboard and mouse.

- The mouse is a pointing device used to input data that has evolved from a mechanical device connected to the computer by a cable to more flexible devices such as a wireless mouse, a thumb mouse, or the mouse panel on a notebook computer.

- Other types of input devices include joysticks, trackballs, graphic tablets, touch display screens, voice recognition devices, scanners, digital cameras, electronic sensors, and remote controls.

- Output devices allow you to see and use the results of processing data. The most common output devices are the monitor and printer.

- Monitors can be monochromatic or full color, and are available in a range of sizes with different screen resolution.

- Printers are used to produce a paper or hard copy of the processed result.

- Printers are classified as either impact (dot matrix) or nonimpact (laser and inkjet).

- Other types of output devices include plotters, projectors, robotic controls, and voice synthesizers.

- To maintain a permanent copy of data, you must store it on some type of storage medium. These may include floppy diskettes, hard disk drives, CDs or DVDs, magnetic tape cartridges, network drives, virtual storage, and flash memory cards.

VOCABULARY *Review*

Define the following terms:

American Standard Code for Information Interchange (ASCII)	Hard disk drive	Nonimpact printers
	Impact printers	Optical storage devices
	Input devices	Output devices
Bit	Instruction cycle (I-cycle)	Plotter
Byte	Keyboard	Pointer
CD-ROM	Main memory	Random access memory (RAM)
Central processing unit (CPU)	Memory	
Controller	Motherboard	Read-only memory (ROM)
DVD	Mouse	Scanner
Execution cycle (E-cycle)	Network drive	System clock

REVIEW *Questions*

MULTIPLE CHOICE

Circle the best response for each of the following statements.

1. Eight _____ make one character.
   A. characters
   B. bits
   C. bytes
   D. codes

2. The _____ contains the CPU, memory, and basic controllers.
   A. memory
   B. motherboard
   C. processor
   D. expansion slot

3. The _____ is considered the brains of the computer.
   A. program
   B. ALU
   C. CPU
   D. control unit

4. Random access memory is _____.
   A. permanent
   B. volatile
   C. nonvolatile
   D. the same as ROM

5. A printer would be considered a(n) _____.
   A. controller
   B. peripheral device
   C. input device
   D. USB

6. Laser, ink-jet, and dot matrix are types of _____.
   A. monitors
   B. printers
   C. storage devices
   D. input devices

7. Monitors and printers are types of _____.
   A. input devices
   B. output devices
   C. storage devices
   D. ports

8. All of the following are sections of the keyboard *except* _____.
   A. alphabetic keys
   B. function keys
   C. Esc key
   D. numeric keypad

9. Floppy diskettes are also called _____.
   A. diskettes
   B. hard drives
   C. CDs
   D. magnetic disks

10. All of the following are types of storage media *except* _____.
    A. network drive
    B. CD-ROM
    C. memory card
    D. graphics tablet

TRUE/FALSE

Circle T if the statement is true or F if the statement is false.

T   F   1. A plotter is a kind of printer that creates output by drawing lines with pens.

T   F   2. The ASCII code is the most widely used standardized coding system.

T   F   3. A bit has eight bytes.

T   F   4. The two primary sections of the CPU are the ALU and the control unit.

T   F   5. You can think of RAM as long-term memory.

T   F   6. The faster the machine cycle, the slower your computer will run.

T   F   7. You can add memory to a computer by inserting it into an expansion slot.

T   F   8. With OCR software and a scanner, a computer can easily translate handwritten text to usable data.

T   F   9. Flash memory is so called because it emits a bright light when data is recorded to it.

T   F   10. Factors that influence the quality of a monitor are screen size, resolution, and dot pitch.

PROJECTS

PROJECT 2-1

Collect information about three or four computer systems advertised for sale. You can look on eBay, check community bulletin boards, or find ads in your local paper. Using either a computer spreadsheet program or paper and pencil, complete a comparison table. Include the following elements in your table: processor speed, amount of memory, number of expansion slots, storage devices, and price. Based on your comparisons, write a short paragraph explaining which computer you would purchase and why.

PROJECT 2-2

If possible, find a computer system with the case removed. Examine the motherboard and the components connected to the motherboard. Locate and count the number of available expansion slots. Locate the RAM chips. See if you can find the CPU. Can you see the chip itself? Look for the hard disk drive and any floppy diskette or CD/DVD drive. Create a drawing of the system and label as many of the components as you can.

PROJECT 2-3

Contact computer vendors, read computer magazines, research the Internet, and use any other resources to collect data concerning the prices of at least five different models of printers. Find sales information for the same product from three vendors. Determine the average cost of each device. Prepare a chart like the one here to show your findings.

Printer	Capabilities	Vendor	Cost	Vendor	Cost	Vendor	Cost	Avg. Cost

 TEAMWORK PROJECT

Your supervisor at the video store is interested in setting up a teleconference with several of the stores throughout the state. However, she would like to get more information on this capability. She has asked you and the assistant manager to research this technology for her and let her know the steps needed to set up such a conference. Working together, research the Internet and any other materials to prepare a step-by-step guide for setting up a teleconference. Include an introduction that gives basic information about teleconferencing.

CRITICAL *Thinking*

ACTIVITY 2-1

Prepare a two-page report describing several applications in which a user would need to use a scanner to input data. Describe the applications and explain why it would be most efficient to use a scanner. Also explore alternatives to a scanner that might be used for the applications, such as using a digital camera or voice recognition device. If you have access to the Internet for your research, try the keyword *optical scanner* with one or two search engines such as Mamma or LookSmart to obtain information.

MAINTAINING AND PROTECTING HARDWARE

OBJECTIVES

Upon completion of this lesson, you should be able to:

- Explain how to evaluate computer hardware to purchase components or upgrades.

- Identify and describe how input and output devices are connected to the computer.

- Describe the routine maintenance tasks necessary to keep your computer in good working condition.

- Explain how to use troubleshooting techniques to solve computer-related problems.

- Understand how to protect the computer system from damage.

- Identify factors that can damage storage media and learn how to safeguard stored data.

Estimated Time: 1 hour

VOCABULARY

Firewall

Hackers

Modem

Parallel ports

Plug and play

Serial ports

Surge protectors

Troubleshooting

Uninterruptible power
 supply (UPS)

Universal serial
 bus (USB)

Virus

Now that you are familiar with what a computer is and what components make up a computer system, it's time to think about what kind of computer is best for the job—whatever that job might be. People and companies often upgrade or buy new components for existing computers, or decide to purchase a whole new computer system. If you get a new printer, a scanner, or some other special input or output device, you will need to connect it to the computer system so you can use it. And when you have your new or upgraded system up and running, you need to take care of it. Some routine maintenance is easy to perform and should be scheduled regularly to keep your computer running well. Of course, sometimes the computer or its peripherals just won't work correctly, and in that case you need to know how to "troubleshoot" to fix small problems or diagnose bigger issues that will require professional computer repair. It is also important to know how to protect your investment in computer equipment and the data it produces by safeguarding hardware and data against theft and damage.

1-1.2.2
1-1.3.1
1-1.3.2
1-1.3.3
1-1.3.4
1-3.1.5

Evaluating Hardware Components and Upgrades

If you or the company where you work are considering upgrading your computer equipment or buying some new components, you need to consider several criteria before you begin to check Web sites or stores to see what is available. If you are buying a computer for your own use, either for school, home, or work, first make a list of the kinds of tasks you want to accomplish with the hardware. If you are part of a decision team investigating new hardware for an office, the company or organization may have a set of standards or requirements that must be met. It is still important to think about what the computer will be asked to do, but certain decisions about the platform or operating system the computer runs, type of output, and backup systems may be dictated by policy, so make sure the hardware you decide to purchase meets the organization's specifications.

When you have an idea of what you need the computer to do, look for software that can be used for the tasks. For example, if you write a lot of letters, make labels for envelopes, and put together a monthly company newsletter, you will obviously need word-processing software. You may also need specialized software for specific tasks like keeping attendance records, tracking payroll deductions, or creating daily menus. Whatever you need to do, there is probably a software program designed to do it. Make sure the software you want to use will run with the operating system on the computer you choose. Application software files must be compatible with the computer's operating system. As we discussed earlier, most personal computers are either Apple Macintoshes that run on a Mac OS platform or IBM PC compatible machines that run Windows. Other operating systems available for personal computers include DOS, a text-based system, and Unix and similar platforms such as Linux and Aix.

Another important consideration when deciding what kind of computer equipment to buy is the expected useful life of the components. Much of the electronic equipment for sale today will quickly be replaced by newer, faster models with more features, but a good dot matrix printer, for example, can last for many years. Do you need the latest features, or do you want to buy a piece of equipment that will work reliably for a long time? Once again, consider the tasks you will ask the computer and peripherals to do before you decide.

Comparing Central Processing Units

The decision you make about the operating system for your new computer will also decide what kind of central processing unit (CPU) it will have. Many Macintosh computers use a Motorola chip, and over the years these chips have had designations such as 601, 603, G3, or G4. In 1993, an alliance was formed by Apple, IBM, and Motorola to produce the PowerPC family of CPUs. New Macs have either a G4 (produced by Motorola and IBM) or a G5 chip (produced by IBM). Both are PowerPC chips that offer very fast processing.

Computers with Windows operating systems will usually have Intel Celeron or Pentium chips. These chips are often designated by a number, such as Pentium 4, and the higher the number, the newer (and faster) the CPU. Intel developed a chip similar to the super-fast PowerPC chip called the Itanium chip, but problems with the chip kept it from being widely available. The newest Intel offering is a Dothan chip, more commonly known as the Celeron M or Pentium M chip. These new chips are so fast their speeds are measured in gigahertz (billion cycles per second), with speeds of more than 2 GHz available.

Recall that the speed of the CPU is based on the system clock, and the speed is usually measured in megahertz (MHz). But if you compare an 800 MHz Macintosh computer and an 800 MHz Windows computer, one may seem to run faster than the other simply because they are designed differently.

In addition to the speed of the CPU, remember that how much RAM, or random-access memory, available for the CPU will also affect the processing speed, and a computer with 512K RAM generally will cost more than a computer with 128K RAM. When you decide which computer to buy, you will have to balance features and performance with price to find the system that is best for you.

Comparing Computer Models

In making a decision about whether to buy a desktop or a notebook computer, and what kinds of output and input devices to purchase, let the tasks you will perform with the system be your guide again. A doctor who moves from one examining room to another may find that a notebook computer streamlines the process of inputting patient data, and it can be uploaded to the healthcare company's computer at the end of the day. Someone whose job is drafting architectural plans using computer-aided drafting software may find that a desktop computer with an oversized monitor and a plotter to output the plans is what she needs (Figure 3-1).

FIGURE 3-1
A desktop computer with a large monitor and a plotter for output makes graphic applications easier to use

Storage Devices

Different kinds of computers have different kinds of disk drives. A desktop computer model may offer a 40GB hard disk drive, a 3½-inch floppy diskette drive, and a CD-ROM drive. A notebook computer may have a larger disk drive but no floppy drive, and another drive that can read and write CD-ROM and DVD disks. The price of different models and the kind and amount of data your work requires should guide you in deciding which kinds of storage devices to look for in your computer.

Peripherals

If you need or want auxiliary speakers, high-quality printers, a graphics tablet, or a scanner, make sure the computer you choose will support these peripherals and also that it will run the software that will make these input and output devices perform properly.

Upgrading Computer Hardware

It is a relatively simple procedure to add RAM to make a computer processor work faster. A computer professional can tell you how much room is available on the computer's motherboard for expansion cards that can add 128K, 256K, 512K or more additional RAM, and the card fits easily into a slot on the motherboard.

If you decide to purchase a more ergonomic keyboard or a new smaller optical mouse, usually all you need to do is plug the device into the appropriate port and an installation wizard will walk you through the steps needed to make the hardware work. Adding a new printer, speakers, a microphone, a scanner, or other new peripheral hardware is equally simple, but you usually need a computer professional to add a new internal disk drive.

Application and Utility Software Included

Many computers come preloaded with software, including popular applications such as word-processing and spreadsheet software and utility software such as antivirus and disk management software. Sometimes the "bundled" software is fully operable and you can register it and use it for the life of the computer. In other cases, this software is offered on a trial basis, and you must pay a fee when you decide to keep it in order to register for updates and continue to use all of the features of the program past a certain date. Consider what

Computer Concepts

Shareware is software you can download from a Web site and use on a trial basis. If you decide you like the software, you pay a registration fee that entitles you to updates and technical support.

kind of application and utility software you need and want before buying a new computer; you may find it is more economical to purchase a model with minimal preloaded software and then purchase the specific programs you want separately.

Warranties and Technical Support

When you buy almost any electronic equipment, it comes with a limited warranty; that is, if the component fails in a given period of time, such as 90 days, the manufacturer will repair or replace it. Most companies or retailers offer extended warranty coverage at an additional cost. Read the terms of extended warranties carefully to make sure they are a good value, and be sure to register new equipment (usually an online process now) so that the manufacturer's warranty is in effect.

1-1.2.6
1-1.2.7

Connecting Devices to the Computer

Input and output (I/O devices) must be physically connected to the computer. There are two ways to connect these devices to a computer. You can plug the device into an existing socket or port located on the back of the computer, or you can install a circuit board with the port you need already included.

 Working in a Connected World

SYSTEM ANALYST

A system analyst works with the computer user to develop information systems. They plan and design new systems, recommend changes to existing systems, and participate in implementing changes. They are also responsible for writing manuals for the programs as well as external documentation. The system analyst is responsible for making sure that all users understand and can use the system effectively as well as keeping management informed.

This position requires a good technical knowledge of the computer. The system analyst should be up to date in the advances in the computer science field, good with details, and comfortable dealing with people. Effective teaching skills are imperative because the analyst will have to teach the system to the users. They have to be self-motivated, a team worker, and a good listener. Many system analysts begin as programmers and work their way up to system analysts. However, having a four-year degree in computer science will enhance chances of obtaining a higher-paying beginning position. Having a certification, which requires five years of experience as an analyst and passing an exam, will also enhance chances of a higher-paying job.

Serial and Parallel Ports

We use ports to connect peripheral devices to the computer. Computers can have several types of ports, including *parallel ports* and *serial ports*. Serial ports transmit data one bit at a time, something like a narrow one-lane road where the traffic can back up. Parallel devices transfer eight bits at a time. Most computers have at least one parallel port and one serial port, and newer computers have several of each plus other specialized ports. If you examine the back of your computer, you will probably find a printer connected to a parallel port and perhaps a mouse connected to a serial port.

Figure 3-2 shows the back view of a computer system case. In addition to power plugs and parallel and serial ports, you see several other connections. One is a *modem*, a device that allows one computer to talk to another via a telephone line or cable connection. There is also an Ethernet plug, a network cable connection plug, a sound card, and a video card. The monitor connects to the video card and auxiliary speakers can be connected to the sound card. The keyboard plugs into a specialized serial port, and a power cord plugs into the power plug to connect the computer to a power supply. Often the monitor's power cord is plugged into the computer and draws its power through the computer. The PS/2 port is used to connect a mouse or keyboard to a PC. Many PCs have a PS/2 port, which is sometimes called a mouse port, so that the serial port can be used by another device, such as a modem. In more recent models, however, a USB port is used for a mouse connection.

FIGURE 3-2
Back view of a PC computer case

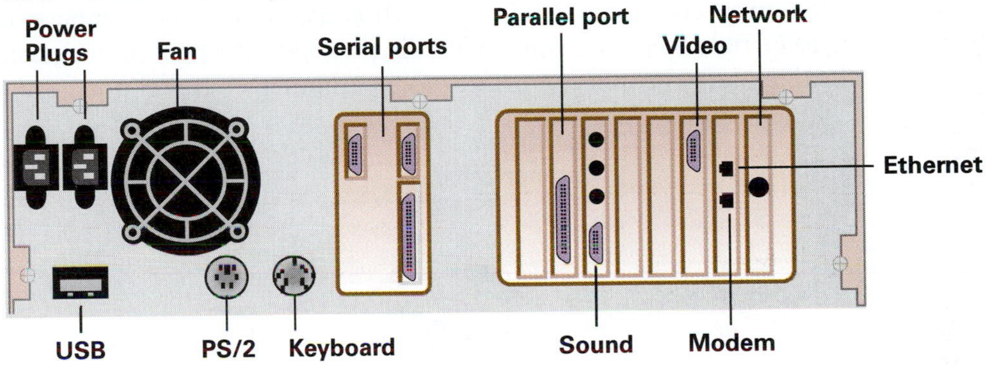

Power Plugs   Fan   Serial ports   Parallel port   Video   Network

USB   PS/2   Keyboard   Sound   Modem   Ethernet

The *Universal Serial Bus (USB)* is a newer standard that supports data transfer rates of up to 12 million bits per second. You can use a single USB port to connect up to 127 peripheral devices. USB is expected to replace serial and parallel ports eventually. Figure 3-3 shows a digital camera with a connection that plugs into a USB port.

FIGURE 3-3
This digital camera is one of many newer computer peripherals that connect easily to a USB port

Special Ports

There are other kinds of ports that are used on older computers or for specific purposes. Briefly, you may find your computer has one of these types of ports:

■ The *SCSI* (pronounced "scuzzy") (for small computer system interface) port is less common in today's computers, but many older models still have a SCSI port for peripherals. One SCSI port can provide connection for one or more peripheral devices; they allow many devices to use the same port.

■ *MIDI* (pronounced "middy") ports are used to connect computers to electronic instruments and recording devices.

■ *PC cards* are used to add memory and to connect peripheral devices to notebook computers. They act as the interface between the motherboard and the peripheral device. The use of expansion cards in notebook computers is impractical because of the size of the notebook computer. Instead, slots for PC cards allow for the attachment of printers, modems, portable disk drives, and CD-ROM drives.

Cable Connections

The cables you use to connect input and output devices to a computer are important, too. Different kinds of cables are required for power cords, computer-to-peripheral connections, and modem-to-telephone line or cable connections. Check that you have the right cable for the job, and make sure the connections are secure on both ends. Some cable connections have thumb screws that have to be tightened, and some will only plug in to the port in one position. Figure 3-4 shows a typical cable used to connect a printer to a computer's parallel port.

FIGURE 3-4
A printer cable

Plug and Play

Most hardware components available today are called *plug and play* because they install so simply. The computer's operating system recognizes the new device when it is plugged in and takes care of all the configuring tasks that once had to be done by the user or the person installing the component. With the plug and play method, a dialog box will appear asking you to confirm the type of new hardware, then the computer takes care of changing all settings and making it ready to use. You may have to install software associated with the device to take advantage of all its capabilities, but sometimes even that is not necessary, such as with a new mouse or modem.

Routine Maintenance

1-1.4.5
1-1.4.6
1-1.4.7

Y ou schedule tune-ups and oil changes for your car, and scheduling routine maintenance tasks to keep your computer in good operating condition is just as important. Hardware is a collection of plastic and metal parts, and it needs some basic care to keep it running well. It's a good idea to schedule routine tasks on your appointment calendar so you won't forget.

The easiest routine maintenance you can perform is a regular visual inspection. Look for loose cable connections; check that every cable and cord is plugged in completely. Damaged cables can keep peripherals from communicating with the computer properly, and a cord that has been bent many times or caught in a piece of office furniture can have a broken wire in it that connects intermittently and can cause problems. If you see a cable that is worn, replace it. There are ribbon cables inside your computer, too, that connect the disk drives to the CPU. If you have had a computer for several years, these cables can become brittle and may need to be replaced by a computer maintenance specialist.

Keeping the system clean is another good way to avoid serious problems. Compressed air that comes in small cans with a straw you can use to direct the spray is a cleaning tool that can clean dust out of a keyboard, but preventive maintenance is even more important. Never eat or drink around your computer to avoid spills that can lead to a "sticky" keyboard or mouse.

FIGURE 3-5
You can keep the computer keyboard clean with a can of compressed air to blow dirt and dust from around the keys

Use wipes made especially for monitors and television screens to clean your monitor. These wipes won't scratch the glass, and they contain an antistatic ingredient that keeps dust from collecting on the screen. The same wipes can be used to clean the glass on a flatbed scanner or the "eye" on a hand-held scanner. Never use a tissue or paper towel to clean the glass surfaces, because they will leave lint behind and may scratch the glass.

You can clean the outside surfaces of printers, scanners, speakers, and the computer case with a sponge or lint-free rag. Printers also need to have their ink cartridge or ribbon replaced periodically; refer to the documentation that came with your printer to perform this maintenance correctly.

> **Note**
>
> Cartridges for inkjet and laser printers can be recycled. Many office supply stores, schools, and community groups collect cartridges for recycling.

It's a good idea to perform "internal" routine maintenance, too. This involves deleting unused or temporary files periodically and running a utility program that cleans up the hard drive and prevents the data stored on it from becoming too fragmented. This will make it easier for the CPU to access data on the hard drive quickly. Also check regularly for updates to your antivirus software so that it will look for the most current versions of viruses.

Troubleshooting

1-1.4.4
1-1.4.8

Even if you carefully perform routine maintenance, you will occasionally encounter problems using your computer, its input and output devices, or the software applications on the computer. *Troubleshooting* involves analyzing problems to correct faults in the system. Keep in mind the following steps to solve computer-related problems:

> **Note**
>
> The Web site *www.everything-computers.com* offers a troubleshooting guide for both Mac OS and Windows computers

- Recognize the problem.

- Replicate the problem by reproducing the steps that cause the problem consistently.

- Attempt basic solutions to correct the problem such as restarting the hardware or checking cable connections.

- Look for available help and advice in manuals or from a technical support Web site or telephone number.

- Communicate the problem accurately to the support technician.

- Follow the instructions the technician gives you carefully.

- Confirm that the problem has been fixed.

- Avoid similar problems in the future.

A simple example of effective troubleshooting is finding and fixing a recurring paper jam in an inkjet printer. First you experience a paper jam every time you try to print an envelope in the printer. Check the manual or online help for the printer and make sure you are loading the envelope correctly in paper tray. You might also lift the cover of the printer to make sure there isn't a small piece of paper or other foreign matter in the printer's feed system. When you are sure the printer feed system is clear, follow the directions carefully to load another envelope correctly. When the envelope prints properly, you know you have solved the problem. Remember to load the envelope the right way the next time, too.

But some problems are not quite so simple to solve. For example, you may have an optical scanner that you are using to scan some original artwork for a Web site you are creating. The scan program gives you an error message every time you click on the Scan button.

- First check that the scanner is on and the power cable is connected.

- Also check the cable that connects the scanner to the computer.

- Restart the computer and try the scan program again.

- If it still doesn't work, contact the technical support department of the scanner's manufacturer. Often this is done by submitting a form found on the company's technical support Web site.

- Explain the problem clearly.

- When you get a response, such as the suggestion to reload the scanner's driver and software, follow the directions carefully.

With good instructions and proper follow-through, chances are you won't see that error message again and you can get back to the job of scanning the graphics.

FIGURE 3-6
Search for information about problems on support Web sites provided for most software and hardware manufacturers

 # *Protecting Computer Systems from Theft and Damage*

1-1.4.1
1-1.4.2
1-1.4.3

There are many threats to computer systems, from power surges that can completely destroy components to hackers who send viruses via e-mail attachments that can disable your system, to a common thief who might switch your laptop computer bag with an empty one while your back is turned for a minute at the café or airport. You (or your company) make a sizable investment in computer equipment, and it is important to protect the equipment from environmental damage and theft.

Keeping Your Hardware Safe

One ever-present danger for a computer system is an electrical power failure. Electricity not only provides the power to operate a computer, but it also is the medium by which data is stored. Computers are vulnerable both to power surges, or spikes in the electric current, and to power outages. Lightning can trigger either condition, for example. A power spike can corrupt computer hardware, rendering it inoperable and making any stored information inaccessible. A power outage can wipe out any data that has not been properly saved.

Computer Concepts

Some companies offer security software for notebook computers that can trace the location of a stolen computer when it is connected to the Internet. The location information is forwarded to the company, and they contact law enforcement officials who may be able to recover the computer.

To safeguard computer systems against power outages, electric cords should be secured so that they cannot be accidentally disconnected. Another option is to install an *uninterruptible power source* (UPS), usually a battery that kicks in if the normal current is interrupted. *Surge protectors*, which plug into electric outlets, can protect against power spikes. They wear out eventually, however, and need to be monitored and replaced as necessary.

FIGURE 3-7
A UPS (uninterruptible power supply) can ensure that your computer hardware is not damaged and data is not lost during a power outage

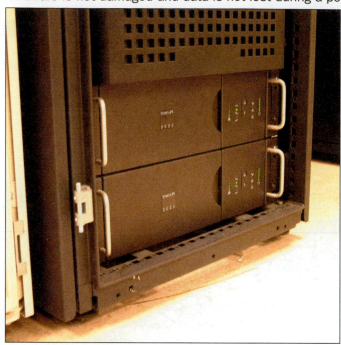

In places that are accessible to the public, you may notice that computer terminals are locked to a desk or table; if you use a notebook computer at school or work, keep it in a locked drawer when you are not using it. Padded bags are available for carrying notebook computers safely from one place to another, and now many of these bags are designed as backpacks, which free your hands and are less likely to catch the attention of a thief looking for a briefcase-type padded bag that obviously is designed for a portable computer.

To safeguard data as it is being entered, active files should be saved frequently. Some programs do this automatically; others require users to do it manually. Even saved data can be lost or damaged by equipment failure, fire or flood, power irregularities, or a *virus*—a program written specifically to cause corruption of data. So it is essential to back up important files regularly. Backing up files entails saving them to removable disks or some other independent storage device that can be used to restore data in the event that the primary system becomes inaccessible. Backup procedures should place a priority on files that would be difficult or impossible to replace or reconstruct if they were ever lost, such as

Note

Never open an e-mail attachment from a sender you do not know. Many computer viruses are spread through e-mail attachments, and sometimes they spread through an e-mail program's address book, so it is important to run antivirus software that can check all attachments for viruses before opening.

users' data files. Secure backup procedures used by large organizations include a regular schedule for backing up designated files and a means of storing backup files off site so that they will survive intact if the main system is destroyed either by natural disaster or by criminal acts.

Hackers are usually skilled computer users who can invade almost any computer that has an Internet connection. Some hackers get into files on another computer to obtain personal information such as credit card and Social Security numbers that they can use for financial gain, others are interested in causing damage through viruses attached to programs or e-mail, and some hack just because they can. In any case, a *firewall* is an essential element in any networked computer today, to create a line of defense against unauthorized entry into your network from outside when you are connected to the Internet.

Caring for Removable Storage Media

Removable storage media require special care to prevent damage that can make the data stored unusable. Here are some safeguards that should be taken:

- Keep away from magnetic and electrical fields such as those contained in televisions and computer monitors.

- Avoid extreme temperatures.

- Never open the data shutter or attempt to disassemble a removable disk cartridge. Never touch the surface of the media itself.

- Remove media from drives and store them properly when not in use.

- When handling CD-ROMs, DVDs, and other optical disks, hold them at the edges.

- Never try to remove the media from a drive when the drive indicator light is on.

- Keep disks in a sturdy case when transporting.

SUMMARY

In this lesson, you learned:

- Decisions about what kind of computer to buy should be based on what you want a computer to do.

- The kind of software you want to run should also help you decide what kind of computer to buy.

- It is important to register new equipment to activate the warranty and technical support.

- Input and output devices are connected to the computer through serial and parallel ports.

- The Universal Serial Bus is a newer standard that is beginning to replace serial and parallel ports.

- There are several types of ports: USB, SCSI, MIDI, parallel, and serial.

- Cables connect peripherals to the computer.

- Many hardware devices today are designed to be plug and play, so the operating system recognizes the new hardware and configures the system for it to work correctly.

- A regular visual inspection of your computer system can help you find loose cables and other potential problems before they affect how the computer runs.

- Keeping your computer system clean is another way to avoid serious problems.

- Troubleshooting involves analyzing problems to correct faults in the system.

- Power outages and power surges can both damage hardware and corrupt data, so it is important to protect your computer system from fluctuations in the power supply.

- Protect your computer from theft, viruses, and hackers by taking basic security precautions.

- To maintain a permanent copy of data, you must store it on some type of storage medium. These may include floppy diskettes, hard drives, CDs, magnetic tape cartridges, and WORM disks.

VOCABULARY *Review*

Define the following terms:

Firewall	Plug and play	Uninterruptible power
Hackers	Serial ports	supply (UPS)
Modem	Surge protectors	Universal serial bus (USB)
Parallel ports	Troubleshooting	Virus

REVIEW *Questions*

MULTIPLE CHOICE

Select the best response for the following statements.

1. Troubleshooting a computer problem involves all of the following *except* _____.
    A. describing the problem accurately
    B. looking for available help from an online technical support Web site
    C. following the computer technician's instructions carefully
    D. opening the back of the computer to make a visual inspection

2. A(n) _____ is a program written to cause corruption of data on a computer.
    A. utility software
    B. virus
    C. antivirus software
    D. defragmenter

3. All of the following are types of ports *except* _____.
   A. MSO
   B. USB
   C. SCSI
   D. MIDI

4. The data stored on removable media can be damaged by all of the following *except* _____.
   A. magnetic fields
   B. extreme temperatures
   C. adhesive labels
   D. fingerprints

5. _____ invade other people's computers.
   A. Hackers
   B. Firewalls
   C. System analysts
   D. Programmers

TRUE/FALSE

Circle T if the statement is true or F if the statement is false.

T   F   **1.** Input and output devices all connect to the computer with the same kind of cable.

T   F   **2.** The software that comes preloaded on a computer includes all the application programs you need.

T   F   **3.** A surge protector will keep your computer powered on even during a blackout.

T   F   **4.** Regular visual inspection is an effective step in routine computer maintenance.

T   F   **5.** USB ports are rapidly replacing both serial and parallel ports.

PROJECTS

PROJECT 3-1

Plug and play components make it easy to add new hardware to your computer system. Visit an electronics store or use the Internet to research what kind of plug and play components are available. If you know someone who has worked with computers for several years, ask them about what kinds of things they had to do to install hardware before plug and play components were available. Write a one-page report comparing the installation of hardware devices when the user had to configure settings to make the hardware run compared to the plug and play process.

PROJECT 3-2

Visit the technical support Web sites of three hardware manufacturers such as Dell Computers, Iomega (disk drives), and Kodak (imaging devices). In a written report, compare the technical support offered by three different companies, considering ease of use and quality of information. Does one site's search feature provide better information than another site's list of frequently asked questions? How can you submit a specific question not covered on the site? How would the technical support offered by a company affect your decisions about purchasing computer components?

PROJECT 3-3

New computer viruses show up almost every day, and they only make the news when they are very destructive and already fairly widespread. Software companies often post information about new viruses on their Web sites. Check *www.symantec.com* and *www.microsoft.com*, or use a search engine such as Yahoo or Excite to search for current virus information. Make a list of the names of the viruses you find, and describe what kind of damage each virus can cause. Try to list at least six viruses with descriptions.

 ## TEAMWORK PROJECT

The computer terminals at the video store are used by many different clerks in the course of a workday. Your supervisor has asked you and another employee to come up with a routine maintenance checklist that any of the clerks can use at the beginning of the day to make sure the terminals are in good working order. Create a checklist that includes daily tasks and weekly tasks to keep the components clean and in good working order.

CRITICAL *Thinking*

ACTIVITY 3-1

Use the Internet and other resources to identify early security measures that were used to protect computers and computer data. Try a search engine with the keyword *early computer security* to locate information. Describe how these measures counteracted the intrusions made. Then, visit the Web sites of some companies that make computer security devices such as *www.pcguardian.com* to find out what kind of technology is available today to protect computers and data. Write a two-page report of your findings.

COMPUTER SOFTWARE

OBJECTIVES

Upon completion of this lesson, you should be able to:

- Distinguish between software and hardware.

- Explain how a computer software program works.

- Understand the steps involved in software development.

- Describe the difference between applications software and systems software.

- Describe the three categories of systems programs.

- Describe operating systems for microcomputers, including network operating systems.

- Define a user interface.

- Explain the difference between a command-line user interface and a graphical user interface.

- Understand the boot process a computer goes through when you start it.

Estimated Time: 1.5 hours

VOCABULARY

Algorithm

Applications software

Boot

Graphical user interfaces (GUIs)

Language translators

MS-DOS

Multitasking

Network operating system

Operating systems

Software development

Systems software

Unix

User interface

Utility software

Over the last 50 years or so, computer technology has changed the world. Not so long ago, workers would not have used computers. Customers would not have ID cards that could be scanned. Accounting was done using ledgers. When most of us think about computers, we think of hardware and how the hardware has changed—computers have become smaller and faster. If we look at the history of computers, however, we find that the early computers were used as little more than high-speed calculators. If computers had not developed the capacity to do so many different tasks so quickly, they would not have had such a major influence on our culture and economy. The reason that computers have had such an impact is through the vision and desire of software developers. These software creators came up with hundreds of ideas and ways in which to use computers. They created programs that affect us in every aspect of our lives.

Hardware vs. Software

You have probably heard the words software and hardware many times. Sometimes it is difficult to distinguish between these two terms. Remember that hardware refers to anything you can touch. This includes objects such as the keyboard, mouse, monitor, printer, chips, disk drives, and CD recorders. You cannot touch software because it has no substance. Software is instructions issued to the computer so that specific tasks may be performed. Another word for software is program. Hardware and software interact as a computer processes data. Input devices, you recall, allow a user to enter data—they are examples of hardware. Then specific programmed instructions tell the computer how to process that data—this is the software component that tells the hardware what to do. Finally, other software instructions format the data correctly so you can understand it when you see it on a monitor or from printer output, or hear it through the speakers.

> **Computer Concepts**
>
> An early computer called the Univac I was a sensation in 1952 when it correctly predicted that Dwight D. Eisenhower would win the presidential election in a landslide victory. The election results were remarkably close to the computer's prediction, but the computer didn't perform a miracle. The programmers who used statistical vote samples (the data) and shrewd analysis techniques (the program commands) deserve the credit for the accurate prediction.

For example, a computer programmer may write a program that lets the user download music from the Internet. The software makes it possible to move a music file from a server somewhere on the Internet, and other software on your computer allows you to play the music. The CPU, the sound card, and the speakers in your computer system are the hardware that makes the sounds you hear as music.

You may have heard someone say he has a problem with how his computer is working. He might say, "It's a software problem." This means there is a problem with the program or data, and not with the computer or hardware itself. A good analogy is a book. The book, including the pages and the ink, is the hardware. The words and ideas on the pages are the software. One has little value without the other. The same is true of computer software and hardware: the way the two interact allows us to use the computer to complete many different tasks.

How a Software Program Works

A computer processes data by applying rules called algorithms. An *algorithm* is a set of clearly defined, logical steps that solve a problem. For example, if you want to explain to someone who has never done laundry how to do it properly, you would explain the process step by step, as shown in Figure 4-1.

FIGURE 4-1
An algorithm lists steps required to accomplish a task

HOW TO DO LAUNDRY
Collect the clothes that need to be washed.
Separate the clothes into light and dark piles.
Take the light pile to the washing machine and put clothes in the machine.
Add laundry detergent to the washing machine.
Set the dial on the washing machine for the correct size load.
Set the dial on the washing machine for warm wash and warm rinse water.
Turn on the washing machine.
When the cycle has finished, take wash out and put clothes in dryer.
Add a dryer fabric softener sheet to the dryer.
Set dryer cycle to Permanent Press.
Set dryer timer to 40 minutes.
Turn on dryer.
When the cycle has finished, take clothes out.
Fold clothes.
Put away clothes.
Repeat all previous steps with dark clothes.

If these steps seem like they offer very detailed instructions for performing a simple task, remember that the person you are instructing has no idea how to do laundry, so you can't assume he or she knows anything about it. In the same way, when a programmer writes software instructions for a computer, every step must give explicit instructions, because a computer can't do anything at all without being instructed to do it through software programmed commands.

So, to tell a computer to perform a simple task such as output the average of three numbers, the program must break this down into many steps. For example:

- Let A equal 95.

- Let B equal 102.

- Let C equal 88.

- Add $A + B + C$.

- Let the sum of $A + B + C$ equal X.

- Divide X by 3.

- Let the quotient equal Y.

- Print the text "The average is" followed by Y.

This is a very simple example of how a programmer would begin to write a software program. After writing an algorithm for solving the problem in plain English (or French, Chinese, or Portuguese, depending on the spoken language of the programmer), the next step would be to rewrite the steps in a formal programming language. Even then the computer won't understand the instructions; a specialized computer program translates the programming language to machine language that the computer will understand.

Software Development

Software development is a multistep process that usually begins when someone recognizes a need to perform a task more effectively or efficiently using a computer. As we have seen, the first thing the programmer must do is break down the task into an algorithm or series of steps that will cover all the individual actions needed to perform the task. Often the programmer works out the logic for the steps in the algorithm by using a flowchart that shows different paths the program will take depending on what data is input.

> **Computer Concepts**
>
> Grace Hooper was a naval officer and computer scientist who first thought of the idea of developing a computer programming code based on English. The language she created, called FLOW-MATIC, led to the development of COBOL, an important programming language for business.

Next, the programmer writes the steps in a computer programming language or code that uses a formal set of terms and *syntax*, or rules for how the words are used together. The computer will then take that code, translate it into language it can understand, and use the translated commands to execute the program.

This isn't the end of the process, however. Computer programs are written by a person or people who can make mistakes. Someone might enter a line of code with a small error in syntax or how a term is spelled, and it can result in very different results than the programmers were expecting. So software development also requires a quality control process that involves running systematic tests, debugging (finding and correcting errors in the code), and beta review, a process that releases commercial software in development to a cross-section of typical users who evaluate the program and report any problems or "bugs" in the software before it is released to the public.

Types of Software

1-2.1.2
1-2.2.1
1-2.2.2
1-2.2.3
1-2.2.4
1-2.2.5
1-2.2.6
1-2.2.7
1-2.2.8

There are two basic types of computer software: *applications software* and *systems software.* Applications software helps you perform a specific task. Systems software refers to the operating system and all utility programs that manage computer resources at a low level. Figuratively speaking, applications software sits on top of systems software. Without the operating system and system utilities, the computer cannot run any applications program.

Applications Software

Applications software is widely referred to as productivity software. Applications software is composed of programs designed for an end user. Some of the more commonly used application programs are word processors, database systems, presentation systems, spreadsheet programs, and graphic design programs. Some other applications categories are as follows:

- Education, home, and personal software—reference, entertainment, personal finance, calendars, e-mail, browsers

- Multimedia software—authoring, animation, music, video and sound capturing and editing, virtual reality, Web site development

- Workgroup computing software—calendars and scheduling, e-mail, browsers, electronic conferencing, project management

Systems Software

Systems software is a group of programs that coordinate and control the resources and operations of a computer system. Systems software enables the many components of the computer system to communicate. There are three categories of systems software: operating systems, utilities, and language translators.

Operating Systems

Operating systems provide an interface between the user or application program and the computer hardware. Figure 4-2 shows how the relationship works. There are many brands and versions of operating systems software. Each of these is designed to work with one or more particular processors. For example, an operating system (abbreviated OS) like Windows is designed to work with a processor made by Intel. Many IBM PC-compatible computers contain this brand of processor. Most Macintosh computers contain a processor manufactured by Motorola. The Windows operating system does not work with this Motorola processor.

FIGURE 4-2
Operating systems: an interface between users and computers

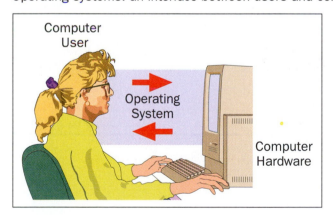

Utilities

Utility software helps you perform housekeeping chores. You use these programs to complete specialized tasks related to managing the computer's resources, file management, and so forth. Some utility programs are part of the operating system, and others are self-contained programs. Figure 4-3 shows a dialog box for a disk cleanup utility. Some other examples of utility program functions are as follows:

- You have an antivirus program that scans the computer disks on a regular basis to look for computer viruses.

- You copy a file from the hard drive to a floppy disk—the file management utility provides the instructions to the computer.

- You convert a graphics file created in one software program so it can be used in another program.

- You use the backup utility to make a copy of the hard drive to archive.

FIGURE 4-3
Disk cleanup utility

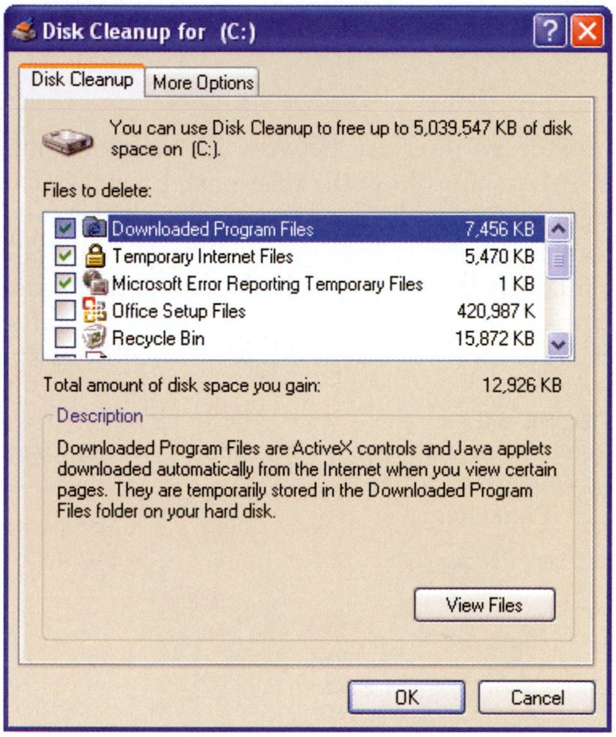

Table 4-1 lists some of the most commonly used utilities and the tasks they perform.

TABLE 4-1
Utility Programs

TYPE OF UTILITY	PURPOSE
File management	Allows the user to perform tasks such as copying, moving, and deleting files
File recovery	Attempts to recover a file that has been erased
Disk defragmentation	Attempts to place the segments of each file on the hard disk as close to one another as possible
Uninstall	Removes an application that is no longer needed
Diagnostic	Provides detailed information about the computer system and attempts to locate problems
File conversion	Converts a file from one format to another
Disk compression	Frees up storage space on a disk by compressing the existing files
Backup	Makes a duplicate copy of the contents of a secondary storage device
Antivirus	Protects the computer system from viruses designed to damage computer hardware or data

Language Translators

Language translators convert code written in a programming language that uses a language based on English into machine language that the computer can understand. For example, the video store might hire a programmer to write a software program to inventory all of the items in the store. The programmer then writes the program statements using a programming language called Visual Basic. A program statement directs the computer to perform a specified action.

The computer, however, cannot read the Visual Basic programming statements because they are written in a language that we understand. This is where the language translator takes over. The translator changes each of the Visual Basic programming statements into machine language. A single statement in a high-level programming language like Visual Basic can represent several machine-language instructions. Now the statements can be executed and the store's inventory can be processed.

Microcomputer Operating Systems

1-1.1.8
1-3.1.1
1-3.1.2
1-3.1.4

There are several popular operating systems for microcomputers. Macintosh and Macintosh clone computers use a version of Mac OS. If your computer is what is commonly referred to as a PC or an IBM PC compatible, you most likely are using one of these three operating systems:

- DOS

- A combination of DOS and Windows

- A standalone version of Windows

Mac OS

The Mac OS is used with Apple's Power Macintosh computers and Power Macintosh clones. The Macintosh was introduced in 1984. One of the main features of this new computer was an interface called Finder that contained icons or symbols representing documents, software, disks, and so forth. To activate the icon, the user clicked on it with a mouse. This operating system was also the first to provide on-screen help or instructions. In 2002, Macintosh released OS v.X.

> **Computer Concepts**
>
> The history of Apple Computer and Steve Jobs and Steve Wozniak is a fascinating story. For an overview of this story, check out the Web site at *http://inventors.about.com/ library/inventors/ blapplecomputer.htm.*

DOS

IBM introduced its first IBM PC in 1981. With the introduction of this new microcomputer came a new operating system. This system was called DOS (Disk Operating System). IBM referred to this operating system as PC DOS. They licensed this software from a small startup company called Microsoft. But Microsoft retained the rights to market its own version of the software. Microsoft called their version *MS-DOS*. This OS was the catalyst that launched Microsoft into the multibillion dollar company it is today.

DOS is a character-based operating system. That is, the user interacts with the system by typing in commands. DOS is a single-user or single-tasking operating system because the user can run only one program at a time.

Windows

In response to the competition from the Macintosh Finder interface, Microsoft introduced its own user-friendly interface in 1987. This OS was called Windows.

- The first versions of Windows contain a graphical shell and were called operating environments because they work in combination with DOS.

- The different applications installed on a computer appear as icons.

- The user activates the icons by clicking on them with a mouse.

- These early versions of Windows are consecutively numbered beginning with Windows 3.0, Windows 3.1, and so forth.

Windows 95 was Microsoft's first true multitasking operating system. *Multitasking* allows a single user to work on two or more applications that reside in memory at the same time. It also supported networking, which allowed two or more computers to be linked, and introduced plug and play technology, explained in Lesson 3, which allows a user to simply plug in a new device and use it immediately, without complicated setup maneuvers.

Windows 98 is easier to use than Windows 95 and has additional features. Some of these new features include the following:

- Internet integration.
- System starts up and shuts down faster.
- Support for the Universal Serial Bus that is used to easily add and remove devices on the computer.

Windows 2000 is an update to the Windows 98 and Windows NT operating systems. Some new features include the following:

- Tools for Web site creation.
- Wizards that guide the user through various operations.
- Monitoring programs.

Computer Concepts

Windows CE is Microsoft's original operating system for handheld devices. More recently, Windows XP Embedded has been introduced as a powerful OS for applications from small mobile devices to large industrial machines. Learn more about these operating systems by searching the Web site at *www.whatis.com*. You can also find additional information at *www.microsoft.com*.

Working in a Connected World

SOFTWARE DEVELOPER

A software developer maintains and helps develop new application and operating systems programs. When you see a job listing for software developer, it could include many requirements. A company may be looking for someone to develop software using a particular programming language such as Visual Basic, C, or C++. Or a company may be looking for someone to develop add-ons to operating systems programs. This could include enhancements to utility programs, updates to language translators, or new additions to the operating system itself. Many companies seek employees with skills in operating systems programs such as Unix and Windows NT.

If you go online to look for software developer jobs, you will find that many of them refer to Oracle, a large information technology software company. Oracle products support database technology, data design and modeling, Web applications, and much more. There is a great variation in salaries and educational requirements for software developers. Educational requirements range from some college to a bachelor's or master's degree or maybe even a Ph.D. Generally, but not always, the more education you have, the higher your starting salary. Most companies require some experience, but a few have entry-level positions.

The most recent update is Windows XP, which provides increased stability and improved device recognition. Even though the Windows versions have changed, some features remain consistent, such as the Start menu, task bar, and desktop. Figure 4-4 shows the Windows XP operating system.

FIGURE 4-4
The Windows XP operating system

Other Operating Systems

Still another operating system is *Unix*. Unix is frequently used by scientists and programmers. This operating system, developed by AT&T, is considered a portable operating system. This means it can run on just about any hardware platform. There are several variants of the language, such as Linux and IBM's AIX.

Network operating systems allow a group of two or more microcomputers to be connected. There are several brands of network operating systems. Three of the most popular are as follows:

- Microsoft Windows NT
- Novell's Netware
- IBM's Warp Server

 ## User Interfaces

1-3.1.3

All computers, from mainframes to microcomputers, have operating systems. Operating systems have become increasingly more user friendly, especially systems for microcomputers. The *user interface* is the part of the operating system that determines how user friendly it is. This is the part of the operating system we interact with when using our computer and is the part with which we are most familiar. The two most common types of user interfaces are command-line interfaces, such as DOS, and graphical interfaces, such as Windows and Mac OS.

Note

If you have a computer, you should have an emergency boot disk. Sooner or later, your computer may not boot from the hard drive. You can use your emergency boot disk (usually a CD) to get your computer started. Each operating system has its own unique way of creating a boot disk. Check your operating system help files for information on how to create this disk.

Command-Line Interfaces

All early computers used command-line interfaces. With this type of interface, you must type the exact command you want to execute. One of the most widely used command-line interfaces for microcomputers is MS-DOS. Using DOS, if you want to look at a list of files on your computer's hard drive, you key the DOS command dir and press the Enter key. Figure 4-5 shows the resulting list of files you would see in the DOS interface. This type of interface is not considered very user friendly. You must memorize the commands and key them without any spelling errors. Otherwise, they do not work.

FIGURE 4-5
Command-line interface

```
C:\>dir
 Volume in drive C has no label.
 Volume Serial Number is E81A-F77B

 Directory of C:\

05/17/2004  07:47 PM    <DIR>          ARCSOFT
05/07/2004  02:04 PM             0 AUTOEXEC.BAT
05/07/2004  02:04 PM             0 CONFIG.SYS
05/07/2004  03:30 PM    <DIR>          DOCS
07/14/2004  09:42 PM    <DIR>          Documents and Settings
05/07/2004  03:25 PM    <DIR>          EZFirewall
07/13/2004  05:18 PM    <DIR>          My Documents
08/16/2004  12:31 PM    <DIR>          Program Files
05/07/2004  03:25 PM    <DIR>          Toshiba
08/05/2004  07:07 PM    <DIR>          unzipped
08/16/2004  12:34 PM    <DIR>          WINDOWS
05/07/2004  02:20 PM    <DIR>          WORKSSETUP
               2 File(s)              0 bytes
              10 Dir(s)  52,593,602,560 bytes free

C:\>_
```

Graphical User Interfaces

As microcomputer technology developed, so did the operating system interface. The next step in this progression was menus that allowed the user to choose commands from a list.

The big breakthrough in ease of use came with the development of *graphical user interfaces (GUIs)*. As mentioned earlier, the first graphical user interface for a microcomputer was Macintosh Finder. Mac OS and Windows are both operating systems that use graphical user interfaces. When the user turns on the computer and starts the operating system, a symbolic desktop is displayed. On this desktop

Computer Concepts

Macintosh popularized the first graphical user interface; however, Apple did not invent the interface. Xerox Corporation developed the idea of using pictorial icons for the interface.

are various objects, or icons (Figure 4-6). These graphical symbols represent files, disks, programs, and other objects. GUIs permit the user to manipulate these on-screen icons. Most people use a pointing device such as a mouse to click the icons and execute the commands.

FIGURE 4-6
Examples of icons in a graphical user interface

Most of today's computers come with some type of GUI. This type of interface lets you interact with your computer using pictures and symbols as opposed to text. A well-designed graphical user interface makes a computer easier to use by freeing you from memorizing complicated text commands. Instead, you point and click with a mouse, or some other type of input device, to activate programs or commands.

A true graphical interface includes standard text and graphic formats. This makes it possible for the user to share data among different programs. For instance, you can create a chart in Excel and copy it into a PowerPoint document.

STEP-BY-STEP 4.1

When you start your computer, operating system commands are loaded into memory. Each operating system starts the computer in its own individual way; when you turn on a computer, you **boot** the system. Understanding the boot process is the key to diagnosing many computer startup problems.

The Step-by-Step given in this example is based on the Windows OS system. Keep in mind, however, that the boot process is similar for all operating systems.

1. Turn on the computer. The first thing that happens is POST, an acronym for Power-on Self Test. This is a series of diagnostic tests to check RAM and to verify that the keyboard and disk drives are physically connected to the computer.

2. The BIOS (Basic Input Output System) searches for the boot record. Drive C, usually the main hard disk drive in the system, is typically the startup drive in today's computers, so that is where the BIOS will look first for the boot record. It is possible to start up the computer with a different drive, however, by changing the startup drive option in the BIOS setup screen. The BIOS is built-in software that is normally placed on a ROM chip. It contains all of the code that controls the monitor, keyboard, disk drives, and other components. This chip comes with your computer when you purchase it.

STEP-BY-STEP 4.1 Continued

3. The boot record is loaded into RAM. The boot record contains several files. These files contain programming configuration instructions for hardware devices and software applications that you may have installed on your computer.

4. Next, the software drivers are loaded. Drivers are what enable you to use your printer, modem, scanner, or other devices. Generally, when you add a new device to your system, drivers are installed for that device.

5. Next to be loaded is the GUI or graphical user interface. In this instance, the GUI is Windows. When loading the GUI, the operating system reads the commands for your desktop configuration. It also loads whatever programs you have previously specified into the Windows Startup Folder.

6. If everything goes as it should, the GUI displays the desktop and the computer is ready to use.

SUMMARY

In this lesson, you learned:

■ Hardware refers to anything you can touch.

■ Software is instructions that tell the computer what to do.

■ Software is also called a program.

■ A computer processes data by applying rules called algorithms.

■ An algorithm creates a logical progression of steps needed to accomplish a task.

■ Software development is a multistep process that includes writing the command code in a programming language, having the computer translate the code into machine language, and then debugging and testing the program.

■ The two basic types of computer software are applications software, also called productivity software, and systems software.

■ Systems software coordinates and controls the resources and operations of a computer system.

■ Three major categories of systems software are operating systems, utilities, and language translators.

■ Operating systems provide an interface between the user and application program and the computer hardware.

■ Utility programs help users complete specialized tasks such as file management.

■ Language translators convert code written in an English-based software programs into machine language.

■ All computers have operating systems.

■ Mac OS is used with Apple's Power Macintosh computers and Power Macintosh clones.

■ DOS was introduced with the IBM PC in 1981 and is a character-based operating system.

- Microsoft introduced the first version of Windows in 1987; this was an operating environment.

- Windows 95 was Microsoft's first true multitasking operating system.

- Unix is a portable operating system.

- Network operating systems allow a group of two or more microcomputers to be connected.

- The user interface is the part of the operating system with which we are most familiar.

- The two most common user interfaces are command-line interfaces and graphical user interfaces.

- Most of today's computers come with some type of graphical user interface.

- Icons are symbols that represent documents, software programs, disks, and so forth.

- A graphical interface includes standard text and graphics so that data processed in one application program can be shared by other applications.

VOCABULARY *Review*

Define the following terms:

Algorithm	Language translators	Software development
Applications software	MS-DOS	Systems software
Boot	Multitasking	Unix
Graphical user interfaces (GUIs)	Network operating system	User interface
	Operating systems	Utility software

REVIEW *Questions*

MULTIPLE CHOICE

Circle the best response for each of the following statements.

1. Another word for software is _____.
   A. hardware
   B. program
   C. algorithm
   D. interface

2. The two basic types of computer software are _____ and _____.
   A. program, applications
   B. productivity, applications
   C. applications, systems
   D. systems, networking systems

3. A group of programs that coordinate and control the resources of a computer system is called _____.
   A. systems software
   B. applications software
   C. language translator
   D. utility program

4. The _____ is the part of the operating system we interact with when using a computer.
   A. formatting utility
   B. programming statement
   C. language translator
   D. user interface

5. DOS was first introduced with the _____.
   A. Apple Macintosh
   B. IBM PC
   C. Unix operating system
   D. Windows

TRUE/FALSE

Circle T if the statement is true or F if the statement is false.

T F 1. The first step in programming is to develop machine language codes.

T F 2. DOS is a multitasking operating system.

T F 3. Debugging a program means looking for errors in the instructions to the computer.

T F 4. Computer hardware is anything you can touch.

T F 5. There are five categories of systems software.

T F 6. The second step in the progression of the operating system interface was icons.

T F 7. Word processing is an example of utility software.

T F 8. Novell NetWare is an example of a network operating system.

T F 9. One of the main features of Apple's Power Macintosh is the command-line interface.

T F 10. Multitasking means a computer user can work in several software applications at the same time.

PROJECTS

PROJECT 4-1

Operating systems have come a long way over the last few years. They are much easier to use and support many more features. If you were going to design an operating system for computers for the year 2020, what features would you include? How would your operating system be different from those that are currently available? Use your word-processing program to write a report or give an oral report to the class.

PROJECT 4-2

Think of a task or problem that a computer could solve, such as finding the answer to a math problem, or printing schedules for people who are attending a conference with different workshops, or keeping track of which costumes are loaned out and who borrowed them from a theatrical costume shop. Write an algorithm that explains the steps in the process needed to perform the task.

PROJECT 4-3

You have been asked to create an icon to represent a new software program that has just been developed. It is an interactive encyclopedia that also contains games to help reinforce the topics presented in the encyclopedia. Think about the icons on your computer's desktop or that you see in the figures showing graphical user interfaces in this chapter. Using graph paper or a computer drawing program, create an icon for this new interactive encyclopedia.

 TEAMWORK PROJECT

Your supervisor at the video store wants to buy a computer for use at home to help her son keep track of customers and billing for his lawn service, which is expanding rapidly. She has been discussing different options with you and another clerk at the store. One person suggests an Apple Macintosh with the Mac OS v.X and the latest software suite, another recommends a PC with the latest version of the Windows OS, and the third considers a PC with the Unix operating system. The supervisor decides they need to do some research to make the best choice. Working with two other people so that each of you can research a different operating system, create a report that sums up the kind of information they would find, listing the positives and negatives for each. Based on your research, decide as a group which computer you would recommend for the lawn care business.

CRITICAL*Thinking*

ACTIVITY 4-1

Recent versions of operating systems include accessibility options for people with visual or hearing disabilities. Research the operating system on your computer and complete a report on the accessibility options you can find. The Control Panel in Windows provides information about the options available.

ESSENTIAL COMPUTER SKILLS

OBJECTIVES

Upon completion of this lesson, you should be able to:

- Start and shut down a computer correctly.
- Use storage media to safely store and access data.
- Open and close a window.
- Name the parts of a window.
- Explain how to change the size of a window and switch between open windows.
- Create and manage files and folders.
- Start and exit a software program.
- Install new software.

Estimated Time: 1.5 hours

VOCABULARY

Desktop

Folder

Icons

Maximize

Menu

Menu bar

Minimize

Pointing device

Restore

Scroll bar

Taskbar

Title bar

Toolbar

Window

You have learned about computer hardware and software, how a computer processes data, inputting and outputting information, storing data, and the ways a user interfaces with a computer. Now it is time to apply this knowledge and learn some essential skills for using a computer. It is important to know how to start and shut down the computer correctly, so that no data is lost and no components are damaged. In addition, managing files and folders that store data and the media where data is stored will ensure that the information you input and process with the computer will be safe and accessible. With a graphical user interface, opening and closing software programs and windows within the programs can be accomplished with a click of your mouse. Installing new software is a straightforward task, too, with step-by-step instructions provided by the software's setup program and your computer's operating system.

1-1.1.8

Starting and Shutting Down the Computer

Starting a computer is simple. Just turn it on, and the operating system does all the work. When you turn on the computer, it first performs a self-test, which was described in Lesson 4. Next, it loads the systems software. Once the computer is up and running, you're looking at the desktop of the graphical user interface (GUI). The two most popular GUIs are the Macintosh OS and Windows.

Getting to Know Your User Interface

To work with a GUI, it is important to understand the associated terminology. Some of the more popular components are as follows:

- *Desktop:* The first screen you see when the operating system is up and fully running. It is called the desktop because the icons symbolize real objects on a real desktop.

- *Icons:* Small pictures that represent a folder, file, command, or some other computer function. You open the file or folder or execute the associated command by clicking or double-clicking an icon.

- *Pointer:* An on-screen symbol that shows the current position of the mouse. It usually appears as an arrow or an I-beam pointer.

- *Pointing device:* A device, such as a mouse or trackball, that allows the user to select objects, such as icons or text.

- *Menu:* A text interface that includes drop-down options; the user clicks on one of the choices to execute a command.

- *Scroll bar:* A horizontal or vertical bar that allows the user to control which part of a list or document is currently in the window's frame. The scroll bar makes it easy to move to any part of a file.

- *Window:* Rectangular area of the screen; used to display a program, data, or other information. Windows can be resized and moved around the screen.

> **Note**
>
> Windows is the name of the operating system for the PC. A *window* is an object within both the Macintosh and Windows operating systems.

Despite the convenience of these GUI features, it is still necessary to use a keyboard for many programs. For instance, trying to enter a document in a word processor with a mouse would be impossible.

Using the Desktop

The desktop contains windows and icons. The desktop is a graphical representation of how someone works at a desk. Working at your desk, you may look at and read documents or files, move the documents around, put them in folders, and store and retrieve them from a file drawer. The computer desktop works in a similar way. You have documents that you can read. You can store those documents in folders and retrieve those documents from folders. These documents and folders are represented by icons. These activities may seem very basic, but they are an essential part of any job. They help you stay organized.

Shutting Down the System

It is important to shut down your computer correctly to prevent damage to the components, software, and data. The operating system may run a cleanup program when you shut down the computer, and it checks to make sure all applications and data files are closed before shutting down. If you turn off the computer or unplug it without going through the shutdown process, you will see a warning screen when you start the computer again. This message will remind you that the system did not shut down properly the last time, and the operating system will check the disk drives for errors. To avoid this, shut down the computer properly every time.

> **Note**
>
> The Turn Off Computer option on the Start menu is available if your computer is configured to show the Windows XP Welcome screen for users to log on. If your computer is not set up for multiple users to log on by clicking their account name, you may instead see the option Shut Down on the Start menu.

In Windows XP, you shut down the computer by clicking the Start button and then selecting Turn Off Computer or Shut Down at the bottom of the Start menu. When the Turn off computer dialog box displays, you will see the options Stand By, Turn Off, and Restart (Figure 5-1). Select Turn Off.

FIGURE 5-1
The Windows Turn off computer dialog box

Working with Storage Media

1-1.1.8
1-1.4.2

Early personal computers used floppy disks to store data and programs. The first floppy disks for microcomputers were 5½-inch magnetic disks in plastic sleeves that really were "floppy." You could bend a disk easily—and possibly destroy what was on the disk. These disks were replaced by 3½-inch disks in a rigid plastic case that are more durable and take up less space to store, but as you learned in Lesson 2, they only store about 1.44MB of data. Other storage media, such as Zip drives and CD-R disks, are portable like floppy disks, but they can store much more data. And hard disk drives, although not portable, have a storage capacity that almost seems limitless.

In the days of true floppy disks, if you wanted to save your work on a disk, you had to format the disk first. Now most storage media, including 3½-inch floppy disks, CD-R and DVD disks, and flash memory, come preformatted and ready to use. If you ever need to format a floppy disk, it is a simple process that you can perform using My Computer.

S TEP-BY-STEP 5.1

1. On the desktop, double-click the **My Computer** icon to open the window. (If there is no My Computer icon on the desktop, click the **Start** button and then click **My Computer** in the Start menu.)

2. Click the **3½ Floppy disk (A:)** icon to select it and then move the mouse pointer over the selected icon and right-click to display the shortcut menu.

3. Select **Format** to display the Format dialog box. Most of the options shown in the dialog box can be left as they are set. You can enter a label or name for the disk in the Volume label text box.

4. To begin formatting the disk, click **Start**.

5. You will see a warning box that tells you all data on the floppy disk will be deleted. Click **OK**. The line at the bottom of the dialog box indicates the format progress.

6. Click **Close** to close the Format Results dialog box. Leave the My Computer window open for the next Step-by-Step.

>
> ### Computer Concepts
> The option Create an MS-DOS startup disk in the Format dialog box will format the disk and copy system files so the computer can be booted from the floppy disk.

> ### Note
> If you have a floppy disk with a lot of data you would like to discard, you can just reformat the disk using the Quick Format option in the Format Dialog box. Keep in mind that when you format a disk, any data contained on that disk is erased.

When a floppy disk is formatted, it is organized into tracks and sectors. A sector is pie shaped and can hold 512 bytes of data. A track is a narrow band that forms a full circle on the surface of the disk. Each track is numbered and labeled in the formatting process, and the file allocation table (FAT) on the disk logs the information about each track.

Remember that it is important to handle all storage media with care. Some precautions to take with any disk include keeping them away from magnetic fields generated by monitors, calculators, telephones, and other electronic devices. Never drink, eat, or smoke near a disk, and do not expose disks to extreme temperatures (never leave a disk in your car for any length of time to avoid this). Don't touch the flexible part of a floppy disk or the surface of a CD or DVD disk, and never set anything on top of a disk if you still want to use the data on it. Take care of your storage media and you will protect the data stored on them.

$\mathcal{O}pening\ and\ Closing\ a\ Window$

IC³
1-3.2.2

Almost everything you do within a graphical user interface requires working with windows. Windows contain the programs you run and the data with which you are working. Opening a window is as easy as double-clicking an icon. This executes a command and opens a window on the desktop. It is easy to open and close windows and to move windows from one place to another on the screen. One of the windows you may want to view often is the Recycle Bin.

To view the Recycle Bin, point to the Recycle Bin icon on the desktop and double-click the mouse. This executes the program and opens a new window. If there is anything in the Recycle Bin, it is represented by either icons or by text (see Figure 5-2). You will see that the icons in the Recycle Bin represent files and folders that have been recently deleted. You can retrieve the data in any file in the Recycle Bin. Point to the file's icon, right-click, and select Restore from the shortcut menu.

FIGURE 5-2
The Recycle Bin window

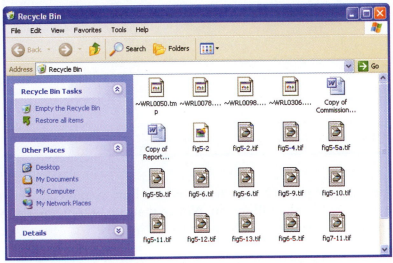

Exploring a Window

A window contains many parts (see Figure 5-3). There is a *title bar* at the top of the window, and then a *menu bar*. Most windows also include a *toolbar* below the menu bar. There may be a ruler below the toolbar and another ruler along the right side of the document window. For longer documents, you will see a scroll bar at the right of the document window that lets you quickly scroll through the file. To help you manage the desktop effectively, you have the following options you can use to manipulate windows:

FIGURE 5-3
The parts of a window

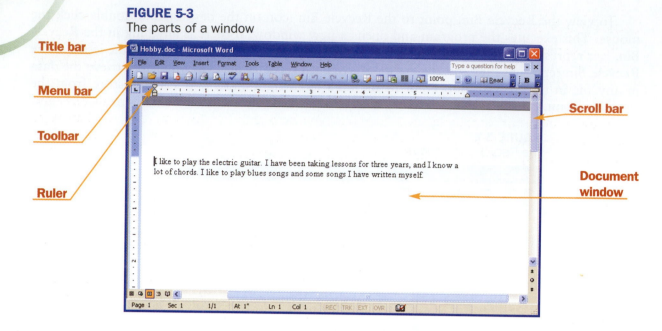

- *Maximize:* Move the mouse pointer over the Maximize button and click the button (Figure 5-4). The window fills the full screen. Notice that the graphic on the Maximize button changes and it now becomes the Restore Down button.

FIGURE 5-4
Maximize button/Restore button

Maximize   Restore Down

- *Restore Down:* Move the mouse pointer over the Restore Down button and click the button. The window returns to its previous size.

- *Minimize:* Move the mouse pointer over the Minimize button and click the button. The window disappears from the screen and is displayed as a button on the *taskbar,* the horizontal bar at the bottom of monitor screen that appears to the right of the Start button. The taskbar is shown with the Recycle Bin window minimized on it in Figure 5-5.

FIGURE 5-5
Recycle Bin displayed as button on the taskbar

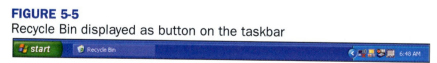

- *Move:* If you don't like where the window is located on the screen, just move it. Move the mouse pointer over the title bar. Hold down the button and drag the window to its new location. A maximized window cannot be moved.

- *Resize:* You can easily change the size of a window. Move the mouse pointer over an edge of the window; hold down the button and drag to make the window smaller or larger. You can change both the width and height of a window at the same time by dragging a corner. A maximized window connot be resized.

Closing a Window

To close the Recycle Bin window, click File to drop down the File menu and then click Close, or click the red Close button in the upper-right corner. You can close any window using either of these methods.

If you have used the Minimize button to reduce an application to a button on the taskbar and you want to close the application window, you have two choices. You can click the button to open the window and then click the Close button, or you can move the mouse pointer over the button, right-click, and then choose Close from the shortcut menu.

Working with Files and Folders

1-1.1.8

When you start using a computer you will quickly accumulate a large number of files. These files can easily become unmanageable. One of the best ways to organize your files is to do what you would do with paper files—create folders for files relating to the same subject or project. *Folders* are represented by icons that look like a traditional manila folder. You can even create and move a folder inside another folder on the Windows desktop.

STEP-BY-STEP 5.2

1. Click the **Start** button.

2. Click **My Documents** in the Start menu.

3. In the left panel of the window, in the box titled File and Folder tasks, click **Make a new folder**.

4. The new folder appears, displaying a temporary name, *New Folder*.

5. Press **Enter**.

6. In the left panel of the window, in the box titled File and Folder tasks, click **Rename this folder**. Type a name for the new folder, such as **Assignments**. (Your instructor may tell you to give the folder a different name.)

7. Press **Enter**.

8. Click the red **Close** button in the upper right of the window to close My Documents.

To delete a folder in the My Documents window, click the folder icon to select it, and then, in the left panel of the window, in the File and Folder tasks box, click Delete this folder. Or you can move the mouse pointer over the selected folder and then right-click. Select Delete from the shortcut menu. In response to the Confirm Folder Delete dialog box, click Yes. Or click the folder, hold down the mouse button, and drag the folder to the Recycle Bin.

> **Note** ☑
>
> In the My Documents window, you can also open the File menu and choose options that include New (to make a new folder), Delete, and Rename.

Managing Files

You can move a file or copy a file from one folder to another or from one disk to another. You cannot, however, have more than one file in a folder with the same name. You can also move, copy, and delete entire folders.

Moving a File

When you move a file, it is copied to a new location. The version in the original location is erased. You will find this feature very useful if you want to organize or reorganize files by moving them into folders.

STEP-BY-STEP 5.3

1. Click the **Start** button.

2. Point to **All Programs** on the Start menu, and then point to **Accessories** to see a list of programs.

3. Click **Windows Explorer**.

4. You will see a list of folders on the left and icons representing folders in the window on the right. Click either the folder name in the list or the folder icon to view the files in the folder.

5. Move the mouse pointer over the icon for the file you want to move and right-click to display the shortcut menu (Figure 5-6). Click **Cut**.

FIGURE 5-6
Moving a file

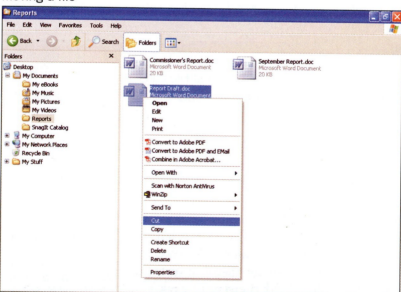

6. Locate the destination folder in the list on the left. Move the mouse pointer over the selected folder and right-click to display the shortcut menu. Click **Paste** to move your file into the destination folder.

You can also click and drag the file from one location to another.

Copying a File

When you copy a file, you create an exact duplicate of your original file. For example, you may want to transfer a copy from your hard disk drive at home to a floppy so you can transport it to a different computer. Or you may want to share a copy of a file with a friend. With one exception, you use the same basic procedure to copy a file as you do to move a file.

STEP-BY-STEP 5.4

1. In the Windows Explorer window, you will see a list of folders on the left and icons representing folders in the window on the right. Click either the folder name in the list or the folder icon to view the files in the folder.

2. Move the mouse pointer over the icon for the file you want to copy and right-click to display the shortcut menu (Figure 5-7). Click **Copy**.

FIGURE 5-7
Copying a file

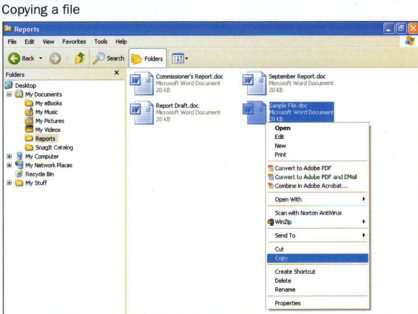

3. Locate the destination folder in the list on the left. Move the mouse pointer over the selected folder and right-click to display the shortcut menu. Click **Paste** to copy your file into the destination folder.

Deleting a File

To delete a file in Windows Explorer, open the folder where the file is located to display the file icons, select the file, right-click to display the shortcut menu, and select Delete. When you delete a file, it is removed from the list of available files and it is sent to the Recycle Bin. Remember, if you discover you have deleted the wrong file or need to retrieve a deleted file, it is easy to recover the file as long as you have not "emptied" the bin. Simply open the Recycle Bin, select the file you want to recover, right-click, and select Restore.

Selecting Files

You've already learned how to copy and/or delete a single file. But what if you have a group of files you would like to delete? It could be a time-consuming chore if you had to do these one by one. Fortunately, you can easily select a group of files. The files can be next to each other or they can be separated by other files.

In the Windows Explorer window, to select a group of adjacent files, click the first file to select it. Then hold down the Shift key and select the last file in the list. The selected files will be highlighted, as shown in Figure 5-8.

FIGURE 5-8
Adjacent selected files

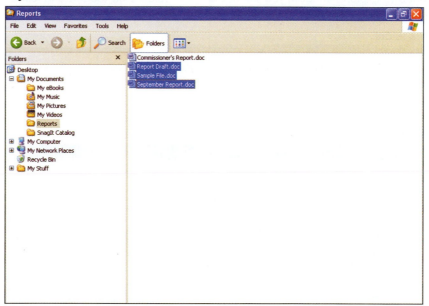

 **Ethics in Technology**

WHAT ARE COMPUTER ETHICS?

Webster's Online Dictionary[1] offers the following definition of ethics:
1. Motivation based on ideas of right and wrong.
2. The philosophical study of moral values and rules.

Ethical judgments are no different in the area of computing than they are in any other field. The use of computers can raise many issues of privacy, copyright, theft, and power, to name just a few. Computer users may be motivated based on ethical or moral judgments, or they may skirt or disregard "correct" behavior. In 1990 the Institute of Electrical and Electronics Engineers created a code of ethics, which you can view at *www.ieee.org* and by selecting About IEEE and then clicking Code of Ethics in the submenu. Many businesses and organizations have adopted this code as ethical guidelines to govern computer use. Remember that this is just a code—not a law. People choose to follow it voluntarily.

1 Webster's Online Dictionary: *www.websters-online-dictionary.org/definition/english/et/ethics.html*

To select a group of nonadjacent files, select the first file, hold down the Control key, and click the remaining filenames you want to select. All the selected files, even though they are separated in the list, will be highlighted, as shown in Figure 5-9.

FIGURE 5-9
Nonadjacent selected files

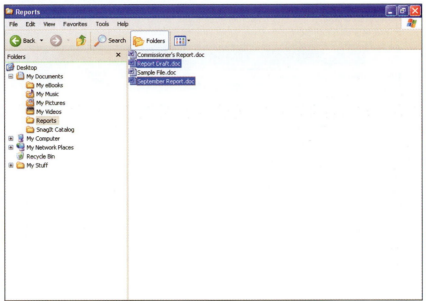

After you select the files, move the mouse pointer over any of the selected filenames, right-click to display the context menu, and then choose Delete or Copy.

Starting and Exiting a Program

1-1.1.8
1-3.2.4

The Recycle Bin is a utility program, so when you opened the Recycle Bin window, you actually started a program. Let's look at how to open a program that is not represented by an icon on the desktop, and that is what most people mean when they talk about computer software—an application program. We will start an application program called WordPad.

STEP-BY-STEP 5.5

1. Click the **Start** button.

2. Point to **All Programs**, then **Accessories**, and then click **WordPad**.

3. Key a sentence or two about your favorite hobby.

4. On the File menu, click **Save**.

STEP-BY-STEP 5.5 Continued

5. The Save As dialog box will open because the file has never been saved before (Figure 5-10). Click the **Save in** drop-down arrow and click the **My Documents** folder if it is not already showing in the text box. You will see the contents of the My Documents folder listed in the window.

FIGURE 5-10
Save As dialog box

6. Double-click the **Assignments** folder; this opens the folder so you can store your data within the folder.

7. In the File name text box, key **Hobby**.

8. In the Save as type text box, click the drop-down arrow and select **Rich Text Format (RTF)** if it is not already in the text box.

9. Click **Save** to save your file and close the Windows Explorer window.

Switching Between Windows

Another advantage of working with a GUI is that you can have many windows open at one time. For instance, suppose you want to open a graphics program and a word-processing program and switch back and forth between the two. This is very easy to do.

S TEP-BY-STEP 5.6

1. Click the **Start** button.

2. Point to **All Programs**, then **Accessories**, and then click **Paint**. The Paint program opens in its maximized state. Click the **Restore Down** button. You now have two programs open on the desktop—WordPad and Paint.

3. To move the window you want to work with to the front, move the mouse pointer over its taskbar button and click the button. Figure 5-11 shows the open WordPad window in the same screen as the open Paint window.

FIGURE 5-11
Two open windows

This example illustrates only two open programs. However, you can have as many open programs as the memory in your computer will support. You can also have more than one instance of the same program open; that is, you can have two or more WordPad document windows open, and so forth.

When you have several windows open at the same time, only one window is active. The title in the active window's title bar will appear in dark or bright lettering; the other windows will have shaded titles in their title bars.

Exiting a Program

Exit a program by closing the program window. Click the Close button in the upper-right corner of the window, or select Close from the program menu. You can access the program menu by clicking the program icon at the far left of the title bar. You can also select the Exit command from the File menu to exit a program. Be sure to save any open documents first; most programs will display a message box warning you to save open documents before exiting the program if you have not done so (Figure 5-12).

FIGURE 5-12
Save changes message box

Installing New Software

1-2.1.3
1-3.3.6
1-3.3.7

Your computer may have many software programs already installed, but at some point you will want to install a new applications program, or perhaps an updated version of a program you already have. Installing new software is a simple procedure that starts by inserting the disk (usually a CD-ROM, but some programs still come on floppy disks) into the appropriate disk drive. You also can download a program from a Web site, and the same basic instructions apply for installing downloaded software.

Computer Concepts

Freeware is software that is distributed to users, usually through a Web site, at no cost. The author of the program still owns the copyright for the software, so if you download a freeware program, you may only use it for your personal use. You cannot legally distribute it to anyone else without the author's permission.

STEP-BY-STEP 5.7

1. Close the WordPad and Paint programs if you have not already done so.

2. Insert the new software disk in the appropriate disk drive.

3. In a CD drive, inserting the disk may automatically open a window showing the files on the disk. If the program is on a floppy disk, open Windows Explorer and click **3½ inch Floppy (A:)** (or a similar designation for the floppy disk drive) to list the files on the disk.

4. Find the file called Setup or Install or a file with a similar name. Double-click the filename to start it.

5. You will see a screen telling you the Installation wizard is preparing to install the new software. You will probably also have to click a button that indicates you agree to the terms of use for the software program you are installing. You can scroll through the terms in a text box and then click the agreement button to continue.

STEP-BY-STEP 5.7 Continued

6. Follow the steps shown in the Installation wizard message boxes (such as the one in Figure 5-13) to completely install the program. You may be asked what elements of the program you want to install, where you want to install it, and other options. It is usually a good idea to accept the options the Installation wizard suggests for these decisions.

FIGURE 5-13
A software Installation wizard message box

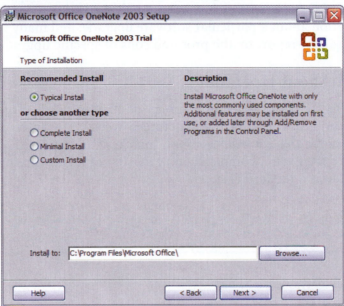

7. When the installation is complete, the Installation wizard may indicate that the computer needs to reboot before the program will be available. If you see this message, be sure all other programs are closed before clicking **OK** or **Finish** to reboot the system.

8. After the computer restarts, you can double-click the shortcut icon for the new program on the desktop (or find the name of the program in the All Programs list and click it) to start the program.

9. You may be asked to register the program. If you have an Internet connection, you can register the program immediately; if not, click the Register Later option to begin using the program. It is a good idea to register a new software program so that you can take advantage of technical support and upgrades offered by the software company.

> **Note** ☑
> Some programs require a key number or code that must be entered to install or register them. You can usually find this code on the program disk or on the software's packaging.

Software Upgrades

Software is always being revised and changed. We have already examined the many versions of operating systems that have been developed in the past few years. In Lesson 4 you learned about Windows 95, Windows 98, Windows 2000, and Windows XP. Sometimes you can upgrade an existing program by installing some additional code, but some upgrades are so extensive they require you to install completely new programs.

Applications software is upgraded also, and like systems software upgrades, the new versions include new features. Software is also upgraded to fix problems (or bugs) that have been reported and to make the software more compatible with other products, such as newer hardware or a new operating system.

It is often beneficial to upgrade software, especially when the new program offers convenient and up-to-the-minute features. But there are also negative aspects of upgrading. For example, you may run into compatibility problems if you try to install newer software on older hardware, or the new program may create conflicts with other software installed on your computer. Sometimes if you upgrade to a new version too soon, you risk problems with software that was released too quickly and may have bugs that were not all worked out yet. A manufacturer's Web site may offer information about a particular software upgrade, and many independent Web sites and industry news regularly report on the pros and cons of specific upgrades.

Staying Informed About Upgrades

If you register software with the manufacturer, you may be notified of upgrades to the program by e-mail. You can also check the manufacturer's Web site for information about the most recent versions of the software. Sometimes minor "patches" and updated material are offered to registered users at no cost. Even a completely new version of a software program may be available to a registered user at a reduced cost.

SUMMARY

In this lesson, you learned:

- When you turn on your computer, the operating system performs all the necessary startup tasks automatically.

- Some of the components of a GUI are the desktop, icons, pointer, pointing device, menus, scroll bar, and windows.

- The desktop is a representation of how people work at a desk and contains windows and icons.

- Shut down the computer using the operating system's Shut Down or Turn Off Computer command to prevent damage to components, software, and data.

- Formatting is the process of preparing a disk so it can be used to write data to and read data from the disk. Most disk media today are preformatted, but you can reformat a disk to erase all the information on it.

- Click or double-click an icon to open a window.

- You can move a window, resize it, maximize it, minimize it, or restore it to its original size.

- Close a window by clicking the Close button at the upper-right corner of the screen.

- Use folders to organize your files.

- Delete folders and files by right-clicking on the folder or filename and using the shortcut menu's Delete command or by dragging it to the Recycle Bin.

- When you move a file, it is moved to a new location.

■ When you copy a file, you create a duplicate of your original file in another location.

■ You can select, move, copy, or delete a group of adjacent or nonadjacent files and folders.

■ You can start a software program by clicking on its name in the All Programs list on the Start menu.

■ You can have several windows and/or programs open at one time and can switch between open windows.

■ The title bar of the active window in your screen has a title in dark or bright lettering; other open windows in the same screen will have shaded titles.

■ To install new software, you start the Install or Setup file and follow the instructions in the Installation wizard.

■ It is a good idea to register new software to take advantage of the technical support and upgrades offered by the software company.

■ Software upgrades can offer new features and fix bugs, but some upgrades may also cause compatibility problems or might be released before they are problem-free.

VOCABULARY *Review*

Define the following terms:

Desktop	Menu bar	Taskbar
Folder	Minimize	Title bar
Icons	Pointing device	Toolbar
Maximize	Restore	Window
Menu	Scroll bar	

REVIEW *Questions*

MULTIPLE CHOICE

Circle the best response for each of the following statements.

1. The _____ is the first screen you see after the operating system is loaded.
   A. WordPad
   B. menu options
   C. desktop
   D. format

2. To keep your files organized, you create_____.
   A. menus
   B. icons
   C. folders
   D. desktops

3. Graphical representations of files and programs are called _____.
   A. icons
   B. menus
   C. pictures
   D. scroll bars

4. To move a window, move the mouse pointer over the _____, press the left mouse button, and drag.
   A. scroll bar
   B. icon
   C. desktop
   D. title bar

5. When you create a duplicate of a file, you are _____ the file.
   A. moving
   B. copying
   C. deleting
   D. executing

6. A small picture representing a file or folder is called a(n) _____.
   A. menu
   B. taskbar
   C. icon
   D. detail

7. The Recycle Bin allows you to retrieve a deleted file by using the _____ command.
   A. Undelete
   B. Undo
   C. Retrieve
   D. Restore

8. A new version of a software program is called a(n) _____.
   A. upgrade
   B. application
   C. bug
   D. wizard

9. Find an Install or _____ program file to install new software.
   A. Configure
   B. Setup
   C. Menu
   D. Format

10. A new software program can be installed from any of the following sources *except* a(n) _____.
   A. downloaded file
   B. output device
   C. CD disk
   D. floppy disk

TRUE/FALSE

Circle T if the statement is true or F if the statement is false.

T F **1.** You can only copy files, not move them.

T F **2.** You can only open one window at a time.

T F **3.** A pointer is usually seen as an I-beam or arrow on the screen.

T F **4.** Formatting a disk erases any data it contained.

T F **5.** To select a group of adjacent files, select the first file, then hold down the Shift key and select the last file in the group.

T F **6.** The toolbar provides drop-down options from which to choose commands.

T F **7.** A window can be resized or minimized to a button on the taskbar.

T F **8.** To close a window, you click its Quit button.

T F **9.** You can close a window that is minimized simply by double-clicking its button on the taskbar.

T F **10.** The Program wizard guides you through the process of installing new software.

PROJECTS

PROJECT 5-1

Examine the desktop of the computer you are using and write a report on the various elements on the desktop. Describe the system you are using and then describe what you think is the best operating system—a visual system with icons or a text-based system.

PROJECT 5-2

If your computer has the Windows XP tour installed (look in the Accessories list in All Programs for a program called *Tour Windows XP*), click on the program name to open it. Your instructor will tell you if your computer can run the animated tour with sound, or if you should choose the non-animated tour with text and images. Click Next to start the tour. Choose Windows XP Basics. When you have finished the tour, write a short report about what you learned.

PROJECT 5-3

Use an Internet search engine such as Google or AltaVista to search for a freeware program that offers a way to keep track of your assignments or work projects. Use a keyword such as *freeware assignment calendar*. With your instructor's permission, download the program (following the instructions on the Web site) and then install it by starting the Install or Setup program.

TEAMWORK PROJECT

You now have some information and knowledge about using a computer. Team up with a friend or coworker and create an outline for a training program. Include all the main elements that you think are necessary for someone to be an effective computer user.

CRITICAL *Thinking*

ACTIVITY 5-1

In a work environment, you often find yourself working with other people as a group. You may be one of a group of food service employees working together in a restaurant or you may work with a group of people who are responsible for restocking shelves in a retail store. Now think about putting groups of files into folders. Are there any similarities between this and people working together as groups? Any differences? Make a table listing similarities and differences between files in folders and people in work groups.

USING TECHNOLOGY TO SOLVE PROBLEMS

OBJECTIVES

Upon completion of this lesson, you should be able to:

- Define problem solving.
- Identify technology tools for solving problems.
- Identify problem-solving steps.
- Identify fundamental concepts of software applications including word processing, spreadsheets, databases, graphics and multimedia, and presentation software.
- Explain how computer software can be used to solve problems.
- Explain how other forms of technology are used to solve problems.

Estimated Time: 1.5 hours

VOCABULARY

Database

Database software

Distance learning

Graphics software

Multimedia software

Personal information management software (PIMS)

Presentation software

Problem solving

Relational database

Search engines

Spreadsheet

Spreadsheet software

Technology

Telecommunications

Teleconferencing

Word-processing software

Did your supervisor ask you to write a report on quarterly sales? Did your math instructor assign you to find the average temperatures for a month in your town? Did your adviser for Future Business Leaders of America ask for a printout of all members who have still not paid their dues or to determine how much candy you would need to sell to make a $250 profit? Do you have a friend who has a disability that prevents him or her from being able to key information into the computer? If you can answer "yes" to even one of these scenarios, technology can provide a solution to your problem!

Problem Solving

Technology is the application of scientific discoveries to the production of goods and services that improve the human environment. The computer is a major element of technology and has aided in improvements in medical research, space travel, and exploration, just to name a few.

Technology provides tools for solving problems. You may encounter situations with problems that can affect business operations as well as how you live your own life. Technology is responsible for transporting us to a make-believe universe when we play video games, and it makes getting cash as easy as locating an ATM machine, any time of the day or night. Technology simplifies business communications when employees send messages, memos, or presentations over networks. The Internet's capabilities are endless.

The computer plays a major role in the technology boom. It addresses and solves many of the technical types of issues and concerns in our society. A basic function of a computer is to solve problems, that is, to answer questions and to provide an easier and better way to perform certain tasks (Figure 6-1). Computer software controls the versatility of the computer. With the appropriate software, you can solve just about any problem or simplify any task.

FIGURE 6-1
Clockwise from upper left: A technician uses a computer to evaluate data; students use a variety of computers for researching and writing papers; a scientist is using a computer containing a special math processor to conduct an experiment; a businessperson is using a computer to keep track of inventory

The amount and kinds of technology available are astounding. You can find technology for almost every situation, from finding and purchasing stock over the Internet to finding personnel for a space shuttle!

Selecting the correct technology to address a specific task or problem requires careful investigation. A logical guideline needs to be followed in order to identify the situation that could use technology to alleviate problems or to enhance a specific task and to identify the exact technology that would address the situation.

Steps in the Problem-Solving Process

*P*roblem solving is a systematic approach leading from an initial situation to a desired situation that is subject to some resource constraints.

To solve a problem successfully, we must apply a logical plan that will act as a guide or road map. It will assist in defining the problem, gathering information concerning the problem, identifying possible solutions, and selecting and implementing the best solution. A guide is listed here.

- Define the problem.

- Investigate and analyze the problem.

- Identify possible solutions.

- Select and implement a solution.

- Evaluate solutions.

Each of the listed steps is very important in the problem-solving process. Each step should be fully completed before going to the next step. Let's explore each step closely.

Define the Problem

In this stage, you ensure that there really is a problem and identify what it is. Sometimes the problem may not be as transparent as you might think. You need to investigate the situation to determine the real issue. Ask questions, use what-if statements, eliminate some facts, include others, clarify the current situation, and identify what the situation should be or perhaps what you would like it to be. If necessary, make notes or sketches.

Investigate and Analyze the Problem

Before you can begin to solve the problem, you need all the facts. Collect all available data regarding the situation. Determine why the problem exists and its possible causes. This step will provide information needed to make an accurate decision. Sometimes during this step, you may decide that a problem really does not exist at all or that what you thought was the problem is actually being caused by something else. However, if there is a legitimate problem or need, your detective work at this stage should provide you with information you need to solve the problem.

Identify Possible Solutions

Once the problem has been pinpointed, possible solutions need to be identified. What can be done to alleviate the problem? What needs to be done differently? What needs to be deleted or added? These are the types of questions that need to be answered as you look for a solution. In exploring possible answers, you may identify several solutions.

Select and Implement a Solution

If more than one possible solution is identified, critique and test each solution to determine what would be the outcome of the situation. Based on this information, choose the solution that provides the best outcome. Once the solution is selected, implement it.

Evaluate Solutions

After putting the chosen solution into place, you will need to evaluate its performance. Did it eliminate the problem? Did it accomplish what you needed to have done? If your answer is yes, you now have a solution to a situation that caused you concern.

Technological Tools Can Help Solve Problems

1-2.2.1
1-2.2.2
1-2.2.3

Now that we have discussed the guidelines for solving problems using technology, let's use it to solve a company's scheduling problem. Employees have been missing meetings, so let's explore how technology can help with this issue.

Define the problem:

What needs to be accomplished? What information is needed and how is it to be presented?

- Select appropriate software to be used

- Eliminate scheduling conflicts

- Know employees' schedules

Investigate and analyze the problem:

- How can a manager know all employees' schedules?

 Ethics in Technology

WHO IS RESPONSIBLE?

Increasingly, computers participate in decisions that affect human lives. Consider medical safety, for instance, and think about the fact that just about everything in a hospital is tied to a computer. So what happens if these machines don't produce the expected results? What happens if they have been incorrectly programmed?

When programmers write a program, they check for as many conditions as possible. But there is always the chance they might miss one. So what happens if a computer malfunctions and applies a high dosage of radiation? What if two medications are prescribed to an individual and the computer doesn't indicate the medications are incompatible? Imagine the consequences if someone called for an ambulance and the dispatch system didn't work. Then the question becomes who is responsible for these mishaps. Is it the programmer? Is it the company who sold the software or hardware? Is it the person who administered the radiation treatment?

The incidents described here actually happened. These are ethical issues that are being decided in court.

- How can a manager notify all employees of a meeting in a timely fashion?

- What type of software is available for these needs?

  Identify solutions:

- Use word-processing software to key a memo to send to all employees announcing a meeting.

- Manually check everyone's schedule to see when they are at work and available for a meeting.

- Identify a software program that can be used to enter and maintain employees' schedules, has the capability to notify employees of meetings, and will let a manager know that they have received the message.

  Select and implement a solution:

  After studying the possible solutions, it was decided that the company would purchase a specialized software program to solve the problem of missed meetings.

Choosing the Right Software

Computers and the Internet have made it much easier to find solutions to many of the tasks that individuals and businesses need to address on a daily basis. Typical software programs used are word processing, database, spreadsheet, utility programs, scheduling, collaboration, telecommunications, and multimedia (graphics, animation, digital video, sound, authoring, presentation).

Once you have learned to use the mechanics of computer software, you can determine how to use this software to perform various types of tasks. Here are some examples:

- *Word-processing software* is used to key data, but it has many applications that it can perform other than just keying. What are these applications and how can you use them to, say, prepare envelopes for a group of customers?

- Web pages can be designed using HTML codes or word-processing software. You have just started a new small business and want to advertise on the Internet. How can you go about having a Web page prepared?

- You know that grades can be averaged in a spreadsheet, but how can you determine what grade you would need to make on the final exam to receive an "A" in your math course?

All of these situations pose problems that need to be solved or at least pose situations that could benefit from some type of technology. Each software application mentioned can solve one of the problems. However, you will need to determine which software program to use and how to use its capabilities to solve the problem at hand. It is important to choose the best application available. For example, use a spreadsheet program to track your company's financial information, and you will discover that the program suits the task and gives you output that is effective and useful. But if you use that spreadsheet program to generate memos to your employees about company sales, you

> ### Computer Concepts
>
> Many word-processing programs have advanced features that allow you to perform spreadsheet and database-like functions. You can create files using mathematical functions similar to those found in spreadsheet programs. Data files can be created that can be sorted, selected, and even merged into other documents.

will be frustrated by the spreadsheet application's lack of appropriate tools for creating a memo. Sometimes software must be developed or at least modified to be effective for a specific task.

Specialized technology is used almost everywhere you look today. It assists in the development of new treatments in the medical field, guides you through tourist attractions such as museums, simulates space travel, assists law enforcement activities, and makes those special effects in movies seem so real.

Software Solutions

There are many different types of software programs available to address various types of applications. Popular software offers programs for general use by students, business people, individuals, and organizations. There is also computer software for specialized areas such as banking, medicine, real estate, insurance, law, and so forth.

Word-Processing Software

There are several word-processing programs. Microsoft Word, WordPerfect, and Lotus WordPro are just a few. Word-processing software allows you to create and modify documents such as the one shown in Figure 6-2. It greatly reduces the need for keying documents. Most word-processing programs have features that make creating various types of documents such as newsletters, memos, reports, and tables an easy task. The merge feature saves hours in preparing multiple documents. Do you need an alphabetical listing of members of an organization? This is a simple task for word-processing software. Footnotes and endnotes can be entered effortlessly. This software addresses many of the document needs of an organization or individual.

FIGURE 6-2
Word-processing document

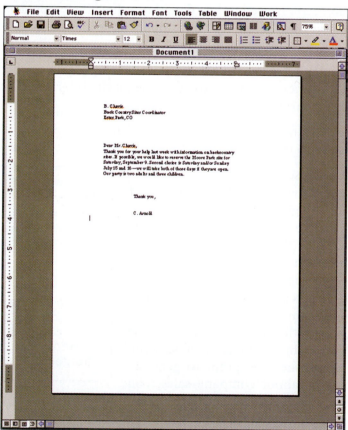

When application software was first developed for microcomputers, desktop publishing was a separate category of software. Now, word-processing programs offer so many formatting options that the two types of software have merged. You can prepare an entire book complete with illustrations, tables, and index using word-processing software. You can even create a Web page using word processing, and then "publish" it to a Web-friendly format automatically.

Spreadsheet Software

Programs that create spreadsheets, such as Microsoft Excel or Lotus 1-2-3, are designed to store and manipulate numeric data. They are used extensively in business to produce financial analyses such as budgets, financial statements, and forecasts (Figure 6-3). Businesses can use spreadsheets to create pricing models that help a company analyze sales of a product or service.

FIGURE 6-3
Spreadsheets are used for documents such as budgets and inventories

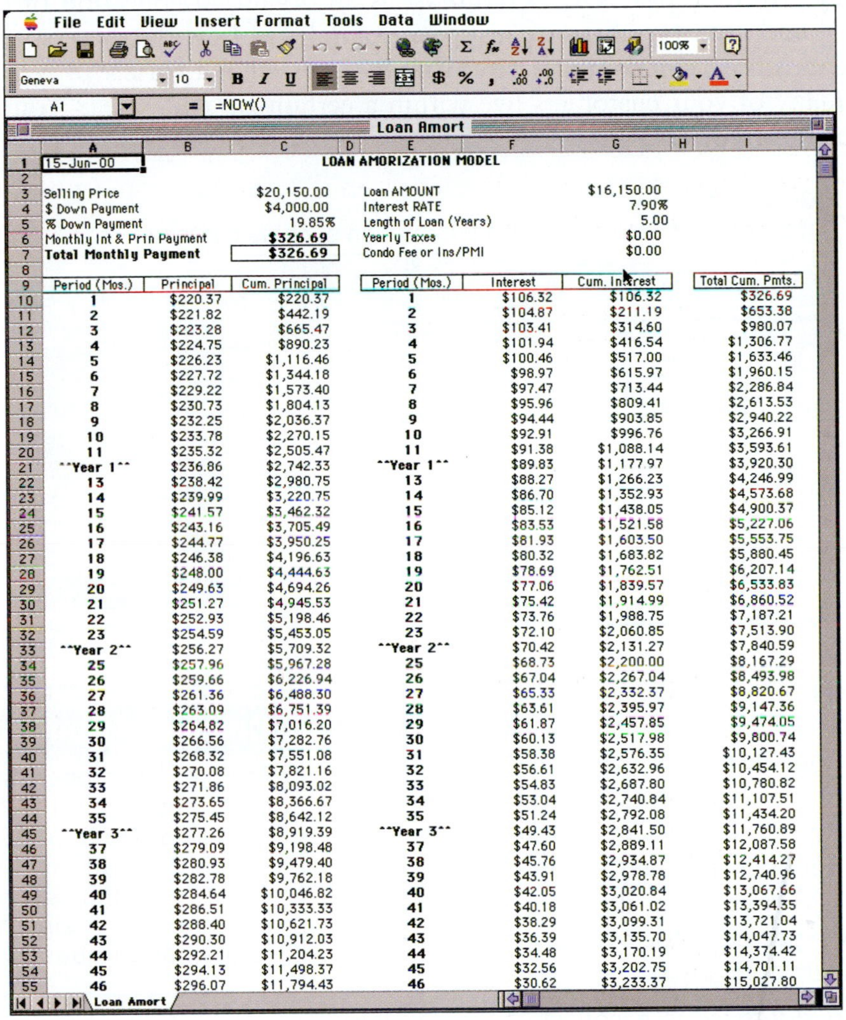

	A	B	C	E	F	G	I
1	15-Jun-00			LOAN AMORIZATION MODEL			
2							
3	Selling Price		$20,150.00	Loan AMOUNT		$16,150.00	
4	$ Down Payment		$4,000.00	Interest RATE		7.90%	
5	% Down Payment		19.85%	Length of Loan (Years)		5.00	
6	Monthly Int & Prin Payment		**$326.69**	Yearly Taxes		$0.00	
7	**Total Monthly Payment**		**$326.69**	Condo Fee or Ins/PMI		$0.00	
8							
9	Period (Mos.)	Principal	Cum. Principal	Period (Mos.)	Interest	Cum. Interest	Total Cum. Pmts.
10	1	$220.37	$220.37	1	$106.32	$106.32	$326.69
11	2	$221.82	$442.19	2	$104.87	$211.19	$653.38
12	3	$223.28	$665.47	3	$103.41	$314.60	$980.07
13	4	$224.75	$890.23	4	$101.94	$416.54	$1,306.77
14	5	$226.23	$1,116.46	5	$100.46	$517.00	$1,633.46
15	6	$227.72	$1,344.18	6	$98.97	$615.97	$1,960.15
16	7	$229.22	$1,573.40	7	$97.47	$713.44	$2,286.84
17	8	$230.73	$1,804.13	8	$95.96	$809.41	$2,613.53
18	9	$232.25	$2,036.37	9	$94.44	$903.85	$2,940.22
19	10	$233.78	$2,270.15	10	$92.91	$996.76	$3,266.91
20	11	$235.32	$2,505.47	11	$91.38	$1,088.14	$3,593.61
21	^^Year 1^^	$236.86	$2,742.33	^^Year 1^^	$89.83	$1,177.97	$3,920.30
22	13	$238.42	$2,980.75	13	$88.27	$1,266.23	$4,246.99
23	14	$239.99	$3,220.75	14	$86.70	$1,352.93	$4,573.68
24	15	$241.57	$3,462.32	15	$85.12	$1,438.05	$4,900.37
25	16	$243.16	$3,705.49	16	$83.53	$1,521.58	$5,227.06
26	17	$244.77	$3,950.25	17	$81.93	$1,603.50	$5,553.75
27	18	$246.38	$4,196.63	18	$80.32	$1,683.82	$5,880.45
28	19	$248.00	$4,444.63	19	$78.69	$1,762.51	$6,207.14
29	20	$249.63	$4,694.26	20	$77.06	$1,839.57	$6,533.83
30	21	$251.27	$4,945.53	21	$75.42	$1,914.99	$6,860.52
31	22	$252.93	$5,198.46	22	$73.76	$1,988.75	$7,187.21
32	23	$254.59	$5,453.05	23	$72.10	$2,060.85	$7,513.90
33	^^Year 2^^	$256.27	$5,709.32	^^Year 2^^	$70.42	$2,131.27	$7,840.59
34	25	$257.96	$5,967.28	25	$68.73	$2,200.00	$8,167.29
35	26	$259.66	$6,226.94	26	$67.04	$2,267.04	$8,493.98
36	27	$261.36	$6,488.30	27	$65.33	$2,332.37	$8,820.67
37	28	$263.09	$6,751.39	28	$63.61	$2,395.97	$9,147.36
38	29	$264.82	$7,016.20	29	$61.87	$2,457.85	$9,474.05
39	30	$266.56	$7,282.76	30	$60.13	$2,517.98	$9,800.74
40	31	$268.32	$7,551.08	31	$58.38	$2,576.35	$10,127.43
41	32	$270.08	$7,821.16	32	$56.61	$2,632.96	$10,454.12
42	33	$271.86	$8,093.02	33	$54.83	$2,687.80	$10,780.82
43	34	$273.65	$8,366.67	34	$53.04	$2,740.84	$11,107.51
44	35	$275.45	$8,642.12	35	$51.24	$2,792.08	$11,434.20
45	^^Year 3^^	$277.26	$8,919.39	^^Year 3^^	$49.43	$2,841.50	$11,760.89
46	37	$279.09	$9,198.48	37	$47.60	$2,889.11	$12,087.58
47	38	$280.93	$9,479.40	38	$45.76	$2,934.87	$12,414.27
48	39	$282.78	$9,762.18	39	$43.91	$2,978.78	$12,740.96
49	40	$284.64	$10,046.82	40	$42.05	$3,020.84	$13,067.66
50	41	$286.51	$10,333.33	41	$40.18	$3,061.02	$13,394.35
51	42	$288.40	$10,621.73	42	$38.29	$3,099.31	$13,721.04
52	43	$290.30	$10,912.03	43	$36.39	$3,135.70	$14,047.73
53	44	$292.21	$11,204.23	44	$34.48	$3,170.19	$14,374.42
54	45	$294.13	$11,498.37	45	$32.56	$3,202.75	$14,701.11
55	46	$296.07	$11,794.43	46	$30.62	$3,233.37	$15,027.80

A *spreadsheet* (or worksheet) is an organized table of financial or other numerical information, arranged in rows and columns. The place where a row and column intersect is called a *cell*. Data and formulas are entered into spreadsheet cells to calculate various conditions. The beauty of the spreadsheet is its ability to recalculate itself when different information is entered. Spreadsheets are organized into workbooks (a group of worksheets) and can include numerical values and textual data as well as formulas, functions, and variables. The output of a worksheet can be configured into charts and graphs that illustrate the data.

Spreadsheet software has become a vital tool to businesses because it helps in predicting the outcome of various situations and factors. There are times when businesses need to know what an outcome will be under certain circumstances. Spreadsheet software offers the ability to forecast with "what-if" statements. The information in a spreadsheet can be sorted, filtered, and analyzed. It is quite evident how this type of software solves problems for businesses. Spreadsheets have other applications as well, such as organizing student grade sheets, tracking household expenses, and preparing a nonprofit group's tax records.

Database Software

Database software makes it possible to create and maintain large collections of data. This type of software is critical to the success of many businesses. A few database products are Microsoft Access, dBASE, and SOL. A *database* is an organized collection of data. Customer lists (Figure 6-4) and inventory lists are just two examples of how database software is used in business. The data stored in a database can easily be accessed in a variety of ways. Do you need to know how many of your customers live within a certain zip code area? Your database software can render this information.

FIGURE 6-4
Database documents organize information such as customer lists

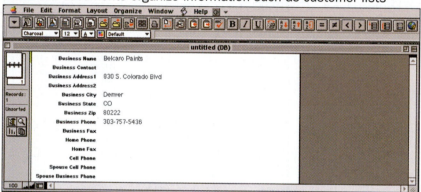

The information in a database is organized into fields (a column of one type of information, such as names or telephone numbers), records (all the data in one row or entry), and tables (a set of fields and entries). Key fields are fields with data used to sort the database. The data can be used to create reports and forms, and the entries in a database table can be queried to find specific information (like those customers within a zip code area).

A *relational database* is a collection of database

> **Computer Concepts**
>
> An IBM researcher named E. F. Codd developed the first relational database in 1970. In 1985, Dr. Codd published a set of 12 rules that serve as guidelines for the design of almost all relational databases today.

tables that are connected to each other. Changing the data in one will change related data in another table, the tables can be cross-referenced, and the entire database can be searched for information without knowing how it is organized. A good example of a relational database is a computerized library catalog. Many databases that hold information about the library's collection of books, movies, audiotapes, and other media make up the catalog, and a library patron can search them quickly and easily to find what they want. A nonrelational database, one consisting of only a single database table, is sometimes called a flat file database.

Enterprise databases are vast and complex relational databases used in industry. For example, an airline reservation system is an enterprise database. A relational database may also be used effectively in a much smaller application, such as a database of church members that includes cross-referenced tables of all registered church members, employees, Sunday school attendees, and other categories.

Presentation Software

Businesses and individuals use *presentation software* to create automated slide shows. Examples of presentation programs include Microsoft PowerPoint and WordPerfect Presentations. A company can create a presentation about their services to show a client, and the program will also generate handouts and speaker's notes to help the person presenting the slide show. You can create animated sequences in a slide and transitions that lead the viewers from one slide to the next. You can also add sound to a slide show presentation. In fact, presentation programs are a type of multimedia software, since they can include both images and sound. A slide show can be shown directly on a computer monitor, or a projector attached to the computer can project the output to a screen. You can even use presentation software to create a slide show that will be viewed on a Web site.

The slides in a slide show are created by using slide masters, which are templates you can use to produce a presentation with a unifying design and a variety of slide types, such as titles, bullet points, text, and graphics such as photographs, clip art, and charts.

The information in a slide show is presented in an active, exciting format to hold an audience's attention. The value of this kind of program for businesses is apparent, as it can be used to advertise products and services, train employees, distribute company reports and statistics, and communicate news and publicity. Slide shows created in presentation software may also be used by an instructor to illustrate a lecture, or by a student to create a multimedia report.

FIGURE 6-5
A slide in a presentation

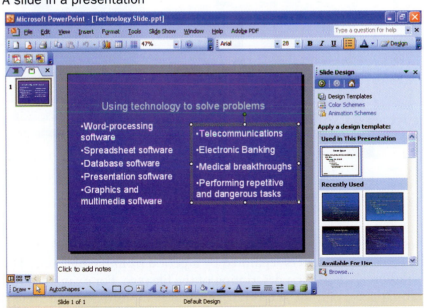

Graphics and Multimedia Software

The category of software referred to as graphics and multimedia software actually encompasses many different kinds of applications. There are programs for creating or editing artwork, including Microsoft Paint, Corel Draw, and Adobe Studio. Applications such as Macromedia's Flash can be used to produce detailed graphics or animation. The output of these kind of software might be used to produce a design for an advertisement, the architectural plans to build a school, or fine art that will be exhibited in a gallery or museum.

Graphics software offers electronic versions of an artist's tools, such as pens and paint brushes, that allow you to draw lines, fill objects with color, and move elements around in a composition. Special tools create curves, add lettering, make perfect circles, and shade areas of a drawing.

You can use *multimedia software* to manipulate digital photographs (Adobe Photoshop and Microsoft Picture It!) and digital video (IMovie and Windows Movie Maker). Then there is sound—music recording has been revolutionized by software such as Pro Tools, which facilitates the creation and manipulation of sounds and music and allows multitrack recordings to be edited with a notebook computer.

> ### Computer Concepts
>
> Country music singer Conway Twitty, who died in 1993, can be heard singing a duet in a digitally created composition released in 2004. Hundreds of hours of recordings of Twitty were scrutinized to find the necessary syllables sung with the right notes to create the vocal track.

FIGURE 6-6

Multimedia software lets you edit digital video on your computer monitor

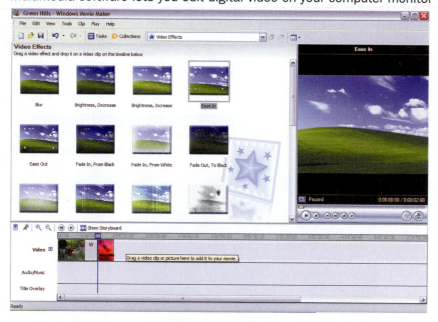

Different types of files store different media output. These file types are often identified by the file extension, the three or four letters separated by a period from the filename. The extensions are often acronyms or abbreviations for a description of the file type. For example, graphic file formats include .BMP (bitmapped), .TIF or .TIFF (tagged image file format), and .JPG or .JPEG (Joint Photographic Experts Group) files. These are used for line art and photographs. Formats such as .GIF (graphic interchange format) and .FPX (FlashPiX) can indicate still art or animation files, and .MOV (short for "movie") and .QT (QuickTime) are used for video files. Music is stored in .WAV (short for "wave") and .MP3 (Moving Pictures Expert Group layer 3—audio) file formats. There are many more multimedia extensions used by other programs, including .AVI (audio-video interleaved), .MPG or .MPEG (Moving Pictures Expert Group), and .RM and .RAM (Real Movie and Real Audio).

Multimedia and graphics software encourage creativity in young artists and open up a world of possibilities to people working in creative fields. For example, with a digital camera and video-editing software, grade school children can produce professional-looking movies with sound and special effects. And in the hands of professionals, a world of virtual reality is emerging in computer games, special effects, music production, and art.

Telecommunications

Telecommunications is electronically transferring data. Two of the most popular features of telecommunications are *distance learning* and *teleconferencing*. Distance learning addresses the problem of not being able to actually attend classes, and teleconferencing reduces the cost of travel, schedule conflicts, and accommodations for busy executives by providing conferencing capabilities without having to leave their offices.

> **Computer Concepts**
>
> George Lucas created the company called Industrial Light & Magic in 1975 to create special effects for the first *Star Wars* movie. In the past 30 years, IL&M have pioneered many processes and technological advances in moviemaking, including combining computer-generated graphics with live-action film to create almost unbelievable effects.

The Internet and e-mail are both forms of electronic data transfer. Users can exchange messages, participate in discussion groups, and transfer files from one location. Electronic mail software allows a user to send, receive, and manage e-mail. Researchers can access information from remote sources, information can be shared around the world, businesses can sell services and products, and so forth. The Internet offers electronic communication, networking, and electronic research tools. These tools are used to collect and analyze data for use in problem-solving activities. As a user, this means you must be adequately familiar with the mechanics or the "know-how" of the software plus how to use search engines and other features available for Internet research.

Search engines allow you to quickly research almost any subject on the Internet. Enter a keyword in a search engine to find sites that contain information that you need. Some popular search engines include Excite, Hotbot, Mamma, AskJeeves, and Google. Figure 6-7 shows a search engine's home page.

FIGURE 6-7
Search engines are helpful in locating needed information on the Internet

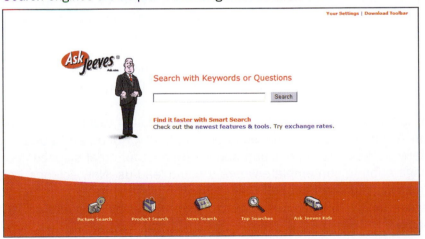

Browsers such as Netscape and Internet Explorer are a kind of software designed to allow people to connect to the Internet and experience the text, graphics, sound, and animation or video on Web pages. There is also software available, such as Microsoft FrontPage or Macromedia Dreamweaver, that simplifies the process of creating Web sites.

Personal Information Management Software

Personal information management software (PIMS) is used to organize appointments, telephone messages, projects, and tasks to be completed. Some examples of PIMS are Microsoft Scheduler+, Microsoft Outlook, and Lotus Organizer.

Other Software Programs

Many other types of software programs on the market provide specific capabilities for specific applications. For example, there is software for real estate agents, engineers, accountants, builders, doctors, musicians, quilters, cooks, and so forth. The list goes on and on.

Integrated software packages are available that combine different productivity applications into one package, so you can easily transfer data from one program to another. For example, a spreadsheet from one application can be imported into a word-processing program easily. Microsoft Office is a suite of integrated applications, as are AppleWorks and the Corel Graphics suite. If you enter a task with the word *software* in a search engine on the Internet, chances are you will find many programs available to accomplish almost any task you can imagine.

Computer Concepts

Voice mail is the most popular example of the combination of telephone technology and computer technology. It has proven to be a very important asset to businesses because it helps to alleviate the many problems caused in trying to make contact with customers and suppliers.

 Technology Timeline

SCIENCE OR SCIENCE FICTION?

New technology can often remind us of gadgets from an old science fiction movie. Some people claim that the resemblance is not because the creators of those fictionalized futuristic shows correctly predicted 21st century trends, however. Instead, some of the inventors and engineers who create today's technology may be science fiction fans who consciously or unconsciously design their devices to imitate what they saw in the movies or read about in books. For example, a cell phone looks a lot like a "communicator" used on spaceships in 1960s television shows, and the Segway scooter provides individual transportation that is a step toward the hovercraft and jetpacks of many tales of the future.

Popular culture has long offered views of a world full of technology, such as those presented in *Twenty Thousand Leagues Under the Sea*; *I, Robot*; and *2001: A Space Odyssey*. Many works of science fiction show a respect for "real science" combined with the imagination to contemplate where it could lead us. Now science imitates science fiction as we flip open our cell phones, swipe our magnetic identification and cash cards, and watch long-deceased actors sell brand-new products on television—or is it a holodeck?

1-2.2.4
1-2.2.5
1-2.2.7
1-2.2.8

Using Other Technologies to Solve Problems

The use of technology has affected our daily lives in so many different ways. As discussed in Lesson 1, microprocessors have computerized many tools and appliances. Cell phones and video games paved the way for even more specialized electronic devices such as tasers and global positioning systems. We will briefly examine some of the situations that have benefited from technological solutions and their benefits to us as individuals and in business.

- *Entertainment:* Computer games can be found in many places including homes, arcades, libraries, and schools. These games range from action games to simulations.

- *Electronic banking:* Nearly every bank offers electronic banking. This service permits customers to bank whenever they want. They can take money out of their accounts at any place there is an ATM machine. They can also do online banking, which allows them to pay bills, check balances, and even reconcile their statements from their home computers.

- *Medical and health care:* For quite some time, computers have been used in hospitals for record keeping. They now have a greater role in the care of patients. Sensors can be attached to patients to indicate when changes occur within their bodies. Tests that used to take a long time to complete can now be done quickly with computers.

- *Dangerous tasks:* Some jobs are too dangerous for humans to perform. Computers can perform these jobs as well or even better than humans. For example, Figure 6-8 shows a robotic arm used to repair a space station instead of sending an astronaut out on a potentially dangerous space walk.

- *Repetitious tasks:* Computers can do repetitive work accurately without getting tired or making mistakes. An example is the manufacture of the microprocessor chip. Each one must be made exactly alike, and computers control the processing equipment down to the exact timing and chemical mixtures.

FIGURE 6-8
Computers can perform tasks in environments too dangerous for humans

SUMMARY

In this lesson, you learned:

■ Technology has made a great impact on our lives.

■ The computer plays a major role in the technology boom.

■ Computer software controls the versatility of the computer.

■ Problem solving involves defining a problem and finding a solution.

■ The sequence of problem solving includes defining the problem, investigating and analyzing the problem, identifying possible solutions, selecting and implementing the best solution, and evaluating the chosen solution.

■ Typical software programs such as word processing, spreadsheet, database management, presentations, graphics, multimedia, and telecommunications are used to solve problems.

■ The Internet offers electronic communication, distance learning, teleconferencing, networking, and electronic research tools to solve problems.

■ Other technology, including devices with microprocessors, have affected our lives by providing solutions to problems and situations in the areas of entertainment, medicine, banking, and the performance of dangerous and repetitious tasks.

VOCABULARY *Review*

Define the following terms:

Database	Presentation software	Spreadsheet software
Database software	Problem solving	Technology
Distance learning	Relational database	Telecommunications
Graphics software	Search engines	Teleconferencing
Multimedia software	Spreadsheet	Word-processing software
Personal information man-		
agement software (PIMS)		

REVIEW *Questions*

MULTIPLE CHOICE

Circle the best response for each of the following statements.

1. Word processing, database, spreadsheets, and telecommunications are types of _____ used to solve problems.
   A. search engines
   B. software
   C. hardware
   D. technology

2. Computer programs used to create and modify video, animation, and music are called _____ software.
   A. personal information management
   B. telecommunications
   C. presentation
   D. multimedia

3. Electronic communication, distance learning, and teleconferencing are examples of _____ tools for solving problems.
   A. software
   B. telecommunications
   C. graphics
   D. hardware

4. _____ software provides the ability to make what-if statements to perform forecasts.
   A. Database
   B. Spreadsheet
   C. Word-processing
   D. Web page design

5. A _____ is a collection of tables that you can search without knowing how it is organized.
   A. relational database
   B. spreadsheet
   C. search engine
   D. list

TRUE/FALSE

Circle T if the statement is true or F if the statement is false.

T F 1. Technology means finding an old-fashioned solution to a modern problem.

T F 2. The first step in the problem-solving process is to select a solution.

T F 3. Telecommunications is electronically transferring data.

T F 4. You use keywords with a search engine to locate information on the Internet.

T F 5. Presentation software is used to create slide shows to present information.

PROJECTS

PROJECT 6-1

Computer games have become a booming business. There are usually two or three that are very popular every year. Locate sales data for the top five computer games over the past two years. Prepare a report indicating the total sales for the two-year period as well as indicating the share of the market each one held. You may find useful information at *www.videogames.about.com*. You may also find information at individual computer games companies.

PROJECT 6-2

You need to take a particular course next semester, but the course is offered at an inconvenient time. You had been told the course was also being offered as a distance learning class, which is sometimes called online learning. Write a report that explains just what this means. How are the computer and other technology involved in making this type of class possible? You may find useful information at *http://www.wested.org* or *http://www.nacol.org/*. Also try using the keyword *distance learning* with several search engines.

PROJECT 6-3

Arthur C. Clarke, who wrote *2001: A Space Odyssey*, said that advanced technology is indistinguishable from what we call magic. And Jules Verne noted that anything one man could imagine, another could invent. If you could invent an advanced technological device that was so wondrous it seemed like magic, what would that device be? How would it work?

TEAMWORK PROJECT

Your manager has asked you and your coworkers for suggestions about an applications suite that will allow employees to prepare payroll information, keep customer records, and produce advertising flyers and Web pages for the company, a small business providing appliance sales and service. Working with two other students, prepare a report that includes information about what kind of software programs you will need for each task. Also consider what other kinds of computer tasks a small business like this might need and what software programs would be needed for those additional tasks.

CRITICAL *Thinking*

ACTIVITY 6-1

Use the problem-solving steps in this lesson to write a strategy for solving a problem that you or a friend have faced, or a problem you have heard about in the news. In a written report, define the problem, then investigate and analyze it, and identify possible solutions that would use a computer program or some other kind of technology. Choose a solution you think will solve the problem. How will you put the solution into action? What could go wrong with the solution you choose? Would the technology need to be updated in a few years, or would the solution remain useful for a long time?

THE WINDOWS OPERATING SYSTEM

OBJECTIVES

Upon completion of this lesson, you should be able to:

■ Describe the general features of Windows XP.

■ Use a mouse to move around the desktop.

■ Identify the parts of the window and what each one does.

■ Work with menus and menu elements.

■ Work with dialog boxes.

■ Manipulate multiple windows.

■ Access the Windows Help feature.

■ Shut down Windows.

Estimated Time: 1.5 hours

VOCABULARY

Active window

Address Bar

Clicking

Command buttons

Commands

Default

Dialog box

Double-click

Dragging

Linking

Log off

Log on

Mouse buttons

Option buttons

Radio buttons

Right-click

Select (highlight)

Shortcut keys

Shortcut menu

Shortcut menu button

Standard desktop

Standard toolbar

Start button

Status bar

Submenu

Windows is a simple, familiar word, which does not sound very high tech. Yet Windows is an accurate name for a rich, powerful, high-tech software program. The Windows operating system is a visual or picture-oriented environment that provides an easy way for users to communicate or interact with the computer using graphic icons and buttons. Remember, Windows offers a graphical user interface, as opposed to the text-based DOS, and Windows' visual environment is the key to understanding and to using this impressive program.

But a graphical user interface does more than make Windows easy to use. One key benefit of a GUI is that it provides a consistent way to work within each program, a consistent way to work with other programs, and a simple and consistent way to switch between programs.

The Windows World

1-3.1.1
1-3.1.3

The Windows environment provides you with an electronic version of your desktop, complete with electronic tools and supplies, all accessible at your fingertips. Its parallels with the physical desktop are not accidental; Windows is designed to be your workplace. Here you will work with your mouse by moving and clicking. You can check your clock (which automatically resets for daylight savings time changes), use your calculator, grab your files and folders, dial your phone, surf the Internet, and open your briefcase. You can instantly see a complete listing of all your tools and supplies, a complete log of all your files and folders—a complete inventory of everything on your computer. And don't forget that wastebasket, which Windows calls a Recycle Bin. You can even decorate your Windows desktop, as you will see later.

You can't appreciate the full potential of Windows until you understand its powerful capabilities, such as file linking and automatic file updating. This powerful yet friendly software is an operating system; that means it manages everything—both the hardware and the software that operate your entire computer system. With Windows, you shift to each new task and open or close programs as effortlessly and quickly as when you use your remote control to switch between TV channels. While one window remains open and active on the desktop, others remain open but inactive—either on the desktop or as buttons on the taskbar.

You learned in Lesson 4 that this capability of running several tasks, or programs, at the same time is called *multitasking*. Multitasking allows you to process data in one program while you are working in another. For instance, while you are working on a spreadsheet in one window, you might be printing a word-processing document in another window.

And with Windows' **linking** features, you can easily transfer data among programs and update the data automatically. For example, if you need to prepare a report every month that includes a financial statement in a spreadsheet, you can put the spreadsheet into a word-processing document and *link* it to the spreadsheet program so that updates made to the spreadsheet will automatically appear in the word-processing report.

Windows Updates

Whether you are new to Windows software or not, adapting to new software—even a new version of familiar software—can be taxing. Learning new tools and unfamiliar features can be time-consuming and may require training. But Windows simplifies the process considerably. Consequently, if you've used an older version of Windows, you'll make the transition easily to Windows XP Professional. As you make the transition, you'll see that Windows XP provides:

- Easier, faster, and more powerful ways to work with application programs, as well as special hardware settings and increased speed for your network connections.

- Greater reliability and built-in support for hardware and software improvements, such as being able to use up to four monitors at a time.

- Enhanced versions of desktop tools, the taskbar, and the Start menu.

- Upgraded support for multimedia that allows you to receive high-quality movies and audio directly on your desktop.

- A single, easy way to have automated access to and delivery of information—whether it is located on your computer, the local area network, or the Internet.

- A mechanism that schedules delivery of information from the Internet that you want to monitor, without requiring that you physically visit the site or even connect to the Internet.

- Advanced capabilities for Internet Explorer and support for all Internet standards.

Starting Windows

1-3.2.3
1-3.2.4
1-3.1.5

Windows XP automatically starts when you turn on your computer. If you are the only person using your computer, Windows XP displays your desktop, ready for you to begin your work. However, Windows may ask you to click a user name before it will give you access to the computer. This is because Windows XP lets many different users create their own accounts. Each account contains all the settings the user likes, such as screen colors, placement of items on the desktop, and other program options. In order to do this, Windows XP needs to know who is going to use the computer. If your computer uses this feature, each time you start the computer, a Welcome screen appears, as shown in Figure 7-1, with each user's account name and an associated icon. You must *log on*, or tell the computer who you are, by clicking one of the user names and, if prompted, entering a password. If you do not follow the correct logon procedure for the computer, you will not be able to access the system. Windows loads all your preferred settings and opens to the Windows *standard desktop*, as shown in Figure 7-2.

FIGURE 7-1
Windows XP may ask users to log on

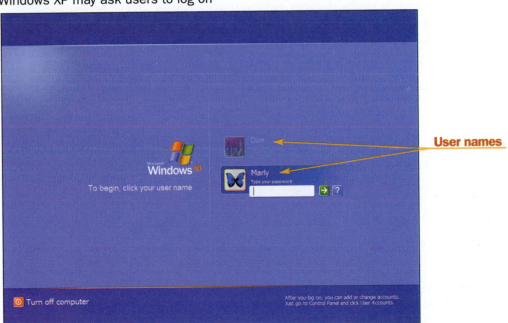

The Windows XP operating system is made up of many specialized computer files that create the Windows environment, including the desktop. Like any computer files, operating system files can become damaged by power surges, viruses, or out-of-date coding. If fundamental operating systems are corrupted, the operating system may need to be reinstalled or updated. A system that frequently locks up and requires rebooting may be a warning sign of unstable operating system files. It's important to reinstall or update the operating system when needed to protect the computer and its data files.

S TEP-BY-STEP 7.1

1. Turn on your computer system.

2. Windows will start automatically.

    a. If prompted, click one of the user names or enter the user name you have been assigned. (You may need to ask your instructor or system administrator for assistance with which user name and password to use.)

    b. If prompted, key your password. As you key your password, the password box will fill with black circles—one for each character in your password. Your password won't display for security reasons, so key your password carefully. If you can't remember your password and you had a password clue entered to help you remember, click the blue box with the question mark to the right of the password box to display a memory clue to your password.

    c. If your system is set up for multiple users, click the green arrow to the right of the password box or press **Enter** on the keyboard or click the **OK** button. Windows should then start.

> **Computer Concepts**
>
> A computer's operating system checks a password by comparing the characters (usually a group of letters or numerals) you enter to a list it stores that associates authorized users with their passwords. If the password you enter matches the one in the computer's list for your user name, you can log on to Windows.

3. Compare your screen with that illustrated in Figure 7-2. Your screen may differ slightly, and there may be more icons on the desktop, but the basic elements should be the same. Spend a few minutes looking at the layout of your screen and the position of the elements. If your screen does not display elements similar to those shown in Figure 7-2, ask for assistance. Remain on the Windows desktop for the next Step-by-Step.

FIGURE 7-2
Windows XP standard desktop

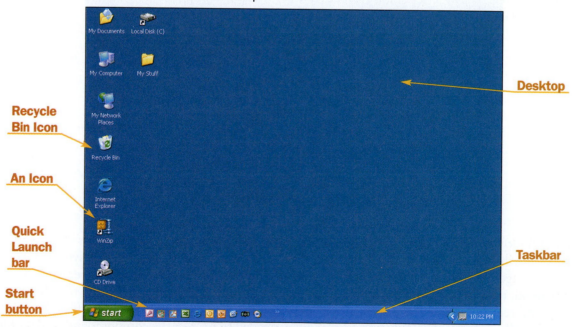

When you open a window, the software determines the window size and location on the desktop. A predetermined software choice or setting is called the *default*. You can change many defaults; for example, you can control the position and size of your windows by changing the default settings. (We will examine changing settings and customizing the desktop in Lesson 8.)

Look again at Figure 7-2, which identifies the main components of the opening Windows screen: the desktop, the taskbar, the Start button (which gives you access to the Start menu), the Quick Launch bar, and icons you can use to work with Windows programs and features.

The Taskbar

Locate the taskbar in Figure 7-2, in its usual default location at the bottom of the screen. You can move it to the top, left, or right side of the desktop to suit your needs. Wherever you choose to position it, you will find the taskbar to be a very convenient helper.

You use the taskbar for two important tasks: to display the Start menu and to switch among currently running programs that you want to keep open. Every program you keep open is represented by a button on the taskbar that offers easy access to all your running programs—just click the button. For example, if you open Excel, the taskbar displays a button for that program. If you then decide to run Paint, the taskbar adds a button for that program. One glance at the icons on the taskbar buttons tells you which programs are running (active).

The Start Menu

You click the *Start button* on the taskbar to display the Start menu, as shown in Figure 7-3. The Start menu contains a list of options you will use throughout this book that enables you to complete frequently performed tasks quickly and easily. For example, you can launch programs from the Start menu, open recently used files, change your system's settings, find files or folders, access Help topics, and close or shut down Windows.

FIGURE 7-3
The Start menu

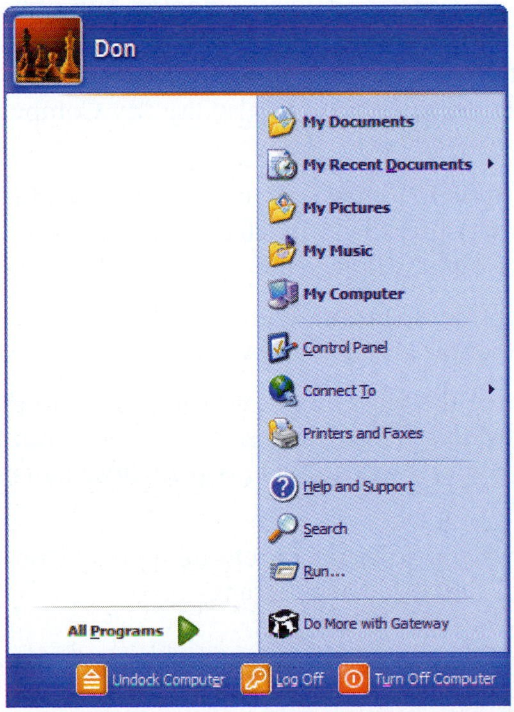

Look closely at the Start menu shown in Figure 7-3. Notice that the items on the menu are placed in one of four sections. These sections are at the top, bottom, left, and right of the menu. The login user name is displayed in large letters in the section across the top of the menu, and options for logging off or shutting down Windows are displayed along the bottom of the menu. A list of folders and programs is displayed on the left and right side of the separator line in the middle portion of the start menu.

The items on the right side of the separator line are known as the pinned items list. These items remain there and are always available for you to click to start them. You can add items to the pinned items list. The list of programs on the left of the separator line is known as the most-often-used-programs list. The programs displayed on the most-often-used-programs list appear there when you use them. Clicking the All Programs item opens a list of programs currently installed on your computer. When you click one of these programs, the program is placed in the often-used-programs list. Windows has a default number of programs that are displayed on this list. When that number of programs is reached, a program you have not opened recently is replaced in the list. You can change the default number of programs displayed on the most-often-used list.

Following is an explanation of the options commonly found on the Start menu:

- *All Programs* contains a complete list of the programs installed on your computer and allows you to launch any program quickly from the desktop.

- *My Documents* contains a list of the documents saved in this folder for quick access.

- *My Recent Documents* contains a list of the documents that were recently opened or created. Your computer may not show this option, but you can add it by customizing your Start menu. Other optional entries in the Start menu include *Favorites*, *My Network Places*, *Printers and Faxes*, and *System Administrative Tools*.

- *My Pictures* contains a list of the digital photos, images, and graphic files saved in this folder.

- *My Music* contains a list of music and other audio files saved in this folder.

- *My Computer* displays the contents of your computer. You can see the hardware devices, resources, programs, and files that are stored on your computer. My Computer also provides information about different system resources, such as the size of the hard disk and how much space is available on it. You can also use My Computer to format disks and to run programs.

- *Control Panel* provides options for customizing the "look and feel" of your desktop. For instance, the Control Panel option lets you change settings, such as the computer's date/time, desktop background, display colors, keyboard language, and mouse controls.

- The *Help and Support* option opens the Windows Help facility, an easy-to-use program that provides you with information about Windows and its programs.

- The *Search* option is one of the most important capabilities in the Windows program. It helps you find files and folders. This option also lets you search for Web sites you visit frequently, plus it provides a quick way to find people whose names are stored in a variety of electronic address books.

- The *Run* command allows you to begin a program quickly from the Start menu. You can also use this command to find a file or program.

■ The *Log Off* option permits you to exit the account you are using and keep the computer on for you or another user to log on at a later time.

■ The *Turn Off Computer* (or *Shut Down*) option provides options for safely shutting down and/or restarting Windows and your computer.

The Quick Launch Bar

The Quick Launch bar on the taskbar displays icons for frequently used programs so they are always visible on your desktop. You will see small icons that represent programs, settings, and other features. The Quick Launch icons let you launch these features quickly—just click to open a window or dialog box. You can find out what each icon on the Quick Launch bar will do by resting the mouse pointer on the icon. A balloon will appear describing what the icon is.

Moving Around the Desktop

1-3.2.4

You have already used the computer's mouse to click and open an application, and you can see the pointer you control with the mouse move around the Windows desktop. The mouse lets you race all over the screen—and, if you want, carry materials with you as you move.

Recall that the mouse is an input device. It allows you to find files, access tools, grab folders you need to move, or place items on the Windows desktop. Of course, you can also use the mouse to put those tools, files, or folders away. But that's not all. The mouse serves a number of other convenient uses. Your desktop is a visual work area, and the mouse is the key to that work area.

Most computers include a mouse as standard equipment. However, some systems, especially portable laptop and notebook models, may have an integrated trackball, touchpad, or Trackpoint on or next to the keyboard. These input devices work like a mouse, but they take less space and don't require a desk to move around on.

Working in a Connected World

ADMINISTRATIVE ASSISTANT

The administrative assistant is responsible for the overall functioning of an office. The position requires the person to work with considerable initiative in the absence of the supervisor and to exercise independent judgment within the framework of established policies and objectives.

The computer is the main tool that the administrative assistant has to complete many of the required tasks, using word-processing, database management, spreadsheet, and personal information software programs daily. The administrative assistant also uses other types of computer capabilities depending on the type of office in which he or she works. The qualifications required to be an administrative assistant include excellent communication skills, both verbal and written; knowledge of modern office practices, systems, and equipment; the ability to handle multiple projects simultaneously; strong math, interpersonal, and organizational skills; and a professional, friendly, and outgoing personality. A college degree is usually preferred. Evidence of some training and impressive experience, however, is sometimes acceptable.

If you're using a conventional mouse, clear an area (at least 1 square foot) next to the keyboard on your computer desktop for moving the mouse. For best performance, use a mouse pad. It's specially designed to sit under your mouse and facilitate its movement. Hold the mouse so the cable extends outward (away from your hand) and the body of the mouse rests under the palm of your hand. Rest your index finger lightly on one of the buttons.

> **Computer Concepts**
>
> A wireless mouse is sometimes called a *hamster* because it has no "tail," or cord, to connect it to the computer. Instead, it transmits information to the computer with infrared impulses.

The Mouse Pointer and Its Shapes

The arrow you see on the desktop is the mouse pointer, a graphical element you move around the screen to select items (such as icons and menu options), issue commands, and move or manipulate screen elements (such as text or windows). Move the mouse and you will see the arrow move.

The pointer changes its appearance depending on the task in which Windows is engaged. Most of the time, it looks like an arrow, but it may assume a number of other shapes. For example:

- When you are working with text, the pointer changes to an I-beam.

- When Windows is working on an instruction and isn't ready to accept further input from you, the pointer changes to an hourglass (or some other icon, like a bouncing ball, if you have chosen a different theme for Windows). This icon means "Wait. Windows is busy finishing a task."

- When an arrow is attached to the wait icon, it indicates that Windows is working on a task but you can still select and move objects.

- When the pointer turns into a circle with a slash through it—the international "no" symbol—the message is "This action is not allowed."

When you move the pointer over parts of a window, the different pointer shapes give you visual clues about how you can move the mouse.

Operating the Mouse

The mouse moves the pointer around the screen, but it does much more than that. The mouse allows you to move windows and to choose various programs by using the *mouse buttons*. Every mouse has one, two, or three buttons, depending on the manufacturer. By default, the button on the left is the primary button (the one you will use most often). It is also referred to as the select/drag button because it is the one you use to select and move elements around the screen. The secondary button, usually the button on the right, is called the *shortcut menu button* (shortcut menus are discussed later in this lesson), and when you use it, you *right-click*. You'll learn when to right-click as you practice using Windows.

Your mouse may also have a "Fast Wheel" located between the primary and secondary buttons or on the side so you can operate it with your thumb. The wheel lets you move through documents quickly by allowing you to roll to scroll. If you click this wheel once, your pointer changes to a large arrow and you can scroll extremely rapidly just by moving the mouse pointer up or down on the screen.

If you are left-handed, Windows allows you to reverse the primary and secondary mouse buttons so you can use the mouse with your left hand. You'll learn how to do this in a later lesson. For the purpose of this book, however, we will always consider the left button to be the primary button and the right button to be the secondary or shortcut menu button.

You use the mouse buttons to select objects and to move objects or icons around the screen. You *select*, or *highlight*, an item by pointing to it and pressing and then releasing the left (primary) mouse button. When you press and then release the left mouse button, the action is referred to as *clicking*; some commands require you to *double-click* (that is, click twice quickly). If you don't double-click the button fast enough, Windows interprets your action as two single clicks rather than one double-click. (With a little experience, you'll double-click expertly.)

Moving objects with the mouse is known as *dragging*. You drag an object by placing the mouse pointer on the item to be moved, then pressing and holding down the primary mouse button while moving the object. When the pointer is at the right location, release the mouse button. Table 7-1 lists and explains five common techniques for using a standard two-button mouse device.

> ### Computer Concepts
>
> You can change your desktop settings so different shapes appear to indicate the different tasks. If you choose a desktop theme, the shapes will be changed automatically to match the theme.

TABLE 7-1
Operating the mouse

TO	DO THIS
Drag	Press and hold the mouse button and move the mouse in the desired direction, then release.
Click	Press and release the left (primary) mouse button.
Double-click	Click the left mouse button twice in rapid succession.
Right-click	Press and release the right (secondary) mouse button.
Select	Point to an item and click the mouse button.

Using the mouse proficiently requires a little practice—and a little patience. In a very short time, you'll use the mouse comfortably and smoothly.

S TEP-BY-STEP 7.2

1. Move the mouse (or other pointing device) on your desk (or mouse pad). As you move the mouse, watch the screen to see how the pointer moves:

   a. Move the pointer to the far left of your screen by sliding the mouse to the left on the desk or mouse pad. Do not lift the mouse.

   b. Move the pointer to the far right of your screen by sliding the mouse to the right.

   c. Move the pointer to the top of your screen by moving the mouse toward the top of your desk or mouse pad.

   d. Move the pointer to the bottom of your screen by moving the mouse toward the bottom of your desk or mouse pad.

2. Display and then close the Start menu:

   a. Point to the **Start** button in the corner of the taskbar.

   b. Click the left mouse button.

   c. Point to a clear area of the desktop and click the left mouse button. The Start menu closes.

STEP-BY-STEP 7.2 Continued

3. Select and rearrange an icon on the desktop:

a. Point to the **Recycle Bin** icon, and hold (do not click) the pointer on the icon for a few seconds. Notice that a small window opens displaying a description of the icon. Click the mouse button. Notice that when you click an icon, it changes color. The change in color means the icon is selected.

b. Click anywhere on the desktop. As you do so, notice that Recycle Bin is deselected (that is, it returns to its original color).

c. Again point to the **Recycle Bin** icon.

d. While holding down the mouse button, drag the icon about one inch to the right and release the mouse button. As you drag the icon, note how a "ghost image" of the icon follows the mouse pointer to indicate where the icon will be placed when you release the mouse button.

e. Drag the Recycle Bin icon back to its original position.

4. Double-click the **Recycle Bin**. The Recycle Bin window opens.

5. Close the Recycle Bin window by clicking the **Close** button.

Identifying the Parts of a Window

1-3.2.1
1-3.2.4

In Lesson 5, you were introduced to the basic parts of the window. Let's take a closer look now at these tools and what they can do. Figure 7-4 identifies the parts of the window by name.

FIGURE 7-4
Parts of a window

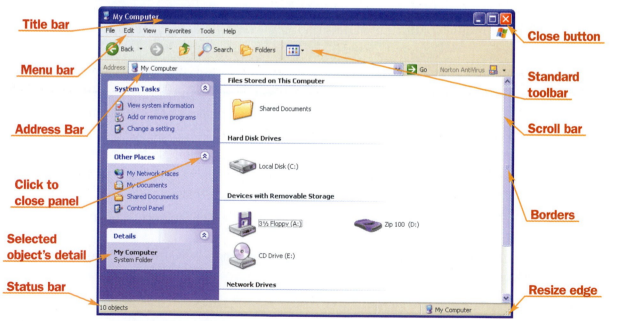

■ The title bar is at the top of the window. It displays the name of the program running in a window—in this case, "My Computer."

■ Directly below the title bar is a menu bar, which lists available menus (the specific choices depend on the program you are running). The menu bar in Figure 7-4 lists six choices: File, Edit, View, Favorites, Tools, and Help.

■ The *Standard toolbar* contains buttons that permit you to access various functions and to issue commands. The toolbar in the My Computer window has buttons for navigating your computer's resources and for changing the display of the objects in the window. If the toolbar is not displayed, open the View menu, select Toolbars, and select Standard Buttons.

■ The *Address Bar* displays the name of the open folder or object. It also permits you to key the address of a Web page quickly without opening your browser. If it is not displayed, open the View menu, select Toolbars, and select Address Bar. Not all applications have an Address Bar option, however. Many programs indicate the name of an open file in the title bar with the program's name.

■ In the rectangular window are icons, which you learned about in Lesson 5. In this window, the icons represent the parts of your computer system and programs to control the system. The icons in your window may be different from those shown in Figure 7-4. When you select an icon, a description of it displays below and to the left of the icon.

■ The Minimize, Maximize/Restore Down, and Close buttons appear at the upper-right corner of the window on the same line as the title bar. Recall that the Minimize button reduces the window to a button on the taskbar, and the Maximize button enlarges the window to fill the screen. Once the window is full-screen size, the Maximize button changes to a Restore Down button, which enables you to restore the window to its previous (smaller) size. The Close button quickly closes the window.

> **Note**
>
> When you load Windows, the default settings on your computer may cause your screen to look slightly different from the screens shown in this text's figures.

■ The borders are the four lines that define the limits of the window.

■ The *status bar* provides information on the currently selected object or the task you are performing. As you choose menu items, select window objects, or issue commands, the actions are described on the status bar.

■ The resize edge provides a large spot to grab when you want to resize a window without moving the upper-left corner.

■ When the window is not large enough to display everything, you will see scroll bars. Clicking the scroll bar moves (scrolls) the contents of a window so you can view objects that are hidden.

Working with Menus

A menu is a list of options or choices. Every window you open in Windows XP contains a menu bar offering menus. The My Computer window in Figure 7-5 has a menu bar with six menus: File, Edit, View, Favorites, Tools, and Help. Each of these menus, in turn, offers a number of *commands* you can issue to perform a task or function.

FIGURE 7-5
Menu in the My Computer window

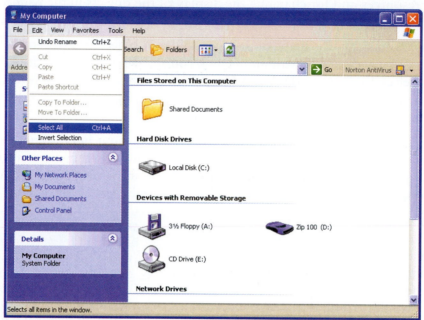

If all these menu choices appeared on the desktop at the same time, your work area would be too cluttered to be useful. Windows' menus organize the choices so they are out of sight but within reach. To find out what choices are available on a particular menu, you display the menu by clicking it. When you click the menu name, the menu drops down, as shown in Figure 7-5. Notice the differences among the listed options. One is highlighted, some are in black letters, some are in a lighter color, and some are followed by three periods. All menu choices have one letter underlined. Each visual element has a special meaning, as explained below.

Highlighting

In Figure 7-5, the Select All menu option is highlighted; that is, the words appear in white letters within a dark box. Highlighting indicates that an option is currently selected.

Colors or Shading

Not all menu options are available to you all the time. The dark or black letters indicate options that are currently available. Light or grayed letters indicate options that are not available. Look closely at the Edit menu in Figure 7-5. Which options are currently available?

Ellipses

An ellipsis is a series of three periods (...) following some commands. See the Copy To Folder and Move To Folder commands in Figure 7-5, for example. An ellipsis tells you that if you choose this option, a second window or dialog box will be displayed, requesting more information from you. (You'll learn more about dialog boxes later.)

Selection Letters

In some applications, each menu option has one underscored letter or number, indicating a keyboard command you can use as an alternative to the mouse. On the keyboard, press the underscored letter or number to choose that command. You can press the selection letters only while the menu is displayed, but in program windows that support selection letters, you can use keyboard commands to display menus, too. For example, in many Microsoft software programs, the file names have an underscored letter (see Figure 7-6). By pressing the Alt key and the underscored letter at the same time, you can display the menu (for example, Alt + E displays the Edit menu in Figure 7-6).

FIGURE 7-6
An application window with menus that support selection letters

Shortcut Keys

Some menu options list *shortcut keys* to the right. Unlike selection letters, shortcut keys can be used even when the menu is not displayed. Shortcut keys also offer the advantage of not having to remove your hands from the keyboard while you are keying.

Shortcut keys generally combine the Alt, Ctrl, or Shift key with a letter key. In this text, such combinations are expressed as follows: Alt + X or Ctrl + O. In Figure 7-6, the shortcut keys for the Select All command are Ctrl + A. To execute this command using the shortcut keys, press the Ctrl key and hold it down while pressing the A key. Then release both keys at the same time.

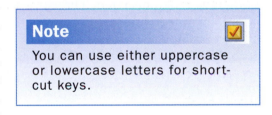

Note

You can use either uppercase or lowercase letters for shortcut keys.

Right-Pointing Arrow

A right-pointing arrow next to a menu option (such as next to Clear in the Edit menu in Figure 7-6) indicates that if you point to that option, another menu will appear with more options. This second menu is a *submenu*. Windows automatically opens submenus after the pointer has been resting on an option for a short period of time. You can click the option to display the submenu immediately.

Selecting an Option from a Menu

To select an option from a menu, first open the menu by clicking the menu name on the menu bar. You'll find that as you move the pointer down the menu, the highlight also moves. Stop the pointer on the option you want to choose, and then click. The command you have chosen will execute.

You can also execute a command using the command's shortcut keys, if available. After you have become familiar with commands, you may find it easier to use shortcut keys for the commands you use most often.

STEP-BY-STEP 7.3

1. Click **Start**, and then click **My Computer** in the Start menu.

2. Display the options in the Favorites menu:

   a. Click the **Favorites** menu name in the menu bar.

   b. Select **Links** or let the mouse pointer rest on the option for a few seconds.

   c. You can click on a link, but if you do not have Internet access available, you will get a message saying the page cannot be displayed or that you do not have an Internet connection. If necessary, click **Work Offline**.

   d. If you do link to a Web page, click the **Close** button.

3. If necessary, restart My Computer and then select all the icons in the My Computer window:

   a. Click the title bar on the My Computer window to verify that it is selected.

   b. Key the shortcut **Ctrl + A**. All the icons are now selected.

   c. Click somewhere in the blank (white) space in the My Computer window to deselect the icons.

4. Close the My Computer window by clicking its **Close** button.

Working with Dialog Boxes

Some menu options, such as the Run... command in the Start menu, need more information before they can be executed. For example, before Windows can run (start) a program, it needs to know the program name. The ellipsis (...) that follows such a command signals that need for additional information. You provide the needed information by responding to a *dialog box*, such as the one shown in Figure 7-7.

FIGURE 7-7
Command buttons, option buttons, and text boxes in a dialog box

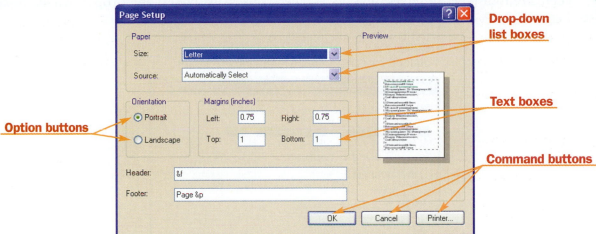

A dialog box is itself a window and has some of the same features as a window, such as an identifying title bar and a Close button. But dialog boxes contain a number of other elements that help you give information to your computer. Let's take a look at the elements you will find most often in dialog boxes.

Buttons

There are two types of buttons: command buttons and option buttons.

- *Command buttons* carry out your instructions using the information selected in the dialog box. Command buttons are always rectangular. When you press a command button, the program accepts your instructions. If there is an ellipsis on the button (for example, Browse...), choosing it will open another dialog box. Typical command buttons are Open, Help, Cancel, and OK. The dialog box in Figure 7-7 contains three command buttons: OK, Cancel, and Printer....

- *Option buttons* (sometimes called *radio buttons*) allow you to choose one option from a group of options (see Figure 7-7). To change a selection, simply choose a different button.

Boxes

There are four types of boxes: text boxes, check boxes, list boxes, and drop-down list boxes (see Figure 7-8). A combo box combines two types of boxes.

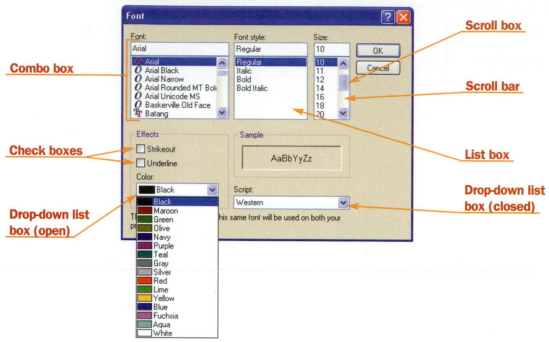

FIGURE 7-8
A dialog box containing several kinds of boxes

- *Text boxes:* Text boxes allow you to key information in the dialog box. A text box may contain a blinking insertion point to show you where to begin keying, or it may already contain text that you can change as necessary. To change existing text, highlight it by double-clicking it and then key the new text.

- *Check boxes:* Check boxes allow you to make choices from a group. However, unlike option buttons, you can check several boxes; that is, you can select a variety of options. Clicking with the mouse selects (✓) or deselects a check box.

- *List boxes:* List boxes present a set of options in list format. When the list of options is too lengthy to fit in the box, scroll bars are available to allow you to scroll through the items. Drag the scroll box to move up or down the list. Figure 7-8 shows scroll bars on the Font list box.

- *Drop-down list boxes:* Drop-down list boxes display only one option and a special arrow symbol. Click the arrow symbol to reveal the entire list box. Figure 7-8 shows two drop-down list boxes, with one of the lists displayed.

- *Combo box:* A combo box is a combination of a text box and a list box. You can select from the list or enter your own choice by keying it in the text box part of the combo box.

STEP-BY-STEP 7.4

1. Open the Start menu by clicking the **Start** button.

2. Move the pointer to the **Run...** command on the Start menu and click. The Run dialog box appears.

3. If the Run dialog box on your screen contains text, make sure the text is highlighted.

4. Key your first name in the text box—do not press Enter.

5. Click the **OK** command button. You now see a message box (another form of dialog box) similar to the one illustrated in Figure 7-9. Windows is telling you that it cannot locate the file you asked to run.

FIGURE 7-9
Message box

6. Click the **OK** command button to cancel the message display.

7. Click the **Cancel** command button to close the Run... dialog box.

Navigating Through Windows

Windows' multitasking ability allows you to perform more than one task at a time. As a result, you may have a lot of windows open on the desktop at one time, and this can be confusing. You can manage those windows and switch between them simply by rearranging the windows on your desktop.

Arranging Windows on the Desktop

In Lesson 5, you learned to drag a window to a different location on the desktop. Dragging can be very time-consuming when you have a number of open windows. A shortcut menu hidden on the taskbar makes it easy to arrange open windows. The *shortcut menu* contains the options that are most commonly performed from the current window display. While the shortcut menu is handy, not all options are included on it. To access the shortcut menu, point to any portion of the taskbar that does not contain a button and right-click. The shortcut menu in Figure 7-10 displays, allowing you to instruct Windows to organize the open windows on your desktop. You can choose one of three different arrangements: Cascade, Tile Horizontally, or Tile Vertically.

FIGURE 7-10
Shortcut menu

- The Cascade Windows option cascades the open windows into a stack with title bars showing; the active window is always in front of the stack, on the top layer.

- The Tile Windows Horizontally option tiles the open windows across the desktop from top to bottom, without overlapping any portion of any window.

- The Tile Windows Vertically option divides the desktop evenly among the open windows and aligns the windows across the screen, left to right, without overlapping any window.

The shortcut menu also contains a Show the Desktop command, which reduces all windows to buttons on the taskbar. You can cancel any option you select by using the Undo command. For example, the shortcut menu would list an Undo Cascade option once you selected the Cascade Windows option. Selecting this option restores the display to its previous arrangement.

At times, you may need to move a window to uncover another window or an object on the desktop. The quickest way is to drag the window by its title bar. If the window is maximized, you must first restore it to its previous size before you move it.

If you want greater control over the position and size of a window, resize it by dragging one of the three types of window borders (horizontal, vertical, or corner) in the direction you prefer.

Switching Between Windows

When multiple windows are open on your desktop, the one you are working with is called the *active window*. Remember that the active window is easy to recognize because its title bar is a different color or intensity. You can make any open window the active window in one of two ways:

- If any portion of the window you want to work with is visible, click it. It will come to the front and become the active window.

- At any time, press and hold down the Alt key; then press Tab. A small window appears in the center of the display. The window contains icons for all items currently open, including items minimized on the taskbar. If you hold down the Alt key and then press and release Tab, you can cycle through all the icons. A box surrounds the item's icon and a description appears at the bottom of the window as it is selected. When the one you want is selected, release the Alt key. That item comes to the front and becomes the active window. This is called the fast Alt + Tab method for switching to a different window.

STEP-BY-STEP 7.5

1. Double-click the **Recycle Bin** icon to open the Recycle Bin window.

2. Click the **Start** button, and then click **My Computer** on the Start menu to open the My Computer window.

3. Click the **Start** button, and then click **Search** on the Start menu to open the Search Results window.

4. Tile the open windows using the shortcut menu:
   a. Point to a blank area in the taskbar and right-click to display the shortcut menu.
   b. Select the **Tile Windows Vertically** option. The windows are now arranged differently, in a tiled format.

5. Right-click on the taskbar and select the **Tile Windows Horizontally** option from the shortcut menu. The windows are rearranged into this tiled format.

6. Right-click on the taskbar and select the **Cascade Windows** option from the shortcut menu. The windows are rearranged into a cascade format.

7. Change the active window:
   a. Click the **My Computer** window. If it wasn't in front, it comes to the foreground and becomes the active window.
   b. Click the **Search Results** window to make it the active window. This window comes to the front as the active window. (You may need to move the windows around on the desktop to see the Search Results Window.)

8. Undo the cascade format and return the windows to the Tile Windows Horizontally format:
   a. Point to a blank area in the taskbar and right-click to display the shortcut menu.
   b. Select the **Undo Cascade** option. The windows are again arranged in a horizontal tiled format.

9. Right-click on the taskbar and select the **Show the Desktop** option on the shortcut menu to minimize all windows to buttons on the taskbar.

10. Open the Search Results window using the Alt + Tab feature:
    a. Press and hold down the **Alt** key.
    b. Press and release the **Tab** key until the Search Results icon is outlined, and then release the **Alt** key.

11. Notice that this window is still in tile format. Display the Search Results window in the cascade format by right-clicking on the taskbar and selecting the **Cascade Windows** option on the shortcut menu.

12. Close all open windows by clicking their **Close** buttons. (You may need to open the other programs on the taskbar to close their windows.)

The Windows Help Feature

IC³
1-3.2.4

Selecting the Help and Support option from the Start menu opens the Help and Support Center window. The Help and Support Center offers support in four categories:

- *Pick a Help topic* contains general information about a topic. For example, clicking What's new in Windows XP displays a list of resources that you can use to learn about Windows XP features.

- *Ask for assistance* provides two ways for getting outside help. The Remote Assistance option allows you to invite someone to help you. Using an Internet connection, anyone running Windows XP can view your screen and, with your permission, work on your computer. The Support option enables you to get help from Microsoft, from product experts, or to discuss your questions with other Windows XP users online.

- *Pick a task* provides access to the latest updates for your computer's operating system, hardware, and software. You can also use this category to find Windows XP–compatible hardware and software, restore your computer to a previous working state, or access helpful tools to keep your computer running smoothly.

- *Did you know?* displays a tip on using Windows XP. Each time the Help and Support Center is opened, the tip that is displayed is selected at random from a group of tips, so be sure to read the tip each time you access the Help and Support Center.

The Help and Support Center is designed to look and work much like a Web page. It has two sections, called panes. When you point to an underlined topic in the left pane, the pointer changes to a hand with the index finger pointing to the topic or word. This indicates that the topic is actually a link. When you click a link, the Help and Support entry is displayed in the right pane. For example, if you click the *Fixing a problem* link in the Pick a Help topic menu, the Help and Support entry will be displayed in the right pane.

Getting Assistance Online

The Help and Support Center's *Ask for assistance* section offers an option called Remote Assistance. Remote Assistance is a convenient way for someone you know to connect to your computer from another computer running Windows XP, chat with you, and observe your computer screen as you work. With your permission, you can receive the remote user's keystrokes as if he or she were keying on your keyboard. In this way, you are able to watch the remote user demonstrate the solution to your problem.

The second option in this section allows you to get support online from a technician who can answer your questions in e-mail or an online chat session. This option also gives you access to newsgroups that can offer tips and guidelines about working with Windows XP.

Using the Windows XP Application Help System

Selecting the Help option and then the Help Topics menu item (or the name of the application's Help, usually the first option) from a Windows XP application menu displays the Help Viewer for that program. For example, when you click Help in the Windows Paint program, and then choose Help Topics, you see the Help Viewer window shown in Figure 7-11. In some programs, the Help Viewer may appear in a narrow pane at the right of the document window; it has two panes when fully opened, as shown in Figure 7-11.

FIGURE 7-11
Windows Paint program's Help Viewer

The three tabs in the left pane of the Help Viewer let you locate and navigate Help topics in different ways.

■ The Contents tab groups topics into general categories so you can browse the table of contents for an application's Help system to locate a topic. Each main topic has a book icon next to it. Click an icon to display a list of topics within that main topic.

■ The Index tab provides an alphabetical listing of key words and terms with topics specific to the application you are using.

■ The Search tab lets you search the Help topics for a term or feature. Again, the available help topics are specific to the application you are using.

STEP-BY-STEP 7.6

1. Click the **Start** button, and then select the **Help and Support** option on the Start menu.

2. Maximize the Help and Support Center window, if necessary.

3. Click the **Fixing a problem** link under the Pick a Help topic menu to display the Help and Support entry.

4. Read the choices in the listing in the left pane, and then click the **Application and software problems** link to display the Help and Support entry for this topic in the right pane. Notice that as you point on the topic, it becomes underlined, indicating that it is a link, and it is highlighted when the topic's entry is displayed in the right pane.

STEP-BY-STEP 7.6 Continued

5. Read the choices for this Help and Support entry in the right pane, and then click **Print Troubleshooter** to display its Help and Support entry.

6. Click the **Close** button to close the Help and Support window.

7. Click the **Start** button, select **All Programs**, select **Accessories**, and then select **Paint** from the menu. When the Windows Paint program opens, click **Help** on the menu bar, then select the **Help Topics** option. The Paint Help Viewer opens, as shown in Figure 7-11.

8. Click the **Show** button, if necessary, to display both panes of the Help window.

9. Click the **Contents** tab, if necessary, to bring it to the front.

10. Click the **Paint** book icon to display its subtopics.

11. Click the **Work with Color** topic and then click the **Paint with a brush** entry in the list of links that drops down. The topic entry is displayed in the Help Viewer's right pane.

12. Click the **Paint** book icon in the navigation pane to close the book.

13. Close the Paint program Help system by clicking the **Close** button on the Help Viewer's title bar.

14. Close Paint by clicking the **Close** button on the title bar.

Shutting Down Windows

1-3.2.3
1-3.1.5

You shut down Windows by using the Start button. You have two choices along the bottom of the Start menu: Log Off or Turn Off Computer (or Shut Down). Each of these choices has options:

■ *Log off*—Selecting this choice keeps your computer running while you log off the computer so someone else can use it. If you select this option (and your system is set up for multiple users), Windows will open a message box asking if you want to Switch User or Log Off, as shown in Figure 7-12. (If your system is not set up for multiple users, the message box gives you the choice between logging off or canceling this action.)

FIGURE 7-12
Log Off Windows message box

- If you choose Switch User, the Welcome screen appears, but Windows keeps your open programs waiting for you. When the new user logs off, Windows switches back to you as the user and everything is just as you left it.

- If you choose Log Off, Windows saves your work and your settings and returns to the Welcome screen for the next user. Windows does not turn the computer off when this option is selected.

- *Turn Off Computer* (or *Shut Down*)—Selecting this choice instructs Windows to prepare to shut down. Each time you select Turn Off Computer, a message box displays, giving you three options:

  - *Stand By*—Select this option if you want to save electrical energy but keep your current programs open so you can resume where you left off.

  - *Turn Off*—This option closes all programs (if you didn't close them first) and shuts down Windows. Depending on how your computer system is set up, your computer's and monitor's power may also turn off. If it is not set up to do this, a message box will appear informing you that it is safe to turn off the power to your computer.

  - *Restart*—This option quits Windows and restarts your computer, opening Windows back up.

STEP-BY-STEP 7.7

1. Click the **Start** button, and select the **Turn Off Computer** option (or the **Shut Down** option if applicable) from the Start menu. Shutting down the computer is good to do each time you are finished working for the day.

2. Select the **Restart** option. Windows will shut down and then automatically start running again. This is helpful if you decide you need to continue working or if your computer locks up.

3. Log on if necessary to start Windows.

4. Shut down Windows again. This time select the **Turn Off** option (or the **Shut Down** option if applicable). The computer may automatically turn itself off, or you will see a message box informing you when it is safe to turn off the computer. Follow your instructor's directions about turning off the computer.

> **Note**
>
> If your Start menu choice is Shut Down instead of Turn Off Computer, your message box will be named Shut Down Windows and it will contain a drop-down list of options. These options are Log off [User Name], Shut down, and Restart. Log off works the same as clicking Log Off from the Start menu. Shut Down is comparable to Turn Off. And Restart functions in the same manner as Restart from the Turn off computer message box.

Sometimes a Windows application will stop functioning or will not respond, and you cannot close the program or perform any other tasks in Windows, such as turning off the computer. Use the Ctrl + Alt + Del key combination (press all three keys at the same time). The Windows Task Manager, shown in Figure 7-13, will appear. There are three options indicated at the bottom of the box—End Task, Switch To, and New Task. End Task will close the nonfunctioning program. To use the Switch To option, highlight one of the programs in the Tasks column that the Status column indicates is Running. The New Task button allows you to launch another program in a dialog box similar to the Run dialog box. If the system has "locked up" and you cannot close any applications, click the Shut Down button at the top of the Windows Task Manager box and you will see options including Turn off and Restart as well as other options. Select Turn off or Restart to safely shut down the computer when the applications are not responding at all.

FIGURE 7-13
The Windows Task Manager dialog box

SUMMARY

In this lesson, you learned:

■ Most Windows activity takes place on the desktop.

■ The Windows opening screen has the following basic components: the desktop, the taskbar, the Quick Launch bar, the Start button, the mouse pointer, and one or more desktop icons.

■ You use the taskbar to open programs and documents and to switch back and forth between running programs.

■ The Start menu options let you launch programs, open recently used files, change your system's settings, find files or folders, access Help topics, and close and shut down Windows.

■ The Quick Launch icons let you open a window or dialog box with a click.

■ The mouse controls an on-screen pointer. The shape of the pointer will change depending on where you are on-screen and what you are doing.

■ Mouse buttons let you make selections by clicking, right-clicking, and double-clicking. The primary button is used most frequently. The secondary button is used for shortcuts.

■ The mouse lets you move (drag) objects.

■ A menu is a list of options or choices. You make selections from a menu by pointing at and clicking an option or using the up or down arrow keys.

■ On a menu, a highlighted option (white letters within a dark box) indicates that this option is currently selected, and light or grayed letters (as opposed to black or dark) mean that an option is not available.

■ A right-pointing arrow next to a menu option indicates that the option has a submenu with more options.

■ A series of three periods (…), called an ellipsis, following a command tells you that if you choose this option, a dialog box will open to request more information.

■ A dialog box is a window. In it you will find command buttons and option buttons. Command buttons are rectangular and you click the button to execute a command. Option buttons (also known as radio buttons) let you choose one option from a group of options.

■ A dialog box may also have check boxes, list boxes, text boxes, and drop-down list boxes, each of which allows you to make selections or key information.

■ Windows' multitasking capability means that more than one window can be open at a time. The windows can be arranged on the desktop in a cascade, horizontally tiled, or vertically tiled format. Click any window or use Alt + Tab to bring a desired window to the front and make it the active window.

■ You can access the Windows Help feature by clicking Help and Support on the Start menu.

■ The *Ask for assistance* option in the Help and Support Center offers a variety of ways to get help, including online help. With Remote Assistance, you can allow someone you know to connect to your computer and demonstrate the answer to a question. The Support page also gives you access to Windows XP newsgroups where you may be able to find an answer to your questions.

■ Every Windows XP application has a Help menu that opens the application's Help Viewer. The left pane of the Help Viewer contains three tabs that provide different options for searching the Help system. When you select an entry on one of the tabs, the right pane displays detailed information about the topic.

■ When you want to shut down Windows, you select either the Log Off or the Turn Off Computer option (or the Shut Down option) from the Start menu.

VOCABULARY *Review*

Define the following terms:

Active window	Linking	Shortcut keys
Address Bar	Log off	Shortcut menu
Clicking	Log on	Shortcut menu button
Command buttons	Mouse buttons	Standard desktop
Commands	Option buttons	Standard toolbar
Default	Radio buttons	Start button
Dialog box	Right-clicking	Status bar
Double-click	Select (highlight)	Submenu
Dragging		

REVIEW *Questions*

MATCHING

Match the correct term in Column 2 to its description in Column 1.

Column 1

Column 2

____ **1.** Desktop component that contains buttons for open programs

A. dragging

____ **2.** Help option that allows someone at another computer to view your screen via the Internet

B. active window

C. Recycle Bin

____ **3.** Graphical element you move around the screen to select, move, and manipulate screen elements

D. taskbar

____ **4.** Act of moving an object with the mouse

E. menu

____ **5.** Icon on the desktop that contains deleted files

F. option buttons

____ **6.** A list of options or choices

G. default

____ **7.** A predetermined choice made by the software

H. command buttons

____ **8.** The window in which you are presently working

I. Remote Assistance

____ **9.** In a dialog box, the buttons that carry out your instructions using the information selected

J. mouse pointer

____ **10.** In a dialog box, the buttons that represent a group of choices from which you can select one

MULTIPLE CHOICE

Circle the best response for each of the following statements.

1. The list of choices on a Windows menu bar _____.
   A. is the same for all programs
   B. will vary according to the program
   C. displays as icons
   D. None of the above

2. Shortcut keys _____.
   A. can be used even when the menu is not displayed
   B. are keystrokes that must be used in place of the mouse
   C. always use the Alt key
   D. cannot be used unless the menu is displayed

3. When a window is not large enough to display everything, _____.
   A. you can click the Restore Down button to enlarge it
   B. the status bar will indicate there is more to be displayed
   C. you should drag its title bar to resize it
   D. scroll bars will be displayed

4. The visual element that indicates whether a menu option is available is _____.
   A. an ellipsis
   B. the color of the option
   C. an underscored letter
   D. highlighting

5. If additional information is needed before a command can be executed, Windows displays a _____.
   A. message box
   B. dialog box
   C. control-menu box
   D. prompt box

PROJECTS

PROJECT 7-1

The local library has computers available with Windows XP Professional installed. You will be using one of these computers but can only spend one hour on it. Develop a strategy to maximize your time. Using the information from this and previous lessons, create a priority list, ranking the most important features to explore and skills to practice.

PROJECT 7-2

1. At the Web site *www.microsoft.com/education/Tutorials.aspx* you can find information about free tutorials for Microsoft software. In the dialog box on the screen, you will see several drop-down list boxes that offer choices about age level, learning area, and product.

2. Select **Windows XP** as the product and choose appropriate options in the other lists.

3. Click the **Search** button at the bottom of the dialog box.

4. One or more tutorials will be listed in the search results. Click on the link to the tutorial that looks most interesting to you and use the information provided to write a summary of the features the tutorial offers. (Do not download the tutorial without your instructor's permission.)

PROJECT 7-3

1. Open the Windows Help and Support feature from the Start menu.

2. Click on the topic **What's new in Windows XP** and continue following links until information about new features in Windows XP opens in the right panel.

3. Click on the link **Related Topics** for more new features.

4. Read the information and make a list of some of the new features of the operating system. You should include at least five new features and what they do in your list.

 ### TEAMWORK PROJECT

In your office, several people share one computer and each must log on using his or her own user name to start Windows. Recently, some workers have noticed that they are missing data, files are not where they should be, and their standard desktop sometimes looks a little different. There is some concern that workers are logging on using other user names. Working with two coworkers, research passwords in the Help and Support feature and online and then write a report suggesting how the computer users can select and use a password that will prevent unauthorized access to individual files and settings.

CRITICAL *Thinking*

In two weeks your computer will be upgraded to Windows XP Professional. This will be your first exposure to this operating system, and you would like to be prepared for the transition. Develop a list of off-line research resources where you can explore the vocabulary and basic procedures of running a Windows PC as well as develop an understanding of some of the pros and cons of desktop automation. These resources can include people, bookstores, and broadcast media. Access at least one of these resources, and write a summary of your findings.

CHANGING SETTINGS AND CUSTOMIZING THE DESKTOP

OBJECTIVES

Upon completion of this lesson, you should be able to:

- Understand the settings on the Control Panel.
- Apply a predefined theme to the desktop.
- Change the Windows desktop background.
- Customize the icons on the desktop.
- Clean up your desktop.
- Explain what a shortcut is and how it is used.
- Create and delete shortcuts.
- Assign a shortcut key to a shortcut.
- Add a program to the Quick Launch bar.

Estimated Time: 1 hour

VOCABULARY

Background

Control Panel

Desktop shortcuts

Desktop theme

Internet Explorer

My Computer

My Documents

My Network Places

Shortcut

Wizard

W indows programs run on the desktop, and objects are placed on the desktop. When you install Windows XP, the original desktop you see may not be the exact desktop you want, but you can customize it to suit your personal tastes. You can also customize the taskbar and Start menu. In addition, you will learn how to use the Control Panel to adjust settings for hardware, find system information, schedule routine maintenance, and change user account information. Another way to customize your desktop environment is to add shortcuts. If you use particular programs or documents frequently, you will learn how to create shortcuts for them so you can access them quickly and easily.

The Control Panel

1-3.3.1
1-3.3.2
1-3.3.4
1-3.3.5

Y ou can open the *Control Panel*, which you will use to change settings on your computer and customize the display, by selecting it on the Start menu. Notice that the Control Panel window, shown in Figure 8-1, has two panes like the Help Viewer and other windows we have seen. The left pane includes a list of tasks you can choose quickly, and other places you can look for information about the Control Panel and Windows. The right pane has nine categories you can pick to change settings and display options. Following are the categories and what you can do with each of them:

- *Appearance and Themes:* Change the background, screen saver, or desktop items; customize the Start menu and taskbar; apply a theme to your display; change the screen display resolution or colors.

- *Network and Internet Connections:* Create a small office or home network; change network, Internet, and phone settings.

- *Add or Remove Programs:* Install, change, or remove software and Windows components; see a list of installed software; control access to certain programs.

- *Sounds, Speech, and Audio Devices:* Change speaker volume and other settings for audio and speech devices; change the sound scheme or individual sounds made by the computer.

- *Performance and Maintenance:* Enable energy-saving features; compress the data on your hard disk drive; schedule routine maintenance tasks, such as disk cleanup and antivirus checking; find system information.

- *Printers and Other Hardware:* Change settings for printers, keyboard, mouse, game controllers, modems, scanners, and cameras; identify the hardware devices on your computer and if they are running properly.

- *User Accounts:* Change user accounts and passwords; change a user's e-mail profile.

- *Date, Time, Language, and Regional Options:* Change the language your system uses or the date, time, or time zone; change the way numbers, currency, dates, and times are formatted and displayed.

- *Accessibility Options:* Adjust hardware and operating system settings for users with vision, hearing, and mobility disabilities.

FIGURE 8-1

The Control Panel in the default Windows XP Category view

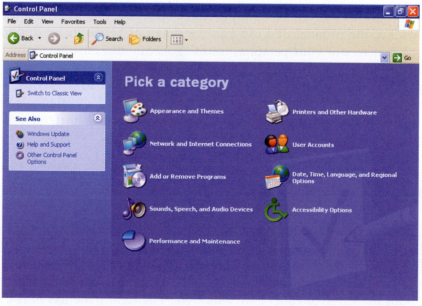

If you are working on a networked computer, you may not be allowed to change all the Control Panel settings. The network administrator can restrict access to some settings to prevent unauthorized users from making changes that can affect other users in a network, such as creating a new user account or altering regional or language settings. Some hardware settings that control how peripherals (printers, modems, and so on) are allocated in a network may also be protected so that changes made by one user will not affect the entire network.

STEP-BY-STEP 8.1

1. Click the **Start** button, and then click **Control Panel** in the Start menu.

2. Select the **Performance and Maintenance** category in the Pick a category area (the window's right pane).

3. In the Performance and Maintenance window, find the Pick a task section and click the **See basic information about your computer** link.

4. The System Properties dialog box opens. If the General tab is not open, click on it to open it. You will see information about the version of Windows you are using under the System heading.

> **Note**
>
> If your Control Panel window is set to Classic view instead of the default Category view, double-click the **System** icon to open the System Properties dialog box.

5. Click **OK** to close the dialog box.

6. Leave the Control Panel window open for the next Step-by-Step.

Technology Timeline

FORMATTING FOR EUROS

Imagine driving from Michigan to Georgia and needing five different currencies for your trip. To purchase items during your journey, you must convert your Michigan dollars to Ohio marks, Kentucky pounds, Tennessee lira, and Georgia francs. It would be inconvenient, and also expensive, because every time you converted the money, the money changers would charge you a fee. This is what tourists traditionally experienced when they traveled in Europe. They had to convert their money to another currency every time they crossed a border. Imagine how difficult it would be to keep track of transactions in financial reports with so many different currencies to convert and different symbols to represent them.

In 1999, 11 European countries embraced one currency unit—the euro. The euro was first introduced in electronic trading—business transactions completed without cash. In January 2002, euro notes and coins started circulating. The changeover to a single currency affects banks, businesses, and consumers. The euro symbol now appears in banks, on financial statements, and on retail price tags. Technology has kept up with the new era. Windows XP allows users to change the default currency format to euros and many applications provide full support for entering, displaying, and printing the euro symbol and for working with values in euro currency.

Changing Control Panel Settings

1-3.3.3
1-3.3.5

You now know many of the settings that can be configured using the Control Panel. Let's look more closely at when you would want to change settings and how to do it.

The computer uses its internal clock to display the correct time, even correcting for Daylight Savings Time, but you may need to change the clock for some reason. For example, if you have a notebook computer and you travel from the west coast to the east coast for an extended stay, you would want to change the time zone setting to correct the time displayed. You can even configure your system to automatically synchronize the time with an Internet time server. Files and folders are date- and time-stamped when you create them and modify them, so having the computer's clock set accurately can be important. Think about any change you make and consider the consequences of the change before you alter a setting. For example, you want files to be date-stamped correctly; therefore, if you set the wrong date or time, you will have inaccurate and misleading information associated with files.

Other settings that you may want to change include the speaker volume control or how the mouse or keyboard works. Sometimes small adjustments can make a computer much easier and more efficient to use. If you are one of several users of one computer, remember to check with a supervisor or other users before making changes. Only make changes if they are needed. It's a good idea to make a note of the original settings so that changes can be modified or reversed if necessary.

STEP-BY-STEP 8.2

1. Click the **Back** button in the toolbar to return to the Pick a category window. Select the **Printers and Other Hardware** category in the Pick a category area.

2. In the Printers and Other Hardware window, click **Mouse** in the *or pick a Control Panel icon* area of the window.

3. The Mouse Properties dialog box opens. You will see several tabs with information about the mouse, including how the buttons are configured, how the pointer appears, and how the "Fast Wheel" scrolls through a document. Click each tab to view the information.

> **Note**
>
> In Classic view, simply double-click the **Mouse** icon to open the Mouse dialog box, and click the **Printers and Faxes** icon to open the associated dialog box.

4. Click **OK** or **Cancel** to close the dialog box without changing any settings.

5. You will be back in the Printers and Other Hardware window again. Click **View installed printers or fax printers** in the Pick a task section to open the Printers and Faxes window. The available printers and faxes appear in the right pane, and the left pane lists tasks under one or more heading.

6. Click **Add a printer** in the Printer Task pane. The Add Printer Wizard will open.

7. In the Add Printer Wizard, you can read information about installing a printer. Read the text and then click the **Next** button.

8. Click the **Next** button in the new dialog box to have the Wizard search for a newly installed printer. Since no printer has been installed, you will see a message that says no new printer was found. Click the **Cancel** button to close the Add Printer Wizard.

9. Close the Printers and Faxes window and then close the Control Panel window.

You can also change some settings by double-clicking the appropriate icon on the right side of the taskbar. Different icons may appear on your taskbar depending on the way your taskbar has been customized. For example, click the time display to open the Date and Time Properties dialog box, and if you see an icon that looks like a bullhorn, you can click it to open the Volume Control dialog box and then adjust the speaker volume. Other icons may open control network connections, printers, and other hardware, depending on what is installed on your computer.

STEP-BY-STEP 8.3

1. Double-click the time display at the right on the taskbar to open the Date and Time Properties dialog box, as shown in Figure 8-2.

FIGURE 8-2
Date and Time Properties dialog box

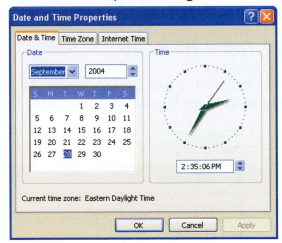

2. Click on each of the three tabs, **Date & Time**, **Time Zone**, and **Internet Time**, to view the different settings you can adjust.

3. Click the **Date & Time** tab and you will see the current month and year displayed in drop-down list boxes, and the current date shaded or highlighted in a calendar grid on the left and a clock with a second hand, and the current time displayed below it on the right.

4. Click on any other day in the calendar grid to select it. Notice the highlight has changed to the new date.

5. Click on the up arrow next to the time displayed in the text box on the right. Notice that the hours number is highlighted, and it increases by an hour every time you click the arrow.

6. Click the **Cancel** button to close the dialog box without changing the settings.

7. Double-click the icon that looks like a bullhorn on the right side of the taskbar to open the Volume Control dialog box. If this icon does not appear on your taskbar, skip steps 7 to 9.

8. In the Volume Control panel, use the slide control to make the volume just a little louder. You may hear a sound when you adjust the setting.

9. Click the **Close** button to close the dialog box and save the change you made to the vol- ume setting.

The Desktop

1-3.2.5

The first thing many people want to do when they start using Windows is to customize the desktop to better suit how they work. For example, when Windows is first installed, the *background* that covers your desktop is usually a picture of a green hill beneath a blue sky with white clouds. (The name of this background is Bliss.) You can change the background to another picture or pattern included with Windows, or you can add your own photograph or artwork. You can also select a theme, which is a coordinated design that carries through all the elements of your desktop and window, changing the colors of windows elements and highlighting and the way icons appear. A screen saver may be included in a theme, or you can choose a different screen saver from Windows' selection, or install a new screen saver program.

The desktop is your work area, and it's easy to customize it just like you would a "real" desk, by adding pictures, rearranging the items you use, making it easy to reach items you use frequently, and even cleaning it up occasionally!

Customizing the Desktop

1-3.2.5

To change the way the desktop looks, you select the Appearance and Themes category in the Control Panel and then click the Display icon to open the Display Properties dialog box.

FIGURE 8-3
Display Properties dialog box

Windows XP theme

Example of current theme

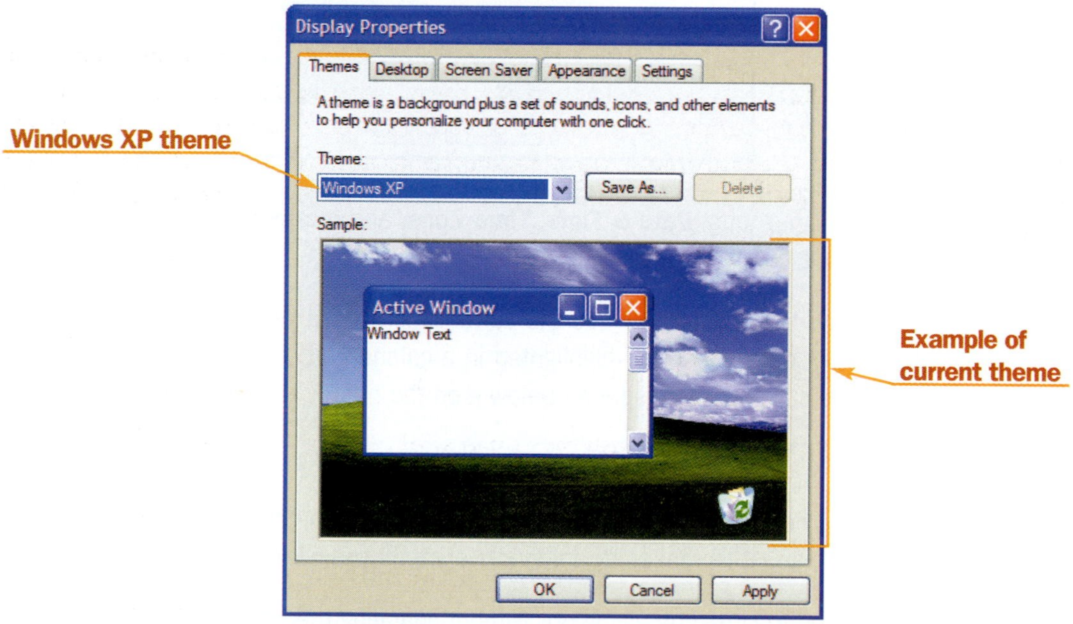

As you see in Figure 8-3, the Display Properties dialog box has several tabs you can use to change the appearance and the behavior of your desktop.

■ The Themes tab assigns a predefined set of icons, fonts, colors, sounds, and other window elements to your desktop. Collectively these elements are called a *desktop theme* and give the desktop a unified and distinctive look.

■ The Desktop tab offers you a selection of pictures and graphics to use as a background on your desktop. You can use one of the backgrounds that come with Windows or create one of your own.

■ The Screen Saver tab permits you to display static or moving graphics or a blank screen when your system is idle.

■ The Appearance tab controls the colors, fonts, and sizes of various screen elements. You can change the appearance of these elements by selecting from a set of predefined schemes or by creating your own scheme.

■ The Settings tab allows you to change the resolution and the number of colors used by the display, change the display type, and change other display characteristics.

>
> **Note**
>
> Right-clicking an empty area on your desktop (a place where there is no folder or icon) and clicking Properties on the short-cut menu will also open the Display Properties dialog box.

Selecting a Desktop Theme

Using the Themes tab, you can quickly modify your desktop background by selecting from a set of predefined themes. If your computer has other users with their own user accounts, each person can have a different theme.

To apply a new desktop theme, simply use the drop-down menu (beneath the word Theme) to select one of the preconfigured themes (see Figure 8-4). The themes that are listed in your Theme drop-down list may differ from the ones in Figure 8-4, but there will probably be several choices in the list. When you click a theme, the new background will appear in the sample window in the center of the Display Properties dialog box. Click the Apply button; after a short wait, the new theme will be set on the desktop.

FIGURE 8-4
Theme drop-down list

The default theme from previous versions of Windows

To access themes from the Internet

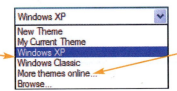

>
> **Note**
>
> If your computer has an Internet connection, you can access a number of themes from the Microsoft Web site by clicking the More themes online option on the drop-down list.

STEP-BY-STEP 8.4

1. Open the Control Panel and click the **Appearance and Themes** link.

2. Click the **Display** icon to open the Display Properties dialog box.

> **Note** ☑
>
> In Classic view, double-click the **Display** icon to open the Display Properties dialog box.

3. Select the **Themes** tab if it is not already selected.

4. On a sheet of paper, write the name of the desktop theme that is currently displayed in the Theme list box.

5. Click the **Theme** drop-down list arrow, and then select **Windows Classic** if it is not already selected. If it is already selected, select one of the other themes in the list.

6. Click the **Apply** button. Your theme will take effect after a short wait. The new desktop background will appear in the Sample window in the Display Properties dialog box and you may see a change in the Active Window displayed there also.

7. Click the **Theme** drop-down arrow, select the desktop theme that you wrote on your paper in Step 4, and then click **Apply**. After a short wait, your desktop background will return to its former appearance. Leave the Display Properties dialog box open for the next Step-by-Step.

Setting a Background Design

You can change a theme's settings by making modifications to the other tabs available on the Display Properties dialog box. For example, to change the background design, click the Desktop tab and select one of the backgrounds. You can select from Windows' preexisting backgrounds, which are listed on the Background list box, or you can use other graphic files (for instance, from a digital camera) as your background. By default, the background is set up to stretch across your screen so it takes up the entire desktop area. You can center the background on the desktop or tile it to fill the entire desktop. You select the option from the Position drop-down list box.

STEP-BY-STEP 8.5

1. Click the **Desktop** tab.

2. Select the Windows XP background:

   a. Click the scroll down arrow in the **Background** list box until the **Windows XP** option appears, and then select it.

   b. Notice that a preview of your selection is displayed in the monitor graphic in the upper portion of the Desktop tab.

   c. Verify that the **Stretch** option is displayed in the Position drop-down list box. The Windows XP background is a picture file, and by default, all picture files are stretched to cover the entire desktop.

STEP-BY-STEP 8.5 Continued

3. Tile the background on the desktop:

 a. Click the **Tile** option from the Position drop-down list.

 b. Click the **Apply** button to reset the background. Notice that the background now fills the desktop by repeating the graphic.

4. Click the **Stretch** option from the Position drop-down list, and then click the **Apply** button to reset the background. Do not click the OK button. Leave the Display Properties dialog box open for the next Step-by-Step.

Windows XP can display any picture or graphic file (usually files with a GIF, JPG, or BMP extension) as a background. If you have picture files already stored on your computer, you can simply browse and select the desired picture. You can also create your own graphic in the Windows Paint program or some other graphics program and use it as a background.

STEP-BY-STEP 8.6

1. Use the **Flowers** file in the Lesson 8 folder of the data files as a background:

 a. Click the **Browse** button on the Desktop tab to open the Browse dialog box.

 b. Select the drive and folder that contain your data files.

 c. Double-click the **Lesson 8** folder, and then double-click the **Flowers.jpg** file. The Browse dialog box closes, and the Display Properties dialog box reappears.

 d. Verify that the **Stretch** option is selected from the Position drop-down list.

 e. Click the **Apply** button to set the background.

2. Reset the background to **Windows XP**:

 a. Scroll the Background list box, locate the **Windows XP** option, and click it.

 b. Click the **Apply** button to set the background to **Windows XP**. Leave the Display Properties dialog box (Desktop tab) open for the next Step-by-Step.

Customizing the Icons on Your Desktop

The Customize Desktop button toward the bottom of the Desktop tab provides a convenient way for you to select which Windows program icons are to appear on your desktop and to determine which icons are used to represent those programs. Click this button, and the Desktop Items dialog box opens (see Figure 8-5). This dialog box contains a General and a Web tab.

> **Note**
>
> You can download a picture or an image from the Web and use it as a background. Simply right-click the picture or image you want to use as a background and click Set As Background.

FIGURE 8-5
The Desktop Items dialog box

On the General tab (see Figure 8-5), you can select the desktop icons you want to appear by checking one or more of the check boxes: My Documents, My Computer, My Network Places, and Internet Explorer. These icons are discussed in detail below.

- *My Documents* is your personal folder where you can save the files you create and use. By default, the My Documents folder contains two additional personal folders: My Pictures and My Music.

- *My Computer* displays the contents of your computer. You can see the hardware devices, resources, programs, and files that are stored on your computer. My Computer also provides information about different system resources, such as the size of the hard disk and how much space is available on it. You can also use My Computer to format disks and to run applications. (You may recall that My Computer is also accessible from the Start menu.)

- *My Network Places* lists all of the computers on your network, if you are connected to a network. It permits you to browse through files on a networked computer.

- With *Internet Explorer*, you get a fast, personalized Web browser with communication capabilities including sending and receiving e-mail, connecting to the Internet, designing your own Web site, and teleconferencing.

Just below the Desktop icons, you will see a window showing the default icons that are used for each of these items, as well as the Recycle Bin icon that is placed on your desktop by default. If you want to use a different icon for any of these items, click the item you wish to change, click the Change Icon button, and select a different icon from the choices provided. If you change your mind or don't like your choice, just click the Restore Default button to return to the Windows XP default icon settings.

STEP-BY-STEP 8.7

1. Click the **Customize Desktop** button. The Desktop Items dialog box (Figure 8-5) is displayed.

2. Click the **General** tab to verify that it is in the foreground.

3. Display the My Documents and My Computer icons on your desktop:

    a. Click the **My Documents** check box in the Desktop icons area. (This will place a check mark in the check box.)

    b. Click the **My Computer** check box.

    c. Click the **OK** button. The Desktop Items dialog box will close.

4. Click the **Apply** button on the Display Properties dialog box to place the selected icons on your desktop. Do not click the OK button on the Display Properties dialog box.

5. Change the My Documents desktop icon:

    a. Click the **Customize Desktop** button to display the Desktop Items dialog box.

    b. Click the **My Documents** icon in the display window, and then click the **Change Icon** button.

    c. Click the folder icon shown in Figure 8-6, and then click the **OK** button. Notice that the icon changes in the display window.

FIGURE 8-6
Folder icon

    d. Click the **OK** button on the Desktop Items dialog box, and then click the **Apply** button on the Display Properties dialog box. Notice that the icon on your desktop has changed to your selection.

6. Remove the My Computer icon from your desktop:

    a. Click the **Customize Desktop** button to display the Desktop Items dialog box.

    b. Click the **My Computer** check box to deselect (uncheck) it, leave the My Documents check box checked, and then click the **OK** button.

    c. Click the **Apply** button on the Display Properties dialog box. Notice that the My Computer icon is no longer displayed on the desktop.

    d. Close the Display Properties dialog box and then close the Control Panel or the Appearance and Themes window if necessary.

Customizing a Toolbar

The standard toolbar is the row of buttons below the menu bar on most windows. Other toolbars appear if you select them in the Toolbars submenu of the View menu. You can easily change the buttons that appear on any toolbar. For example, to change the toolbar in the My Documents window, open My Documents from the desktop. Click on the View menu, and then select the Toolbars option. (The right-pointing arrow tells you a submenu will open.) When you select the Customize option on the Toolbars submenu, the Customize Toolbar dialog box appears. The dialog box has two list boxes: Available toolbar buttons and Current toolbar buttons, as shown in Figure 8-7. The Available toolbar options list box on the left lists the types of buttons available to place on the toolbar. The Current toolbar buttons list box on the right lists the buttons that already exist on the toolbar. To add buttons to the toolbar, select a button from the list box on the left and then click the Add button. To remove buttons from the toolbar, select a button from the right and click the Remove button.

You can change the order in which the buttons appear on the toolbar by selecting a button in the Current toolbar buttons list box and clicking the Move Up button or the Move Down button to change the button's position in the list box.

FIGURE 8-7
The Commands tab of the Customize dialog box

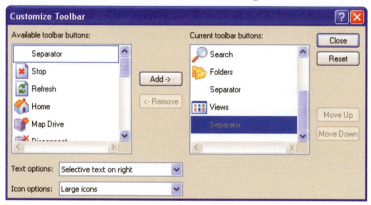

Cleaning Up Your Desktop

Windows XP provides a number of utility programs that help you perform a task quickly and easily. Each of these programs is called a *Wizard* and performs a special function, such as the Add Printer Wizard you encountered earlier in this lesson. For example, as you use work, you will place icons on your desktop. Because these icons function as shortcuts to an application or a document, they are often referred to as *desktop shortcuts*. (You will learn how to create shortcuts in the next section.) Windows XP contains a Desktop Cleanup Wizard that can check your desktop to see which desktop shortcuts you have not used during the previous 60 days; it then lets you decide if you want to remove them. The desktop shortcuts you remove are moved to an Unused Desktop Shortcuts folder from which you can recover them at any time.

Look again at the General tab on the Desktop Items dialog box shown in Figure 8-5. Notice the Desktop cleanup area at the bottom of the sheet. In this area, you can set the Desktop Cleanup Wizard to run automatically every 60 days, or you can run it any time by clicking the Clean Desktop Now button.

Using Shortcuts

A *shortcut* functions as a pointer to an application or a document file, wherever the file is located. When you double-click the shortcut icon, you're opening the actual item to which the shortcut is pointing. The shortcut is represented by an icon on your desktop. A shortcut icon is identified by a small arrow in its lower-left corner (see Figure 8-8). Shortcuts save time because you don't have to open and browse through several folders to find the file you need.

FIGURE 8-8
Shortcut icon

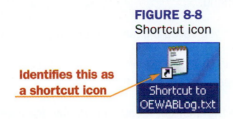

Identifies this as
a shortcut icon

You can create a shortcut by dragging a file to the desktop or by using the Create Shortcut command on the File menu. Shortcut menus also appear when you right-click a file or folder on your desktop, in the right pane of a folder window, or when you right-click an empty space on the taskbar or desktop.

Creating a Shortcut Using Drag and Drop

If you can display an item in the My Computer window, you can create a shortcut for it by dragging and dropping an item to the desktop with the right mouse button:

- Using the right mouse button, right-drag the item (file, program, folder, printer, computer) from its current location to wherever you want the shortcut to appear.

- Drop the item where you want it by releasing the mouse button.

- A shortcut menu appears, giving you several options. Click Create Shortcuts Here.

- The icon appears with the shortcut arrow and a default name.

You may want to change the shortcut's default name to something different. To rename it, right-click the shortcut's icon to display the menu shown in Figure 8-9. Remember that you can often open a task-specific shortcut menu by right-clicking an icon or text; in this case, the shortcut menu options relate to creating shortcuts. Choose Rename, and key the new name in the shortcut icon's text box. You can use this shortcut menu for a number of tasks, such as deleting a shortcut or changing its properties.

FIGURE 8-9
The shortcut menu for creating and managing shortcuts

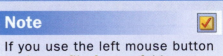

Note ✓

If you use the left mouse button to drag a file from a folder on the C drive to the desktop, you will move the file and its icon to the desktop.

STEP-BY-STEP 8.8

1. Open **My Computer** from the Start menu.

2. Locate the Assignments folder where you saved the file called Hobby created in Lesson 5.

3. Make sure that part of your desktop is visible, and using the right mouse button, drag the Hobby document file icon to the desktop. Release the mouse button.

4. Select **Create Shortcuts Here** from the shortcut menu. The Hobby document shortcut appears on your desktop.

5. Rename the shortcut:
   a. Right-click the **Shortcut to Hobby** icon.
   b. Select **Rename** from the shortcut menu. Notice that the icon's name is now highlighted and has a blinking insertion point.
   c. Key **My Shortcut** and press **Enter** to rename the icon.

6. Close the My Computer window.

Creating a Shortcut Using the File Menu

You can also create a shortcut by selecting the item for which you want (a file, program, folder, printer, or computer) to create the shortcut in My Computer. Then from the File menu select Create Shortcut. Resize the window so you can see the desktop. A shortcut icon for the item appears as the last item in the My Computer window. Drag the new shortcut icon to the desktop. Then you can rename it—as you have already learned.

Assigning a Shortcut Key to a Shortcut

A shortcut key is a keystroke combination that runs a program or opens the dialog box to which it is linked. For example, if you assign the shortcut key Ctrl + Alt + N to your My Shortcut, your new shortcut key will then open the Hobby document. You assign a shortcut key in the shortcut's Properties dialog box, which is accessible from the shortcut menu. You make the assignment by pressing and holding the Ctrl key and then pressing the key you want to complete the shortcut keystroke combination. When you press the Ctrl key, the combination Ctrl + Alt + appears in the Properties dialog box. It ends with + because it is waiting for you to complete the shortcut. Once you select OK, the shortcut keystroke assignment is made, and anytime you press those keys, you will open the document.

You can activate a shortcut in two ways: Double-click the shortcut icon, or issue the shortcut key combination.

STEP-BY-STEP 8.9

1. Right-click the **My Shortcut** icon.

2. Select **Properties** from the shortcut menu. The My Shortcut Properties dialog box appears.

STEP-BY-STEP 8.9 Continued

3. Make sure the Shortcut tab is displayed as shown in Figure 8-10.

FIGURE 8-10
Shortcut tab in the My Shortcut Properties dialog box

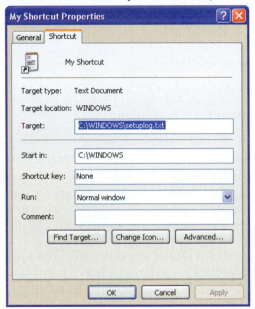

4. Click in the **Shortcut key** text box.

5. Press and hold down **Ctrl**, press **n**, and then release **Ctrl**. The shortcut key Ctrl + Alt + N is displayed in the Shortcut key text box.

6. Click the **OK** button to save the shortcut keystroke combination, and close the My Shortcut Properties dialog box.

7. Double-click the **My Shortcut** icon. Did the Hobby document open?

8. Close the Hobby document window.

9. Issue the shortcut keystroke combination Ctrl + Alt + N:
   a. Press and hold down **Ctrl**.
   b. Press and hold down **Alt**.
   c. Press **n**, and release all keys.

10. The Hobby document once again opens. Close the document.

> **Computer Concepts**
>
> If Windows is already using your selected keystroke combination for another shortcut, it will still allow you to make the assignment. When you enter the keystroke combination, however, Windows will run the other shortcut. In this case, just open the shortcut's Properties dialog box and select a different keystroke combination.
>
> The letter name of your hard disk may appear different from that shown in the Target and Start in text boxes shown in Figure 8-10.

Which method do you prefer—double-clicking the icon or issuing the shortcut key? You probably found the first method simpler, but as you become more familiar with creating shortcuts, you will see that shortcut keys are very useful when the shortcut is not in view or if you prefer to keep your hands on the keyboard.

Deleting a Shortcut

Like most Windows elements, shortcuts can be deleted. There are several ways to delete a shortcut:

- Select the shortcut, then press the Delete key.

- Right-click the shortcut, and then select Delete from the shortcut menu.

- Drag and drop the shortcut in the Recycle Bin.

If you double-click the icon or issue a shortcut, Windows displays a message box asking you to confirm the deletion. Deleting a shortcut deletes only the shortcut, not the file to which the shortcut points. If you drag the shortcut to the Recycle Bin, no confirmation message box appears; the shortcut is simply moved to the Recycle Bin where it will remain until the Recycle Bin is emptied.

Adding a Shortcut to the Quick Launch Bar

With Windows, you have another choice for shortcuts: The Quick Launch bar on the taskbar (see Figure 8-11). Always visible, the Quick Launch bar is great for those items you need to reach fast. If you don't see the Quick Launch bar, right-click in an empty part of the taskbar, point to Toolbars, and then click Quick Launch.

FIGURE 8-11
Quick Launch bar

To add a button to the Quick Launch bar, drag a program, document, or desktop shortcut icon to the Quick Launch bar. To remove a button from the Quick Launch bar, right-click the shortcut and then select Delete from the shortcut menu.

SUMMARY

In this lesson, you learned:

- The Control Panel allows you to find information about system settings, change display options, and customize your desktop.

- You can modify your desktop using the Display dialog box tools and options.

- You can select from Windows' existing themes or choose a different background on the Background tab.

- Windows comes with a number of preexisting desktop themes that give your desktop a unified and distinctive look. A picture can be tiled to fill the whole screen, centered on the screen, or stretched across the screen.

- You can use most any picture or graphic file as a background. For example, you might take a photograph on a digital camera or download a graphic from the Web and then use it as a desktop background.

- The Desktop Cleanup Wizard is used to remove any unwanted or unused desktop shortcuts from the desktop.

- A shortcut functions as a pointer to a file—wherever it is located. Double-click the shortcut icon to open the actual item to which the shortcut is pointing.

- You create a shortcut by dragging and dropping or by using the Create Shortcut option on the File menu. When you no longer need a shortcut, it can be deleted without impacting the original instance.

- You can add a shortcut key to a Windows shortcut. A shortcut key is a keystroke combination that runs a program—or in this case, runs the Windows shortcut to which it is linked. Shortcut keys to Windows shortcuts always use Ctrl + Alt + and one additional character.

- You can place a program, document, or desktop shortcut icon that you plan to use often on the Quick Launch bar.

VOCABULARY *Review*

Define the following terms:

Background	Internet Explorer	My Network Places
Control Panel	My Computer	Shortcut
Desktop shortcuts	My Documents	Wizard
Desktop theme		

REVIEW *Questions*

TRUE/FALSE

Circle T if the statement is true or F if the statement is false.

T F **1.** The Background tab in the Display Properties dialog box lets you change the colors, fonts, and sizes of various screen elements.

T F **2.** By default, your desktop's background is a solid color.

T F **3.** Even though other users share your computer, you must all have the same theme for your desktops.

T F **4.** Windows XP can display any picture or graphic file with a GIF, JPEG, or BMP extension.

T F **5.** Right-clicking a shortcut icon displays the shortcut menu.

MULTIPLE CHOICE

Circle the best response for each of the following statements.

1. You can create a shortcut by using the Create Shortcut command on the _____ menu in My Computer.
   A. Insert
   B. Help
   C. View
   D. File

2. A(n) _____ is a keystroke combination that runs a program or opens the dialog box to which it is linked.
   A. icon
   B. shortcut key
   C. Ctrl key
   D. Wizard

3. The _____ tab in the Display Properties dialog box that lets you assign a predefined set of icons, fonts colors, sounds, and other window elements to your desktop.
   A. Settings
   B. Themes
   C. Appearance
   D. Desktop

4. A _____ is a utility program provided by Windows that helps you perform a task quickly and easily.
   A. Quick Launch
   B. Control Panel
   C. Shortcut
   D. Wizard

5. A(n) _____ is represented by a small arrow in the lower-left corner of its icon.
   A. dialog box
   B. screen saver
   C. shortcut
   D. desktop

PROJECTS

PROJECT 8-1

Before you begin, ask if your instructor wants to see the background you create in this project.

1. Open the Control Panel and click the **Appearance and Themes** link.

2. Click the **Display** icon to open the Display Properties dialog box. (If your Control Panel appears in Classic view, double-click the **Display** icon to open the Display Properties dialog box.)

3. Click the **Themes** tab if necessary, and write down the name of the desktop theme that is currently displayed in the Theme list box.

4. Modify the theme:
    A. Click the **Desktop** tab, select the **Ascent Background**, and then click the **Apply** button.
    B. Click the **Themes** tab, click **Save As**, key **Project 8-1 Theme** in the File name textbox, and then click **Save**.

5. Click the arrow in the **Themes** list box and verify that the Project 8-1 Theme is displayed in the list.

6. Delete the Project 8-1 Theme:
    A. Select **Project 8-1 Theme** from the Theme list box.
    B. Click the **Delete** button.

PROJECT 8-2

1. Verify that the Quick Launch bar is displayed. If not:
    A. Right-click a clear area on the taskbar, then select **Toolbars** from the shortcut menu.
    B. Select the **Quick Launch** option.

2. Move the **My Shortcut** icon on your desktop to the beginning of the Quick Launch bar:
    A. Right-drag the **My Shortcut** icon from the desktop to the Quick Launch bar.
    B. Select the **Move Here** option from the menu.

3. Test the shortcut:
    A. Click the **My Shortcut** icon on the Quick Launch bar to open the Hobby document.
    B. Close the Hobby document.

4. Delete the shortcut from the Quick Launch bar:
    A. Right-click the **My Shortcut** icon on the Quick Launch bar, and then click **Delete** on the shortcut menu.
    B. Click **Yes** in the message box to confirm the deletion.

5. Follow your instructor's directions to log off or turn off your computer.

PROJECT 8-3

Shortcuts are handy tools, but too many shortcuts on the desktop can make it look cluttered and confusing. List other advantages and disadvantages of using shortcuts, including the pros and cons of assigning shortcut keys.

 ## TEAMWORK PROJECT

One of your coworkers is collecting informal inventories of all employees' computer systems. She has requested a list of the system resources and hardware devices on your computer. Working with another student, create a table that includes your name, the system information, such as the computer model, operating system, and registration information, and the hardware devices connected to each of your computers. In a paragraph below the table, explain where you found the information.

CRITICAL*Thinking*

ACTIVITY 8-1

Beyond aesthetics, is there a practical use for applying a desktop background? Include a brief explanation in your answer. If your answer is yes, include an example of a practical application. If your answer is no, cite an example of how a desktop background might impair productivity.

USING WINDOWS EXPLORER

OBJECTIVES

Upon completion of this lesson, you should be able to:

- Define uses for Windows Explorer.

- Identify the parts of the Explorer window and the icons used to represent drives, disks, files, and folders.

- Use Explorer to view the contents of a drive or folder.

- Expand and collapse the folder list.

- Change the view in the Explorer contents pane.

- Sort the information in the contents pane by criteria in the Details view.

- Display information about a file or folder in the Properties dialog box.

- Search for files or folders.

Estimated Time: 1.5 hour

VOCABULARY

Contents pane

Folders bar

Search

Sorting

Tree pane

Wildcard characters

Windows Explorer

The utility program *Windows Explorer* is designed to help you find, view, and manage files easily and effectively. Explorer gives you control over the organization and management of your files and folders. Like My Computer, which you used in earlier lessons, Explorer makes it easy to view the contents of selected disks and folders. In earlier versions of Windows, My Computer and Windows Explorer were separate programs. In Windows XP, My Computer and Windows Explorer are actually the same program; you simply click the Folders button on the toolbar in My Computer to access the Windows Explorer features. All the disk and folder maintenance operations you use with My Computer are available in Windows Explorer. Explorer simply provides additional features to make the tasks easier and faster. In this lesson, you will learn how to use options in Windows Explorer to control the display of files and folders.

The Explorer Window

1-3.2.6

Windows Explorer gives you the capability to search for files and folders, to find details about the contents of the files and folders, and to manage them—deleting, copying, and moving files and folders as necessary. There are three ways to start Explorer:

- Click Start, point to All Programs, point to Accessories, and then click Windows Explorer.

- Right-click over the Start button, and then select Explore from the shortcut menu.

- Click Start, click My Computer, and then click the Folders button on the toolbar.

The right pane of the Explorer window looks similar to and functions like the My Computer window. The major difference between the My Computer window and the Windows Explorer window is how the left pane is used. As you can see in Figure 9-1, My Computer's left pane contains a resource bar that provides links to system tasks and your computer's resources.

FIGURE 9-1
My Computer window

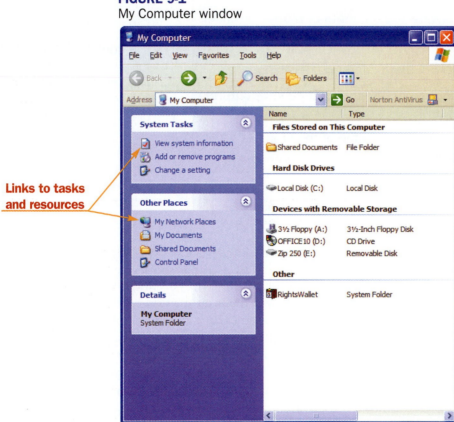

Explorer's left pane (see Figure 9-2) contains the Folders bar, which lets you see the structure of your folders at a glance and allows you to move and copy files by dragging them from one pane to the other. If you've worked in previous versions of Windows, this pane should look familiar to you.

FIGURE 9-2
Windows Explorer window

Currently
selected drive
or folder

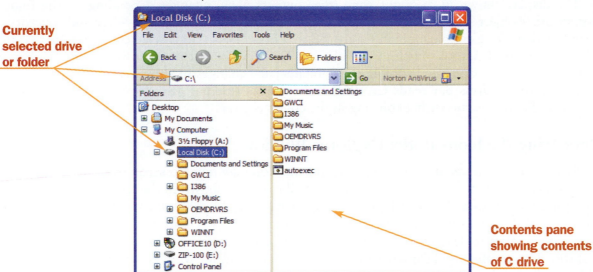

Contents pane
showing contents
of C drive

Note that with either of these windows, because they are really working from the same program, you can alter your view to appear like the other. For example, if you are in the My Computer window and you click the Folders button on the toolbar, the links will disappear and will be replaced by the Folders bar. If you are in the Windows Explorer window and you click on the Close button at the top right of the Folders panel, the Folders bar will disappear and be replaced by the links to System Tasks and Other Places.

S TEP-BY-STEP 9.1

1. Start your computer and launch Windows XP if necessary.

2. Click **Start**, point to **All Programs**, point to **Accessories**, and then click **Windows Explorer**. If Windows Explorer does not appear on the Accessories menu, click the down arrow at the bottom of the menu. Leave this window open for the next Step-by-Step.

Identifying the Parts of the Explorer Window

By now, you should recognize the window features common to many Windows XP screens. If you are new to Windows XP, however, you may not know the function of the two panes in the Explorer window. The *Folders bar* (left pane) is commonly referred to as the *tree pane*. The right pane is called the *contents pane*. These panes are discussed below.

Folders Bar (Tree Pane)

The Folders bar is also called the tree pane because its hierarchical display of all objects on the desktop is like a tree's trunk and branch system. But in this case, the tree is upside down: Its main root (Desktop) is at the top, with folders and subfolders branching off below it.

> **Computer Concepts**
>
> Windows XP continually monitors the programs you use. The programs and files that have not been accessed in some time will not be displayed on a menu until you click the down arrows at the bottom of the menu. The menu listing will expand to show all the options on the menu.

Contents Pane

The display shown in the right pane (the contents pane) changes depending on the folder, disk, or other object selected in the left pane. In other words, the two panes—tree and contents—work together. For example, note in Figure 9-2 that Local Disk (C:) is selected. Also note that the Address Bar says C:\, thus matching the object selected in the left pane. If the WINNT folder is selected in the tree pane, the listing in the contents pane changes to show what's in the WINNT folder and the Address Bar reads C:\WINNT. Explorer's title bar also displays the name of the disk or folder you're currently exploring in the contents pane.

Identifying the Icons in the Explorer Window

At the top of the tree pane is the Desktop icon. You may have to scroll to bring it into view. This icon represents the Windows desktop, and all icons are shown in the tree pane as stemming from the Desktop icon. Look at Figure 9-3. Note how the My Documents, My Computer, and My Network Places icons appear below and to the right of the Desktop icon. The placement of these icons makes it clear that these folders are subordinate to—or down one level from—the Desktop. The graphic used for each icon gives you a clue about what is represented—a drive, a folder, or an application file, for example.

FIGURE 9-3
Icons in the Explorer window

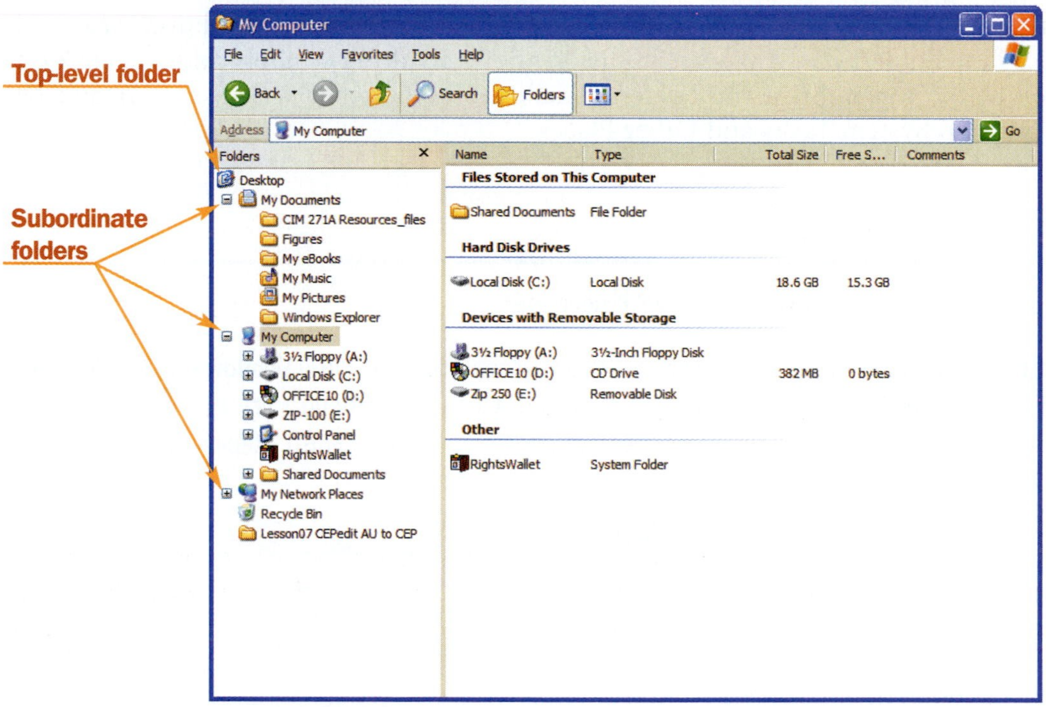

Each of these icons, in turn, has icons below and to the right of them. Under the My Computer icon, for example, you may see an icon for a floppy drive or a CD/DVD drive and an icon for the hard drive. The hard drive icon has a number of folders displayed below and to the right of it. These are the applications and other folders stored on the drive.

Finally, Explorer shows you whether each of these folders has subfolders within it. Notice in Figure 9-3 the small boxes to the left of some icons. Boxes containing a plus sign (+) indicate folders that have subfolders not currently displayed. If a box contains a minus sign (−), the subfolders are displayed below the folder. In Figure 9-3, for example, the minus sign next to the My Computer icon indicates that all subfolders in that folder are displayed below. The plus sign next to the Shared Documents folder indicates that this folder contains subfolders that are not displayed. (See the Expanding and Collapsing the Tree section, which follows.)

Note ✓

If you are displaying the contents of a folder for the first time, you may have to click the **Show Files** or **Show the contents of this folder** link in the contents pane first.

As you can see from a careful look at the tree pane, Explorer uses one view to show the same information that would require several views in My Computer. You'll find this view makes it very easy to handle file-management tasks.

The contents pane also shows several types of icons, depending on the object selected in the tree pane. Look at Figure 9-4. This figure shows that the WINNT folder has been selected. The label *WINNT* is highlighted in the tree pane, and the folder icon appears to be open. The contents pane shows the contents of this folder, which include both subfolders (identified by the yellow folder icons) and files (identified by icons other than that of a folder).

FIGURE 9-4
Displaying the contents of a folder

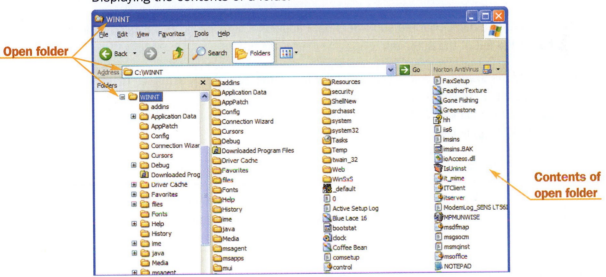

You can see the subfolders in the contents pane even when they are not displayed in the tree pane. Being able to control each pane independently of the other gives you great flexibility when you are copying, moving, viewing, or otherwise manipulating files.

Expanding and Collapsing the Tree

When you open Explorer, it does not display subfolders. If you want to display subfolders for any folder, you must expand the folder list (increase the subfolder display level). To expand the folder list, just click the plus sign in the box to the left of the folder. As the subfolders appear below the folder, the plus sign changes to a minus sign. When you click the minus sign, you collapse the folder list (decrease the subfolder display level).

Collapsing a folder makes it possible to view more objects in the tree. This is useful if you are trying to copy or move files between different folders. Collapsing folders also makes the folder list less cluttered, so it is easier to locate files and folders.

STEP-BY-STEP 9.2

1. Click the **My Computer** icon in the tree pane.

2. Find the drive on which the WINNT or WINDOWS folder is stored (generally drive C). If the box to the left of the drive has a plus sign, click the **plus sign** (+).

3. Locate the WINNT or WINDOWS folder, and note whether there is a plus or a minus sign in the box to the left of the icon.

4. Click the box to the left of the WINNT or WINDOWS folder icon. If the box has a plus sign, the tree will expand, showing the subfolders below the folder; if the box displays a minus sign, the tree will collapse.

> **Note**
>
> On your system, the WINNT folder may have a different name. It may, for instance, be called WINDOWS or Windows. If you are uncertain, ask your instructor for assistance. In this and subsequent Step-by-Step instructions, substitute the appropriate name of your folder wherever you see the name WINNT.

5. If necessary, click again on the box to the left of the folder icon to display the subfolders in the tree pane.

6. Notice that a number of the subfolders have additional subfolders, as indicated by a plus sign in the box to the left of the subfolder.

7. Expand the system32 folder (you may have to use the tree pane's scroll bar to find it), and display all of its subfolders and their subfolders:
   a. Click the **plus sign** in front of the system32 folder.
   b. Click the **plus sign** in front of the drivers folder.

8. Click the **minus sign** (–) in front of the drivers folder. Notice that the drivers folder list collapses.

9. Click the **minus sign** in front of the system32 folder and the **minus sign** in front of the WINNT or WINDOWS folder. Remain in this screen for the next Step-by-Step.

Setting Explorer Options

1-3.2.6

Explorer's View menu is similar to all View menus in other program windows. You can choose to display the Standard toolbar buttons and the status bar, for example, and you can change the view of the contents pane to Thumbnails, Tiles, Icons, List, or Details.

Views

The default view for Windows Explorer displays tiles (large icons) in the right pane, as shown in Figure 9-5. Depending on the task and your goal, you can choose the view option to best meet your objectives.

FIGURE 9-5
Windows Explorer—Tiles view

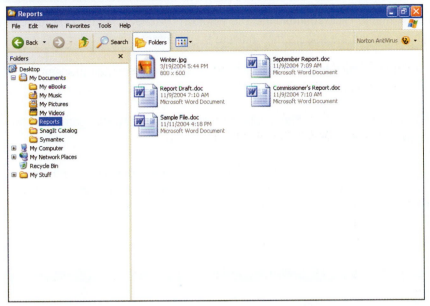

- **Thumbnails:** Displays the images a folder contains on a folder icon so you can identify the contents of the folder quickly. For example, in Thumbnails view, you can see small images of pictures stored within a folder on the folder. By default, four images will be displayed on the folder, and the folder name is displayed under the folder icon.

- **Tiles:** Displays a large icon and filename for each file and provides a visual clue to the type of file and the file contents, such as a musical note for music files or a picture for image files. Information about the file, such as the date it was last modified or the type of file, is displayed below the icons.

- **Icons:** Displays small icons with filenames below them, generally arranged horizontally across the screen.

- **List:** Provides a list of all files and folders. Displays small icons and the filename, usually in a vertical arrangement.

- **Details:** With details, you get much more information than you do with the other view types. Details view can show the file icon, the filename, the file size, the associated application, the date and time the file was created or last modified, and other information depending on the chosen options.

> **Note**
>
> To change the information listed in Details view, click the **View** menu and then click **Choose Details**. Click in the box to the left of each detail name to select it; if you want to eliminate a selected detail, click the box to deselect it. Then click the **OK** button to apply the new details.

Additionally, if a folder contains all graphic files, the Filmstrip view becomes an option as well. With the Filmstrip view, you see a larger image than you do with the Thumbnail view and you can scroll through all the files in the folder.

S TEP-BY-STEP 9.3

1. On the View menu, click **Thumbnails**. The display now shows large icons representing folders and files, with images on the folders that indicate their contents.

2. On the View menu, click **Icons**. The display now shows a horizontal arrangement of folders and files represented by icons and titles.

3. On the View menu, click **List**. The display now shows a vertical arrangement of folders and files represented by icons and titles.

4. On the View menu, click **Details**. The display now shows a detailed list of each folder, and may include information such as name, size, type, and date and time created or last modified (Figure 9-6). Leave this window open for the next Step-by-Step.

FIGURE 9-6
Windows Explorer—Details view

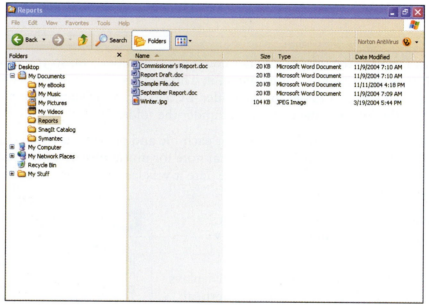

Sorting

To help you more easily locate files and folders, you can also sort the items displayed in a window. *Sorting* is the process of creating a list organized on a specific criterion. For example, you can sort a list of files in alphabetical order by filename, by size from smallest to largest, or by date created or modified, from most recent to oldest files. If you are looking for a file, but you can't remember the name, you might remember that you worked with the file within the last few days. Your best option is to sort by date modified, as shown in Figure 9-7. You can sort files by any details listed in Details view, such as name, size, and type. To sort by any option, just click the column name in Details view.

FIGURE 9-7
Windows Explorer—files sorted by date modified

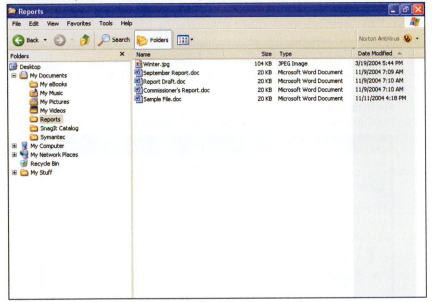

The Toolbar

Explorer's toolbar is similar to the My Computer toolbar. You will see the Back, Forward, and Up navigation buttons that help you navigate in both the tree pane and the contents pane. The Views button at the far right of the toolbar lets you change the way objects are displayed in the contents pane only. The options from the Views button are the same as those listed above: Thumbnails, Tiles, Icons, List, Details, and Filmstrip (for folders containing only graphic files). The Search button opens the Search Companion to help you find specific files or folders, which you will learn about later in this lesson.

Computer Concepts

The arrow that appears next to the column head in Details view indicates whether the list is sorted in ascending order (arrow points up) or descending order (arrow points down).

Remember you can change the Standard toolbar in any window, including the Explorer window, by clicking the Toolbars option from the View menu and then selecting the Customize option from the submenu. In the Customize dialog box, you can add or remove buttons from the toolbar. You can also change how information about toolbar buttons is displayed. In the Text options drop-down list, you can choose to display text identification for each button or to have identifying text appear when you rest the mouse pointer on the button. You can also choose the No text labels option, but you will probably find that the labels help you learn about the available toolbar commands.

Viewing the Contents of a Drive or Folder

1-3.2.6

Most folder and file operations require you first to identify the drive you want to use. In Explorer, icons in the tree pane represent the available disk drives, folders, and other objects. To select a drive, for example, click the appropriate drive icon. The drive is highlighted in the tree pane, and its contents appear in the contents pane (see Figure 9-8).

FIGURE 9-8
Highlighting shows which disk drive is selected

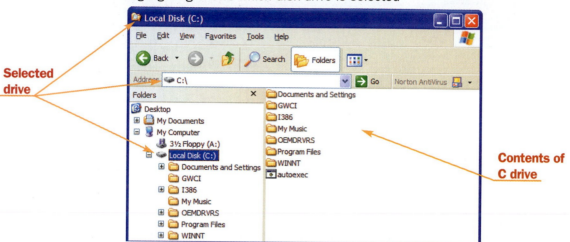

Selected drive

Contents of C drive

You can also select a drive or another desktop object (such as the Recycle Bin) by clicking the object in the Address Bar drop-down list. This action moves you directly to the object in the tree pane. If you have a very large tree displayed, it may be easier to select an object this way than to scroll in search of it.

To view the contents of a folder, click the folder in the tree pane. The folder opens and its contents appear in the contents pane. If the folder has subfolders, you can double-click a subfolder in the contents pane. When you do so, the subfolder's contents are displayed in the contents pane and the tree pane expands to show any subfolders.

Note

If the Address Bar is not visible in your Windows Explorer screen, click on the **View** menu and then open the Toolbars sub-menu. A check mark appears next to selected toolbars. Select **Address Bar** if it is not selected.

STEP-BY-STEP 9.4

1. Click the icon of the drive where your Assignments folder is located. The contents pane shows the contents of the disk or drive.

2. Double-click the **Assignments** folder in the contents pane. Notice that the folder's contents now appear in the contents pane and that the tree pane shows the open folder under the drive icon.

3. Click the **WINNT** or **WINDOWS** folder (usually found on drive C) in the tree pane to display the contents of the folder on your hard drive.

STEP-BY-STEP 9.4 Continued

4. In the contents pane, double-click the **system** folder. (If necessary, click **Show Files** or **Show the contents of this** folder in the contents pane.)

5. Click the **View** button on the toolbar and select **List**. Your display should resemble Figure 9-9.

FIGURE 9-9
Contents of the system folder

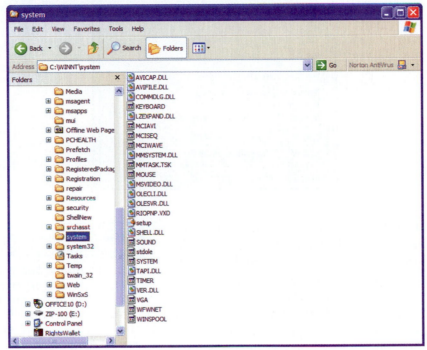

6. Click the **Up** button on the toolbar to select the WINNT or WINDOWS folder again.

7. From the Address Bar drop-down list, select the drive that contains your Assignments folder. (If the Address Bar is not visible, select it from the Toolbars submenu on the Views menu.)

8. Click the **Close** button to close Windows Explorer.

Displaying File Properties

1-3.2.6

The Properties dialog box for a file or folder in Windows displays information about the file or folder, including the type of file, the name of the program that opens the file, the file size, the file location, and the date the file was created and last modified. To display the properties for a file or folder in Windows, right-click the filename or folder in Windows Explorer, and then click Properties. Figure 9-10 shows the properties for a Microsoft Word file named Letter.doc.

FIGURE 9-10
Properties dialog box in Windows

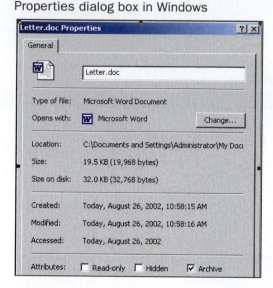

Files created in different programs can have additional properties that are displayed in the Properties dialog box within that program. For example, in addition to General properties, a Microsoft Word document can have Summary, Statistics, Contents, and Custom properties, which might include the document's author, the number of words and paragraphs in the document, and the name of the client for whom the document was created. Figure 9-11 shows the Summary tab of the Properties dialog box in Word for the file Letter.doc.

Note

You can also open the Properties dialog box by right-clicking any icon on the Windows desktop. This will open the shortcut menu so you can select Properties to open the dialog box.

FIGURE 9-11
Summary tab in the Properties dialog box in Microsoft Word

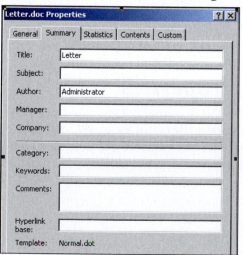

STEP-BY-STEP 9.5

1. Open Windows Explorer. To do this, right-click the **Start** button, and then click **start** and then click **Explore**.

2. Click the **My Documents** icon in the tree pane and look for a data file, such as a word-processing file, an image (or picture) file, or an audio file. Your instructor may direct you to a specific folder to find a data file, or you can open the **My Pictures** folder and find an image file in the **Sample Pictures** subfolder.

3. Right-click the file icon in the contents pane.

4. Click **Properties**. Notice which properties are displayed on the General tab in the dialog box.

5. If there are other tabs in the Properties dialog box, click on each tab and look at the information displayed. Close the Properties dialog box.

6. Close Windows Explorer.

Finding Files and Folders

The Windows XP *Search* feature allows you to find files and folders by specifying a variety of search criteria. For example, you can search for files and folders by name, by date, by type, by size, or by a string of text that they contain. There are three ways to access the Search feature:

- In Windows Explorer, click the Search button on the toolbar.

- If you are not in the Explorer window, click the Start button and then click Search on the Start menu.

- Right-click over the Start button and then select Search… from the shortcut menu.

TECHNOLOGY TIMELINE

LOGICAL SEARCH TOOLS

In the 1840s, George Boole, a self-educated mathematician from England, developed ways of expressing logical processes using algebraic symbols. The Boolean logic uses words called *operators* to determine whether a statement is true or false. This Boolean logic has become the basis for computer database searches. The most common operators used are AND, OR, and NOT. These three simple words can be extremely helpful when searching for data. For example, if you search for "railroad AND models," the results will include documents with both words. If you search for "railroad OR models," the results will include the greatest amount of matches listing documents with either word. A good way to limit the search is to search for "railroad NOT models." The results will then include all documents about railroads but not documents about models.

The Search or Search Results window will open. The left pane is called the Search Companion and offers a list of options to search. Figure 9-12 shows the Search window that opens in the left pane when you click the *All files and folders* option.

FIGURE 9-12
Search Results window

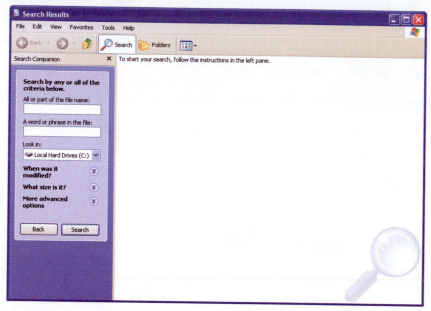

In the *All or part of the file name* text box, type all or part of the name of the file you want to find. You can also use the **wildcard characters** (* or ?) to substitute for characters in a filename. Use * to substitute for zero or more characters and use ? to substitute for only one character.

To search for files containing specific text, type the text you want to find in the A word or phrase in the file text box. Use the Look in list arrow to select the drive or folder you want to search. To specify additional search criteria, click on the down arrow button next to one of the available search options, and then select one or more of the options to narrow your search. Table 9-1 describes the search options available. When you are finished selecting search options, click the Search button at the bottom of the Search Companion pane to start your search.

TABLE 9-1
Search options

SEARCH OPTION	USE TO
When was it modified?	Find files that were created or modified on or between specific dates
What size is it?	Find files of a specific size
Type of file	Find files of a specific type, such as a Microsoft Word document
Search system folders	Search in the folders that contain system information
Search hidden files and folders	Search in files or folders that have the hidden attribute
Search subfolders	Search all the subfolders in a drive or folder

TABLE 9-1 Continued
Search options

SEARCH OPTION	USE TO
Case sensitive	Find files with upper- and lowercase letters that match the filename search criteria
Search slow files or Search tape backup	Find files stored on removable storage devices, such as a tape backup device

STEP-BY-STEP 9.6

1. Click the **Start** button on the taskbar and then click **Search** in the Start menu.

2. Click the **All files and folders** option in the Search Companion (left) pane.

3. Key the name of a file from My Documents for which you would like to search in the All or part of the file name text box.

4. Choose **My Documents** from the drop-down menu of the Look in field if it is not already selected.

5. Click the **down arrow** button next to More advanced options. Make sure that **Search subfolders** is checked.

6. Click the **Search** button.

7. Select the file you want from the list of files and folders in the right pane. Double-click on the file to open it.

8. Close the file.

9. Close the Search window.

SUMMARY

In this lesson, you learned:

- Windows Explorer and My Computer are actually the same program in Windows XP.

- When you start Explorer, you see a window with the familiar title bar, menu bar, display window, and status bar. The display window is divided vertically into two panes—a left pane, which displays the Folders bar, and a right pane, which displays the contents.

- The Folders bar, also referred to as the tree pane, displays all the objects on the desktop in a hierarchical structure, and it displays the folder structure for the currently selected disk. The contents pane displays the contents of the folder selected in the tree pane.

- In the tree pane, the open folder is the active folder. In the contents pane, a folder icon represents a subfolder of the open folder.

- Explorer's View menu options and Views button allow you to control how files are displayed in the contents pane. You can select Thumbnails, Tiles, Icons, List, Details, and sometimes Filmstrip (for graphics files).

- Sorting files in the contents pane organizes the list according to a specific criterion. You can sort files and folders by many specifications including name, size, date modified, and type.

- In the tree pane, you can collapse (decrease the levels shown in) the tree so the folders and subfolders do not appear. You can also expand (increase the levels shown in) the tree so it shows folders of all levels.

- You can display the properties of a file by right-clicking the filename in the Explorer window and then selecting Properties from the shortcut menu to open the Properties dialog box, which provides information about the file including size, type, date, author, and other details.

- The Search feature is available in Windows Explorer by clicking on the Search button on the toolbar, or you can access Search directly from the Start menu.

- Options in the Search Companion allow you to refine your search to find specific files or folders.

VOCABULARY *Review*

Define the following terms:

Contents pane	Sorting	Wildcard characters
Folders bar	Tree pane	Windows Explorer
Search		

REVIEW *Questions*

TRUE/FALSE

Circle T if the statement is true or F if the statement is false.

T   F   1. To start Windows Explorer, you select All Programs on the Start menu and then select Windows Explorer.

T   F   2. In Windows Explorer, the Folders bar is also called the contents pane.

T   F   3. When viewing files as Thumbnails, you can see the date and time the file was modified.

T   F   4. To find a specific file, use the Windows Search feature.

T   F   5. A plus sign next to a folder in Explorer's tree pane indicates folders that have subfolders not currently displayed.

MULTIPLE CHOICE

Circle the best response for each of the following statements.

1. Windows Explorer and _____ are the same program in Windows XP.
   A. Desktop
   B. WordPad
   C. My Computer
   D. Recycle Bin

2. _____ creates a list organized on a specific criterion.
   A. Searching
   B. Sorting
   C. Exploring
   D. Tiling

3. The left pane of Explorer contains a(n) _____ that lets you see the structure of your folders.
   A. tree
   B. icon
   C. link
   D. menu

4. The _____ icon is at the very top of the tree pane.
   A. My Computer
   B. My Explorer
   C. drive C
   D. Desktop

5. All of the following are views you can use to display files and folders *except* _____.
   A. Thumbnails
   B. Rulers
   C. Tiles
   D. List

PROJECTS

PROJECT 9-1

1. Start Windows if it is not already running.

2. Open **My Computer**, and then click the **Folders** button on the toolbar to access the Windows Explorer Folders bar.

3. In Windows Explorer, perform the following steps:
   A. Change the view to **Thumbnails**.
   B. Change the view to **List**.
   C. Change the view to **Icons**.

4. If the Address Bar is not visible, select it from the **Toolbars** submenu of the View menu.

5. Click the **Address Bar** drop-down list arrow, and select **Recycle Bin**.

6. Click the **Back** button to return to Windows Explorer.

7. Click the icon that represents your computer's hard disk in the tree pane.

8. Double-click a folder on your computer's hard disk to view its contents.

9. Right-click a file or subfolder in the folder to open the shortcut menu.

10. Select **Properties** from the shortcut menu to open the Properties dialog box.

11. Look at the information displayed about the file or folder, and then close the dialog box.

12. Click the **Up** button on the toolbar until My Computer appears in the Address Bar.

13. Click the **Folders** button on the toolbar to reopen the resource bar in the left pane.

14. Click the **Close** button to close My Computer.

PROJECT 9-2

1. Open **Windows Explorer,** and display the **Lesson 9** data folder in the contents pane.

2. Open the **Lesson 9** data folder to display its contents with details about the files and folders:
   A. Click the **Lesson 9** folder, then open the Project9-2 folder.
   B. Choose **Details** from the View menu.
   C. Open the **Choose Details** dialog box and select **Name, Size, Type,** and **Date Modified** if these details are not already selected.

3. Print a copy of the Project9-2 Report Form in the Project Reports folder:
   A. Click the **Project Report** folder to open it.
   B. Verify that your printer is accessible and ready.
   C. Select the **Project9-2 Report Form** file, and then select **Print** from the File menu.

4. Using the Project9-2 Report Form you printed in step 3, do the following:
   A. Fill in the heading with the appropriate information.
   B. Answer all questions on the Report Form using Windows Explorer to display the subfolders and files in the Project9-2 folder.
   C. Turn the report in to your instructor if requested.

5. Close Windows Explorer.

6. If instructed to do so, shut down Windows XP and your computer.

TEAMWORK PROJECT

Working with another student, write a list of steps you would follow to use the Windows XP Search feature to find all the JPEG image files in the My Documents folder. Then use the steps to conduct the search individually. When you have the search results, select the List or Details view and click the Name column head to put the list of files in ascending alphabetical order by filename (you may need to click the Name column head twice to put them in A to Z order). On a piece of paper, write the total number of JPEG files you found and the names of the first three files. Compare your results with your partner's results. If there are differences in the list, do you think they are because you have different files on your computer, or because you set up the Search criteria differently?

CRITICAL *Thinking*

ACTIVITY 9-1

During lunch, a coworker asked if you thought there were advantages to working with Windows Explorer rather than My Computer. You told him you would have to think about it and would give him an answer later in the day. Consider features that might be available in Explorer but not in My Computer; determine what, if any, operations are easier to perform in Explorer than in My Computer; and prepare a written response for your coworker.

FILE MANAGEMENT WITH WINDOWS EXPLORER

OBJECTIVES

Upon completion of this lesson, you should be able to:

- Create folders and subfolders.
- Recognize and distinguish between different types of icons.
- Understand how to run an application or open a document file from Windows Explorer.
- Name and rename files and folders.
- Delete folders and restore (undelete) a deleted folder from the Recycle Bin.
- Manage the display and organization of files.
- Copy, delete, and move files from one folder to another.
- Use Disk Cleanup to clear your disk of unnecessary files.
- Run Disk Defragmenter to make your computer operate more efficiently.

Estimated Time: 1.5 hours

VOCABULARY

8.3 alias

Application file icons

Copy

Destination

Disk Cleanup

Disk Defragmenter

Document file icons

Extension

Filename

Fragmented files

Move

Parent folder

Source

Subfolder

1-3.2.6

Creating Folders

As you have learned, folders are used to organize files on a disk, and folders are represented by icons that actually look like file folders. When you want to create a folder to store files, you first must decide where you want to place the new folder. To create a *subfolder,* your decision is in which *parent folder* the new subfolder will be placed. Remember, this is a creation process, a building process. You decide where to create or where to build.

In Lesson 5, you created a new folder in the My Documents window. Windows Explorer gives you the versatility to create and manage files in any location accessible by your computer. This includes hard disk drives, floppy disks, network drives, and folders on those drives. To create a folder in Windows Explorer, select New from the File menu and then click the Folder option in the submenu. A New Folder icon (see Figure 10-1) appears in the contents pane. To create a subfolder, click the folder in the tree pane where you want to place the subfolder (or double-click the folder in the contents pane), then follow the instructions for creating a folder.

FIGURE 10-1
New Folder icon

Recognizing Different Types of Icons

It helps to identify what you are looking at in the Windows Explorer panes, so let's take a moment to learn how to distinguish among the different types of icons used to represent locations, folders, and files. Location icons are graphic images that clearly represent drives, disks, or locations such as My Computer (a computer) or My Desktop (a stylized desktop). Folder icons look like the manila folders used in a filing cabinet, and some folders give a clue to their contents by including a small image such as a musical note, a picture, or a piece of film.

Working with File Icons

There are two basic kinds of file icons—*application file icons* and *document file icons*. Each has distinguishable characteristics.

Application File Icons

An application file icon starts an application. The icon may look like a miniature version of the program icon, or it may look like a miniature window (see Figure 10-2). In both cases, double-clicking an application file icon in the contents pane will start the application program.

> **Computer Concepts**
>
> An easy way to start an application or open a document from Windows Explorer is to use the Open command on the File menu. Select the icon for the file you want to open or run in the contents pane and then choose **Open** from the File menu.

FIGURE 10-2
Application file icons

Document File Icons

Document file icons share the same distinctive feature: a piece of paper with a superimposed graphic (see Figure 10-3). When you create a document file, you can associate that file with an application. For Windows, this means you create a link between a document and an application. This allows you to open a document file directly—you do not need to open the application first.

FIGURE 10-3
Document file icons

1-3.2.6
1-3.2.7

Naming Folders and Files

If you are familiar with DOS or older versions of Windows, you may know that both use a file-naming convention called *8.3* (pronounced "eight dot three"). The "eight" part means that a file's name may be up to eight characters long. The "three" part is an *extension* (no longer than three characters) to the name. And the "dot" is the period that separates the 8 from the 3. Neither spaces nor special characters can be used in the DOS naming system. For example, in the *filename letter.doc*, the name is *letter*, the separator is the standard period, and the extension is *doc*.

Newer versions of Windows, including Windows XP, allow long names (up to 255 characters) for folders and files, and they allow spaces, punctuation marks, and most characters in the names. They allow you to name a folder *JL Smith & Company Contract* instead of a code name such as *jlscocon.doc*. In some cases, extensions are also longer in newer filenames. Examples include the *jpeg* extension used for some graphics files, and the *html* extension, short for hypertext markup language, which is used to designate files in a format used for Web pages.

But only application programs designed specifically for Windows 95 and later versions will permit long filenames. To compensate, Windows (and Windows application programs) assigns a short filename, called an *8.3 alias*. Programs that don't support long filenames see this 8.3 alias as the file's name.

Be extra careful working with programs that don't recognize long filenames:

- If you copy a folder or file with a long filename to a system that doesn't support long filenames, the system will use an 8.3 alias.

- When you open a file that has a long filename in a program that doesn't recognize long filenames, the long filename could get lost.

- Utility programs that back up and restore data and applications may not support long filenames, and using such programs can destroy the long filenames and the backup files may not be accessible.

The same naming conventions apply to folder names. When you create a new folder (before you click anywhere else or press Enter), simply key the folder name. As you key, your folder name replaces the words *New Folder* under the folder's icon. Press Enter to display the new folder name.

S TEP-BY-STEP 10.1

1. Start Windows if necessary, and then start Windows Explorer.

2. If necessary, change the view to **Icons**.

3. Your instructor will tell you whether you will use a floppy disk or a specific location on the hard disk drive to store your practice files.

   a. If you are using a floppy disk, verify that your practice disk is in the appropriate floppy drive, then click the disk's icon in the tree pane (most likely labeled A: or 3½ floppy).

   b. If you are directed to use a location on the hard drive, select the correct drive and folder in the tree pane.

   c. Notice that the drive is now displayed in the Address Bar if it is displayed. (If you do not see the Address Bar, select it from the Toolbars submenu on the View menu to display it.) Notice also that there are few or no icons in the contents pane. You haven't created any folders or files yet, with the exception of the Hobby file in your Assignments folder, which you may see displayed.

4. Create a new folder called Reports:

   a. Click **New** on the File menu, and then select **Folder** on the submenu.

   b. The New Folder icon—with the name *New Folder* highlighted—appears in the contents pane. Key the folder name **Reports**. Be sure to key upper- and lowercase as shown.

   c. Press **Enter**. You should see a new folder named Reports displayed in the contents pane.

5. Create three subfolders in the Reports folder:

   a. Double-click the **Reports** folder icon in the contents pane to open it. The Reports folder icon and name are now displayed in the Address Bar.

   b. Click **New** on the File menu and then select **Folder** from the submenu. A new folder icon appears.

   c. Key the folder name **Monthly**, and then press **Enter**.

   d. Click anywhere in the display window, except on the newly created folder, to deselect it.

6. Following the instructions in Steps 5b–5d, create two additional subfolders in the Reports folder; name them **Quarterly** and **Final**. Your screen should resemble Figure 10-4. Remain in this screen for the next Step-by-Step.

STEP-BY-STEP 10.1 Continued

FIGURE 10-4
Three subfolders in the Reports folder

Renaming a Folder

You may find that after you have used a folder for a time, you need to rename it. This is a simple process; there are actually four ways to rename a folder:

- Click the folder in the contents pane to select it, press the F2 key, and then key in the new name in the text box.

- Click the folder to select it, choose Rename from the File menu, and then key the new name in the text box.

- Right-click the folder name, choose Rename on the shortcut menu, and then key the new name in the text box.

- Click the Folders button on the toolbar to access the My Computer tasks bar. Then click the folder icon to select it, click Rename this folder in the File and Folder Tasks panel, and then key the new name in the text box.

Notice that other folder maintenance tasks appear in the File and Folder Tasks panel of the My Computer window. If no subfolder is selected, the File and Folder Tasks panel includes only Make a New Folder and Publish this folder to the Web. (If you are on a network, you may also see Share this folder.) If a subfolder is selected, the task list includes folder tasks such as Rename this folder, Move this folder, and Copy this folder.

> **Note**
>
> Rename folders with care. Application programs will not work if they cannot locate the folder names for which they are searching.

STEP-BY-STEP 10.2

1. Click the **Up** button on the toolbar to close the Reports folder and return to the drive contents display.

2. Right-click the **Reports** folder icon to display the shortcut menu.

3. Click **Rename** in the shortcut menu.

4. Key the new name **Status Reports**, and then press **Enter**. Leave this window open for the next Step-by-Step.

Deleting a Folder

You can delete a folder in four ways:

- Click the folder to select it and then select Delete from the File menu.

- Click the Folders button on the toolbar, click the folder you want to delete to select it, and then select Delete this folder from the My Computer File and Folder Tasks panel.

- Click the folder to select it and then press the Delete key.

- Right-click the folder and then select Delete on the shortcut menu.

When you delete a folder or subfolder, you also delete all the files in it. Use extreme caution, therefore, before you attempt to delete a folder. To make sure this is what you really want to do, Windows displays a Confirm Folder Delete message box (see Figure 10-5). Windows provides one additional safety net when you are deleting a folder from a hard disk. Folders deleted from a hard disk are transferred by default to the Recycle Bin, from which they can be recovered. But a folder or a file deleted from a floppy disk is gone—period. No Recycle Bin is available.

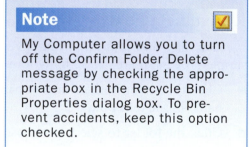

Note ☑

My Computer allows you to turn off the Confirm Folder Delete message by checking the appropriate box in the Recycle Bin Properties dialog box. To prevent accidents, keep this option checked.

FIGURE 10-5
Confirm Folder Delete message box

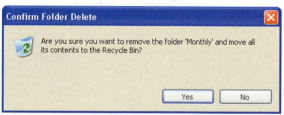

STEP-BY-STEP 10.3

1. Click the **Status Reports** folder in the tree pane (or double-click it in the contents pane) to open the folder and display its subfolders.

2. Delete the Monthly subfolder:
   a. Click the **Monthly** subfolder to select it.
   b. Press the **Delete** key. The Confirm Folder Delete message box appears.
   c. Verify that the correct folder name (Monthly) is shown before you click the **Yes** button. Watch as Windows graphically illustrates the folder being deleted from the Status Reports folder.

3. Click the **Up** button on the toolbar until you return to My Computer.

4. Remain in this window for the next Step-by-Step.

Selecting Files

Windows Explorer permits you to control how your files are organized by allowing you to move and copy files between disks and folders and to delete files. The first step in performing any of these functions is to select the files.

You learned in Lesson 5 that you select a single file by clicking it. To select two or more files that are adjacent to one another, click the first file in the series, press and hold down the Shift key, and then click the last file in the series, and to select files that are not adjacent, press and hold down the Ctrl key and then click each of the files. You can select all the files in a folder with the Select All command on the Edit menu in Explorer.

You can use the scroll bars to move around the display window when selecting files. Don't worry if the selected object moves out of view. An object will remain selected until you select another object or cancel the selection. When you want to cancel all the selections in a window, click a blank area in the window.

STEP-BY-STEP 10.4

1. In the Windows Explorer tree pane, click the drive that contains your data files for this lesson.

2. If necessary, scroll the window of the contents pane until the **Step10-4** folder is in view, then double-click it to open it. (You might have to click the Show files or Show the contents of this folder link in the contents pane first to display the files and folders.)

3. Maximize the window.

4. Select **Details** view if necessary.

5. Select the first file in the contents pane by clicking it once. (Be careful not to double-click, or you may open the file.)

6. Select nonadjacent files:
   a. Press and hold down **Ctrl**.
   b. Click every other filename you currently see in the window.

STEP-BY-STEP 10.4 Continued

7. Deselect the first selected file by pressing **Ctrl** and clicking the file's icon.

8. Deselect all the selected files by clicking once on a clear area in the contents pane.

9. Select adjacent files:
    a. Click the first file in the list.
    b. Press and hold down **Shift**. Then click the tenth file in the listing. All the intervening files will be selected.

10. Deselect all the selected files by clicking once on a clear area in the contents pane.

11. Click **Select All** on the Edit menu to select all the files in the folder.

12. Deselect all the files by clicking once on a clear area in the contents pane. Keep the window open for the next Step-by-Step.

Copying, Moving, and Deleting Files

1-3.2.6
1-3.2.7

One of the key advantages of using Windows is the ease with which you can copy, delete, or move files from one location to another. You move or copy files from a source to a destination. The *source* is the file to be copied, and the *destination* is the location (folder or disk) where the copied or moved file will then reside. Whenever you need to move or copy files, both the source and destination locations should be visible. In this way, you can see what you are moving or copying and where it is going. In Windows Explorer, you can view the source in the contents pane and the destination in the tree pane, or you can use the My Computer option to make the source and destination windows visible at the same time by changing the browsing option in the Folder Options dialog box to *Open each folder in its own window*. Folder Options are available from the Tools menu.

> **Note**
>
> The option to open folders in their own windows is only available when you are in the My Computer screen of Windows Explorer. Click the **Folders** button on the toolbar to close the tree pane on Windows Explorer to access the My Computer window so this option will work.

Copying Files

When you *copy* a file, you place a duplicate of the file in a different location and the original file remains in place. To copy a file to a new location on a different disk, select it. You can select more than one file to copy using the techniques you learned earlier. You can also select a folder to copy.

When you copy folders in Windows Explorer, you must hold down the Ctrl key as you drag the object from its current location and drop it onto its destination; that is, to the folder or drive where you want to copy it. If you are copying a folder from one window to another in My Computer, however, you simply drag the object to a new location to make a copy—you do not need to press any key while you drag to make a copy of the file.

Moving Files

The moving process is similar to the copying process. When you **move** a file, however, you remove it from its original location and place it in the destination location. To move an object to a new location on a different disk in Windows Explorer, simply select it and drag it to the destination. In the My Computer screen, you must hold down the Shift key as you drag the file to its destination to move it without leaving a copy in the source location.

Rather than try to remember when to hold down the Shift or Ctrl key, an alternate method of moving and copying files is to drag the file using the right mouse button. When the file is dropped in the destination, a menu appears; you can then click on your preference: Copy Here or Move Here.

If you attempt to copy or move a file to a destination where an identically named file exists, Windows displays the Confirm File Replace message box, shown in Figure 10-6. Click the Yes button to replace the existing file; click No to cancel the copy or move.

FIGURE 10-6
Confirm File Replace message box

Take special care when moving, copying, deleting, or renaming files so that a file is not lost. You may inadvertently move a file to a location or rename a file and then forget the name or location. Another common error occurs when you rename a file using different application software than that used to create the original file, so the file is no longer associated with that original file and you won't be able to locate it. You may also find that you can no longer open the renamed file in either the original or the new application.

Common problems associated with manipulating and working with files include lost files and file or disk corruption. You can avoid these problems by naming and storing files systematically, backing up data files regularly, and checking compatibility.

STEP-BY-STEP 10.5

1. Select **Tiles** from the View menu.

2. In the tree pane, click the drive where the data files for this lesson are located.

3. Find the **Step10-5** folder in the contents pane and double-click the folder to open it.

4. Double-click the **Status Reports** folder to open it.

5. Double-click the **Final** folder and locate the **10-5Status Qtr 1** file.

STEP-BY-STEP 10.5 Continued

6. Find your **Assignments** folder in the tree pane.

7. Drag the **10-5Status Qtr 1** file from the contents pane to the Assignments folder in the tree pane to move it to the new location.

8. Click the **Assignments** folder in the tree pane to open it in the contents pane.

9. You should see the 10-5Status Qtr 1 file, now in the Assignments folder.

10. Hold down the **Ctrl** key and drag the **10-5Status Qtr 1** file in the contents pane to the Final subfolder in the tree pane to make a copy of the file in the new location.

11. Leave this window open for the next Step-by-Step.

Deleting Files

There are several ways to delete a file in Windows Explorer; in fact, all the ways mentioned earlier that you can use to delete a folder can also be used to delete a file. Select the file and then press Delete, or right-click to open the shortcut menu and then click Delete to quickly delete a file. You will see a Confirm File Delete message box when you delete a file, just as you do when you delete a folder. Click Yes in the dialog box to continue the process of deleting the file. Remember you can also use the Delete command on the File menu or the Delete this file task on the My Computer tasks bar to delete a file also.

STEP-BY-STEP 10.6

1. Click the **Assignments** folder in the tree pane to display its contents in the contents pane.

2. Locate the **10-5Status Qtr 1** file in the contents pane and right-click on the file to open the short-cut menu.

3. Click **Delete** to delete the file. Click Yes to confirm the deletion.

4. Close Windows Explorer.

Restoring a Deleted File

As discussed previously, a file (or folder) deleted from a hard disk goes to the Recycle Bin. The Recycle Bin acts as a temporary storage folder for files you delete and keeps track of where deleted files and folders were originally stored. Then if you need to recover a deleted file or folder, you can use the Recycle Bin to restore it to its original location on the hard disk.

To restore a deleted file from the Recycle Bin, you must restore it before you empty the Recycle Bin because emptying the Recycle Bin permanently deletes all the files currently in the Recycle Bin. Double-click the Recycle Bin icon on the desktop or click the Recycle Bin icon in the tree pane of Windows Explorer to open the Recycle Bin window (see Figure 10-7), which displays files deleted from the hard disk. To restore a file or folder, right-click it and choose Restore from the shortcut menu, or select one or more items you want to restore, right-click any selected item, and then select Restore the selected items from the Recycle Bin Tasks panel or Restore from the File menu.

The selected file will be returned to its original location and it will no longer appear within the Recycle Bin. Use the Restore all items option on the tasks panel to restore all the files and folders in the Recycle Bin to their original locations.

Computer Concepts

If you choose to Empty the Recycle Bin, the files are permanently deleted and cannot be restored.

FIGURE 10-7
Recycle Bin window

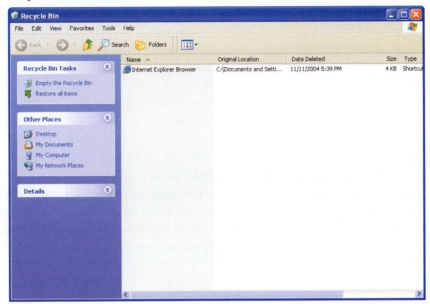

Working in a Connected World

PROJECT MANAGEMENT

Project management is one of the components that a system analyst, a job described in an earlier lesson, might find in a job description. However, because the job of a system analyst can sometimes be so detailed, many companies hire a project manager to work with the analyst and other team members. A project manager might be in charge of a wide array of projects—from Web site development to implementing an entire new computer system. The responsibilities of the project manager would be to manage, guide, keep everyone on task, and coach the team.

People who work in this profession need strong leadership abilities and good organizational skills. Many people use a management software program such as Project Management to help them with this job. Educational requirements vary depending on the company and job requirements—some employers may require a two-year degree, whereas others require a master's degree.

Managing a Hard Drive

1-3.2.7
1-3.2.8

A trouble-free hard disk is extremely important to the Windows operating system. Windows uses your hard disk for temporary storage, and many Windows application programs create temporary files on the hard disk as you use the application. If your hard disk is not in good working order, you may find your system slow in responding or you may have problems running programs and opening documents. Hard disks continue to increase in storage capacity, but a disk on a computer that is used by more than one person or for a long period of time may have many files that are not needed. You can regain disk space using system tools designed to purge the hard disk of unneeded files.

Windows comes with a number of tools to keep your system in good working order. You can review all of these by looking up information about system tools in the Windows Help and Support feature. For the remainder of this lesson, we'll discuss two important disk maintenance tools: Disk Cleanup and Disk Defragmenter. You can open both of these programs from the Start menu.

Disk Cleanup enables you to clear your disk of unnecessary files. *Disk Defragmenter* rearranges the files on your disk, repositioning the files in one place so the disk performs optimally. An error-checking tool that reads a disk's vital signs and either warns you about problems or fixes them is also available. You can access this tool from Windows Explorer by selecting My Computer in the tree pane, and then selecting the icon for the disk you want to check. Click on Properties in the File menu to open the Properties dialog box and you will find the error-checking tool on the Tools tab.

Locating and Deleting Unnecessary Files

You can use Disk Cleanup to help free up space on your hard drive. Disk Cleanup will not work on floppy drives or CD-ROM disks. The Disk Cleanup program searches your drive and then shows you temporary files and unnecessary program files you can safely delete. You can direct Disk Cleanup to delete some or all of those files.

STEP-BY-STEP 10.7

1. Open the **Start** menu.

2. Select the **All Programs** option, select the **Accessories** option, choose the **System Tools** option, and then select the **Disk Cleanup** option. The Disk Cleanup message box appears showing the progress of the scan of your hard drive. Note: If your computer has more than one drive, there will be a prompt asking which drive you want to clean up.

STEP-BY-STEP 10.7 Continued

3. When the scan of the hard drive is complete, the Disk Cleanup for (C:) (or the drive selected) dialog box indicates how much disk space you can gain by cleaning up the disk (see Figure 10-8).

FIGURE 10-8
Disk Cleanup dialog box

4. Only certain file types are selected for deletion by default. Scroll through the list of files to see what other files could be deleted and how much space could be gained on the hard drive by their deletion.

STEP-BY-STEP 10.7 Continued

5. Click the **More Options** tab in the Disk Cleanup dialog box. You will see you have three additional options for cleaning up your disk (see Figure 10-9). The Windows components option permits you to remove optional Windows program components you do not use. The Installed programs option permits you to remove programs you may no longer need or use. The System Restore option tracks changes to your computer and creates a restore point when it detects the beginning of a change. It permits you to remove all but the most recently saved system restoration point or to restore your computer to an earlier state in which your computer was functioning the way you liked.

FIGURE 10-9
Additional disk cleanup options

6. Click the **Cancel** button to close Disk Cleanup without performing any actions.

Each option on the More Options tab launches a separate program to perform the actions described. You would need to select each of these options independently. If you wanted to actually clean up the hard drive on your system (deleting the files listed on the Disk Cleanup tab), you would click OK in the Disk Cleanup dialog box. A message box would ask you to verify that you wanted to perform this action—in which case you would click OK. Then the disk cleanup would proceed. Depending on the number of files involved, the speed of your system, and so on, a disk cleanup can take anywhere from just a couple of minutes up to a half an hour or more.

Defragmenting a Disk

Disks—both hard and floppy—store data in clusters, also referred to as allocation units. A cluster is the smallest amount of disk space the operating system can handle when it writes or reads a file and is usually equal to 512 bytes or the default size of the disk. When you store files on a newly formatted disk, Windows writes each file's data in adjacent clusters. For example, the data for the first file saved might be stored in clusters 3 through 15, the next file's data might use clusters 16 through 30, and a third file's data might use clusters 31 and 32. In this way, Windows stores data in contiguous clusters; that is, in clusters that are adjacent on the disk.

Each time you delete a file, however, you empty clusters and make them available for new data. To optimize your disk space, Windows uses these now-empty clusters as you save new files. First, Windows saves as much data as possible in the first available cluster, then the next available cluster, and the next, and so on, until it has stored all the remaining file data. In this way, Windows splits file data among clusters that are not contiguous. In other words, in its efforts to optimize disk space, Windows creates *fragmented files*, files that are not stored in contiguous clusters. In the normal process of saving new files and deleting old files, your disk becomes quite fragmented.

Fragmentation does not harm a disk, but heavy fragmentation can slow down the disk's read and write times, thus reducing disk efficiency. To enhance disk performance, use Windows' Disk Defragmenter (another option on the System Tools submenu, accessed from the Accessories option on the Start Menu) or a similar program. Disk Defragmenter rearranges disk files, storing each file in contiguous blocks.

First, Defragmenter looks at your disk and tells you what percentage of the disk is fragmented. If the disk is not heavily fragmented, you may not want to proceed; in that case, the Defragmenter gives you an option: continue or quit. If you continue, Disk Defragmenter begins to reposition the files. While Defragmenter is working, you can click the Show Details button to see a graphic display of the program's progress. Note that you cannot use Disk Defragmenter on floppy disks.

STEP-BY-STEP 10.8

1. Open the **Start** menu.

2. Select the **All Programs** option, select the **Accessories** option, choose the **System Tools** option, and then select the **Disk Defragmenter** option. The Disk Defragmenter dialog box appears (see Figure 10-10).

FIGURE 10-10
Disk Defragmenter dialog box

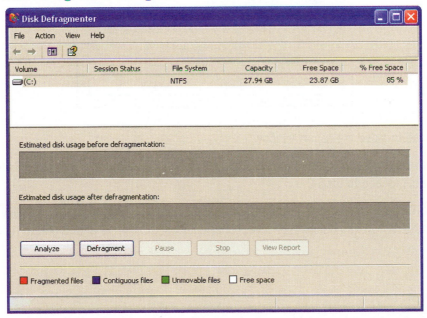

STEP-BY-STEP 10.8 Continued

3. Select your hard disk in the list near the top of the window, and then click the **Analyze** button. Be patient; it may take Windows a minute or two to analyze the disk.

4. A message box like that shown in Figure 10-11 appears, indicating that the analysis is complete.

FIGURE 10-11
Defragmenter message box

5. Click **View Report**. The Analysis Report dialog box opens, as shown in Figure 10-12.

FIGURE 10-12
Analysis Report dialog box

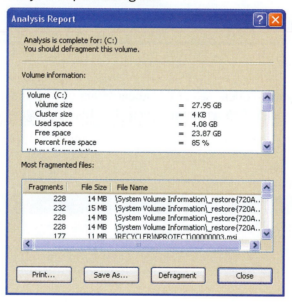

6. Click **Close** to close the report window.

7. If you have permission from your instructor to run Disk Defragmenter, click the **Defragment** button. Otherwise, proceed to step 8.

8. Click the **Close** button to close the Disk Defragmenter. If you are using a floppy disk as your practice disk, remove it from the floppy disk drive. If instructed, shut down Windows and turn off your computer.

SUMMARY

In this lesson, you learned:

■ Folders are used to organize files on a disk. Subfolders can be created within parent folders to build a hierarchy of folders for optimal file organization.

■ An application file icon may look like a miniature version of the program icon, or it may look like a miniature window.

■ It is easy to run an application or open a document file from Windows Explorer by double-clicking an icon.

■ A document file icon looks like a piece of paper with a graphic on it. You can open an associated document file from Windows Explorer without opening the application first.

■ You can assign descriptive names up to 255 characters long to folders and files; however, only Windows 95 and higher can accommodate long filenames. Windows will assign a short filename, called an alias, to each of these files so they can be used with programs that don't support long filenames.

■ You can easily rename folders.

■ Files are moved or copied from a source to a destination. The source is the file to be copied, and the destination is the location (folder or disk) where the moved or copied file will be placed.

■ When you copy a file, you duplicate the original. When you move a file, it is removed from its original location and placed in a new location.

■ Deleting a folder or subfolder deletes all the files within the folder as well. Folders deleted from a hard disk are transferred to the Recycle Bin. Folders deleted from a floppy disk are deleted permanently.

■ You can restore a deleted folder from the Recycle Bin with the Restore this item option on the Recycle Bin Tasks panel or File menu.

■ You can use Disk Cleanup to clear your hard disk of unnecessary files.

■ Disk Defragmenter rearranges the files on a hard disk so the disk performs optimally.

VOCABULARY *Review*

Define the following terms:

8.3 alias	Disk Defragmenter	Move
Application file icons	Document file icons	Parent folder
Copy	Extension	Source
Destination	Filename	Subfolder
Disk Cleanup	Fragmented files	

REVIEW *Questions*

TRUE/FALSE

Circle T if the statement is true or F if the statement is false.

T   F   1. A single cluster is the smallest amount of space on a disk that the operating system can handle when storing data.

T   F   2. You can copy a file in both Windows Explorer and My Computer by holding down the Shift key as you drag the file from its source to its destination.

T   F   3. All application programs can recognize long filenames.

T   F   4. Folders deleted from the hard disk can be retrieved from the Recycle Bin.

T   F   5. You cannot run an application program directly from Windows Explorer.

MULTIPLE CHOICE

Circle the best response for each of the following statements.

1. The _____ is the original location of the file you are moving.
   A. destination
   B. source
   C. recycled
   D. parent

2. In file organization, a subfolder is created within a _____ folder.
   A. manila
   B. source
   C. parent
   D. destination

3. A long filename cannot exceed _____ characters.
   A. 8
   B. 255
   C. 88
   D. 150

4. The Windows program that enables you to clear your disk of unnecessary files is called _____.
   A. Desktop
   B. Disk Defragmenter
   C. Disk Cleanup
   D. Disk Check

5. Removing a file from its original location and placing it in a new location is called _____ a file.
   A. moving
   B. deleting
   C. restoring
   D. copying

PROJECTS

PROJECT 10-1

1. Start Windows if it is not already running, and open **Windows Explorer.**

2. Copy the Project 10-1 folder from the data files to the Desktop location:
   A. Double-click the disk and/or folder containing the data files to display the subfolders in this lesson's data folder in the contents pane.
   B. Locate the Desktop icon in the tree pane (you may need to scroll up to see it).
   C. Hold down the **Ctrl** key and drag the Project 10-1 folder in the contents pane to the Desktop location on the tree pane.

3. Move the Project 10-1 folder to your practice disk or folder:
   A. Insert your practice disk in the floppy drive or locate your practice folder on the hard drive.
   B. Drag the Project 10-1 folder from the contents pane to the floppy disk drive icon or your practice folder on the tree pane.

4. Open the Project 10-1 folder in your practice folder (or on your practice disk), and do the following:
   A. Add a new subfolder called **Special Report #1**.
   B. Copy all the files in the Project 10-1 folder with the words *Sales Manual* in their file-names to the Special Report #1 subfolder.
   C. In the Special Report #1 subfolder, rename the files that contain the word *Chapter* in their filenames by changing the word *Chapter* to **Part**.
   D. Add a new subfolder to the Project 10-1 folder called **Quarterly Reports**.
   E. Move the Progress Reports (Q 1, Q 2, Q 3, and Q 4) files from the Progress Reports subfolder to the Quarterly Reports subfolder.
   F. Delete the Progress Reports subfolder.

5. Leave this window open for the next project.

PROJECT 10-2

1. Open the **Special Report #1** folder from your practice disk or folder.

2. Change the view to **Icons.**

3. Double-click the **Sales Manual Summary** file icon in the contents pane to open the file in its associated application.

4. Close the **Sales Manual Summary** file and the application window.

5. Click **My Documents** in the tree pane.

6. Double-click the **Internet Explorer** icon in the contents pane to run the program. You may see a message that says the page cannot be displayed because there is not an Internet server available, or if your computer does have an active Internet connection, you will see the default home page.

7. Close the Internet Explorer window and then close Windows Explorer.

8. If instructed to do so, shut down Windows XP and your computer.

TEAMWORK PROJECT

The computers in your office are used to track building repair projects that last from a few weeks to a few months, and when a project is finished, many files are deleted from the hard disks. Some workers have noticed that their computers seem to be operating more slowly, and they wonder if it would be a good idea to use the Disk Defragmenter program on a regular schedule. You and a coworker have decided to survey other PC users whose usage could be described as heavy and ask whether they use Disk Defragmenter on their computers. Survey at least two PC users each and then compare your findings. Together, write a written report that summarizes your findings and conclusions. Discuss why it is a good idea (or not) to schedule using Disk Defragmenter regularly. Use the Windows Help and Support feature and online resources if necessary to find out more about defragmenting a hard disk.

CRITICAL*Thinking*

ACTIVITY 10-1

Design a folder structure to organize files you might create for one of the following: your home organization, your job environment, your volunteer work. Create a parent folder and at least two more levels, with at least two folders in each level under one parent. Outline the structure within your practice folder or on your practice disk.

COMPUTING FUNDAMENTALS

REVIEW *Questions*

TRUE/FALSE

Circle T if the statement is true or F if the statement is false.

T F **1.** A local area network connects one computer to other computers and peripheral devices within an office or building.

T F **2.** The GUI is the brains of the computer.

T F **3.** A joystick is a flat drawing surface that can be used to draw or write data for input to a computer.

T F **4.** DOS is a character-based operating system.

T F **5.** Each zero or one used in computer binary code is referred to as a byte of information.

T F **6.** The taskbar is used to display the Start menu and to switch among currently running programs that you want to keep open.

T F **7.** The menu bar contains buttons that permit you to access various functions.

T F **8.** An algorithm is a set of clearly defined, logical steps that solve a problem.

T F **9.** Shortcuts are used to organize files on a disk.

T F **10.** The Windows Search feature allows you to find files and folders by specifying a variety of search criteria.

MATCHING

Match the description in Column 2 to the correct term in Column 1.

Column 1   **Column 2**

___ **1.** Mainframe computers   **A.** Computer programs that help manage a computer's resources and data

___ **2.** RAM   **B.** Used to organize appointments, telephone messages, projects, and other tasks to be completed

___ **3.** Scanners   **C.** Short-term memory found on the motherboard

___ **4.** Software   **D.** An easy way for users to communicate or interact with the computer by way of pictures

___ **5.** PIMS   **E.** Used by large institutions and government installations to process very large amounts of data

___ **6.** Utility software   **F.** A utility program that helps you perform a task quickly and easily

___ **7.** GUI   **G.** The most common experience most people have with the Internet

___ **8.** E-mail   **H.** Also called the Folders bar, it is at left in the Explorer window

___ **9.** Wizard   **I.** Devices that can change images into codes for input to the computer

___ **10.** Tree pane   **J.** Instructions issued to the computer so that specific tasks may be performed

PROJECTS

PROJECT 1

1. Start Windows if it is not already running, and then click the **Start** button.

2. Point to All Programs, then Accessories, and then click **WordPad**.

3. Key a few paragraphs about your favorite volunteer organization.

4. On the File menu, click **Save**.

5. In the Save As dialog box, do the following to save your file:
   A. Locate and select your **Assignments** folder or the folder where you are instructed to save your data files.

    B. Name your file **Volunteer** in the File name box.

    C. Select **Rich Text Format** in the Save as type drop-down list if it is not already selected.

    D. Click **Save** to save the file and return to the WordPad window.

6. Key another sentence or two in your document.

7. On the File menu, click **Save As.**

8. Name your file **Volunteer2** and save it as a Rich Text Format file in the folder designated by your instructor.

9. Close the WordPad file. Close the Appearance and Themes window.

PROJECT 2

1. Click the **Start** button.

2. Click **Control Panel** in the Start menu.

3. Click the **Appearance and Themes** option to open a task panel.

4. Select **Choose a screen saver** from the tasks list.

5. On a piece of paper, write down the current screen saver name shown highlighted in the Display Properties dialog box.

6. Select a different screen saver from the Screen saver drop-down list.

7. If the screen saver does not preview on the computer screen in the dialog box, click **Preview.**

8. Select the original screen saver from the Screen saver drop-down list.

9. Click **OK** or **Cancel** to close the dialog box.

PROJECT 3

1. Right-click the **Start** button and then select **Explore** from the shortcut menu to open Windows Explorer.

2. Locate your assignments data folder and open the **Volunteer2** file from Explorer.

3. Click the **Windows Explorer** button on the taskbar.

4. Open the **Hobby** file in your assignments data folder from Explorer.

5. Right-click in an empty section of the taskbar to open the shortcut menu and click **Cascade Windows.**

6. Close all open files and windows. Follow your instructor's directions about turning off the computer.

KEY APPLICATIONS

 Lesson 11
Using Microsoft Office 2003

2-1.1.1	2-1.1.4	2-1.2.3	2-1.2.6	2-1.2.9
2-1.1.2	2-1.2.1	2-1.2.4	2-1.2.7	2-1.2.10
2-1.1.3	2-1.2.2	2-1.2.5	2-1.2.8	2-1.3.1

Word Processing

 Lesson 12
Word Essentials

2-1.1.1	2-1.3.2	2-2.1.20
2-1.2.4	2-2.1.2	
2-1.2.6	2-2.1.9	

Lesson 13
Editing and Formatting Documents

2-1.3.1	2-1.4.3	2-2.1.7
2-1.3.3	2-1.4.4	2-2.1.8
2-1.3.4	2-1.4.5	2-2.1.10
2-1.3.5	2-2.1.1	2-2.1.11
2-1.3.6	2-2.1.3	2-2.1.12
2-1.3.7	2-2.1.4	2-2.1.18
2-1.3.8	2-2.1.5	2-2.1.19
2-1.4.1	2-2.1.6	2-2.1.21
2-1.4.2		

 Lesson 14
Working with Tables

| 2-2.2.1 | 2-2.2.3 | 2-2.2.5 |
| 2-2.2.2 | 2-2.2.4 | |

Lesson 15
Enhancing Documents

2-1.2.6	2-2.1.13	2-2.1.16
2-1.3.9	2-2.1.14	2-2.1.17
2-1.3.10	2-2.1.15	2-2.1.9
2-1.3.11		

Spreadsheets

Lesson 16
Excel Essentials

2-1.2.1	2-3.1.2	2-3.1.5
2-1.3.4	2-3.1.3	2-3.1.6
2-3.1.1	2-3.1.4	2-3.1.7

Lesson 17
Organizing Worksheets

2-1.4.1	2-3.1.3	2-3.1.8
2-1.4.3	2-3.1.4	2-3.2.1
2-1.4.4	2-3.1.7	

Lesson 18
Creating Formulas and Charting Data

2-3.2.2	2-3.2.6	2-3.2.10
2-3.2.3	2-3.2.7	2-3.2.11
2-3.2.4	2-3.2.8	2-3.2.12
2-3.2.5	2-3.2.9	

Presentations

Lesson 19
PowerPoint Essentials

2-1.2.1	2-1.3.1	2-4.1.4
2-1.2.3	2-4.1.1	2-4.1.6
2-1.2.7	2-4.1.2	2-4.1.10
2-1.2.8	2-4.1.3	2-4.1.11

Lesson 20
Enhancing Presentations with Multimedia Effects

| 2-4.1.3 | 2-4.1.7 | 2-4.1.9 |
| 2-4.1.5 | 2-4.1.8 | |

Databases

 Lesson 21
Access Essentials

 Lesson 22
Managing and Reporting Database Information

USING MICROSOFT OFFICE 2003

Microsoft Office 2003 is an integrated software package that enables you to share information between several applications. The applications available to you depend on the Office 2003 suite that is installed and the selections made during the installation. Microsoft offers several different Office 2003 suites, each with a different combination of applications. Among the Office 2003 applications are Word, Publisher, FrontPage, PowerPoint, Excel, Access, and Outlook. Each application performs specific tasks. Table 11-1 provides a brief description of the uses for available Office applications. Word, Excel, PowerPoint, and Access are covered in depth in this module, and you will find an introduction to Outlook in the last module of this text.

TABLE 11-1
Microsoft Office suite applications

APPLICATION	DESCRIPTION
Word	A word-processing application that enables you to create documents such as letters, memos, and reports.
Publisher	A desktop publishing application that enables you to design professional-looking documents such as brochures, calendars, signs, and posters.
FrontPage	A Web page application that enables you to create and maintain your own Web site.
PowerPoint	A presentation application that enables you to create multimedia slide shows, transparencies, outlines, and organizational charts.
Excel	A spreadsheet application that enables you to work with text and numbers to create tables, worksheets, and financial documents involving calculations.
Access	A database application that enables you to organize and manipulate information such as addresses and inventory data.
Outlook	A schedule/organization application that enables you to efficiently keep track of e-mail, appointments, tasks, contacts, and events.

Starting an Office 2003 Application

2-1.1.1

Depending on your computer setup, you can start Office 2003 applications by double-clicking the application icon on the desktop or by using the Start menu. When you launch most Office applications, a new Office document (word processing document, spreadsheet, database, etc.) is displayed. A *document* is a data file in an application. If you do not see a new blank document window when you open an application, click the New Blank Document button on the toolbar—it looks like a blank page, and is usually located on at far left of the Standard toolbar, as shown in Figure 11-1.

FIGURE 11-1
The New Blank Document button

Each of the applications within the Microsoft Office Suite creates, by default, specific types of files—files in a specific format. Word, for example, creates *doc* files, and Excel creates *xls* files. There are a number of ways that documents can be shared between the applications within the Office 2003 suite. Primarily you can export files from one application to another application's file type or you can import files from one application into another. An Access file can be exported as an Excel file. An Excel file can be saved as a text file and then opened in Word. This kind of data sharing gives you a great deal of flexibility in how you want to view, manage, and use your data.

STEP-BY-STEP 11.1

1. Do one of the following:

   a. Click the **Start** button on the taskbar and point to **All Programs**. When the submenu appears, point to **Microsoft Office**, and then click **Microsoft Office Word 2003** or **Microsoft Word** on the next submenu.

   OR

   b. Double-click the **Microsoft Word** icon on the desktop.

2. If a blank document does not appear on the screen when you open Word, click the **New Blank Document** button (see Figure 11-1) to open a new document window. Leave the Word window open for the next Step-by-Step.

> **Note**
>
> If the Microsoft Office Shortcut Bar is installed, you can use it to open an Office application. The Shortcut Bar floats on the screen and often appears in the upper-right corner of the screen.

Navigating the Windows Application Screens

2-1.1.1
2-1.2.1
2-1.2.3
2-1.2.4
2-1.2.10
2-1.3.1

You can have multiple applications open at the same time. Each open application will display in the taskbar at the bottom of the screen. To switch from one open application to another, click on the application button in the taskbar. The taskbar, with three open applications, is illustrated in Figure 11-2.

FIGURE 11-2
The taskbar with multiple open application buttons

To insert new text or change existing text, you must know how to *scroll* and how to reposition the insertion point. Scrolling enables you to move through the document on the screen without repositioning the insertion point. You can use either the mouse or the keyboard to move the insertion point and scroll.

When you use the mouse to scroll, you use the horizontal or vertical scroll bars. When you use the mouse to reposition the insertion point, you simply move the mouse pointer to the desired location within the document. The pointer changes to an *I-beam*, indicating you can now key text. Position the I-beam where you want the insertion point to be, and then click the mouse button. Figure 11-3 shows an I-beam and some quick ways to scroll using the mouse.

FIGURE 11-3
Ways to scroll with the mouse

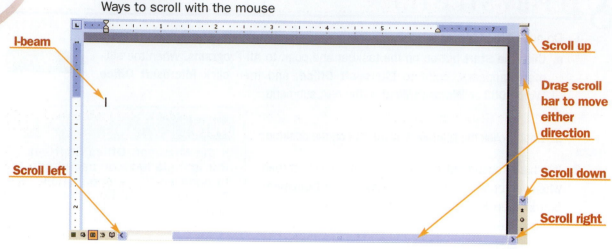

You can also use the arrow keys to move up, down, left, and right in a document, and the PgUp, and PgDn keys move the insertion point up or down about the depth of your screen every time you press one of the keys. If you have good keyboarding skills, learning keyboard shortcuts to move the insertion point can speed your work. Using the keyboard shortcuts eliminates the need to take your hands from the keyboard to navigate through the document. You can find a comprehensive list of keyboard shortcuts in online Help by searching for the keywords *keyboard shortcuts*.

S TEP-BY-STEP 11.2

1. Do one of the following:

   a. Click the **Start** button, point to **All Programs**, point to **Microsoft Office**, and then click **Microsoft Office Excel 2003** or **Microsoft Excel**.

   OR

   b. Right-click in a blank part of the taskbar, click **Show the Desktop** on the shortcut menu, and then double-click the **Microsoft Excel** icon on the desktop.

2. Microsoft Excel is now the active application, although Microsoft Word is still open and running. If you do not see a new blank spreadsheet in the Excel window, click the **New Blank Document** button to open a blank spreadsheet.

3. Move around in the Excel document:

   a. Use the mouse to move the scroll box in the scroll bar at the right of the document window. Notice how the view on the screen moves up and down in the Excel spreadsheet.

   b. Use the arrow keys to move left and right and up and down in the spreadsheet.

   c. Press **PgDn**. Notice you move more than 30 rows down in the spreadsheet (check the row numbers at left in the spreadsheet).

   d. Press **PgUp** to return to the top of the spreadsheet.

STEP-BY-STEP 11.2 Continued

4. Do one of the following:

    a. Click the **Start** button, point to All Programs, point to Microsoft Office, and click Microsoft Office PowerPoint (or Microsoft PowerPoint).

    OR

    b. Click the **Show Desktop** button on the Quick Launch bar if it is visible on the taskbar, and then double-click the **Microsoft PowerPoint** icon on the desktop.

5. Microsoft PowerPoint is now the active application, although Microsoft Word and Microsoft Excel are both still open and running. If you don't see a blank slide document in PowerPoint, click the **New Blank Document** button to open one.

6. The taskbar should show buttons for Word, Excel, and PowerPoint. Click the **Document1 - Microsoft Word** button in the taskbar to switch to that application.

7. Leave the Word, Excel, and PowerPoint applications open for the next Step-by-Step.

Understanding the Information in the Application Window

2-1.2.1

You have learned how to open Microsoft Office applications and how to open a new blank document. When you open a document using the New Blank Document button, it will contain default settings to create a standard data file in the application. You can change these default settings as you work with the document. Figure 11-4 shows the standard features you will find in a document window in any Office application.

FIGURE 11-4
An Office document window

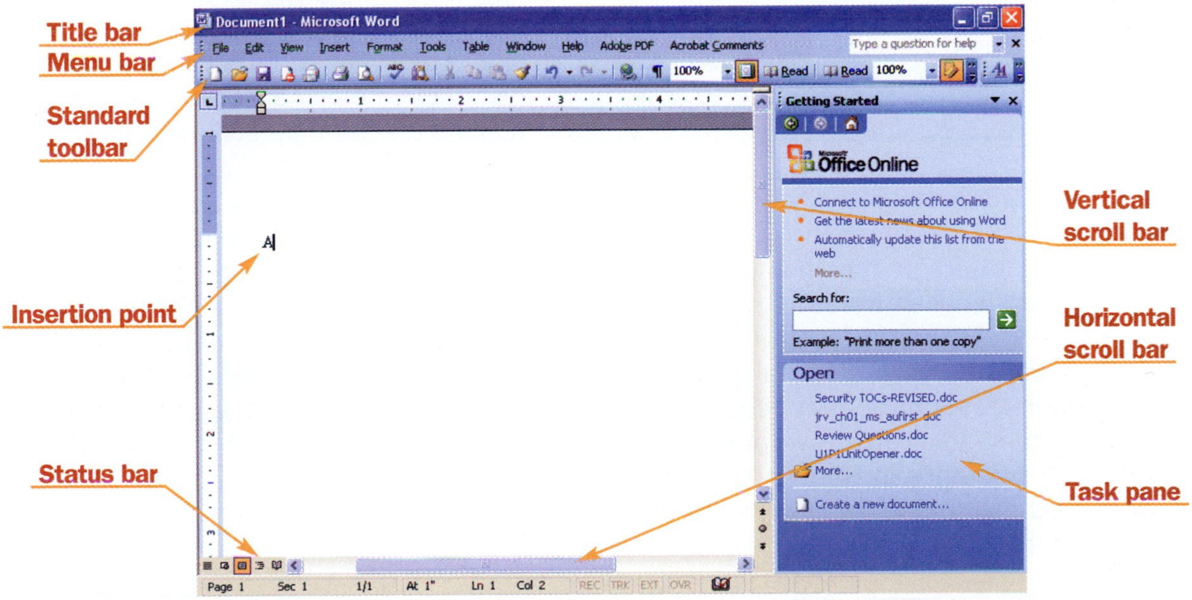

You will probably recognize many of the elements of all Windows 2003 screens, including the following:

- The title bar, which shows the name of the data file and the name of the application you are using.

- The menu bar, which provides access to drop-down menus for the application.

- The Standard toolbar, with buttons to perform frequently needed commands.

- Scroll bars with scroll boxes to help navigate through the document.

- The status bar, which provides information about the current document.

- The taskbar at the bottom of the screen, where you can access other open programs or documents.

Figure 11-4 also shows the task pane that appears when you open an Office document. The tasks listed may differ slightly from one application to another, but you can usually open recently edited documents or open a new document, among other options.

 Technology Timeline

WHY QWERTY?

The arrangement of a standard keyboard on a computer (or a typewriter) is called QWERTY, referring to the first six characters in the top row of letters. But why aren't the letters in alphabetical order, or some other order? Why QWERTY? The most popular story is that the inventor of the typewriter, Christopher Sholes, created the layout of the keyboard in the 1860s to keep commonly used key combinations separated. This was so the typebars, which moved the metal letters to the ribbon when you struck the keys, would not crash into each other. Although no evidence exists to prove this is why the arrangement of keys was chosen, the QWERTY keyboard really does make it more cumbersome to type frequently used letters. And even though electric typewriters and then computers eliminated all possibility of keys crashing together, we still use this old keyboard.

In the 1930s, a university professor named August Dvorak designed a keyboard that would allow faster typing with less finger movement. He placed the most commonly used letters on the "home" keys in the middle row of letter keys, and a typist can key many English words without ever leaving the home keys. It's been estimated that a typist's fingers might travel 16 miles in a day using a QWERTY keyboard but only 1 mile using the Dvorak keyboard. Yet we're still using the QWERTY model. Why? Well, the answer seems to be that people are just set in their ways, and don't want to learn a new system. Also, U.S. government tests in the 1950s actually found that there just isn't a big difference in typing speed between the two keyboards to make it worth changing the standard layout. Good typists type faster than bad typists, no matter what keyboard they use.

Customizing the Document Window

2-1.2.2
2-1.2.5

The Standard toolbar displays right below the menu bar in Office applications by default. You can choose to display other command buttons by using the Toolbars command in the View menu in any application. The choices in the Toolbars submenu may differ slightly from one application to another, but you may find options that will make your work easier in any application. For example, there are toolbars that dis-

Note

If a toolbar displays a title bar, the down arrow near the right side of the title bar allows you to access the Add or Remove Buttons command.

play command buttons for creating forms, reviewing and editing documents, and drawing lines, shapes, and arrows. The Drawing toolbar available in many Office applications is shown in Figure 11-5. Some of the optional toolbars will "float" when they display, overlaying part of the document window, and others appear firmly anchored above or below the document. You can move any toolbar to a position you prefer by positioning the mouse pointer somewhere in the title bar of the toolbar and then dragging it to the new position. If you don't see a title bar in the toolbar, drag on the vertical dashed line at the left of the toolbar (see Figure 11-5).

FIGURE 11-5
The Drawing toolbar

Drag point   **Arrow accesses Add or Remove Buttons**

You may recall that you can add or remove buttons on the Standard toolbar using the Customize command on the Toolbars submenu of the View menu. You can change the button display of any toolbar using this command; simply select the toolbar you want to modify in the list on the left in the Customize dialog box. You can also customize a toolbar by clicking the down arrow at the far right of a toolbar to display the Add or Remove Buttons command for that toolbar (see Figure 11-5). Click on the down arrow in the box and you will see two options. One is usually the name of the toolbar, and if you rest the mouse pointer on that

Note

If you see two small arrows pointing right at the far right of the toolbar, this means not all the buttons available are displayed. Click the arrows to see the other available buttons, or drag the vertical dashed line at the left of the toolbar to expand it.

option, you will see a graphic display of the buttons on the toolbar. You can select or deselect the buttons you want in this graphic display. If you click on the second option, Customize, you will open the Customize dialog box.

You can also change the magnification level of a document—how large or small the text and graphics appear on the screen—with the Zoom command on the View menu. Click the Zoom command to open the Zoom dialog box, which offers set percentages, options for views such as Page width, Whole page, and Many pages, and the Percent text box, where you can enter a specific percentage or click the up and down arrows to find the percentage you prefer for the page display.

STEP-BY-STEP 11.3

1. Click the **Microsoft PowerPoint - [Presentation1]** button on the taskbar to select that application.

2. Open the **View** menu and click **Zoom**. (You may need to click the down arrow at the bottom of the menu to bring the Zoom command into view.)

   a. In the Zoom dialog box, click the option button next to **33%** or the smallest percentage listed.

   b. Click **OK** to close the dialog box and apply the new magnification level.

3. Notice how much smaller the slide layout appears, and then open the Zoom dialog box again.

   a. Click the **up arrow** next to the Percent box in the dialog box until **55%** appears in the box.

   b. Click **OK**.

4. Click the **Document1 - Microsoft Word** button in the taskbar to switch back to that application.

   a. Open the **View** menu and click **Zoom**.

   b. Click the **Many pages** option button and look at the Preview section. You will probably only see one small page displayed, because you do not have a multipage document open.

   c. Click the **Whole page** option button and look at the Preview section again.

   d. Click **Cancel** to close the Zoom dialog box without applying the new magnification level.

5. Leave the Word document window open for the next Step-by-Step.

Opening, Saving, and Printing Documents

2-1.2.7
2-1.2.8

You use the same procedures to open and save documents in all Office applications. Opening a document means to load a file from a disk into the open application. A file is a collection of information saved on a disk. Remember that the terms *document* and *file* are used interchangeably. Each file is identified by a filename.

To *save* a document means to store it on a disk or other storage medium. A file extension is automatically added to the filename when the document is saved. A period separates the filename and the extension. The extension is usually three characters and varies depending on the application used to create the document. For example, Word automatically assigns the extension *doc*, PowerPoint assigns *ppt*, Excel assigns *xls*, and Access assigns *mdb*.

Folders can be used to organize the documents within a disk. The **path** is the route the operating system uses to locate a document. The path identifies the disk and any folders relative to the location of the document. Figure 11-6 illustrates a typical path and identifies the items in the path.

> ### Computer Concepts
>
> You can display file extensions in Windows XP by changing an option in Windows Explorer. Open the **Tools** menu and choose **Folder Options**. Select the **View** tab and turn off the option *Hide extensions for known file types*. The option is turned off when the check mark is removed.

FIGURE 11-6
A typical path to a file location

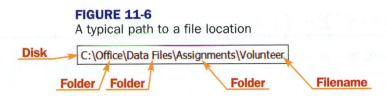

Disk → C:\Office\Data Files\Assignments\Volunteer

Folder / Folder | Folder | Filename

Figure 11-6 illustrates that the Word document called Volunteer is saved in a folder called Assignments. The Assignments folder is, in turn, stored in a folder called Data Files, which can be found in the Office folder on the local (this computer's) hard drive—drive C.

Opening a Document

You have several choices for the way in which you open a file. You can choose Open Office Document on the Start menu; you can choose Open in the File menu of the Office application; or you can simply click the Open button on the Office application's toolbar. All of these procedures display the Open dialog box (Figure 11-7), which enables you to open a file from any available disk and folder. By using the Open dialog box, you can work with multiple files at the same time—in either the same Office program or different programs.

FIGURE 11-7
The Open dialog box

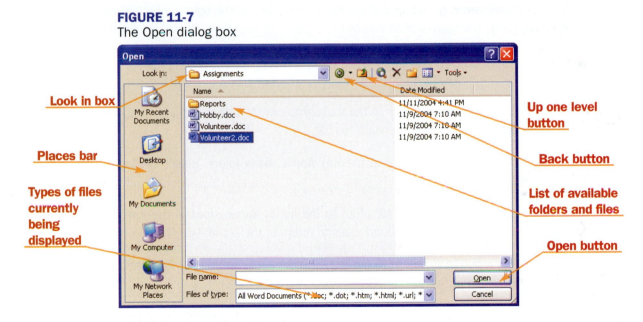

To locate a specific drive or folder, you select from the options available in the Look in box. You can use the Up One Level button (which looks like the Up button in Windows Explorer) to return to the next highest level in the path. Clicking the Back button will return you to the previous drive or folder. When you click the My Recent Documents icon in the left panel of the Open dialog box, called the Places bar, you will see the last 20 to 50 documents and folders that you have accessed listed in the pane to the right. Select a file and then click the Open button at the bottom of the dialog box to open the document.

STEP-BY-STEP 11.4

1. Word should be displayed in the active window. Click **File** in the menu bar, and then click **Open** in the drop-down menu. (To see the Open command in the menu, you may need to click on the double arrow at the bottom of the menu for the full menu to display.) An Open dialog box similar to the one shown in Figure 11-7 will display. Click the **My Recent Documents** icon on the left side of the Open dialog box to go to the folders and locations you use the most.

> **Note**
>
> Word remembers the last file you opened and automatically takes you to the drive and folder where the last file came from, so your Open dialog box may look very different from the one shown.

2. Click the **down arrow** to the right of the Look in box to see the available disk drives. Select the drive that contains your data files.

3. Double-click the **Data** folder. Double-click the **Key Applications** folder. Double-click the **Lesson 11** folder. There is one folder (Lesson 11A) and one Word file (Step11-4a) in the Lesson 11 folder.

4. Click the **down arrow** at the right of the Files of type box at the bottom of the dialog box and select **All Files (*.*)**. The names of all files in the Lesson 11 folder are displayed, including those created in applications other than Word.

5. Click the filename **Step11-4a** once to select it, and then click **Open** in the dialog box.

6. Click the **Microsoft Excel** button in the taskbar to switch to that application and then click the **Open** button on the Standard toolbar.

7. Find the data files again and open the **Key Applications** folder. Select the **Lesson 11** folder and click **Open**.

8. Click the **Up One Level** button to return to the list of folders/files in the Key Applications folder. Click the **Up One Level** button again to return to the list of data file folders.

9. Click the **Back** button to return to the list of folders/files in the Key Applications folder. Click the **Back** button again to see the contents of the Lesson 11 folder.

10. Double-click the filename **Step11-4b** to open it and leave the applications and files open for the next Step-by-Step.

Problems with Opening Files

Within the Office 2003 suite you can usually move files back and forth between applications with relative ease as long as you save them in formats that each application can read. Occasionally, however, you may encounter some problems with opening files. For example, you may use the Open command from the File menu but not see the file for which you are looking. This could be caused by a number of things. First you may need to verify that you are looking in the right drive and the right folder—the file for which you are looking may be stored in a different location. If you are unsure of the location of the file, you can use the Search command (available from the Tools menu in the Open dialog box) to locate the file.

Another reason that you cannot see a file could be that the file is in a format that cannot be read by the application you are using. For example, if you want to open an Access file but you are in Word, you will not see the file listed. You could switch the file type within the Open dialog box to show All Files, so that you could see the file, but that does not necessarily mean that the application you are using will be able to open the file. In general, it is better to open a file in its associated application and then save as or export to the appropriate file format for the application in which you want to open the file.

Occasionally you may encounter a corrupted file or a file that will not open. The application may give you an error message when you try to open the file, it may cause the application to shut down, or it may just not open. In these cases you can try to open the file on a different computer to verify that the file is indeed corrupt and that there isn't something wrong with your computer. You may also want to try to open the file from within Windows Explorer. The file associated with an application may be different than the one in which you are trying to open it.

Yet another problem you may encounter is with *file compatibility*. In most cases, files that were created with older applications can be opened in the newer applications. But sometimes, files created in newer applications are not backwards compatible—meaning that they cannot be opened in older versions of the software. In most cases, you can resolve this issue by opening the file in the newer software and then choosing to save the file in the older application format with the Save As command.

You may also encounter compatibility problems if you are working in a different operating system than the one in which the file was created. For example, if a file was created in PowerPoint on a Macintosh, it may not be able to be opened in PowerPoint on a PC. This problem generally occurs if you are working with different versions of the software across the different platforms. With a little effort, however, you can usually find a way to open and use almost any Office file.

Saving a Document

The quickest and easiest way to save a document is to click the Save button on the toolbar. The document is saved with the same filename and in the same location. To save a file with a new filename or a new location, open the File menu and choose the Save As command. If the file does not already have a name, the application prompts you to name the file upon saving.

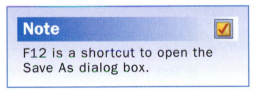

> **Note** ✓
>
> F12 is a shortcut to open the Save As dialog box.

To make it easier to find documents, choose filenames with words that help describe the document. The complete path to the file can include up to 255 characters. Filenames cannot include any of the following characters: /, \, >, <, *, ?, ", |, :, ;.

You should make a habit of saving frequently and after any major changes to your document. If you do this you will avoid the possibility of losing work should there be a power outage or should your computer stop running for some other reason.

It is also important to note that each application offers you a number of choices for formats in which to save your files. The default is always the format for the application in which you are working. Click the down arrow next to the Save as type text box in the Save As dialog box and you will see the list of other file formats in which the current document can be saved.

STEP-BY-STEP 11.5

1. Click the Word **Step11-4a** button in the taskbar to switch to that document.

2. Open the **File** menu and choose **Save As**. The Save As dialog box shown in Figure 11-8 is displayed.

FIGURE 11-8
The Save As dialog box

3. In the File name box, with the filename **Step11-4a** already selected, key **Vehicle Recycling**. (If the text in the File name box is not highlighted, click in the box and select or delete that text and then key the new filename.)

4. Click the **Save** button in the dialog box. The document is saved to the same folder where you opened it, but with a different name. (The original document, with the original name, remains also.)

5. Click the Excel **Step11-4b** button in the taskbar to switch to that document.

6. Open the File menu and choose Save As. Name this document Travel Expenses and change its type to **Text (Tab delimited)**. You may need to scroll down in the Save as type drop-down list to find this option.

7. Save the file in your Assignments folder, if you have one:

   a. Select the **Assignments** folder.

   b. Click **Save**.

   c. If you see a message box warning you that some formats or multiple worksheets may be lost by saving the file as a text file, click **OK** and/or **Yes** to continue.

8. If you do not have an Assignments folder, follow your instructor's directions to create a new Assignments folder first, and then select the folder and click **Save**. Click **Yes** or **OK** in any messages to complete the process of saving the document.

9. Keep the documents and applications open for the next Step-by-Step.

Printing a Document

The quickest and easiest way to print a document is to click the Print button on the Standard toolbar when the document is active. The document is sent to the printer using all the default print settings (such as paper size, paper orientation, number of copies, etc.). If your computer accesses more than one printer, however, you will probably want to print from the File menu. This option displays the Print dialog box shown in Figure 11-9. Here you can view the selected printer and change it, or the printer settings, if necessary. Depending upon which application you are using, your options within the Print dialog box will vary.

FIGURE 11-9
Print dialog box

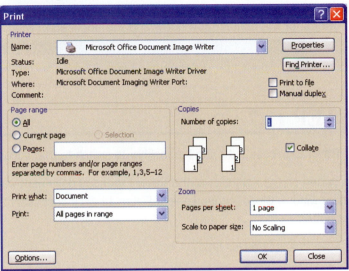

Check with your instructor about the policy for printing documents in this course.

S TEP-BY-STEP 11.6

1. Click the Word **Vehicle Recycling** button in the taskbar to switch to that document.

2. Open the **File** menu and choose **Print**. The Print dialog box shown in Figure 11-9 is displayed. The Print dialog box looks different for each Office application, but most of the print options are similar for all applications.

3. Click the **down arrow** in the Name box. If your computer is connected to more than one printer, the other printers will be listed in this drop-down box. Click to select the printer from which you would like to print this file.

4. Click to select **Current page** in the Page range section. When this option is selected, only the page where you last left the insertion point will print.

5. Click the option for **Pages**. When this option is selected, you can enter a specific page number in the text box (for example, 2). Use hyphens for a page range (for example, 1-3), and use commas to separate pages or page ranges (for example, 1, 3-5).

6. Click **Cancel** to close the dialog box without printing. (To print, you would click **OK**.)

Closing Documents and Applications

2-1.1.2
2-1.2.9

Y ou use the same procedures to close documents and applications in all Office applications. To close a document, you can open the File menu and choose the Close command or you can use the Close button on the document window. To close an application, you can open the File menu and choose the Exit command or you can use the red Close button on the application window. Figure 11-10 shows the document and application Close buttons. When you close a document, the application remains open and so do any other files you have open. If you have no other files open, the application shows a blank screen and is ready for you to open or create another document. When you close an application, you will also close any open files.

FIGURE 11-10
The Close buttons for the document window and the application window

S TEP-BY-STEP 11.7

1. Click the Excel **Travel Expenses** button in the taskbar to switch to that document.

2. Click the **Close** button on the right side of the Travel Expenses document window. Be sure to click the document window Close button. Look at Figure 11-10 if necessary to make sure you click the correct button.

3. Click **No** in the Save Changes dialog box.

4. Open the **File** menu and choose **Exit** to close the Excel application.

5. Click the **PowerPoint** button in the taskbar to switch to that application. Click the **Close** button on the right side of the application window. (Be sure to click the application window Close button.) Keep the Word document **Vehicle Recycling** open for the next Step-by-Step.

Getting Help

2-1.1.3
2-1.1.4
2-1.2.6
2-1.2.10

T he Microsoft Office 2003 applications have some very powerful Help features that will assist you as you work. You have access to online help and documentation as well. You should also not overlook a vital source of help—assistance from others. There may be classmates or coworkers who are familiar with the application you are using. Or perhaps your workplace has a help desk. Additionally, many software manufacturers offer a support line.

The key to using these various sources of help is determining what sort of help you need and the quickest or most efficient way to access that help. The idea is to find the assistance you need without interrupting or delaying your work. Whenever you encounter a problem, your first source of help should be the Help features in each Office application. This is always readily available and is just a few mouse clicks away. For example, you can find out more about most dialog boxes by clicking the Help button in the title bar of the dialog box, which appears as a question mark. This opens a Help window that provides information about the features of that dialog box. The ToolTips, ScreenTips, and the Office Assistant discussed below also can solve many of your problems.

If you have access to the Internet, you can also look there for help. If you can't find the answers you need there and you have technical support available or a classmate or coworker is available to assist you, this should be your next avenue to find the answers you need. Be cautious, however, about asking coworkers or classmates for assistance. You should not interrupt the work they are doing in order to get your work completed.

Use ToolTips and ScreenTips

If you do not know the function of a toolbar button, rest the mouse pointer on the button, but do not click it. After a few seconds, the name of the function appears in a ToolTip. ScreenTips appear in several kinds of situations; for example, when you rest the mouse pointer on a color box in a color drop-down list (such as in the Font dialog box), a ScreenTip tells you what color the square represents. As you key text, you may occasionally see a ScreenTip that suggests how Word can complete a word or phrase for you automatically by pressing Enter. You will learn more about this feature, called AutoComplete, in upcoming lessons.

S TEP-BY-STEP 11.8

1. Position the pointer over the **Print** button on the Standard toolbar. (If the name doesn't display at first, you may need to move the pointer slightly so that it rests fully on the button.) The name of the button (Print), as well as the name of the printer currently selected, will appear in the ToolTip. Point to other buttons on the toolbar to see the name of each button.

2. Open the **File** menu and choose **Print**. Click the question mark icon (the **Help** button) at the upper-right corner of the dialog box. A Help window will open that displays information about the different sections and options of the Print dialog box. Scroll through the information in the Help window and then click the **Close** button to close it.

3. Open the **Format** menu and choose **Font**, then select the **Font** tab if it is not displayed in the dialog box.

4. Click the **down arrow** next to the Font color text box to open a drop-down list of color squares. Rest your mouse pointer on one of the squares. You should see a ScreenTip that indicates what color the square represents.

5. Click the **Close** button to close the Font dialog box. Leave the Word document open for the next Step-by-Step.

Using the Office Assistant

You may have seen the Office Assistant displayed on your screen when you worked with Office applications earlier in this lesson. The *Office Assistant* is an animated Help character that offers tips and messages to help you work more efficiently. For example, if you close a document without saving it, the Office Assistant will ask you if you want to save the changes before closing. If you have a specific question, the Office Assistant will help you search for the answer. To access the Office Assistant, you must have an application open. You can then ask the Office Assistant for help with information about the active Office application.

> **Note**
>
> Sometimes the Office Assistant gets in the way. To move the Office Assistant, simply point to it, hold down the left mouse button, and drag it to a new location on the screen.

STEP-BY-STEP 11.9

1. If the Office Assistant is not displayed on the screen, open the **Help** menu and choose **Show the Office Assistant**.

2. Click the **Office Assistant**. An Office Assistant dialog box similar to Figure 11-11 appears. Your dialog box will look different depending on what application you are using and what information was last requested of the Office Assistant.

3. The existing search text is already selected. Key the following request to replace the existing search text: **How do I use the Office Assistant?**

FIGURE 11-11
The Office Assistant dialog box

4. Click **Search** (or press **Enter**). A list of topics that may provide an answer is displayed in a pane titled *Search Results* at the right of the document window.

5. Click the topic **Display tips and messages through the Office Assistant**.

6. In the Help dialog box that opens, click the topic **View a tip** and read the information about the light bulb that appears next to the Office Assistant. (You may need to close the Search Results pane to view the Help window.)

> ## Computer Concepts
>
> You can change the way the Office Assistant provides help by right-clicking the Office Assistant, selecting **Choose Assistant**, and then making selections on the Gallery and Options tabs. You can also use this shortcut menu to hide the Office Assistant if it gets in the way!

7. Click the **Close** button to close the Help dialog box, and if necessary, click the **Close** button to close the Search Results pane. Leave Word open for the next Step-by-Step.

Online and Internet Help

The Ask a Question box is another alternative to using the Office Assistant. The box appears at the right side of the menu bar in all Office applications. Simply click in the box, key your question, and press Enter. To repeat a question, click the down arrow in the box and select the question.

Although not as convenient as using the Ask a Question box and the Office Assistant, you will find more options in the Help window. You display the Help window by opening the Help menu and choosing Help (i.e., Microsoft Office Word Help) or by pressing the F1 key. You can also access the Help window from the New Document task pane that appears when you open an Office application.

Additionally, you can find answers for frequently asked questions for all Office products at the Microsoft Office Online Web site. You'll also find other information such as important product updates, online services, and clip art. To go to the Microsoft Web site, open the Help menu and choose Microsoft Office Online.

You may need to check with your instructor about how to connect to the Internet from your computer for the following Step-by-Step.

STEP-BY-STEP 11.10

1. If necessary, establish a modem (dial-up) connection to the Internet.

2. Select **Microsoft Office Online** from the **Help** menu. The Microsoft Office Online home page should display in your browser.

> **Note**
>
> You can also access Microsoft's online help from the Help window by clicking the **Connect to Microsoft Office Online** link.

3. From the Search text box drop-down list on the Web page, select **Assistance**, and then key **Printing** in the next text box. Click the **Go** button to start the search.

4. Click the Print a Help topic link in the search results list (you may need to scroll down to find this topic; if it does not display, click a topic that interests you).

5. As you read the information that displays about the topic, you may notice that at the bottom of the page there is a question that asks if the information was helpful, followed by Yes and No buttons. Clicking one of these buttons simply provides feedback about the online help feature to Microsoft.

6. Close your browser. If necessary, disconnect your modem (dial-up) connection.

7. Close the Word document window and the Word application window. (This can be done in one step using the Close button for the application window.)

SUMMARY

In this lesson, you learned:

■ You can start Office applications by clicking the Start button on the taskbar and selecting the application from the Programs folder, or you can double-click the application icon on the Desktop.

■ Navigating through an Office document involves using the mouse, scroll bars, arrow keys, and keyboard shortcuts.

■ Standard features found in every Office application window include the title bar, menus, toolbars, scroll bars, status bar, and taskbar, as well as a task pane that appears when you open an application.

■ You can customize an Office document window by displaying task-specific toolbars and adding or removing buttons from toolbars.

■ The View menu Zoom command allows you to specify exactly what size to display the page.

- The Open dialog box enables you to open a file from any available disk and folder.

- Problems opening files can involve corrupted data or file compatibility issues, such as trying to open a file in a different application, in an earlier version of an application, or in another operating system than was used to create it. There are ways to open and use almost any Office file, however.

- To save a document using a new filename, open the File menu and choose the Save As command.

- To print a document, you can use either the Print button on the application's toolbar or you can open the File menu and choose Print.

- To close document windows and application windows, you click the Close button or open the File menu and choose Close or Exit.

- ToolTips and ScreenTips provide immediate help without interrupting your work. The Office Assistant offers tips and will help you search for answers to specific questions. The Help window and the Office Online Web site are also sources of assistance with Office applications.

VOCABULARY *Review*

Define the following terms:

Document	Office Assistant	Save
File compatibility	Path	Scroll
I-beam		

REVIEW *Questions*

TRUE/FALSE

Circle T if the statement is true or F if the statement is false.

T   F   **1.** You use the same procedures to open and save documents in all Office applications.

T   F   **2.** To save a file with a new filename or to a new location, open the File menu and choose the Save command.

T   F   **3.** The Office Partner is an animated Help character that offers tips and messages to help you work more efficiently.

T   F   **4.** The View menu has options to customize the display in your document window.

T   F   **5.** The light bulb icon in a dialog box displays help topics.

MULTIPLE CHOICE

Circle the best response for each of the following statements.

1. The Office application you would use to organize and manipulate information such as addresses and inventory data is _____.
    A. Outlook
    B. FrontPage
    C. Access
    D. Excel

2. _____ are used to organize the documents within a disk.
    A. Applications
    B. Folders
    C. Icons
    D. Toolbars

3. Rest the mouse pointer on a toolbar button to see the name of the button appear in a(n) _____.
    A. ScreenTips
    B. ToolTips
    C. Help window
    D. Dialog box

4. The _____ command on the View menu allows you to select a specific size for the page display in the document window.
    A. Zoom
    B. Page Layout
    C. Slide Selector
    D. Normal View

5. Click the _____ button on the Standard toolbar to open an empty file in the same application.
    A. Save As
    B. Drawing
    C. View
    D. New Blank Document

PROJECTS

In the following projects, you will become familiar with other Office applications.

PROJECT 11-1

   If you do not have Microsoft Publisher installed, go to Project 11-2.

1. Using a desktop shortcut or the **Start** menu, launch Microsoft Office Publisher. The Microsoft Publisher Start window appears on your screen.

2. You should see a list of new publications in the pane on the left under the heading *New from a design*. Click the **Publications for Print** option and then click the **Flyers** option in the drop-down list. Notice that a list of types of different flyers appears below the Flyers heading and sample flyers display in the window at the right.

3. Click **Event** in the list of flyers at the left to see the different event flyers available.

4. Select other publication types in the New Publications list to see what kinds of publications you can create using Publisher.

5. Close Publisher by clicking the application **Close** button.

PROJECT 11-2

1. Using a desktop shortcut or the **Start** menu, launch Microsoft Outlook.

2. Using a desktop shortcut or the **Start** menu, launch Microsoft PowerPoint.

3. Click **More presentations** (or just **More...**) in the task pane to display the Open dialog box.

4. Open **Project11-2** from the data files. The PowerPoint window displays a slide, an outline of the current presentation, and an area where you can make notes.

5. Move the mouse pointer over some of the toolbar buttons to display a ToolTip for each button.

6. To learn more about the different views you can use in PowerPoint, click the Office Assistant, key **PowerPoint views**, and then click **Search**. In the list of topics that displays, choose **About PowerPoint views**.

7. Read about the different views available in PowerPoint, then close the Help window.

8. Save the PowerPoint presentation as **Three Rs**.

9. Click the **Outlook** button on the taskbar to return to Outlook. Notice the vertical bar at the left of the Outlook window that lists Outlook's tools as shortcut buttons.

10. Click the **Calendar** shortcut. The calendar for the current date opens in the Outlook window. If you wanted to schedule a time to present your Three Rs slide show, you could do so using this Outlook tool.

11. Close Outlook by clicking its application **Close** button.

12. Close PowerPoint by clicking its application **Close** button.

 **TEAMWORK PROJECT**

Your supervisor has decided to assign some projects to teams of employees, and he has asked you and a coworker to investigate what tools Office 2003 offers for collaborative work. Working as a team, use the Office Help features, the Internet, and other resources such as people you know who use Office applications to find out how Office applications allow more than one person to work on a document in Word, PowerPoint, Publisher, and Excel. Make a list of the reviewing, tracking, and other applicable features in each application and indicate how you access the features from the applications.

CRITICAL*Thinking*

ACTIVITY 11-1

In exchange for riding privileges, you have agreed to help the owner of a local riding stable with a number of computer-related tasks. The owner has created the following list of jobs she needs to have done:

■ Write letters to people who board their horses at the stable to tell them feed bills will go up at the beginning of the year.

■ Store information on owners, frequent riders, equipment, and employees.

■ Schedule regular visits by the vet, keep track of regular chores, and plan activities in coming months.

■ Create flyers to place at local clubs with information about riding clinics and other special activities.

■ Create a Web site to provide information on classes, boarding fees, and facilities at the stable.

■ Calculate expenses for running the stable as well as income from riders and boarders.

■ Come up with a presentation that can be used to train new employees and new riders.

What Office applications can you use to complete each of these jobs? Make a table that lists each job and the Office application you would use to complete the task. Are there other jobs you could do for the stable owner using Office applications? List several other tools available in Microsoft Office that might be useful for the riding stable's business tasks.

WORD ESSENTIALS

Word is a powerful, full-featured word processor. You can use Word to create reports, tables, letters, memos, Web pages, and much more. The Word lessons in this course will introduce you to features that enable you to prepare documents efficiently. You will also learn how to edit documents and enhance their appearance.

Creating a New Document

When you first open the Word application, a new blank document is displayed. The document is currently titled Document1. This filename will remain until you open the File menu and choose Save As and assign the document a new filename.

The Getting Started task pane is also displayed (Figure 12-1). This task pane enables you to quickly open documents that you have recently accessed or to create a new document as well as search for information using the Help feature. You can open additional documents on top of the blank Document1. Thus, you can have multiple Word documents open at the same time.

FIGURE 12-1
The Getting Started task pane in Word

When you use the *Create a new document* option in the task pane to open a new document, the document contains **default** settings to create a traditional printed document. Default settings are preset options or variables. Word's extensive formatting options give you many choices about how the finished document will look. You can change the margins, font, spacing between lines, indents for paragraphs, and many other settings. We will learn more about changing document settings in the Word lessons in this text.

After you open an existing document or create a new document, the task pane will disappear. You can open additional documents by using the New Blank Document button or the Open button on the toolbar.

STEP-BY-STEP 12.1

1. Launch the **Word** application and look at the toolbars, menu bar, and other features in the blank document window that opens.

2. If the Getting Started task pane is not displayed, open the **View** menu and click **Task Pane**. Your task pane may look different than the one in Figure 12-1, depending on what documents have been opened recently in Word on your computer.

> **Note**
>
> To display or hide toolbars, open the **View** menu and select the desired toolbar to turn the option on or off. A check mark in front of the toolbar name indicates that the toolbar is displayed.

3. If your screen does not show the Standard toolbar or Formatting toolbar (shown in Figure 12-2), open the View menu and select the appropriate toolbar from the Toolbars submenu. Your Formatting toolbar may be "condensed" and not show all the buttons shown here, but you can expand it or move it to its own row by dragging on the title bar or the dashed vertical bar at far left if there is no title bar displayed.

STEP-BY-STEP 12.1 Continued

FIGURE 12-2
The Formatting toolbar

4. In the Getting Started pane, under Open, click the **Create a new document** option to open the New Document task pane.

> **Note** ✓
>
> Press **Ctrl + F4** as an alternative to using the Close button to close the active document window.

5. Select the option **Blank document** in the New section of the task pane to open a second blank document. Notice that the document title bar displays Document2.

6. Click the **Document1** button in the taskbar to switch to that document and then click the document **Close** button to close the file.

7. The Document2 window should be open. Leave the document open for the next Step-by-Step.

Entering Text in a Document

2-1.3.2

As you enter text in a Word document, the insertion point will move to the right and the status bar at the bottom of the document window will change to reflect the position of the insertion point. As you key, you may see a red or green wavy line under some of the words. Word automatically checks the spelling and grammar in a document as you enter the text. The red wavy line identifies a word that may be misspelled. The green wavy line identifies a possible grammatical error. If you make any errors while keying, press Backspace to remove the errors, and then rekey your text correctly.

If the text you are keying extends beyond the right margin, Word will automatically wrap the text to the next line. This feature is called *word wrap*. Press Enter only to start a new paragraph. To insert a blank line between paragraphs, press Enter twice.

STEP-BY-STEP 12.2

1. Key the sentences below into **Document2**. Notice as you enter the text that the insertion point moves and the status bar reflects the position of the insertion point. Remember: Do not press **Enter** until you reach the end of the paragraph, and then press **Enter** twice to create a blank line between paragraphs.

   Today the majority of the American population lives in cities and suburbs. The people who live in metropolitan areas depend on parks and recreational paths close to their homes for both recreation and contact with nature.

   To preserve acres of green open space, greenways are interconnected open spaces surrounding and running through metropolitan areas. Sometimes these greenways even link cities together.

STEP-BY-STEP 12.2 Continued

2. Open the **File** menu and choose **Save As** to display the Save As dialog box.

3. Click the **down arrow** in the Save in box and locate the folder where you save your work.

4. In the File name box, key **Greenways** followed by your initials, and then click **Save** in the dialog box.

5. Leave the document open for the next Step-by-Step.

Moving Through the Document

In Lesson 11, you learned how to move the insertion point in a document using the mouse and the scroll bars. Move the mouse pointer anywhere in the text visible on your computer screen, click, and the insertion point moves to the place where you clicked. If you want to move beyond the visible part of the document, use the mouse pointer to click and drag the scroll boxes or click the scroll arrows to move up, down, left, or right through your document. The insertion point does not move when you scroll; you must move the mouse pointer to a position in the new screen and then click the left mouse to move the insertion point there.

Using the Keyboard

You can use the arrow keys on the keyboard to move the insertion point one character at a time or one line at a time. If you need to move across several characters or lines, however, the keyboard shortcuts shown in Table 12-1 will make the task easier and quicker.

TABLE 12-1
Keyboard shortcuts for moving the Insertion point

TO MOVE THE INSERTION POINT	PRESS
Right one character	right arrow
Left one character	left arrow
To the next line	down arrow
To the previous line	up arrow
To the end of a line	End
To the beginning of a line	Home
To the next screen	Page Down
To the previous screen	Page Up
To the next word	Ctrl + right arrow
To the previous word	Ctrl + left arrow
To the end of the document	Ctrl + End
To the beginning of the document	Ctrl + Home

STEP-BY-STEP 12.3

1. Press **Ctrl + Home** to move the insertion point to the beginning of the document.

2. Press the **down arrow** twice to move the insertion point down two lines.

3. Press the **right arrow** three times to move the insertion point three characters to the right.

4. Press **End** to move the insertion point to the end of the line.

5. Press the **left arrow** seven times to move the insertion point to the beginning of the last word of the sentence.

6. Hold down **Ctrl** and then press the **left arrow** to move the insertion point to the previous word.

7. Hold down **Ctrl** and then press **End** to move the insertion point to the end of the document.

8. Press **Home** to move the insertion point to the beginning of the line.

9. Hold down **Ctrl** and then press the **right arrow** to move the insertion point to the next word.

10. Leave the document open for the next Step-by-Step.

 Ethics in Technology

DIGITAL WATERMARKS

A watermark was originally a shadowy image embedded in a sheet of paper when the paper was produced; it often showed the name or logo of the paper company. The term is also used to describe a very light image printed in the background of a document that indicates it is an original, a copy, or some other information. Now, a digital watermark is an image embedded within graphics and audio files that is used to identify the owner's rights to these files. In other words, a digital image can be added to music files, pictures, and so forth, to properly identify the creator's work in a way that is invisible to the human eye or not audible to the human ear—until the image or file is copied.

These watermarks also indicate that the work is the original property of its creator. Watermarking technology makes it possible for copyright owners to find illegal copies of the work and take appropriate legal action. For example, if there is a digital watermark in an image on a Web site, you might not be able to see it until you copy the image and paste it in another location. Then the digital watermark would indicate that the image came from a proprietary source. These electronic markers are used to prevent unlawful copying of image and audio files and inhibit copyright infringement.

Selecting Text

2-2.1.2

When you select text, you identify blocks of text you want to move, copy, delete, or replace. The text can be a single character, several characters, a word, a phrase, a sentence, one or more paragraphs, or even the entire document. You can select everything in a document with the Select All command on the Edit menu, or use the keyboard shortcut Ctrl + A. Once you select text, you can edit it by deleting it, replacing it, changing its appearance, moving it, copying it, and so on.

Computer Concepts

Be cautious when working with selected text. If you press any keys on the keyboard when text is selected, the new keystrokes will replace the selected text. Pages of text could accidentally be replaced with a single character.

You can use the mouse or the keyboard to select text. The quickest way to select text using the mouse is to drag the mouse pointer over the desired text. Sometimes it is difficult to select precisely when you are dragging the mouse. The click-Shift-click method makes it easy to select the right text on the first try. Click where you want the selection to begin, hold down Shift, and then click where you want the selection to end. Table 12-2 lists several options for selecting text using the mouse and the keyboard. To deselect the text (remove the selection), click an insertion point anywhere in the document or press an arrow key. If you accidentally delete or replace selected text, or if you just change your mind, click the Undo button.

TABLE 12-2
Ways to select text

TO SELECT TEXT USING THE MOUSE	DO THIS
Any amount of text	Drag over the text.
A word	Double-click the word.
A sentence	Hold down the Ctrl key, then click anywhere in the sentence.
A paragraph	Triple-click anywhere in the paragraph, or double-click in the left margin.
An entire document	Move the pointer to the left of any text. When the pointer changes to a right-pointing arrow, triple-click, or open the Edit menu and choose Select All.
A line	Click in the left margin.
Multiple lines	Drag in the left margin.
One character to the right	Hold down Shift and press the right arrow.
One character to the left	Hold down Shift and press the left arrow.
To the beginning of a word	Hold down Ctrl + Shift and press the left arrow.
To the end of a word	Hold down Ctrl + Shift and press the right arrow.

STEP-BY-STEP 12.4

1. Move the I-beam mouse pointer until it is at the beginning of the first line of text.

2. Hold down the mouse button and drag through the first sentence of text. When all the text is selected, release the mouse button. The sentence is now selected as shown in Figure 12-3.

FIGURE 12-3
Selected text

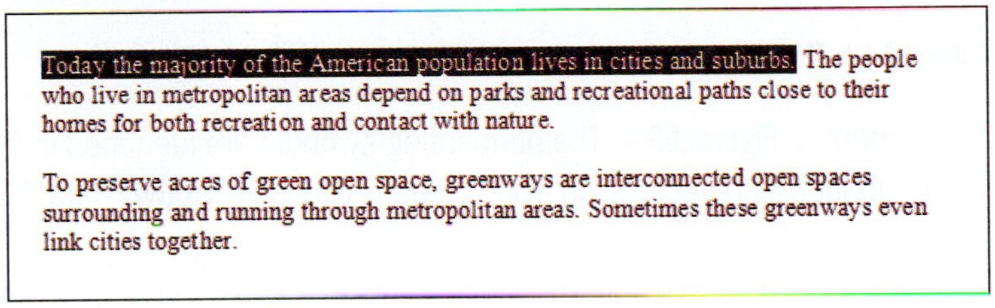

> Today the majority of the American population lives in cities and suburbs. The people who live in metropolitan areas depend on parks and recreational paths close to their homes for both recreation and contact with nature.
>
> To preserve acres of green open space, greenways are interconnected open spaces surrounding and running through metropolitan areas. Sometimes these greenways even link cities together.

3. Double-click the word **recreation** in the last line of the first paragraph to select it and key **leisure activities**. The selected text is replaced with the new text.

4. Press **Ctrl + A** to select the entire document.

5. Click at the beginning of the second paragraph to position the insertion point there. Hold down **Shift**, and then click at the end of the paragraph. The whole paragraph is selected.

> **Note**
>
> If the selected text is not replaced when new text is keyed, open the **Tools** menu and choose **Options**. Make sure *Typing replaces selection* is turned on in the Edit tab.

6. Click at the end of the first paragraph to position the insertion point there. Hold down **Ctrl + Shift** and then press **Home**. All the text from the insertion point to the beginning of the document is selected.

7. Practice other methods of selecting text following the instructions in Table 12-2.

8. Click anywhere in the document window to deselect the text. Then save the changes to a new file named **New Greenways** followed by your initials and close the document. Leave Word open for the next Step-by-Step.

Displaying Nonprinting Characters

2-1.1.1

Word considers characters to be letters, numbers, and graphics. All of these elements are visible on your screen just as they will look when printed. To simplify editing, you can also display some special characters. These characters are known as nonprinting characters because, although you can display these symbols on the screen, they do not print.

The Show/Hide ¶ button on the Standard toolbar enables you to *toggle* the display of these nonprinting characters. Toggling is the process of turning an option on or off using the same procedure, such as clicking a button.

Nonprinting characters include hard returns (or line breaks), blank spaces, page and section breaks, and tab and indent markers. Initially, you may not like displaying nonprinting characters while you work with a document, but give it a try. Once you get used to seeing the nonprinting characters on the screen, you will find them very useful as you create and edit the document.

STEP-BY-STEP 12.5

1. Open the Step12-5 file from the data files for this lesson.

2. Save the document as **Carbohydrates** followed by your initials.

3. Compare your document to Figure 12-4. The nonprinting symbols are identified in the figure. If you do not see the nonprinting characters on your screen, click the **Show/Hide ¶** button on the Standard toolbar.

4. Leave the document open for the next Step-by-Step.

FIGURE 12-4
Document with nonprinting characters displayed

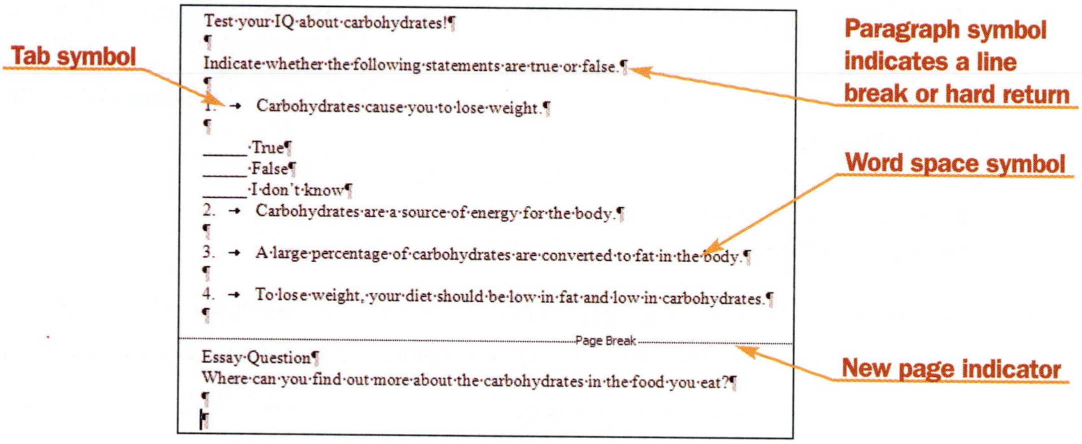

Changing Views

2-1.2.4

Word offers different options for viewing a document. You can change views in any Office application from the View menu; the options vary in different applications. *Normal view* is the default view in Word, and it provides a simple layout so you can enter and edit text quickly. Other frequently used Word view options include *Print Layout view* and *Web Layout view*. Print Layout view shows how a document will look when it is printed, and Web Layout view displays a document as it would appear in a Web browser. As you learn more about each Office application and create documents using the programs, you may find that you prefer one view for certain kinds of tasks and another view for others.

There are two other views available from the View menu in Word, Reading Layout view and Outline view. If they are not displayed in the View menu, click the down arrow at the bottom of the menu to expand it and show all the options. These are views you can use for specialized tasks; the Reading Layout view shows the document as it might appear if you were reading a book, with no status bar, rulers, task panes, and just a few command buttons on the Reading Layout toolbar at the top of the document.

Outline view takes the text in your document and arranges it in classic outline form, using heads in the text as main points in the outline, with subheads and text providing entries in other levels. This view makes it easy to see how a document is structured and to quickly and easily reorganize it. The Outlining toolbar that appears when you select Outline view offers options you can use for restructuring.

Word also provides magnification options to make the text and graphics in a document smaller or larger, and you may find you want to change the magnification level to see how an entire page (or multiple pages) in a document looks, or to read very small text more easily. Use the Zoom command, as you learned in Lesson 11, to open the Zoom dialog box and select from the options there. Word even offers a Preview screen and text preview panel in the Zoom dialog box so you can see how changes you select will display.

S TEP-BY-STEP 12.6

1. Click the **Show/Hide ¶** button to hide the nonprinting characters if you prefer.

2. Open the **View** menu and note which view is selected (the icon representing the view at the left in the menu will have a box shaded in a different color around the icon). Normal view is usually the default view in Word.
   a. Select **Web Layout** view.
   b. Switch to **Outline** view. Notice that the Outlining toolbar appears at the top of the document window when you select this view.
   c. Switch to **Print Layout** view.

3. Open the **View** menu again and click **Zoom** to open the Zoom dialog box.

4. Click the icon below the **Many pages** option to see the different layouts available to view multiple pages.

5. As you move the mouse pointer over the small page icons, you will see the layout description below the icons. When the description says **2 x 2**, click to select it and view the preview windows in the dialog box.

6. Click the option button for **Whole page** to select the option, and then click **OK**. Look at the display of your document now. The text probably looks quite a bit smaller.

7. Open the **View** menu and click the **Zoom** option. In the Zoom dialog box, select the **Text width** option and then click **OK**. Leave the document open for the next Step-by-Step.

Using the Track Changes and Comments Features

2-2.1.9
2-2.1.20

Word offers features that allow several people to collaborate on a document and keep track of who has made changes, where and what the changes are, and even add notes as you would on a paper document. These features include a way to keep track of changes made in a document and a way to add electronic notes that appear in the margin of the document.

A *comment* is a note that the original author of a document, or another person who is reviewing the text, can add in a balloon viewable in the document's margin or in the Reviewing pane. Comments are indicated with highlighting in the text, but they do not print in a document unless you choose to have them print.

You can add a comment anywhere in a Word document by selecting Comment from the Insert menu, or you can click the Comment button on the Reviewing toolbar (Figure 12-5). Display the Reviewing toolbar by selecting it from the Toolbars submenu on the View menu.

> **Computer Concepts**
>
> The Reviewing pane shows changes and comments in a separate window below the document window. You can open the Reviewing pane by clicking the **Reviewing Pane** button on the Reviewing toolbar. Close the pane by clicking the same button again.

FIGURE 12-5
The Reviewing toolbar

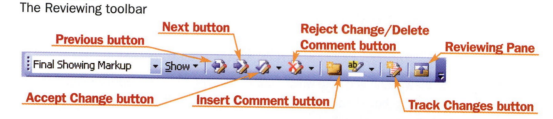

When you add a comment, you will see shading that highlights the text where the insertion point was at the time you clicked the Comment button, and a dashed line leading to the comment balloon in the margin, as shown in Figure 12-6. Key text in the comment balloon to write your note. The initials indicate who has written the comment, and are based on the user information in your computer. The comments are numbered in order in the document.

> **Computer Concepts**
>
> You can view the user information for a computer in the Options dialog box, which is accessed from the Tools menu. Select the User Information tab in the dialog box.

FIGURE 12-6
A comment in a Word document

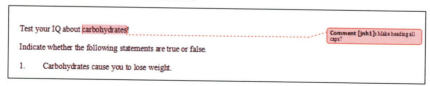

To print the comments in a document, you should be in Print Layout view. On the File menu, click Print. Look for the Print what box at lower left in the Print dialog box, and select Document showing markup from the drop-down list. Then click OK.

The Track Changes feature adds a mark in the margin of a document to show where text has been inserted, deleted, or changed. There are different options for showing deleted text; it may appear crossed out, in *strikethrough* style, or it may be displayed in a deleted text balloon in the margin, depending on the options the user selects and the document view. New text is also clearly indicated in a different color.

To turn on the Track Changes feature, you can select it from the Tools menu, which turns on the feature and adds the Reviewing toolbar to the toolbars above the document window at the same time. The Track Changes button on the Reviewing toolbar also will turn on the feature when click it. You turn off the feature using the same methods; this is another feature that toggles from on to off and from off to on when you select it. You can change the default options in the Track Changes feature (such as the color and style used for insertions and deletions) in the Options dialog box available from the Tools menu. Select the Track Changes tab to see a variety of options for font color and attributes.

> **Note**
>
> You can also turn on the Track Changes feature by right-clicking the **TRK** button in the status bar and then clicking **Track Changes** in the shortcut menu.

Comments and revisions are visible in the document when you use the reviewing tools, adding notes or tracking changes. But you can hide the revisions and comments easily, too, by selecting the Markup command on the View menu. If the changes are visible, clicking Markup will hide them; if they are hidden, clicking the command will show them again.

When changes and notes are added to a document, it is usually passed on to another person, either the original author or another reviewer, to make a decision about the revisions and comments. To do this, display the changes if necessary by clicking Markup in the View menu. You will also need to have the Reviewing toolbar visible (Figure 12-6). The Previous (left arrow) and Next (right arrow) buttons on the toolbar allow you to move forward or backward through the document, viewing revisions and comments one by one. Use the Accept button (with the check mark) to accept a revision and make the change a part of the document; the Reject button (with the red X) allows you reject a change or delete a comment. Notice that both the Accept and Reject buttons provide a drop-down menu that allows you to choose to accept all changes or reject all comments or revisions in a document.

STEP-BY-STEP 12.7

1. Display the **Reviewing** toolbar.

2. Position the insertion point at the end of the first line in the document, and then click the **Insert Comment** button on the Reviewing toolbar.

3. Key **Make heading all caps?** in the comment box.

4. Click somewhere else in the document to finish the comment and then click the **Track Changes** button on the Reviewing toolbar to turn on the feature.

5. In the answers to the first question in the document, select the last answer, **I don't know**, and then key **None of the above** to replace the text. You may see the original text in strikethrough type, or shown in a deleted balloon in the margin of the document. The new text will appear in a different color.

6. In the **View** menu, click **Markup** to hide the comment and revisions in the document. Click **Markup** again to show the comment and revision.

7. Print the document with the comment and changes visible:
   a. Select **Print** from the **File** menu.
   b. Select **Document showing markup** in the Print what box.
   c. Select Current page in the Page range section.
   d. Click **OK** to print the document page.

STEP-BY-STEP 12.7 Continued

8. Position the insertion point at the beginning of the document

   a. Click the **Next** button on the Reviewing toolbar to move to the comment.

   b. Click the **Next** button again to the move to the revision.

   c. Click the **Previous** button to return to the comment, and then click the **Reject Change/Delete Comment** button to delete the comment.

   d. Add a new comment to the end of the first line: **Heading okay**.

9. Save the file as **Carbohydrates Markup** followed by your initials and then close the document and close Word. (You can close both at the same time by clicking the application **Close** button.) Follow your instructor's directions about turning off the computer.

SUMMARY

In this lesson, you learned:

- A blank Word document opens when you open the Word application, and you can open additional documents from the Getting Started task pane or by using the New Blank Document button on the Standard toolbar.

- Word automatically wraps text to the next line when the line of text extends beyond the right margin.

- When you scroll through the document, the insertion point does not move. To reposition the insertion point, you can use either the mouse or the keyboard.

- You can use the mouse or keyboard shortcuts to move through a document.

- Text must be selected before you can move, replace, copy, or delete it. Text can be selected using the mouse or the keyboard.

- The Show/Hide ¶ button on the Standard toolbar toggles the display of nonprinting characters such as tab and indent symbols, blank spaces, page and section breaks, and paragraph marks.

- The View menu has several options you can choose to change the display of a document.

- Comments are electronic notes that can be added to a document to provide information that is not part of the text. The notes appear in balloons in the margin of the document.

- The Track Changes feature allows you to clearly see changes made to a document, and you can hide or show comments and changes using the Markup command on the View menu.

- You can print a document with or without visible revisions and comments by selecting different options in the Print dialog box.

VOCABULARY *Review*

Define the following terms:

Comment	Print Layout view	Web Layout view
Default	Strikethrough	Word wrap
Normal view	Toggle	

REVIEW *Questions*

TRUE/FALSE

Circle T if the statement is true or F if the statement is false.

T　F　**1.** A task pane provides an easy and quick way to open a recently accessed document or create a new document.

T　F　**2.** Word offers five different views for the document window.

T　F　**3.** As you key a paragraph of text, you should press Enter to stop each line at the right margin.

T　F　**4.** The Track Changes feature shows changes and deletions made to the text.

T　F　**5.** To move quickly to the beginning of a document, click the Home key.

MULTIPLE CHOICE

Circle the best response for each of the following statements.

1. Preset options already in place in a new document are called _____ settings.
   A. default
   B. factory
   C. user
   D. standard

2. The _____ feature automatically moves text to the next line when you reach the end of the current line.
   A. outline
   B. track changes
   C. strikethrough
   D. word wrap

3. To relocate the insertion point in a document, point the _____ at the proper location and then click the left mouse button.
   A. Reviewing pane
   B. scroll bar
   C. window
   D. mouse pointer

4. To move to the next word in a document, press _____ and then the right arrow key.
   A. Shift
   B. Ctrl
   C. Home
   D. Word Up

5. The Show/Hide ¶ button, which shows or hides nonprinting characters in a document, is an example of an option that _____ by using the same procedure to turn it on or off.
   A. word wraps
   B. comments
   C. toggles
   D. defaults

PROJECTS

PROJECT 12-1

1. Launch Word and open a new Word document.

2. Open **Project12-1** from the data files. Save the document as **Tiger** followed by your initials.

3. Click the **Document1** button in the taskbar to return to the new blank document you created when you started Word. (Note that if Word was already open, the new blank document you created in step 1 may be named Document2, Document3, or so on.)

4. Key the following text:

```
Someone Else's Fault

Almost everyone knows about the San Andreas Fault in California. Shifting
along this fault line resulted in numerous damaging earthquakes throughout
the twentieth century.

Relatively unknown by comparison, the New Madrid Fault in the central
United States caused three of the most powerful earthquakes in U.S. history
in the nineteenth century. One earthquake along this fault line was so
powerful it caused the Mississippi River to run backward for a brief
stretch. Damage from the earthquake was reported as far away as Charleston,
South Carolina, and Washington, DC.
```

5. Save the document as **New Madrid** followed by your initials. Print the document and then close it.

6. Leave the **Tiger** document open for the next Project.

PROJECT 12-2

1. The document **Tiger** should still be open. Position the insertion point following the period after the number *1,000* in the second paragraph of the document.

2. Press the spacebar once and key the following sentences:

   ```
   The South China tiger is dangerously close to extinction. Only 20 to 30
   tigers are thought to be alive in a few isolated areas. Because there have
   been no recent sightings of this tiger, some people believe it might
   already be extinct.
   ```

3. Use **Ctrl + End** to move to the end of the document. Key the following sentence:

   ```
   They state that only an immediate, widespread effort by concerned
   individuals and support from governments of countries where tigers still
   exist will keep tigers alive in the wild.
   ```

4. Navigate to the top of the document. If you are not already in Print Layout view, change to this view.

5. Position the I-beam pointer so that it is in the white space immediately above the first paragraph and in the center of the document. Double-click to insert the insertion point, and then key **Tiger, Tiger** to create a title for the document. After you key the title, press **Enter** to insert a blank line between the title and the first paragraph of text.

6. Save your changes and close the document.

TEAMWORK PROJECT

As you worked through this lesson, you learned that Word offers a total of five views to help you work with specific types of documents. Learn more about the different Word views in this project.

1. Divide into five groups. Each group should be assigned a different Word view: Normal, Web Layout, Print Layout, Reading Layout, or Outline.

2. Each group should use observation and the Word Help system to learn as much as possible about its assigned view. Be sure to answer these questions as you gather information:
   A. How can you tell where the top and bottom of the page are in this view?
   B. This view is designed for working with what kinds of documents?
   C. What happens to the document window when you change to this view?
   D. Are there any objects that will not display in this view?
   E. How many ways can you find to switch to this view?

3. Each group should write a short report on the information it has gathered on its view. One member of the group should summarize the group's findings in a brief presentation.

CRITICAL *Thinking*

ACTIVITY 12-1

Use the Word Help system to find information on Word's personalized menus and toolbars. Write a brief summary of this feature and state whether you feel this feature will be useful to you in this course.

EDITING AND FORMATTING DOCUMENTS

OBJECTIVES

Upon completion of this lesson, you should be able to:

■ Delete and insert text using the Backspace and Delete keys and Insert and Overtype mode.

■ Use the Undo and Redo features.

■ Edit text using drag-and-drop editing and the cut, copy, and paste commands.

■ Find and replace text.

■ Format text with fonts, line spacing, alignment, tabs and indents, page breaks, and bulleted and numbered lists.

■ Check and correct spelling and grammar.

■ Display document statistics such as word count.

■ Use Print Preview and format a document for printing.

Estimated Time: 2 hours

VOCABULARY

Alignment

Attributes

Clipboard

Drag-and-drop

First line indent

Font

Format

Format Painter

Hanging indent

Hard page break

Insert mode

Landscape orientation

Overtype mode

Points

Portrait orientation

Soft page break

Word is designed to handle many kinds of word-processing documents. Editing and formatting features give you the ability to refine your documents and determine how they will look on the screen, on the Web, or as printed pages. Editing involves adding, deleting, changing, or moving text in a document. Editing enables you to correct errors and refine the appearance of the document. You can also check the spelling and the grammar in your document with Word. Formatting features enable you to change the appearance of a document so you can make it more attractive and easier to read. Word offers a number of formatting options that can be applied to as much text as desired, from a single character to the entire document. When your document is edited and formatted the way you want it, Word provides document statistics about the file and also allows you to preview the document before printing it.

Deleting and Inserting Characters

2-1.3.3

When you edit documents, you often need to delete and replace existing text. This is very easy to do in Word. You can quickly delete characters one at a time by using either the Backspace or the Delete keys. The Backspace key deletes the character to the left of the insertion point. The Delete key removes the character to the right of the insertion point. If you hold down either of these keys, the characters will continue to delete until you release the key. You can also select a character, word, sentence, or paragraph and then press Delete to delete the selected text.

By default, Word enters text in a document using the *Insert mode*. In this mode, when you type new text in front of existing text, the existing text shifts to the right to make room for the new text. When the Insert mode is turned off, the *Overtype mode* is activated. In the Overtype mode, new text you key replaces the existing text. You can toggle between the Insert mode and the Overtype mode by double-clicking OVR in the status bar or by pressing the Insert key (on the keyboard). Regardless of how you toggle, when OVR is dimmed, Insert mode is on; when OVR is dark or bold, Overtype mode is on.

S TEP-BY-STEP 13.1

1. Open **Step13-1** from the data files for this lesson. Save the file as **Diet** followed by your initials and then position the insertion point right before the period at the end of the last sentence in the first paragraph.

2. Press **Backspace** several times to erase the last four words in the sentence (*instead of losing weight*).

3. Move the insertion point to the beginning of the word *complex* in the first sentence after the heading. Double-click the word **complex** to select it, and then press **Delete** to erase the word.

4. Make sure *OVR* in the status bar is dimmed. If the option is bold in the status bar, double-click it to toggle off the Overtype mode.

5. Position the insertion point right before the word *Answers* in the heading. Key **Carbohydrate** and then a space. In Insert mode, Word inserts the text between the existing characters.

6. Double-click **OVR** in the status bar to toggle on the Overtype mode.

7. Make sure the insertion point is in front of the word *Answers* in the heading. Key **Knowledge**. The new word replaces the word *Answers* with the new text.

8. Double-click **OVR** in the status bar to switch back to the Insert mode. Save the changes and leave the document open for the next Step-by-Step.

Undo, Redo, and Repeat

2-1.3.4

Sometimes you may delete or replace text unintentionally. Whenever you perform an edit that you want to change back, you can use the Undo command. If you undo an edit and then change your mind, you can reverse the undo action by using the Redo command. You can undo and redo multiple actions at one time by choosing from the Undo or Redo drop-down list on the Standard toolbar (shown in Figure 13-1). When you undo or redo an action from the drop-down list, Word will also undo or redo all the actions listed above it on the list.

FIGURE 13-1
The arrows next to the buttons access
drop-down lists for each command

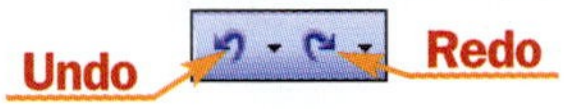

Undo Redo

There may be times when you want to repeat your last action. For example, you may enter your name in a document and then want to add your name in other locations in the document. You can use the Repeat command to repeat your last action. You can access the Repeat command in the Edit menu, or you can use the shortcut key combination Ctrl + Y to execute the command. If you can't repeat the last action, the Repeat command in the Edit menu will change to *Can't Repeat.*

> **Note** ☑
>
> The shortcut key combination for the Undo command is **Ctrl + Z**; for the Redo command, use **Ctrl + Y**.

STEP-BY-STEP 13.2

1. Position the insertion point at the end of the document and press **Enter** three times.

2. Key your name and then position the insertion point at the beginning of the document.

3. Open the **Edit** menu and choose **Repeat Typing**. Your name is inserted before the heading in the document.

4. You change your mind. Click the **Undo** button on the Standard toolbar. The blank lines and your name disappear from the top of the document.

5. Click the **down arrow** next to the Undo button and select **Typing "Carbohydrate."** (*Hint*: You may have to scroll down through the list to see this in the list.) All the previous actions will remain highlighted, as shown in Figure 13-2. The last 12 actions are reversed.

FIGURE 13-2
Select multiple actions in the Undo list box

6. Click the **Redo** button on the Standard toolbar to undo only the last undo. The word *Carbohydrate* is reinserted in the heading. Save the changes and keep the document open for the next Step-by-Step.

Copying and Moving Text

2-1.3.1
2-1.3.3

Selected text can be copied or moved from one location in a Word document to a new location in the same document, to a different Word document, or even to a different document in another application program. There are several ways to copy and move text. You can use the mouse to drag selected text from the existing location and then drop the selected text in its new location. This is called **drag-and-drop** editing. You can also use the Cut and Paste commands to relocate selected text.

Use Drag-and-Drop Editing

Drag-and-drop editing makes moving text quick and easy, especially when you are moving the text short distances. You simply drag selected text to the new location and then release the mouse button. You can also copy text using drag-and-drop editing. Hold down Ctrl as you drag, and the selected text will be copied instead of moved.

S TEP-BY-STEP 13.3

1. Select all of the text in the third paragraph of the document. Make sure you include the tab character before the first word and the blank paragraph after the last sentence. (*Hint*: Click the **Show/Hide ¶** button to see the tab and paragraph characters.)

2. Point to the selection and hold down the left mouse button. You will see a dotted insertion point displayed.

3. Drag the dotted insertion point in front of the tab character that precedes the word *Each* at the beginning of the second paragraph in the document, and then release.

STEP-BY-STEP 13.3 Continued

4. With the paragraph still selected, hold down **Ctrl** and use the left mouse button to drag the text to the end of the document. The text is copied to the new location.

5. Click **Undo** and then click to deselect the text.

6. Save the changes and close the document. Leave Word open for the next Step-by-Step.

> **Computer Concepts**
>
> To drag text beyond the current screen of text, drag the pointer toward the top or bottom of the screen. As you hold the pointer at the edge, the document will automatically scroll in that direction.

Use the Cut, Copy, and Paste Commands

You can access the Cut, Copy, and Paste commands by clicking the appropriate buttons on the Standard toolbar (Figure 13-3). You can also access the commands by right-clicking the selected text. Then choose the desired command from the shortcut menu that is displayed.

FIGURE 13-3
The Cut, Copy, and Paste buttons

When you use the Cut, Copy, and Paste commands, Word stores the selected text in the *Clipboard*. The Clipboard is a temporary storage place in your computer's memory. The Clipboard is a shared item between all the Office applications. It can store data of all Office types and that data can be pasted from the Clipboard to other documents in the same application or to documents in other Office programs. You send selected contents of your document to the Clipboard by using the Cut or Copy commands. Cutting removes text from the document and stores it in the Clipboard. Copying also stores the text on the Clipboard, but it leaves the text in the document. You can retrieve the contents of the Clipboard by using the Paste command.

> **Note**
>
> The shortcut keys for Cut are **Ctrl + X**; for Copy, **Ctrl + C**; and for Paste, **Ctrl + V**. The Cut, Copy, and Paste commands can also be found on the Edit menu.

The Clipboard will store up to 24 items. If you display the Clipboard task pane (Figure 13-4), you can see items stored in the Clipboard. To display the Clipboard task pane manually, select Clipboard or Office Clipboard from the Edit menu. The shortcut key combination to open the Clipboard task pane requires you to press Ctrl + C twice. Make sure that nothing is selected when you press Ctrl + C. If text is selected, the shortcut will copy the selected text to the Clipboard instead of opening the Clipboard task pane. It is not necessary to display the Clipboard task pane when you are cutting or copying text, however. The Clipboard still functions even if the task pane is not displayed.

> **Computer Concepts**
>
> If you cut or copy text and fail to leave a blank space between sentences, Word will automatically adjust the spacing by adding a blank space.

FIGURE 13-4
Clipboard task pane

You can select any one of the items in the task pane and paste it, or you can choose the Paste All button to paste all the Clipboard items at once. If you choose the Clear All button, all the contents are removed from the Clipboard.

When you use the Paste command, items are inserted at the location of the insertion point. Pasting the contents of the Clipboard does not delete the contents from the Clipboard. Therefore, you can paste Clipboard items as many times as you want. When you turn off the computer, the Clipboard contents are lost.

S TEP-BY-STEP 13.4

1. Open **Step13-4** from the data files for this lesson and save the file as **Quiz** followed by your initials.

2. Press **Ctrl + C** twice to display the Clipboard task pane. If any items are displayed in the task pane, click the **Clear All** button in the task pane.

3. Select the three lines of text and the blank paragraph following the text under Question 1. Be sure to include the paragraph symbol in your selection.

4. Click the **Copy** button on the Standard toolbar. Word copies the selected text to the Clipboard and displays the item in the task pane, as shown in Figure 13-4.

STEP-BY-STEP 13.4 Continued

5. Position the insertion point in the blank paragraph below Question 2.

6. Click the **Paste** button on the Standard toolbar. Word pastes the contents of the Clipboard at the location of the insertion point. Notice that the item is still displayed in the Clipboard task pane.

7. Position the insertion point in the blank paragraph below Question 3, and then click the item in the task pane.

8. Select the entire line of text for Question 4, and then click the **Copy** button.

9. Select the entire line of text for Question 3, and then click the **Copy** button again.

10. You should see three items in the Clipboard task pane. Position the insertion point in the blank paragraph below Question 4. Click on the last item in the Clipboard task pane with the____*True*____*False* contents.

11. Click the **Clear All** button to remove the items from the Clipboard.

12. Save the changes and leave the document open for the next Step-by-Step.

> **Computer Concepts**
>
> Word offers many options for using the Clipboard. Use the Help feature to find out more about the Clipboard and to determine which options best meet your needs.

Inserting Special Text: Date, Time, and Special Characters

2-2.1.7
2-2.1.8

The Insert menu in Word has options available to quickly insert the current date, time, or special symbols in your document. Click the Date and Time command to open the Date and Time dialog box (Figure 13-5), where you can choose from many different formats for the inserted text. Select the format you prefer in the Available formats list and then click OK to insert the date or time you have chosen. The text will be inserted at the place in the document where the insertion point is positioned, so be sure you have the insertion point in the place where you want the date or time to appear, or you will have to cut and move the inserted text.

FIGURE 13-5
The Date and Time dialog box

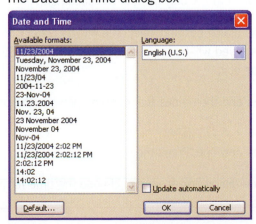

The options in the Date and Time dialog box enter the current date and time as text that remains as it was entered in your document, so if you open it the next day, the previous day's date will appear in the document. You also have the option to insert a field in your document that will always show the current date or time. To insert a date field, position your insertion point where you want the date information to appear, and then select Field from the Insert menu. Choose Date from the Field names list and then select the date or time format you want to insert from the Date formats list. Click OK to insert the field.

Use the Symbol command on the Insert menu to open the Symbol dialog box (Figure 13-6). You can use the scroll bar to scroll through all the available symbols, or choose a subset of symbols from the Subset drop-down list. For example, if you are looking for an arrow symbol or a mathematical operator, select the applicable option from the list and you will see the symbols in that group in the dialog box window.

The Special Characters tab in the Symbol dialog box gives you access to characters such as dashes, copyright and trademark symbols, and nonbreaking spaces. Select the character you want and then click Insert to place the character in your text at the position of the insertion point.

FIGURE 13-6
The Symbol dialog box

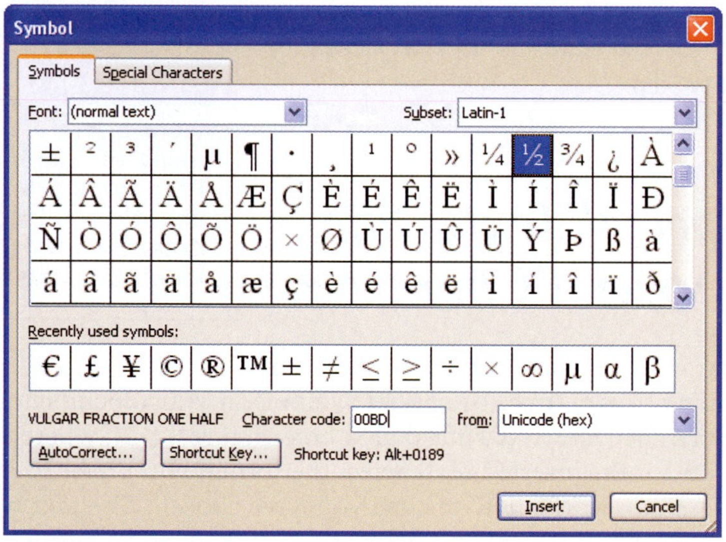

STEP-BY-STEP 13.5

1. Position the insertion point at the beginning of the document.

2. Open the **Date and Time** dialog box and select the MM/DD/YYYY date format from the Available formats list. (The date displayed will be the current date, such as 4/18/2008.) Click **OK** to insert the text and close the dialog box.

3. Press **Enter** three times and then move the insertion point to the beginning of the blank line under the date.

4. Key **Time of test:** on the new line. Press the spacebar.

5. Open the **Date and Time** dialog box again and choose the time format that includes AM or PM, and then click **OK**.

STEP-BY-STEP 13.5 Continued

6. Move the insertion point to a blank line at the end of the document and press **Enter**.

7. Open the **Symbol** dialog box and click the **Special Characters** tab. Select the copyright symbol (©) from the list and then click **Insert** to insert the character in the text. Following the copyright symbol, key the current year and your name (for example, ©2009 Your Name). Close the Symbol dialog box.

8. Press **Enter** and then select **Field** from the **Insert** menu.

9. In the Field names list, select **Date**, and then select the format of your choice in the Date formats list.

10. Save the changes and close the document. Leave Word open for the next Step-by-Step.

2-1.3.5
2-1.3.6

Using Find and Replace

Scrolling through a long document to locate a specific section of text is time-consuming and not very efficient. The Find feature in Word makes searching for text and/or formats much easier. When you need to replace or reformat multiple occurrences of the same text, you can use the Replace feature to replace each occurrence automatically.

Find Text

You use the Find command to search a document for every time a specific word or phrase occurs. The search will begin at the location of the insertion point. If you want to search only a specific portion of a document, you can select the desired text before beginning the search. The Find command on the Edit menu opens the Find and Replace dialog box, where you enter the text you want to find.

Find and Replace Text

If you want to replace the search text with new words, you choose the Replace command. The replacements can be made individually, or all occurrences can be replaced at once. Use the Find command to open the Find and Replace dialog box, and click the Replace tab to display text boxes you can use to enter the text to find and the text you want to use to replace it. The Replace tab is shown in Figure 13-7.

> **Note** ☑
>
> The shortcut keys to execute the Find command are **Ctrl + F**. Use **Ctrl + H** to execute the Replace command.

FIGURE 13-7
The Replace tab in the Find and Replace dialog box

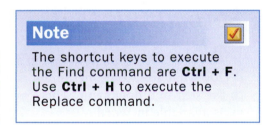

S TEP-BY-STEP 13.6

1. Open **Step13-6** from the data files. Save the document as **Treadwall** followed by your initials. If necessary, move the insertion point to the top of the document.

2. Open the **Edit** menu and choose **Find**. The Find tab in the Find and Replace dialog box is displayed.

3. In the Find what box, key **workout**, and then click **Find Next**. Word locates the first occurrence of the word, and the word is selected in the document window. The dialog box remains open.

4. Click **Find Next** again. Word finds the next occurrence of the word in the open document. Click **Cancel** to close the dialog box.

5. Move the insertion point to the beginning of the document. (*Hint:* Hold down **Ctrl** and press **Home**.)

6. Open the Edit menu and choose **Replace**. The Replace tab in the Find and Replace dialog box is displayed, as shown in Figure 13-7. Notice the word *workout* from your last search is still displayed in the Find what box.

7. Key **tread wall** in the Find what box.

8. Click in the **Replace with** box and key **Treadwall**.

9. Click **Replace All**. Word replaces all occurrences of the search text with the replace text. A message box displays indicating that four replacements were made. Click **OK** to close the message box.

10. Click **Close** in the Find and Replace dialog box. Save the changes and close the document. Leave Word open for the next Step-by-Step.

IC³ *Formatting Text*

2-1.3.8
2-2.1.1
2-2.1.3
2-2.1.4
2-2.1.5
2-2.1.6
2-2.1.10
2-2.1.11
2-2.1.12

Formats are applied to text in a document to manipulate the appearance of the text. You can decide what size, font, attributes, indents, or list styles you want to use when you add a *format* to the text in a document. There are character formats, paragraph formats, and document formats available in Word.

■ Text color and underline are examples of *character formats*. You can apply more than one character format at a time. For example, you can format characters in both bold and italic formats.

■ A *paragraph format* is applied to an entire paragraph and cannot be applied to only a portion of a paragraph. For example, you cannot single-space part of a paragraph and double-space the rest. Word defines a paragraph as any amount of text that ends with a paragraph mark—which is caused by a *hard return* (pressing the Enter key).

- *Document formats* apply to an entire document. For example, margins and paper size are document formats. You can position the insertion point anywhere in a document to change the entire document format. Document formats can be applied either before or after you key text in your document.

We will learn more about character formats and paragraph formats in this section. Document formats are discussed in the last section of this lesson, Formatting a Document for Printing.

Character Formats

Fonts and Point Sizes

A *font* is the design of the typeface in your document. Fonts are available in a variety of styles and sizes, and you can use multiple fonts in one document. The size of the font is measured in *points*. The larger the points number, the larger the font size will be.

You can quickly change the font and point size by using the buttons on the Formatting toolbar. However, when you open the Font dialog box from the Format menu to change the font, you can also apply other font options such as outline, superscript, and shadow. The Font dialog box (Figure 13-8) can be very useful when you want to make several font changes at one time, or if you want to explore what options are available and what they would make the text look like.

> **Computer Concepts**
>
> If you change the format *before* you enter text, all the text you enter will be formatted with the new format until you change the format again. If you have already entered the text, you can change the paragraph formats by clicking in the paragraph and then applying the new format. To change a paragraph format in more than one paragraph or for more than one character, select all the text before applying the format.

FIGURE 13-8
The Font tab in the Font dialog box

![The Font tab in the Font dialog box showing Font, Character Spacing, and Text Effects tabs. Font: Times New Roman; Font style: Regular; Size: 12. Effects checkboxes for Strikethrough, Double strikethrough, Superscript, Subscript, Shadow, Outline, Emboss, Engrave, Small caps, All caps, Hidden. Preview shows "Times New Roman". Note: "This is a TrueType font. This font will be used on both printer and screen." Buttons: Default..., OK, Cancel.]

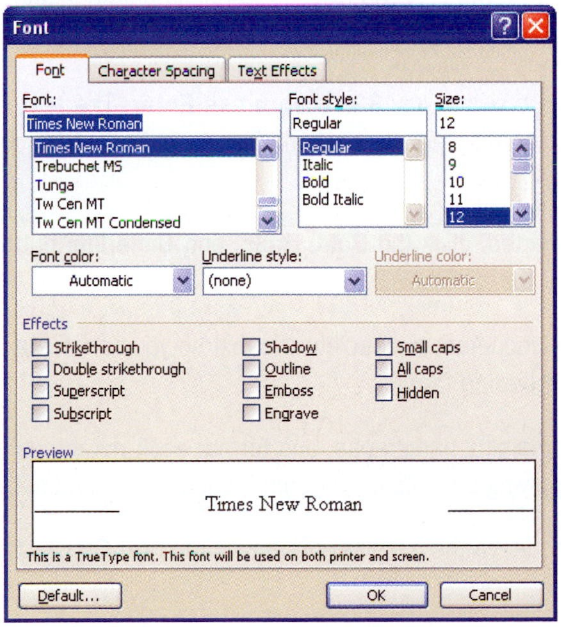

Font Attributes

The Font dialog box lists font styles, also called *attributes*, such as Regular, Italic, Bold, and Bold Italic, and options for underlining text and font color. You can also apply many of these attributes quickly by selecting the text and then clicking the appropriate button in the Formatting toolbar. The Bold, Italic, and Underline buttons immediately apply the attribute to the selected text; you can apply the currently selected alternate font color by clicking the Font Color button, or click the down arrow next to the button to open the Font Color dialog box.

The Font dialog box also offers many other attribute options, such as small caps, strikethrough, and underline color options. When you select font attributes in the Font dialog box, click OK to apply the styles or Cancel to close the dialog box without applying the changes.

STEP-BY-STEP 13.7

1. Open **Step13-7** from the data files and save the document as **Wild Things** followed by your initials.

2. Select the first line of text, then open the **Format** menu and choose **Font**. If necessary, click the **Font** tab to display the Font sheet.

3. In the Font list box, scroll up and select **Arial**. In the Font style list box, scroll down if necessary and select **Bold Italic**. Notice the text in the Preview box changes as you select different character formats.

4. In the Size list box, scroll down and select **48**. Click **OK**.

5. Select the second line of text, and then click the **down arrow** at the right of the Font box in the Formatting toolbar. A list of fonts appears. The fonts you used most recently are shown at the top of the list, and they are separated by a double line from the rest of the font list.

6. Select any font style from the list. The text in the document changes, and the name of the selected font displays in the Font box.

7. Click in the Font Size box and key **32**. Then press **Enter**. The text in the document is enlarged, and the size of the font displays in the Font Size box. Do not be concerned if the text wraps to the next line.

8. With the text still selected, click the **Bold**, **Italic**, and **Underline** buttons on the Formatting toolbar.

9. Click anywhere in the document to deselect the text so you can see all the font changes. Click **Undo** once to remove the underline format.

10. Select each of the remaining paragraphs, and format each paragraph with a different font and point size. Also practice applying bold, italic, underline, superscript, and subscript formats.

11. Save the changes and leave the document open for the next Step-by-Step.

Paragraph Formats

Line Spacing and Alignment

The default line spacing in Word is single spacing. When text is double-spaced, there is a blank line between each line of text. The blank line between each line of text is half the space for 1½-line spacing. You can choose from several line spacing options by using the Line Spacing button on the Formatting toolbar (shown in Figure 13-9) or by opening the Format menu, choosing Paragraph, and selecting from the line spacing options in the Paragraph dialog box. You can also adjust the spacing both before and after the paragraph itself in the spacing section of the Paragraph dialog box.

FIGURE 13-9
Line spacing and alignment buttons on the Formatting toolbar

Alignment options — — **Line Spacing**

Alignment refers to how text is positioned between the left and right margins. Text can be aligned in four different ways: left, center, right, or justified. The Alignment options each have a button on the Formatting toolbar, as shown in Figure 13-9. The default setting is left alignment. Center alignment is often used for titles, headings, and invitations. Right alignment is often used for page numbers and dates. You can quickly apply any of these alignments using the buttons on the Formatting toolbar.

Note

The shortcut key combination for single spacing is **Ctrl + 1**. For 1½ spacing, the shortcut key combination is **Ctrl + 5**; and for double spacing it is **Ctrl + 2**.

 Technology Timeline

TYPEWRITING VERSUS KEYBOARDING

Before computers and word-processing programs, typewriters were used to create formal documents. The first machines typed only in capital letters. The Remington Company was the first to offer a typewriter that could print both upper- and lowercase letters with the addition of the Shift key. The action was called a *shift* because the carriage on a typewriter would actually shift the position of the typebar to print either of two letter cases. Modern electronic machines such as computers no longer use a mechanical shift to print upper- and lowercase letters, but the Shift key remains on keyboards for this process.

On typewriters, it was also common practice to include two blank spaces between sentences. The extra blank space created more white space and made it easier to read the text. However, today's word-processing applications are more sophisticated and the extra spaces are not necessary because the fonts generally allow for proportional spacing, which eliminates excess white space between characters. Therefore, the white space between sentences is more obvious. Consequently, you need only key one blank space between sentences.

S TEP-BY-STEP 13.8

1. Select the entire document, and then click the **down arrow** on the Line Spacing button on the Formatting toolbar. Select 2.0. The lines are now double-spaced.

2. With the entire document still selected, click the **down arrow** on the Line Spacing button and select 1.5. The spacing between lines is reduced to 1½ line spacing.

3. With the entire document still selected, click **Format** on the menu bar and then click **Paragraph**.

4. Select the **Indents and Spacing** tab if necessary and then set both the Before and After spacing to **6pt**. Click **OK**.

5. Click **Undo** on the Standard toolbar.

6. Click in the first line of the document, and then click the **Center** button on the Formatting toolbar.

7. Select all the remaining lines in the document and then click **Center**. All the lines are centered on the page.

8. Position the insertion point in the paragraph of the document that begins *Join us in...* Click the **Justify** button on the Formatting toolbar.

9. Position the insertion point in the last line of text in the document and click the **Align Right** button to align the text at the right margin.

10. Save the changes and close the document. Leave Word open for the next Step-by-Step.

Displaying the Ruler

In most of the available views in Word, you will usually see a ruler at the top of the document window. The Ruler displays as the default setting, but if you do not see it, make sure that Ruler is selected in the View menu. The Ruler is a handy reference to see the "true" size of your text and document, and it can also be used to quickly set tabs, indents, and margins in your document.

Changing Tabs and Indents

Tabs are useful for indenting paragraphs and lining up columns of text. Word's default tabs are set at every half inch. You can, however, set custom tabs at other locations. When you set new tabs, the default tab(s) to the left of the new tab stop are automatically removed. The default tab style is left-aligned. When you begin to enter text at the tab, the text lines up at the left and extends to the right. With a center-aligned tab, the text is aligned evenly on either side of the tab position. With a right-aligned tab, the text lines up at the right and extends to the left. A decimal tab can be used to align numbers or text. Numbers with decimals are all aligned at the decimal point; text aligns on either side of the tab.

To set custom tabs, position the insertion point in the paragraph where you want to set a tab stop. Then choose the alignment by clicking the tab alignment symbol at the left edge of the Ruler. Next, click the Ruler where you want to set the tab. A tab marker appears on the Ruler to show the tab setting. Figure 13-10 shows the Ruler with some tab markers and what each of the tab markers looks like for different alignment settings. Dragging any tab marker to a new position on the Ruler changes the location of the tab. To remove the tab setting, drag and drop the marker off the Ruler. If you want to set precise measurements for tabs, open the Format menu and choose Tabs.

FIGURE 13-10
Tab symbols on the Ruler

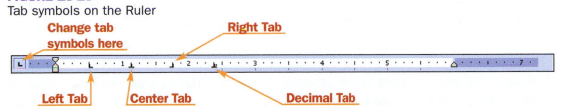

An indent is a space insert between the margin and where the line of text appears. You can indent text from the left margin, from the right margin, or from both the left and right margins. For example, to draw attention to specific paragraphs in a document, you can indent all the lines of the paragraph from the left and right margins. If you are creating a long document and you want the first line of all the paragraphs to be indented, you can format a first line indent. A *first line indent* can make a document easy to read, because a person can easily tell where a new paragraph begins. If you are creating a bibliography for a report, you can format a *hanging indent*. In text formatted with a hanging indent, the first line of text begins at the left margin, and all other lines of the paragraph "hang," or are indented, to the right of the first line. To quickly format an indent, position the insertion point in the paragraph to be formatted and then drag the indent markers on the Ruler. Figure 13-11 shows the Ruler's indent markers.

> **Note**
>
> If you drag the bottom half of the Hanging Indent marker, the First Line Indent marker will also move. If you point to the middle of these markers, a two-headed arrow will display and you can drag to change the left margin.

FIGURE 13-11
Indent markers on the Ruler

First Line Indent marker
Hanging Indent marker
Left Indent marker

STEP-BY-STEP 13.9

1. Open **Step13-9** from the data files and save the document as **Parks** followed by your initials. If necessary, open the **View** menu and choose **Ruler** to display the Ruler.

2. Position the insertion point anywhere in the line that begins *Mount Rushmore....* and then click the tab symbols at the left end of the Ruler until the **Right Tab** symbol is displayed.

3. Click near the 5-inch mark on the Ruler (just to the left of the Right Margin marker). Then drag the **Right Tab** marker on the Ruler and position it exactly at the right indent marker.

4. Position the insertion point in front of *April 11* and press the **Tab** key. The date is now aligned at the right margin.

STEP-BY-STEP 13.9 Continued

5. Position the insertion point in the paragraph beginning *Yellowstone....* Notice that there are no tab markers displayed on the Ruler. The tab you set in the *Mount Rushmore* paragraph was applied to that paragraph only. Format a right tab at the right margin, and then insert a tab character in front of the date in the *Yellowstone...* paragraph to align the date at the right margin.

6. Format a similar right tab for the date for the Glacier National Park documentary.

7. Position the insertion point in the paragraph that begins *This national memorial....* Drag the **Left Indent** marker to the ½" mark on the Ruler. (Notice that the First Line Indent and Hanging Indent markers move also.)

8. Drag the **Right Indent** marker to the 5" mark on the Ruler.

9. Click in the paragraph that begins *The park was established....* Notice that the Left Indent marker is positioned at the 0" mark on the Ruler. When you moved the Left Indent marker in step 9, the indent format was applied only to that paragraph. Format this paragraph and the one that begins *This national park . . .* with left and right indents similar to the ones you applied in steps 9 and 10.

10. Position the insertion point in the paragraph that begins *Each documentary....* Drag the **First Line Indent** marker to the ½" mark on the Ruler. Notice that just the first line of the paragraph is indented from the left ½".

11. Position the insertion point in the last paragraph in the document. Point to the **Hanging Indent** marker and drag the marker to the ½" mark on the Ruler. All lines but the first line are indented from the left ½".

12. Save the changes and close the document. Leave Word open for the next Step-by-Step.

Page Breaks

Word begins new pages when needed by inserting *soft page breaks*. A soft page break is automatically inserted for you when you fill a page with text or graphics. You can also break pages manually by inserting *hard page breaks*. A hard page break forces a page break at a specific location, regardless of how full the page of text is. The location of a soft page break will change if you add or delete text so that each page remains completely filled with text. A hard page break will remain where you insert it until it is deleted. To insert a hard page break, select Break from the Insert menu and then select the Page break option in the Break dialog box. Or you can use the shortcut key combination for inserting a hard page break, Ctrl + Enter.

In Normal view, you will see a page break as a dotted line; in Page Layout and Reading Layout views, the pages actually look like separate sheets of paper, so you will clearly see where page breaks are located. You may not see any indication of page breaks at all in Web Layout and Outline views.

In addition to hard page breaks, you can also insert section breaks in your documents. Whereas a page break just forces the start of a new page, a section break allows you to vary the layout of a document within a page or between pages. For example, you may want part of your document to appear as a single column and then have a portion of it appear in two columns. Or you may want different portions of your document to have different headers or footers.

Bullets and Numbers

Bullets and numbers are easy to add using the Bullets and Numbering buttons on the Formatting toolbar. In general, you should use a numbered list for steps that must be completed in a specific order. This is sometimes referred to as an ordered list. Bullets are used to list items whose order does not matter—an unordered list.

Bulleted and numbered lists are automatically formatted with a hanging indent. Word automatically calculates the best distance for the hanging indent. You can change the bullet symbol, the number style, or the distance for the hanging indent in the Bullets and Numbering dialog box. If you apply the bullet or number format before you enter text, each new paragraph will be formatted with the bullet or number. To end the format, press Enter a second time and backspace over the unwanted bullet or number, or click the button on the toolbar to toggle the option off.

S TEP-BY-STEP 13.10

1. Open **Step13-10** from the data files and save the document as **Expo** followed by your initials.

2. Select all the lines (paragraphs) in the list below the first heading that begins *Displays and Demonstrations*.... Click the **Bullets** button on the Formatting toolbar. Each paragraph in the selection is formatted with a bullet symbol. The symbol will vary depending on the symbol last used for bullets.

3. Select the list below the second heading that begins *A Look at*.... Open the **Format** menu and choose **Bullets and Numbering**. If necessary, click the **Bulleted** tab to display the bullet options. Select one of the bullet symbols and then click **OK**.

4. Select the list below the third heading *Seminars and Films*. Click the **Numbering** button on the Formatting toolbar.

5. Position the insertion point at the beginning of the first paragraph of text (just below the three-line centered heading), and then press **Ctrl + Enter** to add a hard page break. Notice that the three lines of the document heading are now on a separate page.

6. Click **Undo**. Make sure the insertion point is still at the beginning of the first paragraph, and click **Break** on the **Insert** menu.

7. Select the **Page break** option if it is not already selected and then click **OK**. The three lines of the document heading are again on a separate page.

8. Save the changes and close the document. Leave Word open for the next Step-by-Step.

Using Format Painter

2-2.1.18

Whenyou apply multiple character formats to text, you can use the *Format Painter* button to quickly copy the formatting to other text. Select the text with the formatting you want to copy. Double-click the Format Painter button on the Standard toolbar (shown in Figure 13-12). When the pointer changes to a paintbrush, click the text where you want to apply the formatting. If you want to apply the formatting to a group of words, drag the pointer across the words to select them. To turn off the feature without applying the format to other text, click the Format Painter button again or press the Esc key. Format Painter will apply font and size formatting as well as some basic graphic formatting, such as borders, fills, and shading, which you will learn more about in Lesson 15.

FIGURE 13-12
The Format Painter button

STEP-BY-STEP 13.11

1. Open **Step13-11** from the data files. Save the document as **Hummingbirds** followed by your initials.

2. Format the document as described in the following steps. Use the Format Painter wherever possible to repeat formatting that is the same.

   a. Change the first line to Arial 10 pt and make the paragraph align right.

   b. Change the second line to Arial 14 pt bold and center the line.

   c. Make the three subheads Arial 11 pt bold and underlined.

   d. Justify the two paragraphs of text (under the heading *Attracting Hummingbirds . . .*), change the line spacing to 1½ lines, and make the type 10 pt Arial.

   e. Format the text following the *Creating an "Attractive" Garden* heading in the same way as the first two paragraphs.

   f. Change the first line of text following the *Tips for Attracting Butterflies and Hummingbirds* heading to 10 pt Times Roman (or Times New Roman) italic.

   g. Make the rest of the text in this section a bulleted list. Choose the bullet type you prefer.

   h. Format the two lines of text following the *Modifying an Existing Garden* heading in 10 pt Times Roman italic, and change the alignment to justify the text.

   i. Make the rest of the text in this section a numbered list.

   j. For every text paragraph (not the headings, the bulleted paragraphs section, and the numbered list section), create a first line indent of 0.5 inches.

3. Notice that the formatting changes have made the document more than one page, and Word automatically added a soft page break.

4. Use the **Many pages** option in the Zoom dialog box to view your document at the 1 x 2 setting. Save your changes and close the document.

2-2.1.21

Using the Document Statistics Tools

The Word Count command on the Tools menu in Word opens the Word Count dialog box, which provides statistics about your document that include the number of pages, sentences, lines, and characters as well as how many words are in your document. If you click the Show Toolbar button in the Word Count dialog box, the Word Count toolbar shown in Figure 13-13 will float in your document window, and you can click Recount at any time to view updated statistics about how many pages, lines, sentences, or words are in the document. You can see all the options for available statistics in the drop-down list in the Word Count dialog box. To hide the Word Count toolbar, click the Close button in the toolbar's title bar.

FIGURE 13-13
The Word Count toolbar with drop-down list of document statistics

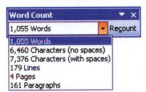

2-1.3.7
2-2.1.19

Checking Spelling and Grammar

Spell checking a document can significantly reduce the amount of time you spend proofreading and editing. Word can help you with both spell checking and proofreading. Word has a standard dictionary that you can use to check your spelling. You can check the spelling of one word, a selected group of words, or the entire document. To spell check the entire document, use the Spelling and Grammar dialog box.

Good proofreading skills also include checking grammar. When you check for the grammar in a document, you read for content and make sure each sentence makes sense. Word can also help you find grammatical errors such as incomplete sentences, the wrong use of words, and capitalization and punctuation errors.

As you enter text in a document, Word automatically checks the spelling of each word against its standard dictionary. If Word cannot find the word in its dictionary, it will underline the word with a wavy red line. This does not always mean the word is misspelled. It simply means the word is not listed in Word's dictionary. To view suggestions for alternative spellings of the word, you can right-click the underlined word to display a shortcut menu. You can select an alternative spelling from the shortcut menu, or you can choose to ignore the misspelling. In any case, once you have indicated your preference, the red wavy line disappears until you close and reopen the document.

Computer Concepts

Although the spell checker is very helpful for identifying spelling errors, you still need to proofread. The spell checker simply verifies that the word is spelled correctly; it does not confirm that you have used the correct word. For example, if you use the word *their* instead of *there*, the spell checker will not identify the error.

Computer Concepts

The grammar checker is a helpful tool, but you still need to have a good working knowledge of English grammar. The grammar checker can identify a possible problem, but it's up to you to decide if the change should be made depending on the context of the sentence.

Word also automatically checks for grammar errors as you enter text. When it finds a possible error, Word underlines the word, phrase, or sentence with a wavy green line. You can then access a shortcut menu to view suggestions for changes. If you prefer not to have Word check for spelling or grammar errors as you key text in a document, you can turn off this feature by clicking the Options button in the Spelling and Grammar dialog box. Click the *Checking spelling as you type* and/or the *Check grammar as you type* options to deselect them. The red or green underlines are only visible when you display your document. They will not appear when you print the document.

STEP-BY-STEP 13.12

1. Open a new document. Open the **Tools** menu, choose **Options**, and click the **Spelling & Grammar** tab. Make sure the selected options match those shown in Figure 13-14 and then click **OK**.

2. Key the following text: **In the erly 1700s,** Notice that as you press the spacebar after *erly*, Word underlines the word with a red wavy line.

FIGURE 13-14
Spelling and Grammar Options dialog box

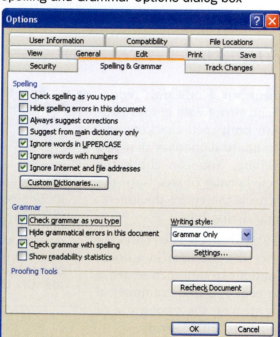

3. Point to the word *erly* and right-click. A shortcut menu is displayed and several word choices are displayed at the top of the menu.

4. Select **early** in the shortcut menu. The correct spelling replaces the original spelling in the document.

5. Position the insertion point after the comma you keyed and press the spacebar. Then key **Potawatomi Indians**. Notice that as you press the spacebar after *Potawatomi*, Word underlines the word with a red wavy line.

STEP-BY-STEP 13.12 Continued

6. Right-click on the word *Potawatomi*. The proposed spelling *Pottawatomie* in the shortcut menu is an alternative way to spell the name of the Indian tribe. However, the spelling you entered is also correct. Click **Ignore All** in the shortcut menu. The red wavy line is removed, and the word *Potawatomi* will not be flagged as misspelled again in this document until you check the Recheck Document (or Check Document) button in the Spelling and Grammar dialog box.

7. Position the insertion point after the word *Indians*. Key a period and then press **Enter**. The entire sentence is underlined with a green wavy line.

8. Point to any part of the green underlined portion of the sentence and right-click. A shortcut menu is displayed, and the words *Fragment (consider revising)* appear at the top of the menu.

9. Click outside the shortcut menu to close it. Then edit the sentence to read *In the early 1700s, the Potawatomi Indians lived near Green Bay, Wisconsin.*

10. Select **Word Count** from the **Tools** menu to open the Word Count dialog box and then look at the statistics for the document. Click the **Show Toolbar** button in the dialog box, and then click **Close**.

11. Key **They were friendly with the French but fought with the British in the War of 1812.** and then click **Recount** in the Word Count toolbar. Notice that the word count displayed in the text box changes.

12. Click the **down arrow** in the text box to display other changes in the document statistics, and then click the toolbar's **Close** button. Leave the document open for the next Step-by-Step.

Formatting a Document for Printing

2-1.4.1
2-1.4.2
2-1.4.3
2-1.4.4
2-1.4.5

Document formats are formats that are applied to an entire document. These include margins, the orientation of the page, text columns, and borders and shading. We will look at how to adjust a document's margins and page orientation in this lesson. More advanced document formats will be covered in Lesson 15.

Change Page Orientation and Margins

Portrait orientation formats the content of the document with the short edge of the page at the top. This is the default setting, and most printed documents are formatted this way. You can change to landscape orientation in the Page Setup dialog box, which is accessed with the Page Setup command on the File menu. *Landscape orientation* formats the content of the document sideways with the long edge of the page at the top. Your on-screen document will accurately reflect the page orientation you choose.

> **Note**
>
> You can also change margins by dragging the margin markers on the Ruler.

Margins are the blank space around the edges of the page. In general, text only appears in the printable area inside the margins. The default settings are 1 inch for top and bottom margins, and 1.25 inches for left and right margins.

Use Print Preview to Display a Document

To avoid wasteful printing, it is a good idea to preview your document and make adjustments before you print it. Print Preview is an on-screen, reduced view of the layout of a completed page or pages. In Print Preview, you can see such things as page orientation, margins, and page breaks. If you find errors or necessary changes, you can edit the document in Print Preview or you can change back to Normal view to make the corrections.

Select a Printer

The default printer for your computer system is listed in the text box at the top of the Print dialog box. You can temporarily change the printer you use to print a job, however, by clicking the down arrow to the right of the text box and then clicking the name of another printer. Your system may have several printers available to users such as an inkjet printer, a laser printer, and perhaps a fax program that also serves as a kind of printer. Selecting a different printer from the list gives you the flexibility to use any printer available to your system to print a job.

S TEP-BY-STEP 13.13

1. Open the **File** menu and choose **Page Setup**. If necessary, click the Margins tab to display the Page Setup dialog box as shown in Figure 13-15. Notice that the top and bottom margins are 1" and the left and right margins are 1.25".

FIGURE 13-15
Margins sheet in the Page Setup dialog box

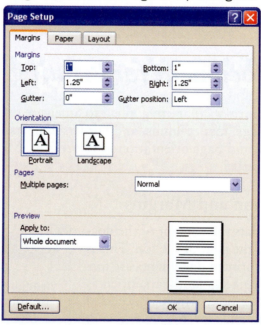

2. Select the **Landscape** option under Orientation. When you select landscape orientation, Word automatically reverses the default margins settings. The top and bottom margins are now 1.25".

3. Select the text in the Top box, then key or select **1**. It is not necessary to key the inch symbol. Then, change the value in the Bottom text box to 1 and click **OK**.

STEP-BY-STEP 13.13 Continued

4. Click the **Print Preview** button on the Standard toolbar. The Print Preview toolbar similar to the one shown in Figure 13-16 is displayed.

FIGURE 13-16
Print Preview toolbar

You can print directly from Print Preview

One page button

Click to close Print Preview

5. If necessary, click the **One Page** button on the Print Preview toolbar to display the entire page in Normal view.

6. On the **File** menu, click **Print**, and when the Print dialog box opens, notice the printer name shown in the Name text box in the Printer section of the dialog box. This is your system's default printer.

7. Click the **down arrow** to the right of the Name text box to access a list of other printers available on your system. Click any of the printer names to change from the default printer to a different printer for this job. Then click **Cancel** to close the dialog box without printing.

8. Click the **Close** button on the Print Preview toolbar to return to the document window.

9. Close the document without saving the changes. Close Word and follow your instructor's directions about turning off your computer.

Common Printing Problems

Even when using the Print Preview, there are times when what you think will print out and what you actually get on the printed page are different. This could be due to a variety of different things.

Sometimes the font in your document might not be available on the printer you are using. Change the font in your document to a TrueType font, which looks the same on the printed page as it does on the screen, or change the font to one that is available on your printer. Check to make sure you are using valid print settings, such as margins that are within the area your printer will print.

If the layout of your page looks wrong when you print it, you may be printing a document that was created with a different version of Microsoft Word or was formatted for a different paper size. To have Word format the document to your printer's paper size for this printing session only, click Print on the File menu. Under Zoom, select the paper size you want to use in the Scale to paper size box. Word will scale the page to fit the paper size you choose, similar to the reduce/enlarge feature on a photocopy machine.

You may try to print a document and it appears that nothing happens. First make sure your printer is online and is correctly connected to your computer, and open the Print dialog box to confirm that the correct printer is selected in the Printer Name text box. If all connections and settings are okay, the problem may be in the Windows settings. Printing from your computer is primarily controlled by settings in Windows, so you need to determine if your printer setup in Windows is correct by using the Windows Printing Troubleshooter. To access the Troubleshooter, click Help and Support on the Windows Start menu. Key *printing troubleshooter* in the Search box and then select the problem or problems you are having and follow the instructions in the Printing Troubleshooter pane. If the Microsoft Windows printer setup looks correct, check the Word printer settings to make sure that the selected printer matches the printer you're using. Lastly, make sure that the page range you've selected in the Print dialog box corresponds to the pages you want to print.

If, when you try to print, you not only do not get a printed document, but Microsoft Word itself stops responding, it is likely that you do not have the correct printer driver. You can try installing an updated printer driver from the printer's manufacturer to resolve this problem.

SUMMARY

In this lesson, you learned:

- The Delete key and the Backspace key can be used to delete characters.

- When you add new text in Insert mode, the new characters are inserted between existing text. When text is entered in Overtype mode, the new text replaces existing text.

- The Undo and Redo commands make editing easy when you make mistakes or change your mind.

- The Repeat command lets you repeat your most recent action.

- Selected text can be copied or moved from one location in a Word document to a new location in the same document, to a different Word document, or to another application. Drag-and-drop editing is especially helpful when you are moving or copying text short distances.

- When you use the Cut, Copy, and Paste commands, Word stores the selected text in the Clipboard. The Clipboard stores up to 24 items.

- The Find command makes searching for text and/or formats easy. The Replace command replaces multiple occurrences of text automatically.

- Fonts are available in a variety of styles and point sizes.

- Attributes such as bold, italic, underline, small caps, and color can be added to text, and more than one attribute can be applied to the same text.

- You can adjust the line spacing in a paragraph to create more or less white space between the lines of text.

- Formatting the paragraph alignment for left, center, right, or justified positions the text appropriately between the left and right margins.

- Custom tabs can be set by clicking on the Ruler.

- Options for indenting text include left indents, right indents, first line indents, and hanging indents.

- Word automatically adds a ~~hard~~ *SOFT* page break when you fill a page, but you can add a ~~soft~~ *HARD* page break to force a new page to start at any point in a document. *SEE P. 256*

- The Bullets and Numbering feature automatically adds and formats bullets and numbers in lists.

- Document statistics provide information about the number of words, pages, lines, paragraphs, and sentences in the Word Count dialog box.

- Word checks spelling and grammar as you key text. Misspelled words are marked with red wavy lines and possible grammar errors are marked with green wavy lines. Spelling and grammar errors can be corrected as you enter text by using a shortcut menu.

- To check all spelling and grammar at once, use the Spelling and Grammar dialog box.

- The page orientation determines how the document will print on the page. Adjusting the margins affects the white space around the edges of the page.

- Print Preview shows a reduced view of the layout of a document. You can also reduce the view of a document by changing the zoom. Print Preview can help eliminate wasteful printing.

VOCABULARY *Review*

Define the following terms:

Alignment	Format	Overtype mode
Attributes	Format Painter	Points
Clipboard	Hanging indent	Portrait orientation
Drag-and-drop	Hard page break	Soft page break
First line indent	Insert mode	
Font	Landscape orientation	

REVIEW *Questions*

TRUE/FALSE

Circle T if the statement is true or F if the statement is false.

T   F   **1.** You can find the Cut, Copy, and Paste buttons on the Formatting toolbar.

T   F   **2.** In Overtype mode, new text is inserted between existing text.

T   F   **3.** To duplicate your last action, you can use the Repeat command.

T   F   **4.** To copy text using drag-and-drop, hold down the Ctrl key as you drag.

T   F   **5.** The Clipboard stores up to 10 items.

T   F   **6.** It is possible to apply more than one attribute to the same text.

T   F   **7.** Landscape orientation prints sideways with the long edge of the page at the top.

T   F   **8.** You can edit a document while in Print Preview.

T   F   **9.** When you set a tab, you position the tab marker on the Formatting toolbar.

T   F   **10.** Bulleted and numbered lists are automatically formatted using a first line indent.

MATCHING

Match the correct term in Column 1 to its description in Column 2.

Column 1	Column 2
____ **1.** font	**A.** Space you insert between the margin and the line of text
____ **2.** indent	**B.** How text is positioned between the left and right margins
____ **3.** margin	**C.** Break you insert manually to end a page
____ **4.** alignment	**D.** Break Word automatically inserts when a page is full
____ **5.** hard page break	**E.** Design of a typeface
	F. Blank space around the edges of a page

PROJECTS

PROJECT 13-1

You've been helping out at your local community center. Today, the director of programs gave you a file containing a description of some of the courses offered at the center. She admitted she created the document in a hurry and asked you to edit the document for her using her file and her notes.

1. Open **Project13-1** from the data files. Save the document as **Languages**, followed by your initials.

2. Display the Clipboard task pane and clear all items from the Clipboard.

3. Scroll down the page and notice that there is a course title separated from its description. Cut the *Japanese for Beginners* title from its current location and paste it above the course description that begins *Build a solid foundation for communicating in Japanese...*

4. Remove the extra blank line that remains above the *English as a Second Language* heading after you moved the *Japanese for Beginners* heading. (Display nonprinting characters, if necessary, to see the paragraph symbol for the blank line.)

5. According to the director's notes, Spanish for Beginners and Japanese for Beginners are offered on the same day and time and for the same number of weeks. You need to add information to both class descriptions.
   A. First, copy the class dates (*September 25–November 13*) that appear below the Japanese instructor's name. Do not include the paragraph symbol at the end of the dates in the selection.

   B. Then, position the insertion point below the Spanish instructor's name and paste the dates. Press **Enter** to insert a blank line below the dates.

   C. Next, position the insertion point after the Spanish instructor's name (*Ken Grazzi*) and press **Enter** to insert a new line. Key **Tuesday, 6–8 p.m.**

   D. Position the insertion point after the Japanese instructor's name (*Hiroki Sasaki*) and use the Repeat command. Word should move to a new line and insert the same day and time you keyed for the Spanish class.

6. Clear all the items from the Clipboard. Copy to the clipboard the name of the German for Beginners instructor and the fee for the German for Beginners class.

7. Paste the German instructor's name after the course number for *Continuing German for Beginners*.

8. All classes have the same fee, so you can paste the class fee after the dates for each class.

9. The director's notes indicate that Ken Grazzi may not be able to teach the Spanish class. Delete his name.

10. After checking with the director, you learn that Mr. Grazzi will be able to teach the class after all. Use Undo to restore his name.

11. Using cut and paste and/or drag-and-drop, reorganize all information for the classes to be in alphabetical order by the class title.

12. At the bottom of the document, press **Enter** and then insert the copyright symbol.

13. Insert today's date following the copyright symbol. Select a date format that includes only the month and year.

14. Save your changes. Print and close the document.

PROJECT 13-2

Your good work at the community center has convinced the director to give you another assignment. Help her create the title and contents pages for the Recreation Commission's fall program guide.

1. Open **Project13-2** from the data files. Save the document as **Contents** followed by your initials.

2. Change the page orientation to landscape. Change the top and bottom margins to **1 inch**, and change the left and right margins to **2 inches**.

3. Center the first eight lines of text, beginning with *Oak Creek Recreation Commission* and ending with *Mt. Washington Recreation Center*.

4. Format the centered text as follows:
   A. Change the font style of the first line (*Oak Creek Recreation Center*) to bold and the font size to 28 point.
   B. Change the size of the next two lines (*Community Center* and *Program Guide*) to 20 point.
   C. Change the size of the next line (*Fall*) to 20 point and apply bold style.
   D. Change the size of the last four centered lines to 20 point.

5. Position the insertion point in front of the word *Contents* and insert a page break. On the new page, format the word *Contents* as 20 point bold.

6. Select all the text below the *Contents* heading and then set a right tab at the 6.5-inch mark on the ruler. Format the program listings as follows:
   A. Apply bold and italic formatting to the first three lines below the *Contents* heading (*Registration*, *Memberships*, and *Hours*) and the last two lines (*Special Events* and *Community Meetings*). Change the size of these lines to 12 point and the font to Arial. Include the page numbers in all formatting changes.
   B. Apply bold and underline formatting to the headings (including the page number) for each age group (*ELEMENTARY PROGRAMS*, *TEEN PROGRAMS*, and *ADULT PROGRAMS*). Change the size of these headings to 11 point and the font to Arial.
   C. Apply a 0.25-inch left indent to the lists of programs under each age group heading and change their point size to 12.

7. View the document in Print Preview. You decide that the first page could be spread out a little to fill up more of the page. Close Print Preview and display the first page. Add blank lines as desired to improve the look of the first page. Check your adjustments using Print Preview.

8. Save your changes and close the document and Word. Follow your instructor's directions concerning turning off your computer.

TEAMWORK PROJECT

The fonts you use to format a document can be divided into two types: serif and sans serif. Serif faces are often used for the main body of a document, and sans serif faces are used for headings and other display items. Learn more about the differences between these two types of typefaces with a partner.

1. With your partner, decide who will research serif typefaces and who will research sans serif typefaces.

2. Use the Web, an online encyclopedia, or other reference to read about typography, the art of designing typefaces. Concentrate on your chosen type, either serif or sans serif.

3. You and your partner should be able to answer these questions after your research:
   A. What is a serif?
   B. What is the main difference between a serif typeface and a sans serif typeface?

4. Select a paragraph of text and a heading from any source and key the material using the type of typeface you have been studying (you key in serif, for example, and your partner keys in sans serif). Copy the text several times and apply different fonts of either serif or sans serif to each copy.

5. With your partner, decide which of the fonts is most readable and appropriate for each type of text.

CRITICAL *Thinking*

ACTIVITY 13-1

You have been copying multiple items to the Clipboard. You learned in this lesson that the Clipboard will hold up to 24 items. What do you think will happen when you copy the 25th item? Use the Help feature to see if your answer was correct.

WORKING WITH TABLES

Suppose you have a document in Word that includes information you want to arrange in several lines across two or three columns. How can you create the columns you need in Word? If your answer is "Set tab stops," you're correct. However, there's also an easier and faster way. The table features in Word make the task of arranging text and numbers in columns both quick and easy.

Creating a Table

2-2.2.1

A table consists of cells (boxes) to which you add text or graphics. A *cell* represents one intersection of a row and a column in a table. In a table, rows go across and columns go down.

By default, Word formats a border around all the cells in a table. If you don't want this border to print, you can remove the border. However, the boundary lines for each of the cells still remain. These boundary lines in a table are called *gridlines*. Gridlines are used for layout purposes; they do not print.

Inserting a Table

To create a table, you must first decide how many columns and rows you want in the table. Then you create a table grid and enter the data. The Insert Table button on the Standard toolbar (Figure 14-1) will display a grid of table cells when you click it. You use the grid to determine how many rows and columns will be in your table. You can also manually enter the table size (number of columns and rows) through the Insert Table dialog box. To open the dialog box, select Insert on the Table menu, and then select Table in the submenu.

Computer Concepts

The Insert Table button also appears on the Tables and Borders toolbar. However, the button on the Tables and Borders toolbar will not display a grid. Instead, it will open the Insert Table dialog box. Or, if you click the down arrow next to the button, it will display the options available in the Insert Table command.

FIGURE 14-1
The Insert Table button

S TEP-BY-STEP 14.1

1. Launch Word and open a blank document. Click the Insert Table button on the Standard toolbar. A grid of table cells appears.

2. Click in the first cell in the grid and drag down the grid until seven rows of cells are displayed; then drag across until the bottom of the grid reads *7 x 3 Table*, as shown in Figure 14-2. Then release the mouse button and the table will appear in the document.

3. Leave the document open for the next Step-by-Step.

FIGURE 14-2
Table grid

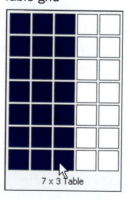

7 x 3 Table

Inserting and Deleting Rows and Columns

2-2.2.3

After you create a table, you may decide to change it. For example, you may need to add more rows or delete a column. Word has many features that make these changes easy.

Changing the Number of Rows and Columns

If you want to insert a new row at the end of the table, you can position the insertion point in the last table cell and press Tab. To insert a new row anywhere else in the table, use the Insert command in the Table menu.

If you select the content in a cell or group of cells and press Delete, the text is deleted but the cells are still there. To remove rows or columns, you must choose the Delete command in the Table menu. When you delete a row or column, the text is also deleted.

STEP-BY-STEP 14.2

1. Position the insertion point in the last cell in the table (at the lower right). Press **Tab** to create a new row.

2. Move the insertion point to the top cell in the middle column. Open the **Table** menu and choose **Insert**, then select **Rows Below** in the submenu. The table now has nine rows.

3. Position the insertion point in any cell in the second row. Open the **Table** menu and choose **Delete**, then select **Rows** in the submenu. As you can see, one row has been deleted from the table.

4. Position the insertion point in any cell in left column. Open the **Table** menu and choose **Delete**, then select **Columns** in the submenu.

5. Click **Undo** to restore the column you deleted.

6. Move the insertion point to the second cell in the third column. Open the **Table** menu and choose **Insert**, then select **Columns to the Left** in the submenu.

7. Leave the document open for the next Step-by-Step.

> **Note**
>
> To insert or delete multiple rows and columns at one time, first select the desired number of rows or columns. For example, if you want to insert or delete three rows, select three rows in the table. Then choose the **Table Insert** or **Table Delete** command.

Merging and Splitting Table Cells

When you remove the boundary between two cells, it is called *merging cells*. You can merge cells horizontally or vertically. You can merge cells when you want to create a heading to span across two or more columns. To merge cells, the cells must be selected.

When you convert a cell into multiple cells, it is called *splitting cells*. You can split a cell into two or more rows and/or two or more columns. To split a cell, the insertion point must be positioned in the cell.

You can also split a table into two separate tables by selecting Split Table from the Table menu. A new table will begin with the row in which you have placed your insertion point. You will practice this in Step-by-Step 14.7.

STEP-BY-STEP 14.3

1. Position the insertion point in the first cell in the table.

2. Open the **Table** menu and choose **Insert**, then select **Rows Above**. A new row is added and the four cells in the new row are selected.

3. With the new row still selected, open the **Table** menu and choose **Merge Cells**. (*Hint:* You may need to expand the menu to see the Merge Cells command.)

4. Click anywhere in the window to deselect the row. The four cells have been converted into a single long cell.

5. Position the insertion point in the new blank row, then open the **Table** menu and choose **Split Cells**. (*Hint:* You may need to expand the menu to see the Split Cells command.) The dialog box shown in Figure 14-3 is displayed.

FIGURE 14-3
Split Cells dialog box

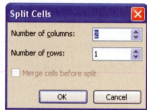

6. Change the number in the Number of columns box to **1**. Change the number in the Number of rows box to **2**. Click **OK**. Click anywhere in the window to deselect the row. You will see that the row is split into two rows.

7. Close the document without saving it and leave Word open for the next Step-by-Step.

Formatting Tables

2-2.2.4

There may be occasions when you need to create and customize a more complex table. For example, the table may require cells of different heights or a varying number of columns per row. The Draw Table tool is very useful for creating complex tables. You use the Draw Table tool much the same way you use a pen to draw a table on a sheet of paper. When you use the Draw Table tool, you draw the table using the mouse. The document must be displayed in Print Layout view when you use the Draw Table tool.

The Eraser tool enables you to remove cell boundaries. Click on the Eraser button, and the pointer changes to an eraser. When you point and click on a cell gridline, the line will be selected. When you release, the gridline is deleted. The Eraser tool is especially useful if you want to delete a gridline or if you want to change the layout by moving a gridline.

STEP-BY-STEP 14.4

1. Open a new blank document. If necessary, open the **View** menu and choose **Ruler** to display the Ruler at the top of the document. (The Ruler is displayed when there is a check mark to the left of the command in the menu.)

2. If necessary, display the **Tables and Borders** toolbar. Open the **View** menu, choose **Toolbars**, and turn on the **Tables and Borders** toolbar shown in Figure 14-4.

FIGURE 14-4
Tables and Borders toolbar

3. Click the **Draw Table** button on the Tables and Borders toolbar. The pointer changes to a pencil and Word automatically changes to Print Layout View.

4. To draw the outside boundary of the table grid, position the pointer at the left margin. Then click and drag down and to the right to create a table boundary. Release when the table (box) is approximately 6 inches wide by 2½ inches high.

5. Create the vertical and horizontal lines inside the table. Position the point of the pencil where you want the line to begin. Then click and drag to the point where you want the line to end. A broken line will display as you drag the mouse. Repeat to draw all of the lines illustrated in Figure 14-5. Note that there are four horizontal lines ½ inch apart, and three vertical lines at approximately 1 inch, 4½ inches, and 5½ inches on the ruler.

> **Computer Concepts**
>
> Sometimes when you display a toolbar, it is floating on the screen. You can move a floating toolbar anywhere on the screen by dragging the title bar. If you drag the toolbar to the edge of the program window or to a location beside another docked toolbar, it becomes a docked toolbar. To move a docked toolbar, drag the move handle (the vertical dashed line at the left side of the toolbar).

FIGURE 14-5
Table grid for Step-by-Step 14.4

STEP-BY-STEP 14.4 Continued

6. Click the **Draw Table** button to deselect it.

7. Click the **Eraser** button. The pointer changes to an eraser.

8. Point the eraser on the first vertical line in the first row. When the bottom corner of the eraser is positioned over the line, click to select the line and delete it. Figure 14-6 shows the eraser with a selected line. If you click and the line is not selected, reposition the eraser and try again. The line will only be deleted if it is selected when you click.

FIGURE 14-6
Eraser with selected line

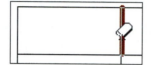

9. Erase two more lines in the first column.

10. Click the **Eraser** button to deselect it.

11. Leave the document open for the next Step-by-Step.

As you worked with the table you created, you probably thought you were looking at the gridlines for your table. But the lines you saw on the screen are actually borders. You can go to the Help screen to find out more about borders.

You can use the Answer Wizard in Help to ask a question or key search words. A list of topics related to your question is displayed, and when you click on one of the proposed topics, details about the topic are provided in the same dialog box at the right.

STEP-BY-STEP 14.5

1. If necessary, display the Office Assistant by opening the **Help** menu and choosing **Show the Office Assistant**.

2. Click the **Office Assistant**, key **table gridlines**, and press **Enter**. In the list of topics, click on **Display or hide gridlines in a table**. Read the information about the gridlines.

3. You decide you want to remove the default border, but you don't know how. Click in the **Type a question for help** text box in the upper-right corner of the Word window and key **Remove default table border**, then press **Enter**. Notice the list of topics that display in the Search Results pane.

4. Click the link **Remove a border** and then choose the **Remove a border from a picture, a table or text** link in the Word Help window.

5. Study the directions in steps 1–3 in the Help window. Click the hyperlinks for **table** and **cells** in step 1 of the directions. The first time you click on a hyperlink in the Help window, a definition will display. When you click on the hyperlink again, the definition will be hidden.

STEP-BY-STEP 14.5 Continued

6. Close the Help window after you read the information, and then change the text in the Help question text box to **select cells**. Press **Enter**. Then click the link **Select text and graphics** in the Search Results pane. In the Help Window, click the **Select items in a table with the mouse** link. Study the examples. Be sure to read the section *Multiple cells, rows, or columns*.

7. Close the Help window and the Search Results pane.

8. If you prefer to hide the Office Assistant, select **Hide the Office Assistant** from the Help menu. Leave the document open for the next Step-by-Step.

Removing Table Borders

Now that you have read about how to remove borders from a table, give it a try. In the following Step-by-Step, you will practice one of the Tips provided in the Help screen. However, you can explore the other methods of removing table borders on your own.

STEP-BY-STEP 14.6

1. Position the insertion point anywhere inside the table.

2. Open the **Format** menu and choose **Borders and Shading**. If necessary, select the **Borders** tab to display the dialog box shown in Figure 14-7.

FIGURE 14-7
Borders and Shading dialog box

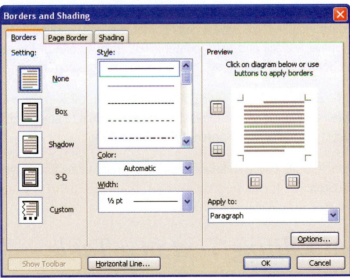

3. Under **Setting**, select **None** and then click **OK**.

4. Your document should now display lines that indicate the cell boundaries. If you don't see any lines in your document, open the Table menu and choose Show Gridlines. The gridlines are similar to the borders you removed, but they are much lighter in color. (If you do see gridlines, the menu item on the Table menu would read Hide Gridlines.)

5. Close the document without saving changes and leave Word open for the next Step-by-Step.

Formatting Borders and Shading in a Table

Borders and shading can greatly enhance the appearance of a table and even help to make the table easier to read. The default setting for tables is to print with a ½-point single-line border around all cells. Generally, this border will be appropriate for the tables you create. However, there may be occasions when you want to customize the border and add shading to some of the table cells. You may even want to remove the border completely. Word makes it easy to format borders and change the shading of cells in your table.

STEP-BY-STEP 14.7

1. Open a new blank document and check to make sure the Ruler and the Tables and Borders toolbar are displayed.

2. Use the **Insert Table** button, the Insert command on the Table menu, or the **Draw Table** button on the Tables and Borders toolbar to create a table with four columns and six rows.

3. Select the first row of cells. (*Hint:* Point to the left side of the first row. When the pointer changes to a right-pointing arrow, double-click.)

4. Click the **down arrow** next to the **Line Weight** button on the Tables and Borders toolbar. In the drop-down list, select **1½ pt.**

5. Click the **Outside Border** button on the Tables and Borders toolbar. The border line becomes heavier.

6. With the row still selected, click the down arrow next to the **Shading Color** button on the Tables and Borders toolbar. If you have a color printer available, choose a light color. Select **Gray-10%** if you have a black and white printer. (*Hint:* Point to one of the shading options and wait for the ScreenTip to display so you know you have the correct option.)

7. Select the column of cells at the left edge of the table. (*Hint:* Click in the second cell of the first column and then press Shift and click in the last cell in the column to select the entire column under the first row.) Repeat the shading color format. (*Hint:* Press **F4**.)

8. Save the changes in a file called **Calories** followed by your initials and leave the document open for the next Step-by-Step.

Inserting and Editing Text in a Table

2-2.2.2

Adding and changing text in the cells of a table is a similar process to entering characters in a document. You can use the keyboard, and the Cut, Copy, and Paste commands are available as you insert and edit the text in a table. You can also use drag-and-drop editing, and there are some other shortcuts available to enter table text.

Computer Concepts

You can use the number pad on your keyboard to enter numbers. Make sure that NUMLOCK is turned on.

Entering Text in the Table

To move the insertion point from one cell to another, you can press the arrow keys or Tab. If the text that you enter is wider than the column, Word automatically wraps the text to a new line within the cell. When you reach the end of a row and press Tab, the insertion point moves to the first cell in the next row.

> **Note**
>
> To move the insertion point to the cell that is to the left of the current cell, press **Shift + Tab**.

S TEP-BY-STEP 14.8

1. Position the insertion point in the first cell of your table. Key **Activity**.

2. Press **Tab** to move the insertion point to the next cell to the right in the same row. Key **20 Minutes**. Press **Tab** and then key **40 Minutes**. Press **Tab** again and key **60 minutes.**

3. Press **Tab** to move the insertion point to the first cell in the next row.

4. Press the **down arrow** to move the insertion point down to the third row.

5. Key the rest of the table as illustrated in Figure 14-8. Use **Tab** or the arrow keys to move from one cell to another.

FIGURE 14-8
Completed table for Step-by-Step 14.8

Activity	20 minutes	40 minutes	60 minutes
Cross-country skiing	192	384	576
Golf	132	264	396
Mountain biking	204	408	612
Running: 9 min/mi	264	528	784

6. Save the changes and leave the document open for the next Step-by-Step.

Editing Table Text

Editing table text is similar to editing other document text. You can insert, delete, copy or move text within the table cells. You can also apply several formats to change the font and alignment of the text within a cell. To make text in a cell bold, italic, or underlined, or change the color of the text, use the same formatting procedures you use for regular document text. Select the text you want to change, or select an entire row or column, and then apply the formatting.

S TEP-BY-STEP 14.9

1. Click in the last cell in the table (*784*). Change the number to **792**.

2. Add a row below the row that begins with *Cross-country skiing* and key **Downhill skiing** in the first column of the new row.

STEP-BY-STEP 14.9 Continued

3. Press **Tab** to move to the next column and key **144**. Key **288** in the third column and key **432** in the last column of the row.

4. Position the insertion point immediately after the word *Golf* in the first column of the fifth row and key the following text in the cell:

   : carrying clubs

5. Select the third row (*Cross-country skiing*). Hold the left mouse button down and drag the selected row down so the dotted insertion point is in front of the word *Golf*.

6. Release the mouse button to move the row to a new position above the *Golf* row.

7. Save the changes and leave the document open for the next Step-by-Step.

Aligning Text Within Table Cells

The Tables and Borders toolbar displays several buttons you can use to align text within the cells. You can align text at the top, center, or bottom of a cell, as well as left or right. You can quickly change the direction of text in a table cell by clicking the Change Text Direction button. The direction of the text toggles between three text positions: top to bottom, bottom to top, and horizontal (the default position with which you began).

STEP-BY-STEP 14.10

1. Click in the first cell to the right of *Downhill skiing* (*144*).

2. Click the **Align Right** button on the Formatting toolbar. The number shifts to the right edge of the cell.

3. With the insertion point still in the *144* cell, hold down **Shift** and then click in the last cell of the table (*792*). All of the cells containing numbers are selected.

4. Click the **Align Right** button.

5. Position the pointer to the left of the first row. When the pointer changes to a right-pointing arrow, double-click to select the entire row. Apply the **Center** and **Bold** formats to the row.

6. Select the entire table. (*Hint:* Place the insertion point somewhere within the table, then open the **Table** menu, choose **Select**, and then choose **Table** in the submenu.)

7. Click the **down arrow** next to the cell alignment button (the ScreenTip shows **Align Top Left** as the default option for this button) on the Tables and Borders toolbar. A box with nine alignment options is displayed, as shown in Figure 14-9.

STEP-BY-STEP 14.10 Continued

FIGURE 14-9
Cell Alignment options

8. Select the **Align Center Left** option in the second row of options. (*Hint:* Point to the option and wait for the ScreenTip to display so you know you have the correct option.) The text in each cell is centered between the top and bottom boundaries of the cell.

9. Click outside the table to deselect it, and then select the first row of the table.

10. Click the **Change Text Direction** button on the Tables and Borders toolbar. The text in the first row rotates to the right and is displayed from top to bottom.

11. Click the **Change Text Direction** button again. The text rotates to the right and is now displayed from bottom to top.

12. Notice that several of the buttons on the Formatting toolbar are altered to reflect the new text direction. Click the **Center** button on the Formatting toolbar. The text in the first row is centered between the top and bottom boundaries of the cells.

13. Select rows three through seven in the second, third, and fourth column. (*Hint*: Click in the *144* cell and then hold down the left mouse button and drag to the last cell in the table, *792*.)

14. Select the **Align Center Right** option from the cell alignment options on the Tables and Borders toolbar and then click outside the table to deselect the cells.

15. Save the changes and leave the document open for the next Step-by-Step.

Modifying the Table Structure

2-2.2.3

When you create a table grid, Word makes all the columns the same width. Sometimes, you'll want to adjust the column widths or the row heights in a table to make the text easier to read or to fit a certain style or content. If you want to specify an exact column width or row height, you should use the Table Properties command on the Table menu. However, it's usually easiest to drag a border to a new position. You can also adjust the width of each column automatically using the AutoFit feature. Word offers five AutoFit options. In this lesson, you will learn and practice AutoFit to Contents. With AutoFit to Contents, Word automatically adjusts all column widths and heights as needed to accommodate the contents within the cells.

> **Note**
>
> If you want rows or columns to be spaced evenly throughout the table, select the particular rows or columns and then click the Distribute Rows Evenly or Distribute Columns Evenly button on the Tables and Borders toolbar.

To align a table on the page horizontally, you must first select the entire table. Then you format the alignment in the same way you align text paragraphs.

If a table cell is formatted for AutoFit, Word will automatically adjust the cell width each time the cell contents change.

S TEP-BY-STEP 14.11

1. Position the insertion point on the first column. Open the **Table** menu and choose **Table Properties**. Select the **Column** tab, click in the **Preferred width** text box, and set the width to **1** inch. Click **OK**.

2. Position the insertion point in the last row. Open the **Table** menu and choose **Table Properties**. Select the **Row** tab, click in the **Specify height** text box, and set the height to **0.5** inches. Click **OK**.

3. Position the insertion point anywhere within the table. Open the **Table** menu and choose **AutoFit**. In the submenu, choose **AutoFit to Contents**. The text in the first column no longer wraps within the cell, and the extra white space in the other three columns is eliminated. Notice that the last row remains .5 inches high, because you set that height in the Specify height text box, and that format supersedes the AutoFit command.

4. With the insertion point still positioned in the table, open the **Table** menu and choose **Select**. Then select **Table** in the submenu. All the cells in the table are selected.

5. Click the **Center** button on the Formatting toolbar. The table is now positioned in the middle between the left and right margins.

6. Click anywhere in the second row. Open the **Table** menu and select **Split Table**. The heading row is now a separate table that is centered between the left and right margins.

7. Click **Undo** to return the two tables to one table. If you notice that the heading row is now too narrow to align correctly over the rest of the rows in the table, click **Undo** again.

8. Save the changes and leave the document open for the next Step-by-Step.

Sorting Data in a Table

2-2.2.5

Tables organize material to make it easier to read, and you have discovered how formatting the table and the characters in the table can add clarity to the information. You can also sort the information in a table on different search criteria to organize the table contents to emphasize data in different ways.

The Sort command on the Table menu opens the Sort dialog box shown in Figure 14-10. You can also sort data in a table by using the Sort Ascending and Sort Descending buttons on the Tables and Borders toolbar. Sorting data in ascending order rearranges it into alphabetical order from A to Z or numerical order from lowest number to highest number. A descending sort rearranges the data in alphabetical order from Z to A or numerical order from highest number to lowest number.

FIGURE 14-10
The Sort dialog box

STEP-BY-STEP 14.12

1. Click anywhere in the second row of the table and then select **Delete** from the **Table** menu and **Rows** from the submenu to delete the blank row in the table.

2. Select **Sort** in the **Table** menu to open the Sort dialog box.

3. In the dialog box, make sure *Activity* appears in the Sort by text box (to sort the rows in alphabetical order by the name of the activity) and *Text* appears in the Type text box. The word *Paragraphs* should display in the Using text box.

4. Click the option button for **Descending** to the right in the Sort by section.

5. Click **OK** to sort the data in descending alphabetical order according to the entries in the Activity column. The entries in first column of the table now appear sorted in reverse alphabetical order. Notice that the other columns in the rows were rearranged so that the correct entries for each row are in the second, third, and fourth columns also.

6. Click in any row in the second column of the table and then click the **Sort Ascending** button on the Tables and Borders toolbar. The table is now arranged so that the numerals in the second row are in order from lowest to highest, and the other columns in the rows were rearranged also to keep the entries in rows together.

7. Save the changes and then close the document. Leave Word open for the next Step-by-Step.

Converting Text to a Table and a Table to Text

Assume that you've already created a multicolumn list using tab settings. You decide that you want to organize the data in a table because it will be easier to format. In Word, it isn't necessary to key all the data again. Word can quickly convert text separated by paragraph marks, commas, tabs, or other characters into a table with cells.

When converting text to a table, Word determines the number of columns needed based on paragraphs, tabs, or commas in the text. When converting a table to text, Word inserts tabs to show where the column breaks are.

Whether you have converted a text file into a table or created a new table using any of the methods in Word, the AutoFormat feature provides several built-in table styles that include borders, background shading, and character formats. You can apply a table style by opening the Table menu and choosing Table AutoFormat. When you select a style in the dialog box, a preview area shows the effect of the style you select.

STEP-BY-STEP 14.13

1. Open **Step14-13** from the data files. Save the document as **Scores** followed by your initials.

2. Select the entire document. (*Hint:* Press **Ctrl + A**.)

3. Open the **Table** menu and choose **Convert**. In the submenu, select **Text to Table**. The dialog box shown in Figure 14-11 is displayed.

FIGURE 14-11
Convert Text to Table dialog box

4. Under Table size, the number of columns should already be set to **3**. Under AutoFit behavior, select **AutoFit to contents**. Under Separate text at, make sure **Tabs** is selected. Click **OK**. Click anywhere in the window to deselect so you can see the revised table.

5. Position the insertion point in the table, then open the **Table** menu and click **Table AutoFormat**. The dialog box shown in Figure 14-12 is displayed.

STEP-BY-STEP 14.13 Continued

FIGURE 14-12
Table AutoFormat dialog box

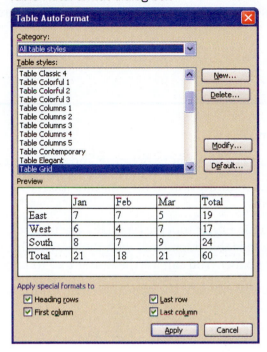

6. Select **Table Colorful 2** in the Table styles list. Notice that the Preview box shows approximately how your table will be formatted.

7. In the *Apply special formats to* section at the bottom of the dialog box, deselect **Last column** if it is selected. Click **Apply**.

8. With the insertion point still positioned in the table, center the table horizontally on the page by selecting the entire table and clicking the **Center** button on the Formatting toolbar.

9. Select the entire table and then select **Convert** on the **Table** menu.

10. Click **Table to Text** and then make sure the **Tabs** option is selected in the Convert Table To Text dialog box shown in Figure 14-13. Click **OK**.

FIGURE 14-13
Convert Table To Text dialog box

STEP-BY-STEP 14.13 Continued

11. Click **Undo** to return the document to table format.

12. Save the document and then close it. Follow your instructor's directions about turning off your computer.

SUMMARY

In this lesson, you learned:

- The table feature in Word enables you to organize and arrange text and numbers easily.

- If you need to change the organization of information after you create a table, you can remove rows and columns.

- The Draw Table tool and the Eraser tool are especially useful when you need to create a complex table. You can draw the table boundaries with the Draw Table tool much like you would draw a table on a sheet of paper. You can use the Eraser tool to remove cell boundaries.

- Borders and shading greatly enhance the appearance of a table and often make the table easier to read.

- Format fonts and text alignment in table cells the same way you apply those formats in other Word documents.

- You can edit the text in table cells using the same editing methods used for other Word text.

- The AutoFit feature automatically adjusts the width of a column based on the contents of the cells in a column.

- Sort the information in a table to organize the table contents to emphasize data in different ways.

- Word will convert text to a table or a table to text.

- The AutoFormat feature automatically adds borders and shading to your table.

VOCABULARY *Review*

Define the following terms:

Cell	Merging cells	Splitting cells
Gridlines		

REVIEW *Questions*

TRUE/FALSE

Circle T if the statement is true or F if the statement is false.

T   F   1. Table rows go across a page, and columns go down a page.

T   F   2. You can choose to hide or display a table's gridlines.

T   F   3. When you remove the boundary between two cells, you are splitting the cells.

T   F   4. The AutoAdjust command automatically adjusts all column widths in a table.

T   F   5. Word can create a table from text in which data is separated by paragraph marks, tabs, or commas.

MULTIPLE CHOICE

Circle the best response for each of the following statements.

1. If you wanted to add a new row in the middle of a table beneath the row in which your insertion point is located, you would choose the _____ menu, click Insert, and then select Row Below.
   A. Tools
   B. Insert
   C. Table
   D. Edit

2. Converting one cell into multiple cells is called _____ cells.
   A. merging
   B. splitting
   C. combining
   D. realigning

3. To create a complex table, use the _____ tool to position gridlines just where you want them.
   A. Complex Table
   B. Insert Table
   C. Create Table
   D. Draw Table

4. Sorting a table in _____ order arranges text entries in alphabetical order.
   A. ascending
   B. descending
   C. paragraph
   D. heading

5. The _____ feature automatically adds borders and shading to a table.
   A. AutoFit
   B. AutoFormat
   C. AutoBorder
   D. AutoAdjust

PROJECTS

PROJECT 14-1

1. Open **Project14-1** from the data files. Save the document as **Population** followed by your initials.

2. Position the insertion point in the last blank line of the document and use the **Insert Table** button to create a grid for a 6-row by 3-column table.

3. Complete the table by entering the data shown in Figure 14-14.

FIGURE 14-14
Data for Project 14-1 table

	2000	2010
18 – 24	30,388	28,513
25 – 34	52,697	44,248
45 – 54	27,157	40,347
55 – 64	42,802	50,938
65+	33,640	39,048

4. You realize you left out the data for the 35–44 age group. Insert a row in the proper location and key the following data: **35–44   23,864   25,890**

5. It would be helpful to see the percent change in population. Add a column to the right of the *2010* column and key the column heading **% Change** in the first row. Insert the following information in the cells of the new column:

   –6.2
   –16.0
   8.5
   48.6
   19.0
   16.0

6. Insert a new row above the first row of the table and merge all cells in it. Key the table title **Population by Age**. Center and bold the first two rows of the table.

7. Use AutoFit to adjust column widths, and then center the table in the page.

8. The data in the *% Change* column would look better if the decimal points were aligned. Right-align the numbers (but not the column head) in this column.

9. Remove all the borders in the table, then shade alternate rows of the data beginning with the *18–24* row.

10. Save your changes and close the document.

PROJECT 14-2

1. Open **Project14-2** from the data files. Save the document as **Hurricanes** followed by your initials. You have compiled the information in this document while doing research on hurricanes, and you decide you could format the information more clearly and attractively if you converted it to a table.

2. Select only the tabbed data (not the blank line or the source line) and convert the text to a table. Accept the suggested number of columns, select AutoFit to contents, and separate the text at tabs.

3. AutoFormat the table using the **Table Web3** format.

4. Insert a new row at the top of the table and merge all cells in it. Key the title **Costliest U.S. Hurricanes of the Past 50 Years**, and then press **Enter** and key **(In Billions)**. Center and boldface the first two rows of the table.

5. Center the data in the *Category* column, and right-align the data in the *Damage* column.

6. You keyed the wrong year for Hurricane Andrew. Change the year for Andrew to **1992**.

7. The data in the table is currently arranged in ascending order according to the *Ranking* column, which also orders the hurricanes from costliest to least costly storm. Sort the table on the data in the *Year* column to rearrange the data so that the storms are listed in chronological order, with the most recent storms last.

8. Rearranging the table draws attention to the dates of each storm, but you decide the ranking by cost is the aspect of the information you want to emphasize. Click the Undo button to return to the original order.

9. You decide the first ten entries in the table give enough information about the destructive power of hurricanes. Delete the last two rows in the table.

10. Center the table horizontally.

11. Save your changes. Print and close the document.

TEAMWORK PROJECT

If you completed Project 14-2, you learned how costly hurricanes can be in terms of property damage. The data shown in the Hurricanes table was compiled by the National Oceanic and Atmospheric Administration and is current only through 1996. You have probably heard about several powerful and costly hurricanes in the United States since then, such as Floyd, Bonnie, Charley, and Frances. With a partner, see if you can update the table with more recent data.

1. Write down the years from 1997 to the last complete hurricane season (hurricane season begins in June and ends in November, so if you are working on this project before the end of November, do not include the current year in your list).

2. Split the years with your partner so that you each have half of them to research.

3. Using Web search tools or other research tools, try to locate a summary of hurricane damage for each year.

4. If any of the years you research total more dollar damage than the hurricanes shown in the Hurricanes table, insert new rows to add the data you have found.

5. When you have compiled the data, experiment with sorting the rows using different criteria and applying different formats to the column heads, borders, cells, and text.

6. With your partner, decide which format presents the data the way you prefer, and then add your names and the current date to the bottom of the document page.

7. Print a copy of the finished document.

CRITICAL *Thinking*

ACTIVITY 14-1

The owner of the stable where you ride horses has been complaining about the comings and goings of her part-time staff and unpaid helpers (of whom you are one). She'd like a way to keep track of names, phone numbers, what days and hours each worker is scheduled, and hourly salary (if any). Use what you have learned in this lesson to create a table that will help the stable owner organize the information about her staff. Key several fictitious entries in the table (including yourself) to test your solution.

ENHANCING DOCUMENTS

Publishing a professional-looking newsletter or report a few decades ago could only be accomplished with the combined efforts of several people. Artists created the graphics and artwork, typesetters set the text, and designers prepared the finished page layouts for the printer. The process was often quite expensive. Today, with personal computers and inexpensive software, you can prepare attractive, professional-looking documents on your desktop computer. *Desktop publishing* is the process of using a computer to combine text and graphics to create an attractive document. In the early days of personal computers, there were separate applications for desktop publishing, but today you can accomplish these kinds of formatting tasks with most word-processing programs.

Word provides a number of features to enhance documents. You can format text in columns, add borders and shading, and include page numbers, headers, and footers on each page. For research papers, it is easy to add endnotes or footnotes; for design jobs like newsletters or brochures, you can import pictures, draw your own pictures, use WordArt to shape and rotate text, and add styles or themes to give the project consistency. In addition, templates and text tools such as AutoText and the Thesaurus feature enable you to create professional documents quickly and efficiently.

Using Columns, Borders, and Shading

2-2.1.16

One common application for desktop publishing is newsletters. Newsletter text is often formatted in multiple columns. The text flows down one column and begins again in the next column if necessary. Usually, the heading (or title of the newsletter) is formatted as a single-column *banner*—the heading spreads the full width across the multiple newsletter-style columns.

It is easy to apply columns in Word, and there are a few different ways to do so. You can use the Columns button on the Standard toolbar to select from several column options, or select Columns from the Format menu to access the preset options in the Columns dialog box. When you apply the column format, the columns are usually balanced so that the column lengths are approximately equal. There may be occasions, however, when you want to control where columns break. To adjust where a column ends, you can insert a *hard column break*.

Borders and shading also can help enhance the appearance of a document such as a newsletter or flyer. Word offers many options for line styles, line weights, colors, and shading effects. To access these borders and shading features, you can open the Format menu and choose Borders and Shading to display the Borders and Shading dialog box. Or you can quickly access most of the features by displaying the Borders and Shading toolbar. To display the toolbar, right-click on any toolbar on your screen and choose Tables and Borders in the shortcut menu.

> **Note**
>
> A check mark before the toolbar name indicates that the toolbar is already displayed. Clicking on the toolbar name will then turn off the shortcut menu and close the toolbar you selected.

S TEP-BY-STEP 15.1

1. If necessary, launch Word. Open **Step15-1** from the data files and save the document as **Newsletter** followed by your initials. If necessary, click **Show/Hide ¶** to display nonprinting characters.

2. Select the paragraph of text under the heading *PROTECTION FROM THE SUN*. Do not include the blank paragraph marks above or below the text in the selection.

3. Click the **Columns** button on the Standard toolbar. A grid displaying four columns appears.

4. Drag across the grid to select two columns, as shown in Figure 15-1. When you release the mouse button, the selected text is formatted in two columns of equal width.

FIGURE 15-1
Columns grid

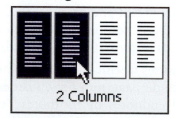

5. Select the three paragraphs of text under the heading *THE HEALTH RISKS OF LIVING ALONE*. Click the **Columns** button and select three columns in the grid, then release. The selected text is formatted in three columns of equal width.

STEP-BY-STEP 15.1 Continued

6. Select the paragraph of text below the heading *HIKING AND BIKING ADVENTURES*.

7. Open the **Format** menu and choose **Columns**. The dialog box shown in Figure 15-2 is displayed.

FIGURE 15-2
Columns dialog box

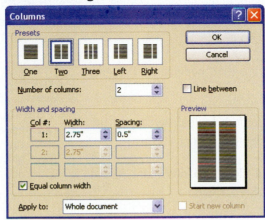

8. Select **Right** under **Presets** and select the option **Line between**. Word automatically adjusts the column widths under Width and spacing and updates the Preview.

9. Click **OK**. The text is formatted in two columns of unequal width, with a vertical line between the columns.

10. Position the insertion point in front of the third paragraph in *THE HEALTH RISKS OF LIVING ALONE*. The paragraph begins *Ironically,....* Open the **Insert** menu, choose **Break**, then select **Column break** and click **OK**.

11. Position the insertion point in front of the second paragraph in the same article that begins *Studies show that....* Insert a column break.

> **Computer Concepts**
>
> Use the shortcut key combination **Ctrl + Shift + Enter** to insert a hard column break quickly.

12. Position the insertion point in the blank paragraph above the first line of text *PROTECTION FROM THE SUN*.

13. Right-click on any toolbar and choose **Tables and Borders** in the shortcut menu to display the Tables and Borders toolbar. Click the down arrow on the **Line Weight** button on the Tables and Borders toolbar and select **3 pt**.

14. Click the **down arrow** on the **Border** button (the ScreenTip for this button probably says *Outside Border*) just to the left of the Shading Color button. Select **Top Border**.

15. Position the insertion point in the blank paragraph at the end of the document. Click the **down arrow** alongside the **Border** button and select **Bottom Border**.

STEP-BY-STEP 15.1 Continued

16. Position the insertion point in the first heading *PROTECTION FROM THE SUN* and then click the **down arrow** next to the **Shading Color** button on the Table and Borders toolbar. Select the color **Tan**. (*Hint:* Point to a color in the color palette and wait for the ScreenTip to display the name of the color.) A tan shade format is applied to the entire heading.

17. Position the insertion point in the second heading *THE HEALTH RISKS OF LIVING ALONE*, then click the **Shading Color** button. (Note that the color *Tan* is already selected and is showing on the Shading Color button.)

18. Repeat the format for the third heading *HIKING AND BIKING ADVENTURES*.

19. Close the Table and Borders toolbar by clicking the **Close** button in the upper-right corner.

20. Save the changes and close the document. Leave Word open for the next Step-by-Step.

> **Note**
>
> If the toolbar is docked, you will not see a Close button. Right-click anywhere in the toolbar, and then click **Tables and Borders** in the shortcut menu to close it.

 Working in a Connected World

STAGE TECHNICIAN

Have you ever seen a community theater musical, attended a concert, or enjoyed a touring company's production of a popular Broadway show? The performers on stage couldn't entertain you without the help of a talented group of stage technicians who depend on computer technology to do their jobs in twenty-first century theater.

The lighting, sound, and stage sets of a theatrical production all use specialized computer programs to create the special effects we've become accustomed to seeing. The lighting designer may use a proprietary software application such as Litewrite to program the light board, and the production's sound is enhanced with a MIDI (musical instrument digital interface) mixing board that uses sophisticated computer technology to produce digital sound effects, amplified voices, or perhaps even a "virtual" orchestra. The set designer uses a computer-aided drafting program such as AutoCADD to design the set and may also employ computer-assisted robotics to move the set pieces during the production.

But stage technicians also use more common types of computer software to do their jobs. For example, the property manager, who tracks the props used in a show, can keep track of hundreds of small items using a database program that tells her which actor uses a prop in which scene, as well as where the prop is stored. The stage manager depends on a note-taking program such as Lotus Notes or Microsoft OneNote to keep track of the director's staging instructions. Long-distance collaboration is common, and a designer may work with technicians across the country using Microsoft's NetMeeting to view designs and get input from the design team and e-mail and instant messaging to quickly contact coworkers as work on a production proceeds.

2-2.1.13
2-2.1.14

Page Numbers, Headers, and Footers

When your document has multiple pages, you may want to insert page numbers. The Page Numbers command on the Insert menu is a quick way to add page numbers that do not need accompanying text. (What this actually does is create a *header* or *footer* with a page number as the only text.)

Headers and footers are information and/or graphics that print in the top and bottom margins of each page. Your document can have a header, a footer, or both. Headers and footers can be a single paragraph or multiple paragraphs. Creating a header or footer is another way to add page numbers to a document. The advantage of formatting a header or footer rather than just using the Insert Page Numbers command is that you can include text with the page number. (Note that you can always edit the header or footer—and hence the page number—if you change your mind about how you want them to appear.)

S TEP-BY-STEP 15.2

1. Open **Step15-2** from the data files and save the document as **Walking** followed by your initials. Select the entire document and change to double-spacing.

2. Position the insertion point in front of the second heading that begins *The Right Clothes....* Open the **Insert** menu and choose **Break**. Select **Page break** and click **OK**.

3. Open the **Insert** menu and choose **Page Numbers** to open the dialog box shown in Figure 15-3.

FIGURE 15-3
Page Numbers dialog box

4. In the Position text box, verify that **Bottom of page (Footer)** is selected. In the Alignment text box, select **Center**. Click **OK**.

5. If necessary, select **Print Layout** from the **View** menu, and then scroll to the bottom of the first or second page to see the page number. These are dimmed because they are part of the footer and you must open the header or footer pane to edit them.

STEP-BY-STEP 15.2 Continued

6. Open the **View** menu and choose **Header and Footer**. The Header and Footer toolbar and a blank header pane appear. The document pane is dimmed as shown in Figure 15-4. This indicates that you can now edit the header (and footer) but not the document.

FIGURE 15-4
Header and Footer toolbar and header pane

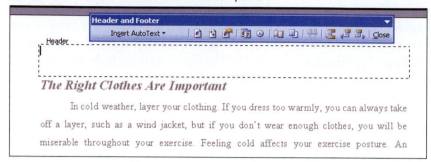

7. Key **Walking in Hot and Cold Weather** and then press **Tab** twice. (Notice that, by default, the headers and footers have a left-align tab, a center tab, and a right-align tab.) The insertion point is now positioned at the right margin in the header pane.

8. Click the **Insert Date** button on the **Header and Footer** toolbar. The current date is inserted in the header pane. This will automatically be updated each time the document is opened.

9. Click the **Switch Between Header and Footer** button. The footer pane is displayed and you can see the page number that you inserted previously.

10. Click **Close** in the Header and Footer toolbar to close it and to return to working in the document.

11. View the document in **Print Preview** or change the zoom to view the document in a reduced image.

12. Close the Print Preview window if necessary, save the changes, and leave the document open for the next Step-by-Step.

Footnotes and Endnotes

2-2.1.15

Notes are added to documents to show the source of borrowed material or to provide extra or explanatory information about the text. *Footnotes* are inserted at the bottom of the page on which the note is referenced in the document, and *endnotes* are placed together at the end of a document. Both kinds of notes are linked to their in-text reference symbol—usually a letter or numeral set above the text base line, called a *superscript*. That is, if you double-click the superscript numeral or letter in the document, the insertion point will move to the associated footnote or endnote.

If you format your document with footnotes and then decide to change the notes to endnotes, Word provides a conversion feature that quickly changes all footnotes to endnotes or vice versa. Notes are also automatically renumbered if you add or delete a note in the text.

S TEP-BY-STEP 15.3

1. Delete the blank paragraph following the main head of the document and then position the insertion point at the end of the first paragraph of text (following *...90 degrees or higher.*).

2. Select **Reference** from the **Insert** menu, and then click **Footnote** in the submenu to open the Footnote and Endnote dialog box shown in Figure 15-5.

FIGURE 15-5
The Footnote and Endnote dialog box

3. In the dialog box, check to make sure the **Footnotes** option is selected in the Location area and **Bottom of page** is the option in the list box across from Footnotes.

4. In the Format area, select **1, 2, 3** in the Number format list box if it is not already selected. Leave the other options in the dialog box as they are.

5. Click **Insert** to add the note to your document. A superscript numeral *1* will appear in the text and the insertion point should move to a position following another superscript numeral *1* at the bottom of the first page. There may be a rule above the numeral.

6. Following the superscript numeral, key **32 degrees Celsius**.

7. Move the insertion point to just after the comma following the text *5 degrees or more below zero* in the third paragraph of text and insert another footnote. A superscript numeral 2 appears in the text and a superscript 2 for the note also appears. This note may appear at the bottom of a new page.

8. The insertion point should be positioned to key the footnote text. Insert a minus sign (*Hint*: Select **Symbol** on the **Insert** menu and then look in the Mathematical Operators subset to find the minus sign.) and then key **20 degrees Celsius**.

9. If the second footnote appears on a new page, you reformat the document to eliminate the new page with nothing on it but the second footnote. Position the insertion point in front of the heading *The Right Clothes Are Important*, and then press the **Backspace** key. Both of the footnotes should now appear at the bottom of the first page.

STEP-BY-STEP 15.3 Continued

10. Double-click on the footnote reference **1** in the document. Notice that the document window scrolls down and the insertion point moves to the first footnote at the bottom of the page.

11. Select **Reference** from the **Insert** menu and then click **Footnote**.

12. In the Footnote and Endnote dialog box, click the **Convert** button (see Figure 15-5).

13. In the Convert dialog box that opens, select **Convert all footnotes to endnotes** if the option is not already selected and then click **OK**.

14. Back in the Footnote and Endnote dialog box, select **1, 2, 3** in the Number format drop-down list if it does not already appear there and then click **Close** or **Apply**. You should see the notes now positioned at the bottom of the second page of the document.

15. Select both of the endnotes and change the font to **Arial 9 pt**. (*Hint:* Use the Font and Font Size drop-down lists on the Formatting toolbar to format the footnotes.)

16. Save the changes and close the document. Leave Word open for the next Step-by-Step.

2-1.3.9
2-1.3.10

Inserting Graphics

You can use graphics to illustrate an idea presented in the document, to enhance the appearance of the document, or to make the document more functional. *Graphics* are items other than text and can include photos, borders, clip art, and drawing objects. *Clip art* is artwork that is ready to insert in a document. *Drawing objects* are Word tools that enable you to create your own artwork.

> **Computer Concepts**
>
> You may find it easier to work with graphics in a document by reducing the view of the document. For example, you can change the zoom of the document view to 75%.

Inserting Clip Art

Word has numerous clip art images and photos that are stored in the Office Collections folder. You can also access clip art that you have saved (in the My Collections folder). If you have an Internet connection open, you can search for clip art at the Microsoft Web site. Search results are displayed in the task pane as *thumbnails*, which are miniature representations of a picture.

> **Computer Concepts**
>
> If you click the down arrow on the right side of a clip art thumbnail, a shortcut menu will display and provide options for copying and pasting, deleting the clip from the Clip Organizer, copying the clip to a Collection folder, and so on.

Inserting a Picture from a File

You can also insert photos and clip art that are stored in other folders. This is called importing a picture. To import a picture, position the insertion point where you want the picture inserted, open the Insert menu, choose Picture, and select From File in the submenu. When the Insert Picture dialog box opens, browse to locate and select the graphics file.

STEP-BY-STEP 15.4

1. Open the **Newsletter** document you created in Step-by-Step 15.1 and save it as **Health Newsletter**.

2. Position the insertion point in front of the paragraph in the second article that begins *Doctors now believe....*

> **Note**
>
> You can leave the Insert Clip Art task pane open as you work so you can quickly access additional Clip Art images.

3. Open the **Insert** menu, choose **Picture**, and then select **Clip Art** from the submenu. The Clip Art task pane is displayed.

4. Select the text in the Search for text box and key **doctor**. If there is no text to be selected, just position the insertion point within the box.

5. Specify where Word should search for clip art. Click the **down arrow** next to the **Search in** list box. Click in the box next to the option **Everywhere** to select it. The option is selected when a check mark is displayed in the box to the left of the option name.

> **Computer Concepts**
>
> If there is a plus sign in front of the Everywhere option, click it to expand the list and display the option where clip art can be found. If there is a minus sign in front of the Everywhere option, the list of options is already expanded.

6. In the Results should be list box, select **All media file types** if that option is not already selected.

7. Click the **Go** button next to the Search for text box in the task pane. The results should display at least one clipart image as a thumbnail, as shown in Figure 15-6.

FIGURE 15-6
Clip Art task pane displaying results that match the search word *doctor*

8. Click the clip shown in Figure 15-6 (or any clip of a doctor) to insert the image in the document at the location of the insertion point, and then close the task pane.

9. Position the insertion point in front of the paragraph beginning *Are you looking....*

> **Note** ☑
>
> You can drag and drop a clip art image from the task pane to anywhere in your document.

10. Open the **Insert** menu, choose **Picture**, and then select **From File** in the submenu. The Insert Picture dialog box is displayed.

11. Locate the Lesson 15 data files in the Look in box. Select the file **Biking** and click **Insert**. The picture is inserted at the location of the insertion point. The document may wrap to a second page.

12. Save the changes and leave the document open for the next Step-by-Step.

Changing the Size of a Graphic

Once you have inserted a graphic or picture in a document, there are many ways to manipulate the picture. To work with a graphic, you must click on it to select it. You will know it is selected when you see eight small squares on the border of the graphic. These squares are called *sizing handles*. When a graphic is selected, you can cut, copy, paste, delete, and move it just as you would text.

The easiest way to change the size of a graphic is to drag one of the sizing handles. As you drag the sizing handle, you can see the effects of the change on your screen. If you want to change the size to exact measurements, you need to use the Format Picture command. Right-click on the graphic, select Format Picture from the shortcut menu, and then choose the Size tab in the Format Picture dialog box to enter exact measurements.

> **Note** ☑
>
> You can also click the **Format Picture** button on the Picture toolbar to access the Format Picture dialog box.

When you scale a graphic proportionally, you change all dimensions of the graphic (height and width) approximately equally. Use a corner sizing handle to reduce or enlarge a graphic proportionally. You can also scale a graphic just vertically or just horizontally, which distorts the image.

Cropping a Graphic

When you *crop* a graphic, you cut off portions of the graphic that you do not want to show. You might want to crop extra white space around an image or actually remove part of the image altogether. The Crop button on the Picture toolbar, which opens when you select a graphic, allows you to quickly crop a picture to remove any unwanted part of the image.

S TEP-BY-STEP 15.5

1. If necessary, turn on the display of the Ruler. (*Hint:* Open the **View** menu, and choose **Ruler**.)

2. Click on the clip art image of the doctor in the newsletter. When the picture is selected, the Picture toolbar is displayed. Eight sizing handles appear on the outside border of the image as shown in Figure 15-7.

FIGURE 15-7
Picture with sizing handles

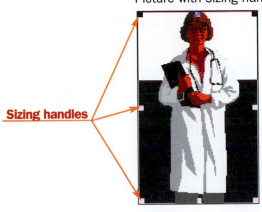

Sizing handles

3. Point to the lower-right corner of the image. When the pointer changes to a two-headed arrow, drag the corner sizing handle toward the center of the picture. When the picture is approximately 1½ inches high and 1 inch wide, release the mouse. Use the rulers at the top and left edges of the document to judge the picture size.

4. Click the biking graphic. The nonprinting border around the picture is displayed as well as the sizing handles. Notice that there is excess white space on the right side and bottom of the picture.

5. Click the **Crop** button on the Picture toolbar. The pointer changes to a cropping box.

6. Position the cropping box on the sizing handle on the middle right of the picture. Then click and drag the sizing handle to the left to trim the white space. Figure 15-8 shows how the cropping line displays. When you release the mouse button, the portion of the picture you cropped is gone.

FIGURE 15-8
Cropping a picture

7. Point to the sizing handle on the middle bottom of the picture and crop the white space at the bottom of the picture.

STEP-BY-STEP 15.5 Continued

8. Click the **Crop** button to turn off the cropping feature.

> **Note** ✅
>
> If the Picture toolbar is not displayed, open the **View** menu and choose **Toolbars**, then select **Picture**.

9. Resize the picture so it is approximately 1 inch high and 1 inch wide. (*Hint:* Be sure to drag a corner handle so you will resize the image proportionately.)

10. Save the changes and leave the document open for the next Step-by-Step.

Wrapping Text Around a Graphic

By default, Word inserts graphics in the line of text. This means that the graphic is positioned directly in the text at the insertion point. Instead of being in the line of text, however, you can format the text in the document to wrap around the graphic. By changing the wrapping style, you can drag and drop the graphic anywhere within the printable area of the page.

To create a tighter wrap around the graphic, you can edit the wrap points for the graphic. The wrap points identify the edge of the graphic. You can drag these wrap points to reposition them.

Moving a Graphic

A text-wrapping format must be applied to the graphic before you can reposition it in your document. You can then move the graphic by selecting it and dragging it to a new location. You will practice applying a wrapping style and moving a graphic in the following exercise.

STEP-BY-STEP 15.6

1. If necessary, click on the biking picture to select it.

2. Click the **Text Wrapping** button on the Picture toolbar. A drop-down list of wrapping options appears. Figure 15-9 provides a description of each of the options displayed in the drop-down list.

FIGURE 15-9
Text-wrapping options

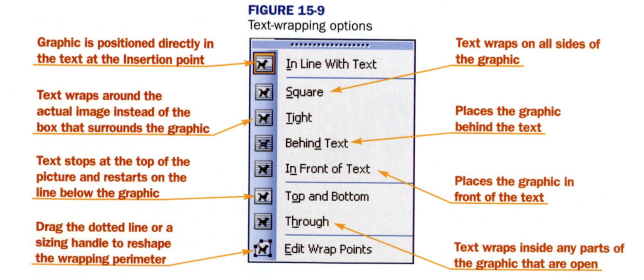

STEP-BY-STEP 15.6 Continued

3. Select the **Square** option. The text now wraps along the right side and bottom of the picture.

4. With the biking picture still selected, click the **Text Wrapping** button and then click **Edit Wrap Points**.

> **Note**
>
> You cannot drag and drop a picture until after you have applied a text-wrapping style.

5. Point to the sizing handle on the bottom right of the picture and drag the handle to the left to create a diagonal line as shown in Figure 15-10. When you release the mouse button, the text shifts to the left along the diagonal line.

FIGURE 15-10
Editing the Wrap points of a picture

6. Point to the center of the picture. When the pointer changes to a four-headed arrow, drag the picture to the left so it aligns with the left margin.

7. Select the doctor picture, click the **Text Wrapping** button, and select the **Tight** option. The text wraps tightly around the actual image instead of the rectangle boundary of the image. The way the text wraps will depend on the clip art image you selected.

8. Drag the picture to the right margin of the article.

9. Save the changes and leave the document open for the next Step-by-Step.

Creating WordArt Objects

WordArt is a feature that enables you to transform text into a graphic. You can create your own styles or you can choose from several predefined styles in the WordArt Gallery. When you create a WordArt object, the WordArt toolbar is displayed.

STEP-BY-STEP 15.7

1. Position the insertion point at the beginning of the document at the first paragraph mark.

2. Click the **Drawing** button on the Standard toolbar to display the Drawing toolbar. The Drawing toolbar is automatically docked at the bottom of your Word document window, above the Status bar.

> **Note**
>
> If the Drawing toolbar is already displayed, clicking the Drawing button on the Standard toolbar will close it.

STEP-BY-STEP 15.7 Continued

3. Click the **Insert WordArt** button on the Drawing toolbar. The dialog box shown in Figure 15-11 is displayed.

FIGURE 15-11
WordArt Gallery dialog box

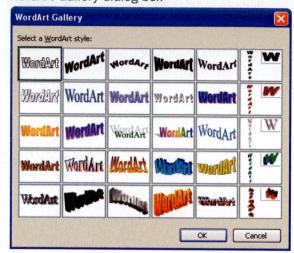

4. Select the fourth style in the second row and then click **OK**. The Edit WordArt Text dialog box displays.

5. Key **Health News** in place of the text in the text box and click **OK**. Word formats the text as a WordArt object and positions the object in your document.

6. Click on the object to select it. Then, point to the sizing handle in the lower right corner and drag it to the right edge of the document. The WordArt object will expand to the width of the document, leaving a one-inch margin on the right.

7. With the object still selected, point to the object and right-click. Choose **Format WordArt** from the short-cut menu. If necessary, click the **Color and Lines** tab to display the dialog box shown in Figure 15-12.

FIGURE 15-12
Format WordArt dialog box

STEP-BY-STEP 15.7 Continued

8. In the Color list box under Fill, click the **down arrow** to display a grid of colors. At the bottom of the grid, select **Fill Effects**. The Gradient tab in the Fill Effects dialog box is displayed.

9. For Color 1, select **Orange**. For Color 2, select **Tan**. Under Shading styles, select **Diagonal up**. Click **OK**. The Fill Effects dialog box closes, and the Format WordArt dialog box is still open.

10. In the Color list box under Line, select **Orange**. Click **OK**. The border lines and the fill colors for the WordArt object are formatted with the new colors.

11. With the WordArt object selected, click the **WordArt Shape** button on the WordArt toolbar. Choose a different shape. Notice that the shape changes but the text, fill color, and line colors remain unchanged. Explore other shapes and choose one that is appropriate for this newsletter.

12. Delete some of the blank lines under the WordArt object, and make other adjustments if necessary to fit the document on one page.

13. Save the changes and close the document.

Using Drawing Tools

2-1.3.11

Sometimes you may need to create your own artwork. For example, you may want to illustrate a map with directions. You can use the Drawing toolbar in Word to create drawing objects. When you insert a drawing object in Word, a *drawing canvas* displays. The drawing canvas helps you arrange your drawing and keep parts of your drawing together, while also providing a frame-like boundary between your drawing and the rest of the document. If you don't want the drawing canvas to display, press Esc after you select a drawing tool but before you begin drawing.

> **Computer Concepts**
>
> You can format a background or border for the drawing canvas. You can also add a picture by choosing the floating wrapping style and then dragging the picture onto the drawing canvas.

Once you have drawn objects in your document, they can be manipulated in a variety of ways. As you place objects on the page, the most recent ones are placed on top—they are layered. You can select any object and choose to have it placed at the very back layer, the very front layer, or moved forward or backward one layer at a time, using the options from the Draw menu on the Drawing toolbar. You can also select multiple objects and group them together to become one object that can be moved and manipulated as such.

Resizing the Drawing Canvas

The drawing canvas is especially helpful if your drawing contains several shapes, because it keeps your shapes together as one object. You will practice resizing the drawing canvas and using the drawing canvas to scale your drawing in the following exercise.

STEP-BY-STEP 15.8

1. Open a new document and, if necessary, display the **Drawing** toolbar.

2. Click the **Line** button on the Drawing toolbar. The pointer changes to a crosshair and the drawing canvas is displayed as shown in Figure 15-13. Notice, too, that the Drawing Canvas toolbar is displayed. These toolbar buttons enable you to adjust the canvas size and fit the drawing within the drawing canvas.

FIGURE 15-13
Drawing Canvas and Drawing Canvas toolbar

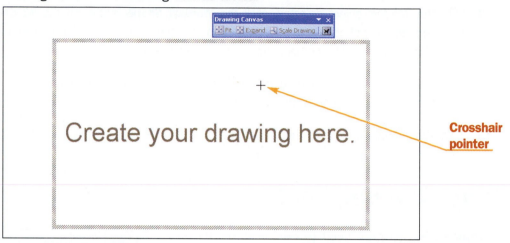

Crosshair pointer

3. Point to the upper-left corner of the drawing canvas and drag the crosshair across the width of the canvas. Do not release the mouse button until the line is straight, even, and the length you want.

4. Click the **Line** button again and draw a second line, this time running diagonal across the drawing canvas.

5. With the second line still selected (the sizing handles on each end of the line indicate that the line is selected), click the **Line Style** button on the Drawing toolbar and select **3 pt** (the 3-pt single line, not the double line). The weight of the selected line is now heavier.

6. With the line still selected, click the **down arrow** next to the **Line Color** button on the Drawing toolbar. Select **Green**. The color of the selected line changes.

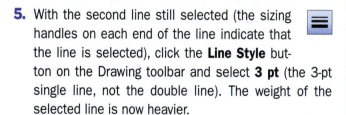

> **Note** ✓
>
> If the drawing canvas does not display, open the **Tools** menu, choose **Options**, select the **General** tab, and make sure there is a check mark for the option **Automatically create drawing canvas when inserting AutoShapes**.

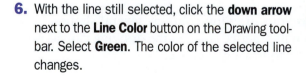

> **Computer Concepts**
>
> An object must be selected before you can choose an option from the Drawing toolbar. If the format you want to apply is dimmed, make sure the object you want to format is selected.

STEP-BY-STEP 15.8 Continued

7. Click the **Rectangle** button on the Drawing toolbar. Position the crosshair in the middle of the screen and drag the crosshair down and to the right to create a box approximately one inch high and one inch wide. (This box should overlap the diagonal line at some point.)

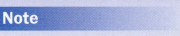

Note

To create a perfect square, hold down **Shift** as you drag the crosshair, or just click once in the document without dragging after selecting the Rectangle tool.

8. With the rectangle object still selected, click the **down arrow** to the right of the **Fill Color** button on the Drawing toolbar and select **Blue**. The rectangle is filled with the blue color.

9. With the rectangle object still selected, open the **Draw** menu on the Drawing toolbar. Point to **Order** and select **Send Backward**. The rectangle is moved behind or under the diagonal line.

10. With the rectangle object still selected, hold down the **Ctrl** key and click on the diagonal line so that both the rectangle and the line are selected.

11. Open the **Draw** menu and click **Group**. This makes the rectangle and the line one object. Note how it can be moved and resized as a single object.

12. With the object still selected, open the **Draw** menu and choose **Ungroup**.

13. Drag one of the sizing handles to resize the drawing canvas. For example, drag a marker inward to eliminate excess white space around the drawing objects.

14. Click the **Fit** button on the Drawing Canvas toolbar. The boundary area of the drawing canvas automatically adjusts to fit the drawing objects and all excess space is eliminated.

15. Click the **Expand** button. The drawing canvas is enlarged in increments each time you click the expand button.

16. Click the **Scale Drawing** button. The boundary of the drawing canvas changes to display eight round sizing handles. Drag a corner handle to resize the drawing canvas just as you would resize a drawing object or a picture. The drawing objects are resized as a unit.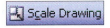

17. Click the **Text Wrapping** button on the Drawing Canvas toolbar and select the **Square** option. The text- wrapping format is applied to the canvas just as it is applied to any drawing object. You can reposition the drawing canvas, and all the objects will move as a unit.

18. Close the document without saving the changes. Leave Word open for the next Step-by-Step.

Inserting Text Boxes

A text box is a graphic that enables you to add text to your artwork. Because the text box is a graphic, you can resize and position it the same way you resize and reposition pictures and drawing objects. Within the text box, you can change the font and the alignment of the text. To insert a text box, click the Text Box button on the Drawing toolbar. A drawing canvas opens, and you can drag the crosshair to create a box anywhere within the drawing canvas. When you release the mouse button, the insertion point will be inside the text box, ready to key text, and the Text Box toolbar will appear. You can learn more about text boxes with the Help or Office Assistant. Search for the phrase *text box* to find out more about inserting, formatting, and resizing text boxes.

Using AutoShapes to Create Objects

The AutoShape feature in Word enables you to create a variety of predesigned drawing objects. Stars, arrows, shapes, and callouts (text that describes something in an image) are among the AutoShape designs from which you can choose on the Drawing toolbar.

You create an AutoShape the same way you create other drawing objects. Select the AutoShape that you want to draw from the toolbar. The pointer changes to a crosshair which you drag to the desired size of the AutoShape. When you choose Callouts from the AutoShapes menu, the AutoShape is automatically formatted as a text box so you can add text inside the object. You can resize and reposition AutoShapes in the same way you change the size and position of pictures and drawing objects.

2-1.2.6
2-2.1.17

Templates and Styles

It can be a time-consuming task to come up with a pleasing design and then format all the characters in every document you create. Fortunately, Microsoft Office has predesigned documents for almost any purpose you can imagine. In addition, there are preset style choices available that make formatting and designing the perfect document easy for anyone.

Using Templates

Every Word document is based on a template. A *template* is a file that contains document, paragraph, and character formats for documents that you create frequently. The template saves all standard text and formatting choices so all you need to do is enter the variable text. This can greatly increase the speed and efficiency of your work since you do not need to spend time setting up the details of the page. It can also increase the quality of your work since it can ensure that all documents you produce have the same settings and formats.

> **Computer Concepts**
>
> All of the documents that were written to create this entire text were created by using a template containing a specific set of styles.

The default settings for the "blank" or new document margins and fonts are stored in a template. Depending on your Word installation, many types of document templates may be available to you. You can see the available templates in the Templates dialog box when you open a new document.

STEP-BY-STEP 15.9

1. Click **New** on the **File** menu. This opens the New Document task pane.

STEP-BY-STEP 15.9 Continued

2. In the Template section, click the **On my computer...** link to open the Templates dialog box.

3. In the Templates dialog box, switch to the **Letters & Faxes** tab, shown in Figure 15-14, and then select **Contemporary Letter** and click **OK**. This opens a new document that is already formatted in a letter style that has areas in which you can click to enter information. (The choices shown in your dialog box may differ from those shown here.)

FIGURE 15-14
The Letters & Faxes tab of the Templates dialog box

4. Click in the upper-right corner and enter your address.

5. Highlight *Company Name Here* and key a company name.

6. Click in the area below the date and key the following address:
   Josh O'Brien
   5020 Balsam Court
   Endicott, NY 13760

7. Select **Sir or Madam** in the salutation line and key **Josh**.

8. Select the paragraph in the body of the letter and key **Thank you so much for agreeing to meet with me on September 30. I am really looking forward to discussing the possibility of combining our two businesses. I think we could make a great team!**

9. Click the line below *Sincerely* and key your name.

10. Click the line for your job title and press the **Delete** key.

11. Save your document as **Merger Letter**. Close the document, but leave Word open for the next Step-by-Step.

Using Styles

Another way in which you can quickly and easily change the appearance of a section of text is to apply a style. A *style* is a set of formatting characteristics that you can apply to text, tables, and lists in your document. When you apply a style, you apply a whole group of formats in one simple step.

For example, instead of taking three separate steps to format your title as 14 pt, Arial, bold, and center-aligned, you can achieve the same result in one step by applying a title style.

There are four general types of styles you can create and apply:

- A paragraph style controls all aspects of a paragraph's appearance, such as text alignment, tab stops, line spacing, and borders, and can include character formatting.

- A character style affects selected text within a paragraph, such as the font and size of text, and bold and italic formats.

- A table style provides a consistent look to borders, shading, alignment, and fonts in tables.

- A list style applies similar alignment, numbering or bullet characters, and fonts to lists.

You can create, view, and reapply styles from the Styles and Formatting task pane. Direct formatting that you apply is also stored in this pane so that you can quickly reapply it.

Styles are also included in templates. The blank document template contains a set of styles already created for you. You can also create your own styles and include them in a template. As you work in the document based upon that template, all of the styles associated with that template will then be available to you. This again can ensure consistency across multiple documents. By selecting the Add to template check box in the New Style dialog box, the style you create will always be available with the template.

> **Note**
>
> If you want to use text that you've already formatted as the basis of a list style, paragraph style, or character style, select it, and then base the new style on the formatting and other properties applied to the selected text.

STEP-BY-STEP 15.10

1. Open a new blank document.

2. Open the **Format** menu and select **Styles and Formatting** to open the Styles and Formatting task pane. Note the styles that are already available to you.

3. In the Styles and Formatting task pane, click **New Style**.

4. In the Name box, key **TX**.

5. In the Style type box, select **Paragraph** if necessary.

6. In the Style based on box, select **Body Text** from the drop-down menu.

7. In the Style for following paragraph box, note that TX has already been selected. The style you are creating is the default style for the following paragraph. If this were a heading, you would likely want the following paragraph to be a paragraph style.

STEP-BY-STEP 15.10 Continued

8. In the Formatting section, change the font style from Times New Roman to **Arial**. Leave all of the other Formatting options set as they are (based on the Body Text style). Click **OK**.

9. Key or insert today's date in your document and press **Enter**.

10. Select **TX** from the Styles and Formatting task pane and key **This is an example of what you can do with a style.** Press **Enter**. (Note that the new paragraph is automatically formatted in the TX style.)

11. Close the document without saving it. Leave Word open for the next Step-by-Step.

Enhancing Your Document with Text Tools

2-2.1.19

Υou learned how to check the spelling and grammar in your document in Lesson 13, but Word offers other features to enhance the content of your document and create quality results competently and effectively. The language tools available in Word include a Thesaurus that helps you find just the right word, and the AutoText and AutoComplete features literally take over the sometimes tedious task of keying text.

Finding the Right Word

The Thesaurus feature in Word can help you compose professional documents. A *thesaurus* is a compilation of alternative words or synonyms. In Word, you can let the software do the searching for a perfect synonym by selecting Thesaurus from the Language submenu on the Tools menu. If you have already selected a word to look up in the document, the Research pane will open with a list of alternative words already displayed (Figure 15-15). Or you can enter a word in the Search for text box at the top of the task pane, and then click the Start searching arrow to the right of the text box.

FIGURE 15-15
A Thesaurus entry in the Research pane

When you point to an equivalent in the list, a drop-down arrow gives you access to a short-cut menu that allows you to insert the new word, copy it, or look up more synonyms for the new word. If you have selected a word in your document, when you choose Insert from the shortcut menu, the new word from the Thesaurus replaces your original word choice.

Creating Documents More Efficiently

By now you have undoubtedly encountered Word's AutoComplete feature. This feature suggests the spelling for frequently used words and phrases. AutoComplete will fill in days of the week, months, salutations, and complimentary closings commonly used in letters. As you begin to key the first few characters of these frequently used words, Word suggest the entire spelling in a box on the screen (often referred to as a ScreenTip). You can accept the suggested spelling by pressing Enter. If you do not wish to accept the suggested spelling, continue keying and the Screen Tip will disappear.

> **Computer Concepts**
>
> By default, the AutoRecover feature automatically saves a temporary copy of your document every 10 minutes. The temporary copy will open automatically when you start Word after a power failure or similar problem.

What can you do about words or phrases that are common to your documents but are not included in the AutoComplete set of words? For this, Word provides AutoText. With AutoText you can create your own text entries which are then added to the AutoComplete set of words. AutoText entries must be at least five characters long if you want to insert the entry by using AutoComplete.

S TEP-BY-STEP 15.11

1. Open **Step15-11** from the data files and save the document as **History** followed by your initials.

2. Double-click the word *important* in the last line of the text to select it.

3. Open the **Tools** menu, select **Language**, and then select **Thesaurus**. The Research task pane opens and displays a list of alternative choices for the word *important*, similar to the task pane shown in Figure 15-15.

4. Click the **minus sign** to the left of the first word in the list to hide the sublist and bring any other synonyms with their own lists into view.

5. Display any sublists again by clicking the **plus sign** next to each main entry, and then click on a word in one of the sublists you would like to use instead of *important*.

6. Click the **down arrow** to the left of the word you have chosen and click **Insert** on the drop-down menu. Word replaces *important* with the synonym you have chosen.

7. Close the Research pane.

8. Open the **Tools** menu and select **AutoCorrect Options**.

9. Switch to the **AutoText** tab.

10. In the Enter AutoText entries here text box, key your full name.

STEP-BY-STEP 15.11 Continued

11. Click **Add** and then click **OK**.

12. Position the insertion point in the blank paragraph following the text in the document, and then begin to key your first name. After you have keyed the fourth letter in your name, the Screen Tip with your complete name will appear. Press **Enter** to accept the AutoComplete entry.

13. Press **Enter** to begin a new paragraph. Key **Westmoreland Historical Society**.

> **Note**
>
> To store paragraph formatting with the AutoText entry, include the paragraph mark in the selection.

14. Select the entire name of the organization. Open the **Insert** menu, point to **AutoText**, and select **New**.

15. In the Create AutoText dialog box, accept the name Word proposes or key a new one. (If you plan to insert the entry by using AutoComplete, make sure the name contains at least four characters because Word inserts an entry only after four characters have been typed.) Click **OK**.

16. Press **Enter** and then begin to key the current date. After you have keyed the fourth letter of the month, the complete month's name will appear in a ScreenTip. Press **Enter** to accept the AutoComplete entry.

17. As you key the space and the day, the AutoComplete ScreenTip will display the complete current date. Press **Enter** again to accept the entry. Format the three lines of text you have entered using the **Byline** style.

18. Position the insertion point at the end of the heading *How to Collect an Oral History* and press **Enter**.

19. Open the **Insert** menu, point to **AutoText**, and then select the name of the AutoText entry you created in steps 13 through 15. The phrase *Westmoreland Historical Society* inserts under the heading.

20. Save the changes and then close the document. Follow your instructor's directions about turning off the computer.

SUMMARY

In this lesson, you learned:

- Text can be arranged in a variety of multicolumn formats, all within the same document.

- Borders and shading are also important tools for desktop publishing. You can choose from a variety of options for line styles, colors, and shading effects.

- The Insert Page Number command automatically numbers all the pages in a document. You can include text with the page number by formatting a header or footer.

- Footnotes and endnotes are used in a document to show the source of borrowed material or to provide extra or explanatory information about the text; footnotes appear at the bottom of each page and endnotes are added to the end of a document.

- Clip art and other pictures help to enhance the appearance and effectiveness of a document.

- When you format a picture for text wrapping, you can position the graphic anywhere on the page by dragging it to a new position.

- WordArt enables you to convert text to a graphic. WordArt objects can be positioned and resized the same as pictures.

- You can create your own artwork using the drawing tools.

- The drawing canvas helps you arrange, position, and resize your drawing objects. You can format and move the drawing canvas just as you format other objects.

- AutoShapes provide predesigned drawing objects such as stars, shapes, and callouts.

- Microsoft Office templates and styles provide a uniform appearance for your documents and can increase the speed and quality of your work by providing predesigned documents and preset formats.

- The Thesaurus provides a list of alternative words and synonyms to help you compose professional documents effectively.

- AutoText and AutoComplete make entering repetitive phrases simple and easy.

VOCABULARY *Review*

Define the following terms:

Banner	Endnote	Sizing handles
Clip art	Footer	Style
Crop	Footnote	Superscript
Desktop publishing	Graphics	Template
Drawing canvas	Hard column break	Thesaurus
Drawing objects	Header	Thumbnails

REVIEW *Questions*

TRUE/FALSE

Circle T if the statement is true or F if the statement is false.

T F **1.** Page numbers are added to a Word document as headers or footers without any other text.

T F **2.** Drawing objects are predrawn artwork ready to insert in a document.

T F **3.** When you size a graphic proportionally, you change all the dimensions approximately equally.

T   F   **4.** You will find drawing tools on the Formatting toolbar.

T   F   **5.** Endnotes appear on the page on which they are referenced.

MULTIPLE CHOICE

Circle the best response for each of the following statements.

1. The process of using a computer to combine text and graphics is called _____.
   A. desktop publishing
   B. graphics
   C. clip art
   D. pasting

2. _____ are small squares on the border of a graphic that let you know it is selected.
   A. Crops
   B. Footers
   C. Sizing handles
   D. Selection marks

3. When you _____ a graphic, you remove a part of the graphic that you don't want to show.
   A. select
   B. crop
   C. resize
   D. move

4. The _____ feature helps you find synonyms for words in your document.
   A. AutoText
   B. AutoComplete
   C. Thesaurus
   D. Grammar

5. The _____ helps you arrange and size your drawing objects.
   A. drawing object
   B. drawing preview
   C. Drawing toolbar
   D. drawing canvas

PROJECTS

PROJECT 15-1

1. Open **Project15-1** from the data files. Save the document as **Garden News** followed by your initials.

2. Select the first two lines in the document. Apply a green shading to the selected headings. If necessary, select the text and change the font color to white. Note that if you choose a dark color, Word will automatically change the font color so it will display against the dark shading.

3. Position the insertion point in the *Fall Gardening* heading. Insert a 2¼-point border below the heading. Use the **Repeat** command to insert borders below the other two headings.

4. Position the insertion point at the beginning of the second paragraph below the *Fall Gardening* heading. Insert a clip art picture that relates to autumn. Resize the picture proportionately so it is about 1½ inches tall. Choose an appropriate text-wrapping option. Adjust the position of the picture so that the top of the picture lines up with the first line of the second paragraph.

5. In the last sentence of the same paragraph, double-click the word **profit** to select it and then open the Thesaurus in the Research pane.

6. From the list of synonyms, select an alternative word (be sure you choose a word that replaces *profit* used as a verb, such as *gain* or *benefit*). Insert the word you choose in the document to replace *profit*.

7. Select the text (but not the blank line above the text) that describes the Annual Tree Sale. Apply a yellow shading to the selected text.

8. Position the insertion point at the beginning of the second paragraph under the *Gardening Today Spotlight* heading and insert the picture file **flower** from your data files. Crop the white space on the right side of the picture. Resize the picture to approximately 1½ inches high and 1 inch wide.

9. Apply a square text-wrapping option to the new picture. Move the picture to the right side of the page and position it so the top of the picture lines up with the first line of the second paragraph under the *Gardening Today Spotlight* heading.

10. Select the last paragraph in the document and apply the same green shading you used for the two headings at the top of the document. If necessary, change the font color to white.

11. Add a footer to the document that includes your name at the left margin and the current month and year at the right margin.

12. Save your changes and close the document.

PROJECT 15-2

1. Open a new document. Save it as **Map** followed by your initials.

2. Use the **Line, Rectangle,** and **Fill Color** drawing tools to create the lines and box illustrated in Figure 15-16. The Rulers on the edges of the screen are displayed in the figure to help you judge the size and position of the objects.

FIGURE 15-16
Drawing objects for Project 15-2

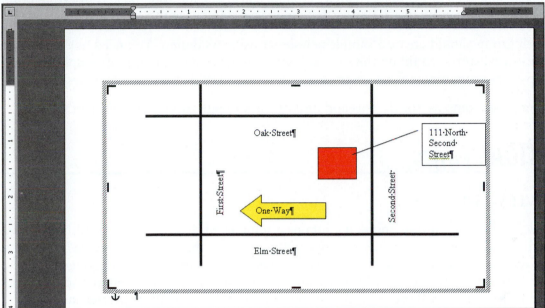

3. Fill the rectangle with the bright red color.

4. Create four text boxes for the street names:
    A. To create the First Street and Second Street text boxes, draw tall, narrow boxes. Then use the **Text Direction** button on the Text Box toolbar to change the direction of text in the text box.
    B. Remove the borders from the text boxes.

5. Use an **AutoShape** to create the One Way arrow in the map. Fill the AutoShape with the bright yellow color.

6. Create the callout that points out the exact address of the red rectangle.

7. Rescale the drawing object by resizing the drawing canvas so that the map fills the width of the page. Then apply the **Square** text-wrapping format and position the map in the center of the page horizontally.

8. Save your changes and close the document. Follow your instructor's directions about turning off your computer.

TEAMWORK PROJECT

In this lesson, you have learned some ways to enhance a document. Put your knowledge into practice by designing a newsletter for your class, school, or workplace. Follow these steps:

1. The class should divide into three or four groups.

2. Each group should brainstorm ideas for the layout of the newsletter, appropriate graphics, and what kinds of stories to use in the newsletter. Use features you have learned about in this lesson, such as borders, shading, columns, headers and footers, and inserting graphics, to make your newsletter design visually interesting and easy to read.

3. Each group should create a sample newsletter using its design. You need not write a number of real stories to fill up the spaces. Instead, write one paragraph of sample text and copy it as many times as necessary to show how text will appear in the newsletter.

4. As a class, compare the designs and discuss the strengths and weaknesses of each.

CRITICAL *Thinking*

ACTIVITY 15-1

You have created a drawing that contains a number of drawing objects. Although you have worked as carefully as you can, you cannot place some of the objects as precisely as you would like. Is there any way to move the objects in small increments without dragging them using the mouse? Is there any way to specify that your drawing object be positioned in a specific location? Use the Help system in Word to find answers to these questions. Write a brief summary of what you learn.

EXCEL ESSENTIALS

OBJECTIVES

Upon completion of this lesson, you should be able to:

- Identify the parts of the Excel screen.

- Create and navigate through a worksheet.

- Use the AutoCorrect and AutoComplete features in Excel.

- Insert and delete rows and columns.

- Change column width and row height, including using AutoFit to fit the column width to the cell contents.

- Copy, clear, move, and delete data.

- Use AutoFill to copy the same data into a range of cells.

- Format the contents of a cell and add shading and border formats to a range of cells.

- Use the Undo and Redo features.

Estimated Time: 1 hour

VOCABULARY

Active cell

Cell reference

Fill handle

Filling

Range

Workbook

Worksheet

Excel is an electronic spreadsheet application designed to replace the tedious work of using pencils, paper, and calculators. A *spreadsheet* is used to gather, organize, and summarize text and numeric data. Spreadsheets are called *worksheets* in Excel. The worksheet consists of a grid of rows and columns into which you can enter numbers, text, and formulas. The worksheet in Excel is also used to perform calculations. In the past, people manually created ledgers that served the same function as today's electronic spreadsheets. When changes were necessary, the process of making corrections to the ledger was painstaking. With an electronic spreadsheet, changes are relatively easy.

Identifying the Parts of the Excel Screen

When you first launch the Excel application, a blank worksheet is displayed. Remember, Excel refers to a spreadsheet as a worksheet. The new worksheet is titled *Book1*. This filename will remain until you choose Save As from the File menu and assign the document a new filename. The worksheet is always stored in a *workbook* that contains one or more worksheets.

Excel has its own unique menus, screen parts, and toolbars. The mouse pointer displays as a thick plus sign when it is within the worksheet. When you move the pointer to a menu, it turns into an arrow.

The Getting Started task pane is also displayed when you open Excel. This task pane enables you to quickly open workbooks that you have recently accessed or to create a new workbook. After you open an existing

workbook or create a new workbook, the task pane will disappear. If Excel is already launched, you can click the New button on the Standard toolbar to open the New Document task pane and create a new blank worksheet.

The worksheet is divided into columns and rows. Columns of the worksheet appear vertically and are identified by letters at the top of the worksheet window. Rows appear horizontally and are identified by numbers on the left side of the worksheet window. The intersection of a single row and a single column is called a *cell*. The **cell reference** identifies the column letter and row number (for example, A1 or B4). Usually, the top row of a worksheet is used for explanatory text or column headings that identify the type of data in each column.

S TEP-BY-STEP 16.1

1. Start Excel.

2. Compare your screen with Figure 16-1.

FIGURE 16-1
The Excel window

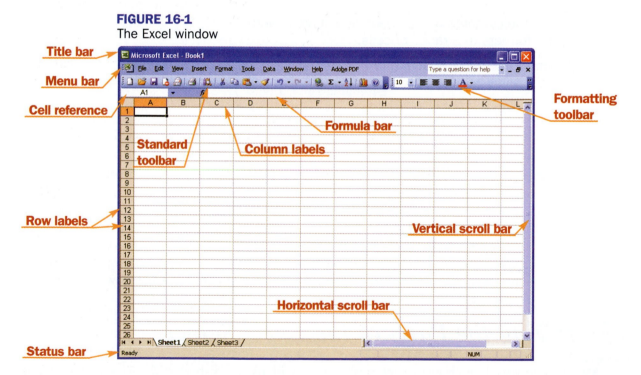

3. Note the various components of the Excel screen and their names. Leave the workbook open for the next Step-by-Step.

2-3.1.1
2-3.1.2

Navigating Through a Worksheet

To create a worksheet, you enter information into the cells. Before you can enter data into a cell, you must first select the cell. When the cell is selected, a dark border appears around the cell. You can select a cell using either the mouse or the keyboard. When a cell is selected, it is called the *active cell*, shown in Figure 16-2. The active cell is identified in the Name Box at the top of the worksheet screen. You can change the active cell by using the mouse or the keyboard.

FIGURE 16-2
Active cell in worksheet

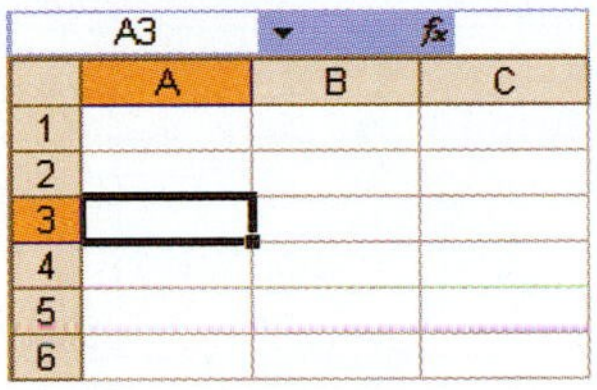

Entering Data and Moving Around in the Worksheet

You enter data by keying text or numbers in the active cell and then either pressing Enter on the keyboard or clicking the Enter button (green check mark) on the Formula Bar. You can also press Tab to enter the information and then move to the next cell in the row. By default, Excel displays approximately eight characters in each cell. As you begin keying text, you will see the insertion point indicating where the next character of text will appear. When text is too long for a cell, it will spill over into the next cell—if the next cell is empty. If the next cell is not empty, the text that does not fit into the cell will not be displayed—but it is still contained within the cell. Numerical data may appear as a series of number signs (####) if the number does not fit in the cell.

> **Note**
>
> In Excel, pressing **End** will not take you to the end of a row. Use the shortcut key combination **Ctrl + right arrow** to move to the last cell with data in a row.

Many of the keyboard shortcuts you learned to use in Word will move the insertion point in Excel in similar ways. For example, the arrow keys will move the insertion point one cell in any direction, and Page Up or Page Down moves the insertion point one screen up or down. Table 16-1 includes other keyboard shortcuts you can use to move the insertion point in an Excel worksheet.

Selecting a Range of Cells in the Worksheet

To select an entire row in a worksheet, click the row number at the left of the screen. To select an entire column, click the column letter at the top of the document. You may notice that the entire row or column has a dark border, and the row number or column letter is shaded, along with all the other cells in the row or column except the first cell. The first cell is still the active cell, even when the entire row or column is selected, and the lack of shading in the cell indicates it is the active cell. If you enter data with a row or column selected, it will be entered in the first cell.

> **Computer Concepts**
>
> The arrow keys also can be used in combination with the Shift key to select cells in a range. Hold down the **Shift** key and press the **up arrow** or **down arrow** to select cells in a column; use the **left arrow** and **right arrow** keys with **Shift** to select cells in a row. If you use **Shift + left arrow** to select a row of data cells and then press the **up** or **down arrow** without releasing the Shift key, you can select a range of cells with the keyboard.

You can also select a row, column, or section of a worksheet by clicking and dragging the mouse to highlight the area you want to select. When you select a group of cells, the group is called a *range*. All cells in a range touch each other and form a rectangle. The range is identified by the cell in the upper-left corner and the cell in the lower-right corner, separated by a colon (for example, A1:D4).

TABLE 16-1
Keyboard shortcuts for moving the Insertion point in Excel

TO MOVE THE INSERTION POINT	PRESS
Right one cell	Tab
Right one cell	right arrow
Left one cell	left arrow
To the next row	down arrow
To the previous row	up arrow
To the beginning of a row	Home
To the next screen	Page Down
To the previous screen	Page Up
To the last cell with data in a row	Ctrl + right arrow
To the first cell in a row	Ctrl + left arrow
To the cell after the last cell with data in the document	Ctrl + End
To the beginning of the document	Ctrl + Home

S TEP-BY-STEP 16.2

1. Click the **Create a new workbook** link at the bottom of the Getting Started task pane to open the New Workbook pane.

2. Click **Blank Workbook** in the New section of the task pane. A new workbook titled *Book2* is opened.

3. Click in cell **A3** to select it. You will enter column headings in row 3 to identify the data that will appear in each column.

4. Key **Days**. Notice that the text you enter is displayed in the cell and in the Formula Bar.

5. Press **Tab**. The insertion point moves to the next cell in the third row, B3. Key **Cruise**.

6. Press **Tab** and key **Price**. Press **Tab** and key **Dates**. Press **Enter**. The insertion point moves to the first cell in the fourth row, A4.

> **Note**
>
> The Enter and Cancel buttons will not display in the Formula Bar unless you enter data in a cell or position the insertion point in the Formula Bar.

STEP-BY-STEP 16.2 Continued

7. Click in cell **A3**. It currently displays *Days* in the cell and in the Formula Bar. To change the text in the Formula Bar, click in the **Formula Bar** and position the insertion point in front of the word *Days*, as shown in Figure 16-3.

FIGURE 16-3
Insertion point positioned in the Formula Bar

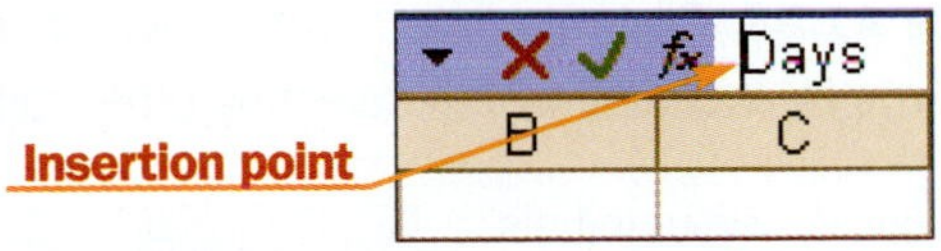

Insertion point

8. Key **#** and then press the **spacebar**. Click the **Enter** button (the green check mark) on the Formula Bar. The change is made in the Formula Bar and in cell A3. (The green check mark in the Formula Bar only enters the data. It does not allow for the automatic movement to A4.)

9. Press the **right arrow** to move to cell **B3**. It currently displays *Cruise*. Key **Destination** and press **Enter**. The contents of the cell are replaced with the new text you entered.

10. Click in cell **C3**. It currently displays *Price*. Press **F2**. Notice that the insertion point is now positioned at the end of the text in the cell.

11. Use the **Backspace** key to delete the existing text and key **Cost**. Press **Enter**. All the contents in the cell are replaced with the new text you entered, and the cell below, C4, becomes active.

12. Press the **left arrow** two times to move to cell **A4**. Key **6** and press **Enter**. The cell below, A5, becomes active.

13. Key the following numbers, pressing **Enter** after each number. When you are done, your worksheet should look like Figure 16-4.

4

5

7

4

FIGURE 16-4
Worksheet with data entered

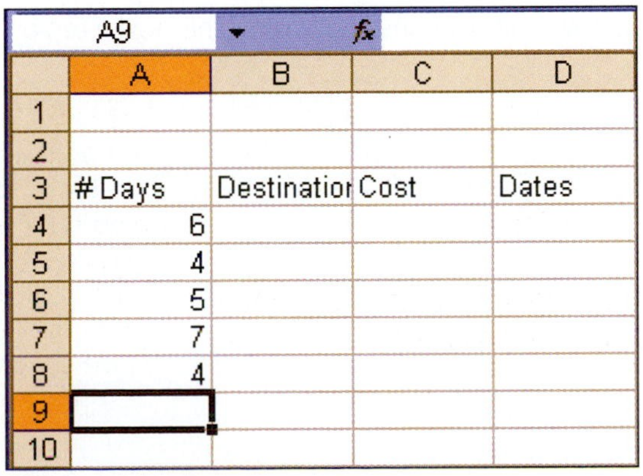

	A	B	C	D
1				
2				
3	# Days	Destination	Cost	Dates
4	6			
5	4			
6	5			
7	7			
8	4			
9				
10				

STEP-BY-STEP 16.2 Continued

14. Click on the column letter to select column **A**. Notice that the column is shaded except for the first cell, which is the active cell now.

15. Click on the row number to select row **4**. Key **7** and notice that this new data replaces the data in the active cell, A4.

16. Click and drag to select the range **A1:B8**. Click elsewhere in the worksheet to deselect the range. Use the Shift key with the arrow keys to experiment with selecting other ranges in the worksheet.

17. Save the worksheet as **Cruises** followed by your initials. Leave the worksheet open for the next Step-by-Step.

> **Note** ☑
>
> If you choose not to enter the data you have keyed, you can press **Esc** or click the **Cancel** button (the red X) in the Formula Bar.

Using the AutoCorrect and AutoComplete Features in Excel

The AutoCorrect feature in Excel corrects common mistakes as you enter data. For example, if you key *hte*, Excel will automatically change the text to read *the*. With the AutoComplete feature, Excel compares the first few characters you key in a cell with existing entries in the same column. If the characters match an existing entry, Excel proposes the existing entry. You can press Enter to accept the proposed entry.

STEP-BY-STEP 16.3

1. Click in cell **B4**. Key **Caribbean** and press **Enter**.

2. Key **Bahamas** in cell B5 and press **Enter**.

3. Key **C**. Notice that Excel suggests *Caribbean* because you entered it earlier in the column. Press **Enter** to accept the proposed text.

4. Key **Alaska** and press **Enter**.

5. Key **Belize adn**. Then look at the active cell as you press **spacebar**. Excel automatically corrects the spelling of *and*. Key **Cozumel** and press **Enter**.

6. Save the changes and leave the worksheet open for the next Step-by-Step.

Inserting and Deleting Rows and Columns

2-3.1.4

When you insert or delete a row or a column in Excel, it affects the entire worksheet. All existing data is shifted in some direction. For example, when you add a new column, the existing data shifts to the right. When you add a new row, the data shifts down a row. One of the beneficial features of Excel is that it automatically updates the cell references whenever you do this. If the data in one cell is dependent on the data in another cell, when these cells are adjusted, Excel will keep straight what information is required where. When you delete rows and columns, the cells and all their contents are removed, and the cell references are also automatically updated.

To insert or delete multiple columns and rows in a single step, select the desired number of columns or rows before executing the command.

STEP-BY-STEP 16.4

1. Select any cell in column **D**. Open the **Insert** menu and click **Columns**. A new column is inserted before column D, and the data that was labeled *Column D* is now labeled *Column E*.

2. Click in cell **D3** and key the column heading **Agent**. Press **Enter**, and then key the following list of travel agent initials in cells D4 through D8. Use Excel's AutoComplete feature to complete repeated entries, and remember to press **Enter** after each entry to move to the next cell in the column.

   JRK

   AMF

   JRK

   AMF

   AMF

3. Select any cell in column D. Open the **Edit** menu and choose **Delete**. The Delete dialog box shown in Figure 16-5 is displayed.

FIGURE 16-5
Delete dialog box

4. Select the option **Entire column** in the dialog box, and then click **OK**. The column of data you just entered is deleted from the worksheet. What was labeled *Column E* is again labeled *Column D*.

5. Click in any cell in row 7. Open the **Insert** menu and choose **Rows**. A new row is inserted above the row you had selected and it becomes row 7. The existing data shifts down, and the row labels are updated to reflect the change.

STEP-BY-STEP 16.4 Continued

6. Key **10** in cell A7 and then key **Panama** in cell B7.

7. Click on the row number for row 8 and drag down to include row 9 in the selection. Both rows should be selected.

8. Open the **Insert** menu and choose **Rows**. Two new rows are inserted above the selected rows.

9. Key the following information in the first two columns of the new rows:

14	**Mediterranean**
4	**Caribbean**

10. Click on the label for row 9. The whole row should be selected. Open the **Edit** menu and choose **Delete**. Because you selected the entire row before choosing the Delete command, the Delete dialog box does not display but the entire row is deleted.

11. Save the changes and leave the workbook open for the next Step-by-Step.

 Working in a Connected World

SIMULATION ANALYSTS

Simulation analysts work with large and small organizations. Their primary job is to investigate different options to determine which would be the best for a particular situation. For instance, health care company administrators might want to implement a new system for filing and processing insurance claims. Before spending a huge amount of money, they may hire a simulation analyst to determine which system would best meet their needs. Perhaps a bank is going to bring in a new system to process checks. It hires an analyst to do simulation modeling of what the system might and might not do.

Simulation analysts work with all types of companies and industries. Some necessary skills include the ability to see detail in a system and to be a good technical writer. The person should be a logical thinker and have good analytical skills. A good memory is an additional asset. Expertise using spreadsheet software, which is often used to calculate the results of different scenarios involving numbers, is also a plus, and analysts may find they need high-security clearance to perform their jobs. A spreadsheet simulation may analyze military air and missile defenses, inputting variables such as number of missiles, location, and time-critical targeting to present multiple warfare scenarios.

Opportunities and the need for simulation analysts are increasing. One of the reasons for the increase is that simulation is being applied to a larger variety of problems by more and more companies. Generally you need at least a bachelor's degree in computer information systems or computer engineering to find a job as a simulation analyst.

2-3.1.4

Changing Column Width and Row Height

Sometimes the data you enter in a cell is wider than the column. When the data is too wide for the cell, Excel displays a series of number signs (####), cuts off the data, or allows the data to run outside of the column, depending on the type of data in the cell. You can widen the column in two ways. You can drag the right edge of the column letter to the desired size. Or, an alternative way to change the column width is to select the cells you want to change and then use the Column command on the Format menu. Then you can select Width from the submenu to specify the exact width, or you can let Excel find the best fit by clicking the AutoFit Selection option on the same submenu. Likewise, you can change the height of a row to meet the requirements of the data within the row.

Computer Concepts

In Excel, the number that appears in the Standard column width box is the average number of digits 0-9 that fit in a cell. The default unit of measurement for row height is points, the same measurement used to indicate font size. There are 72 points in 1 inch.

STEP-BY-STEP 16.5

1. Point to the boundary on the right side of the column letter B. When the pointer changes to a double-headed arrow, drag the boundary to the right about one-half inch to widen the column. Figure 16-6 illustrates how you can drag a column boundary to change the column width.

Note

You can also find the best fit by positioning the mouse pointer on the right edge of the column letter and double-clicking when the double-headed arrow appears.

FIGURE 16-6
Dragging a column boundary to change the column width

Drag the column border to resize a column

	A	B	C	D
1				
2				
3	# Days	Destination	Cost	Dates
4	7	Caribbean		
5	4	Bahamas		
6	5	Caribbean		
7	10	Panama		
8	14	Mediterranean		
9	7	Alaska		
10	4	Belize and Cozumel		
11				
12				

Width: 15.43 (113 pixels)

B11

2. Click the column letter **B** to select the entire column.

3. Open the **Format** menu and choose **Column**, then select **AutoFit Selection** in the submenu. Excel automatically adjusts the cells in the column to fit the cell with the most content—in this case, *Belize and Cozumel.*

4. Click the row heading **3** to select the entire row.

5. Open the **Format** menu and choose **Row**. Select **Height** and change the height to **25**. Click **OK**.

STEP-BY-STEP 16.5 Continued

6. Observe the change in row 3. The row is now about twice as high as the other rows.

7. Click anywhere in the worksheet to deselect the row. Save the changes and leave the worksheet open for the next Step-by-Step.

Working with Data in Worksheet Cells

Sometimes after entering data in a worksheet, you need to reorganize it. You may even want to remove some of the data and not replace it. Or, you may want to move or copy existing data from one location to another. Excel also offers a way to fill an entire column or row with the same data repeated in each cell, with a feature called AutoFill.

You can edit, replace, or clear existing data in the worksheet cells. You learned in Step-by-Step 16.2 that you can edit the data directly in the cell, or you can make the necessary changes to the cell contents in the Formula Bar. To replace cell contents, you can select the cell and key the new data. If you want to clear the cell contents but not replace it with other data, select the cell and then press the Delete key or the Backspace key.

Clearing and Deleting Data

The process for deleting data can be as simple as pressing the Delete or Backspace keys. When you delete the contents of a cell this way, the formats for the cell remain in the cell. Therefore, if you enter new data in the cell, the existing formats will apply to the new contents. (You will learn about formatting cells in the next section of this lesson.)

If you want to remove the contents and the formats, you need to clear the cell. Clearing the cell leaves a blank cell in the worksheet. You can clear the contents and the formats from the cell, clear just the contents, or clear just the formats.

When you use the delete feature, you remove the cell entirely. With the delete feature, you have four options. You can delete an entire row or an entire column. Or you can delete just a single cell and then shift the cells to the left or shift the cells up. Likewise, you can insert a single cell and shift the surrounding cells to the right or down. However, use caution when using the shift feature. The results may misalign data in your rows and columns.

Copying and Moving Data

Copying data saves you from having to key the same data into another location. The process, as in all Office applications, is easy. First, you must copy the data from one location. To copy the data, select it and then click the Copy button on the Standard toolbar. The data is placed in the Clipboard, a temporary storage location in your computer's memory. Then, select the destination cell where you want to place the data, and paste the data into the new location. The data remains in the Clipboard.

Moving data is similar to copying data, except you cut the data from one location and paste it in the destination location. When you move or copy all the data in a cell, the formats are also moved or copied. Unlike a word-processing table, if you move data to a cell that already has data in it, that data doesn't move to make room for the new data. If you don't want to lose information, you have to move data into empty cells; otherwise, the data in the destination cells will be replaced.

You can copy or move multiple cells of data at the same time. First select the range, then click the Copy or Cut button. Select the first cell in the destination range and click the Paste button.

Using AutoFill

The AutoFill command is another time-saving feature that enables you to copy data from one cell to another. AutoFill also provides several options for entering certain series of data, such as months or days of the week.

> **Note**
>
> If you want to add the same contents to multiple cells, you can select all the cells before you enter the content. After you key the content, press **Ctrl + Enter**. The content you keyed will then be entered into each of the selected cells.

Filling data is another method for copying data in a worksheet. It is faster than copying and pasting because filling requires only one step. However, the Fill command can only be used when the destination cells are adjacent to the original cell. You can fill data up or down in the same column, or right or left in the same row.

STEP-BY-STEP 16.6

1. Click in cell **A8**. The cell currently displays *14*. Press **Delete** to remove the contents.

2. With cell A8 still selected, key **10** and press **Enter**.

3. Click in cell **B6**. Open the **Edit** menu and choose **Delete**. The Delete dialog box will open. Select **Shift cells up** and then click **OK**. The contents in cells B7, B8, and B9 are shifted one cell up.

4. Open the **Insert** menu and choose **Cells**. The Insert dialog box is displayed. Select **Shift cells down** and then click **OK**. The contents in cells B6 through B8 are each shifted down one cell and there is now a new empty cell B6.

5. Click in cell **B4**. Click the **Copy** button on the Standard toolbar. The contents of the cell (*Caribbean*) are copied to the Clipboard. Also, an animated border (a dotted-line marquee) is displayed around the selected cell as shown in Figure 16-7.

> **Note**
>
> If you want to see the objects on the Clipboard, select **Office Clipboard** from the **Edit** menu, or press **Ctrl + C** two times to open the Clipboard pane in Excel. However, you do not have to have the Clipboard pane open to copy and paste data.

STEP-BY-STEP 16.6 Continued

FIGURE 16-7
Marquee around a selected cell

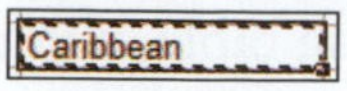

6. Click in cell **B6**. Then click the **Paste** button on the Standard toolbar. The copied data is pasted in the destination cell.

7. Press **Esc** to remove the marquee around the copied cell.

8. Click in cell **D3**. The cell currently displays *Dates*. Open the **Edit** menu and click **Cut**. The contents of the cell are stored in the Clipboard and a marquee appears around the cell border.

9. Click in cell **E3**, and then click the **Paste** button on the Standard toolbar. The contents that were cut from cell D3 have been moved to cell E3.

10. Click in cell **D3** to make it the active cell and then key **Vacancy**.

11. Select cell **D4** and key **Yes**.

12. Position your mouse pointer over the small square in the bottom right corner of the active cell. This square, shown in Figure 16-8, is called the ***fill handle***. When you point to the fill handle, the pointer changes to a bold plus sign.

FIGURE 16-8
Fill handle in a selected cell

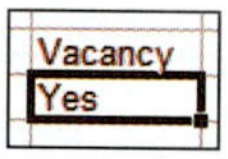

13. Drag the fill handle down to cell D8. The range of cells D4:D8 is selected. A ScreenTip displays the cell contents that will be copied to the range of cells.

14. Release the mouse button, and the contents of D4 (*Yes*) now appear in cells D5 through D8.

15. Click in cell D10 and key **No**. Then point to the fill handle. Drag up to select cell **D9**. When you release, the cell contents from D10 (*No*) are copied to cell D9.

16. Deselect the cells and save the changes. Leave the workbook open for the next Step-by-Step.

> **Note**
>
> To quickly fill to the right, click in the destination cell and press the shortcut keys **Ctrl + R**. This copies the contents of the cell at left to the destination cell. To quickly fill down, click in the destination cell and press the shortcut keys **Ctrl + D**. The contents of the cell above will be copied. To fill multiple cells, select the cell containing the contents, and then drag to create a range of cells before pressing the shortcut keys.

Formatting the Contents of a Cell

2-3.1.5
2-3.1.6
2-3.1.7

Formatting the contents of a cell, like formatting in other Windows applications, changes the way it appears. For example, you may want to change the alignment of the text or use commas in numbers to separate the thousands. To apply formats, you must first select the cell(s) containing the data to be formatted.

Changing Fonts and Font Sizes and Align Text

You learned in the lessons about Word that a *font* is the design of the typeface in your document. Fonts are available in a variety of styles and sizes, and you can use multiple fonts in one document. The font size is a measurement in points that determines the height of the font. Bold, italic, underline, and color formats can also add emphasis to the contents of a cell. By default, Excel aligns text at the left of the cell and numbers at the right of the cell. However, you can change the alignment.

Computer Concepts

When you clear the contents of a cell, the formats applied to the contents of that cell are not removed. To remove the formats without removing the data, choose **Clear** from the **Edit** menu and select **Formats** in the submenu.

Note

To change the font color, choose **Cells** from the **Format** menu, and then click on the **Font** tab, or click the **Font Color** button on the Formatting toolbar.

S TEP-BY-STEP 16.7

1. Click in cell **A3**, and then drag to the right to select a range of cells containing the other four cells in the same row (B3, C3, D3, and E3). The range A3:E3 is selected.

2. Click the **Italic** button on the Formatting toolbar. The text in each of the cells is formatted with the italic attribute.

3. With the cells still selected, click the **down arrow** at the right of the **Font** box on the Formatting toolbar. Scroll down and select **Times New Roman**.

4. With the cells still selected, click the **down arrow** at the right of the **Font Size** box. Select **14**.

5. With the cells still selected, click the **Center** button on the Formatting toolbar. Each of the labels in the row is centered.

6. Click in cell **A4** and drag down to cell **B10** to select a range of cells. Click the **Center** button.

7. Select **column D** and then click the **Center** button on the **Formatting** toolbar. Notice that the contents of cells D4 through D10 changed from left alignment to center alignment, but the text in D3 did not change because it was already formatted with center alignment in step 5.

8. Deselect the cells and save the changes. Leave the worksheet open for the next Step-by-Step.

Adding Shading and Borders to Cells

You can highlight a cell, a row of cells, or a column with color, shading, or borders. Select the cells you want to format, and then open the Format Cells dialog box. You can access this dialog box by selecting Cells from the Format menu. The Format Cells dialog box has six tabs, including Number, Alignment, Font, Border, Patterns, and Protection. Use the Patterns tab to add a fill color or shading pattern to cells. The Border tab gives you options for outlining a cell or range of cells.

Note

Ctrl + 1 is a shortcut for accessing the Format Cells dialog box. You can also access the Format Cells dialog box by right-clicking an active cell or range and then selecting **Format Cells** in the shortcut menu.

Formatting Numbers and Dates

Generally, numbers are displayed with no formatting and are aligned at the right side of a cell. However, dates and times are automatically formatted in the default styles dd-mmm (date, month) and hh:mm (hour:minute), respectively. You can change the format of any number data by selecting the cells and then selecting options from the Number tab of the Format Cells dialog box.

Format Painter

You can use the Format Painter to copy the format of a worksheet cell without copying the contents of the cell. For example, after formatting one cell as a date, you may format other cells for dates by painting the format. To paint a format, select a cell that has the format you want to use. Click the Format Painter button on the toolbar, and then select the range of cells that you would like to format in the same way.

Computer Concepts

After changing the font or font size of cell contents, you may find it necessary to adjust the column width, even if you previously used the AutoFit feature.

STEP-BY-STEP 16.8

1. Click in cell **C4** and key **599**, then press **Enter**. Notice that the numbers are automatically aligned at the right edge of the cell.

2. Key the following numbers, pressing **Enter** after each number:

   299

   399

   799

   999

   899

   399

3. Click in cell **C4** (599) and use **Shift + down arrow** to select the range C4:C10.

4. Open the **Format** menu and choose **Cells**. If necessary, click the **Number** tab in the Format Cells dialog box that displays.

Note

You can magnify or reduce the view of the worksheet by using the **Zoom** button on the Standard toolbar. The default magnification is 100 percent. To get a closer view, select a larger percentage from the drop-down list or key in your own percentage and click **Enter**.

STEP-BY-STEP 16.8 Continued

5. Under Category, select **Currency**. The dialog box changes to display the currency format options, as shown in Figure 16-9.

FIGURE 16-9
Currency format options in the Format Cells dialog box

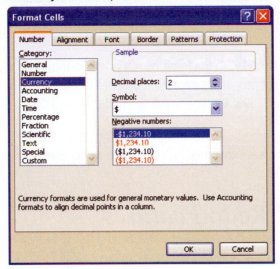

6. In the Decimal places box, click the down arrow until **0** is displayed. Click **OK**. The numbers are all formatted with dollar signs.

7. Click in cell **E4**. Key **March 3** and press Enter. Notice that Excel automatically changed the format to *3-Mar*. Click in cell E4 to select it again.

8. Open the **Format** menu and choose **Cells**. Because you just accessed it, the Number tab should be displayed, but if necessary, select the Number tab.

9. Under **Category**, select **Date**. Under **Type**, select **3/14/01** (not *3/14/2001). Click **OK**. The date format in cell E4 changes.

10. Click the Format Painter button on the toolbar. Notice that the dotted-line marquee appears around the active cell.

11. Click in cell **E5** and drag down to cell **E10**. When you release the mouse button, the format from E4 will be copied to E5 through E10. Notice there is no content in the cell—you copied only the formatting.

12. Enter the following dates in cells E5 through E10, pressing **Enter** after each date. The dates are automatically formatted with the date format used in cell E4.

   3/10
   3/18
   3/25
   3/31
   4/5
   4/9

STEP-BY-STEP 16.8 Continued

13. Select the cell range **A3:E3** and open the **Format Cells** dialog box. (*Hint:* Right-click the selected cells and then click **Format Cells** in the shortcut menu.) Click the **Patterns** tab and choose a light pink fill color. Click **OK** to apply the fill color and close the dialog box.

14. With the same cell range still selected, open the **Format Cells** dialog box again and click the **Border** tab. Click the **Outline** button to add an outside border to the cell range and then click **OK** to apply the border.

15. Select the cell range **D9:D10**. In the Patterns tab of the Format Cells dialog box, click the **down arrow** next to the **Pattern** list box and select **25% Gray**. (A ScreenTip appears when you rest the mouse pointer on each pattern; find the one in the top row that says *25% Gray*.) Click **OK** to apply the gray shading.

16. Deselect the cells and save the changes. Leave the worksheet open for the next Step-by-Step.

The Undo and Redo Features

I f you make a mistake, or if you change your mind, you can use the Undo command to reverse your most recent changes. If you undo an action and then change your mind, you can reverse the undo action by using the Redo command. You can undo and redo multiple actions at one time by choosing from the Undo or Redo drop-down lists on the Standard toolbar, just as you did in Word. When you undo or redo an action from the drop-down list, Excel will also undo or redo all the actions listed above it on the list.

> **Computer Concepts**
>
> There is a limit of 16 actions that you can undo and redo. Furthermore, the Undo and Redo actions are cleared from the drop-down list when you save the worksheet. Therefore, you should always undo an action as soon as you realize you have made a mistake.

S TEP-BY-STEP 16.9

1. Click in cell **A11**. Key **4** and press **Tab**.

2. Key **Baja California** and press **Tab**.

3. Key **299** and press **Tab**.

4. Key **Yes** and press **Tab**.

5. Key **4/2** and press **Enter**. (Notice that the format remains 2-Apr, because you only copied the date format in cell E4 down to cell E10.)

6. Click the **Undo** button on the Standard toolbar. The date is removed.

7. Click the **down arrow** to the right of the **Undo** button. The Undo list is displayed.

STEP-BY-STEP 16.9 Continued

8. Click on the third action in the list (*Typing "Baja California" in B11*) to undo the last three actions. Cells B11 through D11 are empty now.

9. Click the **down arrow** to the right of the **Redo** button on the Standard toolbar to display the Redo list. Click on the fourth action in the list to redo all four. The content in cells B11, C11, D11, and E11 is restored. Format cell E11 so the date format is the same as in the cells above it.

> **Note**
>
> If the Redo button is not displayed on the Standard toolbar, click the **Toolbar Options** button (the **down arrow** at the right side of the toolbar) and then click the **Redo** button.

10. Save the changes and close the worksheet. Follow your instructor's directions about turning off your computer.

SUMMARY

In this lesson, you learned:

■ The Excel screen has its own unique screen parts, menus, and toolbars.

■ To enter data in a cell, the cell must be selected. You can use the mouse or the keyboard to move from one cell to another.

■ As you enter data, Excel will automatically correct some of your keyboarding errors. If the data you are entering matches characters of existing entries, Excel will propose the existing entry to save you time.

■ When you insert or delete rows and columns, all existing data is shifted up, down, left, or right.

■ There are several options for changing the column width. You can drag a column border, use the AutoFit feature, or specify an exact measurement.

■ To reorganize a worksheet, you can delete, clear, copy, or move the data.

■ The AutoFill command enables you to copy data from one cell to another or enter certain series of data such as months or days of the week.

■ When you format the contents of a cell, you change the appearance of the text or numbers in the cell.

■ The Undo command reverses a previous action. The Redo command reverses an undo.

VOCABULARY *Review*

Define the following terms:

Active cell	Filling	Workbook
Cell reference	Range	Worksheet
Fill handle		

REVIEW *Questions*

TRUE/FALSE

Circle T if the statement is true or F if the statement is false.

T F **1.** A worksheet is the same as a spreadsheet.

T F **2.** Within the worksheet, the mouse pointer displays as a hand with a pointing finger.

T F **3.** When data is too wide for a cell, the part of the data that will not fit is automatically deleted.

T F **4.** By default, text aligns at the left of a cell.

T F **5.** The AutoComplete feature fills a column or row with the data in the first cell automatically.

MATCHING

Match the correct term in Column 2 to its description in Column 1.

Column 1	**Column 2**
___ 1. Identifies the column letter and row number	A. active cell
___ 2. The selected cell where you can enter data	B. Cells
	C. AutoFit
___ 3. A selected group of cells	D. cell reference
___ 4. The command on the Format menu used to change a date format	E. range
___ 5. Automatically adjusts column width to display data in cells	

PROJECTS

PROJECT 16-1

1. If necessary, launch Excel. If Excel is already launched, click the **New Button** on the Standard toolbar to create a new worksheet.

2. In cell A1, key **Running vs. Walking** and press **Enter**.

3. Beginning in cell A3, key the data shown below. If you would like, you can use AutoComplete to help you complete the entries, but you will then have to edit the entry to change *stroll* to **brisk** in the second entry. Do not be concerned if the columns are too narrow for the content. You will fix that in the next step.

Activity	Speed	Calories/Hour
Walking (stroll)	**2 mph**	120
Walking (brisk)	**3.5 mph**	360
Jogging	**4 mph**	600
Running (moderate)	**10 mph**	1020

4. Save the worksheet as **Exercise** followed by your initials.

5. Adjust the column widths to display all text.

6. Center the content in cells A3:C3. Format the range of cells with a fill color of your choice.

7. Edit the speed for Jogging to **5 mph**. In cell A1, change the word *vs.* to **versus**.

8. Undo the last change.

9. Format the text in cell A1 as **16-point bold**. Format the range A3:C3 as **12-point bold italic**. (Adjust cell widths as necessary after changing the text size.)

10. Insert a row between rows 5 and 6 and enter the following data in columns A through C in the new row:

Walking (fast)	5 mph	480

11. Select the cell range A4:C8 and change the font to Times New Roman. Make the font color red.

12. Select the cell range **B4:B8** and center the content.

13. Select the cell range **C4:C8** and apply the **Number** format with the 1000 separator and no decimal places.

14. Save the changes and close the worksheet.

PROJECT 16-2

1. Open **Project16-2** from the data files. Save the worksheet as **Mensa Groups** followed by your initials.

2. Select column **A** and change the column width to **25** characters wide.

3. Select cell **A1** and change the font to **14 pt blue**.

4. Use AutoFit to make columns B and C wide enough to view all the text.

5. Select row 4 and change the font to **12 pt bold**.

6. Center the text in row 4 and then center the entries in column C.

7. Add a new column between columns B and C.

8. Key **Membership** in cell C4 in the new column and then enter the following data in the rest of the cells in the column. Remember to press **Enter** after each entry.
   133
   203
   377
   114
   177
   225
   344
   161
   185
   267
   336
   97

9. Change the format of the Membership column data to display **0** decimals.

10. Click in cell **A2**. Change the date format to the **March-01** style. Add the **bold** and **italic** formats and **center** the text in the cell.

11. Add a column after column D with information about when the groups meet. All the groups meet biweekly except the Lubbock and Memphis groups, which meet monthly. Use the heading "Meetings" and format it like the other column heads, increasing the column width if necessary to accommodate the heading. Use AutoFill to enter the data in this column and then apply center alignment.

12. Save your changes and close the worksheet. Follow your instructor's directions about turning off your computer.

 TEAMWORK PROJECT

Worksheets are excellent tools to organize information so you can make easy comparisons between sets of data. For this project, assume you need to set up a home office with new communications equipment. Because you're not yet sure of your budget, you need several price options for each piece of equipment. With a teammate, gather and organize information as follows:

1. Identify a list of at least 16 pieces of equipment that a state-of-the-art home office needs. Some of these may be a desktop computer, scanner, printer, fax (or all-in-one unit that includes scanning, copying, printing, and faxing functions), cordless phone, answering machine, and so on.

2. Create a worksheet to store the list of equipment you decide on. Create column headings for "Low End," Moderate," and "High End" so that you can store three prices for each equipment item.

3. Using computer catalogs or Web resources, find low-end, moderate, and high-end options for each equipment item. For example, low-end options for a copier would include 3 pages per minute and black and white copies. Moderate options for a copier would include 8 pages per minute and an automatic document feeder. High-end options would include 12 pages per minute, color copies, and zoom capability. Divide the research work so that you find information on half of the items and your teammate finds information on the other half. Key your results in one worksheet.

4. Format the worksheet so that you can clearly see all data you have entered. Highlight cells, rows, or columns with color fill, shading, or borders to indicate the items you think are most important. Compare your worksheet with those of other teams to see what equipment items are considered most important for a home office.

CRITICAL *Thinking*

ACTIVITY 16-1

While formatting a worksheet, you have changed the default font in a few cell ranges from Arial to Times New Roman. Selecting each cell range is tedious, however. Is there a way you can select an entire worksheet and apply a new font to all cells at one time? Use the Help files in Excel to find the answer and then write a brief report on what you learn.

ORGANIZING WORKSHEETS

<table>
<tr><td>

OBJECTIVES

Upon completion of this lesson, you should be able to:

- Merge cells.

- Fill a data series in adjacent cells.

- Use AutoFormat to format a worksheet.

- Create multiple worksheets.

- Sort data in a worksheet.

- Change the page setup.

- Add headers and footers to a worksheet.

- Preview and print a worksheet.

Estimated Time: 1 hour

</td><td>

VOCABULARY

Ascending order

Descending order

Gridlines

Header row

Merge

</td></tr>
</table>

A key feature of Microsoft Excel is the ease with which you can change and organize the data in a worksheet. You can change the appearance of the spreadsheet to emphasize specific data using formatting or sort the information to highlight significant data. You will also find it useful to print completed worksheets and there are many options you can use to make your printed spreadsheets intelligible and professional looking.

Merging Cells

2-3.17

There will be times when you want text to span across several columns or rows. To do this, you can merge cells. When you *merge* cells, you combine several cells into a single cell. You can use merged cells to create a title or other informational text for your worksheet. The Merge and Center button on the Formatting toolbar automatically centers the text in merged cells.

S TEP-BY-STEP 17.1

1. Open file **Step17-1** from the data files. Save the worksheet as **Tallest Structures** followed by your initials. (*Note*: The worksheets in this lesson contain data about the tallest manmade towers and buildings in the world. These lists are not intended to be official, and the data contained in them may be inaccurate or out of date.)

2. Select cells **A1:D1**.

3. Click the **Merge and Center** button on the Formatting toolbar. Excel combines the four cells into a single cell (A1).

4. Key **Tallest Manmade Structures in the World**, and then press **Enter**.

5. Click in cell **A1** to select it again. Change the font to **Times New Roman** and change the font size to **16**.

6. With the cell still selected, click the **Bold** button on the Formatting toolbar.   **B**

7. With the cell still selected, click the **down arrow** to the right of the **Fill Color** button on the Formatting toolbar and select the color **Light Green**.

8. Select the range **D4:D24** and open the Format Cells dialog box. (*Hint*: Right-click the selected range and choose **Format Cells** from the shortcut menu.)

9. Click the **Number** tab if necessary and then click in the check box by the option *Use 1000 separator (,)* to add a comma to the numeric data in this column. Click **OK** to close the dialog box and apply the format.

10. Deselect the range and save the changes. Leave the worksheet open for the next Step-by-Step.

 Ethics in Technology

COMPUTER VIRUSES

The word "viruses" can put fear into anyone who uses the Internet or exchanges files on disk or via e-mail. How can such a small word cause such fear? It is because a virus can cause tremendous damage to your computer files!

A *virus* is simply a computer program that is intentionally written to attach itself to other programs or disk boot sectors and duplicates itself whenever those programs are executed or the infected disks are accessed. A virus can wipe out all of the files that are on your computer. Viruses can exist on your computer for weeks or months and not cause any damage until a predetermined date or time code is activated. Not all viruses cause damage. Some are just pranks; maybe your desktop will display some silly message. Viruses are created by persons who are impressed with the power they possess because of their expertise in the area of computers, and sometimes they create them just for fun.

To protect your computer from virus damage, install an antivirus software program on your computer and keep it running at all times so that it can continuously scan for viruses.

Entering Data with the AutoFill Command

2-3.1.3

Y ou've seen how Excel will fill adjacent cells with the same content. The AutoFill command will also allow you to fill a series of numbers and increase or decrease the cell contents in increments based on the pattern of the original contents. In the following exercise, you will use the Excel Help feature to find out more about what AutoFill can do.

S TEP-BY-STEP 17.2

1. Click **Microsoft Excel Help** on the **Help** menu to open the **Excel Help** task pane.

2. Key **fill** in the Search for text box.

3. Click the **Start searching** button (the green arrow to the right of the text box) to display a list of links in the Search Results task pane, similar to Figure 17-1.

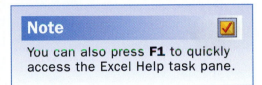

> **Note**
>
> You can also press **F1** to quickly access the Excel Help task pane.

FIGURE 17-1
Search Results task pane in Microsoft Excel Help

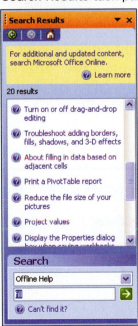

4. Scroll down if necessary so you can click the link **About filling in data based on adjacent cells**.

5. Read the information under the heading *Fill in a series of numbers, dates, or other items* and look at the examples of series that can be extended. The examples illustrate that you can fill times, days of the week, months, quarters, and text. Notice, too, that if the initial selection includes the months January and April, the extended series will indicate a span of four months. (July is the third month after April, and October is the third month after July.)

6. Click the **Close** button in the upper-right corner of the screen to close the Help screen and then click the **Close** button in the Search Results task pane to close the pane.

AutoFill Options

In Lesson 16, you used the fill handle on a cell to copy the same data into several cells. You may have noticed as you released the mouse button after dragging the fill handle that a small button appeared below and to the right of the fill handle. This is the AutoFill Options button. When you point to the AutoFill Options button, the button expands to show a down arrow. If you click the down arrow, a shortcut menu appears with options to copy the content of the cells, fill the selected cells with formatting only, or fill the cells without the formatting. Figure 17-2 shows the AutoFill Options button with its shortcut menu open.

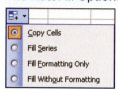

FIGURE 17-2
The AutoFill Options button and shortcut menu

Fill a Data Series in Adjacent Cells

You can use the AutoFill feature to quickly fill in a series of numbers and dates. To fill in a series, a pattern must be established in the initial selection of cells. Then when you drag the fill handle, the pattern is continued. When you drag the fill handle down or to the right, the series increases. However, if you drag the fill handle up or to the left, the series will decrease. If you select a range of cells that include data in a new series and then click the down button on the AutoFill Options button, a new option called Fill Series will be available and selected in the menu. This option is now available because the selected cells indicate a pattern.

S TEP-BY-STEP 17.3

1. Insert a column before the Building column and enter **Ranking** as the heading in cell A3.

2. Click cell **A4**. Key **1** and then press **Enter**.

3. Cell A5 is now the active cell. Key **2** and press **Enter**. You have now established a pattern where your numbers increase in increments of **1**.

4. Select cells **A4** and **A5**, and then click the **Center** button to center the cell contents.

5. With the cells still selected, point to the fill handle at the bottom of cell A5. When the pointer changes to a bold plus sign, drag down to cell **A18** to select a range of cells. Notice the ScreenTip indicates what will appear in each cell as you drag down. When you release the mouse button, Excel fills the cells with the numbers 3 through 15 and you see the AutoFill Options button.

6. Notice that the numbers in the cells are centered because the AutoFill default option fills the series and copies the formatting. Click the **AutoFill Options** button and you will see the Fill Series button is selected on the shortcut menu. Click the **Fill Without Formatting** option and the numbers in cells 3 through 15 are now aligned at right within the cells (the default format for numbers).

STEP-BY-STEP 17.3 Continued

7. Select cells **A4** and **A5** again and fill cells A6 to A24. The default option Fill Series once again fills the numbers and formats them according to the selected cells, so you will see the numbers 3 through 21 centered in the cells.

8. Deselect the cells. Then, select cells **A4:A22** and press **Delete**.

9. Select cells **A23** and **A24**. Point to the fill handle at the bottom-right corner of cell A24 and drag up to cell A4. The cells will fill with a series of numbers in decreasing order from 21 through 1.

10. Deselect the cells. Notice that in rows 7 and 8, the towers are exactly the same height. Click in cell **A8** and change the ranking from 5 to **4** and press **Enter**.

11. Save the changes and leave the workbook open for the next Step-by-Step.

Applying AutoFormats

Excel offers numerous AutoFormats that you can use to give your worksheet a professional look. These AutoFormats instantly format the entire worksheet with borders, shading, and data formatting. To apply an AutoFormat, you must first select the range to be formatted. The AutoFormat may override existing formats that you have applied. If desired, you can modify the formats after they are applied.

STEP-BY-STEP 17.4

1. Select all the range of cells **A3:E24**. (*Hint:* Click in the left corner of cell A3 and drag down to cell E24.)

2. Open the **Format** menu and choose **AutoFormat**. The dialog box shown in Figure 17-3 is displayed.

FIGURE 17-3
AutoFormat dialog box

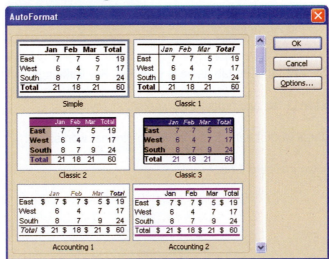

STEP-BY-STEP 17.4 Continued

3. Scroll down and select the **List 2** option. Click **OK**. Notice the font attributes, shading, and borders that have been applied to the worksheet. The bands of shading in the body of the spreadsheet help to draw your eye across the rows so you can read associated data a little more easily now. You may also see that the title of the worksheet is obviously no longer centered over the data since the new column was added at the left of the worksheet.

4. Select cells **A1** and **B1** and then click the **Merge and Center** button on the Formatting toolbar to center the title over the entire worksheet. (You may need to click **Merge and Center** twice to center the title.)

5. Deselect the cell and save the changes. Keep the worksheet open for the next Step-by-Step.

Creating Multiple Worksheets

2-3.1.4

Whenever you open a new worksheet in Excel, you automatically open a workbook with three sheets (or worksheets) in it. In Excel, the document you create is called a workbook, and each workbook contains the individual worksheets—just as a notebook contains many sheets of paper. To switch to a different worksheet, simply click on the worksheet tab at the bottom of the screen.

Excel automatically assigns the name Sheet and a sequential number to each new worksheet. If desired, you can rename the worksheet. You can also add additional worksheets to a workbook or remove unnecessary ones.

STEP-BY-STEP 17.5

1. Click the **Sheet2** tab at the bottom of the screen as shown in Figure 17-4. A new blank worksheet is displayed.

FIGURE 17-4
Worksheet tabs

2. Double-click the **Sheet2** tab. The tab name is selected. Key **Buildings** and press **Enter**.

3. Double-click the **Sheet1** tab and rename the worksheet **Towers**.

4. Click on the **Buildings** worksheet tab to switch back to that worksheet.

5. Enter the data shown in Figure 17-5.

STEP-BY-STEP 17.5 Continued

FIGURE 17-5
Data for Buildings worksheet

Building	Location	Height in Feet	# Stories
Empire State Building	New York, USA	1,250	102
Sears Tower	Illinois, USA	1,454	110
Bank of China Tower	Hong Kong, PRC	1,209	70
Central Plaza	Hong Kong, PRC	1,227	78
Petronas Tower 2	Kuala Lumpur, Malaysia	1,483	88
Petronas Tower 1	Kuala Lumpur, Malaysia	1,483	88
Jin Mao Building	Shanghai, PRC	1,379	88
The Centre	Hong Kong, PRC	1,149	73
Emirates Tower #1	Dubai, UAE	1,149	54

6. Center and bold the column headings and center the numbers in the third column. Select all four columns and then format the columns using the AutoFit Selection command.

7. Click the **Sheet3** tab. Click the **Edit** menu and select **Delete Sheet**. The unused sheet is deleted.

> **Note**
>
> An alternative way to rename a worksheet is to right-click the worksheet tab, select **Rename** in the shortcut menu, key the new name, and press **Enter**.

8. Open the **Insert** menu and select **Worksheet**. A new worksheet, automatically named **Sheet1**, is inserted.

9. Rename the new worksheet **Sheet3**.

10. Save the changes and leave the workbook open for the next Step-by-Step.

2-3.2.1

Sorting Data

You can quickly sort data in a worksheet. To sort Excel data, you must indicate the column you want to base your sort on. The information in that column will be sorted, and all the data in corresponding rows will also move appropriately. Excel lets you sort alphabetically or numerically. *Ascending order* sorts alphabetically from A to Z or numerically from the lowest to the highest number. *Descending order* sorts alphabetically from Z to A or numerically from the highest to the lowest number.

Excel has two toolbar buttons (Sort Ascending and Sort Descending) that make sorting quick and easy. You simply click in the column you want to sort by and then click one of the sort buttons. Excel will automatically determine if you have a *header row* (headings at the top of your columns), and it will not include this row in the sort.

> **Computer Concepts**
>
> The Sort buttons are available on both the Standard toolbar and the Formatting toolbar in Excel.

> **Note**
>
> If the Sorting Ascending and Sort Descending buttons are not displayed on the Standard toolbar, click the **Toolbar Options** arrows at the right side of the toolbar and then select the Sort button you want.

If you have a worksheet with multiple columns of data, you can base the sort on data in three different columns. For example, you can sort the Buildings worksheet first by height, then by building name, and then by city. When you want to sort by multiple criteria, you must open the Sort dialog box, which is available on the Data menu in Excel.

STEP-BY-STEP 17.6

1. Switch to the **Buildings** worksheet.

2. Click in any cell in column **A**. Then click the **Sort Ascending** button on the Standard or Formatting toolbar. The building names are arranged in ascending alphabetical order, and the data in the other columns moves with the building name.

3. Click the **Sort Descending** button. The building names are now arranged in descending alphabetical order, and the building data again moves with the building name.

4. Open the **Data** menu and choose Sort. All the data in the worksheet (except the headings) is selected and the dialog box shown in Figure 17-6 is displayed.

FIGURE 17-6
Sort dialog box

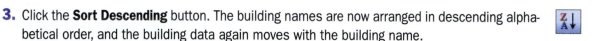

5. Select **Height in Feet** in the list box under Sort by. If necessary, select **Descending** at the right of the Sort by option.

6. Click the **down arrow** in the list box under the first Then by option. Select **Location** and then, if necessary, select **Ascending** at the right of the Then by option.

7. Click the **down arrow** in the list box under the second Then by option. Select **Building** and then, if necessary, select **Ascending** at the right of the Then by option.

8. Click **OK**. The worksheet data is rearranged from highest to lowest height in column C. If any two buildings are the same height, they are sorted in alphabetical order by the city. If the two buildings are in the same location, they are sorted in alphabetical order by building name.

9. Save the changes and leave the workbook open for the next Step-by-Step.

Printing a Worksheet

2-1.4.1
2-1.4.3
2-1.4.4

Before you print the worksheet, you will want to look at it in Print Preview. Print Preview enables you to preview the worksheet on the screen to see what it will look like when it is printed. This can save you time and paper. If the worksheet does not display correctly on the page, you can make adjustments in the Page Setup dialog box.

Changing the Page Setup

If the worksheet is large and the columns or rows wrap to a second page, you can sometimes fit the worksheet on one page by changing the page orientation. Recall that in Lesson 13 you learned that *portrait* orientation formats the content of the document with the short edge of the page at the top. This is the default setting. You can change to *landscape* orientation in the

> **Note** ✓
>
> The page setup settings apply only to the current worksheet. They do not apply to all the worksheets in the workbook.

Page Setup dialog box. Landscape orientation formats the document sideways with the long edge of the page at the top.

Another option for fitting the worksheet on one page is to turn on the Fit to command. This feature scales the worksheet up or down as necessary so it fits on the number of pages you designate.

S TEP-BY-STEP 17.7

1. Switch to the **Towers** worksheet.

2. Click the **Print Preview** button on the Standard toolbar. Click the **Next** button on the Print Preview toolbar to see the column on the second page. Notice that the *Height in Feet* column displays on page 2. (This was indicated in the worksheet itself by the dotted line between columns D and E.)

3. Click the **Close** button in the toolbar at the top of the screen to close Print Preview.

> **Note** ✓
>
> If your worksheet appears on one page, this may be because landscape orientation has already been selected in the Page Setup dialog box, or scaling has been adjusted to fit the worksheet on one page. Try clicking the **Portrait** option before going on with the steps in this excercise.

STEP-BY-STEP 17.7 Continued

4. Open the **File** menu and choose **Page Setup**. If necessary, click the **Page** tab to display the dialog box shown in Figure 17-7.

FIGURE 17-7
Page tab in the Page Setup dialog box

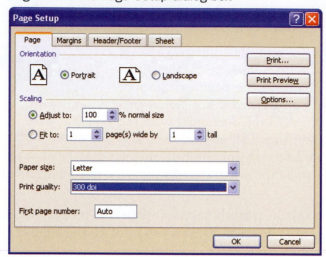

5. Note that the Scaling is set at *Adjust to: 100% normal size* by default. Turn on the **Fit to** option in the Scaling section and accept the default settings of 1 page wide by 1 page tall.

6. Click **OK**. The dialog box closes and you return to the worksheet. (Notice that the dotted line no longer appears between columns D and E.)

7. Click the **Print Preview** button again. The worksheet appears slightly smaller than it was, but all the columns now fit on one page, as shown in Figure 17-8.

STEP-BY-STEP 17.7 Continued

FIGURE 17-8
Worksheet in portrait orientation and scaled to fit

8. Click the **Setup** button on the Print Preview toolbar to open the Page Setup dialog box. On the Page tab, select **Landscape** in the Orientation section.

9. If necessary, in the Scaling section, select **Adjust to** and change the percentage in the % normal size box to **100**.

10. Click the **Margins** tab to display the dialog box shown in Figure 17-9.

FIGURE 17-9
Margins tab in the Page Setup dialog box

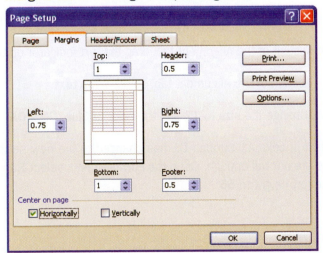

11. In the Center on page section at the bottom of the dialog box, select **Horizontally**. Click **OK**. Notice that this time the preview of the worksheet shows the page turned sideways, and the worksheet is centered horizontally on the page. Close the Print Preview screen.

12. Switch to the **Buildings** worksheet, change the page orientation to landscape, and center the worksheet horizontally on the page.

13. Click the **Print Preview** button in the dialog box to preview the Buildings worksheet, and then close the Print Preview screen.

14. Save the changes and leave the workbook open for the next Step-by-Step.

Changing Alignment and Wrapping Text in Cells

In Lesson 16 you learned about basic cell alignment, including center-, left-, and right-aligning the content of a cell in reference to its horizontal position within the cell. There are several other options, however, for aligning cells. There are additional horizontal positions including centering across selected cells, justifying the content of a cell, and distributing the content. You can adjust the alignment of the content of a cell vertically as well. Your choices for vertical alignment are top, center, bottom, justified, and distributed.

If you examine the Alignment tab of the Format Cells dialog box, you will also find some other interesting choices such as changing the orientation of text within a cell so the text sets at an angle, shrinking the content to fit within the cell, or allowing the text to wrap to new lines within a cell if the contents don't fit on one line.

STEP-BY-STEP 17.8

1. In the **Buildings** worksheet, select the cell range **A1:D1**.

2. Right-click to open the shortcut menu and select **Format Cells** to open the Format Cells dialog box.

3. Click the **Alignment** tab. Set the Horizontal position to **Left** and the Vertical position to **Center**.

4. In the Orientation section of the Alignment tab, drag the text indicator up to **45 Degrees**.

5. In the Text control section of the Alignment tab, select **Wrap text**.

6. Click the **Font** tab. Change the size to **12** and the color to **Blue**. Click **OK**.

7. Notice that the text in cells A1 through D1 has changed to the new settings, but you can't read it because the cells are not tall enough. Open the **Format** menu, select **Row**, and select **Height** in the submenu. Set the row height to **55**.

STEP-BY-STEP 17.8 Continued

8. Click **OK** to apply the row height change and close the dialog box. Notice that you can now see that the new alignment options have been applied to the header row, with text set at an angle, and in column C the text has wrapped to set on two lines.

9. Save your changes and leave the workbook open for the next Step-by-Step.

Gridlines

By now you have probably noticed that the *gridlines* you see in the worksheet do not appear in the Print Preview screen. The gridlines do not appear in the printed worksheet, either. If you want certain lines to appear in the printed worksheet, you need to add borders. The borders you specify will be placed in the locations of the current gridlines. But what if you just want to print all of the gridlines as they appear in the on-screen worksheet? Or what if you do not want to see the gridlines in the on-screen worksheet? You can handle both of these situations by turning the gridlines on or off.

To remove gridlines from the on-screen worksheet, open the Tools menu, select Options, and then choose the View tab. In the Window options section, deselect Gridlines, and then click OK. The gridlines will no longer appear on the screen—although the cells still exist and any borders you have placed will still be present.

To add gridlines to the printed document, open the Page Setup dialog box, choose the Sheet tab, and then select Gridlines in the Print section.

Add a Header and a Footer

Headers and footers are a means of providing useful information on a printed worksheet. The header is text that is printed in the top margin of every worksheet page. The footer is text that is printed in the bottom margin of every page. Neither headers nor footers are displayed in the worksheet window. You must preview or print the worksheet to see them. Headers and footers are set up from the Page Setup dialog box.

Among other things, headers and footers can include the date a worksheet was printed, the name of the person or company that created the worksheet, and the filename of the workbook. You can choose one of the standard (pre-made) headers or footers or you can create your own customized headers and footers. In Excel, formatting codes are used in headers and footers to represent the items you want to appear. With these you can insert dates, times, filenames, and page numbers automatically. By using the formatting codes instead of manually keying these items, the information is always updated automatically. For example, if you use the date and time formatting codes, whenever you print the worksheet, the date will reflect the current date and the time will be the exact time of the printing.

STEP-BY-STEP 17.9

1. Switch to the **Towers** worksheet.

2. Open the **File** menu and choose **Page Setup**.

3. Click the **Header/Footer** tab to display the dialog box shown in Figure 17-10.

FIGURE 17-10
Header/Footer tab in the Page Setup dialog box

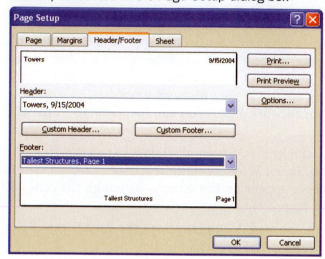

4. Open the **Footer** drop-down list, scroll down, and select **Tallest Structures, Page 1**. An example of the footer appears in the lower portion of the dialog box.

5. None of the standard headers in the list meets our needs, so we will create a custom header. Click the **Custom Header** button.

6. The cursor should be in the Left section. Click the **Sheet name** button. The &[Tab] formatting code appears.

7. Click in the **Right** section. Click the **Date** button. The &[Date] formatting code appears.

8. Click **OK**. The Page Setup dialog box now shows examples of both the header and the footer selected.

9. Click the **Print Preview** button. Your page should appear similar to Figure 17-11.

STEP-BY-STEP 17.9 Continued

FIGURE 17-11
Preview of Towers worksheet with a header and a footer

Towers 9/15/2004

Tallest Manmade Structures in the World

Ranking	Building	Use	Location	Height in Feet
1	KTHI-TV Tower	TV tower	North Dakota, USA	2,063
2	KXJB Tower	TV tower	North Dakota, USA	2,060
3	KZFX Radio Tower	Radio tower	Texas, USA	2,018
4	WITN Tower	TV tower	North Carolina, USA	2,000
4	KATV Tower	TV tower	Arkansas, USA	2,000
6	Senior Road FM Site	TV tower	Texas, USA	1,977
7	WFMY TV Tower	TV tower	North Carolina, USA	1,912
8	Coweta TV Tower	TV tower	Oklahoma, USA	1,909
9	Canadian National (CN) Tower	TV/Tourist tower	Toronto, Canada	1,814
10	Ostankino Tower	TV/Tourist tower	Moscow, Russia	1,772
11	Oriental Pearl Tower	TV tower	Shanghai, China	1,535
12	Menara Kuala Lumpur	TV/Tourist tower	Kuala Lumpur, Malaysia	1,379
13	Tianjin TV Tower	TV tower	Tianjin, China	1,362
14	Gerbrandy Tower	TV tower	Ysselstein, Netherlands	1,253
15	Fernsehturm	TV/Tourist tower	Berlin, Germany	1,197
16	WRLT Tower	TV tower	Tennessee, USA	1,180
17	Tokyo Tower	TV tower	Tokyo, Japan	1,092
18	Sky Tower	TV/Tourist tower	Auckland, New Zealand	1,076
19	AMP Tower	TV tower	Sydney, Australia	1,065
20	Nanjing Television Tower	TV tower	Nanjing, China	1,017
21	Emley Moor TV Tower	TV tower	Emley Moor, England	1,000

Tallest Structures Page 1

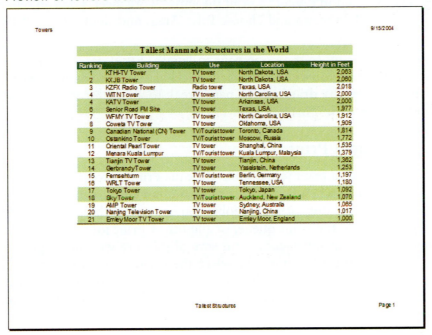

10. Close the Print Preview screen and then select the **Buildings** worksheet.

11. Open the **Page Setup** dialog box again and select the **Sheet** tab.

12. In the Print section, select the **Gridlines** option.

13. Click the **Print Preview** button. Your worksheet should appear similar to the one shown in Figure 17-12.

FIGURE 17-12
Preview of Buildings worksheet with gridlines applied

Building	Location	Height in Feet	# Stories
Petronas Tower 1	Kuala Lumpur, Malaysia	1,483	88
Petronas Tower 2	Kuala Lumpur, Malaysia	1,483	88
Sears Tower	Illinois, USA	1,454	110
Jin Mao Building	Shanghai, PRC	1,379	88
Empire State Building	New York, USA	1,250	102
Central Plaza	Hong Kong, PRC	1,227	78
Bank of China Tower	Hong Kong, PRC	1,209	70
Emirates Tower #1	Dubai, UAE	1,149	54
The Centre	Hong Kong, PRC	1,149	73

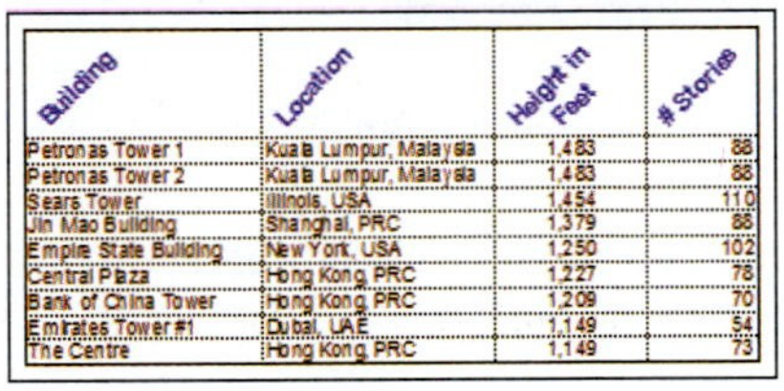

14. You decide that the worksheet appears better without the gridlines. Click the **Setup** button to return to the Page Setup dialog box and then deselect the **Gridlines** option and click **OK**.

15. Click the **Close** button on the Print Preview toolbar and then save the changes and leave the workbook open for the next Step-by-Step.

Printing a Worksheet

When you click the Print button on the Standard toolbar, Excel prints the active worksheet with the default print settings. If you want to change any of the print options, you need to open the Print dialog box. If you don't want to print the entire worksheet, you can select the range you want to print. Open the File menu and choose Print Area, and then select Set Print Area in the submenu.

When the worksheet is more than one page in length, Excel determines where to break the page and begin a new one. If you don't like where Excel has split the data between pages, you can create your own page break by dragging the page break to a new location. You can also insert a manual page break in a location of your choice.

Pausing or Canceling a Print Job

To check the progress of a print job, double-click the Printer icon that appears on the taskbar at the bottom of your screen when you are printing. If it is a short print job, note that the Printer icon may only appear briefly, but for longer jobs, you can access the print queue box by clicking the icon. There you will see the print queue, or the list of print jobs currently in progress. You may only see one job in the print queue, but if several jobs are waiting to print, they will all be listed in the queue. To cancel a print job, select the document name and then click Cancel Printing on the Document menu. Select the Pause Printing command on the Document menu to stop the print job temporarily; to restart printing, deselect the Pause Printing command.

S TEP-BY-STEP 17.10

Before you print your Buildings worksheet, you want to explore the options of printing it as two pages—one page with the top five buildings and the second page with the remaining buildings—or just printing all buildings in the list on one page.

1. Click in cell **A7**.

2. Open the **Insert** menu and select **Page Break**. A dotted line appears above row 7 indicating a page break.

3. Open the **File** menu and select **Print Preview**.

4. Select the **Next** button to see the second page.

5. You decide that you prefer to keep all of the information on one page. Click the **Close** button to return to the worksheet.

6. With cell A7 still selected, open the **Insert** menu and select **Remove Page Break**.

7. Select the range of cells from A1 through C10. This is all of the information for the buildings in the list except the *# Stories* column.

>
> **Note** ☑️
>
> You can also click the **Undo** button on the Standard toolbar to undo the last action in the worksheet.

STEP-BY-STEP 17.10 Continued

8. Open the **File** menu, select **Print Area**, and then select **Set Print Area** in the submenu. Click anywhere in the worksheet and notice that the area you had selected now has a dotted line around it to indicate the print area.

9. You decide it would still be best to print the entire worksheet. Open the **File** menu, select **Print Area**, and then select **Clear Print Area** in the submenu.

10. Open the **File** menu and choose **Print** to display the Print dialog box. Click **OK**, and you will see the Printer icon appear on the taskbar at the bottom left of your screen. Quickly double-click the **Printer** icon and then select the document name from the print queue. (There should only be one document listed in the print queue.)

Computer Concepts

The options available in the Print dialog box vary according to the type of printer available.

11. From the **Document** menu, select **Pause Printing** to stop the print job temporarily. Notice that a check mark next to the Pause Printing command indicates the command is selected, and under the Status head in the print queue, the message *Paused – Printing* is partially visible.

12. Click **Pause Printing** again to deselect the command and start the print job again.

13. Click the **Cancel Printing** command from the **Document** menu to cancel the print job. The Status message *Deleting Printing* appears. Click the **Close** button (the red X in the upper-right corner of the box) to close the print queue box.

14. Select **Print** from the **File** menu again, and when the Print dialog box opens, under Print what, select **Entire workbook** as shown in Figure 17-13. (Your dialog box will probably not match exactly.)

FIGURE 17-13
Print dialog box

15. If you are permitted to print, click **OK** to print both worksheets in the workbook. If you are not permitted to print, click **Cancel** to close the Print dialog box.

16. Save your changes and close the workbook.

17. Close Excel and follow your instructor's directions about turning off your computer.

SUMMARY

In this lesson, you learned:

■ If you want text to span across several rows or columns, you can merge multiple cells into a single cell.

■ The AutoFill feature can recognize a pattern in numbers or text and fill a series based on the pattern.

■ You can use AutoFill to fill cells with or without formatting from the source cells.

■ Applying AutoFormats can give your worksheet a professional look quickly and can make reading the data easier.

■ You can delete or add one or several worksheets to a workbook, and you can rename each worksheet.

■ The Sort feature provides options for organizing worksheet data numerically or alphabetically. You can sort the data based on a single column, or you can sort the data based on multiple criteria.

■ The Alignment tab of the Format Cells dialog box offers advanced alignment options for cell contents including wrapping text to new lines and orienting text vertically or at an angle.

■ Before you print, you can preview the worksheet on the screen to see what it will look like when it is printed.

■ You can change the page orientation or use the Fit to feature to fit all the data on one page.

■ Gridlines normally appear on screen in worksheets but do not appear when the worksheets are printed. You can hide the gridlines on screen or have the gridlines appear in a printed worksheet by selecting appropriate options.

■ Headers and footers can be added to worksheets to provide information such as the source and date of the data.

■ Inserting page breaks manually or selecting part of a worksheet as a print area control the appearance of the print output.

■ You can choose to print the active worksheet only, or you can choose to print all worksheets in the workbook.

VOCABULARY *Review*

Define the following terms:

Ascending order   Gridlines   Merge
Descending order   Header row

REVIEW *Questions*

TRUE/FALSE

Circle T if the statement is true or F if the statement is false.

T F **1.** When you use AutoFill to fill a data series in a range of cells, you can choose to complete the series either with or without the formats.

T F **2.** You can sort a worksheet based on data in up to four columns.

T F **3.** The header row in a worksheet is excluded when worksheet data is sorted.

T F **4.** A workbook can contain a maximum of three worksheets.

T F **5.** When an AutoFormat is applied to a worksheet, no additional changes can be made to the formatting.

MULTIPLE CHOICE

Circle the best response for each of the following statements.

1. Merging cells automatically applies _____ alignment.
   A. left
   B. right
   C. center
   D. justified

2. The Print button on the standard toolbar _____.
   A. prints the active worksheet
   B. prints the entire workbook
   C. opens the Print Preview screen
   D. opens the Print dialog box

3. A collection of related worksheets is called a(n) _____.
   A. volume
   B. spreadsheet
   C. file
   D. workbook

4. The Header/Footer tab in the Page Setup dialog box provides codes to insert _____.
   A. the current date
   B. the filename
   C. the page number
   D. all of the above

5. To sort from the largest number to the smallest, you would sort in _____ order.
   A. ascending
   B. descending
   C. alphabetical
   D. landscape

PROJECTS

PROJECT 17-1

1. Open **Project17-1** from the data files. Save the worksheet as **Classes** followed by your initials.

2. Rename *Sheet1* as **Languages**. Rename *Sheet2* in the workbook as **Fitness**.

3. Switch to the **Languages** worksheet. Select the cell range **A4:F9** and AutoFit the column width to selection.

4. Someone has mistakenly formatted the class numbers with 1000s separators. Use the **Clear** command on the **Edit** menu to clear only the formats from these cells. Then center the values again.

5. Copy the cell range **A1:F4**. Switch to the **Fitness** worksheet. With cell **A1** selected, paste the copied cells.

6. Enter the following fitness class information:

Class	Class #	Winter	Spring	Summer	Fall
Low Impact Aerobics	5105	10	12	15	9
Bench Step Aerobics	5100	9	11	14	12
Combo Aerobics	5290	8	11	13	11
Nautilus	5309	13	14	18	15
Beginning Yoga	4380	10	9	8	7
Tai Chi Chuan	4300	11	9	8	12

7. Switch to the **Languages** worksheet. Insert a new column to the left of column B. The new column will be very wide since it defaults to the width of the column before it. Do not be concerned. You will adjust the width later. In cell B4, enter the column heading **Fee**.

8. Click in cell **B5** and enter the value **120**. Format this value as currency with zero decimal places and center the value in the cell.

9. Fill cells B6:B9 with the value in cell B5. Select the cell range **B5:B9** and AutoFit the column to selection.

10. Insert a row above row 8. Insert the following information in the new row:
    German for Beginners $120   7044   18   17   19   15

11. Select the cell range **A1:G10** (all the cells in the data table) and apply the AutoFormat **Colorful 1**. Notice that the format has changed the title to a smaller type and the alignment of text in some cells has changed.

12. Select cell **A1** and change the font to **16 pt**, and then select cell **A2** and change the font to **12 pt**.

13. Select the cell range **C5:G10** and center the cell contents.

14. Switch to the **Fitness** worksheet. Insert a new column to the left of column B and enter the column heading **Fee**.

15. The fee for all fitness classes is $95. Enter that value in cell B5. Format the cell for Currency with 0 decimal places. Then fill the value in the cell range B6:B10. Select the cell range **A5:B10** and AutoFit the column to selection.

16. Select the entire **Fitness** worksheet and apply the **Colorful 1** format using the AutoFormat command.

17. Change the title in cell A1 to **16 pt** and then change the title in cell A2 to **12 pt**.

18. Change the alignment in the cell range C5:G10 to **Center**.

19. Center both worksheets horizontally on the page. Preview each worksheet in Print Preview.

20. Save your changes. If you are permitted to print, print both worksheets in the workbook. Close the workbook.

PROJECT 17-2

1. Open **Project17-2** from the data files. Save the worksheet as **Tutoring** followed by your initials.

2. Click in cell **G1** and key **September**. Use the AutoFill handle to automatically fill cells H1:J1 with the month names **October, November,** and **December**. Select the cell range **A1:J15** and adjust column widths to display the content.

3. You decide that last names should come first in this worksheet:
   A. Insert a new column to the left of column A.
   B. Select all data in column C (the *Last Name* column) and move it into the new column A. Adjust the width of column A to display all data.
   C. Delete the now empty column C.

4. To make it easier to find information about specific students, sort the data in the worksheet. Use the **Sort** dialog box and specify a sort by last name and then by first name, both in ascending order.

5. Harris Patrick has decided not to continue in the tutoring program. Delete the row that contains his data.

6. Preview the worksheet. Notice that it does not fit on one page. Open the **Page Setup** dialog box and click the **Page** tab if necessary.

7. In the Scaling section, select the **Fit to** option and leave the default option of 1 page wide by 1 tall.

8. Close the Print Preview screen and then change the orientation to **Landscape** and change the percentage in the Adjust to text box to **100%**.

9. Center the worksheet horizontally on the page.

10. Add a custom header to the worksheet that includes the current date at left and the filename of the worksheet at right.

11. In the Sheet tab of the Page Setup dialog box, select the option that will print the gridlines of the worksheet.

12. Check the worksheet in Print Preview. If you have permission to print, print the worksheet.

13. Save your changes and close the workbook.

TEAMWORK PROJECT

With a partner, explore voting statistics for your state in U.S. presidential elections from 1980 through the most recent presidential election. Follow these steps:

1. Create a worksheet to hold your data. In column A, key **1980** in one cell and then **1984** in the cell below it. Use AutoFill to add the remaining presidential election years up to and including the most recent presidential election.

2. Create columns for **Republican, Democrat,** and **Independent** candidates.

3. Using an almanac or Web search tools, find information on the popular vote for Republican, Democrat, and independent candidates for your state in each election. If there is more than one independent candidate, add together all the votes for all independent candidates. Collect data from 1980 through the most current presidential election. Divide the research assignment evenly so that both you and your partner gather the data.

4. Add a column to your worksheet and title it **Winning Party**. Insert the political party of the candidate who won each election nationally. Use the fill command to insert parties if the same party won two or more consecutive presidential elections. Which party won most often in the years you studied?

5. Format the worksheet table to make it easy to read and professional looking. If you have permission to print, preview the worksheet and adjust the page setup as necessary to make it fit on one page. Then print the worksheet.

CRITICAL *Thinking*

ACTIVITY 17-1

You have created a very large worksheet. You would like to be able to work in several parts of the worksheet simultaneously and be able to scroll in each part. Is there a way to create panes in a worksheet that would allow you to scroll in each pane independently? Use the Help files in Excel to discover the answer to this question and then write a brief description of what you learn.

CREATING FORMULAS AND CHARTING DATA

<table>
<tr><td>

OBJECTIVES

Upon completion of this lesson, you should be able to:

- Understand and create formulas in a worksheet.
- Identify and correct formula errors.
- Use the AutoSum feature.
- Understand and use function formulas.
- Understand and use relative and absolute cell references.
- Create a chart from worksheet data.
- Edit chart data and change chart formats and options.
- Interpret data from worksheets and charts.

Estimated Time: 1.5 hours

</td><td>

VOCABULARY

Absolute cell reference

Argument

Chart

Embedded chart

Formulas

Function formula

Mathematical functions

Mixed cell reference

Operand

Operator

Order of evaluation

Relative cell references

Statistical functions

</td></tr>
</table>

One of the primary uses of a spreadsheet is to solve problems that involve numbers. The worksheet is often used to complete complex and repetitious calculations accurately, quickly, and easily. Instead of using a calculator to perform mathematical calculations, Excel will perform the calculations for you. Excel has more than 300 built-in functions for performing calculations, or you can create your own formulas. Excel also comes with tools that can help you communicate worksheet data more effectively. For example, you can create a chart from data to enhance the information contained in the worksheet.

Formulas

2-3.2.3
2-3.2.4
2-3.2.5
2-3.2.6
2-3.2.8

The equations used to calculate values in a cell are known as *formulas*. A formula uses numbers and cell references to perform calculations such as addition, subtraction, multiplication, and division. A formula consists of two components: an *operand* and an *operator*. The operand is a number or cell reference. The operator is a symbol that tells Excel what mathematical operation to perform with the operands. For example, in the formula =B5+6, the operands are B5 and 6; the operator is the plus sign. Figure 18-1 lists some of the mathematical operators used in Excel.

FIGURE 18-1
Operators used in Excel

Mathematical Operation	Operator
Addition	+ (plus sign)
Subtraction	— (minus sign)
Multiplication	* (asterisk)
Division	/ (forward slash)
Percent	% (percent sign)

All formulas begin with the equal sign. This tells Excel that you are entering a formula instead of a numeric value.

A formula can be as simple as a single cell reference. For example, if you enter the formula =B3 in cell C4, the cell will display the same contents as cell B3. If you then change the value in cell B3, cell C4 will automatically be updated to reflect the change.

Formulas containing more than one operator are called *complex formulas*. For example, the formula =A4*B5+10 will perform both multiplication and addition. The sequence used to calculate the value of a formula is called the ***order of evaluation***. Formulas are evaluated as follows:

- Multiplication and division are performed before addition or subtraction.

- Calculations are performed from the left side of the formula to the right side.

- You can change the order of evaluation by using parentheses. Calculations enclosed in parentheses are performed first.

> **Computer Concepts**
>
> You can find all the mathematical operator symbols on the number keypad.

> **Note** ✓
>
> When creating formulas, there must be a closing parenthesis for every opening parenthesis. Otherwise, Excel will display an error message when you enter the formula.

Figure 18-2 provides examples to illustrate the order of evaluation.

FIGURE 18-2
Examples of order of evaluation

Formula	Result
=8+4*4	8 + 16 = 24
=8*4+4	32 + 4 = 36
=(8+4)*4	12 * 4 = 48
=8–4/4	8 – 1 = 7
=8/4–4	2 – 4 = -2
=(8*4)-(4/4)	32 – 1 = 31

Creating a Formula

There are two ways to enter a cell address into a formula. You can key the cell address or you can point to the cell. When entering the cell reference, the column letter can be keyed in either uppercase or lowercase. In the Step-by-Steps in this text, the column letters you must key are shown in lowercase. As you enter the cell references, Excel color-codes the borders around the cells and the cell references in the formula.

Computer Concepts

Generally, cell references are used in formulas rather than the actual value in the cell. That way, if the value in the cell changes, the formula does not need to be updated.

The formula is displayed in the Formula Bar as you enter it in the cell. However, once you press Enter or click the Enter button on the Formula Bar, the result of the formula will display in the cell. To see the formula, you must click in the cell and then view the formula in the Formula Bar.

Editing a Formula

You can choose from three methods to edit a formula: (1) you can double-click the cell and then edit the formula in the cell, (2) you can select the cell, press F2, and then edit the formula in the cell, or (3) you can select the cell and then edit the formula in the Formula Bar.

Note

You can also simply click in a cell and type a new formula in the cell. The new formula replaces the formula that was originally in the cell.

S TEP-BY-STEP 18.1

1. Open **Step18-1** from the data files. Save the workbook as **Regional Sales** followed by your initials.

2. Click in cell **E3**. Key **=b3+c3+d3**. Compare your screen to Figure 18-3. Notice that each cell you referenced in the formula is selected with a color, and the color matches the color of the cell reference in the formula. Also, notice that the formula is displayed in the cell and in the Formula Bar.

FIGURE 18-3
Entering a formula in a cell

	A	B	C	D	E	F
SUM ▼ X ✓ *fx* =b3+c3+d3						Formula
1			Sales by Region			
2		July	August	September	*Total*	
3	Eastern Region	$15,888	$14,645	$19,780	=b3+c3+d3	
4	Central Region	$17,750	$15,404	$18,322		
5	Southern Region	$18,931	$17,932	$20,003		
6	Western Region	$20,050	$21,435	$23,112		
7	*Total*					
8						

Formula Bar

Cell references are color coded

3. Press **Enter** or click the **Enter** button on the Formula Bar. The result of the formula, *$50,313*, is displayed in cell E3.

STEP-BY-STEP 18.1 Continued

4. Click in cell **E3**. Compare your screen with Figure 18-4. Notice that the formula is still displayed in the Formula Bar.

FIGURE 18-4
Result of a formula displayed in a cell

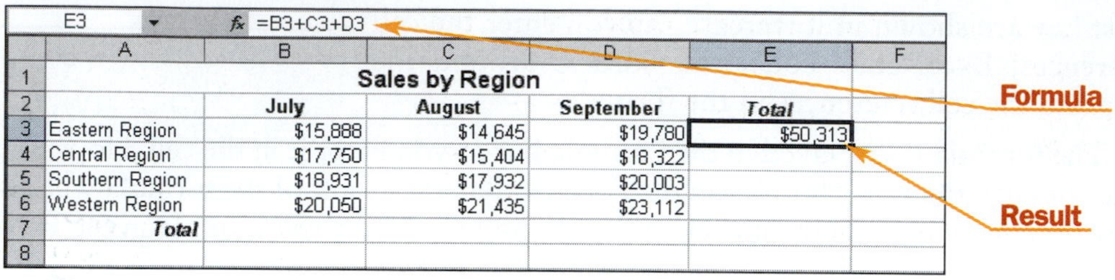

E3	▾	*fx* =B3+C3+D3			
	A	B	C	D	E	F

	A	B	C	D	E	F
1		Sales by Region				
2		July	August	September	Total	
3	Eastern Region	$15,888	$14,645	$19,780	$50,313	
4	Central Region	$17,750	$15,404	$18,322		
5	Southern Region	$18,931	$17,932	$20,003		
6	Western Region	$20,050	$21,435	$23,112		
7	Total					
8						

Formula

Result

5. Click in cell **E4**. Key **=**. Then click in cell **B4**. Notice that the cell reference B4 now displays following the = in both the Formula Bar and in cell E4.

6. Key **+** and then click in cell **C4**. Key **+** and click in cell **D4**. Both the cell and the Formula Bar now display the formula =B4+C4+D4.

7. Press **Enter** or click the **Enter** button on the Formula Bar. The result $51,476 is displayed in cell E4.

8. Double-click in cell **B4**. Change the amount to **16,750**. Then press **Enter** or click the **Enter** button on the Formula Bar. Notice that the result in cell E4 changes to $50,476 to reflect the change.

9. Click in cell **E5**. Enter the formula **=b4+c4+d4** and then press **Enter**. The result $50,476 should display in cell E5. Notice that this is the same number that appears in cell E4 because you used cell references for the cells in row 4 in your formula.

10. Double-click in cell **E5** and then change the first cell reference from *B4* to **b5**. Press **Enter** or click the **Enter** button on the Formula Bar.

11. Click in cell **E5**, press **F2**, and then change the second cell reference in the formula from *C4* to **c5**.

12. Click in the Formula bar to change the third cell reference from *D4* to **d5** and press **Enter**. The result ($56,866) displays in cell E5.

13. Click in cell **E6** and key **=**. Then click in cell **B6**, key **+**, click in cell **C6**, key **+**, and click in cell **D6**. Press **Enter** and look at the number displayed in cell E6. You should see the result $64,597.

14. Save the changes and leave the workbook open for the next Step-by-Step.

Formula Errors

When Excel cannot properly perform a calculation, an error value will display in the cell where you entered the formula. The error may exist because the cell contains text instead of a numeric value. An error value will display if the cell referenced in the formula contains an error or if a formula tries to divide by zero. An error value will also display if the cell is not wide enough to display the result. There are a number of common errors that occur—and common causes for those errors. Table 18-1 lists these common errors, their typical causes, and some possible solutions.

Fortunately, Excel provides help to solve formula errors. You may have noticed that when you entered incorrect cell references in cell E5 in the last Step-by-Step, a small triangle appeared in the upper-left corner of the cell, and an exclamation point within a diamond displayed next to the cell. This is the Trace Error button, which appears when a cell may contain a formula error. Point to the Trace Error button to see a ScreenTip that explains the potential error. Then, you can click the down arrow on the Trace Error button to select help with the error, edit the formula, ignore the error, or other options.

> **Note**
>
> Excel has an AutoCorrect feature that automatically checks a formula for common keyboarding mistakes. Sometimes Excel is able to identify the error. If so, a suggested correction appears in an alert box.

TABLE 18-1
Common errors, their causes, and solutions

ERROR	TYPICAL CAUSE/SOLUTION
#####	Occurs when the column is not wide enough or if a negative date is entered. If the column is not wide enough, widen the column or change the number format so that the number will fit within the column. Negative dates usually occur when there is an incorrect formula calculating a date. Check and correct your date formula.
#VALUE!	Occurs when the wrong type of argument (defined on page 370) or operand is used. It could result from entering text when a formula requires a number of a logical value such as TRUE or FALSE. Trace the error to determine which of these is the cause and correct it.
#DIV/0!	Occurs when a number is divided by zero. Most often caused by using a cell reference to a blank cell or to a cell that contains zero. Trace the error and correct the reference.
#N/A	Occurs when a value is not available to a function or formula. This can be caused by missing data or by referencing a cell that contains #N/A instead of data (you can use this as a placeholder for data that is not yet available). Trace the error and replace the missing data with a real value. Can also be caused by giving an inappropriate value for a lookup. To resolve this, make sure the lookup value argument is the correct type of value—for example, a value or a cell reference, but not a range reference.
#REF!	Occurs when a cell reference is not valid. Often caused by deleting cells referred to by other formulas or pasting moved cells over cells referred to by other formulas. To correct this error, trace the error and then change the formulas. Or, if you notice the error right after deleting or pasting cells, restore the cells on the worksheet by clicking Undo immediately after you delete or paste cells which caused the error. This can also be caused by running a link to a program that is not running. To resolve the error in this case, start the program to which the worksheet is trying to link.

TABLE 18-1 Continued
Common errors, their causes, and solutions

ERROR	TYPICAL CAUSE/SOLUTION
#NUM!	Occurs with invalid numeric values in a formula or function. This can be caused by using an unacceptable argument in a function that requires a numeric argument. To correct this, make sure the arguments used in the function are numbers. For example, even if the value you want to enter is $1,000, enter 1000 in the formula. This error can also be caused by using a worksheet function that iterates, such as IRR or RATE, and the function cannot find a result. To resolve the error in this case, use a different starting value for the worksheet function or change the number of times Microsoft Excel iterates formulas.
#NULL!	Occurs when you specify an intersection of two areas that do not intersect. The intersection operator is a space between references. Typically caused by an incorrect range operator. Trace the error and make sure that the correct range operators are used. To refer to a contiguous range of cells, use a colon (:) to separate the reference to the first cell in the range from the reference to the last cell in the range. For example, SUM(A1:A10) refers to the range from cell A1 to cell A10 inclusive. To refer to two areas that don't intersect, use the union operator, the comma (,). For example, if the formula sums two ranges, make sure a comma separates the two ranges (SUM(A1:A10,C1:C10)).

S TEP-BY-STEP 18.2

1. Click in cell **E5**. Enter the following formula: **=a5+c5+d5**.

2. Press **Enter** or click the **Enter** button on the Formula Bar. You will see a small triangle in the upper-right corner of the cell, and *#VALUE!* is displayed in cell E5. This is the error value. Excel cannot perform the calculation because cell A5 does not contain a numeric value.

3. If necessary, click in cell **E5** in the worksheet. Now you can find out more about the error in the formula:

   a. Point to the **Trace Error** button that is displayed to the left of the cell.

   b. A ScreenTip displays, showing *A value used in the formula is of the wrong data type.*

   c. Click the **down arrow** on the Trace Error button to display the menu shown in Figure 18-5.

FIGURE 18-5
Error menu

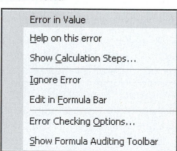

STEP-BY-STEP 18.2 Continued

d. Select **Show Calculation Steps**. The Evaluate Formula dialog box shown in Figure 18-6 is displayed. Now you can clearly see that the problem is that you are trying to add text (*Southern Region*) with numbers.

FIGURE 18-6
Evaluate Formula dialog box

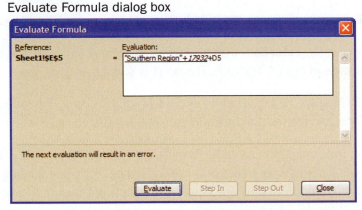

4. Click the **Close** button in the Evaluate Formula dialog box and then correct the formula in cell E5 to **=b5+c5+d5** and press **Enter**. Check to make sure the result $56,866 appears in cell E5.

5. Save the changes and close the workbook. Leave Excel open for the next Step-by-Step.

Relative and Absolute Cell References

2-3.2.2
2-3.2.4

By default, when you create formulas, the cell references are formatted as *relative cell references*. That means when the formula is copied to another cell, the cell references will be adjusted relative to the formula's new location. This automatic adjustment is helpful when you need to repeat the same formula for several columns or rows.

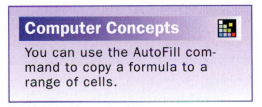

Computer Concepts

You can use the AutoFill command to copy a formula to a range of cells.

There are times, though, when you don't want the cell reference to change when the formula is moved or copied to a new cell. For example, you may be calculating expenses for auto mileage. The number of miles should always be multiplied times a fixed amount that represents the cost per mile. To create this formula, you format an absolute cell reference. An *absolute cell reference* does not change when the formula is copied or moved to a new location.

To create an absolute cell reference, you insert a dollar sign ($) before the column letter and/or the row number of the cell reference you want to stay the same. To illustrate, =A1 is a formula with an absolute reference.

A cell reference that contains both relative and absolute references is called a *mixed cell reference*. For example, you can have an absolute column reference and a relative row reference. Or, you can have a relative column reference and an absolute row reference. To illustrate, =$A1 is a formula with a mixed cell reference. The column reference is absolute and the row reference is relative. When formulas with mixed cell references are copied or moved, the row or column references that are preceded by a dollar sign will not change. However, the row or column references that are not preceded by a dollar sign will adjust relative to the cell to which they are moved.

STEP-BY-STEP 18.3

1. Open **Step18-3** from the data files. Save the workbook as **Mileage** followed by your initials.

2. Click in cell **E3**. Enter the formula **=d3*c10**. (The asterisk symbol is used to indicate multiplication.)

3. Press **Enter** or click the **Enter** button on the Formula Bar. Excel multiplied the value in cell D3 (*81*) times the value in cell C10 (*$0.33*). The result is *$26.73*.

4. Click in cell **E3**. Drag the fill handle down to cell E7. AutoFill copies the formula in cell E3 to all the cells in the range, and the results display in each of the selected cells.

5. Click in cell **E4**. Notice the formula in the Formula Bar displays *=D4*C10*. When you filled the formula down, Excel automatically changed the cell references for D3 in the original formula. However, because the cell reference for C10 was absolute, Excel did not change that cell reference.

6. Save the changes and keep the workbook open for the next Step-by-Step.

Using AutoSum

2-3.2.7

Although it is easy to enter a formula, if the formula consists of several cells, it could take you a long time to enter all the cell references. A shortcut for entering cell references is to identify a range of cells. For example, B5:D5 includes the cells B5, C5 and D5.

The AutoSum feature enables you to quickly identify a range of cells and enter a formula. When you use the AutoSum button, Excel scans the worksheet to determine the most logical column or row of adjacent cells containing numbers to sum. Excel identifies those cells as a range. For example, if the active cell is E7 and there are numbers in cells A7 through D7, Excel will identify the range A7 through D7.

After identifying the range of cells, the AutoSum feature creates a function formula to calculate the sum of the range. A *function formula* is a special formula that names a function instead of using operators to calculate a result. In this case, the function is SUM. The SUM function formula is the most frequently used type of function formula. Figure 18-7 illustrates the parts of the SUM function formula. A function contains three parts—the equal sign, the function name, and the arguments. The equal sign tells Excel that a formula follows. The function name tells Excel what to do with the data. The *argument* is a value, cell reference, range, or text that acts as an operand in a function formula. The argument is enclosed in parentheses after the function name. You will learn about other function formulas in the next section of this lesson.

FIGURE 18-7
Parts of a function formula

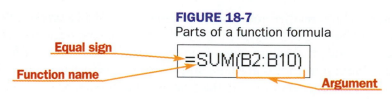

Equal sign

Function name

=SUM(B2:B10)

Argument

Sometimes Excel does not identify the correct range when you use the AutoSum feature. To identify a different range of cells, drag to select the desired cell range. Then click Enter to display the sum in the cell.

Note

When you insert or delete a new row or column that affects a range of cells identified in a formula, Excel will automatically update the range in the formula to reflect the change(s) in the range.

STEP-BY-STEP 18.4

1. Click in cell **B8**, and then click the **AutoSum** button on the Standard toolbar. (If you do not see the AutoSum button, click the Toolbar Options button on the toolbar to display it.) Excel displays a marquee (an animated border) around the cell range B3:B7 and proposes the formula =SUM(B3:B7). A ScreenTip also displays showing that the formula involves adding numbers, as shown in Figure 18-8. Press **Enter** to accept the formula.

FIGURE 18-8
Proposed AutoSum formula

SUM	▼ X ✓ fx	=SUM(B3:B7)		
	A	B	C	D	E
1		JULY MILEAGE REPORT			
2	Date	Odometer Start	Odometer End	Total Miles	Expense
3	1-Jul	78,541	78,622	81	$26.73
4	2-Jul	78,904	78,991	87	$28.71
5	7-Jul	79,106	79,165	59	$19.47
6	8-Jul	80,155	80,352	197	$65.01
7	9-Jul	80,394	80,457	105	$34.65
8	Total	=SUM(B3:B7)			
9		SUM(number1, [number2], ...)			
10		Cost per mile	$0.33		

Proposed formula

2. Click in cell **C8**. Click the **AutoSum** button and, since it is correctly summing the cell range C3:C7, press **Enter** or click the **Enter** button on the Formula Bar. The result $397,587 displays in cell C8.

3. Use the **AutoSum** button to enter a formula to calculate the column total in cell D8. Notice that Excel automatically summed the range of cells E3:E7 in cell E8 at the same time. Click in cell E8 to display the formula in the Formula Bar.

Computer Concepts

To quickly preview the sum of a range of cells, select the range of cells. The sum is displayed in the status bar at the bottom of the screen.

4. Save the changes and close the workbook. Leave Excel open for the next Step-by-Step.

Function Formulas

2-3.2.3

Excel has more than 300 built-in functions for performing calculations. In fact, you have already used one of Excel's built-in mathematical and trigonometric functions—the SUM function. *Mathematical functions* perform calculations that you could do using a scientific calculator. When you used the AutoSum button, Excel used the SUM function to calculate the results. *Statistical functions* are functions that describe large quantities of data. For example, a statistical function can determine the average of a range of data. Excel provides other types of functions, including trigonometric and logical functions, that are beyond the scope of this course.

Table 18-2 describes some of the most common mathematical and statistical functions available in Excel.

TABLE 18-2
Common Excel functions

MATHEMATICAL FUNCTIONS	
=PRODUCT	Multiplies values in the specified cells
=ROUND	Rounds the value to the nearest value in one of two ways: with the specified number of decimal places or to the nearest whole number
=ROUNDUP	Rounds the value up to the next higher positive value (or the next lower negative value) with the number of specified decimal places
=ROUNDDOWN	Rounds the value down to the next lower positive value (or to the next higher negative value) with the number of specified decimal places
=SUM	Adds the values in the specified range of cells
STATISTICAL FUNCTIONS	
=AVERAGE	Totals the range of cells and then divides the total by the number of entries in the specified range
=COUNT	Counts the number of cells with values in the specified range
=MAX	Displays the maximum value within the specified range of cells
=MEDIAN	Displays the middle value in the specified range of cells
=MIN	Displays the minimum value within the specified range of cells

There are several methods for entering functions in the worksheet. If you know the function name and argument, you can key an equal sign, the function name, and the argument. Or, if you want help entering the formula, you can use the Insert Function button on the Formula Bar, shown in Figure 18-9, to open the Insert Functions dialog box, where you can choose a function. Then the Function Arguments dialog box guides you through the process of building a formula that contains a function.

FIGURE 18-9
The Insert Function button on the Formula Bar

The Average and Sum Function

The Average function is a statistical function. It displays the average of the range identified in the argument. For example, the function =AVERAGE(B2,G2) calculates the average of the values contained in cells B2 and G2. As you already know, the Sum function is a mathematical function. The AutoSum button automatically inserts the Sum function in your worksheet. You can also select the Sum function from the Insert Function dialog box. If you used the Sum function instead of the average function, that is, =SUM(B2,G2), the total (instead of the average) of the values contained in cells B2 and G2 would be calculated.

Computer Concepts

The Insert Function dialog box makes it easy for you to browse through all of the available functions to choose the one you want. Furthermore, when you select a function, a brief explanation of that function is displayed. If you want help on the function, click the link at the bottom of the dialog box.

Figure 18-10 illustrates an example of a formula containing an Average function. The equal sign tells Excel that a formula follows. The function name AVERAGE tells Excel to calculate an average of the three cells included in the argument—B4, B6, and B8.

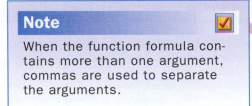

> **Note** ✓
>
> When the function formula contains more than one argument, commas are used to separate the arguments.

FIGURE 18-10
Average function formula

Equal sign

Function name

Argument

STEP-BY-STEP 18.5

1. Open **Step18-5** from the data files. Save the workbook as **Weather** followed by your initials.

2. You want to calculate the average high temperature for the week. Click in cell **C12**. Key **=average(c2:c8)**. This formula tells Excel to calculate the average of the values in the cell range C2:C8.

> **Computer Concepts** ▦
>
> It is not necessary to key the function name in all caps.

3. Press **Enter** or click the **Enter** button on the Formula Bar. The result *24* is displayed in cell C12.

4. Now you want to calculate the average low temperature for the week. Click in cell **B12**. Click the **Insert Function** button on the Formula Bar (see Figure 18-9). An Insert Function dialog box similar to the one shown in Figure 18-11 is displayed. (Your dialog box may look a little different.) *fx*

FIGURE 18-11
Insert Function dialog box

5. In the Search for a function box, key **calculate average** and click **Go**. The display of options under Select a Function changes and AVERAGE is already selected. Notice that a brief explanation of the Average function is displayed at the bottom of the dialog box.

STEP-BY-STEP 18.5 Continued

6. Click **OK**. The Function Arguments dialog box shown in Figure 18-12 is displayed. Notice that Excel identified the range B10:B11 in the Number 1 text box. Also, Excel proposes a formula with the AVERAGE function in the Formula Bar.

> **Note**
>
> If you do not know which category to choose from, click the **down arrow** in the *Or select a category* list box and then select **All**. The complete list of function names will display.

FIGURE 18-12
Function Arguments dialog box

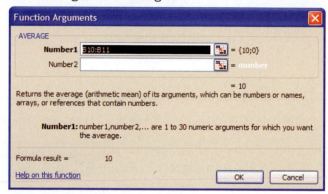

7. The range in the Number 1 text box is not correct. Click in the text box and change the range to **b2:b8**.

8. Click **OK**. The result 9 is displayed in cell B12.

9. Save the changes and leave the workbook open for the next Step-by-Step.

> **Computer Concepts**
>
> The purpose of the Function Arguments dialog box is to help you construct a function formula.

The Count Function

The Count function is a statistical function that displays the number of cells with numerical values in the argument range. For example, the function =COUNT(B4:B10) displays the number 7 when all the cells in the range contain a numeric value.

You can edit a range of cells in the Function Arguments dialog box by selecting the cells. Although the intent of the Function Arguments dialog box is to guide you in creating formulas, the dialog box can get in the way when you are creating the formula. That is why the collapse and expand features are available in the Function Arguments dialog box. They allow you to minimize and maximize the dialog box as you work with it.

STEP-BY-STEP 18.6

1. Click in cell **B11** and then click the **Insert Function** button to display the Insert Function dialog box. Under Select a function, select **COUNT**.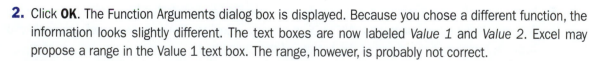

2. Click **OK**. The Function Arguments dialog box is displayed. Because you chose a different function, the information looks slightly different. The text boxes are now labeled *Value 1* and *Value 2*. Excel may propose a range in the Value 1 text box. The range, however, is probably not correct.

STEP-BY-STEP 18.6 Continued

3. Click the **Collapse Dialog** button at the right side of the Value 1 text box. The dialog box minimizes so that you only see its title bar and the range of cells. (The proposed formula is still displayed in the Formula Bar.)

4. If necessary, drag the minimized dialog box out of the way and then select the range B2:B8. The formula in the dialog box is updated and now shows the new range you selected. Notice, too, that the formula in the Formula Bar is also updated.

5. Click the **Expand Dialog** button at the right side of the Function Arguments title bar, or press **Enter**. The dialog box is maximized. Notice that the Value 1 text box now displays the range *B2:B8*. Click **OK**. The result 7 is displayed in cell B11.

6. Click in cell **B15**. Click the **Insert Function** button and select **SUM** under Select a function. Click **OK**.

7. The Function Arguments dialog box displays. The range in the Number 1 text box is not correct. Minimize the Function Arguments dialog box. Click in cell D2 and drag to select the range D2:D8. Then maximize the dialog box and click **OK**. The result *12* displays in cell B15.

8. Save the changes and leave the workbook open for the next Step-by-Step.

The Minimum and Maximum Functions

The Minimum (MIN) and Maximum (MAX) functions are also statistical functions. The MIN function displays the smallest number contained in the range identified in the argument. The MAX function displays the largest number contained in the range identified in the argument.

S TEP-BY-STEP 18.7

1. Click in cell **B13**. Click the **Insert Function** button to display the Insert Function dialog box.

2. In the Search for a function text box, key **minimum**. Under Select a function, select **MIN** and click **OK**.

3. Collapse the Function Arguments dialog box and then select the range **B2:B8**.

4. Expand the dialog box and then click **OK**. The result –2 is displayed in cell B13.

5. Click in cell **B14**. Click the **Insert Function** button to display the Insert Function dialog box. Under Select a function, select **MAX** and click **OK**.

6. Collapse the dialog box and select the range **C2:C8**.

7. Expand the dialog box and click **OK**. The result *30* is displayed in cell B14.

8. Save the changes and close the workbook. Leave Excel open for the next Step-by-Step.

2-3.2.10
2-3.2.12

Create a Chart

A *chart* is a graphic representation of your worksheet data. Charts help to make the data more interesting and easier to read and understand. Before you can create a chart, you must decide what type of chart you want to create. Excel provides several options for chart types. The chart type you select will depend on the data you want to represent. Table 18-3 lists some of the Excel chart types and a description of the types of data you can illustrate with each chart.

TABLE 18-3
Chart types

Area chart	Effective for emphasizing trends because it illustrates the magnitude of change over time.
Bar chart	Helpful when you want to make comparisons among individual items.
Column chart	Useful in showing changes over a period of time, or for making comparisons among individual items.
Doughnut chart	Similar to a pie chart in that it shows comparisons between the whole and the parts. However, a doughnut chart enables you to show more than one set of data.
Line chart	Illustrates trends in data at equal intervals.

TECHNOLOGY TIMELINE

BUILDING A BETTER VEGETABLE

You may have learned in a biology class about Gregor Mendel, the nineteenth-century monk credited with introducing the science of genetics. Mendel spent years cross-breeding sweet peas and other plants to discover the secrets of heredity, or how certain traits in parents are passed on to offspring. Mendel's experiments were definitely "low-tech" and involved planting seeds, waiting for them to grow and mature, then planting seeds from the new plants and waiting again for them to grow. Because of the time it took to breed generations of plants or animals, knowledge about genetics advanced slowly for decades.

But, more recently, computer simulation has allowed cross-breeding experiments to be done in hours instead of days by inputting data in a program for the various parent organisms' genes and attributes and then tracking the simulated progeny, or offspring. This has led to swift progress in the science of genetics, but even greater strides are coming soon as a result of many "genome projects" that are currently underway.

These projects use computer science to identify and sequence—or map—every gene of an organism, from fruit flies to human beings. The data then can be used to research many kinds of inherited traits in the progeny. For example, work is underway to create vaccinations that can be given by eating a banana instead of getting a shot, and there is ongoing research to create a tomato that tastes homegrown but can be stored, shipped, and sold at a grocery store. Computer simulation programs shorten the experimental stage of such research so much from the years it took Mendel to breed sweet peas that the applications of genetic research in the future are limited only by scientists' imaginations.

TABLE 18-3 Continued
Chart types

Pie chart	Compares the sizes of portions as they relate to a whole unit and illustrates that the parts total 100 percent. Effective when there is only one set of data.
Scatter chart	Illustrates scientific data, and it specifically shows uneven intervals—or clusters—of data.

After you decide which chart type you want to create, you must decide which chart options you want to use. To do this, you must first understand the parts of a chart. Figure 18-13 describes the parts of a chart. Take time to study this illustration and become familiar with the various parts.

FIGURE 18-13
Parts of a chart

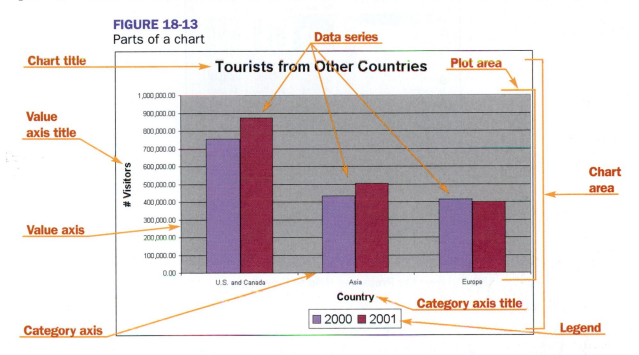

Use the Chart Wizard to Create a Chart

The Chart Wizard in Excel makes it easy for you to create professional-looking charts. The Chart Wizard will ask you questions about several chart options. You can create the chart on a separate sheet, or you can create the chart on the worksheet that has the data you want to chart. If the chart will not fit on the same sheet with the

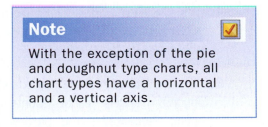

Note

With the exception of the pie and doughnut type charts, all chart types have a horizontal and a vertical axis.

data or if you want to create more than one chart from the same data, you will probably want to create the chart on a separate sheet. An *embedded chart* is a chart created on the same sheet as the data used in the chart. One advantage of embedding a chart on the same page as the data is that the data and the chart can be viewed at the same time.

Before you begin the Chart Wizard, you must first select the data you want to be represented in the chart. You do not always need all the worksheet data to create the chart, so you need to select the range of cells that you want to illustrate in the chart before you use the Wizard.

S TEP-BY-STEP 18.8

1. Open **Step 18-8** from the data files. Save the workbook as **News** followed by your initials.

2. Select the range **A5:B9** and then click the **Chart Wizard** button on the Standard toolbar. The dialog box shown in Figure 18-14 is displayed.

FIGURE 18-14
Chart Wizard—Step 1 of 4—Chart Type dialog box

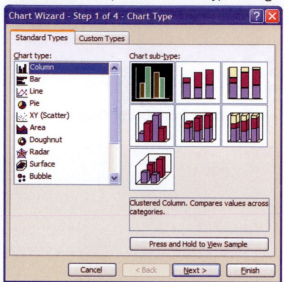

3. Under Chart type, select **Pie**, then select the second chart sub-type in the first row (*Pie with a 3-D visual effect*). Click and hold the **Press and Hold to View Sample** button in the dialog box. A preview of the chart is displayed.

4. Release the button and click **Next**. A preview of the chart is shown in the Chart Source Data dialog box. Notice also that the data range you selected is displayed in the Data range text box.

5. Click the **Next** button to display the Chart Options dialog box. Click in the **Chart title** text box and key **Where People Get the News**.

6. Click the **Data Labels** tab to change the dialog box options. Under Label Contains, select the option **Percentage**. The preview of the chart is updated to show the labels. Compare your screen to Figure 18-15.

> **Note** ☑
>
> Click the **Back** button to return to the previous Chart Wizard dialog box if, for instance, you want to make a change to a previous selection.

STEP-BY-STEP 18.8 Continued

FIGURE 18-15
Data Labels tab in Step 3 of 4—Chart Options dialog box

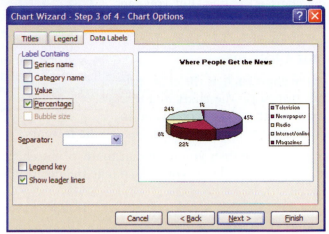

7. Click **Next**. The Chart Locations dialog box is displayed. Select the **As new sheet** option to place the chart on a sheet by itself. The new sheet will be named *Chart1*.

8. Click **Finish** in the Chart Wizard dialog box. The wizard closes and the chart is displayed in a new sheet in the workbook. You may notice that the Chart toolbar also appears in the window.

9. Save the changes and leave the workbook open for the next Step-by-Step.

Edit Chart Data

2-3.2.10

There may be occasions when the data used to create the chart changes after the chart has been created. Fortunately, you do not need to create a new chart. When you edit the data in the worksheet, Excel will automatically update the chart to reflect the changes.

Computer Concepts

You can create an instant chart by selecting the data you want to chart and then pressing **F11**. A two-dimensional column chart is created. However, notice that there are no data labels or chart title in this chart.

STEP-BY-STEP 18.9

1. Notice that the chart currently displays *24%* for Internet/online. Click the **Sheet1** tab to switch to the worksheet containing the data for the chart.

2. Click cell **B8** and key **555**, and then press **Enter**. The value in cell C8 is updated from *24%* to *25%*.

3. Click the **Chart1** tab. Notice that the chart has also been updated and it now shows *25%* for Internet/online. (Also note that the other percentages changed accordingly.)

4. Save the changes and close the workbook. Leave Excel open for the next Step-by-Step.

Editing Chart Formats and Options

2-3.2.10

You've already seen that you can easily update chart data, even after the chart is created. But you can also change the chart options after you create a chart.

Changing Formats or Options

Many of the parts of the chart such as the chart title and the axis titles are positioned on the chart in a text box. If you click the part of the chart you want to change, the text box will display and then you can change the formats.

The Chart Options command enables you to change many of the chart features. For example, you can change the text in the chart title, or you can change the position of the legend.

STEP-BY-STEP 18.10

1. Open file **Step18-10** from the data files. Save the workbook as **Demographics** followed by your initials.

2. Select the range **A2:E7** and then click the **Chart Wizard** button. Under Chart type, select **Bar**. Under Chart sub-type, select the first option in the second row (*Clustered bar with a 3-D visual effect*).

3. Click **Next**. For Series in, select the option **Columns**, if necessary.

4. Click **Next**. If necessary, click the **Titles** tab to display the Titles sheet. In the Chart title text box, key **Centerville Demographics**. In the Category (X) axis text box, key **Year**. In the Value (Z) axis text box, key **Census Count**.

5. Click **Next**. Leave the option *As object in* selected. Then click **Finish**. The chart is displayed below the worksheet data. Do not be concerned if the chart overlaps some of the worksheet data.

6. Point to any white area in the chart. When a ScreenTip displays *Chart Area*, click and drag the chart down to the lower-left corner of the worksheet. Then click the chart title. The text box surrounding the title is displayed.

7. With the text box selected, click the down arrow in the Font Size box on the Formatting toolbar and select **14** (or a font size that is not already selected). The text box is resized to accommodate the new font size.

8. Right-click the axis labels at the bottom of the chart (0, 20,000, 40,000, and so on). Select **Format Axis** in the shortcut menu. The Format Axis dialog box is displayed.

STEP-BY-STEP 18.10 Continued

9. If necessary, click the **Font** tab. Change the font size to **9** (or a font size that is not already selected) and click **OK**.

10. Right-click the value axis title **Census Count**. Select **Format Axis Title** in the shortcut menu. From the Font tab in the Format Axis Title dialog box, change the font size to **12** and click **OK**.

11. If necessary, click the chart to select it. (*Hint:* It is selected when you see the eight sizing handles around the border of the chart.) Drag the upper-right sizing handle to resize the chart until it is about as wide as the five columns of data above it. Then drag the sizing handle in the middle of the bottom edge of the chart to make the chart about as high as it is wide.

12. With the chart selected, open the **Chart** menu and choose **Chart Options**. The Chart Options dialog box shown in Figure 18-16 is displayed.

FIGURE 18-16
Chart Options dialog box

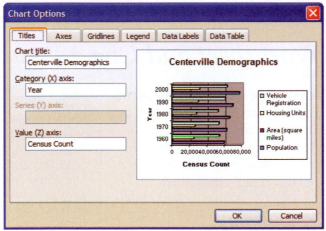

13. Click the **Legend** tab. Select **Bottom** in the Placement section. The preview in the dialog box now shows the legend below the chart.

14. Click the **Titles** tab. Under Chart title, change the title in the text box to **Centerville Growth Trends**.

15. Click **OK**. The chart title is changed, and the legend is repositioned at the bottom of the chart.

16. Save the changes and leave the workbook open for the next Step-by-Step.

Changing the Chart Type

Now that you have created a bar chart and edited some of the chart parts, you realize a bar chart is not the best chart type for displaying the demographic data. A line graphic would be more effective for illustrating trends in data. Fortunately, you can change the chart type easily—and without starting over!

STEP-BY-STEP 18.11

1. With the chart selected, open the **Chart** menu and choose **Chart Type**. The Chart Type dialog box opens.

2. Under Chart type, select **Line**. Under Chart sub-type, the first option in the second row is already selected. Click **OK**. The bar chart is converted to a line chart.

3. Click outside the chart to deselect it and then save the changes.

4. Close the workbook and follow your instructor's directions about closing Excel and turning off your computer.

Interpreting Worksheet and Chart Data

2-3.2.9
2-3.2.11

Worksheets and charts can be an excellent means of conveying information. But they can also be confusing or misleading if they are not set up correctly. As you continue your work with worksheets, you will become more comfortable with interpreting the data within them and more adept at analyzing charts created from them.

> **Computer Concepts**
>
> You can enlarge or reduce the display of a chart on your screen with the Zoom command. Open the **View** menu, choose **Zoom**, and select a smaller or larger percentage under Magnification in the Zoom dialog box.

Drawing Logical Conclusions from Worksheets

The results of a worksheet are only accurate if correct data and formulas have been entered. If you are certain of the accuracy of the content of the worksheet, then the next questions are: What does this worksheet tell me? What logical conclusions can I draw from it?

Obviously a worksheet can contain a great deal of information. The easiest way to summarize that information is to use the tools within Excel to obtain the information required. For example, if you want to know the average of a set of values, you would use the AVERAGE function. When using tools such as this, you can be certain of the results. But there are other ways in which you can draw conclusions from the worksheet. For example, you may notice in a column that the values are continually increasing. If this column is a chronological listing of your company's sales, you could conclude that there is a trend—that your company's sales are increasing each year. On the other hand, if this same column was not a chronological listing of sales, but rather a listing of sales by region, it is not logical to interpret a trend. If the regions are listed alphabetically, it does not make sense to conclude that the sales are higher because a region's name appears later in the alphabet.

Interpreting Graphical Data

As you recall, Excel provides many different chart types that you can choose from to display data. But what use are these charts? Again, like the worksheets themselves, you must be careful to ensure that the data within them is accurate and that the values represented in the charts are correctly labeled. If the values and their representation are correct, charts are extremely useful for spotting and interpreting trends, summarizing data, highlighting the most important data (or, at least, the data that you feel is most important), and for making facts clear that would perhaps not be clear when looking at the worksheet.

In all cases, you must carefully weigh both where values within a worksheet or chart are coming from as well as what each value actually represents.

SUMMARY

In this lesson, you learned:

- One of the primary uses for Excel spreadsheets is to perform calculations. Formulas are equations with numbers, cell references, and operators that tell Excel how to perform the calculations.

- All formulas begin with =. To enter the cell references in a formula, you can key the cell address or you can point and click the cell you want to reference.

- If Excel cannot perform a calculation, an error value will display. The Trace Error button will display and can help guide you in troubleshooting the problem. Then, you can edit the formula directly in the cell or in the Formula Bar.

- If you do not want the cell reference to change when the formula is moved or copied to a new location, the cell reference must be formatted as an absolute cell reference.

- The AutoFill feature enables you to quickly copy formulas to adjacent cells. The cell references are adjusted relative to the formula's new location.

- The AutoSum feature enables you to quickly identify a range of cells and enter a formula.

- Functions are special formulas that do not require operators. Excel provides more than 300 built-in functions to help you perform mathematical, statistical, and other functions.

- The Average function displays the average of the range identified in the argument. The Sum function totals the values in the specified range of cells.

- The Count function displays the number of cells with numerical values in the argument range.

- The Minimum and Maximum functions display the smallest or the largest number contained in the range identified in the argument.

- A chart displays the worksheet data visually and often helps the audience understand and interpret the information more clearly.

- When the worksheet data is changed, the chart is automatically updated to reflect those changes.

- Chart formats, options, and types can be changed at any time, even after the chart has been created.

- Excel worksheets and charts convey information and allow you to draw logical conclusions from the data, but you must ensure that the data is accurate and that you know what the values represent to make a correct assessment.

VOCABULARY *Review*

Define the following terms:

Absolute cell reference	Function formula	Order of evaluation
Argument	Mathematical functions	Relative cell references
Chart	Mixed cell reference	Statistical functions
Embedded chart	Operand	
Formulas	Operator	

REVIEW *Questions*

TRUE/FALSE

Circle T if the statement is true or F if the statement is false.

T F **1.** A formula must consist of more than one cell reference.

T F **2.** You can enter a cell reference in either uppercase or lowercase.

T F **3.** An absolute cell reference will automatically adjust when moved or copied.

T F **4.** A function contains two parts: the function name and the arguments.

T F **5.** When entering a function name, you must use all capital letters.

T F **6.** The Function Argument dialog box displays only when you have an error in a function formula.

T F **7.** Once you create a chart using the chart wizard, you cannot edit the chart.

T F **8.** Not all chart types can be used to graph any kind of data.

T F **9.** If the data changes after the chart is created, you must create a new chart.

T F **10.** You can reposition a chart easily by dragging the selected chart to another section of the worksheet.

MATCHING

Match the correct term in Column 1 to its description in Column 2.

Column 1	Column 2

____ **1.** argument

____ **2.** embedded

____ **3.** statistical

____ **4.** Minimum

____ **5.** operand

____ **6.** formula

____ **7.** mixed

____ **8.** Count

____ **9.** axis

____ **10.** operator

A. Describes a chart created on the same sheet with data

B. Function that displays the smallest number in a range

C. Cell references that contain both relative and absolute references

D. Provide data to a formula

E. Type of functions used to describe large quantities of data

F. Symbol that tells Excel what mathematical operation to perform

G. Used to calculate values in a spreadsheet cell

H. Function that displays the number of cells with numerical data in an argument range

I. Value, cell reference/range, or text used as an operand in a function formula

J. A line bordering a chart that is used as a reference, to measure data in the chart

PROJECTS

PROJECT 18-1

1. If necessary, launch Excel, and then open **Project18-1** from the data files. Save the workbook as **Pies** followed by your initials.

2. Click in cell **E6** and create a formula that will multiply the total number of deep-dish apple pies by the price for all fruit pies in cell C5. (*Hint*: The formula should include an absolute cell reference for cell C5.)

3. Use AutoFill to copy the formula for the other fruit pies.

4. In cells D11 and E11, use **AutoSum** to sum the total number of fruit pies and the fruit pie revenue.

5. Using the same procedure, calculate revenues and subtotals for the remaining pie categories.

6. In cell D33, create a formula that will add each of the subtotal values in the D column (cells D11, D17, D24, and D31).

7. In cell E33, create a formula that will add each of the subtotal revenue values in the E column (cells E11, E17, E24, and E31).

8. In cells D35 and E35, create formulas to subtract last year's numbers and revenues from the Grand Total amounts for this year. Is Melissa gaining or losing business?

9. In cell E37, use a function formula to calculate the average price of Melissa's pies (average the values in cells C5, C13, C19, and C26). What is the average pie price?

10. Change the price for Tropical Treats to $15.00. How did the change impact Melissa's gain/loss? How did the change impact the average pie price?

11. Save the changes and close the workbook.

PROJECT 18-2

1. Open **Project18-2** from the data files. Save the workbook as **Tree Sale** followed by your initials.

2. Use the Chart Wizard to chart the data in cell range A5:E12 as follows:
   A. In the Step 1 of 4 dialog box, select the first column chart in the second row of chart options (*Clustered column with a 3-D visual effect*).
   B. In the Step 2 of 4 dialog box, select the **Rows** option to chart the data by rows.
   C. In the Step 3 of 4 dialog box, key the Value (Z) axis label **Total Sales**. Click the **Legend** tab and select the **Bottom** placement option.
   D. In the Step 4 of 4 dialog box, accept the default option to embed the chart on the same sheet.

3. Position the chart so that it is below the worksheet data. Enlarge or reduce the chart as necessary to make it about the same width as the columns of data.

4. You have just noticed an error in the data. Change the value for Tulip poplar in Week 1 to **$4,150** and observe the change in the chart.

5. Display the Chart Options dialog box and add the title **Fall Tree Sale** to the chart. Change the title point size to **16**.

6. Click the legend and increase the size of the legend text to **9** point (or a small font size that is not already selected).

7. Save your changes and close the workbook.

TEAMWORK PROJECT

As you have learned in this lesson, functions can help you analyze data in a number of ways. Excel includes hundreds of functions to help you with financial, statistical, mathematical, and other problems. In this project, explore two functions of your choice with a partner to learn how they can be applied to specific data analysis situations. Make sure your functions are not covered in this or the previous lesson. Follow these steps:

1.   In a blank Excel worksheet, open the Insert Function dialog box. Review the functions in each category to find two you are interested in exploring with your teammate. (Your functions should come from two different categories.)

2.   Read the Microsoft Excel Help files for the functions you have chosen to find out what kind of data the function can analyze and what kinds of information you must supply as arguments for the functions.

3.   Construct worksheets containing data appropriate for each function and then use the functions to analyze the data.

4.   After you are sure you are using the function correctly, make a team presentation to share what you have learned about your functions.

CRITICAL *Thinking*

ACTIVITY 18-1

You have created a three-dimensional pie chart with a number of slices. Some of them are hard to see because the three-dimensional chart is rather flat. Can you tilt the chart in any way so you can see the pie slices better? Use Excel to find the answer and then write a summary on what you learned.

POWERPOINT ESSENTIALS

OBJECTIVES

Upon completion of this lesson, you should be able to:

- Open and save an existing presentation.
- Identify the parts of the PowerPoint screen.
- Navigate through a presentation.
- Change the slide view.
- Create a new presentation.
- Apply a design template.
- Add, delete, copy, and move slides.
- Preview a presentation.

Estimated Time: 1 hour

VOCABULARY

Normal view

Placeholders

Presentations

Slide design

Slide Finder

Slide layout

Slide Show view

Slide Sorter view

PowerPoint helps you create, edit, and manipulate professional-looking slides, transparencies, or on-screen presentations. The presentations you create can include text, drawing objects, clip art, pictures, tables, charts, sound, and video clips. Creating a presentation may seem like an overwhelming task, but PowerPoint provides many features that make that task easy and fun.

2-1.2.7
2-1.2.8

Opening and Saving an Existing Presentation

When you first start PowerPoint, the Getting Started task pane is displayed at the right. As in other Office applications, this task pane provides several options for opening an existing document or for creating a new one. In PowerPoint, the document files are called *presentations*. The most recently opened presentations are displayed in the Open panel near the bottom of the task pane, but you can also search for additional files by using the Open command. In PowerPoint, the Open, Save, and Save As commands you have used in Word and Excel are again available on the File menu. You can also access the Open dialog box from the Getting Started task pane.

STEP-BY-STEP 19.1

1. Start **PowerPoint**. A blank slide will open and the Getting Started task pane should display at right.

2. At the bottom of the Open panel in the task pane, click the option **More . . .** to display the Open dialog box.

3. Locate and select the file **Step19-1** from the data files. Click **Open**.

4. Save the presentation as **The 3Rs** followed by your initials. Leave the presentation open for the next Step-by-Step.

> **Note**
>
> If the Getting Started task pane does not open, it is not selected as an opening option. Select Open on the File menu to display the Open dialog box.

> **Computer Concepts**
>
> You can save a presentation so it can be viewed using a Web browser. To save the presentation in HTML format, open the **File** menu and choose **Save as Web Page**.

 Identifying the Parts of the PowerPoint Screen

2-1.2.1

The presentation window in Figure 19-1 displays many familiar-looking parts, including the title bar, menu bar, toolbars, and status bar. Scroll bars appear when your presentation includes more than one slide so you can scroll through the presentation.

Working in a Connected World

CAREER COMMUNICATION SKILLS

Chances are that you have given some thought to the kind of career or job you want when you finish school. Are you interested in entering the corporate world, perhaps as an account manager in a marketing or advertising firm? Or maybe you've always wanted to teach, in a classroom or training workers on the job. If you like science, you may be considering a career as a researcher for a large company or a university. In any of these careers, individuals most likely to be promoted and succeed have something in common—they have good oral and written communication skills. The ability to make formal presentations is an increasingly important skill for many different occupations. In fact, communication skills can greatly enhance one's success in the classroom or on the job.

Many jobs require that an employee be able to organize, analyze, and communicate information. Moreover, employees are often called on to formally present information. For example, an account manager may use a presentation to "pitch" a new idea to a client. An instructor plans and presents material to other people every day. And a research scientist may be called on to report findings to a board, create a presentation on future projects for a grant application process, or even conduct a press conference to introduce a scientific breakthrough! The audience may be as small as one or two coworkers, or it may be a much larger group of people, and the presentation may be in person or on camera. To deliver an effective presentation, you must possess the confidence to deliver the presentation competently.

Some features unique to PowerPoint include the Outline pane, the Slide pane, and the Notes pane. You use the Outline pane to organize the content of your presentation. You can view the content of your presentation in outline format or in slide format. You can also move through your presentation quickly by clicking the slides in the Outline pane.

The Slide pane in the center of the PowerPoint window allows you to see the slide as it will appear in your presentation. Click in the Slide pane and then select a percentage in the Zoom drop-down list on the Standard toolbar to make the slide appear larger or smaller. You can click in the Notes pane and add notes and information to help you with your presentation.

FIGURE 19-1
Main PowerPoint window

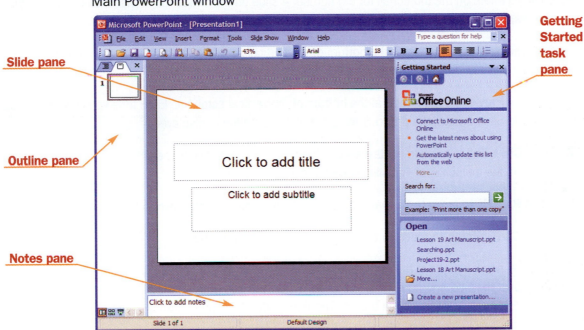

Navigating Through a Presentation

2-1.2.3
2-1.3.1
2-4.1.11

> **Note** ☑️
>
> If the Outline tab is selected in the Outline pane, the slide icon next to the slide number in the Outline pane changes to gray to indicate the current slide.

You learned that you can move to a different slide by clicking on the slide in the Outline pane. You can also use the scroll bar or shortcut keys to navigate through a presentation. In PowerPoint, the Next Slide and Previous Slide buttons at the bottom of the vertical scroll bar (shown in Figure 19-2) give you another way to navigate through the presentation easily. You will also recognize some of the shortcut key combinations in the following exercise; the same shortcut keys perform similar maneuvers when navigating through documents in many different Office applications.

FIGURE 19-2
The Next Slide and Previous Slide buttons

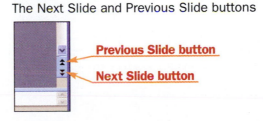

STEP-BY-STEP 19.2

1. Compare your screen to Figure 19-1 and take time to identify the three panes on the screen. Notice that the current slide displayed in the Slide pane is the first of six slides.

2. Look at the contents in the Outline pane. If necessary, click the **Outline** tab to display all of the text contained on each of the six slides in the presentation.

3. In the Outline pane, click the **Slides** tab. The display changes to show thumbnail images of the slides.

4. Click anywhere on the thumbnail for the number 4 slide on the Slides tab in the Outline pane (*Rights*). The display in the Slide pane changes to show the fourth slide.

5. Click the **Next Slide** button at the bottom of the vertical scroll bar on the right. Each time you click the Next Slide button, the next slide in the presentation is displayed.

6. Click the **Previous Slide** button at the bottom of the vertical scroll bar. Each time you click the Previous Slide button, the previous slide in the presentation is displayed.

7. Press **Ctrl + End** to move to the last slide in the presentation. Notice that each time you move to a different slide, the thumbnail of that slide is selected in the Outline pane.

8. Press **PageUp** to move to the previous slide, and then press **PageDown** to move to the next slide.

9. Press **Ctrl + Home** to move to the first slide in the presentation.

10. Drag the scroll box down the vertical scroll bar. As you drag the box, a label to the left of the scroll bar shows the title and number of the slide. When you see *Slide: 3 of 6 The Three Rs*, as shown in Figure 19-3, release the mouse button. The third slide of the presentation is displayed.

FIGURE 19-3
Slide label on scroll bar

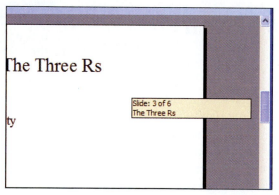

11. Leave the presentation open for the next Step-by-Step.

Changing the Slide View

2-4.1.4

PowerPoint offers three different ways to view your presentation. *Normal view* is the default view and the one you've seen in PowerPoint so far. This view provides the Outline pane, the Slide pane, and the Notes pane.

>
> **Note**
>
> To adjust the size of the panes in Normal view, point to the pane borders and, when the pointer changes to a double-headed arrow, drag the pane border.

You can change the view by clicking the buttons at the lower left of the PowerPoint window, shown in Figure 19-4. The other two views are *Slide Sorter view* and *Slide Show view*. Slide Sorter view gives you an overall picture of your presentation by displaying your slides as thumbnails (miniature versions of each of the slides in the presentation). Slide Sorter view makes it easy to add and delete slides and change the order of the slides. In Slide Show view, the current slide fills the whole computer screen. You use this view when you present the show to your audience. You will learn more about using Slide Show view at the end of this lesson.

FIGURE 19-4
The buttons at the lower left of the PowerPoint window change the view

Normal View button ⟶

⟵ Slide Show View button

Slide Sorter View button ⟋

STEP-BY-STEP 19.3

1. Click the **Slide Sorter View** button at the bottom of the screen. The display changes to show all the slides in the presentation, as shown in Figure 19-5. Notice that the third slide has a blue border around it, indicating that it is selected.

FIGURE 19-5
Presentation displayed in Slide Sorter view

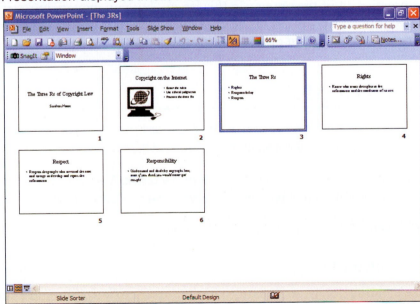

2. Click the **Normal View** button at the bottom of the screen to return to Normal view.

3. Close the presentation and leave PowerPoint open for the next Step-by-Step.

Creating a New Presentation

2-4.1.1

PowerPoint provides several options for creating a new presentation:

- You can create a new blank presentation and apply a design template. Design templates, which you will learn more about in the next section, provide a preformatted slide design with colors, styles, and layouts. If you want to create a presentation without a preset design and without any existing content, you can create a new blank presentation. You can then apply your own design and slide layouts.

- You can choose the AutoContent Wizard to guide you through a series of questions about the presentation you want to create. Based on your answers, the Wizard will organize ideas and create a presentation customized from your responses. You will not be instructed to use the AutoContent Wizard to create a presentation in this lesson, but you will have the opportunity to experiment with the feature in the Teamwork Project at the end of the next lesson if you are interested in learning more about this process.

- PowerPoint provides several presentations when you choose General Templates in the New Presentation task pane. These presentations already contain content that was previously organized and formatted on slides. You can modify the content to customize the presentation for your needs.

- You can create a new presentation based on an existing presentation. All the slides from the existing presentation are opened in a new presentation. Save the new presentation with a new filename.

You will not practice all of the options in this lesson, but you may want to try using some of these features on your own. Regardless of the way you create your presentation, PowerPoint provides placeholders for easy insertion of text and graphics.

STEP-BY-STEP 19.4

1. Open the **View** menu and choose **Task Pane**. If the task pane is open but not showing the New Presentation options, click the **down arrow** in the title bar of the task pane and choose **New Presentation**.

2. Under New in the task pane, click the link **Blank presentation**. A new, blank title slide appears in the Slide pane and the Slide Layout pane now displays in the task pane at right.

3. Leave the presentation open for the next Step-by-Step.

Effective Presentation Design

When you are creating a new presentation, it's important to keep in mind a few basic principles for effective design. PowerPoint offers so many templates and slide layouts that it is tempting to use many different layouts and formats in your presentation. But if your presentation is too "busy," the formatting can detract from your content. You want the slide layouts and design features you choose to emphasize your information, not overwhelm it. Following are a few design guidelines to keep in mind when you are creating a presentation.

- Don't overload a slide with too much content—include only essential information to keep your message clear and concise.

- Use bullets to present lists of information when the data does not need to be in any particular order.

- Use numbered lists to show the steps in a process or data that should be examined in order.

- Limit the number of special features, such as bullets, graphics, or numbered items, on one slide.

- Tables and charts can illustrate numerical data or trends, but keep the charts simple and easy to read.

- Use graphics or charts only to highlight relevant information. Don't use graphics just to "decorate" a slide.

- Select only one or two fonts to use in each slide, and use the same fonts for the same features in all the slides in a presentation to create a consistent appearance.

A good presentation holds your audience's attention without distracting them from understanding the information you are presenting. PowerPoint allows you to use color, design, graphics, sound, data, and even animation to illustrate your points effectively. These options can all be used to emphasize your points and clarify your information, but don't let your message get lost by overloading your slide show with the abundant "special effects" available.

Speaker Notes

Look back at Figure 19-1 to locate an area in the Normal view window below the Slide pane with a message that reads *Click to add notes.* As you know, this is the Notes pane, and it provides a place for you to write speaker notes, which you can use to remind yourself of what information you want to emphasize, or even include the dialogue you want to use when you present your slide show to an audience. Adding speaker notes to a presentation is a simple click-and-enter process: Click in the notes area and then key the text you want to include.

> **Computer Concepts**
>
> You can only add text in the Notes pane. To add graphics or other elements to the speaker notes, select **Notes Page** from the **View** menu. This view also allows you to change the notes layout and background.

Applying a Design Template

2-4.1.3
2-4.1.6

You can easily give your presentation a professional look by applying a slide design. A *slide design* specifies a color scheme, text format, backgrounds, bullet styles, and graphics for all the slides in the presentation. As you saw in the last Step-by-Step, PowerPoint provides several professionally designed templates from which you can choose. The design template you choose for your presentation, if possible, should reflect the theme of the presentation topic. Moreover, the design should not detract from the message you want to deliver.

> **Note**
>
> PowerPoint provides numerous design templates from which you can choose. Some of the templates are not installed during a typical installation. If you choose a design that is not installed, you may be able to open the design from the application CD.

Each design template has a specific look and feel. You can apply a different slide design at any time to change the look of your presentation. However, the content of your slides does not change. You can edit the content of slides before or after you apply a new design template; that is, the information on the slide can be changed independently of its design and formats.

To apply a slide design template, open the Format menu and choose Slide Design. The Slide Design task pane will display, showing the template currently used in this presentation, recently used designs, and designs that are available for use.

If you like a slide design but you don't like the colors used in the design, you can easily change the color scheme of the design. PowerPoint offers several standard color schemes for each slide design. You can apply a new color scheme to all the slides or apply it only to selected slides.

> ### Note
>
> If you'd like to create your own color scheme, click the **Edit Color Schemes** link that appears at the bottom of the Slide Design task pane after you select the Color Schemes link. The Edit Color Scheme dialog box will display. If necessary, click the **Custom** tab, select the item you want to edit (such as Title text or Fills), and then click the **Change Color** button. Select the new colors and click **OK**. When you're done selecting the new colors, click **Apply** in the Edit Color Scheme dialog box.

S TEP-BY-STEP 19.5

1. Open the **Format** menu and choose **Slide Design**. The Slide Design task pane shown in Figure 19-6 is displayed at the right of your screen. (The designs shown in your task pane may not be exactly like the ones shown in Figure 19-6, but they will be displayed in a similar way.)

FIGURE 19-6
Slide Design task pane

2. Under Available For Use, scroll down to view all the thumbnails for the available designs. Then, locate and click the design titled **Balance**. (*Hint:* The design has a brown background. When you point to the thumbnail of the slide design, a ScreenTip will display with the design name.) The new design appears in the Slide pane, replacing the blank slide that was displayed.

STEP-BY-STEP 19.5 Continued

3. At the top of the task pane, click the link **Color Schemes**. Several color schemes are displayed in the task pane, as shown in Figure 19-7.

FIGURE 19-7
Task pane with color scheme options

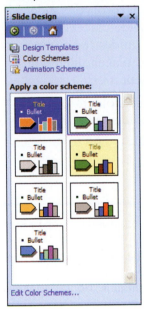

4. Click the **down arrow** on the right side of the first option. A drop-down menu with three options displays. Select **Show Large Previews**.

5. Use the scroll bar to view the color scheme options. Click some of the options to view the different color schemes. The new colors are applied to the slide in the presentation, and the new colors appear in the Slide pane and in the Outline pane. Notice that not only does the background color change, but the text color also changes.

6. Select a color scheme that you prefer. Click the **down arrow** to display the drop-down menu, and then select **Apply to All Slides**.

7. Close the presentation without saving it and leave PowerPoint open for the next Step-by-Step.

Adding, Deleting, and Duplicating Slides

Y ou can add new slides, copy slides, or delete slides in Normal view or Slide Sorter view. In the next two Step-by-Steps, you will practice inserting, cutting, and duplicating slides in both views.

Adding Slides

To add a new slide, open the Insert menu and choose New Slide, or click the New Slide button on the Formatting toolbar. When you add a slide, the design that you have already applied to the presentation is automatically applied to the new slide. The *slide layout* used in the previous slide is also applied. The slide layout refers to the way things are arranged on the slide. All but one of the layout options provide placeholders. The *placeholders* provide placement guides for adding text, pictures, tables, or charts. The placeholder will not print or display in the actual presentation.

You can resize and move the placeholders on the slide. You can even format the placeholders with fill colors and borders. And, if you do not use a placeholder, you can delete it.

> **Computer Concepts**
>
> Some placeholders for text automatically format a bullet at the beginning of each paragraph. The bullet color and symbol are formatted based on the design template. To remove the bullet, position the insertion point in the paragraph containing the bullet, and then click the Bullet button on the Formatting toolbar.

S TEP-BY-STEP 19.6

1. Open **The 3Rs** presentation that you saved in Step-by-Step 19.1

2. From the **Format** menu, select **Slide Design** and then apply a design template of your choice.

3. Go to the fourth slide in the presentation. (*Hint:* Use the scroll bar or click the number 4 slide text in the Outline pane.)

4. Click the **New Slide** button on the Formatting toolbar. A new blank slide is created and placed after slide number 4. Notice that the Outline pane is updated to show that the new slide has been added.

5. Notice that the Slide Layout task pane is now displayed at the right of your screen. The new blank slide is formatted with the same layout that was used for the number 4 slide. This layout is also selected under *Text Layouts* in the task pane. The ScreenTip in the task pane describes this layout as *Title and Text*.

6. Select the **Title** and **2 Column Text** option in the task pane. (*Hint:* It is directly to the right of the currently selected layout. When you point to the option, the ScreenTip will show the option name.) The slide layout for the new slide will change to display a text box for a title with two columns for text below.

7. Switch to **Slide Sorter** view. (*Hint:* Click the Slide Sorter View button at the bottom left corner of the screen.) Notice the new blank number 5 slide.

STEP-BY-STEP 19.6 Continued

8. Click between slides number 3 and number 4 to position the insertion point between the two slides. The insertion point will be displayed as a long vertical line between the two slides.

9. Open the **Insert** menu and click **New Slide**. A new slide is created. You now have a total of eight slides in your presentation.

10. Save the changes and leave the presentation open for the next Step-by-Step.

Deleting and Duplicating Slides

You can delete slides in Normal view or Slide Sorter view. It is easy to delete multiple slides in Slide Sorter view, and this view also makes it easy to copy and move slides. You can use the Cut, Copy, and Paste commands to copy or move slides.

When you use the Cut, Copy, and Paste commands, PowerPoint stores the slide content and design in the Clipboard. Remember that the Clipboard is a temporary storage place in your computer's memory. You send selected slides to the Clipboard by using the Cut or Copy commands. Then you can retrieve those contents by using the Paste command. The contents remain in the Clipboard until you copy or paste something new, or when you turn off your computer. You can paste Clipboard items as many times as you want. To view the contents of the Clipboard at any time, select Office Clipboard from the Edit menu. You can also display the Clipboard in the task pane by clicking the down arrow to the right of the current task pane title and then selecting Clipboard from the menu of other task panes that displays.

> **Computer Concepts**
>
> You can select multiple slides before you move, copy, or delete. To select multiple slides in Slide Sorter view, click the first slide, hold down the **Ctrl** key, and click each additional slide to be included in the selection. Or, you can select a series of slides by clicking the first slide in the series and then holding down the **Shift** key while clicking the last slide in the series. All slides between and including the two slides you clicked will be selected.

> **Computer Concepts**
>
> The shortcut keys for the Cut command are **Ctrl + X**. Use **Ctrl + C** for the Copy command and **Ctrl + V** for the Paste command. These are the same shortcut keys for performing these functions in other Microsoft Office applications.

S TEP-BY-STEP 19.7

1. Click slide number **6** to select it. Then press **Delete**. The slide is removed and the following slide numbers are revised to reflect the change.

2. Click slide number **3** to select it. Click the **Copy** button on the Standard toolbar. The slide content and design are copied to the Office Clipboard.

> **Note**
>
> To remove a slide in Normal view, you must open the **Edit** menu and choose **Delete Slide**. To delete a slide in the Outline tab, click the slide icon to the right of the slide number to select the slide number and its contents, and then press **Delete**.

STEP-BY-STEP 19.7 Continued

3. Position the insertion point after slide number 7. Click the **Paste** button on the Standard toolbar.

4. Switch to Normal view and click slide number **4** (the blank slide) to select it. Open the **Edit** menu and click **Delete Slide**.

5. The remaining slides are out of order. The number 6 slide should follow slide number 4. Switch back to Slide Sorter view to make it easier to move slides.

6. Select slide number **6** and click the **Cut** button on the Standard toolbar. The number 6 slide is removed and all subsequent slides are renumbered.

7. Position the insertion point between slide number 4 and slide number 5, and then click the **Paste** button. The slides are rearranged and automatically renumbered.

8. Save the changes and close the presentation. Leave PowerPoint open for the next Step-by-Step.

Using the Slide Finder

The *Slide Finder* enables you to quickly find and copy slides from one presentation to another. You can copy selected slides one at a time or you can copy all of the slides at once. When slides are copied to a second presentation, they automatically adopt the format applied to the second presentation. You can access the Slide Finder either in Slide Sorter view or in Normal view.

STEP-BY-STEP 19.8

1. Open a new presentation using the From design template option in the New Presentation pane.

2. Select the **Ocean** template and save the presentation as **Global Students** followed by your initials.

3. The Slide pane shows a slide layout for a Title Slide. Click in the first placeholder and key **A New Country**. Press **Enter**, and then key **A New Experience**.

4. Click in the second placeholder and key your first and last names.

5. Switch to **Slide Sorter** view. There is only one slide in the presentation, and it is selected.

6. Open the **Insert** menu and choose **Slides from Files**. The Slide Finder dialog box shown in Figure 19-8 is displayed.

7. Click the **Browse** button in the dialog box. The Browse dialog box opens. Locate and select the file Step19-8a in the data files.

8. Click **Open** in the Browse dialog box. Miniature versions of the first three slides in the Step19-8a presentation are displayed at the bottom of the Slide Finder dialog box.

STEP-BY-STEP 19.8 Continued

FIGURE 19-8
Slide Finder dialog box

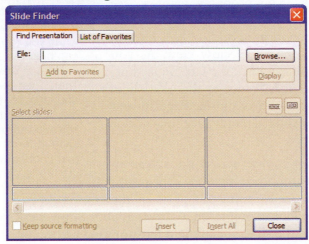

9. Click slide number **2** to select it. Then click the **Insert** button. You can probably see that in the screen behind the dialog box, the slide is inserted into your *Global Students* presentation after the first slide. (You can also see that the inserted slide converts to the design template for the current presentation.)

10. The Slide Finder dialog box remains open. Click slide number **2** again to deselect it. Then click slide number **3** to select it, and click **Insert**.

11. Click the **Browse** button in the Slide Finder dialog box again and locate and select the file **Step19-8b**. Click **Open**.

12. Click the **Insert All** button. All the slides in the Step 19-8b file are inserted in the *Global Students* presentation after the current slide.

13. Click the **Close** button in the Slide Finder dialog box to close it.

14. Notice that there are now ten slides in the presentation. Save the changes and leave the document open for the next Step-by-Step.

Previewing a Presentation

Now that you have had some practice creating PowerPoint presentations, you probably want to see what a slide show looks like when you present it to an audience. You can see how a presentation will look in full-screen view by choosing Slide Show view. As you view the presentation, you can click the left mouse button or press the spacebar to advance to the next slide. You can also use the arrow keys or the PageUp and PageDown keys on the keyboard to advance forward or backward.

When you move your mouse across the screen in Slide Show view, an arrow mouse pointer appears on the screen that you can use to point out parts of the slide. After you move the mouse pointer in a screen in Slide Show view, you will see several icons in the lower-left corner of the slide, including a left-pointing arrow, a pen icon, a menu icon, and a right-pointing arrow. When you click the arrows, the display moves to the previous (with the left-pointing arrow) or next (with the right-pointing arrow) slide in the presentation.

Click the pen icon to display a menu of options to change the mouse pointer to different kinds of pens. You can then use the mouse pointer as a pen to draw or write on the screen. The pen marks overlay the slide and you can choose whether to save the pen annotations or discard them when you close the presentation preview.

The menu icon opens a shortcut menu that offers options to navigate through the slide show, close it, change the display color or appearance, and access Help.

Any speaker notes you have added to your presentation are not visible in Slide Show view unless you make them appear. To display a note in Slide Show view, click the menu icon or right-click anywhere in the slide to open a shortcut menu. On the shortcut menu, select Screen and then click Speaker Notes in the submenu. The note for that slide will appear in the middle of the screen, in front of the slide information.

> ## Computer Concepts
>
> If you don't want a slide to appear when you run the presentation, you can hide the slide. Select the slide in Normal view or Slide Sorter view. Then open the **Slide Show** menu and choose **Hide Slide**. To restore the slide so it does display when you run the presentation, select the slide, open the **Slide Show** menu, and choose **Hide Slide** again to toggle the feature off.

STEP-BY-STEP 19.9

1. Switch to Normal view and go to slide number 1. Click the **Slide Show View** button in the lower-left corner, just above the status bar. (Refer back to Figure 19-4 if necessary.) The first slide shows in full-screen view.

2. Click the left mouse button to advance to the next slide. Experiment with using the arrow keys and the PageUp and PageDown keys to move from slide to slide.

3. Move the mouse pointer across the screen, and when the arrows and icons appear, click one of the arrows to move to the previous or next screen.

> ## Note
>
> You can start the slide show on any slide by displaying or selecting the slide you want to begin with before switching to Slide Show view.

STEP-BY-STEP 19.9 Continued

4. Click the pen icon to display a shortcut menu. The Arrow option is the default selection and is checked in the menu. Choose **Felt Tip Pen**. Experiment writing on the screen with the pen, then advance to the next slide.

5. Click the pen icon again and select **Highlighter**. Use the new mouse pointer to highlight some of the text on the slide, then press **Esc** to turn off the pen and bring back the arrow pointer.

6. Click the menu icon to open another shortcut menu. Click **Go to Slide** in the menu, and then click slide number **7**, *Countries you can visit . . .*

7. Right-click to open the shortcut menu again, click **Screen**, and then select **Speaker Notes** from the submenu. The speaker note for this slide appears in a message box in the middle of the screen, similar to Figure 19-9. Click **Close** to close the Speaker Notes message box.

FIGURE 19-9
Speaker notes message box

8. Click the menu icon again, click **Go to Slide** in the menu, and then click slide number **10**, *Global Students*.

9. Click the right-pointing arrow, which will take you to a black screen with directions displayed at the top that say *End of slide show, click to exit*. Notice that the arrows and icons in the lower-left corner of the screen still appear. Click the left-pointing arrow to return to the last slide in the presentation.

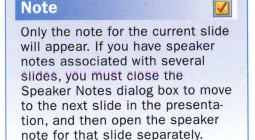

Note ☑

Only the note for the current slide will appear. If you have speaker notes associated with several slides, you must close the Speaker Notes dialog box to move to the next slide in the presentation, and then open the speaker note for that slide separately.

10. To exit the slide show, press **Esc**. A message box will appear, as shown in Figure 19-10, asking if you want to keep the ink annotations you made with the pen and highlighter.

FIGURE 19-10
Keep or Discard Slide Show annotations message box

11. Click **Discard** to exit without saving the pen marks. The current slide will display in Normal view.

12. Click the application close box in the upper-right corner of the screen (the red X) to close the presentation and the application. Follow your instructor's directions about turning off your computer.

SUMMARY

In this lesson, you learned:

■ When you start PowerPoint, you can choose to create a new presentation or open an existing presentation.

■ In addition to using the Outline pane to move to a different slide, you can also use the scroll bar or shortcut keys to navigate through a presentation in Normal view.

■ PowerPoint offers three different views to display a presentation. You work in either Normal view or Slide Sorter view as you create and edit your presentation. In Slide Show view, the current slide fills the full computer screen. You use this view to preview your presentation and when you present the show to your audience.

■ There are several ways to create a new presentation in PowerPoint, including opening a blank presentation or a design template, using the AutoContent Wizard, selecting a presentation with content, and modifying existing presentations.

■ You can add speaker notes to slides in the Notes pane that appears below the Slide pane in Normal view.

■ The slide design automatically formats slides with color schemes, bullet styles, and graphics. A design template ensures that all slides in a presentation have a consistent look. You can apply a design at any time without affecting the contents of the slides.

■ You can add a new slide in Normal view or Slide Sorter view. When you add a new slide, you can select a slide layout or use the default layout.

■ It is easy to delete and copy slides in Slide Sorter view. You can use the Cut, Copy, and Paste commands to delete, move, or copy slides in a presentation.

■ The Slide Finder enables you to find and copy one or more slides from one presentation to another quickly and easily.

■ In Slide Show view, you can preview your presentation, move through the slide show using the mouse, spacebar, or shortcut keys, and even draw or write over the slides.

VOCABULARY*Review*

Define the following terms:

Normal view	Slide design	Slide Show view
Placeholders	Slide Finder	Slide Sorter view
Presentations	Slide layout	

REVIEW *Questions*

TRUE/FALSE

Circle T if the statement is true or F if the statement is false.

T   F   **1.** You can use the Outline pane to quickly navigate through a presentation.

T   F   **2.** You can add new slides in Slide Show view.

T   F   **3.** To move to the first slide in a presentation, you can press Ctrl + Home.

T   F   **4.** When you apply a design template to a slide, you cannot change the text on the slide.

T   F   **5.** To see your presentation as a slide show, you use Normal view.

MULTIPLE CHOICE

Circle the best response for each of the following statements.

1. The _____ enables you to copy slides from one presentation to another.
    A. Design template
    B. Slide Show
    C. Slide Finder
    D. task pane

2. _____ view displays a miniature version of each of the slides in the presentation.
    A. Slide Show
    B. Slide Sorter
    C. Normal
    D. Web Layout

3. A(n) _____ specifies a uniform color scheme, background, bullet style, text format, and graphics for a presentation.
    A. color template
    B. slide layout
    C. application design
    D. design template

4. _____ provide(s) guides for adding text, pictures, tables, and charts.
    A. Formats
    B. Sizing handles
    C. Slide Finder
    D. Placeholders

5. _____ view allows you to preview a presentation, move from slide to slide, and write temporarily or permanently on the slides.
    A. Slide Show
    B. Normal
    C. Slide Sorter
    D. Notes Page

PROJECTS

PROJECT 19-1

1. If necessary, start PowerPoint. Open **Project19-1** from the data files. Save the presentation as **Gettysburg** followed by your initials.

2. Change to Slide Sorter view. Cut slide number 2 and then paste the slide at the end of the presentation.

3. Change to Normal view and navigate to the first slide in the presentation.

4. Click in the subtitle placeholder and key **Three Days in July**.

5. Choose and apply a slide design to the presentation.

6. Save your changes and then preview the presentation.

7. In Slide Show view, turn on the Highlighter option.

8. Use the highlighter to highlight *Seminary Ridge* on slide number 3 and *Cemetery Ridge* on slide number 4.

9. Exit the slide show, and click **Keep** in the message box that asks *Do you want to keep your ink annotations?*

10. Close the presentation.

PROJECT 19-2

1. Open **Project19-2** from the data files. Save the presentation as **Searching** followed by your initials.

2. Change the color scheme of the current slide design to the scheme in the Color Scheme dialog box that has a purple title.

3. Delete slide number 2.

4. Insert a new slide after the newly renumbered slide number 2 and apply the **Title Only** slide layout to the new slide.

5. Click the placeholder in the new slide number 3 and key **Then, Choose a Tool**.

6. Add a slide at the end of the presentation with the Title and Text layout. In the title placeholder, key the title **Other Resources**.

7. Key the following items in the text placeholder:
   Resource lists
   Guides
   Clearinghouses
   Virtual libraries

8. Delete slide number 6.

9. Save your changes and preview the presentation.

10. Close the presentation and then close PowerPoint.

 TEAMWORK PROJECT

One of the best uses of a PowerPoint presentation is to persuade an audience to adopt a particular point of view. With a partner, explore both sides of a specific issue. Follow these steps:

1. As a class, brainstorm some topic issues of interest to the entire class (such as a proposal for a new community park or a school dress code policy). Or, your instructor may have a list of issues already prepared.

2. Form groups of two students who have different opinions on one topic. The students in each group will create separate presentations that illustrate each of their positions.

3. Gather information on the issue from surveys or research and then create a presentation to support your own particular point of view.

4. Design the slides to emphasize your points clearly. Select a design template and slide layouts that do not detract from your content and distribute your information effectively on the slides in your presentation.

5. If possible, present the slide shows for both sides of each issue and have the class critique each presentation for design, content, and persuasiveness.

CRITICAL *Thinking*

ACTIVITY 19-1

You have applied a design template to a presentation. Several of the slides in the presentation need special emphasis so your audience will really pay attention. You wonder if you can change the color scheme for those particular slides. Can you do this in PowerPoint?

Use the Help files in PowerPoint to find the answer. Write a brief summary of what you learn.

ENHANCING PRESENTATIONS WITH MULTIMEDIA EFFECTS

OBJECTIVES

Upon completion of this lesson, you should be able to:

- Add information to a slide.
- Format text.
- Insert pictures and other graphics.
- Change the slide layout.
- Use Slide Masters.
- Create transitions between slides.
- Change the order of slides in a presentation.
- Print handouts and notes to accompany a slide show.

Estimated Time: 1 hour

VOCABULARY

Clip Organizer

Exit effect

Slide Master

Transitions

To create an effective presentation, you must consider all the text and graphics you enter on the slides. Changing the color of the text or changing the style for the text can make the slides easier to read. Adding pictures can help communicate your message and help your audience remember the information you present. The layout you choose for the slides and the transitions you add between the slides add interest and can help keep the attention of your audience focused on the presentation. You can also use PowerPoint to create and print speaker's notes and audience handouts.

Adding Information to a Slide

2-4.1.3

To add text to a slide or to edit a slide, you must display the slide in Normal view. If the slide contains a placeholder for text, you simply click inside the placeholder and enter the text. You can add text to a slide in three additional ways, however, including adding text in an AutoShape, in a text box, and WordArt text.

- Slide layouts contain text and object placeholders in various combinations. You can type titles, subtitles, and body text in the text placeholders. You also can resize the placeholders, move them to another position in the slide, and add formatting to the text.

- PowerPoint provides AutoShapes such as callout balloons and block arrows that you can use to emphasize text. When you enter text in an AutoShape, the text is attached to the shape and moves with it.

- Text boxes allow you to place text anywhere on a slide, even outside a placeholder. Text boxes also can have a border, fill, shadow, or three-dimensional (3-D) effect.

> **Computer Concepts**
>
> Use the PowerPoint Help feature to find out more about using WordArt in presentations.

- Use WordArt to create ornamental text effects. With WordArt, you can stretch, curve, and rotate your text to add even more elaborate effects.

You have already entered some text in placeholders in the exercises in Lesson 19. In the exercises in this lesson, you will practice adding text if the slide does not have a placeholder for text, and find out how to add interest to your slides with AutoShapes. You will also edit text already on a slide and change the slide layout to accommodate the text you want to add. When you add and edit text, the contents in the Outline pane are automatically updated.

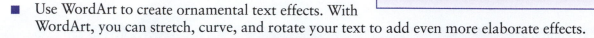

STEP-BY-STEP 20.1

1. Open **Step20-1** from the data files and save the presentation as **International Club** followed by your initials.

2. Click slide number **3** in the Outline pane so you can add text. Click in the placeholder in the middle of the slide that says *Click to add text*. Key **Area team leaders** and then press **Enter**.

3. You will see another bullet appear, ready for you to enter another item. Key **Host coordinators** and press **Enter**, then key **District representatives** after the new bullet that appears.

> **Computer Concepts**
>
> PowerPoint automatically adjusts the layout if you insert items that don't fit the original layout. For example, if you fill a text box with several lines of text and keep entering text, PowerPoint will reduce the font size as needed so all the text will fit inside the text box.

4. Click outside the placeholder to deselect it. Then press **Ctrl + Home** to move to the first slide.

5. Click **Student Name** to move to that placeholder. Move the placeholder to the lower-right corner of the slide. You can reduce the text box by using the sizing handles so the text box fits in the right half of the slide at the bottom.

6. Select the words **Student Name** and replace the words with your first and last names.

7. Open the Insert menu and select Text Box. A small arrow appears in the slide. Position the arrow about an inch below the slide title and click to open a text box. In the text box, key **An International Club Presentation**.

8. Move the mouse pointer over the text box until it changes to a two-pointed arrow. Use the sizing handles to stretch the text box so the text fits on one line if necessary. Move the mouse pointer until it changes to a four-pointed arrow, and then drag the text box to center it under the title.

STEP-BY-STEP 20.1 Continued

9. Click outside the text box to deselect it and then, if necessary, display the Drawing toolbar by selecting it from the Toolbars submenu on the View menu.

10. Navigate to slide number 8 and click **AutoShapes** on the Drawing toolbar.

11. Point to **Callouts** in the pop-up menu and then select the first callout option. (The ScreenTip for this option reads *Rectangular Callout*.)

12. Drag the crosshair pointer that appears to place a rectangular "balloon" to the right of the telephone number text on the slide, as shown in Figure 20-1.

FIGURE 20-1
Positioning an AutoShape on a slide

13. Key **Toll-free number!** in the AutoShape callout balloon and then click outside the AutoShape to deselect it.

14. Save the changes and leave the presentation open for the next Step-by-Step.

Formatting Text

When you use a design template, the format of the text on each of the slides is predetermined. There may be occasions, however, when you want to alter the text format. You may want to change the font style or point size. A font is the general shape and style of a set of characters. Fonts are available in a variety of styles and sizes, and you can use multiple fonts in one document. The size of the font is measured in points.

You can quickly change font style and point size by using the Formatting toolbar. However, when you open the Font dialog box to change the font, you can also apply other font options such as color, outline, superscript, and shadow. The Font dialog box is also more useful if you want to make several font changes at one time or if you want to explore what options are available and what they would make the text look like.

Computer Concepts

The higher the point size is, the larger the font size is. One inch equals approximately 72 points.

Selecting Text

You must first select text to be able to change the font, point size, or to apply any other text format such as boldface. You can use the mouse or the keyboard to select text. When you select text, you identify text or blocks of text for editing or formatting. You can select a single character, several characters, a word, a phrase, a sentence, one or more paragraphs, or even the entire document. Once you select text, you can delete it, replace it, change its appearance, move it, copy it, and so on. Table 20-1 shows some shortcuts you can use to select text in a presentation. Some of these shortcuts will look familiar because they are similar to those used to select text in other Office applications.

TABLE 20-1
Ways to select text in a presentation

TO SELECT TEXT	DO THIS
A word	Double-click the word.
A paragraph and all its subordinate text	Triple-click anywhere in the paragraph.
All text on a slide	On the Outline tab in Normal view, click the slide icon after the slide number.
Text in a placeholder, AutoShape, or text box	Position the insertion point in the object and press Ctrl + A.
Text in all the placeholders in a presentation	Position the insertion point on the Outline tab in Normal view and press Ctrl + A.

Changing the Appearance of Text

You can change the appearance of the text in your presentation by changing the font style, the font size, and the font color. You can also add special emphasis by changing the text to italics, bold, or small capitals. However, using too many fonts or too many different formats generally makes the text harder to read. You want to use formats in moderation.

Serif typefaces (such as Times Roman) have embellishments or curls at the ends of the letters. Sans serif typefaces (such as Arial) have plain strokes with clear and simple curves. Serif typefaces are easiest to read and should be used when there are many words on a screen. Sans serif typefaces are usually heavier and bolder and are appropriate for titles and subtitles.

To quickly increase the font size to the next increment in the Font Size box, select the text and press Ctrl +] (closing square bracket). Continue pressing the keys for additional increases. Press Ctrl + [(opening square bracket) to decrease the font size to the previous increment. This is quite helpful when you want to grow or shrink the text to fit within a specified area on the slide.

> **Note**
>
> You can position the insertion point in the Font size box, key the size, and press **Enter**. This method enables you to enter font sizes that do not appear in the list. However, there is a limit to the maximum and minimum size you can enter.

STEP-BY-STEP 20.2

1. Go to slide number 1 and triple-click the text in the first placeholder in the slide pane to select it (*A New Country A New Experience*).

2. With the text selected, click the **down arrow** next to the **Font** box on the Formatting toolbar. Select **Times New Roman** in the drop-down list.

STEP-BY-STEP 20.2 Continued

3. With the text still selected, click the **down arrow** in the **Font Size** box on the Formatting toolbar. Scroll down and select **60** in the drop-down list. The selected text is enlarged to the bigger font size.

4. With the text still selected, press **Ctrl +]** (closing square bracket) three times to increase the font size. Notice that the text no longer fits in two lines.

5. Press **Ctrl + [** (opening square bracket) one time to decrease the font size.

6. With the text still selected, click the **Bold** button on the Formatting toolbar, and then open the **Format** menu and choose **Font**. The Font dialog box shown in Figure 20-2 displays.

FIGURE 20-2
Font dialog box

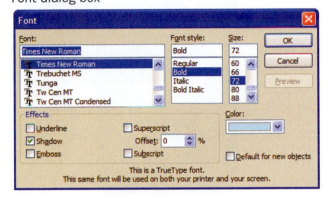

7. Click the **down arrow** in the box beneath **Color**. A box of color options is displayed. The set of colors shown here are all used in the template design and are, therefore, good choices.

8. Select the last color in the row of color options, the **gold** color. Then click **OK** to close the Font dialog box.

9. Click anywhere on the slide to deselect the text so you can see the change in the font color.

> **Computer Concepts**
>
> You can use the Undo and Redo commands in PowerPoint to reverse or repeat one or more of your recent actions.

10. Click the **Undo** button on the Standard toolbar. The last edit—changing the text color—is reversed and the text reverts to its original color.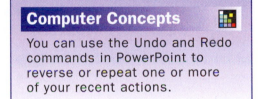

11. Save the changes and leave the document open for the next Step-by-Step.

2-4.1.3

Inserting Graphics

There may be times when you want to add clip art and graphics to your presentation. Pictures can help your audience remember your message. PowerPoint allows you to place pictures inside special graphic placeholders. When you insert a picture in a placeholder, the picture replaces the placeholder. You can insert pictures from the *Clip Organizer* (a wide variety of pictures, photographs, sounds, and video clips that you can insert in your presentations). You can also insert a picture from a scanned photo or from a file.

When a clip art image is selected, eight small squares called *sizing handles* appear on the border of the graphic. When it is selected, you can cut, copy, paste, delete, move, and resize the picture. To resize the picture, drag a sizing handle. You will see the effects on the screen as you drag. If you drag a corner sizing handle, the picture will be resized proportionally.

Computer Concepts

Sometimes photos, clip art, and graphics can be much more powerful than words. Print media and television news provide examples of how visual images can enhance the message being communicated.

STEP-BY-STEP 20.3

1. Go to slide number 2 and display it in Normal view. Notice that the slide layout includes title, content, and text. The content placeholder on the left displays six different icons as shown in Figure 20-3.

FIGURE 20-3
Placeholder for graphics content

2. Point to each of the icons to display the ScreenTip. Notice that you can insert tables, charts, clip art, pictures, diagrams or organization charts, and media clips.

3. Click the **Insert Clip Art** icon. A Select Picture dialog box similar to the one shown in Figure 20-4 is displayed. Do not be concerned if the clip art images in your dialog box are different.

FIGURE 20-4
Select Picture dialog box

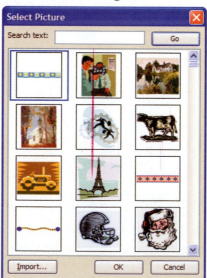

STEP-BY-STEP 20.3 Continued

4. Click in the **Search text** box and key **globe**, and then click **Go**. PowerPoint will search the Clip Organizer for all pictures related to this word. A dialog box then displays images that match the word, as shown in Figure 20-5.

FIGURE 20-5
Picture search results

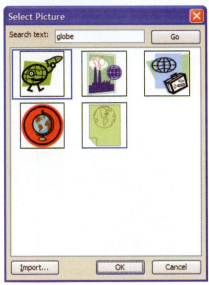

5. Click the picture of the image illustrated at the end of the first row in the search results pane shown in Figure 20-5, or find one that is similar. You may need to scroll down through the pictures to find a suitable image.

6. After you select the clip art image you want to use, click **OK**. The image is inserted in the slide and the Select Picture dialog box closes.

7. Eight sizing handles should appear around the picture, similar to Figure 20-6. Point to the sizing handle at the upper-left corner of the image. When the pointer changes to a two-headed arrow, drag the sizing handle up and to the left to make the picture bigger.

FIGURE 20-6
Selected picture with sizing handles

8. Point to the center of the picture. The pointer will change to a four-headed arrow. If necessary, drag the picture to reposition it to the left of the bulleted list.

9. Save the changes and leave the document open for the next Step-by-Step.

Changing Slide Layout

2-4.1.5

You can change the slide layout of a slide in a presentation, before or after you add information. Choose Normal view to change or add a slide layout. If the Slide Layout task pane is not displayed, open the Format menu and select Slide Layout. The Slide Layout task pane, shown in Figure 20-7, appears at the right of the window. There are four categories of slide layouts available:

■ Text Layouts

■ Content Layouts

■ Text and Content Layouts

■ Other Layouts

FIGURE 20-7
Slide Layout task pane

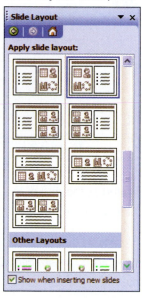

The Content Layouts options include one for a blank slide, and the Other Layouts category includes options for inserting specialized contents such as tables, charts, media clips, and organizational charts.

When you add a new slide to a presentation, a default layout with placeholders for a title and text is applied, but you can select any slide layout to apply it to the new slide. To change the layout of an existing slide, select the slide in Normal view and then select the new slide layout in the Slide Layout task pane. Your content and formatting will remain as they were; only the layout of the slide will change. You may find that if you select a layout that does not have placeholders for all the text and content in the original slide, elements of the slide may appear overlapping. You can move any placeholder to change the arrangements of elements on a slide.

S TEP-BY-STEP 20.4

1. Go to slide number 9. You want to add more information to this slide, which will display at the end of your presentation.

STEP-BY-STEP 20.4 Continued

2. Open the Slide Layout task pane and select the **Title Slide** option. This provides another placeholder for text, but you may have too much information to add it as a subtitle.

3. The information you want to add is shown below. Select the **Title and Text** slide layout and enter the text in the bulleted text placeholder. (The title that originally appeared on the slide should display in the title placeholder on the slide.)

> Thank you for attending this meeting of the International Club
>
> Our club meets every Wednesday at 3:00 pm in Room 124
>
> For more information about the Global Students program, visit www.GlobalStudents.com

Computer Concepts

The AutoCorrect feature in PowerPoint can automatically correct errors as you key text in a presentation. You can set the options for the AutoCorrect feature in the AutoCorrect dialog box.

4. Save the changes and leave the presentation open for the next Step-by-Step.

Slide Masters

A *Slide Master* is an element of the design template that stores information about the template. You can keep formats such as font styles and background design in a Slide Master, and you can also add text or insert graphics that will appear on every page. Then you can make a global change or addition, such as selecting a different background color or updating a logo, and have that change reflected on all the slides in your presentation.

Ethics in Technology

PROTECTING INTELLECTUAL PROPERTY

The term *intellectual property* is used to refer to information, material, or processes that were created by and belong to a person or corporation. The types of things included in the definition of intellectual property include books, poems, plays, and other works of literature; music and artwork; inventions and ideas; product names and logos; and scientific or business procedures. Computers make it much easier to copy and disseminate art, documents, inventions, music, and ideas in cyberspace, which has made legal concerns about the rights of a creator—to ensure that the original output of a human mind is considered valuable and entitled to protection—a hot topic.

Often people think that any information available on the Internet is in the public domain and free for the taking. This is not always the case. There are protections for intellectual property, including copyright for literary works, art, and music; patents for inventions and procedures; trademarks for company and product logos; and trade secrets, which include recipes, codes, and manufacturing processes. Be careful not to use protected material in your own work without permission from the person who owns the material.

A Slide Master is automatically provided with every design template in PowerPoint. To view a Slide Master for a presentation, open the View menu, click Master, and then select Slide Master from the submenu. You can make changes to a Slide Master just as you would to any slide, but the actual slide text, such as text, titles, and lists, is typed on individual slides in Normal view. The only text that should be entered on the Slide Master is entered in the **Header and Footer** dialog box.

Note

When you change the Slide Master, any changes you have made to individual slides are preserved.

S TEP-BY-STEP 20.5

1. On the **View** menu, point to **Master**, and then click **Slide Master**. The Slide Master, similar to Figure 20-8, displays in the Slide pane. Notice that the Slide Master View toolbar also is visible.

FIGURE 20-8
Slide Master with Slide Master View toolbar

2. Look at the Outline pane. There are no tabs for Slides and Outline in Slide Master View, and you may also notice more than one thumbnail displayed in the pane. Some design templates have multiple Slide Masters.

3. Click the first slide in the Outline pane to select it if it is not already selected. This is the Slide Master for slides 2 through 10 in this design template. The second master slide is the Title Master, which will apply changes only to slide number 1, the title slide in this presentation.

4. Click the box at the bottom of the Slide Master labeled *Footer Area* to select it, and then click in the box again to select the placeholder text.

Note

Most design templates in PowerPoint have two master slides, one for the title or first slide, and one for the other slides in the presentation. If you open a new blank presentation, you may find there is only one Slide Master for all of the slides. You can use the Slide Master View toolbar to add a new Slide Master or Title Master to any presentation.

STEP-BY-STEP 20.5 Continued

5. Key **International Club** and then click outside the box to deselect it.

6. Click the **Date Area** box at the lower left of the slide. Click in the box again to select the placeholder text.

7. Select **Date and Time** from the **Insert** menu to open the Date and Time dialog box.

8. In the dialog box, select the format with the month spelled out, followed by a two-digit year (such as *November 08*) from the list of available formats, and then click **OK** to add the date format to the slide and close the dialog box.

9. Click **Close Master View** on the Slide Master View toolbar to return to your presentation and navigate through the slides to see the text and date that now appear on every slide (except the first slide).

10. Save the changes and leave the presentation open for the next Step-by-Step.

Transitions

2-4.1.7

S lide *transitions* determine the changes in the display that occur as you move from one slide to another in Slide Show view. For example, you can format the transition so the current slide fades to black before the next slide is displayed. Or you can choose to have the next slide automatically appear after a designated number of seconds. You can even choose a sound effect that will play as the transition occurs. You can apply the transition choices to a single slide or to all the slides in the presentation. To apply a slide transition, you must work in the Slide Transition task pane.

S TEP-BY-STEP 20.6

1. Open the **Slide Show** menu and choose **Slide Transition**. The Slide Transition task pane shown in Figure 20-9 is displayed. Make sure the AutoPreview option at the bottom of the task pane is turned on.

FIGURE 20-9
Slide Transition task pane

STEP-BY-STEP 20.6 Continued

2. Under Apply to selected slides, scroll down and select **Strips Right-Down**.

3. Under Modify transition in the Speed drop-down box, select **Medium**.

4. Under Advance slide, deselect **On Mouse Click**. Then, select **Automatically after**. In the box below, key or select **00:03**.

5. Click the **Apply to All Slides** button.

6. Go to slide number 1 and then click the **Slide Show** button in the task pane to view the presentation in full screen. Each slide should automatically advance after three seconds.

7. Press **Esc** or click the **End of slide show, click to exit** message at the top of the screen to exit the slide show.

8. Save the changes and leave the presentation open for the next Step-by-Step.

> **Note**
>
> You can also open the Slide Transition task pane by clicking the **down arrow** at the top of the task pane and choosing **Slide Transition** in the menu.

Applying an Exit Effect

You can apply an *exit effect* to make text or objects leave the slide. For example, you can make text disappear very subtly by fading it away, or you can make an object disappear with a much more dramatic exit such as making it disappear quickly.

PowerPoint also provides features for entrance effects, emphasis effects, and other animation effects. You can also add sound to a slide show, and even add special "triggers" to start a sound effect or animation segment. Use the PowerPoint Help feature to find out more about these features.

STEP-BY-STEP 20.7

1. Go to slide number 9 in Normal view. Open the **Slide Show** menu and choose **Custom Animation**. The Custom Animation task pane now displays to the right of the Slide pane.

2. Click the title **Global Students** to select it. Hold down **Shift** and click the subtitle containing the bulleted text. Both items should be selected.

3. Click the **Add Effect** button in the task pane, choose **Exit**, and then select **More Effects**. The Add Exit Effect dialog box shown in Figure 20-10 is displayed. If necessary, turn on the **Preview Effect** option.

STEP-BY-STEP 20.7 Continued

FIGURE 20-10
Add Exit Effect dialog box

4. Under the Basic category, select **Peek Out**. Click **OK** to apply the effect and close the dialog box. Notice there are several number tags on the slide, *1* to the left of the title and *1*, *2*, and *3* to the left of the bulleted items. There are two *1* tags because you applied the effect to both items at the same time.

5. Go to slide number 1 and then click the **Slide Show** button in the task pane to view the presentation in full screen. When the last slide displays, you will see the exit effect as the title and first bulleted item move down and disappear, followed by the second bulleted item and then the third bulleted item. The title and first bulleted item disappear at the same time because they are both tagged as the number 1 effect.

6. Press **Esc** or click the **End of slide show, click to exit** message at the top of the screen to exit the slide show. Save the changes and leave the presentation open for the next Step-by-Step.

Changing the Order of Slides in a Presentation

2-4.1.8

You can rearrange one or more slides by using drag-and-drop editing as well as by using the cut and paste method you used in the last lesson. It may be a little easier to use drag-and-drop editing in Slide Sorter view, where all the slides are arranged in rows in one screen, but you can also rearrange slides in the Outline pane in Normal view. Select the slide(s) to be moved, and then drag the slide(s) to the new location. The insertion point will be displayed as a long vertical line between the two slides. When you release the mouse button, the slide(s) will be repositioned at the new location of the insertion point.

STEP-BY-STEP 20.8

1. Switch to Slide Sorter view. You may notice that there is some new information included on the line with the slide number under each thumbnail, as shown in Figure 20-11. The star symbol indicates that the slide has a special effect associated with it, and the *00:03* tells you that the slide show is set up to move from one slide to the next after three seconds.

FIGURE 20-11
Slide Sorter view

2. You have decided that you want to put the list of countries an exchange student can visit (slide number 6) right after the slide about becoming an exchange student (slide number 4). Select slide number **6** and drag it so the insertion point appears between slides 4 and 5.

3. Release the mouse button. The *Countries you can visit* slide is now slide number 5 and the following slides have been renumbered.

4. It makes sense to have the slide titled *Benefits* (slide number 7) closer to the slides about becoming an exchange student, too. Select slide number **7** and drag it to a position between slides 4 and 5. The slide is renumbered as slide number 5.

5. Save the changes and leave the presentation open for the next Step-by-Step.

$)C^3$ *Printing Handouts and Speaker Notes*

2-4.1.9

PowerPoint offers several options for printing your presentation. You can print individual slides, handouts, speaker notes, an outline of the presentation, and more. The PowerPoint Help feature will allow you to learn about the available options.

S TEP-BY-STEP 20.9

1. If the Office Assistant is not displayed, open the **Help** menu and choose **Show the Office Assistant**.

2. Click the **Office Assistant**. Key **print** in the text box, and then click **Search**.

3. A list of topics displays in the Search Results task pane. Select **Print handouts**.

4. Read the steps involved in printing handouts based on a PowerPoint presentation. You can leave the Help screen open for reference as you complete the following steps to print handouts.

5. Open the **File** menu and click **Print Preview**.

   a. Click the **down arrow** in the Print What text box to see the options available.

   b. Select the option **Handouts (4 slides per page)** from the drop-down list.

   c. Click the **Landscape** button on the Print Preview toolbar if necessary to change to a horizontal page layout. The handout layout appears in the preview window, as shown in Figure 20-12. Notice that the mouse pointer is a magnifying glass with a plus sign.

FIGURE 20-12
Handouts for a slide show

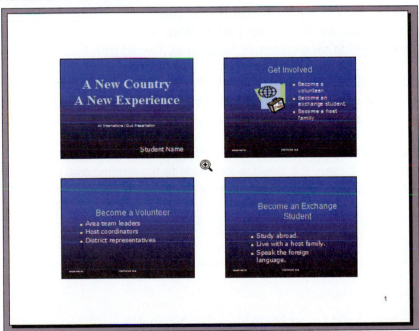

   d. Click in the window to increase the size of the print preview display. The pointer changes to a magnifying glass with a minus sign. Click again to return the display to the original size.

6. If you have permission to print, click the **Print** button in the Print Preview toolbar. Accept the default settings in the Print dialog box and click **OK** to print the three pages of handouts.

STEP-BY-STEP 20.9 Continued

7. Click the **Portrait** button on the Print Preview toolbar to change back to a vertical page layout.

8. Click the **down arrow** in the Print What text box, select **Notes Page**, and then scroll through the preview window to slide number 6. Notice the speaker note for that slide appears beneath the slide.

9. Click the **Options** button on the Print Preview toolbar and point to **Color/Grayscale**.

10. Select the **Grayscale** option in the submenu that appears and notice how the display has changed. Scroll up to slide number 2 to see how the clip art appears with the Grayscale option selected.

11. Click the **Print** button on the Print Preview toolbar to open the Print dialog box. Notice that *Grayscale* is now selected in the Color/Grayscale text box at the bottom of the dialog box.

12. Click **Cancel** to close the Print dialog box without printing.

> ### Computer Concepts
> You can also select other color options for printing in the Print dialog box or in the Options drop-down list on the Print Preview toolbar. Select the Grayscale or Pure Black and White options to print output that will be duplicated on a copier.

13. Click the **down arrow** in the Print What box on the Print Preview toolbar, and then select **Outline View**. The outline of the slide show content is displayed as it would print.

14. Click the **Close** button on the Print Preview toolbar and then close the Help window. (If the Help window has automatically minimized, click the taskbar button that says *Microsoft Office PowerPoint Help*, with a question mark, and then close the Help window.)

15. Click the application close box to close the presentation and PowerPoint. If a message box displays asking if you want to save the changes you made to the *International Club* presentation, click **No**. Follow your instructor's directions about turning off your computer.

SUMMARY

In this lesson, you learned:

■ To add or edit text, a slide must be displayed in Normal view. When you add text or edit text, the slide contents are automatically updated in the Outline pane.

■ If you want to change the way text looks on a slide, you can select the text and apply different formats. For example, you can change the font style, font size, and font color.

■ Pictures help to clarify the message of your presentation. Graphics can make your audience remember your message and PowerPoint makes it easy for you to add a picture to a slide.

■ At any time in the process of creating a presentation, you can change the layout of one or all the slides in the presentation by selecting a new slide layout in the Slide Layout task pane.

- A Slide Master is part of a design template and is used to make uniform changes to slide characteristics such as background color and font, or to add repeated text or graphics to all the slides in a presentation.

- The slide transition affects how each new slide appears. You can apply transition settings to a single slide or to all the slides in the presentation.

- PowerPoint provides special effects that can enhance how a slide opens or closes or add emphasis, animation, or sound.

- You can use drag-and-drop editing to quickly change the order of slides in a presentation in Slide Sorter view.

- PowerPoint provides several options for printing a presentation, including handouts, notes pages, and an outline of the slide show content.

VOCABULARY *Review*

Define the following terms:

Clip Organizer   Slide Master   Transitions
Exit effect

REVIEW *Questions*

TRUE/FALSE

Circle T if the statement is true or F if the statement is false.

T F 1. To reposition a graphic or picture on a slide, the sizing handles must be displayed.

T F 2. AutoShapes are arrows, balloons, and other graphics in which you can add text.

T F 3. When you format a slide transition, it must be applied to all slides in the presentation.

T F 4. The font dialog box provides many font options that are not available on the standard (default) toolbars.

T F 5. You can rearrange slides using either the Cut and Paste toolbar buttons or drag-and-drop editing.

MULTIPLE CHOICE

Circle the best response for each of the following statements.

1. To add information to a slide or to edit a slide, you must display the slide in _____ view.
   A. Slide Show
   B. Slide Sorter
   C. Normal
   D. Print Preview

2. To print handouts for a presentation, you must open the _____ window.
   A. Slide Show
   B. Slide Sorter
   C. Normal
   D. Print Preview

3. The _____ is a part of a design template that stores slide characteristics such as background color, font, and footer information.
   A. Slide Sorter
   B. Slide Master
   C. Transition Master
   D. Notes Page

4. You can find pictures, photographs, sounds, and video clips in the _____.
   A. Art Folder
   B. Clip Organizer
   C. Notes Page
   D. Slide Sorter

5. PowerPoint's slide entrance and exit effects are accessed in the _____ task pane.
   A. New Presentation
   B. Slide Transition
   C. Custom Animation
   D. Color Scheme

PROJECTS

PROJECT 20-1

1. If necessary, start PowerPoint. Create a new presentation with the **Stream** design template. Accept the Title Slide layout for the first slide. Save the presentation as **Refuge Inn** followed by your initials.

2. In the title placeholder, key **Refuge Inn**.

3. In the subtitle placeholder, key the following text exactly as shown: **Yuor Refuge from Stress**. PowerPoint will correct the misspelling for you.

4. You've thought of a better phrase for the subtitle. Click **Undo** to remove all but the first word.

5. Key **Island Retreat** as the new subtitle. The subtitle should now read *Your Island Retreat.*

6. Add a new slide and change the slide layout to Title and Text, if necessary. Key the title **About the Refuge Inn.** Key the following bullet items in the text placeholder:
Family owned since 1952
Double rooms, suites, and efficiencies
Excellent restaurants nearby
Hiking, boating, and biking in the Massassoit National Wildlife Refuge

7. Add another Title and Text slide and key the title **Visit Us Soon!** Key the following bullet items on the slide:
Open year round
Packages available
Call 555-555-4509 for more information

8. Use the Slide Finder to open **Project20-1** from the data files. Insert slides 4 and 5 to the end of your presentation.

9. Change the order of slides so that the current slide number 5 appears before current slide number 4.

10. Move slide number 3 to the end of the presentation.

11. Choose an appropriate slide transition. Set the speed for the transition to medium and format the slides to advance automatically after five seconds. Apply the transition formats to all slides in the presentation.

12. Save the changes you've made to the presentation and then preview it from the beginning.

13. Display the presentation outline in Print Preview, and if you have permission to print, print the outline.

14. Close the presentation.

PROJECT 20-2

1. Open **Project 20-2** from the data files and save the presentation as **Refuge Inn 2** followed by your initials.

2. On slide number 1, format the title as Arial, 48 pt, bold and change the color to pale yellow. Format the subtitle as Arial italic and change its color to the same pale yellow as the title.

3. Format the title on each slide as Arial, 48 pt bold, and pale yellow. (*Hint:* If you learned how to use the Format Painter in Word, you can use it the same way in PowerPoint to complete this task quickly.)

4. Choose appropriate clip art pictures for slides 3 and 4. Resize and position the pictures as needed.

5. Open the Slide Master for slides 2 through 6 and key **Refuge Inn Marketing Presentation** in the Footer Area text box.

6. Format the footer text as Times New Roman, 14 pt, and pale yellow.

7. Go to slide number 2. Select the bulleted list text and add an exit effect as follows:
   A. Format an exit effect so items in the bulleted list leave the slide with the Fly Out effect.
   B. Set the speed at Medium.
   C. Format an exit effect so the title exits with the Dissolve Out effect set at Slow speed.

8. Use the Play button in the task pane to see the exit effects for slide number 2.

9. Add a fast Dissolve transition that advances the slides automatically after three seconds, and apply the transition to all the slides in the presentation.

10. Save the changes and then preview the slide show from the beginning.

11. Display handouts for the presentation with three slides on a page and scroll through the handouts to see all the slides in the presentation.

12. Close Print Preview without printing the handouts and then close the presentation.

 TEAMWORK PROJECT

In these two lessons about PowerPoint slide shows, you have worked with fairly simple presentations. If you wanted to make a more complex presentation on a specific subject, you could use the AutoContent Wizard in PowerPoint to create the slides for you. With a partner, explore the AutoContent Wizard using these steps:

1. With your partner, begin the AutoContent Wizard. (*Hint*: Click **New** on the **File** menu and then select **From AutoContent Wizard** in the New Presentation task pane to get started.) Select a presentation type from the list of all presentations. Choose a presentation type with a subject you know a little bit about, such as Selling Your Ideas or Communicating Bad News. It will also be helpful to imagine a particular situation that matches your presentation type. For example, if you choose the Communicating Bad News presentation, imagine that you and your teammate are the management team of a small company, and you have to tell your employees that none of them will receive bonuses this year.

2. Answer the questions the Wizard asks you. If necessary, use the Help feature in PowerPoint to find out what options the Wizard is giving you.

3. After the presentation appears, examine the sample slide material in the outline pane. You will need to replace the sample text with your own text.

4. Replace the text as necessary to fit the situation you have imagined. Both partners should contribute in creating new text (you can alternate slides to share the work). Delete any unnecessary slides and add slides if necessary.

5. Run your presentation, showing it to the entire class if possible.

CRITICAL*Thinking*

ACTIVITY 20-1

You have created a presentation to convince fellow citizens to support a local clean-up campaign. You have included as the last slide a list of several phone numbers and contact names for more information on the campaign. You anticipate that your audience will want to see this information a number of times during the presentation. It will be time-consuming to click through the slides each time to reach the last slide. PowerPoint offers several ways that you can jump directly to a specific slide during a presentation. Research this topic using Help and write a brief report discussing at least two methods of moving between slides. Create a short presentation to demonstrate the two methods.

ACCESS ESSENTIALS

A database is a collection of related information organized for rapid search and retrieval. Databases can contain all types of data from an address list to schedules for a soccer tournament. Access is the Microsoft Office database program that enables you to organize and manipulate data in many ways.

You might wonder what the difference is between a spreadsheet and a database. Actually, they are very similar. Like spreadsheets, databases are composed of rows and columns. Both enable you to organize, sort, and calculate the data. Although a spreadsheet is great for calculating data, a database offers much more comprehensive functions for manipulating the data. Access is a powerful program that offers many features, most of which are beyond the scope of this course. The Access lessons in this module will introduce you to some of the basic features for entering, organizing, and reporting data in Access. Then as you continue to learn and use Microsoft Office, you will have the building blocks you need for utilizing this powerful program.

Identifying the Parts of the Access Screen

The Access screen is similar to other Office 2003 applications, with a title bar, a menu bar, and a status bar. Unlike Word and Excel, Access does not have a standard document view. The Access screen changes based on the features you are using as you work with the database. Many of the menu options and toolbar buttons are unique to the Access application.

When you open a Database Objects window in Access, you will notice that the Objects bar at the left of the window displays several objects: Tables, Queries, Forms, Reports, Pages, Macros, and Modules. These objects work together to help you organize and report the information that you store in the database. Every database file contains each of these objects. Tables are the primary objects in the database, and each of the objects and everything you do in a database relies on the data stored in the tables. Access also refers to a database table as a *datasheet*. A database can contain multiple or tables.

The following list describes the purpose of each of the objects. You will learn to create tables in this lesson, and you will learn to create queries, forms, and reports in Lesson 22. Although you will not learn how to create pages, macros, or modules in the scope of this course, the following explanations help to describe the potential of the features that are available to you in Access.

■ **Tables:** Tables store data in columns and rows. All database information is stored in tables, and all other database objects rely on the existence of the table(s).

■ **Queries:** A query is a way to ask a question about the information stored in the table. Access searches for and retrieves data from the database table(s) to answer your question.

■ **Forms:** Forms make it easy for you to enter data into a table.

■ **Pages:** Pages enable you to design other database objects so they can be published on the Web.

■ **Macros:** Macros enable you to perform a series of operations with a single command.

■ **Modules:** Modules enable you to perform more complex operations that cannot be completed with macros.

S TEP-BY-STEP 21.1

1. Launch Access. The Microsoft Access window and the Getting Started task pane shown in Figure 21-1 are displayed. Do not be concerned that the files listed in the Open section of your task pane are different.

Computer Concepts

The files listed above More . . . in the Open section of the Getting Started task pane in Access are the documents most recently accessed.

STEP-BY-STEP 21.1 Continued

FIGURE 21-1
Microsoft Access window with the Getting Started task pane

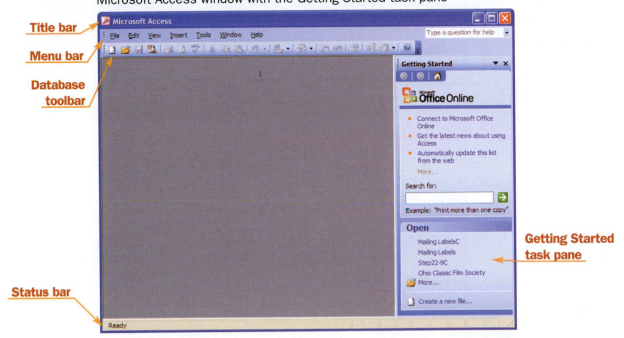

Title bar

Menu bar

Database toolbar

Getting Started task pane

Status bar

2. In the task pane, under Open, select **More**. The Open dialog box displays.

Note

You may receive a warning about the safety of the Access data files for exercises when you open them in Access 2003, depending on what updates to Windows XP have been installed on your computer. Normally you can ignore this warning and click **Yes**, **Open**, or **OK** to continue opening a file. If you see a warning screen, however, check with your instructor first before going on.

STEP-BY-STEP 21.1 Continued

3. Locate and open the file **Step21-1** from the data files. The Step21-1: Database window, similar to that shown in Figure 21-2, is displayed. Compare your screen with Figure 21-2 and identify the parts of the Access screen to familiarize yourself with the program.

FIGURE 21-2
Step 21-1: Database window displayed

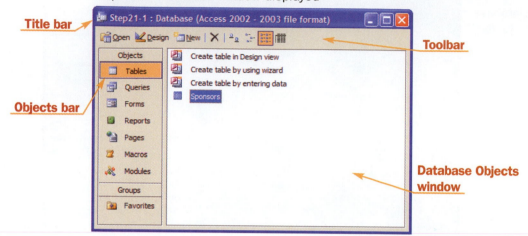

4. Select **Tables** on the Objects bar if necessary. The Sponsors table in the Database Objects window will already be selected.

5. Click the **Open** button in the Database window toolbar. The Sponsors: Table shown in Figure 21-3 is displayed.

Computer Concepts

A default setting tells Access 2003 to save files in the Access 2000 file format. A file in Access 2000 file format can be opened in Access 2000, Access 2002, and Access 2003. You can choose to save your Access files in Access 2002-2003 file format, but then you will be able to open those files only with Access 2002 or Access 2003. To change the default setting, an Access file must be open. Open the **Tools** menu, choose **Options**, and then click the **Advanced** tab. In the Default File Format box, select the desired Access file format.

STEP-BY-STEP 21.1 Continued

FIGURE 21-3
Sponsors: Table

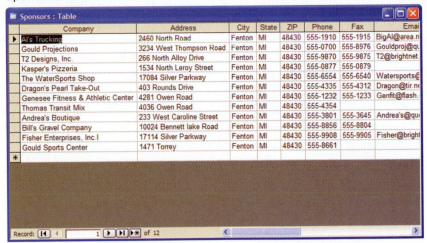

6. Click the right arrow on the horizontal scroll bar (at the bottom of the screen) to view the columns to the right. This table provides data about companies that currently provide sponsorship for a club as well as companies that potentially could become sponsors.

7. Open the **File** menu and choose **Close** to close the table. The Database window is visible again.

8. Click **Queries** on the Objects bar. There is one query object named *Prospective Sponsors Query*, and it should already be selected.

9. Double-click the query object to open it. This query locates and displays the companies that are considered to be prospective sponsors. The information comes from the Sponsors table.

> **Note**
>
> You can also close the table by clicking the Close button at far right in the Sponsors: Table title bar. Be sure you click the table Close button and not the Access application Close button, which is at the far right of the Microsoft Access title bar.

10. Open the **File** menu and choose **Close** to close the query. The Database window is still displayed.

11. Click **Reports** on the Objects bar. There is one report object named *Prospective Sponsors Report*, and it should already be selected. Double-click the report object to open it. The report displays the data contained in the Prospective Sponsors Query.

12. Click the **Close** button in the Prospective Sponsors Report window to close the report, and then click the **Close** button in the Database window. Leave Access open for the next Step-by-Step.

Creating a Database Table

When you create a new database, the first object you need to create is a table. It is the primary object because it contains the data. You can create as many tables as you need to store the information. An Access table contains fields and records. A *field* is a single piece of database information, such as a first name, a last name, or a telephone number. A *record* is a group of related fields in a database, such as all the information about the person, including first and last name, address, postal code, telephone number, and so forth.

When you create a table in Access, you will be prompted to create a primary key. The *primary key* uniquely identifies each record in a table. The primary key tells Access how your records will be sorted, and it prevents duplicate entries. For example, you may have a student ID number, and no other student has exactly the same number as you.

You can display the table in Datasheet view or in Design view. *Datasheet view* displays the table data in a row-and-column format. *Design view* displays the field names and what kind of values you can enter in each field. You define or modify the field formats in Design view.

If this sounds like a lot to remember, do not be concerned. Access provides a Wizard that simplifies the task of creating and entering data in the table.

Saving a Database File

In all other lessons in this module, you have saved data files using a new filename. However, you can only use the Save As command for naming and saving parts of an Access database. You cannot use the File Save As command to save the entire database under a new name. To rename an Access file, you can open My Computer (or Windows Explorer) from the desktop or the Start menu. Then locate and select the filename, open the File menu, and choose Rename. You can copy or save the file in a new location before you rename it.

Creating a Table Using a Wizard

When you create a table using a Wizard, you respond to a series of questions about how you want to set up the table. The Wizard guides you through the process, and it formats the table based on your answers.

STEP-BY-STEP 21.2

1. Click the **New** button in the Database toolbar. The New File task pane displays at the right.

2. In the task pane under New, select **Blank database**. A File New Database dialog box displays, similar to the one shown in Figure 21-4. Your dialog box may look different.

STEP-BY-STEP 21.2 Continued

FIGURE 21-4
File New Database dialog box

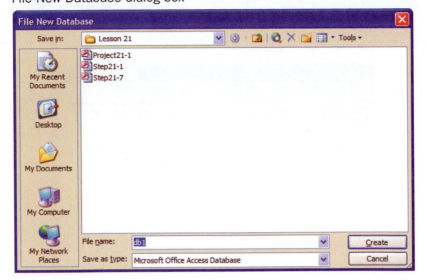

3. Locate the folder where you save your documents. Then delete the proposed filename in the File name: box and key **Addresses** followed by your initials. Click **Create**. A new database window like the one shown in Figure 21-5 is displayed.

FIGURE 21-5
Addresses: Database window

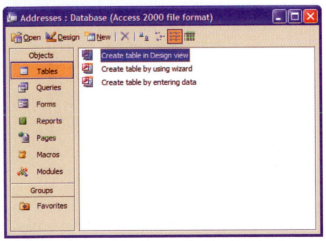

STEP-BY-STEP 21.2 Continued

4. Double-click **Create table by using wizard**. The Table Wizard dialog box opens. Select **Personal** to display the dialog box shown in Figure 21-6.

FIGURE 21-6
Table Wizard dialog box

Select Personal here

Adds the selected field to the list of fields for the new table

5. Identify the fields to be included in the table. In the Sample Fields list, select FirstName. Then click the single right arrow to add the field in the Fields in my new table list.

6. Using the same procedure, select the following fields in the Sample Fields list and add them to the Fields in my new table list.

LastName

Address

City

StateOrProvince

PostalCode

Country/Region

> **Note**
>
> If you click the right double arrows (>>), all the fields are added to the Fields in my new table list. If you click the left single arrow (<), the selected field will be removed from Fields in my new table list. If you click the double left arrows (<<), all the fields will be removed from the Fields in my new table list.

7. Click **Next**. The Wizard will ask you to name your table. The proposed name *Addresses* appears in the text box, and this name is appropriate. This step of the Wizard also asks if you want the Wizard to set a primary key for you. The answer *Yes, set a primary key for me.* is already selected. Click **Next** to accept the settings on this page of the Wizard.

8. The Wizard then asks what you want to do after the Wizard creates your table. If necessary, select **Enter data directly into the table.** and click **Finish**.

9. The table is created and the columns display the field names. Because there are no records entered in the table, a single blank row is displayed.

STEP-BY-STEP 21.2 Continued

10. Notice that in the first row in the *AddressesID* field, *(AutoNumber)* is displayed. This field contains the primary key, and Access will automatically number each record that you enter.

11. Click the **Save** button on the Database toolbar and leave the table open for the next Step-by-Step.

Entering Records in Datasheet View

The Addresses table is currently displayed in Datasheet view. In this view, the table display is similar to a spreadsheet. The intersection of a row and a column is called a *cell*, just as in an Excel worksheet. Fields appear as columns, and each column has a *field name*. The field name is a label that helps you identify the fields. Each row in the table contains one single record of the entire database.

When you enter data into a cell, it is called an *entry*. To move from one cell to another, you can use the mouse to click in a cell. You can also use the keyboard to navigate in a table. Table 21-1 describes the keys you can use to move around in a table in Datasheet view.

TABLE 21-1
Keys for navigating in Datasheet view

KEY	DESCRIPTION
Enter, Tab, or right arrow	Moves the insertion point to the next field.
Left arrow or Shift + Tab	Moves the insertion point to the previous field.
Home	Moves the insertion point to the first field in the current record.
End	Moves the insertion point to the last field in the current record.
Up arrow	Moves the insertion point up one record and stays in the same field.
Down arrow	Moves the insertion point down one record and stays in the same field.
Page Up	Moves the insertion point up one screen.
Page Down	Moves the insertion point down one screen.

STEP-BY-STEP 21.3

1. Enter the first record. Click in the first empty cell (the *First Name* field), and key **Jaimey**. Notice that as you enter the text in the first field, Access automatically assigns the primary key *1* in the *AddressesID* field.

2. Press **Tab** to move to the next field, and complete the entry by entering the following information in the respective fields:

Last Name	**McGuirk**
Address	**610 Brae Burn**
City	**Mansfield**
State/Province	**OH**
Postal Code	**44907-9122**
Country/Region	**USA**

STEP-BY-STEP 21.3 Continued

3. Press **Tab** twice to move to the *First Name* field in the next row. Enter the following data for two more records:

First Name	**Jesse**
Last Name	**Bain**
Address	**288 Silvercrest Drive**
City	**Lexington**
State/Province	**OH**
Postal Code	**44904-9007**
Country/Region	**USA**
First Name	**Matt**
Last Name	**Smith**
Address	**4645 Rule Road**
City	**Bellville**
State/Province	**OH**
Postal Code	**44813-0987**
Country/Region	**USA**

4. Click the **Save** button to save the changes and leave the database open for the next Step-by-Step.

Modifying a Database Table

Although it is usually easier to change your table design before you enter data, you can refine the design at any time. You can modify the table in Datasheet view or Design view.

Changing the Column Width

The default column widths are often too wide or too narrow for the data in the table. This is the case with your database. The Address field is not wide enough to display all the text in the street address, and there's a lot of white space in the StateOrProvince field. You can adjust the column width easily by dragging the column border or by entering a specific width in the Column Width dialog box accessed from the Format menu. You can also use the Best Fit command to let Access select the appropriate column width.

STEP-BY-STEP 21.4

1. Point to the right edge of the field name (the heading cell) in the Address column. The pointer changes to a two-headed arrow. Drag the column border to the right to increase the width of the column. Continue to drag the column border until you get the correct width so that the complete address for all entries is visible.

2. Point to the right edge of the *State/Province* field name and drag the border to the left to decrease the width of the column so there is no wasted space in that column. Do not be concerned that the entire field name does not display after you resize the column width.

STEP-BY-STEP 21.4 Continued

3. Point to the field name *First Name*. When a down arrow displays, click and drag to the right until all the columns in the table are selected.

4. Open the **Format** menu and choose **Column Width** to display the dialog box shown in Figure 21-7.

FIGURE 21-7
Column Width dialog box

5. Click **Best Fit**. Notice that the width of each column is adjusted to accommodate the contents within the column, including the field name at the top of each column.

6. Save the changes and leave the database open for the next Step-by-Step.

Adding and Deleting Fields in Design View

Often, after you create a table and enter data, you decide you want to add or delete fields. You can add fields in either Datasheet view or Design view. Design view, however, provides toolbar buttons that make the task easier.

STEP-BY-STEP 21.5

1. Click the **View** button on the Table Datasheet toolbar. The table is displayed in Design view as shown in Figure 21-8.

FIGURE 21-8
Addresses: Table displayed in Design view

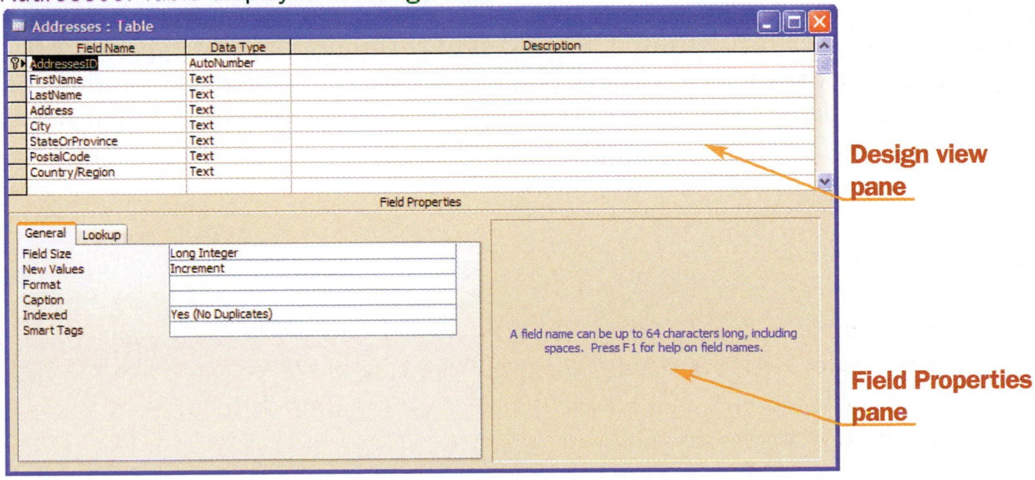

STEP-BY-STEP 21.5 Continued

2. Click in the first blank row directly below the field name *Country/Region*. Key **Birthdate** and press **Enter**. The new field is entered.

3. Click the **Country/Region** field. A right-pointing arrow displays to the left of the field name. This arrow indicates that the row is the current row.

4. Open the **Insert** menu and click **Rows**. A new row is inserted above the selected row.

5. Key **e-mail** and then press **Enter**.

6. Select the row containing the *Country/Region* field. Click the **Delete Rows** button on the toolbar.

7. When prompted to delete the field and all the data in the field, click **Yes**. The field and all the data entered in the field are removed from the table.

8. Save the changes and leave the database open for the next Step-by-Step.

Computer Concepts

The View button is a toggle button. This means when you're viewing the table one way, the button changes to make it easy to switch quickly to the other view. So, when the table is in Datasheet view, the View button shows Design view. If you click the View button, the table switches to Design view and the View button now indicates Datasheet view.

Note

Use caution when deleting rows in Design view. Once you confirm the deletion, you cannot undo the deletion.

Changing Field Properties

In Design view, you can specify the data type for each field. For example, you can specify text, numbers, currency, and even Yes/No. The default data type for a field is regular text, which is appropriate for most of the fields in your table. However, in a field like the Birthdate field in your database table, you may want to specify that the data type be formatted to hold date/time data instead of text.

When you select a data type, a dialog box displays several options for field properties. *Field properties* are specifications that allow you to customize the data type settings. The field properties available depend on the data type selected. One of the most common field properties is field size. The default field size is 50 characters, but you can specify that the field allow up to 255 characters. Another common field property is format. The format specifies how you want Access to display numbers, dates, times, and text.

S TEP-BY-STEP 21.6

1. Your database should still be displayed in Design view. Click in the **Data Type** cell next to the field *Birthdate*. The current data type is Text, and when you click in the cell, a down arrow will display.

2. Click the down arrow to display the options shown in Figure 21-9 and then select **Date/Time**.

FIGURE 21-9
Data Type options

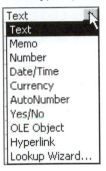

3. Notice that the Field Properties that are displayed in the pane at the bottom of the Design view window change to show the values for the Date/Time data type.

4. In the Field Properties pane at the bottom of the window, click in the text box next to *Format*. When the down arrow displays, click it to display the list of options shown in Figure 21-10. Select **Short Date**.

FIGURE 21-10
Date/Time format options

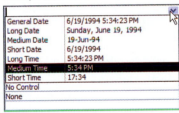

5. In the Design view pane, click in the **Data Type** cell for the *StateOrProvince* field. The data type is set for Text.

6. Click in the **Field Size** text box in the Field Properties pane. The field size is currently set at *20*. Change the field size to **2**. This will require that the user use two-letter state abbreviations when entering the state name in the table.

7. Click the **View** button on the toolbar to switch to Datasheet view. When prompted to save the changes, click **Yes**. When prompted that data may be lost, click **Yes** to continue.

STEP-BY-STEP 21.6 Continued

8. Enter the following data in the *Birthdate* and *e-mail* fields. Notice that as you enter the birthdate data, Access will automatically format the date using the short date format you specified.

First Name	e-mail	Birthdate
Jaimey	**JMcGuirk@nets.com**	**March 13, 1978**
Jesse	**JBain@LFSC.com**	**April 11, 1979**
Matt	**MSmith@qry.com**	**June 18, 1980**

Note

As you enter the e-mail addresses, you may find that the AutoCorrect option automatically changes the capital letters you key to lowercase. To have the entries appear as they are shown here, rest the mouse pointer on the AutoCorrect Options icon, and then click the **down arrow** that appears at the right of the icon. Select the first option in the list, **Change Back to...** to reverse the AutoCorrect action.

9. Enter the following new record. Remember that as you enter the state name, Access will not permit you to enter more than two characters. You will need to enter the two-letter state abbreviation for Ohio.

First Name	**Kelsey**
Last Name	**Erwin**
Address	**2038 Leiter Road**
City	**Lucas**
State/Province	**Ohio**
Postal Code	**44843-9880**
e-mail	**KErwin@csfa.com**
Birthdate	**October 6, 1979**

10. Format the *e-mail* and *Birthdate* columns width for best fit. (*Hint*: Select the columns, open the **Format** menu, choose **Column Width**, and then select **Best Fit** in the dialog box.) Save the changes.

11. Open the **File** menu and choose **Close**. The Datasheet Objects window is displayed. Notice that your Addresses table is now displayed as an object in the Database objects window.

12. Click the **Close** button in the Database window to close the database file.

Note

Press **F6** to move the insertion point between the Field Properties pane and the Design view pane.

Editing Database Records

It is common for data to change after you've entered it in your database. For example, people move, so you have to change their addresses and probably their phone numbers. Access provides several navigation features that make it easy for you to move around in a datasheet table so you can make necessary edits. These features are especially useful when you're working in large databases. Figure 21-11 shows the navigation buttons that are displayed at the bottom of a table shown in Datasheet view.

FIGURE 21-11
Navigation buttons

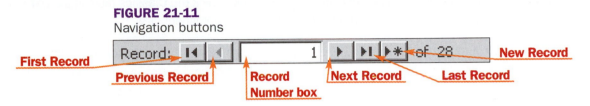

First Record

Previous Record

Record Number box

Next Record

Last Record

New Record

If you make a mistake adding or editing data, you can choose the Undo command to reverse your last action. As soon as you begin editing another record, however, the Undo command is no longer available.

Ethics in Technology

SOFTWARE PIRACY

One of the biggest problems facing the computer industry today is software piracy, the illegal copying or use of programs. Copying software is very easy. Some people believe it is all right to copy software and use it for free. They think software is too expensive. And it can be. Some low-level software costs less than $25, but more specialized software can cost hundreds or even thousands of dollars. When users copy the software, they are only giving up access to documentation and tech support, so they decide it is worth it to copy it illegally.

You may be surprised to know that not only individual users copy software illegally—so do businesses. Billions of dollars are lost every year as a result of pirated software. Software can be pirated in many ways. Of course, the easiest is to copy from the original disks. But software can also be copied from the server of a network and via e-mail. *Shareware*, free software that can be used for a given period of time, is also being abused. Many people use it with no intention of purchasing it.

You, too, may ask, "What is the big deal about copying software?" Developing a software program is an expensive process that takes highly trained programmers hundreds of hours to develop. It is a form of intellectual property and the creators of software own the rights to it just as an author owns the rights to what he or she writes. The Copyright Act of 1976 was passed to govern software piracy. In 1983, a Software Piracy and Counterfeiting Amendment was added. It is no longer a misdemeanor to copy software illegally—it is a felony.

S TEP-BY-STEP 21.7

1. Open **My Computer** and find the file **Step21-7** in the data files.

2. Copy the **Step21-7** file to the location where you save your documents and then rename the copy **Classics** followed by your initials.

3. Close **My Computer** and then open the file **Classics** from your saved documents folder.

4. If necessary, click **Tables** in the Objects bar, and then double-click the **Classics** table in the Database Objects window to open the table. The table is displayed in Datasheet view.

5. The first cell in the table *(ID number 1)* is selected. The right-pointing arrow to the left of the first row indicates that this is the current row. Click the **Next Record** button in the bottom left corner of the screen. The selection moves to the ID number 2 in the second row in the table.

6. Click the **Previous Record** button. Notice that even though the selection changes rows, the selection remains in the same field—*ID*.

7. Select the number **1** in the Record number box in the middle of the navigation buttons and key **22**. Press **Enter** (or **Tab**). The selection moves to the ID *22* in the twenty-second row in the table.

8. Press **Tab** twice to position the insertion point in the *Author First* field in the same row. Key **James** to change the entry. Notice that a pencil displays at the left edge of the row, indicating that the record is being edited.

9. Click the **Next Record** button. The selection (or insertion point) moves to the next row in the table. Notice that the selection stays in the *Author First* field. Also notice that the pencil is no longer displayed to the left of row 22. This is because when you pressed Next Record, the edit was completed. (This is true whether you click a navigation button, press the **Enter** key, use the **Tab** key to move to the next row, use the arrow keys, or relocate the insertion point with the mouse. As soon as you move out of the row, the entry is completed.)

> When you edit a record in Datasheet view, Access automatically saves the changes to the record.

10. Click the **First Record** button. The insertion point moves to the *Author First* field in the first row in the table.

11. Click the **Last Record** button. The insertion point moves to the *Author First* field in the last row in the table.

12. Press **Tab** twice to move to the *Cover* field in the same row. Key **Paperback** to replace the current entry.

STEP-BY-STEP 21.7 Continued

13. Click the **Previous Record** button to move to the row above. Key **Paperback** to replace the entry. Press **Tab** (or **Enter**).

14. The last change was not necessary. Click the **Undo** button on the toolbar. The action is reversed and the cell should display *Hardcover*. Leave the database open for the next Step-by-Step.

Computer Concepts

You can also execute the Undo command by pressing **Ctrl + Z** or opening the **Edit** menu and choosing **Undo**.

Adding and Deleting Records

To add a record, you must enter the data in the blank row at the end of the table. To delete a record, you must first select the record. To select a record, point to the *record selector*, which is the box located at the left edge of each row. You use the record selector to select the row. When you see a right-pointing arrow in the record selector, you can click, and the entire row is selected. You can select more than one record by dragging down several rows. This means you can delete multiple rows at once.

Computer Concepts

You can also select multiple, consecutive records by selecting the first record, holding down the **Shift** key, and then clicking on the last record. All the fields in between the first selected record and the last record will be selected.

After a record is selected, you can press the Delete key to remove the data. Access will display a message box to ask you if you are sure about the deletion. Once you've deleted a record, you cannot use the Undo command to restore it.

Selected data also can be copied or moved from one location in an Access table to a new location within the same table, or to a different table. The Cut, Copy, and Paste commands you have used in other Office applications are also available in Access. Access stores cut or copied text in the Clipboard. You can access the Cut, Copy, and Paste commands by clicking the appropriate buttons on the toolbar, choosing the commands from the Edit menu, or right-clicking the selected data and then choosing a command from the shortcut menu.

STEP-BY-STEP 21.8

1. Click the **New Record** button. The insertion point is positioned in the first available blank row at the end of the table.

STEP-BY-STEP 21.8 Continued

2. Press **Tab** to move to the *Title* field. Access will automatically insert an ID number for the primary key when you begin to enter data. Enter the following data for the new record:

Title:	**Crime and Punishment**
Author First:	**Fyodor**
Author Last:	**Dostoyevsky**
Cover:	**Hardcover**
# Pages:	**499**
Publisher:	**HarperCollins Publishers, Inc.**
Price:	**6.99**

3. Point to the left of the *ID* field 26. (The record is fourth from the bottom in the table.) When the pointer changes to a right-pointing arrow, click to select the entire row.

4. Press **Delete**. When prompted to confirm the deletion of the record, click **Yes**. The record is deleted from the table.

5. Point to the left of the *ID* field 27, *Emma* by Jane Austen. When the pointer changes to a right-pointing arrow, click to select the entire row.

6. Click the **Copy** button on the standard toolbar, point to the left of the ID field in the empty row at the bottom of the table. When the pointer changes to a right-pointing arrow, click to select the entire row.

Note

As in all Office applications, the shortcut keys for Cut are **Ctrl + X**; for Copy, **Ctrl + C**; and for Paste, **Ctrl + V**.

7. Click **Paste** to paste a copy of the *Emma* record in the new row. Change the title to **Northanger Abbey**, the number of pages to **220**, and the publisher to **Modern Classics Library**.

8. Select the **Paperback** entry from record 28 (*The Red Badge of Courage*) by double-clicking in the cell, and then press **Ctrl + C** to copy the entry.

9. Double-click the **Hardback** entry in the new *Northanger Abbey* record and then press **Ctrl + V** to replace it with the data on the Clipboard (*Paperback*).

10. Open the **File** menu and choose **Close**. (Remember that Access automatically saves your changes when you edit records.)

11. The Database Objects window is now visible again. Click the **Close** button in the Database window to close the database file.

12. Close Access and follow your instructor's directions about turning off the computer.

SUMMARY

In this lesson, you learned:

- Many parts of the Access screen are similar to other Office XP applications. However, Access also has several different toolbar buttons and menus to perform tasks unique to Access.

- Database objects work together to help you organize and report the information stored in the database.

- Tables are the primary objects in a database. All other objects are based on data stored in tables.

- You use Datasheet view to enter records in a table.

- A table can be modified after it is created, even after data records have been entered into it. You can edit a table in Datasheet view or in Design view.

- In Design view, you can specify the data type for each field. The field properties are specifications that allow you to customize the data type settings. Text is the default field property for a cell.

- Access provides several navigation buttons to make it easy for you to move around in a table. If you make a mistake adding or editing data, you can choose the Undo command to reverse your last action.

- You can add and delete records in a table while working in Datasheet view. New records are added at the end of the table. To delete a record, you must first select the entire row containing the record.

- Selected data can be copied or moved from location to another in an Access table, or to another table, using the Cut, Copy, and Paste commands. The cut or copied data is stored in the Clipboard.

VOCABULARY *Review*

Define the following terms:

Datasheet	Field	Record
Datasheet view	Field name	Record selector
Design view	Field properties	
Entry	Primary key	

REVIEW Questions

TRUE/FALSE

Circle T if the statement is true or F if the statement is false.

T   F   **1.** All database information is stored in tables.

T   F   **2.** You cannot add or delete fields after you have entered data in a table.

T   F   **3.** Tables are the main objects in a database because they store the data.

T   F   **4.** Databases are similar to spreadsheets.

T   F   **5.** You must add new records at the end of the table.

MULTIPLE CHOICE

Circle the best response for each of the following statements.

1. A _____ is a single piece of information in a database, such as a first name, a last name, or a telephone number.
   A. entry
   B. field
   C. record
   D. column

2. _____ view displays the table data in a row-and-column format.
   A. Table
   B. Design
   C. Normal
   D. Datasheet

3. The _____ uniquely identifies each record in a table.
   A. primary key
   B. field name
   C. entry number
   D. column head

4. _____ are specifications that allow you to customize a field beyond choosing a data type.
   A. Record selectors
   B. Field properties
   C. Primary keys
   D. Navigation buttons

5. A(n) _____ is a group of related fields, such as all the information about an employee.
   A. column
   B. entry
   C. record
   D. database

PROJECTS

PROJECT 21-1

1. Open Windows Explorer and copy the file **Project21-1** from the data files to the location where you save your documents, and then rename the file **Films**.

2. Close Windows Explorer and launch Access if necessary.

3. Open the **Films** database file. This database stores membership information and the current video collection of the Oak Creek Film Society (OCFS), a club for lovers of classic films.

4. Notice that this database contains two tables: Collection and Members. Open the **Collection** table to see the films the OCFS has collected so far.

5. Close the table and click the **Forms** object in the Objects bar. Open the **Members** form to see the form used to insert member data.

6. Close the form and click the **Queries** object in the Objects bar. Double-click the **Suspense** query to see the films in the collection that belong to the *Suspense* category. Close the query.

7. You need to create a new table for the database to store information on special events that the OCFS sponsors. Click the Tables **object** in the Objects bar. Create a new table using the Wizard:
   A. Select the **Business** category if necessary and then select the sample table **Events**.
   B. Add the following sample fields to your new table: **EventName, Location, StartDate,** and **EventDescription**.
   C. Accept the table name **Events**.
   D. Let the Wizard set a primary key for you.
   E. There is no relationship between this new table and existing tables. So, when prompted about the relationship, simply click **Next**.
   F. When prompted about what you want to do after the Wizard creates the table, select **Enter data directly into the table**, if necessary, and click **Finish**.

8. Enter the following data in Datasheet view:

Event Name	Location	Start Date	Event Description
Holiday Classics	Odeon Theatre	12/15/07	Christmas theme
Horror Classics	Odeon Theatre	1/17/08	Horror theme
Hitchcock Classics	Odeon Theatre	2/22/08	Suspense theme

9. You decide your table needs some modifications. With the **Events** table open, switch to Design view.

10. The *EventDescription* field doesn't add much to the table because the subject of each event is clear from the event name. Delete the **EventDescription** field and all contents.

11. It would be helpful to see the time for each event. Insert a new field following the *StartDate* field named **Start Time** with the Date/Time data type. Specify the **Medium Time Format** field property.

12. Each event includes clips from classic films. Insert a new field named **Films** following the *StartTime* field. Because each event includes more than one film, change the field size for the Films field to **200**.

13. Save your changes to the design and return to Datasheet view. Insert the following data in the new fields:

Event	Start Time	Films
Holiday Classics	7:00 PM	A Christmas Story, A Christmas Carol
Horror Classics	7:00 PM	Dracula, Frankenstein
Hitchcock Classics	6:30 PM	The Birds, Vertigo

14. Add one more event with the following information. Note that all three movies fit in the *Films* field now that you have changed the field size.

Event:	**Spoofing the Classics**
Location:	**Odeon Theatre**
Start Date:	**3/17/08**
Start Time:	**4:00 PM**
Films:	**The Pink Panther, Young Frankenstein, Dr. Strangelove**

15. Adjust the column widths to display all text in the fields. Save your changes.

16. Close the Events table and, if you are going directly to Project 21-2, leave the Films database open.

PROJECT 21-2

1. Open the **Films** database if necessary, and then open the **Collection** table.

2. Make the following corrections to the data in the table:

   A. Go to record 24 (*The Haunting*). You think the title of this film is incorrect. It should be *The Haunting of Hill House*. Key **of Hill House** in the *Title* field.

   B. Whoops, you were wrong. That was the title of the book, not the film. Your original title was correct after all. Click **Undo** to return the title to *The Haunting*.

   C. Go to record 26 (*Casablanca*) and scroll, if necessary, so you can see the *Award* field. To save space, you are not including the word *Best* for all Academy Awards. Delete the word *Best* and the space that follows in this field.

3. You need to add several films that were acquired for recent events. (You do not have to enter a number in the *ID* field; Access will supply a number automatically when you key an entry in the *Title* field.)

Title:	**Vertigo**	Title:	**Dr. Strangelove**
Year:	**1958**	Year:	**1964**
Length:	**128**	Length:	**93**
MPAA:	**NR**	MPAA:	**NR**
Color/BW:	**Color**	Color/BW:	**BW**
Director:	**Hitchcock**	Director:	**Kubrick**
Category:	**Suspense**	Category:	**Comedy**
Actor:	**James Stewart**	Actor:	**Peter Sellers, George C. Scott**
Actress:	**Kim Novak**		

4. You have another new film to add. To save time, copy record 29 (*Star Wars*) and paste it in a new record. Change the title to **The Empire Strikes Back**, the year to **1980**, the length to **124**, and the director to **Kershner**. Remove *Alec Guinness* from the list in the *Actor* field and add **Billy Dee Williams** to the list. Delete the existing text in the *Award* field and then enter **Special Effects**.

5. You have discovered that the 1969 version of Hamlet is damaged. Delete this record (14) from the table.

6. Close the table and save changes when prompted, and then exit the database.

TEAMWORK PROJECT

Databases are ideal for storing statistics such as those of sports teams. With a partner, create a database to record stats for a sports team. Follow these steps:

1. With your teammate, choose a team for further study.

2. Collect the statistics you will need for your database. Some of the pieces of information you might collect would be players' names, number of games, and individual or team statistics for each game. Divide up the players and/or games with your teammate so you each have half the work to do.

3. Create a database to store the data you collect.

CRITICAL*Thinking*

ACTIVITY 21-1

You want to insert two new fields in a database. One field—named *Notes*—will hold complete sentences of text. In some cases, the sentences are fairly lengthy. The other field, named *Values*, has to hold numbers containing decimals. However, it is important that these numbers are not rounded off during calculations. What data types and field properties will you need to specify in order to display data properly in these new fields? Experiment in Access to find the answers, and then check your answers using the Access Help screens.

MANAGING AND REPORTING DATABASE INFORMATION

OBJECTIVES	VOCABULARY
Upon completion of this lesson, you should be able to:	Field selector
■ Change the datasheet layout.	Orientation
■ Create a form.	Query
■ Enter and edit data in a form.	Report
■ Sort data in Datasheet view.	
■ Find and replace data in Datasheet view.	
■ Create a query.	
■ Print a report.	
■ Create mailing labels.	
Estimated Time: 1 hour	

As the amount of data in a database increases, it becomes more difficult to manage records and find information. Access has several useful features that help you work with larger databases. These features help you order the data, find the data, and summarize and report the data.

Changing the Datasheet Layout

If you want to rearrange the fields in Datasheet view, you can drag them to a new location. To select a field, point to the field name at the top of the column. The box containing the field name is also a *field selector*. You use the field selector to select the column. When you see a down-pointing arrow in the field selector, click, and the entire column is selected. After you select the field, point to the field selector and drag the selection to the new location. As you drag, a vertical bar will follow the mouse pointer to indicate where the field will be moved. When you release the mouse button, the field is inserted in its new location.

STEP-BY-STEP 22.1

1. Open Windows Explorer and copy the file **Step22-1** from the data files to the location where you keep your document files.

2. Rename the copy of the file **Books** and then close Windows Explorer.

3. Launch Access and open the **Books** file from your document files.

4. Select **Tables** in the Objects bar if necessary, and then double-click the **Book List** table in the Database Objects window to open it.

5. Scroll to the right until the *Cover* column, the *# Pages* column, the *Publisher* column, and the *Price* column are all visible on the screen.

6. Point to the field name *Cover*. When the pointer changes to a down-pointing arrow, click and drag to the right to select the *Cover* and *# Pages* columns.

7. Release the mouse button when the two columns are selected. Then point to either of the field names and drag the columns to the right. As you drag, a bold vertical line will display. When that vertical line is positioned on the border between the *Publisher* column and the *Price* column as shown in Figure 22-1, release the mouse button.

FIGURE 22-1
Dragging columns to a new location

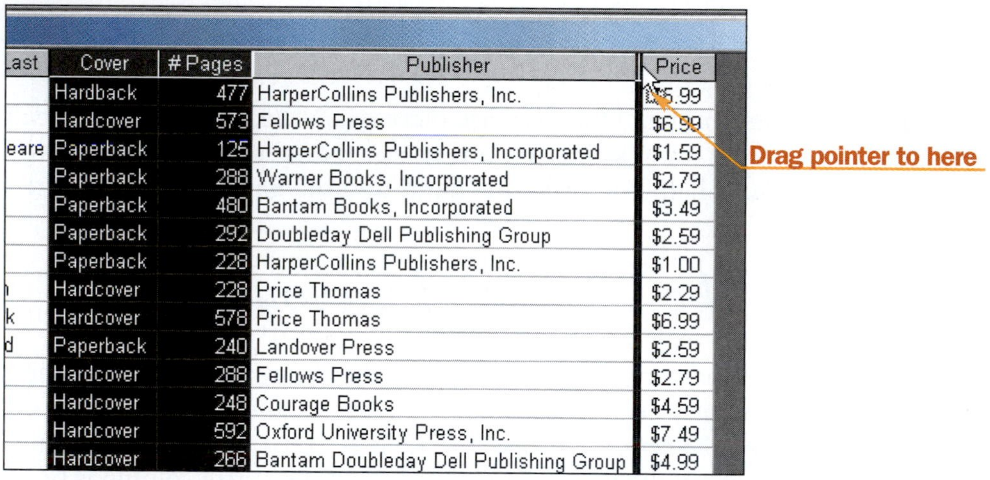

Last	Cover	# Pages	Publisher	Price
	Hardback	477	HarperCollins Publishers, Inc.	$5.99
	Hardcover	573	Fellows Press	$6.99
eare	Paperback	125	HarperCollins Publishers, Incorporated	$1.59
	Paperback	288	Warner Books, Incorporated	$2.79
	Paperback	480	Bantam Books, Incorporated	$3.49
	Paperback	292	Doubleday Dell Publishing Group	$2.59
	Paperback	228	HarperCollins Publishers, Inc.	$1.00
1	Hardcover	228	Price Thomas	$2.29
k	Hardcover	578	Price Thomas	$6.99
d	Paperback	240	Landover Press	$2.59
	Hardcover	288	Fellows Press	$2.79
	Hardcover	248	Courage Books	$4.59
	Hardcover	592	Oxford University Press, Inc.	$7.49
	Hardcover	266	Bantam Doubleday Dell Publishing Group	$4.99

Drag pointer to here

8. Click anywhere in the table to deselect the columns. The two columns are moved and now display after the *Publisher* column and before the *Price* column.

9. Compare your screen to Figure 22-2. If the columns are not in the correct order, try again. Select the column(s) you need to move and drag it to the new location.

STEP-BY-STEP 22.1 Continued

FIGURE 22-2
Table with columns rearranged

ID	Title	Author First	Author Last	Publisher	Cover	# Pages	Price
1	Moby Dick	Herman	Melville	HarperCollins Publishers, Inc.	Hardback	477	$5.99
2	Little Women	Louisa	Alcott	Fellows Press	Hardcover	573	$6.99
3	Romeo & Juliet	William	Shakespeare	HarperCollins Publishers, Incorporated	Paperback	125	$1.59
4	To Kill a Mockingbird	Harper	Lee	Warner Books, Incorporated	Paperback	288	$2.79
5	Uncle Tom's Cabin	Harriet	Stowe	Bantam Books, Incorporated	Paperback	480	$4.59
6	The Adventures of Huckleberry Finn	Mark	Twain	Doubleday Dell Publishing Group	Paperback	292	$2.59
7	Oliver Twist	Charles	Dickens	HarperCollins Publishers, Inc.	Paperback	228	$1.00
8	The Scarlet Letter	Nathaniel	Hawthorn	Price Thomas	Hardcover	228	$2.29
9	The Grapes of Wrath	John	Steinbeck	Price Thomas	Hardcover	578	$6.99
10	The Great Gatsby	F. Scott	Fitzgerald	Landover Press	Paperback	240	$2.59
11	Pride and Prejudice	Jane	Austen	Fellows Press	Hardcover	288	$2.79

10. Click the **Close** button in the Book List table window and click **Yes** when you are prompted to save the changes made to the layout of the table. Leave the Database Objects window open for the next Step-by-Step.

Creating a Form

Access offers another way to enter data in a table. You can create a data-entry form. A form offers a more convenient way to enter and view records. When you create a form, you are adding a new object to the database. Although you can create a form manually, the Form Wizard makes the process easier. The Wizard asks you questions and formats the form according to your preferences.

STEP-BY-STEP 22.2

1. Click **Forms** in the Objects bar.

2. Double-click **Create form by using wizard** in the Database Objects window. The Form Wizard dialog box shown in Figure 22-3 is displayed.

FIGURE 22-3
Form Wizard dialog box

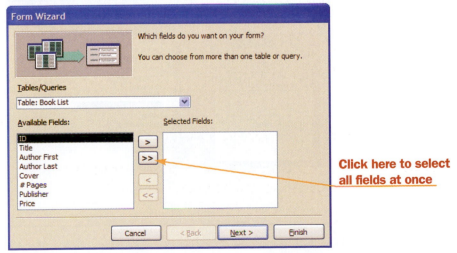

Click here to select all fields at once

STEP-BY-STEP 22.2 Continued

3. Notice that *Table: Book List* is already selected under *Table/Queries*. Also notice that all the fields available in the table are listed under *Available Fields*.

4. You need to identify the fields you want on your form. Click the double arrows button (>>). All of the field names are displayed in the Selected Fields list. This tells Access to include all the fields in the form.

5. Click the **Next** button. The Form Wizard dialog box changes so you can select a layout for the form, as shown in Figure 22-4.

FIGURE 22-4
Selecting a layout for a form

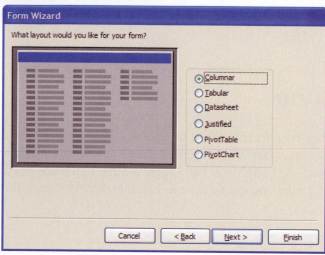

6. If necessary, select **Columnar** for the layout, and then click **Next**. The dialog box changes so you can select a style for the form, as shown in Figure 22-5.

FIGURE 22-5
Choosing a style for a form

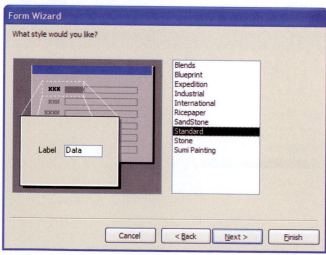

STEP-BY-STEP 22.2 Continued

7. If necessary, select the **Standard** style. The preview box shows you what this form style looks like.

8. Select some of the other styles to see what they look like. Then select the **Stone** style and click **Next**. The final Form Wizard dialog box changes so you can create a title for the form.

9. Key **Classic Books**.

10. If necessary, click the **Open the form to view or enter information.** option to select it. Then click **Finish**. Access creates and displays the form similar to that shown in Figure 22-6. Notice that data from the first record is displayed in the form. Leave the form and the database open for the next Step-by-Step.

FIGURE 22-6
Customized form

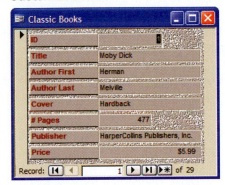

Entering and Editing Data in a Form

Entering data in a form is similar to entering data in a table in Datasheet view. You use the same keys to move the insertion point among the fields. Furthermore, the same navigation buttons are available at the bottom of the form. To add a new record, go to the blank record at the end of the database or click the New Record button. To edit an existing record, display the record and make the changes in the fields of the form.

Note

When you enter or edit a record in Form view, Access automatically updates the records in the table.

STEP-BY-STEP 22.3

1. Click the **New Record** button at the bottom of the form. A new form is displayed with labels, but there is no data entered in the form.

2. Press **Tab** to position the insertion point in the field *Title*. Access will assign an ID number when you begin to enter data. Key **A Room with a View**. Notice that the pencil icon is displayed at upper left in the form, indicating that you are editing the record.

3. Press **Tab** and key **E. M.**

4. Press **Tab** and enter the following information into the form:

   Author Last: **Forster**
   Cover: **Paperback**
   # Pages: **355**
   Publisher: **Bagshot Press**
   Price: **5.99**

5. Press **Enter** (or **Tab**). A new blank form is displayed.

6. Select the number **31** in the Record Number box at the bottom of the form, key **8**, and press **Enter**. A form containing the data for the eighth record is displayed.

7. The author's last name is misspelled. It should be Hawthorne. Click in the *Author Last* field, position the insertion point at the end of the entry, and key the letter **e**.

8. Open the **File** menu and choose **Close**. Notice that the Database Objects window displays the new form *Classic Books* in the list of objects.

9. Click the **Tables** button in the Objects bar, and then double-click the **Book List** table to open it.

10. Scroll down to the end of the table. Notice that the new record has been added to the table. Go to record 8. Notice that the name *Hawthorne* has been corrected.

11. Close the table and leave the Database Objects window open for the next Step-by-Step.

Sorting Data in Datasheet View

Often you will want records in a database to appear in a specific order so you can access data easier and more quickly. Databases often contain numerous records. Access provides toolbar buttons that will help you sort the records in a table quickly. You can sort text and numbers in either ascending or descending order. As you may recall, ascending order sorts alphabetically from A to Z and numerically from the lowest to the highest number. Descending order sorts alphabetically from Z to A and numerically from the highest to the lowest number.

Unfortunately, the Undo command is not available after you perform a sort. However, if you change your mind after sorting data, you can open the Records menu and choose Remove Filter/Sort to revert to the original order of the database.

STEP-BY-STEP 22.4

1. Click **Tables** in the Objects bar, and then double-click **Book List** in the list of objects to open the table.

2. Click in any row in the field *Title*. Click the **Sort Ascending** button on the toolbar. The records in the table are rearranged and placed in alphabetical order from A to Z by book title.

3. Open the **Records** menu and choose **Remove Filter/Sort**. The records are returned to the original order.

4. If necessary, scroll to the right and click in any row in the *Price* field. Click the **Sort Descending** button on the toolbar. The records are rearranged in numerical order with the highest priced book listed first.

5. Click in any row in the *Author Last* field, and then click the **Sort Ascending** button. The records are arranged in alphabetical order from A to Z by the author's last name. Leave the database table open for the next Step-by-Step.

Finding and Replacing Data

There may be occasions when you need to locate a particular value, one record, or a group of records in a database. Locating this data can be simple if the database is not large. However, if the database is quite large, finding a particular record or value can be tedious.

Scrolling in a Datasheet or Form

You learned in the last lesson how to move around in a large database table using the navigation buttons at the bottom of the table. You also used the navigation buttons in Form view in this lesson. If your database is not large, however, you may find it more expedient to locate data by scrolling in a datasheet table or form. Use the horizontal and vertical scroll bars and scroll buttons in Datasheet view to move quickly through a table. If you have a form with a lot of fields, you will also see a vertical scroll bar and scroll buttons in Form view. You can use these to scroll through the list of fields in a form.

Using the Find Command

Let's assume that you want to see if there are any books about Huckleberry Finn included in the database. You could sort the records in alphabetical order by title and then scroll down through the list to look for the title. However, if the database had hundreds, or even thousands of records, this method could be time-consuming. The Find command, available on the Edit menu, provides a much faster way for you to locate specific records or find certain values within fields quickly.

> **Note**
>
> If you only want to search a specific section of the table, you can select the section before you execute the Find command. Access will look for the search text only in the selected cells.

S TEP-BY-STEP 22.5

In this exercise, you will first practice scrolling through a database table, and then you will use the Find feature to find a specific book in the datasheet.

1. Use the scroll bars to practice scrolling. Then scroll and locate the following book titles:

    The Great Gatsby

    Little Women

    A Tale of Two Cities

    Dr. Jekyll and Mr. Hyde

2. Scroll up to the first record in the database table and position the insertion point in the first row in the *Title* field. Be careful, though, not to select any text in a cell.

3. Open the **Edit** menu and choose **Find**. The Find and Replace dialog box shown in Figure 22-7 is displayed. Do not be concerned if your dialog box does not match exactly.

FIGURE 22-7
Find and Replace dialog box

4. With the insertion point already positioned in the Find What text box, key **Huckleberry Finn**. If there is already text in the box, it will be replaced when you key the new search text.

> **Note**
>
> The shortcut keys for displaying the Find dialog box are **Ctrl + F**.

5. Notice that *Title* is displayed in the Look In box. This option is correct as is. It tells Access to look for all occurrences in the *Title* column.

> **Note**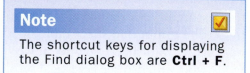
>
> If you want Access to search the entire database, select the name of the database table in the Look In box.

6. Change the options, if necessary, to match those illustrated in Figure 22-8:

    a. Click the **down arrow** in the Match box and select **Any Part of Field**. Access will locate any book title that has the words *Huckleberry* and *Finn* in it.

    b. If necessary, select **All** in the Search box.

    c. The *Match Case* and *Search Fields As Formatted* options should not be selected. If they are selected, point to the option and click once to uncheck the box and turn the option off. When these options are turned off, Access ignores capitalization and data formats when searching for matching text.

STEP-BY-STEP 22.5 Continued

FIGURE 22-8
Completed Find and Replace dialog box

7. Click the **Find Next** button in the dialog box. Access scrolls to the first record that matches the search criteria and highlights the book title in the *Title* field.

8. Click the **Find Next** button again. A message displays indicating that there are no more occurrences of the search text.

9. Click **OK** in the message box to close the message. Then click the **Cancel** button in the Find and Replace dialog box. Leave the database table open for the next Step-by-Step.

> **Note**
>
> You can use the shortcut keys **Shift + F4** to execute the Find command without opening the Find and Replace dialog box. Access will search for the text and values that were entered in the Find What box for the last search.

Using the Replace Command

If you are working with a large database and you want to replace existing data with new data, the task can be tedious. However, like the Find command, the Replace command makes the task easy. The Replace command locates the search text and replaces it with new text that you specify. For example, in the Classics database there is no consistency in the spelling of the word Incorporated. Sometimes it is spelled out completely, and sometimes it is abbreviated (Inc.). You can search for all the occurrences when the word is abbreviated and then automatically replace those abbreviations with the complete spelling.

> **Note**
>
> The shortcut keys for displaying the Replace dialog box are **Ctrl + H**.

STEP-BY-STEP 22.6

1. Click in the first row in the *Publisher* field. Be careful not to select the text.

2. Open the **Edit** menu and choose **Find**. Click the **Replace** tab to display the dialog box shown in Figure 22-9.

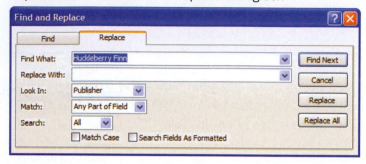

FIGURE 22-9
Replace tab in the Find and Replace dialog box

3. Notice that the Find What box still contains the text from your last search. Key **Inc.** to replace the old search text.

4. Click in the **Replace With** text box to select it and key **Incorporated**.

5. The Look In box should display *Publisher*. The Match box should display *Any Part of Field*. The Search box should display *All*.

6. Click the **Find Next** button. Access selects the entry *Random House, Inc.* in the second record in the *Publisher* column because it contains the abbreviation *Inc.* Do not be concerned that the entire entry is selected.

7. Click the **Replace** button in the dialog box.

8. If necessary, click the **up arrow** in the vertical scroll bar so you can see the second record in the *Publisher* column. Notice that *Inc.* was replaced with *Incorporated*, but the remaining text in the entry (*Random House,*) did not change.

9. Notice, too, that the next occurrence of *Inc.* is selected. When you pressed the Replace button in step 7, Access automatically replaced the appropriate text and performed the Find Next function.

Computer Concepts

If you change your mind about a replacement, you can use the Undo command to reverse the action. Remember, you must choose the Undo command before editing another record.

Note

There may be times when you do not want to replace the selected text. On those occasions, simply click the Find Next button to go to the next occurrence. No changes are made unless you click the Replace button.

STEP-BY-STEP 22.6 Continued

10. Click the **Replace All** button. A message is displayed warning that you will not be able to undo the replace operation. Click **Yes**. Access replaces all occurrences of *Inc.* with *Incorporated* throughout the column.

11. Scroll up and down to view all the entries in the column. Notice that there are no more abbreviations for *Incorporated*.

12. Click the **Cancel** button to close the dialog box, and then close the table. When prompted to save the changes to the design of the table, click **Yes**. Leave the Database Objects window open for the next Step-by-Step.

> **Computer Concepts**
>
> When you use the Replace option, you can view each change and confirm the replacements individually. You should use the Replace All option only when you are confident about making all the replacements without reviewing them first. You can use the Match Case option to aid in preventing inadvertent replacements. Match Case allows you to be more specific in what you replace, and you won't need to approve each replacement individually.

Creating Queries and Reports

Although the Find command provides an easy way to find data, you may need to locate multiple records, all containing the same values. If you have a large database, and several records contain the value you are searching for, this is another task that can be tedious. In this case, you can use a *query*, which enables you to locate multiple records matching specified criteria. Remember, you learned in Lesson 21 that Query is one of the database objects displayed in the Objects bar. The query provides a way for you to ask a question about the information stored in a database table(s). Access searches for and retrieves data from the table(s) to answer your question.

To illustrate, consider the following example. Suppose you just read a book by Charles Dickens. You really enjoyed the book and you would like to read another book authored by him. You could locate the books by Charles Dickens one at a time in the Classics database by using the Find command. But a query makes your task easier, and also creates a list of the titles for you.

When you create a query, you must identify all the fields for which you want to display information. For example, you might want only the title and the author name to display. The order in which you select the fields will be the order in which the information is displayed in the query results.

S TEP-BY-STEP 22.7

1. Click the **Queries** button on the Objects bar. The query objects are displayed in the Database Objects window. Note that there are currently no query objects for this database.

2. Double-click **Create query in Design view**. The Show Table dialog box shown in Figure 22-10 is displayed.

FIGURE 22-10
Show Table dialog box

3. Click the **Add** button in the dialog box. This adds the fields from the selected table (*Book List*) to your new query.

4. Click the **Close** button in the dialog box to close the Show Table dialog box. The fields available from the *Book List* table are listed in a dialog box and the query grid shown in Figure 22-11 is displayed.

Computer Concepts

Because databases often include more than one table, you can choose the table you want to use for the query. In this case, the database has only one table—*Book List*—and it is already selected.

FIGURE 22-11
Query window

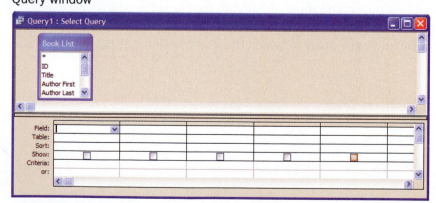

5. In the query grid, click the **down arrow** in the first column next to *Field*. Choose **Author Last** from the drop-down list.

6. Click in the first column next to *Criteria*. Key **Dickens** and press **Enter**. This tells Access to display any records written by authors with the last name *Dickens*. Access places quotations around the text.

STEP-BY-STEP 22.7 Continued

7. Click in the second column next to *Field*, click the **down arrow**, and then select **Title** from the drop-down list. Your screen should match Figure 22-12.

FIGURE 22-12
Completed query grid

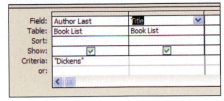

8. Click the **Save** button on the toolbar. Because the query has not yet been saved, the Save As dialog box is displayed. Key **Dickens Query** to replace the text in the Query Name text box and then click **OK**.

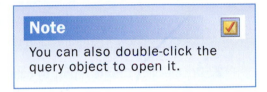

> **Note**
>
> You can also double-click the query object to open it.

9. Open the **File** menu and choose **Close**. The query Design view is closed and the Database Objects window is displayed. The Dickens Query is in the list of Query objects.

10. Select **Dickens Query** in the list of objects and then click the **Open** button in the Database Objects window. The results of the query are displayed as illustrated in Figure 22-13.

FIGURE 22-13
Dickens Query

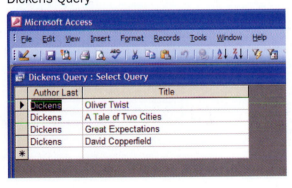

11. Close the query. Leave the Database Objects window open for the next Step-by-Step.

Printing a Report

You can print a database in Datasheet view, but when you do, all of the data contained in the database is printed. This can be very cumbersome if the database is large or if you only need certain information from the database. A *report* is a database object which allows you to organize, summarize, and print all or a portion of the data in a database. You can create a report based on a table or a query.

Although you can prepare a report manually, the Report Wizard provides an easy and fast way to design and create a report. The Wizard will ask you questions about which data you want to include in the report and how you want to format that data. Most of the format options that the Wizard will present are beyond the scope of this lesson. When the options are presented in the Wizard dialog boxes, you probably will not need to use them here, but if you are interested in learning more about Access features, you may want to take an advanced Access course.

One of the format options you will apply in the report is page orientation. Remember, you learned in earlier lessons that the *orientation* determines how the report will print on the page. Landscape orientation formats the report with the long edge of the page at the top. Portrait orientation formats the report with the short edge of the page at the top.

STEP-BY-STEP 22.8

1. Click the **Reports** button on the Object bar. The report objects are displayed in the Database Objects window. There are currently no reports to display for this database.

2. Double-click **Create report by using wizard**. The Report Wizard dialog box shown in Figure 22-14 is displayed. If necessary, click the **down arrow** in the text box under Tables/Queries and select **Table: Book List**.

FIGURE 22-14
Report Wizard dialog box

3. Choose the field names to be included in the report:
   a. Select **Author First**, then click > to move the field name to *Selected Fields*. The field name is displayed under *Selected Fields*.
   b. Select **Author Last** and then click >.
   c. Select **Title** and then click >.
   d. Select **Price** and then click >.

4. Then click the **Next** button. A dialog box displays, with options for grouping a report by fields. With this report, these options are not needed.

STEP-BY-STEP 22.8 Continued

5. Click the **Next** button. Another dialog box opens, offering options for the sort order of the records. Click the **down arrow** in the first box and select **Author Last**. Click the **down arrow** in the second box and select **Title**. Leave the order at the default setting *Ascending*. If there are two or more books by the same author, the titles will be ordered first by author last name, then by the book title.

6. Click the **Next** button. The next dialog box offers options for layout and orientation. If it is not already selected, click the **Tabular** option. Then select the **Landscape** option under Orientation. Notice that the option to adjust the field width to fit all fields on a page is selected.

7. Click the **Next** button. The dialog box that displays offers options for styles. Your dialog box may have a different style selected. Select the **Casual** style.

8. Click the **Next** button. The last dialog box for the Report Wizard, shown in Figure 22-15, asks you what title you want to use for the report. The title currently displayed is *Book List*, because that is the name of the table. Change the title to **Classic Books**.

FIGURE 22-15
Title dialog box

9. If necessary, click the option **Preview the report** to select it. Then click **Finish**. A preview of the report is displayed in Print Preview.

10. Click the **down arrow** to the right of the Zoom box on the Standard toolbar and select **75%**. The preview of the report is reduced. If necessary, reduce the zoom more so you can see the entire page.

11. Use the navigation buttons at the bottom of the Print Preview window, shown in Figure 22-16, to view the second page of the report, and then return to the first page.

FIGURE 22-16
Navigation buttons in Print Preview window

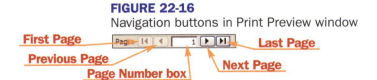

STEP-BY-STEP 22.8 Continued

12. If you have your instructor's permission to print, click the **Print** button on the Print Preview toolbar to print the two-page report.

13. If the Save As dialog box opens automatically, click **Save** in the dialog box to save the report and then accept the default options in the Print dialog box and click **Print** or **OK** to print the report.

14. If the Save As dialog box did not open automatically, open the **File** menu and click **Save**, then close the Print Preview window if necessary.

15. Click the **Close** button in the Classic Books report window to close the report.

16. Notice that the Classic Books report is listed in the Database Objects Reports window. Close the database but leave Access open for the next Step-by-Step.

Mailing Labels

Because databases often contain data regarding names and addresses, it is common to create mailing labels based on the database information. For example, if you maintain your friends' names and addresses in a database file, you can quickly print labels to mail greeting cards. You can print labels for selected friends or for the entire database. In the next Step-by-Step, you will use the report feature to create mailing labels. You will create a new report using a different Wizard.

S TEP-BY-STEP 22.9

1. Open My Computer and copy the file **Step22-9** from the data files to the location where you keep your document files.

2. Rename the copy of the file **Mailing Labels** and then close My Computer.

3. Open the file **Mailing Labels** from your document files.

4. If necessary, click the **Reports** button on the Object bar. There are no reports to display for this database.

5. Click the **New** button in the Database Objects toolbar. The New Report dialog box is displayed.

6. Select Label Wizard. Then click the **down arrow** in the list box below and select **Mailing List**. Click **OK**.

STEP-BY-STEP 22.9 Continued

7. The Label Wizard dialog box is displayed. If necessary, select **Sheet feed** under Label Type and select **Avery** in the Filter by manufacturer list box. Scroll down in the top list box (*What label size would you like?*) and select Product number **3110** (or another product number with three labels across and no larger than 1¼" × 2⅜"). When your dialog box looks like Figure 22-17, click **Next**.

FIGURE 22-17
Label Wizard dialog box displaying selected label options

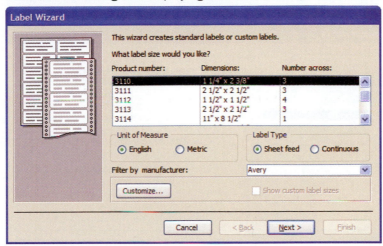

8. The next step in the Wizard is to describe the text appearance on the mailing label. If necessary, change the Font size to **10** and change the other options so your dialog box looks like the one shown in Figure 22-18. Then, click **Next**.

FIGURE 22-18
Label Wizard dialog box displaying selected font options

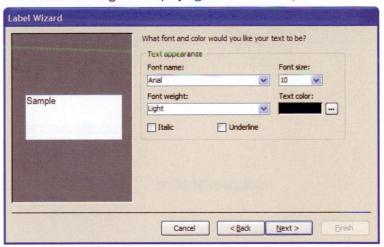

STEP-BY-STEP 22.9 Continued

9. The next step in the Wizard is to choose the fields. From the Available Fields list, construct a proto-type (a sample) for the labels. Select the fields as shown in Figure 22-19. (*Hint:* Select the field name from the Available Fields list, and then click >. Leave a blank space between fields, and press **Enter** to move to the next line. It is not necessary to key a comma after the field *City*.) When your dialog box looks like Figure 22-19, click **Next**.

FIGURE 22-19
Label Wizard dialog box displaying a prototype label

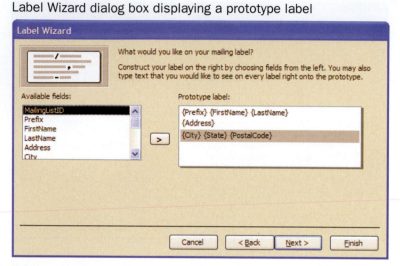

10. The next step in the Wizard is to sort the labels. Scroll down and select the PostalCode field from the Available Fields list and then click >. The field name is moved to the Sort by list. When your dialog box looks like Figure 22-20, click **Next**.

FIGURE 22-20
Label Wizard dialog box displaying the selected sort options

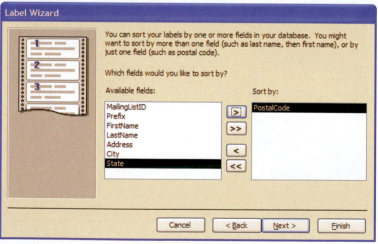

STEP-BY-STEP 22.9 Continued

11. The last step in the Wizard is to name the report. You can assign a name to the report if desired, but the proposed name *Labels Mailing List* is good. Click the option **See the labels as they will look printed** if it is not selected, and then click **Finish**.

12. If you get a message indicating that some data may not be displayed, click **OK**. The labels are displayed as they will print. If you were printing the labels, you would put the label sheets in your printer and choose the command to print.

13. Click the Close button in the Labels Mailing List: Report window to close the report. Notice that the Labels Mailing List report is listed in the Database Objects Reports window.

14. Close the database and then close Access. Follow your instructor's directions about turning off your computer.

SUMMARY

In this lesson, you learned:

- To rearrange database fields in Datasheet view, you must select the columns containing the fields and then drag them to a new location.

- The Form Wizard helps you create a professional-looking, customized form for entering data.

- Entering and editing data in a form is similar to entering and editing data in a table in Datasheet view. You use the same navigation buttons to move from one record to another.

- You can sort records in Datasheet view in either ascending or descending order.

- The Find command can save you time looking for records and specific values in a table. The Replace command can save you time finding and replacing specific text.

- You can create a query to find records that match specified criteria. Access searches for and retrieves data from the table(s) that match the criteria you identify.

- A report allows you to organize, summarize, and print all or a portion of the data in a database. You can choose a Wizard to guide you through the process in creating and formatting a report.

- When you want to create mailing labels, you create a report object and use the Label Wizard.

VOCABULARY *Review*

Define the following terms:

Field selector	Query	Report
Orientation		

REVIEW *Questions*

TRUE/FALSE

Circle T if the statement is true or F if the statement is false.

T   F   **1.** A form makes it easy to enter new data into a table.

T   F   **2.** You use the same navigation controls in a form as you use in a datasheet.

T   F   **3.** If you change your mind after you sort data, you can choose the Undo command to return the data to its original order.

T   F   **4.** You can use the Find command to make a list of multiple records that match specific criteria.

T   F   **5.** The Report Wizard guides you through the process of organizing and summarizing data in a database.

MATCHING

Match the correct term in Column 1 to its description in Column 2.

Column 1	Column 2
___ **1.** query	**A.** Navigation control used to go directly to a specific record
___ **2.** descending	**B.** Box containing the field name
___ **3.** Form Wizard	**C.** Determines how a report will appear on a page
___ **4.** orientation	**D.** Inserts new data in place of old in a database table
___ **5.** field selector	**E.** Change the layout of a database table in this view
___ **6.** record number box	**F.** Tool used to create a new form easily
___ **7.** Replace command	**G.** Locates data you are searching for in a database
___ **8.** New Record button	**H.** Enables you to locate multiple records that all match the same criteria
___ **9.** Datasheet	**I.** Sort order to arrange data with most recent date at the top of the list
___**10.** Find command	**J.** Displays a blank form

PROJECTS

PROJECT 22-1

1. Open My Computer and copy the file **Project22-1** from the data files to the location where you keep your document files. Rename the copy of the file **Ohio Classic Film Society**.

2. Close My Computer and launch Access.

3. Open **Ohio Classic Film Society** from the data files.

4. Select **Forms** in the Objects bar. Use the **Form Wizard** and the following information to create a new form using the **Members** table: select all the fields (*Hint:* Click the >> button), the **Columnar** format, and the **Sumi Painting** style. Finish using the Form Wizard by naming the form **OCFS Members**.

5. Add a new record using the form. (You do not need to enter a number in the *Member ID* field. Simply press **Enter** or **Tab**. Access will add the Member ID automatically after you key an entry in the *First Name* field.)
   First Name: Sam
   Last Name: Martin
   Address: Old Ferry Rd
   City: Oak Creek
   State: OH
   Zip: 43211
   Phone: 555-1216

6. Go to record 8 and change Judith Schuyler's phone number to **555-5005**.

7. Go to record 14. Brian Tannenbaum has moved. Change his street address to **7140 Cascade Street** and leave all other information the same.

8. Close the form and leave the Database Objects window if you are immediately moving on to Project 22-2.

PROJECT 22-2

1. Click **Tables** in the Objects bar and then open the **Members** table.

2. You want to make sure that you added a new member to the database. Find the record for Sam Martin.

3. Oak Creek is growing rapidly and has earned another zip code. Find all the 43210 zip codes in the table and change them to **43213**.

4. You would like to have a list of member names and phone numbers to hand out to all members. Create a report as follows:
   A. Go to the Database Objects window and click Reports in the Objects bar.
   B. Start the Report Wizard and choose the **Members** table.
   C. Select only the **First Name, Last Name,** and **Phone** fields.
   D. Do not group the report.
   E. Sort the report by **Last Name** in ascending order.
   F. Use the **Tabular** format and **Portrait** orientation.
   G. Choose the **Bold** style.
   H. Name the report **Members Phone List** and preview the report.

5. Close the preview, and then, if necessary, close the Members Phone List: Report window and the Members: Table window.

6. In the Database Objects window, click **Tables** in the Objects bar and then open the **Collection**.

7. Go to record 8 and correct the spelling of the last word in the title from *Arc* to **Ark**.

8. Sort the table by **Category** in ascending order. How many adventure films do you have in the collection?

9. Sort the table by **Length** in descending order. What is the longest film in the collection? How long is it?

10. Close the table without saving design changes. (Remember that the change to the data in record 8 was saved automatically by Access.)

11. For an upcoming society meeting, you want to see the titles, directors, and lengths of all foreign films in the collection. Follow these steps to create your query:
    A. Create a new query in Design view using the **Collection** table.
    B. Add the **Category, Title, Director,** and **Length** fields to the query, in that order.
    C. In the Category Criteria box, key **Foreign**.
    D. Save the query as **Foreign Query**.

12. Open the query. How many foreign titles do you have in the collection? Close the query results.

13. You are considering doing a special event on several directors. Create a report that will show you what films you have by each director. Follow these steps to create the report:
    A. Create a new report using the Report Wizard based on the **Collection** table. Select the **Director, Title,** and **Year** fields for the report, in that order.
    B. Do not add any grouping levels.
    C. Sort the report in Ascending order by **Director**.
    D. Choose the **Columnar** layout and **Portrait** orientation.
    E. Use the **Compact** style.
    F. Name the report **Directors Report** and preview the report.

14. Close the preview and then close the database.

TEAMWORK PROJECT

Create a roster for your computer class or workgroup to record the names, addresses, phone numbers, e-mail addresses, and other information about your classmates or coworkers. Follow these steps:

1. With a teammate, determine what information you want to gather and organize.

2. Divide the names of your classmates or coworkers so that each of you will gather information for half the group.

3. After you have gathered the information, create a new database and a table with the fields you identified in step 1. Then use the Form Wizard to create a form to make data entry easier. Select the options you think will present the information you've collected in the best way, and give your form a relevant title.

4. Enter the information into the form.

CRITICAL*Thinking*

ACTIVITY 22-1

Creating a query isn't the only way you can display specific records in a database. You can use what is called a filter. Open the **Ohio Classic Film Society** database and then open the **Collection** table. Click in any Category field that reads *Shakespeare*. Click the toolbar button just to the right of the Sort Descending button. What happens to the table? (When you are finished, close the database table without saving changes to the design.)

Use the Help files in Access to find out what kind of a filter you just applied. How do you redisplay all the records in the table?

KEY APPLICATIONS

REVIEW *Questions*

TRUE/FALSE

Circle T if the statement is true or F if the statement is false.

T F   1. In Word, to manually move text to a new page, you can insert a hard page break.

T F   2. Alignment refers to the white space between the edge of the paper and the text.

T F   3. If you need to create a complex table in Word, you should use the Draw Table tool.

T F   4. When data is too wide to fit in a cell, Excel displays a series of asterisks (*****).

T F   5. You can easily change a column chart to a bar chart if you wish.

T F   6. As you create a presentation, PowerPoint automatically checks for and corrects misspelled words.

T F   7. When you use Slide Finder, you must choose to insert all slides.

T F   8. Databases and spreadsheets are very similar in structure.

T F   9. You can insert a new record anywhere in an Access table.

T F 10. You can adjust column widths in Excel, but not in Access.

MATCHING

Match the correct term in Column 1 to its description in Column 2.

Column 1	Column 2

Column 1

___ 1. Absolute cell reference

___ 2. AutoComplete

___ 3. Clip Organizer

___ 4. Workbook

___ 5. Template

___ 6. Slide transition

___ 7. Query

___ 8. Argument

___ 9. Sizing handles

___ 10. Report

Column 2

A. Small squares surrounding a graphic or object, indicating that it is selected

B. A file that contains formatting and text that you can customize to create a new document similar to, but slightly different from, the original

C. An object that allows you to select, format, and print only specific fields from a table

D. Collection of pictures, photographs, sounds, and videos

E. Determines the changes in the display that occur as you move from one slide to another in Slide Show view

F. An object that allows you to locate multiple records matching specified criteria

G. Cell reference that does not change when moved

H. Word suggests the spelling of frequently used words or phrases

I. A collection of related worksheets

J. A value, cell reference, range, or text that acts as an operand in a function formula

PROJECTS

PROJECT 1

1. Start Word and open **Project1** from the data files. Save the document as **Refuge** followed by your initials.

2. Change the page orientation to landscape. Then position the insertion point in the blank line at the top of the document and specify three columns.

3. Position the insertion point in the second blank line below the heading *National Wildlife Refuge* and insert an appropriate clip art image for the topic. Resize the picture to be about 2 inches high. Center the picture, but do not wrap text around it.

4. Insert a 3-point blue-gray border below the *National Wildlife Refuge* heading. Use **Repeat** to insert the same border for the first blank paragraph beneath the clip art picture.

5. Create a WordArt heading for the first column of text using the word **Massassoit**. Size the graphic so it is as wide as the column. Move the WordArt graphic to the top of the first column and wrap text above and below it. Adjust the graphic if necessary so that it is at the top of the column, with the blank line and the words *National Wildlife Refuge* below it. Change the color of the graphic if desired to coordinate with the clip art picture.

6. Use drag-and-drop to move the first paragraph of text (the description of the National Wildlife Refuge System) to the last blank line in the document. Be sure to include the empty line before the paragraph when you drag and drop.

7. Use bullets to format the entries beneath the *Wildlife and Ecosystem*, *Public Use*, and *Safety Information* headings. (*Hint:* Align the bullet with the left edge of the column, if necessary, by opening the Bullets and Numbering dialog box and clicking the **Customize** button. Then change the Bullet position indent to 0, the Tab space after indent to **0.25**, and the Text position indent to **0.25**.)

8. Under the *Wildlife and Ecosystem* heading, delete the bullet that reads *Do not remove any plant life from the Refuge*. Then, in the bullet that reads *Do not remove any animals from the Refuge*, use **Overtype** to replace the word *animals* with **species**.

9. You're pretty sure you misspelled Lyme when keying information about ticks and Lyme disease. Find the word *Lime* and replace it with **Lyme**.

10. Find the list of unusual bird visitors to the Refuge in column 3. Select these bird names and insert a left-aligned tab at approximately 1½" on the Ruler above the column. This tab should line up the second column of names.

11. Use **Find** to locate the phrase *Enjoy all wildlife from a distance*, and then use a light blue background as a highlight to emphasize the entire sentence.

12. Insert another appropriate picture that fits the content. Resize the picture to be about 1 inch square. Wrap text around the picture and move it to the end of the document so that the last paragraph of text wraps around it. Make sure the picture aligns at the bottom with the last line of text and with the right edge of the column.

13. Create a footer with the current date left aligned (make sure the date will update automatically).

14. Preview the document to see if any changes need to be made in the layout. If necessary, resize pictures and the WordArt graphic to fit all text on one page. Insert column breaks if any headings fall at the bottoms of columns.

15. Save your changes and close the document, and then close Word.

PROJECT 2

1. Start PowerPoint and open **Project2** from the data files. Save the presentation as **Everest** followed by your initials.

2. Apply the **Mountain Top** design template.

3. On slide #1, click to the left of the first word in the title placeholder. Key **Mt. Everest:** and then press **Enter**.

4. Change the font of the title to **Times New Roman 54 pt**. Change the size of the font for the author of the quote (**—Ed Viesturs**) to **24 pt** and **Italic**.

5. Change the titles of the remaining slides in the presentation to **Times New Roman 54 pt**.

6. Change the layout of slide 6 to **Title and 2-Column Text**. In the new right-hand column, key the following text:
   First ascent by an American: Whittaker, 1963
   First ascent by an American woman: Allison, 1988

7. Add the **Newsflash** slide transition, **Medium** speed, deselect the option to advance slide on mouse click, and set the option to advance automatically after three seconds (**00.03**). Apply the transition to all the slides in the presentation.

8. Go to slide number 1 and then run the presentation. After you have finished viewing the slides, save your changes, close the presentation, and close PowerPoint.

PROJECT 3

1. Open Windows Explorer and copy **Project3** from the data files to the location where you save your documents. Rename the copy of the file **Zoo Data**.

2. Start Access and open the **Zoo Data** file. Open the **Specimens** table.

3. Several people have recently asked you some specific questions about the zoo's specimens. Use the sort feature to find the answers to these questions:
   A. How many Reptile specimens does the zoo have?
   B. Does the zoo have any ring-tailed lemurs and, if so, how many?
   C. What species has the largest population? (*Hint*: Sort in the Number field in descending order and then find the common name at the top of the table.)
   D. Sort in ascending order on the ID field to return the table to its original order.

4. You want to know how many members of the Carnivora order the zoo currently has. Create a query in Design view as follows:
   A. Add the **Order**, **Common Name**, **Species Name**, and **Number** fields to the query.
   B. In the Order column, click in the **Criteria** box and key **Carnivora**.
   C. Save the query as **Carnivores Query** and close it.

5. Open the **Carnivores Query**. How many different species does the zoo have? How many carnivores are there altogether? Close the query.

6. Create a report to show all the animals in each group. Follow these steps:
    A. Start the Report Wizard and select the **Specimens** table for the report.
    B. Select the **Group**, **Common Name**, **Endangered**, and **Number** fields for the report.
    C. In the next dialog box, select **Group** and then click the > button to group the records by this field.
    D. In the next dialog box, choose to sort by **Common Name**.
    E. Choose the **Stepped** layout and the **Compact** style.
    F. Name the report **Animals by Group** and preview the report. Use the navigation controls at the bottom of the report to view the second page of the report.

7. Close the preview window, and then close the database and Access.

SIMULATION

You volunteer at the local Rails-to-Trails organization, which converts old, unused railroad beds into trails for public use. These trails can be used for a variety of activities including walking, biking, running, and in-line skating. You have been asked to help the organization distribute information about rail-trails in your area. You may want to prepare a press release in Word, print mailing labels using Access, and create a slide show in PowerPoint to present at local community gatherings. First, however, you have decided to gather some data, and decide that Excel is the best application to organize the data.

JOB 1

You are always being asked about rail-trails in neighboring states. You have decided to prepare a fact sheet about current and projected trails in the five-state area.

1. Start Excel and open **Job1** from the data files. Save the workbook as **Trail Miles** followed by your initials.

2. Apply the **Number** format with the 1000 separator and zero decimals for the number values.

3. Insert a row above row 4. In cell B4, enter the heading **Open**. Merge and center this data over cells B4 and C4. In cell D4, enter the heading **Projected**. Merge and center this data over cells D4 and E4. You have just received the data for West Virginia's rail-trails.

4. In row 10, add the information for West Virginia. Widen columns as necessary to display all information.
    51 open trails totaling 376 miles
    23 projected trails totaling 446 miles

5. In cell A11, key **Totals**. In cells B11:E11, total the numbers of trails and miles.

6. Sort the data in ascending order by state.

7. Apply the **List 2** AutoFormat to the data.

8. Change the size of the two lines in the title to **14 pt** and center both lines of the title.

9. Save your changes. Close the workbook and exit Excel.

LIVING ONLINE

Module

Estimated Time for Unit: 8.5 hours

LIVING ONLINE

 Lesson 23
Networks and Telecommunication

3-1.1.1	3-1.1.5	3-1.2.4
3-1.1.2	3-1.2.1	3-1.2.5
3-1.1.3	3-1.2.2	3-1.2.6
3-1.1.4	3-1.2.3	

 Lesson 24
E-Mail and Effective Electronic Communication

3-2.1.1	3-2.2.2	3-2.3.3
3-2.1.2	3-2.2.3	3-2.3.4
3-2.1.3	3-2.2.4	3-2.3.5
3-2.1.4	3-2.2.5	3-2.3.6
3-2.1.5	3-2.2.6	3-2.3.7
3-2.1.6	3-2.3.1	3-2.3.8
3-2.2.1	3-2.3.2	3-4.2.4

 Lesson 25
Internet Essentials

3-1.1.1	3-3.1.3	3-3.2.3
3-1.2.6	3-3.1.4	3-3.2.4
3-1.2.7	3-3.1.6	3-3.2.11
3-3.1.1	3-3.2.1	3-3.2.12
3-3.1.2	3-3.2.2	3-4.3.4

 Lesson 26
Researching on the Internet

3-3.2.5	3-3.2.9	3-3.3.2
3-3.2.6	3-3.2.10	3-3.3.3
3-3.2.7	3-3.3.1	3-3.3.4
3-3.2.8		

 Lesson 27
Evaluating Online Information

3-3.3.5	3-4.1.1	3-4.3.2
3-3.3.6	3-4.3.1	

Lesson 28
Technology and Society

3-4.1.1	3-4.1.3	3-4.3.4
3-4.1.2	3-4.1.4	

Lesson 29
Security, Privacy, and Ethics Online

3-1.1.6	3-4.2.4	3-4.3.5
3-3.1.5	3-4.3.1	3-4.3.6
3-4.2.1	3-4.3.3	3-4.3.7
3-4.2.2	3-4.3.4	3-4.3.8
3-4.2.3		

NETWORKS AND TELECOMMUNICATION

As companies grow and purchase more computers, they often find it advantageous to connect those computers through a network. This allows users to share software applications and to share hardware devices such as printers, scanners, and so forth. Networks and networking software are being used increasingly to connect employees in different offices, even in different cities all over the world, so they can work together effectively wherever they are.

Networks

3-1.1.1
3-1.1.4
3-1.2.4

When most people think of networks, they envision something fairly complicated. At the lowest level, networks are not that complex. In fact, a *network*, as explained in Lesson 1, is simply a group of two or more computers linked together. As the size of a network increases and more and more devices are added, the installation and management does become more technical. Even so, the concept of networking and the terminology remain basically the same regardless of size.

An endpoint of a network connection is referred to as a node. That is, any device attached to a network, including computer terminals or workstations, peripherals such as printers, and file servers, is a node on a computer network.

In this lesson we discuss local area networks (LANs) and wide area networks (WANs). The primary difference between the two is that a LAN is generally confined to a limited geographical area, whereas a WAN covers a large geographical area. Most WANs are made up of several connected LANs.

Most organizations today rely on computers and the data stored on the computer. Many times they find they need to transmit that data from one location to another. The transmission of data from one location to another is *data communications*. To transmit that data requires the following components, as illustrated in Figure 23-1:

> **Computer Concepts**
>
> When computers are connected in a network, there are opportunities for unauthorized access from outside the network. Software and hardware devices that safeguard a network and provide security from unauthorized entry are called *firewalls*.

- A sending device, which is generally a computer

- A communications device, such as a modem, that converts the computer signal into signals supported by the communications channel

- A communications channel or path, such as telephone lines, cable, or a wireless transmission link, over which the signals are sent

- A receiving device that accepts the incoming signal, which is generally a computer

- Communications software

FIGURE 23-1
Communications components

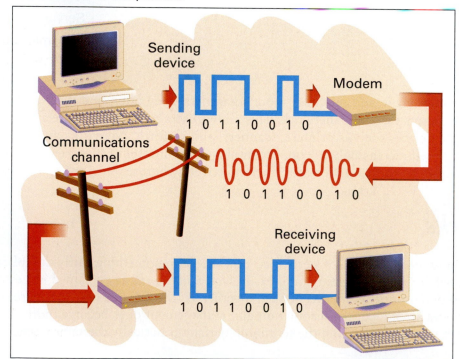

Most networks have at least one server and many clients. A *server* is a computer that manages network resources, and a *client* is a computer on the network that relies on the server for resources.

Network Benefits

To consider the topic of network benefits, you might first think about the biggest network of all, the Internet. Think about some of the changes that have occurred in our society because of the Internet. Perhaps the most profound of all of these changes is electronic mail, which we will cover in Lesson 24. A network provides almost instant communication and e-mail messages are delivered almost immediately. Other benefits include the following:

- *Information sharing:* Authorized users can use other computers on the network to access and share information and data. This could include special group projects, databases, and so forth.

- *Hardware sharing:* No longer is it necessary to purchase a printer or a scanner or other frequently used peripherals for each computer. Instead, one device connected to a network can serve the needs of many users.

- *Software sharing:* Instead of purchasing and installing a software program on every single computer, it can be installed on just the server. All of the users can then access the program from one central location. This also saves companies money because they purchase a site license for the number of users. This is much less expensive than purchasing individual software packages.

- *Collaborative environment:* Enables users to work together on group projects by combining the power and capabilities of diverse equipment.

Communications Media

3-1.1.1
3-1.2.1
3-1.2.3

To transfer data from one computer to another requires some type of link through which the data can be transmitted. This link is known as the *communications channel*. The worldwide telephone network is an important player in this channel. The telephone system is actually a collection of the world's telephone networks, including cellular, local, long-distance, and communications satellite networks. Although it was originally designed to handle voice communications, it is now used to transmit data, including fax transmissions, computer-to-computer communications such as e-mail, and live audio and video from the Web.

At one end of the communications channel, you have a sending device, such as a computer or fax machine. A communications device, such as a modem, connected to the sending device converts the signal from the sender to a format that transmits over a standard dial-up telephone line or a dedicated line. A dial-up line provides a "temporary" connection, meaning each time a call is placed, the telephone company selects the line to transmit it over. A dedicated line, on the other hand, provides a permanent or constant connection between the sending and receiving communication devices. The transmission is moved or "switched" from one wire or frequency to another. A switch is a device located at the telephone company's central office that establishes a link between a sender and receiver of data communications. At the receiving end, another modem converts the signal back into a format that the receiving device can understand.

To send the data through the channel requires some type of *transmission media*, which may be either physical or wireless.

Physical Media

Several types of physical media are used to transmit data. These include the following:

■ *Twisted-pair cable:* This is the least expensive type of cable and is the same type used for many telephone systems. It consists of two independently insulated copper wires twisted around one another. One of the wires carries the signal and the other wire is grounded to absorb signal interference. Figure 23-2 shows an example of a twisted-pair cable.

FIGURE 23-2
Twisted-pair cable

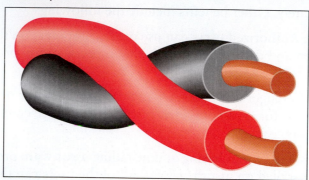

■ *Coaxial cable:* Coaxial cabling is the primary type of cabling used by the cable television industry and it is also widely used for computer networks. Because the cable is heavily shielded, as illustrated in Figure 23-3, it is much less prone to interference than twisted-pair cable; however, it is also more expensive.

FIGURE 23-3
Coaxial cable

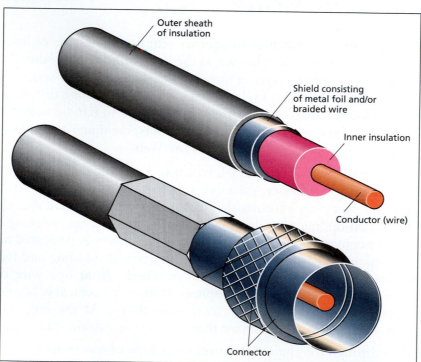

■ *Fiber-optic cable:* Fiber-optic cable is made from thin, flexible glass tubing (Figure 23-4). Fiber optics offer several advantages over traditional metal communication lines. The bandwidth is much greater, so it can carry more data; it is much lighter than metal wires; and it is much less susceptible to interference. The main disadvantage of fiber optics is that it is fragile and expensive.

Computer Concepts

Telephone companies are continually replacing traditional telephone lines with fiber-optic cables. In the future, almost all wired communications will use fiber optics.

FIGURE 23-4
Fiber-optic cable

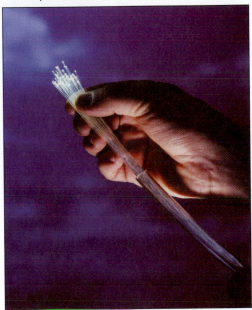

Wireless Media

Just like physical media, several wireless options are also available:

■ *Radio signals:* Transmissions using radio signals require line of sight; that is, the signal travels in a straight line from one source to the other. For radio transmission, you need a transmitter to send the signal and a receiver to accept the signal.

■ *Microwaves:* A microwave signal is sent through space in the form of electromagnetic waves. Just like radio signals, they must also be sent in straight lines from one microwave station to another, as illustrated in Figure 23-5. To avoid interference, most microwave stations are built on mountaintops or placed on the top of large buildings.

FIGURE 23-5
Microwave tower

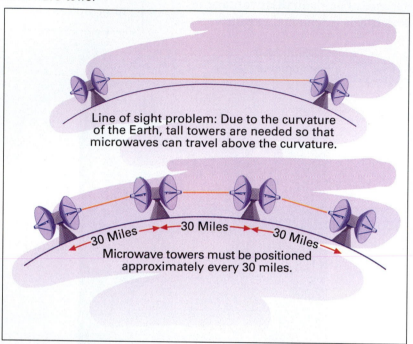

Line of sight problem: Due to the curvature of the Earth, tall towers are needed so that microwaves can travel above the curvature.

30 Miles → ← 30 Miles → ← 30 Miles

Microwave towers must be positioned approximately every 30 miles.

■ *Satellite transmissions:* Communication satellites are placed in orbit 22,300 feet above the surface of the Earth. This allows the satellite to maintain a constant position above one point on the Earth's surface by rotating at the same speed as the Earth. The satellite contains equipment that receives the transmission, amplifies it, and sends it back to Earth, as shown in Figure 23-6.

Computer Concepts

Wireless communications are becoming more widely available every day. Your favorite coffee shop may advertise "Free Wi-Fi," a wireless network you can access using a connector card in your notebook computer. Office buildings, college campuses, and even city parks offer wireless Internet connections now, freeing computer users to work almost anywhere.

FIGURE 23-6
Satellites

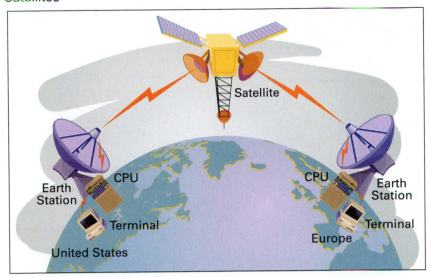

The type of communications media an organization may select to use within a network is determined by several different factors: the type of network, the size of the network, and the cost.

Network Hardware

3-1.1.3
3-1.2.2
3-1.2.3
3-1.2.5
3-1.2.6

Most networks consist of a network server and computer clients. In addition to the server and the client, there are two other categories of network hardware: communication devices and devices that connect the network cabling and amplify the signal.

Communication Hardware

Communication hardware devices facilitate the transmitting and receiving of data. When we think about communication hardware, the first thing that generally comes to mind is the desktop computer and modem. However, all types of other devices send and receive data. Some examples are large computers such as supercomputers, mainframe computers, and minicomputers; hand-held and laptop computers; and even fax machines and digital cameras. Two of the more commonly used transmitting devices for personal use are as follow:

- *Modem:* The word *modem* is an acronym for *modulate-dem*odulate, which means to convert analog signals to digital and vice versa. This device enables a computer to transmit data over telephone lines. Computer information is stored digitally (in binary code of zeros and ones), whereas information sent over telephone lines is transmitted in the form of analog waves. Both the sending and receiving users must have a modem. The speed at which modems can transmit data has increased dramatically in the past few decades. The first modems introduced in the 1960s could send data at a rate of about 300 bits per second (bps). By the early 1990s, the speed of data transmission via modem had increased to 9600 bps, and today the standard modem has a speed of 56 Kbps (kilobits per second). There are special modems capable of transmitting data as fast as 8 Mbps (megabits per second) over telephone lines. Figure 23-7 shows a computer with a modem attached; many modems in newer computers are internal devices.

FIGURE 23-7
Computer with modem attached

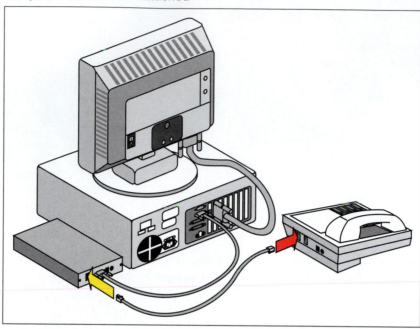

- *Cable modem:* A cable modem uses coaxial cable to send and receive data. This is the same type of cable used for cable TV. The bandwidth, which determines the amount of data that can be sent at one time, is much greater with a cable modem than with a dial-up modem connection. Cable modems allow as many as a thousand users to transmit data on one 6 MHz (megahertz) channel, capable of transmitting data at speeds of 30 to 40 Mbps. A cable modem can be connected directly to your computer or connected to a set-top box used with your television. With a set-top box, you can access and surf the Web from your TV.

> **Note**
>
> Recall that a *bit* is the smallest measurement of computer binary code, a single 0 or 1. A *kilobit* equals 1000 bits, and a *megabit* is 1000 kilobits.

Network Transmission Hardware

Modems work well for personal computers and a small one- or two-person office. However, when it comes to transmitting data across LANs and WANs, the devices are considerably different. Some of the more widely used of these devices are as follows:

- *Network interface cards (NICs):* This is an add-on card for either a desktop PC or a laptop computer. Each computer on a network must have a NIC. This card enables and controls the sending and receiving of data between the PCs in a LAN.

> **Computer Concepts**
>
> Cable companies allocate a 6 MHz channel for *downstream* Internet transmissions—data coming from the Internet to your computer—but only a 2 MHz channel for *upstream* transmissions, because Internet users download much more information than they upload.

■ *Hub:* You may have heard the word *hub* applied to airports. Travelers make connections through various hubs to go from one location to another. In data transmission, a hub works similarly. It is a hub or junction where data arrives from one or more directions and is forwarded out in one or more other directions (Figure 23-8). Hubs contain ports for connecting computers and other devices. The number of ports on the hub determines the number of computers that can be connected to a hub.

FIGURE 23-8
Computers connected to a hub

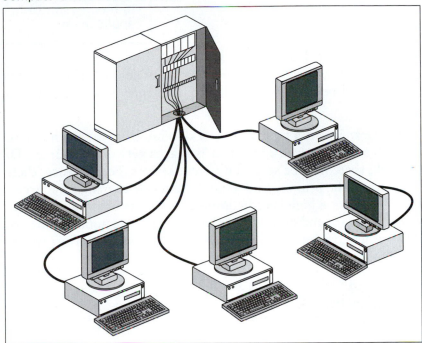

■ *Bridge:* A bridge is a special computer that connects one LAN to another LAN. Both networks must use the same protocol, or set of rules. Think about the bridge as a device that determines if your message is going to the LAN within your building or to the building across the street.

■ *Gateway:* A gateway is a combination of software and hardware that links two different types of networks that use different protocols. For instance, gateways between electronic mail systems permit users on different systems to exchange messages.

Computer Concepts

Network *architecture* refers to how the computers in a network communicate with each other—directly, or through a server. The *topology* of a network describes the geometric arrangement used to connect the devices.

■ *Router:* A router is like a traffic policeman—this intelligent device directs network traffic. When you send data through a network, it is divided into small packets. All packets don't travel the same route; instead one may go in one direction and another in a different direction. When the packets reach their final destination, they are reassembled into the original message. A router connects multiple networks and determines the fastest available path to send these packets of data on their way to their correct destination. And, just like our traffic policeman, in the event of a partial network failure, the router can redirect the traffic over alternate paths.

Types of Networks

3-1.1.2
3-1.1.5

Many types of networks exist, but the most common types are local area networks (LANs) and wide area networks (WANs), which were introduced in Lesson 1. As explained earlier, a LAN is generally confined to a limited geographical area and a WAN covers a wide geographical area.

> **Computer Concepts**
>
> For definitions of networking terminology, visit *www.novell.com/info/glossary/glossary.html*. Look up some of the terms used in this lesson to find out more about them.

Local Area Networks

Most LANs connect personal computers, workstations, and other devices such as printers, scanners, or other devices. There are two popular types of LANs—client/server and peer-to-peer. The basic difference is how the data and information are stored.

■ *Client/server network:* This is a type of network architecture in which one or more computers on the network act as a server. The server manages network resources. Depending on the size of the network, there may be several different servers. For instance, there may be a print server to manage the printing and a database server to manage a large database. In most instances, a server is a high-speed computer with lots of storage space. The network operating system software and network versions of software applications are stored on the server. All of the other computers on the network are the clients. They share the server resources (Figure 23-9).

FIGURE 23-9
Client/server network

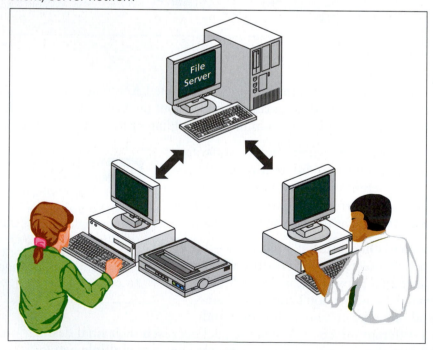

■ *Peer-to-peer network:* In this type of architecture, all of the computers on a network are equal. There is no computer designated as the server. People on the network each determine what files on their computer they will share with others on the network. This type of network is much easier to set up and manage. Many small offices use peer-to-peer networks. Figure 23-10 illustrates a simple peer-to-peer network.

FIGURE 23-10
Peer-to-peer network

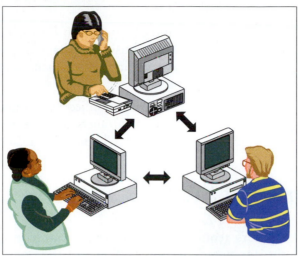

Working in a Connected World

BUILDING COMMUNITIES WITH COMPUTERS

Computer modeling is a term that describes the use of computers to create a mathematical model of a real-life system or process and then test it under different conditions. If you have ever played the computer game SimCity, you already have some experience with computer modeling. When you play the game, create a city, and then change certain data, such as the population or the layout of a utility system, you can see what changes occur in different situations.

Professions such as urban planning and civil engineering use more sophisticated computer-modeling programs to create models of many features in a community. Urban planners may make models to determine the best use of a community's land and resources. Civil engineers may test a groundwater clean-up plan, a storm sewer system, or even a transportation corridor by creating a computer model of the process or system. Geographical information systems (GIS) are another type of computer program used by engineers and planners to store and share information about a community. GIS maps show the location of structures, streets, underground pipes and wires, and geological features in an area.

Urban planners and civil engineers must have a college degree and, after they receive their degree, they serve an internship and take a test to acquire state licensure. But government agencies and consulting companies also employ technicians who assist the professional-level employees in their work. A technician needs to have working knowledge of computer modeling and GIS computer programs, good communication skills, and the ability to work well with a team. As a professional or a technician, you could be part of a team using computer technology to build a better community where you live and work.

Wide Area Networks

A WAN covers a large geographical network. This area may be as large as a state or a country or even the world, since the largest WAN is the Internet. Most WANs consist of two or more LANs and are connected by routers. Communications channels can include telephone systems, satellites, microwaves, or any combination of these.

Two variations on a WAN are intranets and extranets. An *intranet* is designed for the exclusive use of people within an organization. Many businesses have implemented intranets within their own organizations, on which they make available files such as handbooks and employee manuals, newsletters, and employment forms.

An *extranet* is similar to an intranet, but it allows specified users outside of the organization to access internal information systems. Like the Internet, intranets and extranets utilize and support Web technologies, such as hyperlinks and Web pages coded in hypertext markup language (HTML).

Network Operating Systems Software

As you know, all computers require an operating system. The operating system, among other functions, manages the computer's resources. Some of the operating systems with which you may be familiar are Windows XP, Mac OS, and Unix.

Two types of operating systems are necessary in computer networking. The first is the desktop operating system, such as Windows XP or Mac OS. The second is the networking operating system. Some desktop operating systems, such as Windows, Unix, and Mac OS, have built-in networking functions. These functions work adequately within a very limited environment. To really utilize a network, however, full-function network operating systems (NOS) software is required.

Network operating systems run on the server and provide features such as administration; security; file, print, communications, and database management; and other services to personal computer clients.

SUMMARY

In this lesson, you learned:

■ A network is a group of two or more computers linked together.

■ A local area network is generally confined to a limited geographical area.

■ A wide area network is made up of several connected local area networks.

■ Data communications is the transmission of data from one location to another.

■ The Internet is the biggest network of all.

■ You can use a network for information sharing, hardware sharing, software sharing, and as a collaborative environment.

■ The link through which data is transmitted is the communications channel.

■ Transmission media can be either physical or wireless.

■ Physical media includes twisted-pair cable, coaxial cable, and fiber-optic cable.

- Wireless media includes radio signals, microwaves, and satellite transmission.
- Most networks consist of a network server and computer clients.
- A modem is a type of communication device.
- Network interface cards enable the sending and receiving of data between PCs in a LAN.
- A hub is a device that controls the incoming and forwarding of data.
- A bridge connects one LAN to another.
- A gateway links two different types of networks.
- A router directs traffic on the Internet or on multiple connected networks.
- The two popular types of LANs are the client/server network and the peer-to-peer network.
- Networks require network operating system software.

VOCABULARY *Review*

Define the following terms:

Bridge	Gateway	Peer-to-peer network
Client	Hub	Router
Client/server network	Intranet	Server
Communications channel	Modem	Transmission media
Extranet	Network interface cards (NICs)	

REVIEW *Questions*

TRUE/FALSE

Circle T if the statement is true or F if the statement is false.

T   F   **1.** Coaxial is the most expensive type of cable.

T   F   **2.** Microwave signals must be sent in straight lines.

T   F   **3.** Fiber-optic cable is made from flexible glass tubing.

T   F   **4.** A hub is an add-on card that allows a computer to connect to a network.

T   F   **5.** Software sharing is one of the benefits of networking.

MULTIPLE CHOICE

Circle the best response for each of the following statements.

1. A _____ is confined to a limited geographical area.
    A. wide area network
    B. local area network
    C. tiny area network
    D. metropolitan area network

2. The least expensive type of physical communications media is _____.
    A. twisted-pair cable
    B. fiber-optic cable
    C. coaxial cable
    D. radio signals

3. A _____ changes analog signals to digital signals and digital signals to analog.
    A. satellite
    B. NIC
    C. bridge
    D. modem

4. A _____ is a combination of software and hardware that links two different types of networks.
    A. hub
    B. bridge
    C. gateway
    D. router

5. A(n) _____ is a computer on a network that relies on another specialized computer for resources.
    A. server
    B. hub
    C. extranet
    D. client

PROJECTS

PROJECT 23-1

Keep a record of the different types of data communications devices you use in a day or week. For instance, did you use the telephone, the computer, a fax machine, and so forth? Create a graph illustrating the data you collect.

PROJECT 23-2

Your work supervisor has asked you to prepare a proposal for a new copier for the office. You are to work with several of your coworkers. However, it is difficult for everyone to get together at the same time. Write a report that gives a short overview of the proposal you have been assigned to prepare and an explanation of how using a computer network would help your group accomplish its goal.

TEAMWORK PROJECT

Two of the most popular networking operating systems are Microsoft NT and Novell Netware. Working with a partner, search the Web for information on both of these network operating systems, with each partner focusing on one of the two systems. Using the information you find in your online research, work together as a team to prepare a report and chart comparing the features of these two network operating systems.

CRITICAL *Thinking*

ACTIVITY 23-1

As a result of computers and networks, more and more people are working from home. These people are called telecommuters. Prepare a paper describing some jobs you think people could do at home. Then add two paragraphs, one on the advantages of working at home and a second on the disadvantages of working at home.

E-MAIL AND EFFECTIVE ELECTRONIC COMMUNICATION

OBJECTIVES

Upon completion of this lesson, you should be able to:

- Understand and use e-mail features in Outlook.
- Send and receive e-mail.
- Organize and manage e-mail you receive.
- Write effective and professional e-mail.
- Manage an address book.
- Explain other types of electronic communication.

Estimated Time: 1.5 hours

VOCABULARY

Address book

Archive

Contacts

Electronic mail

Emoticons

Instant messaging

Packets

Spam

E-mail, or *electronic mail*, is one of the most popular services on the Internet. You can use e-mail to stay in touch with your family and friends, conduct business, and send attachments such as text and image files. You can even check your e-mail when you're on vacation or a business trip.

Microsoft Outlook is an Office application you can use to manage e-mail, and Web browsers usually come with a built-in e-mail program. For example, Outlook Express is the name of Internet Explorer's program. The e-mail features of Outlook are very similar to the features of Outlook Express, so after you practice using Outlook in the exercises in this lesson, you will find that you are able to use Outlook Express also.

Electronic Mail

3-2.1.1
3-2.3.1
3-2.3.2
3-2.3.7

E-mail is not that different from regular mail. You have a message, an address, and a carrier that figures out how to get it from one location to another. You may send e-mail to other people on a network at an organization, or you can use an Internet service provider to send e-mail to any computer in the world. Unless a technical problem occurs, e-mail travels much faster than regular mail (sometimes referred to as "snail mail"). When you send someone an e-mail message, it is broken down into small chunks called *packets*. These packets travel independently from server to server. You might think of each packet as a separate page within a letter. When the packets reach their final destination, they are recombined into their original format. This process enables the message to travel much faster. In fact, some messages can travel thousands of miles in less than a minute.

Accessing E-Mail

As e-mail has become a widespread way of communicating in our business and personal lives, the methods used to access e-mail have multiplied. There are a number of Web sites and Internet service providers that offer e-mail included in a monthly fee or even at no charge. America Online, Hotmail, and AltaVista are examples of companies that provide Web-based e-mail services. After you set up an e-mail account with one of these services, you can easily access your account by way of the company's Web page by entering your account name (usually your e-mail address) and a password. The Web page will often direct you to a built-in e-mail program that will let you read mail, send messages, and manage your electronic communication.

Wireless communication, which you learned about in Lesson 23, has also expanded the ways e-mail can be transmitted and retrieved. Many people have cell phones or hand-held computers that can send and receive e-mail almost anywhere. There are also integrated applications, such as Lotus Notes and Microsoft OneNote, that let you send e-mail directly from a note-taking application simply by clicking the E-Mail button on the toolbar. In addition, application programs such as PowerPoint and Excel also have an E-Mail button on the Standard toolbar that allows you to open Microsoft Outlook and send a message with a file from the application as an attachment. (You will learn more about attachments later in this lesson.)

Microsoft Outlook

The Microsoft Office program Outlook is a versatile application that can organize appointments, tasks and to-do lists, addresses, and e-mail. If you have the opportunity, use the Help feature to find out more about how you can use the application to organize many aspects of your work effectively. This lesson will concentrate on sending, receiving, and managing e-mail with Outlook.

When you launch Outlook, a screen similar to the one shown in Figure 24-1 is displayed. The default opening window is the Outlook Today window, which gives you an overview of the calendar, tasks, and mail features of the program.

FIGURE 24-1
The Outlook window

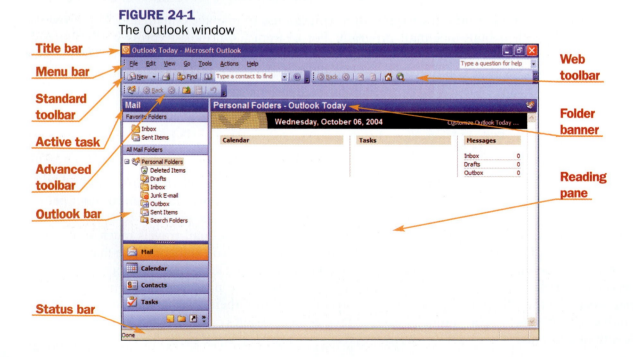

The current task selected in the Outlook bar at the left of the window is Mail. The name of the selected task appears in the task banner at the top of the Outlook bar. In Mail, you will see there are a number of standard folders, including Inbox, Deleted Items, Drafts, Junk E-Mail, and Outbox. When you select a folder in Mail, such as Inbox, the names of items in the folder appear in the Navigation pane to the right of the Outlook bar, as shown in Figure 24-2. Click an item in the folder to see the full text in the Reading pane, the large window at the right of the Outlook screen. In Outlook's other tasks, the task window opens directly in the Reading pane.

FIGURE 24-2
Navigation pane and Reading pane in Mail window

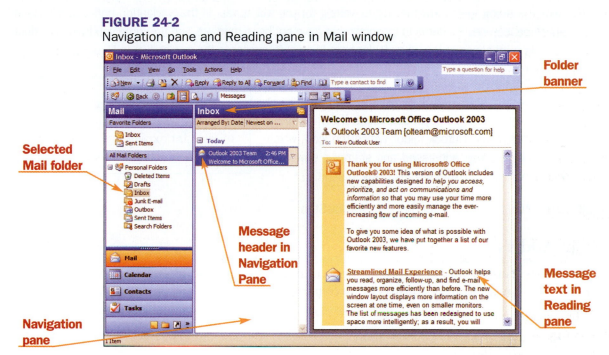

You will not use all of Outlook's folders in this lesson, but in the following Step-by-Step you will take a short tour of Outlook by opening several Outlook folders. Most Outlook folders can be customized to display information in a folder in a number of different ways. When you open a folder, you will see the view that was used the last time that folder was opened.

STEP-BY-STEP 24.1

1. Launch Outlook. If your computer is on a network, you may be prompted to enter your profile name and a password when launching Outlook. If a dialog box appears asking you to make Outlook your default program for e-mail, Calendar and Contacts, click **No**.

2. Click **Calendar** in the Outlook bar. This feature is used to set up appointments and meetings. If no one has entered any meetings in Outlook yet, this folder will be empty.

3. Click **Contacts** in the Outlook bar. This feature stores information about personal and business contacts. If no one has entered any contacts in Outlook yet, this folder will be empty. (You will use the Contacts feature later in this lesson to create an address book for your e-mail.)

4. Click **Tasks** in the Outlook bar. A grid used to organize information about tasks you want to accomplish displays in the Reading pane. If no one has yet entered any tasks in Outlook, this folder will be empty.

STEP-BY-STEP 24.1 Continued

5. Click **Mail** in the Outlook bar and then click the **Deleted Items** folder in the All Mail Folders list in the Outlook bar. The Deleted Items folder opens in the Navigation pane. Any time you delete items from other mail folders, the items are stored here until you delete them permanently. If no one has deleted any items in Outlook, this folder will be empty.

6. Click the **Inbox** folder. Any messages waiting for you will appear in the Navigation pane, with a closed envelope icon next to items in the inbox that have not been read yet. The first time you launch Outlook, there is a message in the inbox folder from Microsoft, similar to the one shown in Figure 24-2.

7. Click the **Outbox** folder. There may not be any messages in this folder, which is used to hold completed messages that have not yet been sent. If there are any messages in the Outbox folder, notice the icon, which looks like a small addressed and stamped envelope, which indicates the message is ready to send.

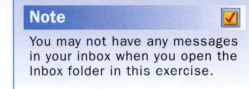

Note

You may not have any messages in your inbox when you open the Inbox folder in this exercise.

8. Leave this folder open for the next Step-by-Step.

E-Mail Addresses

When you send postal mail to someone, you must know the address. The same thing is true for e-mail. An e-mail address consists of three parts:

■ The user name of the individual

■ The "@" symbol

■ The user's domain name

For instance, Mary Smith's e-mail address could be msmith@AOL.com.

Creating a Message

Regardless of the e-mail program used, all e-mail messages contain certain standard elements, as shown in Figure 24-3. The header contains information on the address(es) of the receiver(s). The header also has a Cc field, where you can enter e-mail addresses for individuals who are to receive a "carbon copy" of the message. The subject field in the header section contains a brief description of the content of the message. The body contains the text of the message.

3 Mod Lesson 24   C5338   33912   Page 506   12/20/04cb

FIGURE 24-3
Standard elements in an e-mail message

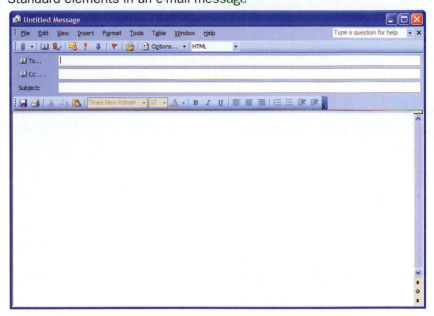

 Sending and Receiving E-Mail

3-2.1.1
3-2.1.2
3-2.1.3
3-2.1.5
3-2.2.1
3-2.2.2
3-2.3.2
3-2.3.6
3-2.3.8
3-4.2.4

If your computer is set up to handle e-mail, you can use the Inbox folder in Outlook to send and receive e-mail messages. An advantage to using Outlook as your e-mail application is that, as you create messages, you have easy access to the other Outlook folders. You can quickly address the message to someone on your contacts list, check your calendar to make sure you are available for a meeting, or add a task to your task list when a message requests further action. In addition to sending a message, you can include attachments such as pictures or documents.

Receiving E-Mail

When Outlook launches, it sends a request to your mail server to find out if you have any messages waiting. If you do, Outlook receives them and displays them in the Inbox folder. The Navigation pane displays message headers for any new messages. The message header tells you who sent the message, the subject of the message, and the date and time your server received it. The Reading pane of the Inbox window displays the actual text of the message. If you have a number of messages, you can read each one by clicking its message header to display the message text in the Reading pane.

If you are already working in Outlook, you can check your e-mail at any time. Open the Inbox folder and click the Send/Receive button on the Standard toolbar. After you have finished reading your messages, if you do not need to keep the messages, you can delete them by selecting each message header and clicking the Delete button on the Standard toolbar.

Sending E-Mail

Sending e-mail is as easy as clicking a few buttons and keying your message text. You enter an e-mail address in the To text box, either by keying the address or by inserting an address stored in your address book. You also enter e-mail addresses in the Cc text box if you are sending copies of the message to other recipients.

You can add another field labeled *Bcc* to enter e-mail addresses for recipients who are to be "blind" copied, meaning the primary addressee does not see that others are copied on the message, and a From field to add your own name. To add these fields, click the Options button on the toolbar and select the field you want to add to the message form from the drop-down list.

It is good e-mail etiquette to include a subject for your mail message. The subject should be brief, yet it should be descriptive enough to tell the recipient what the message is about. Then key your message.

After you have entered the addresses, subject, and text of your message, click the Send button on the toolbar to send the e-mail message. In the following exercise, you will practice creating an e-mail message that you will send to yourself. Check with your instructor if necessary to find out what your e-mail address will be for the exercises in this lesson.

> **Computer Concepts**
>
> Before you can use Outlook for e-mail, you must have messaging capability on a network or a mail account set up with an ISP (Internet service provider) and Outlook must be configured to send and receive e-mail. If you encounter any problems with the following exercises, consult your instructor to make sure your computer is correctly configured to receive and send e-mail.

If you send a copy of a file attached to your e-mail message, you should also see a field or icon in the header section to indicate that the message has an attachment. You can attach just about any kind of file to an e-mail message—word-processing documents, pictures or graphics files, sound files, and video files. Sending files as attachments is an easy way to transfer data from one computer to another. The addressee can then open the attachment and view it on their computer, save it to disk (referred to as downloading), or delete it.

Another way to send information in an e-mail message is to include an embedded Web site address or URL (uniform resource locator) in the body of your message. Most e-mail programs recognize the format of a URL and automatically format it as a hyperlink, which will connect directly to the referenced Web page when the link is clicked. This is a good way to send someone a link to information that may change (for example, a link to a newspaper's Web site or to a Web page that regularly updates financial information).

> **Note**
>
> E-mail attachments can contain viruses. Never download or open files from people you don't know. And, most importantly, be sure to keep your antivirus software up to date.

S TEP-BY-STEP 24.2

1. Click the **New Mail Message** button in the Inbox folder. The Untitled Message form (shown in Figure 24-3) appears.

2. You will send a message to yourself. If you do not know the e-mail address you should use to receive a message on the computer you are using, check with your instructor for this information. Then click in the **To** text box and enter your e-mail address.

STEP-BY-STEP 24.2 Continued

3. Click in the **Subject** text box and key **George Washington Information**.

4. Click in the message area. As soon as you do, the title of the window changes to *George Washington Information - Message*.

5. For the body of the message, key the following:

Here is some information on the first president of the United States, George Washington. I found the information at www.whitehouse.gov. Please review and let me know if you have any questions.

Notice that when you key the Web page reference, it is underlined, and it also may appear in a different color. Depending on the e-mail program you use, you may have to click, double-click, or hold down the Ctrl key and click to activate the link and open the associated Web page.

6. Press **Enter** twice and key your name to sign the e-mail. Your screen should look similar to Figure 24-4.

FIGURE 24-4
Completed message form

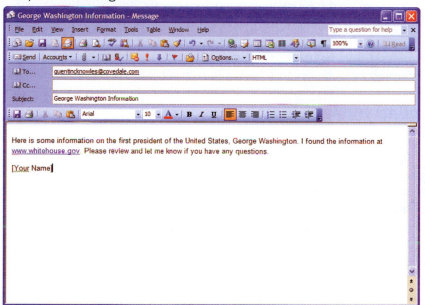

7. Attach the file **Step24-2a** from the data files to your message.

   a. Click the **Insert File** button on the toolbar.

   b. In the Insert File dialog box that opens, locate the **Step24-2a** file in the data files location.

   c. Click the filename, and then click the **Insert** button.

8. Click the **Send** button on the Outlook toolbar to send the message.

> **Note** ✅
>
> You will see a new text box labeled *Attachment* in the heading of the message after the Insert File dialog box closes. The text box displays information about the attachment, including an icon representing the type of file, the name of the file, and the size of the file.

STEP-BY-STEP 24.2 Continued

9. Create another simple message to yourself and attach the file **Step24-2b** to the message.

10. Delete the attachment by selecting the filename in the Attachment text box and then pressing **Delete**. Click the **Send** button on ther Outlook toolbar to send the message.

11. Leave Outlook open for the next Step-by-Step.

Troubleshooting Problems with E-Mail

Some e-mail service providers limit the size of attachments to e-mail messages. You may receive a message when you try to send an e-mail with an attachment saying that it cannot be sent because it exceeds the size the program can handle. Even if your e-mail provider and program can send a large attachment, you may find that the recipient cannot receive the message or open the attachment.

Other technical problems can prevent messages from being sent or received, or you may occasionally receive a message saying a program could not be delivered. This message usually means that the recipient's address was entered incorrectly or no longer exists. However, other errors may be caused by a problem in the server that handles the mail for your e-mail provider or for that of the recipient. If you receive a message that says your e-mail could not be delivered or sent, check the address and try to send it again. Sometimes the problems with a server are temporary, and the message can be sent successfully if you try again.

Encoding or Encrypting E-Mail

Some communication is not suitable for e-mail. For example, legal documents or other information that requires a traditional signature may not be considered legally binding without a handwritten signature, and so need to be sent through more traditional delivery methods. Some business or government correspondence may be sensitive or secret, and it is impossible to send e-mail that is completely secure. In this kind of situation, some e-mail messages are encoded or encrypted. Microsoft Outlook's cryptographic features are used to ensure the integrity of data—that is, to make sure no one changes the information before the intended receiver sees it—as well as to keep the contents of the message secret. The process involves *encrypting* the information in the message by "scrambling" it so that it cannot be understood. Then, when the intended recipient opens the message, he or she uses a key for *decryption* that unscrambles the information and returns it to the original text.

 # Organizing and Managing E-Mail

3-2.2.1
3-2.2.3
3-2.2.4
3-2.3.2
3-2.3.5
3-2.3.7
3-2.3.8

You can imagine that if you receive and send numerous e-mail messages every day, you need some way to manage and organize the message. You may want to delete unneeded or spam messages, for example. *Spam* is unsolicited e-mail, essentially electronic junk mail, that may take up a lot of space in your inbox. In other circumstances, you will want to reply to some messages you receive, and *archive*, or save, some important messages for future reference. Outlook offers simple methods to organize, save, and even search for messages in your e-mail folders.

Working with Messages You Receive

When you receive an e-mail message, you have a number of options on what you can do with it. You can send a reply to the message, forward the message to someone else, save the message to a specified location, or delete the message. Before you can perform an action on a message, you must first select it.

■ *Replying to a message:* You can reply to an e-mail message in one of two ways. Click the Reply or Reply All button, key your reply message, and then send the message. With this type of reply, the original message is included along with your reply message. This type of reply is appropriate when you're answering a question or responding to specifics in the original message. Or, you can create a new mail message in response to a message. With this type of reply, only the text of your reply message is included, unless you copy text from the original e-mail message and paste it into the new message. If you copy information from another e-mail message, the > character often precedes each line of the copied information to identify that it came from another source. Some e-mail programs automatically apply default formats to text that you paste into a message. When you reply to an e-mail message, the recipient(s) normally sees the letters "Re" preceding the text in the subject line to indicate that it is a reply message.

■ *Forwarding a message:* This is similar to replying to a message. Forwarding messages helps cut down on the time you spend keying messages from scratch. It's also a quick way to share information with a number of people. When you forward a message, the recipient(s) normally sees the letters "Fw" preceding the text in the subject line to identify it as a message that's being forwarded.

■ *Saving a message:* You can save an e-mail message in various formats (including text and HTML formats) to disk so that you can open and read it later. You can also save and organize e-mail messages in folders within your e-mail program. In Outlook, for example, you can create folders within your local folders (Inbox, Outbox, Sent Items, Deleted Items) to further organize your messages. To copy or move a message into a folder, simply right-click the message header in the Navigation pane, select the Move to Folder or Copy to Folder option, and then select the folder to which you want to move or copy in the dialog box that opens.

■ *Deleting a message:* You can delete an e-mail message easily by selecting it and then pressing the Delete key or clicking the Delete button on the e-mail program's toolbar. In some e-mail programs, such as Outlook, this moves the message into a deleted mail folder. To delete it permanently, you must delete it from this location.

Icons in the message headers listed in the Navigation pane offer clues about each message. For example, an icon that looks like the back of a sealed envelope indicates a message that has been received but not read; an exclamation point icon means the sender considers it an urgent or high priority message; a paper clip icon means that the message has a file attached to it. You can also manually mark a message as read or unread, or add a flag icon to remind yourself to follow up on the message. Use the keywords *message icons* in Microsoft Outlook Help to find out more about the icons in message headers.

STEP-BY-STEP 24.3

1. To complete this exercise, you must have sent yourself an e-mail as instructed in Step-by-Step 24.2. From your inbox, select the *George Washington Information* e-mail message to view it.

2. Open the attachment. An attachment is usually identified by an icon of a paper clip to the left of the sender's name in the message header, as shown in Figure 24-5. (*Note:* Your Inbox may appear different than the one shown in Figure 24-5. Regardless of the screen layout, the attachment will be indicated in the same way.) Click the paper clip icon and then double-click the attachment in the Reading pane. It should open in Word. (If the Reading pane is not visible, click on the View menu, select Reading Pane, and click Right in the drop-down box.)

FIGURE 24-5
An e-mail message header indicating an attachment

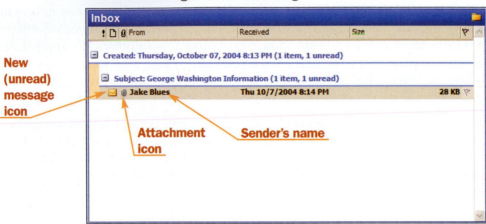

New (unread) message icon

Attachment icon   Sender's name

3. You can save the attachment to disk from within the application in which you opened it, or you can save it from the e-mail message as follows:

   a. Close the attachment file and return to Outlook.

   b. Make sure the e-mail message is selected in your inbox.

   c. Click the paper clip icon and then choose to save the attachment by right-clicking the filename and selecting **Save As** from the shortcut menu. Save the file to the location where you keep your assignments.

> **Note**
>
> When you save this attachment, it may overwrite the original data file of the same name. In this case, if you see a message box asking you if you want to replace the file, click **Yes**.

4. Reply to the e-mail message. Make sure the e-mail message is selected in your inbox, and click the **Reply** button. The original sender's e-mail address (yours!) should automatically appear in the To field. In the subject line, you should see *Re* to indicate that you are sending a reply. Close the e-mail message without saving or sending.

5. Click the **Reply to All** button. The original sender's e-mail address should automatically appear in the To field. Although it does not apply in this Step-by-Step, the e-mail addresses of anyone else who received the e-mail should automatically appear in the To field as well or in the Cc field if they were copied on the original e-mail.

STEP-BY-STEP 24.3 Continued

6. Key in the following text for your reply:

> **Thanks. I'll let you know if I have any questions.**
>
> **[Your Name]**

7. Click the **Send** button on the toolbar to send the e-mail.

8. Now, forward the e-mail to yourself. Select the e-mail message in your inbox and click the **Forward** button.

9. Key your e-mail address in the To field. Notice the *Fw* in the subject line. The recipient will be able to identify the message as one that is being forwarded.

10. Forward the e-mail by clicking the **Send** button on the toolbar.

11. Save the original *George Washington Information* e-mail message to disk. Select the message in your inbox. Open the **File** menu and select **Save As**. In the Save As dialog box, select the location where your assignments are saved as the location where you want to save the file, enter the filename **GWashington Info** for the message, accept or select the **HTML** format to save the message, and click **Save**. Remain in this screen for the next Step-by-Step.

> **Note**
>
> By default, Outlook saves the file in HTML format. To change the format, open the **Tools** menu in the Outlook window, select **Options**, click the **Mail Format** tab, and select **Rich Text** or **Plain Text** from the Message format drop-down list.

Managing Your Inbox

Most e-mail programs give you a number of options for managing and organizing e-mail messages. You can sort e-mail according to the name of the sender, by subject, or by the date received. It's a good idea to delete spam or other unnecessary messages regularly to prevent an "Inbox overflow" message, which indicates that there is no more room in your Inbox folder for any new messages.

You can use the search feature to find e-mail messages from a certain person or received on a certain date. You can organize mail into different folders that you create within your e-mail program. For example, you might have a folder for personal correspondence and, within that folder, you might have individual folders for your personal contacts.

STEP-BY-STEP 24.4

1. You should now have several versions of the *George Washington Information* e-mail message in your inbox. Use the sort feature to sort the messages by the Subject field.

a. Click the **Arranged By** button at the top of the Navigation pane.

b. Select **Subject** from the pop-up menu.

STEP-BY-STEP 24.4 Continued

2. Click the **Find** button on the toolbar to open the Find bar, shown in Figure 24-6.

   a. To search your inbox for the message that you forwarded, key **Fw** in the Look for text box. Be sure that **Inbox** is selected in the Search In text box.

   b. Click **Find Now** on the Find bar. All messages that have been forwarded will display in the Navigation pane.

FIGURE 24-6
The Find bar in Outlook

3. Create a new folder within your Inbox folder and name it **George Washington**.

   a. Right-click the **Inbox** folder in the Outlook bar's *All Mail Folders* list.

   b. Select **New Folder** in the shortcut menu.

   c. In the **Create New Folder** dialog box, key **George Washington** in the Name text box.

   d. Click **OK** to create the folder and close the dialog box.

4. Right-click any one of the *George Washington Information* e-mail messages in your inbox. On the shortcut menu, click **Move to Folder** and select the **George Washington** folder. Click **OK**. The message is removed from the inbox and placed in the George Washington folder.

5. Right-click another of the *George Washington Information* e-mail messages in your inbox. On the shortcut menu, click **Copy to Folder** and select the George Washington folder. A copy of the message remains in the inbox and is also placed in the George Washington folder.

 Ethics in Technology

E-MAIL/E-ACHES

Although e-mail is one of the more popular services of the Internet, its widespread use has ushered in a number of problems. One of the most nagging problems is simply the overflow of e-mail messages many users find in their inboxes. Like your telephone number, your e-mail address can get into the address books of marketers and newsgroups, enabling them to send you many unwanted e-mails, or spam, as these messages are commonly called.

E-mail communication can also lead to confusion and misinterpretation. Receivers are often guilty of not thoroughly reading an e-mail message before they reply, or they may not use the Reply All option correctly. It's important to pay close attention to whom your messages and replies are going. You don't want to automatically reply to all addressees if the content of the message is not relevant to all of them, but you also need to be sure to reply to all parties who have an interest in your reply.

STEP-BY-STEP 24.4 Continued

6. Select all the *George Washington Information* e-mail messages in your inbox by selecting one, holding down the **Ctrl** key, and clicking the others. Click the **Delete** button on the toolbar or press the **Delete** key to delete the messages from your inbox.

7. Leave Outlook open for the next Step-by-Step.

3-2.3.2
3-2.3.3
3-2.3.4
3-2.3.5
3-2.3.7
3-2.3.8

Professional and Effective Electronic Communication

E-mail has become a prevalent form of communication for both personal and business users. While it can be informal in nature—much like a telephone conversation—e-mail communication should be courteous and professional, especially among business users. E-mail messages can be printed and saved, so they can serve as "written proof" of what has transpired, much like a signed letter or other official document. Keep in mind the following elements of professional and effective electronic communication when you compose your e-mail messages:

- Proofread your messages before sending them. Most e-mail programs have spell checkers that can help identify spelling and grammatical mistakes.

- Limit your use of *emoticons* (keyboard symbols used to show emotion, such as :-o to show surprise), humor, and jokes in your messages. They can easily be misunderstood and misinterpreted.

- Keep your messages short and to the point. If you're soliciting a response from the receiver of the message, you'll find that a brief message with a pointed list of questions is most effective in getting that response.

- Try to limit each message to a single subject. For work-related communications, your message may become part of someone's file on the subject, and it is easier to track the information if it is subject specific.

- Double-check the addresses in the To and Cc/Bcc text boxes before sending a message to avoid sending inappropriate or irrelevant messages. If you use the Reply All feature, you may accidentally embarrass yourself by sending a message to the wrong person or inconvenience the recipient with unwanted and unneeded communications.

- Remember that e-mail sent through company networks or Internet e-mail sites is not private.

- Use the appropriate mail format to send your messages. Sometimes excessive formatting in a specific word-processing format or in HTML format can prevent the receiver from reading a message if they do not have the appropriate application to view it.

> **Computer Concepts**
>
> The use of all capital letters in an e-mail message is considered to be SHOUTING, and it also makes a message harder to read. Try to avoid using capital letters for emphasis.

Special E-Mail Features

IC³

3-2.1.4
3-2.2.3
3-2.2.6
3-2.3.6
3-2.3.7

Most e-mail programs come with a variety of features and options that make it easy to generate an automatic reply or forward mail, block messages from specific senders, copy a message to other recipients, and customize the look and feel of your messages. For example, to customize your messages, click the down arrow next to the Options button on the toolbar in the message window. Then select the E-mail Signature option on the drop-down menu to open the E-mail Options dialog box, shown in Figure 24-7. You enter and format an automatic signature in the E-mail Signature tab.

FIGURE 24-7
E-mail Options dialog box

Copying to Multiple Recipients

You can insert more than one name in the To text box. The message will go to all the names on the list at the same time. Add people you would like to receive a copy of this e-mail to the Cc list. If you want someone to receive a copy of the e-mail without letting the other message recipients know who else is receiving the e-mail, add the Bcc (blind copy) text box and then insert the addresses for the blind copy recipients. If sending or copying an e-mail to more than one person, each e-mail address should be separated by a semicolon.

Adding Formatting to a Message

The e-mail messages you have created in this lesson may have looked rather plain and boring to you. While you don't want your e-mails to be distracting or silly (particularly if you are sending them to business contacts), you can still add some visual interest. Open the E-mail Options dialog box and select the Personal Stationery tab to create a custom look for your messages. Keep in mind, however, that sometimes added formatting cannot be read if the recipient has a different e-mail program to read mail than was used to create your message.

Automatic Message Responses

It is possible to configure e-mail programs such as Outlook to deal automatically with e-mail messages you receive. The automatic controls you can set in Outlook include the following:

- An automatic "out of the office" response that replies to all e-mail messages received when you are unable to reply to messages yourself.

- A forwarding command that will redirect your mail to another e-mail address.

- A "block senders" list that will keep messages from certain addresses from being placed in your inbox, which is particularly useful to block unwanted advertisements that are often sent repeatedly to the same e-mail address.

Some of these features are only available in Outlook if you are using a Microsoft Exchange Server e-mail account. Use the Outlook Help feature to find out more about how to block, forward, or automatically respond to messages. Use the key terms *automatic message* and *block senders* to generate a list of topics in Help.

> **Computer Concepts**
>
> Blocked messages in an e-mail program are actually saved in a separate folder rather than the inbox folder. In Outlook, the folder is named Junk E-mail. You can still access the messages if needed, and you should regularly check the folders of blocked and deleted messages and clear out messages you really don't want to keep to make space for new messages that will be saved to those folders.

Managing an Address Book

You can manually key in e-mail addresses, or you can insert them from your address book. An *address book* is an electronic list of your contacts that works in conjunction with your e-mail program. Once you enter an e-mail address in your address book, all you have to do is click the name and the address is inserted automatically in the header of your message. This eliminates the possibility of keying in the wrong e-mail address.

The *Contacts* folder in Outlook allows you to create an address book to store many kinds of information about people you work with or communicate with on a regular basis. As you insert information about a contact, Outlook creates an address card for that contact. Outlook arranges the address cards in alphabetical order so you can easily locate each one. Figure 24-8 shows two address cards in the Contacts folder.

FIGURE 24-8
Business and personal contacts in the Contacts folder

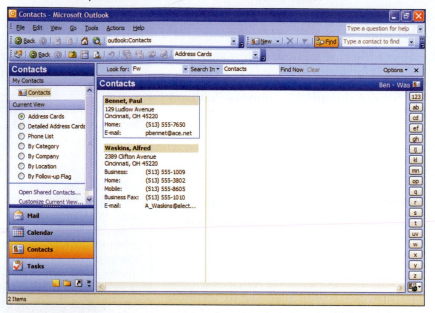

If you want to send a message to a contact stored in the Contacts folder, click the To button. A dialog box opens to allow you to select a contact name. Because you have already stored the e-mail address for that contact in the Contacts folder, you do not have to rekey the address. The contact's name appears in the To text box, and the message will automatically be sent to the e-mail address you previously stored. If you want to send a copy of the message to another person, click the Cc button to open the dialog box with contact names again. If an e-mail address is not in your address book, you can also type it in the Cc box.

Computer Concepts

You can also use the Address Book feature in Outlook Mail to create or edit a list of e-mail addresses. On the **Tools** menu, select **Address Book** to open the Address Book dialog box. You can edit or select from entries in the Outlook Address Book or your Contacts list from this dialog box.

Adding and Deleting Contacts

To add a new contact, choose New Contact from the Actions menu. Outlook displays a dialog box with a number of tabs. You can fill in as much or as little information on these tabs as you like. After you complete the dialog box, Outlook adds a new address card to the Contacts folder.

Note

You can also double-click in any blank space in the Contacts Reading pane to display the *Untitled - Contact* form or you can click the **New** button on the toolbar.

You can easily remove an address card from the contacts list. In the following exercise, you will add a contact, create an e-mail message to the contacts, and then remove the contact you added.

STEP-BY-STEP 24.5

1. Click **Contacts** to open the Contacts folder.

2. In the Outlook bar, you should see a list of options in a list headed Current View. Select the **Address Cards** option if necessary.

3. Open the **Actions** menu and choose **New Contact**. The *Untitled - Contact* form opens.

4. Click in the **Full Name** text box and key **Jane Treadway**.

5. Press **Tab** to move the insertion point to the next text box. Notice the dialog box name changes to *Jane Treadway – Contact* and the File as text box below automatically fills in *Treadway, Jane*. Key **Office Manager** in the Job title text box.

6. Press **Tab** to go to the next text box and key **Williston Associates**.

7. Click in the **Address** text box and key the address shown in Figure 24-9. Then key the remaining information shown in the figure.

FIGURE 24-9
Contact information for Jane Treadway

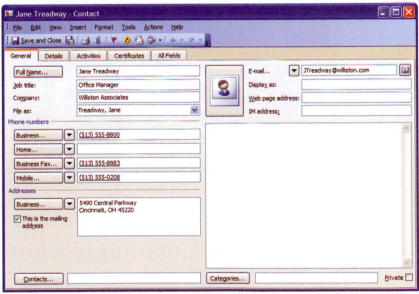

8. When you have finished entering the information, click the **Save and Close** button. The form closes and the contact information appears in the Reading pane.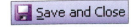

9. Notice that the Address Card view does not show all the details for the contact you just added. You can view them with the Detailed Address Cards view. On the Outlook bar, select **Detailed Address Cards** from the Current View options. You can now see all information on the address card.

STEP-BY-STEP 24.5 Continued

10. You just learned that Ms. Treadway's business telephone numbers have changed. Double-click the header in the **Treadway** address card to open her contact form and change the business phone number to **(513) 555-7777** and the business fax number to **(513) 555-7779**. Then click the **Save and Close** button to close the form and return to the Detailed Address Cards view.

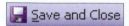

> **Note** ☑️
>
> If there are many address cards in your Contacts folder, you may want to click the alphabet buttons at the right of the Reading pane to find the new entries. Click the **t** button, if necessary, to view the Jane Treadway card.

11. Click **Mail** in the Outlook bar and then select the **Inbox** folder if necessary.

12. Click the **New Message** button and then click the **To** button to open the Select Names dialog box.

> **Computer Concepts** 🔳
>
> You can also right-click an address card in Contacts and then select **New Message to Contact** in the shortcut menu to open a new message form already addressed to the contact.

13. If **Contacts** is not in the *Show Names from the* text box, select it from the drop-down list, and then click on the e-mail entry for **Jane Treadway** in the list. Be sure not to click on the business fax entry.

14. Click **OK** to close the dialog box and insert Jane Treadway's e-mail address in the To text box.

15. Close the Untitled Message window and click **No** when you are prompted to save the changes to the message.

16. Click **Contacts** on the Outlook bar, and then select the **Address Cards** option in the Current Views list.

17. Click the address card for **Jane Treadway** to select it. The bar behind the name changes to a color to indicate it is the active card. (If this contact is the first or only one in the list, it may already be selected.)

18. Click the **Delete** button on the toolbar to remove the contact. Then close Outlook and follow your instructor's directions about turning off your computer.

3-2.1.5
3-2.1.6

Other Forms of Electronic Communication

As mentioned earlier, it is now possible to send e-mail using a cell phone or a personal digital assistant or hand-held computer. There are also other forms of text messaging available besides e-mail, and these methods are available on many kinds of electronic devices. *Instant messaging* is becoming a popular medium for correspondence in business as well as social settings. The Instant Messaging feature in Outlook, for example, enables you to send messages in real time. In other words, you can send and receive messages while you and the contact are both logged on to the Internet. Each contact must have an instant messaging account, available through many Internet service providers. Figure 24-10 shows an instant messaging screen in the program available from America Online.

FIGURE 24-10
America Online Instant Messenger screen

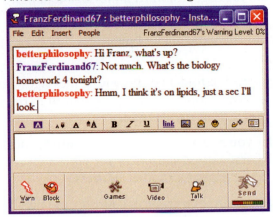

Instant messaging does not save or archive messages, but there are some blocking features that can filter out messages from specific senders. More and more cell phones and personal digital assistants support instant messaging or text messaging as well as e-mail, utilizing wireless connections to access the Internet and make the connection between the people sending messages. Keep in mind that instant messaging is direct, "real-time" communication using text messages. Because it is so immediate, you should use care when using instant text messaging for business purposes. Make sure your messages are professional and brief, and remember that you will probably not be able to access any record of messages sent or received this way.

SUMMARY

In this lesson, you learned:

■ Microsoft Outlook includes features to manage appointments, tasks, and e-mail. The Outlook bar displays shortcuts that give you quick access to each of the Outlook folders.

■ Electronic mail is similar to regular mail because it requires an address, a message, and a carrier to get it from the sender to the receiver.

■ E-mail messages are broken into smaller portion of electronic data called packets, which are sent independently and then reorganized into the original message.

■ You can access e-mail on a computer using a program like Microsoft Outlook, or you can send and receive e-mail messages using a Web site with a built-in e-mail program, such as American Online or Hotmail.

■ Wireless communication makes it possible to send and receive e-mail using a hand-held computer or cell phone with e-mail capabilities.

■ E-mail addresses consist of three parts: the user name, the "@" symbol, and the domain name.

■ An e-mail message header includes the address of the recipient, the subject of the message, and information about to whom the message is sent as a copy.

- You can use the Inbox folder in Outlook to send and receive e-mail messages.

- An attachment is an application file that is sent with an e-mail message and can be opened by the recipient.

- You can reply to an e-mail message, forward a message to a new recipient, delete a message, or save a message.

- Spam, or junk e-mail, consists of unsolicited messages that take up space in your inbox unnecessarily.

- E-mail messages are organized in folders of incoming messages, sent messages, deleted messages, and junk e-mail that was blocked from being placed in the inbox. You can also create additional folders to organize your own e-mail.

- Special e-mail features let you add an automatic signature to messages, block messages from certain addresses, create personalized stationery for your messages, and set up an automatic response or forward your messages to another address.

- Professional electronic communication requires courtesy and brevity. Always check that the spelling and grammar is correct, and that the message is being sent to the intended recipient(s).

- The Contacts folder is designed to store information about business and personal contacts with whom you communicate often.

- You can create address cards that hold information such as name, address, phone number, e-mail address, and so on. Address cards are listed in alphabetical order in the Contacts folder.

- Other forms of electronic communication are available using a desktop or laptop computer, cell phone, or personal digital assistant, such as instant messaging, which allows you to send messages in real time.

VOCABULARY *Review*

Define the following terms:

Address book	Electronic mail	Packets
Archive	Emoticons	Spam
Contacts	Instant messaging	

REVIEW *Questions*

TRUE/FALSE

Circle T if the statement is true or F if the statement is false.

T   F   **1.** Each Outlook folder organizes a different type of information.

T   F   **2.** The first part of an e-mail address is called the domain name.

T   F   **3.** As you add contacts to your address book, Outlook arranges them in alphabetical order.

T   F   **4.** You can sort e-mail messages by subject or by date received.

T   F   **5.** Long messages are appropriate for e-mail if you cover several topics in one message.

MATCHING

Match the correct term in Column 2 to its description in Column 1.

Column 1	Column 2
____ 1. To send an e-mail message on to another recipient	**A.** Emoticon
____ 2. A file sent with an e-mail message	**B.** Spam
____ 3. A keyboard symbol used to convey a tone or feeling in an electronic communication	**C.** Packet
	D. Blind copy
____ 4. A small chunk into which an e-mail message is broken as it is sent to the recipient	**E.** Attachment
	F. Instant message
____ 5. Junk e-mail marketing a product or service	**G.** Forward

PROJECTS

PROJECT 24-1

1. If necessary, launch Outlook. Open the **Contacts** folder. Enter and save the following personal and business contacts. Use your own city or town, state, and zip code for the addresses.

Full Name:	Marian Teodorescu	Full Name:	Rose Golding
Job Title:		Job Title:	Career Counselor
Company:		Company:	Careers Plus
Address:	18 Baldwin Way	Address:	451 Rhodes Hall
Business Phone:		Business Phone:	555-8825
Home Phone:	555-9834	Home Phone:	
E-mail:	teodorm@netlink.com	E-mail:	rgolding@careers.org

2. Create an e-mail message to send to a contact in your address book and copy it to yourself. Do not send the message to one of the fictitious contacts that you created in Step 1. Write a message that relates to a subject you are interested in researching.

3. Attach the file Project 24-1 from the data files and send the message.

4. Create a folder at the same level as your inbox folder and name it **Research**. When you receive the message you sent, open the attachment.

5. Close the attachment file, and then copy the e-mail message to the **Research** folder you created in step 4.

6. Delete the message from your inbox.

PROJECT 24-2

1. If necessary, open the **Inbox** folder in Outlook.

2. Create the following e-mail messages:
   A. Create a message to Marian to confirm that you will be going to the library with her next Tuesday. (*Hint:* Remember to click the **To** button in the new message window to locate her name in your contacts list.) The subject of the message should be **Library Research**. Key your name at the end of the message. Save the message as **Marian** and do not send it.
   B. Create a message to Ms. Golding to confirm your appointment with her at 10:00 a.m. on Friday. The subject of the message should be **Confirm Meeting**. Thank her for taking the time to see you. Key your name at the end of the message. Save the message as **Confirm Meeting** and do not send it.

3. Exchange e-mail addresses with another student in your class, and then add the other student's name and e-mail address to your Contacts folder.

4. Create a brief e-mail message to the other student that mentions the subject matter of the attachment you opened in Project 24-1. (If you haven't completed Project 24-1, write a brief message that says you are working on Project 24-2.)

5. Send the message.

6. You should receive a message from the student with whom you exchanged addresses. Forward the message you receive back to the other student. When you receive a forwarded message from the other student, open it, read it, and then delete it.

7. Go back through the Outlook folders and delete all the items you added in Project 24-1 and Project 24-2, including the Research folder and its contents.

8. Close Outlook.

TEAMWORK PROJECT

Individuals who use e-mail for frequent communication are often annoyed by unwanted e-mail called *spam*. Spam is unsolicited e-mail messages that can be obnoxious, offensive, and a waste of your time. Some countries have laws against spam. Your Internet service provider may try to block spam before it reaches your mailbox. However, you may still be inconvenienced by junk e-mail.

Working with a partner, research spam to learn more about what it is used for, how marketers get addresses, how effective spam is, and ways you can stop spam. Then, you and your teammate should each select one of the two positions—pro spam, how effective it is and what it is meant to do; or against spam, if it is a nuisance or problem and how you can stop it before it reaches your e-mail inbox. Write a brief summary of your findings and compare them with your partner. Then, at the end of your report, answer the following questions together: Is spam ever useful? Should there be laws to restrict spam? Do you think you can block all spam from reaching your inbox?

CRITICAL *Thinking*

ACTIVITY 24-1

If you don't have a personal e-mail address, how would you go about opening a free account for personal e-mail? There are a number of Web sites that provide free access to e-mail, and even if you don't have a computer, public libraries, schools, and even some "Internet cafes" offer free or inexpensive computer access to the World Wide Web that you can use to check incoming messages and send your own e-mail. If you wanted to set up a personal e-mail account, what kind of features would you like to have for your account? You might want to investigate some Web sites, such as www.hotmail.com, www.usa.net, or www.yahoo.com, to find out about the options available and then list the ones you think are most important. Why do you believe you would need these features for your e-mail account?

INTERNET ESSENTIALS

OBJECTIVES

Upon completion of this lesson you should be able to:

- Explain the origin of the Internet.

- Explain how to connect to the Internet and how it works.

- Understand how to use a browser to surf the Internet.

- Understand how to customize browser settings.

- List the major features of the Internet and explain what they do.

- Access a recently visited Web site using the History feature.

- Refresh a Web page by reloading it directly from the Web site.

- Explain how a Web site's security makes it possible to safely provide private information.

- Understand how to troubleshoot problems encountered when browsing Web pages.

Estimated Time: 1.5 hours

VOCABULARY

Browser

Cache

Cookies

Domain name

File transfer protocol (FTP)

Home page

Hyperlinks

Hypertext markup language (HTML)

Hypertext transfer protocol (HTTP)

Newsgroup

Uniform resource locator (URL)

Web server

Each day millions of people "surf," or explore, the information superhighway—the Internet. It is compared to a highway system because it functions much like a network of interstate highways. People use the Internet to research information, to shop, to go to school, to communicate with family and friends, to read the daily paper, to make airplane reservations, and so forth. They use the Internet at work, at school, and at home. Anyone with access to the Internet can connect with and communicate with anyone else in the world.

How the Internet Works

The Internet is a worldwide network of smaller networks that allow for the exchange of data, information, and e-mail messages. Even though no one person or organization can claim credit for the Internet, we can trace its early origins to the 1960s and the U.S. Department of Defense. The birth of the Internet is closely tied to a networking project started by a governmental division called the Advanced Research Projects Agency (ARPA). The goal was to create a network that would allow scientists to share information on military and scientific research.

The original name for the Internet was ARPANET. In 1969 ARPANET was a wide area network with four main host node computers. A host node is any computer directly connected to the network. These computers were located at the University of California at Santa Barbara, the University of California at Los Angeles, the Stanford Research Institute, and the University of Utah.

Over the next several years, the Internet grew steadily but quietly. Some interesting details are as follow:

- The addition of e-mail in 1972 spurred some growth.

- By 1989 more than 100,000 host computers were linked to ARPANET.

- The World Wide Web began in 1989 when Tim Berners-Lee, working with a European organization known as CERN, wrote a small computer program that allowed pages to be linked through a formatting process known as hypertext markup language (HTML).

- In 1990 ARPANET ceased to exist, but few people noticed because its functions continued.

- The thousands of interconnected networks were called an Inter-Net-Network and became known as the Internet, or a network of smaller networks that included small organization LANs, Internet service providers, and online services.

- In 1993 the world's first browser, Mosaic, was released by Marc Andreessen, working for the National Center for Supercomputing Applications at the University of Illinois. Mosaic provided a graphical interface for the Internet.

- The Mosaic browser made it so easy to access the Internet that there was a 340% growth rate in Internet use during the year it was introduced.

- The Internet is still growing at an unprecedented rate.

The Internet's Impact on Society

The use of the Internet in American homes has spread quickly among all demographic groups and across geographic regions. It has been spurred by increasing computer use in schools and workplaces. By 2004, two-thirds of all Americans, nearly 200 million people, used the Internet at home, work, or school. Usage levels among children were even higher. Common uses at home include e-mail, operating home offices, managing household budgets and financial planning, obtaining information on products and services, making online purchases, playing games, and searching for health information.

The benefits of the Internet are so numerous and widespread that their value is almost incalculable. Businesses have automated record-keeping tasks that used to require countless hours, freeing workers for more productive activities. Marketers instantaneously send information via the Internet to prospective customers anywhere in the world, incurring no incremental cost beyond maintaining a Web site and e-mail list. Buyers can compare products, prices, and services offered by dozens or even hundreds of possible sellers, all without making a single phone call.

People who have difficulty moving around physically can now conduct many activities via the Internet that previously would not have been possible. The Internet is creating new opportunities every day—to learn and research, to keep in touch with distant friends and family members, to stay informed about political developments and make views known to government officials, and to nurture relationships that bridge and break down national, ethnic, and cultural barriers in an increasingly interconnected world.

The Internet Is Never the Same Place Twice

It is important to realize that the Internet is transitory, ever changing and reshaping itself. It is a loose association of thousands of networks and millions of computers across the world that all work together to share information. The beauty of this network of networks is that all brands, models, and makes of computers can communicate with each other. This is called *interoperability*.

So how do we communicate across the Internet? Think about our postal service. If you want to send someone a letter anywhere in the world, you can do that—as long as you know the address. The Internet works in a similar fashion. From your computer, you can connect with any other networked computer anywhere in the world—as long as you know the address.

> **Computer Concepts**
>
> Because the Internet changes constantly, you may find that a Web site address that worked previously no longer connects you with a working site. Sometimes you will be redirected to a new address, but sometimes an address will simply no longer work.

Computers on the Internet communicate with each other using a set of protocols known as TCP/IP, or Transmission Control Protocol and Internet Protocol. A *protocol* is a standard format for transferring data between two devices. TCP/IP is the agreed-on international standard for transmitting data. It is considered the language of the Internet. The TCP protocol enables two host computers to establish a connection and exchange data. A host computer is simply a computer that you access remotely. The IP protocol works with the addressing scheme. It allows you to enter an address and sends it to another computer; from there the TCP protocol takes over. Returning to our postal service analogy, this is similar to what happens when you take a letter to the post office. You deliver the letter to the post office and then the post office takes over.

Postal addresses usually contain numbers and street names. Likewise, when we access another computer on the Internet, we are accessing it using a number. However, you don't have to remember or type in that number. Instead you can enter the *domain name*. The domain name identifies a site on the Internet. An example of a domain name is *microsoft.com*. If we want to access the Microsoft Corporation's computers that are connected to the Internet, we start our browser and type *www.* (for World Wide Web), followed by the domain name.

3-1.1.1
3-1.2.6
3-1.2.7
3-3.2.2

Accessing the Internet

Before you can even begin to surf the Net, you have to be connected. If you connect to the Internet from an office or academic setting, you are probably connecting through a local area network (LAN). You connect to the Internet using a network interface card (NIC). This is a special card inside your computer that allows the computer to be networked. A direct connection is made from the LAN to a high-speed connection line leased from the local telephone company.

> ### Computer Concepts
>
> High-speed digital telephone lines such as ISDN (Integrated Services Digital Network) or DSL (Digital Subscriber Lines) use special hardware that allows data transmission at far greater speeds than standard phone wiring.

For the home user, common ways to connect to the Internet include using a dial-up modem and a telephone line, a dedicated high-speed digital telephone line ("dedicated" means it is always available for Internet access), a cable modem, or a wireless connection. Refer back to Lesson 23 to refresh your memory about the different methods of connecting to a network.

Getting connected to the Internet is fairly simple, but there are a few steps you need to take:

- **Step 1:** Locate an Internet service provider (ISP) or an online service. There are thousands of Internet service providers. Most are small local companies. Their service is primarily a connection or "on ramp" to the Internet. Online services are large national and international companies, such as America Online and MSN. Generally, the local ISP is less expensive, but many people use the online services because of the additional information and services they offer.

- **Step 2:** Once you find an ISP, you must install some type of telecommunications software. This software enables your computer to connect to another computer. Your ISP or online service company will provide this software, or you may be able to use software already installed on a newer computer, especially if it is set up for a wireless connection.

- **Step 3:** You will need a software application called a Web browser in order to surf the Web. The Web is one component of the Internet (see later in this lesson). Two of the most popular browsers are Netscape's Navigator and Microsoft's Internet Explorer. Most computers purchased today come with a browser already installed.

Once you have contracted with your ISP and you have telecommunications software and a browser, then you are ready to connect to the Internet. This is the easy part. You may have to give instructions to your computer to dial a local telephone number if you are using a dial-up modem, but if you have a high-speed dedicated phone line, a cable connection, or a wireless service, you simply launch your browser. This connects you to your ISP's computer, which in turn connects you to the Internet. Figure 25-1 shows an application that searches for available wireless hookups. Once you are connected and launch your browser, you can go anywhere on the Internet. You're online with the world.

FIGURE 25-1
A wireless Internet service provider allows access to the Internet

Different types of Internet connections provide a range of options. Individuals and organizations should be prepared to balance the features they want, such as connection speed and reliability, with the cost and availability of the different options. For example, broadband connections allow multiple channels of information to be transmitted over a single link so more than one channel of video, voice, and computer data can be carried simultaneously. Cable modems, DSL (Digital Subscriber Lines), and T1 lines offer high bandwidth, as opposed to a dial-up telephone modem, which has only a single bandwidth that can transmit voice or data, but not at the same time. A T1 line is a high-speed digital telephone line, usually leased from a communications company, that can transmit more than 1.5 million bytes per second via 24 channels. T1 lines, also referred to as leased lines, are often used by companies that need to transmit large amounts of data quickly; they are usually too expensive for home use. Broadband cable connections, however, do allow many home computer users to enjoy the benefits of faster connection speed and multiple channels to transmit data.

Browser Basics

3-3.1.1
3-3.1.2
3-3.2.2
3-3.2.3
3-3.2.4

A *browser* is the software program that you use to retrieve documents from the World Wide Web and to display them in a readable format. The Web is the graphical portion of the Internet. The browser functions as an interface between you and the Internet. Using a browser, you can display both text and images. Newer versions of most browsers can also support multimedia information, including sound and video.

The browser sends a message to the *Web server* to retrieve your requested Web page. Then the browser renders the HTML code to display the page. *HTML*, or *hypertext markup language*, is the language used to create documents for the Web. You navigate through the Web by using your mouse to point and click on hyperlinked words and images. Figure 25-2 shows an example of a Web page.

FIGURE 25-2
A Web page displayed in Internet Explorer

Although most browsers have very similar features, the menu options to select these features may be somewhat different. The major differences you will see involve special built-in tools. These tools include programs for mail, chat, viewing and listening to multimedia, and so forth. If you are not using Internet Explorer, use your browser's Help feature to find out more about how to use its specific tools.

The Parts of the Browser Window

Understanding the parts of the browser window is the key to using a browser effectively. Review Figure 25-3 to familiarize yourself with the names of each part of the browser window. Table 25-1 contains a definition of each part of the screen.

FIGURE 25-3
Browser window terminology

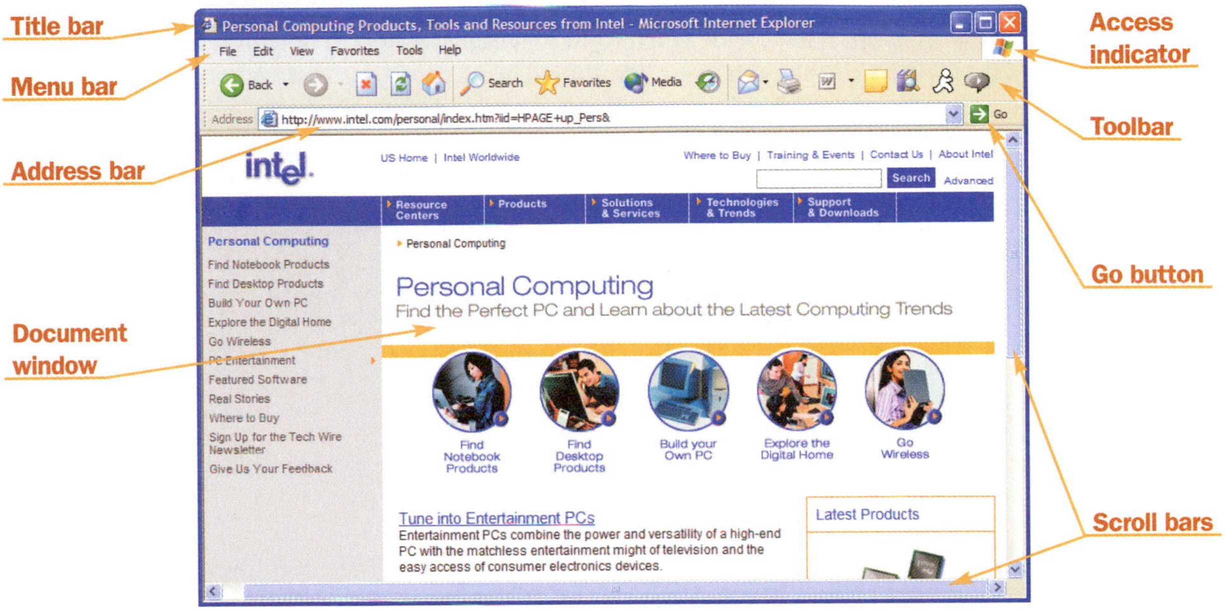

TABLE 25-1
Parts of the browser window

ITEM	DEFINITION
Title bar	The bar at the top of the window that contains the name of the document.
Menu bar	Contains menu names that you can click to display various commands and options.
Toolbar	Contains icons for single-click access to most commonly used menu commands.
Address bar	Contains the URL, or address, of the active Web page; also where you enter the location for the Web page you want to visit.
Go button	Connects you to the address displayed in the Address bar.
Document window	Displays the active Web page.
Status bar	Located at the bottom of the browser window; shows the progress of Web page transactions.
Access indicator	A small picture in the upper-right corner of the browser; when animated, it means your browser is accessing data from a remote computer.
Scroll bars	Vertical and horizontal scroll bars; let you scroll vertically and horizontally if the Web page is too long or wide to fit within one screen.

Launching the Browser

In this lesson it is assumed that you have an Internet connection—either dial-up or direct connection. To connect to the Internet, you may have to launch a program that dials the Internet connection first if you have a dial-up modem. If you have a direct high-speed connection or a wireless connection, however, you will simply launch your Web browser to access the Internet. In most instances, you can double-click the browser icon located on your computer's desktop. If the icon is not available, open the browser from the Start menu.

When your browser is installed, a default home page is selected. The *home page* is the first page that is displayed when you launch your browser. The address bar located near the top of the browser window contains the address of the current page. This address is called the *uniform resource locator (URL)*. The URL tells the browser where to locate the page. A unique URL identifies each Web page.

If you want to visit a specific Web site, you need to know the address. The address bar is also where you enter the address of the Web site you want to visit. After you key the URL, you can press Enter to go to the Web site. Once you are at a Web site, you can use a variety of navigation tools to link to information available on the site.

STEP-BY-STEP 25.1

1. Launch your Internet browser. The first page you see is your home page.

2. In the address bar, key the following URL: **www.whitehouse.gov**. Then click the **Go** button next to the address bar or press **Enter**. This takes you to the home page of the White House, the home of the U.S. President.

3. You can navigate through the pages of the site using a number of navigation tools:

Note
Web pages are often updated, so the content and appearance of the sites you visit may differ from those shown in the illustrations in this lesson.

   a. Notice the list of links on the left side of the home page. Click a link of your choice and review the information on the page you jumped to. Click the **Home** link near the top of the page to return to the White House home page.

   b. Notice the links across the top of the page. Click the **Kids** link. Review the information on the page, and then click the **Back** button on your browser's toolbar.

   c. Click the **Site Map** link at the top of the page. You are jumped to a page that illustrates in outline form the various Web pages contained within the site, as shown in Figure 25-4.

STEP-BY-STEP 25.1 Continued

FIGURE 25-4
Site Map page at *www.whitehouse.gov*

d. You should see a Search box on the Site Map page, probably near the top of the page. In the box, key **Thomas Jefferson** and then click **Search** or press **Enter** to begin the search.

e. Click a link in the search results list to find more information on Thomas Jefferson. If necessary, click additional links on the pages to find more detailed information on Jefferson. This is referred to as "drilling down" in a Web site to find information. For example, you may see the name of Jefferson's wife, Martha Wayles Skelton Jefferson, as a hyperlink in the text on a page about Jefferson. Click the hyperlink to jump to the page about Mrs. Jefferson.

4. Review the information you find, and then click the **Back** button several times to return to the White House home page.

5. Click the **Forward** button to jump back to the Site Map for the White House Web site.

6. Click the **Home** button on the toolbar to return to your browser's home page. Keep the browser open for the next Step-by-Step.

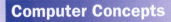

Customizing Browser Settings

3-3.2.11
3-3.2.12

Y̲ou can change some of the settings on your browser, including privacy settings and other settings such as a browser's default home page. It is easy to change your home page so you can display a Web page you want to view frequently.

Computer Concepts

Many people create a custom home page. If you have access to the Internet and can upload your own Web page, you may want to create a page with hyperlinks you visit frequently.

Internet Explorer provides access to browser settings from the Tools menu on the browser toolbar. Select the Internet Options menu entry to open a dialog box with tabs that display settings for security, privacy, connections, and the programs your browser automatically uses for Internet services such as e-mail, newsgroups, and online conferencing. (You will learn more about newsgroups and online conferencing later in this lesson.)

As you become an experienced Internet user, you may find that you want to change how your browser handles cookies, for example. *Cookies* are small text files that are created by some Web pages when you visit the site. The files may include information about your preferences for the Web page, and these files are stored on your computer. You must balance the ease of use provided by cookies, which remember Web sites and settings for you, with security issues and storage space available. For the most part, the default settings for cookies and stored pages are appropriate for the majority of Internet users, but you can find out more about optimizing settings by using the Internet Explorer Help feature. Use *cookies* as a keyword and select topics such as *Understanding cookies* and *Customize your privacy settings for all Web sites* to navigate to Help screens that will explain how these settings work.

Some Internet files are temporarily stored in a folder on your hard disk as you view them. This storage location is referred to as a *cache*, and it is useful because it speeds up the display of pages you frequently visit or have already seen, because Internet Explorer opens these files from your hard disk instead of from the Web. The size allotted to your cache can affect how quickly a Web page you have previously viewed is loaded into your browser. You can set the size of the temporary Internet files folder or empty the files stored in it by clicking the Settings button in the Temporary Internet files section of the General tab in the Internet Options dialog box. You will view the Settings dialog box for temporary Internet files in the next exercise.

S TEP-BY-STEP 25.2

1. Your browser should be open to your home page. Click the **Tools** menu and then select **Internet Options** from the menu to open the Internet Options dialog box shown in Figure 25-5.

FIGURE 25-5
Internet Options dialog box

STEP-BY-STEP 25.2 Continued

2. On the General tab of the dialog box, you will see the top section relates to the browser's home page. The current home page appears in the Address text box. Click the **Use Default** button and notice if the URL in the Address text box changes.

3. Click the **Use Current** button to display the current home page's address in the text box again. On a piece of paper, carefully write down the URL of the current home page.

4. Click some of the other tabs in the Internet Options dialog box to investigate the settings for security, privacy, and the Internet connection. Do not change any of the settings.

5. Click the **General** tab again and look at the section in the middle of the tab called *Temporary Internet files*. You can delete cookies, delete temporary files, and change the way your browser saves Web pages with these settings.

   a. Click the **Settings** button to view the available settings, including options for checking for newer versions of stored pages, the amount of disk space to allocate to your cache, and the location of the folder for temporary Internet files.

   b. Click **Cancel** to close the Settings dialog box without changing any settings.

6. In the Home page section of the General tab, select the address in the text box and then key **http://www.olympic.org** to change your home page to the official Olympic Movement Web site's home page.

7. Click **OK** to close the dialog box, and then click the **Home** button on the browser's toolbar to jump to your new home page.

8. Key **www.whitehouse.gov** in the address bar and click the **Go** button to return to the White House Web site.

9. Open the Internet Options dialog box again by selecting **Internet Options** from the **Tools** menu in your browser.

10. On the General tab of the dialog box, click the **Use Current** button in the Home page section of the tab. Notice that the URL in the Address text box changes to *www.whitehouse.gov*. You can make any Web page currently displayed by your browser your home page by using the Use Current button to set a new home page.

11. Key your browser's original home page address, which you wrote down in step 3, in the Address text box and then click **OK**.

12. Leave the browser open for the next Step-by-Step.

Communicating on the Internet

So far in this lesson, we've discussed how to browse Web pages. The Internet, however, is made up of many services. Some of the more popular of these services include e-mail, chat rooms, mailing lists, FTP, and newsgroups. You learned about e-mail in the previous lesson, but before we move on to the other services available on the Internet, let's look more closely at the World Wide Web.

The World Wide Web

Many people use the terms World Wide Web, or Web for short, and Internet interchangeably. In reality, they're actually two different things. The Web is a subset or an application that makes use of the Internet. It consists of a collection of electronic files, referred to as Web pages, which contain information and built-in *hyperlinks*, which you have already used when you accessed the information about Thomas Jefferson on the White House Web site. When you click a hyperlink, you are transferred to another electronic file. A series of related Web pages is referred to as a Web site. There are thousands (if not millions) of Web sites functioning on the Web.

Businesses have Web sites where they advertise and sell products and services, provide information to investors, or post job openings. The Web sites for schools, universities, and other educational institutions often list course offerings, supply electronic enrollment forms, and even offer distance-learning opportunities. And there are a multitude of sites hosted by businesses, professional and nonprofit associations, churches, medical organizations, and so forth that exist solely to provide information. In addition, there are a number of Web sites designed to access data from electronic databases that are stored on a server. Your local library stores data on books, videos, newspapers, and journals in an electronic database that you can access through the library's Web site anytime of the day.

> ### Computer Concepts
>
> There are hundreds or even thousands of online tutorials to help you become more familiar with Internet features. You can find several tutorials at *www.northernwebs.com* when you click the **Beginners' Central** tutorial link. Topics covered include learning while you surf, offline operations and file downloading, configuring e-mail and news readers, FTP, and myths of the Internet.

The Web has its own underlying protocols. One protocol is known as *HTTP*, or *hypertext transfer protocol*. This protocol, or standard, defines how messages are formatted and transmitted. You can send and receive Web pages over the Internet because Web servers and browsers both understand HTTP. For instance, when you enter a Web site address in your browser, this sends an HTTP command to the Web server to tell it to locate and transmit the requested Web page. A Web server is a computer that contains Web pages. By installing special software, any computer can become a Web server. Every Web server has its own IP address and most have a domain name. The domain name identifies the IP address.

The Web site address, or uniform resource locator (URL), uniquely identifies a Web page, as you learned previously. The first part of the address indicates what protocol to use, and the second part specifies the IP address or the domain name where the resource is located. For example, in the URL *http://www.smithsonian.org*, shown in Figure 25-6, the first set of letters in the address bar, *http*, is the protocol and indicates that this is a Web page. The letters *www* indicate that the site is located on the World Wide Web, and the domain name is *smithsonian.org*. The *.org* at the end of the name indicates that this is a nonprofit organization. Table 25-2 lists other examples of domain abbreviations.

FIGURE 25-6
Smithsonian Institution home page

TABLE 25-2
Domain extensions indicate what type of organization sponsors a Web site

DOMAIN ABBREVIATION	TYPE OF ORGANIZATION
edu	Educational institutions
com	Commercial businesses, companies, and organizations
gov	Government institutions, such as the IRS
mil	Military organizations, such as the army
net	Network provider
org	Nonprofit organization

Web sites located outside the United States may include a domain abbreviation that includes a country code, such as *uk* for the United Kingdom or *jp* for Japan. For example, the URL for the government of Canada's home page is *http://canada.gc.ca*, and the *ca* extension is the domain abbreviation for Canada.

Chat Rooms

You can call someone through the Internet and "talk" to them the way you do on the phone, only you are writing and reading on your computer rather than talking and listening with a phone in your hand. You are using the computer to create real-time communication between yourself and another user or a group of users. To participate in a chat, you enter a virtual chat room. Once a chat has been initiated, users enter text by typing on the keyboard, and the message appears on the monitor of the other participants. Chat rooms provide an opportunity for people with a common interest to talk together about the subject, although many chat rooms are more general in nature and provide a place for people to meet and talk. You should always be cautious in chat rooms and not give away information of a personal nature.

Mailing Lists

A mailing list is a group of people with a shared interest. Their e-mail addresses are collected into a group, and this group is identified by a single name. Whenever you send a message, everyone on the list receives a copy. Some mailing lists are called LISTSERVs, named after a mailing list software program. There are mailing lists for every imaginable topic. Many professional groups and associations utilize mailing lists as an effective way of communicating with members and potential members. You can subscribe to a mailing list just as you would subscribe to a magazine. A list owner is the person who manages the list.

There are several variations of mailing lists, such as the following:

- Announcements are one type of mailing list. For example, you could subscribe to the IBM mailing list and receive announcements of new products.

Working in a Connected World

A WIDE WEB OF CAREER OPPORTUNITIES

If you want a career that involves working on Web sites, you may need to consider your strengths and interests before you decide what kind of position you want. The jobs of a Web developer, a Web designer, and a Webmaster sound similar, but each has different responsibilities. A Web designer usually has strong graphic design skills, deciding how a Web site will look and work. The designer may use a graphics program, such as Adobe Studio, to create the elements of the Web page. Some Web designers may also do the programming, but many turn that task over to a Web developer. The Web developer needs technical knowledge of computer programming languages, such as C++, Java, and Visual Basic. In addition, a background in database development is important. Oracle and SQL are two widely used database interfaces. Other skills needed include experience with applications, such as JavaScript or Macromedia Flash to create actions and animation, and Active Server Pages or Perl to create the framework that makes the site work. Web designers and developers both need to know how to use an HTML editor, such as Microsoft FrontPage, to produce the code that displays the pages correctly in a user's Internet browser. The Web designer and Web developer also work together to make a site efficient and appealing to users.

A Web site has to be maintained and kept up to date. The Webmaster is responsible for this task. A typical Webmaster manages a Web site, making sure the programming is working, fixing problems, and running the Web server software. The Webmaster is the person that users contact if they have problems with the site, so the position calls for good interpersonal communications skills as well as management ability and technical expertise.

Employment opportunities in Internet site development and management fields are increasing every day. Web designers and developers may work for a large corporation with a major Internet presence or for a company that specializes in creating Internet sites, and Webmasters are needed in any organization that has a Web site. Such organizations include educational institutions, museums, libraries, government agencies, political campaigns, and of course, businesses.

- A discussion list is another type of list. Members use this type of list to ask questions and share information on a particular topic. For instance, let's assume you belong to a mailing list for people interested in creating professional computer-based presentations. You want to include a special feature in a presentation you are working on, but you're not sure how to do this. You can send your question to the list members. Most likely, if the list is an active list, you will receive several responses to your question.

- Some lists are public lists and some are closed or private lists. With a public list, anyone can subscribe. A private list limits subscribers to members of a particular organization or group.

- Some mailing lists have a summary or digest version. Instead of receiving each individual message posted to the list, the list manager or list owner groups the postings. Generally this is for a designated time period, such as a day or a week. Then the postings are sent as a batch to all subscribers.

Before you start subscribing to mailing lists, do your homework. Many of these lists produce a huge volume of e-mail messages. You could end up receiving hundreds or even thousands of messages a day.

Newsgroups and Bulletin Boards

A *newsgroup* is a discussion forum or a type of bulletin board. Each board is dedicated to discussion on a particular topic. Figure 25-7 shows a sports newsgroup with a message board sponsored by the British Broadcasting Corporation (BBC). The difference between a newsgroup and a mailing list is that with a newsgroup you can select the topics you want to read. These messages are stored on a news server, which is a computer that contains the necessary newsgroup software.

FIGURE 25-7
BBC newsgroup posting

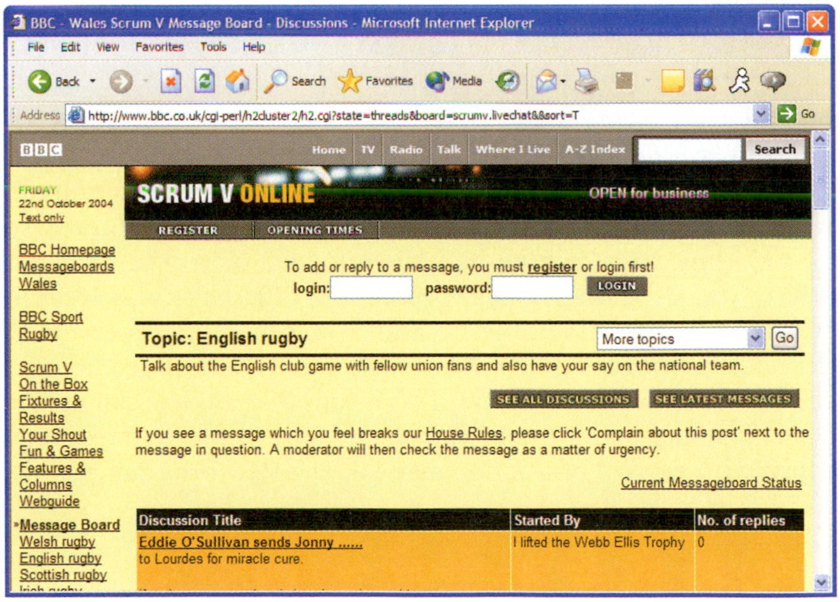

Some newsgroups are moderated, meaning any messages or information sent to the group are first read and reviewed by a moderator. The moderator determines whether the information is appropriate and relevant and, in some cases, may edit the material before posting to the group.

Computer Concepts

There are over 50,000 different newsgroups, and the number is increasing each day.

Online Conferencing

Technology now provides businesspeople, students taking long-distance classes, members of a national organization, and even far-flung family members with the hardware and software needed to connect online to discuss issues, earn degrees, or just have a reunion. Freeware and commercial versions of software such as CU-SeeMe are available that provide a chat setting with audio and video. Hardware requirements for online conferencing include a microphone and speakers for audio and a digitizing camera for video. Video and audio on the Internet require high-speed connections. Windows NT users have access to Microsoft Netmeeting with audio and video, and the commercial program Timbuktu provides a link to Netmeeting for Macintosh users.

Computer Concepts

During recent election campaigns in the United States, Great Britain, and other counties, online conferencing has allowed campaign volunteers and prospective voters to interact directly with candidates and campaign organizers.

Online conferencing can offer many benefits, including the ability to confer with people all over the world without travel costs, providing equal time for all participants, and the automatic creation of a permanent record of the meeting if required. This last benefit may also be a drawback, however, as some issues raised in a discussion may be better left unrecorded, and it is also sometimes more difficult to interpret subtle emotional moods as easily as in an in-person meeting. However, for companies, organizations, and individuals with access to a computer and the Internet, online conferencing will continue to be used in new and exciting ways to make the world a more connected place.

File Transfer Protocol

At one time or another, you may have been on the Internet and tried to access a special feature such as an audio file. You receive a message that a plug-in is required. A plug-in is an add-on software application that adds a specific feature to your Web browser or other programs. You click on a link and the plug-in is downloaded or transmitted to your computer. You most likely have just used *file transfer protocol* (FTP). This is an Internet standard that allows users to download and upload files to and from other computers on the Internet.

Many FTP servers are connected to the Internet. Some of these require user IDs and passwords. Others permit anonymous FTP access. This means that anyone can upload and download files from the server. The files on the server can be any type of file. Some examples are software updates for your printer, a revised instruction manual, or a new program that is being tested.

Working with Web Pages

3-3.1.3
3-3.1.4
3-3.2.1
3-3.2.4
3-4.3.4

Browsing the Web can be fascinating, but it can also be confusing. You may work your way through a maze of linked pages or use the navigation tools to move from page to page and back. Your browser provides some tools to keep track of where you have been and to "refresh" or reload a page to get the most current version or to update the information.

Recent History

Your browser tracks the sites you have visited for a certain period of time. The default setting in Internet Explorer, for example, is to keep track of sites visited for approximately three weeks. You can access the list of sites you have visited by clicking the History button on the browser toolbar. This will open the History pane to the left of your browser window, and you can see the sites you have visited organized by date (3 Weeks Ago, 2 Weeks Ago, Last Week, Today), as shown in Figure 25-8. Click a folder under one of the headings to access the Web addresses you visited, and then you can return to the site by clicking one of the addresses, which are hyperlinks.

FIGURE 25-8
History pane

You can also clear the History list by clicking the Clear History button on the General tab of the Internet Options dialog box in Internet Explorer.

Reloading and Refreshing a Web Page

If you get a message that a Web page cannot be displayed, or you want to make sure you have the latest version of the page, click the Refresh button on the browser's toolbar to reload the page directly from the Web site. Sometimes your cache has an outdated version of a page that is loaded when you try to access a site, so the Refresh button is available to update the page.

> **Note**
>
> You can change the setting for how many days to keep sites in the History list in the General tab of the Internet Options dialog box. In the History section of the tab, use the spin arrows to select how many days you want to keep sites in the list.

S TEP-BY-STEP 25.3

1. The White House Web site home page should still be displayed in your browser window. Click the **Home** button to return to your original home page.

STEP-BY-STEP 25.3 Continued

2. Click the **Refresh** button to make sure the most recent version of your home page is loaded. Do you notice any changes to the page after it has reloaded?

3. Click the **History** button to open the History pane.

4. Click the **Last Week** icon in the History pane to display a list of folders of Web pages accessed on the computer in the past week. With your instructor's permission, click a folder that looks interesting and then click a hyperlink for a Web page to open the page in your browser.

5. Click the **Today** icon and look for the folder with the Olympic Movement Web pages.

6. Click the link to open the Olympic Movement home page, and then click the **Refresh** button to reload the page.

7. Click the **Close** button in the History pane.

8. Follow your instructor's directions about disconnecting from the Internet if necessary, and then close your browser. Turn off your computer if your instructor tells you to do so.

Secure Web Pages

Some Web sites, such as those used for financial transactions or e-commerce, are more secure than sites that simply provide information. Web sites are secured through encrypted communication, which was also discussed in relation to e-mail in Lesson 24. Some Web sites also require you to log in using an account or user name and a password. You may see a message indicating that you are now entering (or leaving) a secure Web site, and you will often see a padlock icon or another indicator in the status bar of a Web page to indicate the information is secure. Occasionally you may get a message questioning the security of a site you are entering. Read the information in the message carefully before deciding whether or not to provide sensitive information on such a site.

You may also be required to provide a password for an Internet Web site that limits the access to members or subscribers. For example, if you access a university's Web site, you may be able to browse and link to many parts of the site, but you may need a password to access a professor's class-specific Web sites or your student account. Or, you may be able to read the current online edition of a newspaper, but if you want to search the paper's archives, you would need to provide a password to show that you are a subscriber.

Problems Accessing Web Pages

One of the most common problems you will encounter when browsing Web pages is a Page Not Found error. As mentioned earlier, the Internet is never the same place twice; Web pages and whole sites come and go every day, so a link that worked the last time you used it may be gone when you try it again. The Page Not Found error message sometimes provides you with advice about how to trace a link; for example, if you return to the home page of the Web site, you may be able to find a new link to the information you are trying to access.

Some other problems you may encounter include slow or interrupted page loading, which may be the result of a Web page with many graphics or special features; Web page content that looks like nonsense, which can sometimes be resolved by refreshing the page; and Web-based applications that do not work because you are using an outdated browser or are missing a plug-in program needed to run the application.

In addition, if you encounter a large number of pop-up ads that appear as you browse the Web, or in extreme cases, if your browser seems to automatically redirect to a different page or the browser does not respond to commands from your keyboard or mouse, you may have spyware on your computer. *Spyware* is programming that is installed on your computer without your knowledge. It may be used to gather information about your Web browsing habits or it can allow "remote control" access to your computer by a hacker. In many cases it is used to direct you to a Web site you would not otherwise visit; no matter what its purpose, you do not want spyware on your computer. A firewall and other security measures can prevent spyware gaining access to your computer. You should also be careful about files you download from the Internet. If you are not confident that the site is trustworthy, think twice about downloading files, because they may include a piggybacked spyware program.

SUMMARY

In this lesson, you learned:

- Origins of the Internet can be traced to the U.S. Department of Defense. The original name for the Internet was ARPANET.

- Mosaic was the Internet's first browser, providing a graphical interface to information on the Web.

- To connect to the Internet from a business or academic setting, you probably have a direct connection via a local area network and a network interface card.

- For the home user, the most common types of Internet connection include a modem and telephone line, a cable modem connection, and a wireless connection.

- To connect to the Internet, you need an Internet connection, telecommunications software, and a browser.

- A browser is a software program you use to retrieve documents from the World Wide Web.

- Two popular browsers are Microsoft's Internet Explorer and Netscape's Communicator.

- *Interoperability* means that all brands, models, and makes of computers can communicate with each other.

- A protocol is a standard format for transferring data between two devices. TCP/IP is the agreed-on international standard for transmitting data.

- The domain name identifies a site on the Internet.

- Microsoft's Internet Explorer and Netscape's Navigator are two of the most popular Web browsers.

- The HTTP protocol defines how Web messages are formatted and transmitted.

- Web pages are linked through hypertext.

- The Web site address is referred to as the URL, or Uniform Resource Locator. Every Web page on the Internet has its own unique address.

- Your home page is the first page that displays when you launch your browser.

- The Web and e-mail are two important applications that make use of the Internet. Other features of the Internet include chat rooms, mailing lists, newsgroups and bulletin boards, online conferencing, and file transfer protocol.

- You can access a list of recently visited Web sites by clicking the History button on the browser toolbar.

- The Refresh button on the toolbar reloads a Web page directly from the Web site to provide the most up-to-date version of the page.

- Secure Web sites encrypt information and require you to provide account information and/or a password for access to protect private data.

- Problems accessing Web pages can involve compatibility issues with your software, Web pages that are no longer available, and spyware, a kind of software installed on your computer without your knowledge that can track your Web use or even control your computer.

VOCABULARY *Review*

Define the following terms:

Browser	Home page	Newsgroup
Cache	Hyperlinks	Uniform resource locator
Cookies	Hypertext markup language	(URL)
Domain name	(HTML)	Web server
File transfer protocol (FTP)	Hypertext transfer protocol	
	(HTTP)	

REVIEW *Questions*

TRUE/FALSE

Circle T if the statement is true or F if the statement is false.

T F **1.** Educational institutions normally use the .aca domain name.

T F **2.** A mailing list owner manages virtual chat rooms.

T F **3.** The History button on the toolbar will reload the Web page you are currently viewing.

T F **4.** You must use a modem to communicate over a regular telephone line.

T F **5.** The home page is the first page that displays when you launch your browser.

MULTIPLE CHOICE

Circle the best response for each of the following statements.

1. A software program used to retrieve documents from the WWW is called a _____.
   A. packet
   B. home page
   C. browser
   D. Web server

2. An URL is the _____.
   A. Web site address
   B. same as the location bar
   C. same as the address bar
   D. toolbar

3. Which of the following is *not* a navigation tool you might find at a Web site?
   A. bookmark
   B. site map
   C. navigation bar
   D. search box

4. The first graphical browser was named _____.
   A. Internet Explorer
   B. Navigator
   C. Avatar
   D. Mosaic

5. If you wanted to talk to several people about a specific subject in real time on the Internet, you would use _____.
   A. e-mail
   B. a newsreader
   C. a chat room
   D. a list manager

PROJECTS

PROJECT 25-1

1. Start your browser and connect to the Web.

2. In the address bar, key the URL **www.noaa.gov** and then click the **Go** button or press **Enter** to connect to the Web site of the National Oceanic and Atmospheric Administration. Use the links or the search box on the page to find the weather report for your city (or a large city close by).

3. Return to your home page and open the Internet Options dialog box.

4. If necessary, write down the current home page's URL and then change your home page to the Web page with your city's weather report.

5. Use the History feature to return to the Olympics Web site you visited in this lesson, and then click the **Home** button. You should return to the weather report page.

6. With your instructor's permission, visit another Web page in the History list that looks interesting.

7. Change your browser's home page back to the original URL that you wrote down in step 4.

8. Keep your browser open if you are continuing immediately with Project 25-2.

PROJECT 25-2

Visit the National Zoo Web site at *www.nationalzoo.si.edu*. Tour the site and then write a summary of what you found. Include the following topics: (1) information on the Web Cams and what animals you could view; (2) days and hours the zoo is open; and (3) classroom resources for students and teachers. What is your overall opinion about this site?

TEAMWORK PROJECT

In this lesson, several Internet features were described. Work with a partner and discuss which of these features each of you would you most likely use and why you would use it. Make a list that includes all the features that were mentioned in this lesson and make two columns, one for each member of your team. Then use a ranking scale of 1 to 5 (1 means you would probably never use this feature and 5 that you would definitely use it) to rank how important you and your partner think each feature is. Work together to prepare a report that explains your rankings and why you ranked each feature as you did.

CRITICAL *Thinking*

ACTIVITY 25-1

Do you think the government will ever be able to regulate the Internet? That is, will any agency ever be able to control and limit what someone puts online? Write a page on your thoughts on this issue.

RESEARCHING ON THE INTERNET

The Internet contains a wealth of information. In fact, you can find information on just about any topic you can imagine. The problem is that the Internet contains so much information, it can be difficult to locate just what you need. In this lesson, you learn how to conduct searches on the Internet that get you to the information you need.

Searching Online

3-3.2.5

We live in the information age, and the amount of information continues to grow at a fast rate. To conduct an effective online search on a particular topic can be a real challenge. It is easy to be overwhelmed by the overabundance of raw data. With the right tools, however, the task becomes easier. One key to a successful Internet search is an understanding of the many tools available. Certain tools are more suitable for some purposes than others.

When searching online, the main tool you will use to find information is a *search engine*. You use a search engine to search for keywords. Search engines are automated indexes, so you may find that sometimes your search results include information that is irrelevant, but you will learn how to refine your search in this lesson.

It's important to understand that no single Web tool indexes or organizes the whole Web. When using an online search tool, you are searching and viewing data extracted from the Web. This data has been placed into the search engine's database. It is the database that is searched—not the Web itself. This is one of the reasons why you get different results when you use different search engines.

You might ask yourself, "Why would I want to search the Internet? What's out there that can help me?" The following are just a few examples of how the Internet can help you:

- You need to do some research for that paper due in your continuing education class next week.

- Your grandfather is losing his hearing and has asked you to help him find some information on hearing aids.

- You plan to take a trip to Mexico this summer and would like to get information on some of the best places to stay.

As you can see from these examples, there can be hundreds of reasons why you might want to conduct an Internet search. Perhaps you have already used the Internet to find information for a school project; you may also want to pursue research related to work, hobbies, health questions, government issues, or a host of other subjects.

Search Engines

A search engine is a software program. There are hundreds of search engines throughout the Internet. Each search engine may work a little differently, but most of them have some common search features. For example, all search engines support keyword searches. Although keyword searches may not always be the most effective way to search, this is the search method most individuals use.

Some search engines support an additional enhancement called concept-based searching. The search engine tries to determine what you mean and returns hits on Web sites that relate to the keywords. *Hits* are the number of returns or Web sites based on your keywords. If you search for "video games," the search engine may also return hits on sites that contain Nintendo and Playstation. One of the best-known search engines using concept-based searching is Excite. Its search engine uses ICE (intelligent concept extraction) to learn about word relationships.

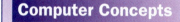
Computer Concepts
Some search engines such as AltaVista can translate your search results into another language.

Another feature supported by some search engines is stemming. When you search for a word, the search engine also includes other "stems" of the word. For example, you enter the search word *play*, and you may also get back results for *plays*, *playing*, and *player*.

Keyword Searches

Keyword searches let you search for keywords within a Web document. The Web page author can specify these *keywords* using meta tags within the Web page document. Meta tags are special tags embedded within the Web page document. They do not affect how the page displays. Many search engines use these tags to create the index. For example, if your Web site is about Nintendo 64, your meta tag may look something like this:

<meta name="keywords" content="Nintendo 64, Mario, James Bond, Donkey Kong">

With this meta tag in your Web site, search engines may include it in searches for Mario, James Bond, and Donkey Kong as well as in searches for Nintendo 64.

What if the Web page author doesn't specify meta tags? Then the search engine evaluates the document and indexes "significant" words. Depending on the search engine, significant words may be those words mentioned at the beginning of a document or words that are repeated several times throughout the document.

To search using keywords, the process is as follows:

> **Computer Concepts**
>
> All hypertext markup language (HTML) tags are set within brackets (for example, <body>), and they control Web site formats such as background and font color, font size and attributes, and graphics and hyperlinks. You can see HTML codes, including meta tags, by viewing an HTML file in a Web editor such as Microsoft FrontPage.

- Launch your Web browser and go to a search engine Web site.

- Submit an online form to the search engine. This form contains your keywords. These keywords describe the information you are trying to locate.

- The search engine matches as many keywords as possible by searching its own database. A database is a collection of organized information.

- The search engine then returns a list of hyperlinks to Web site addresses where the keywords are found. You can click the hyperlinks to view the Web sites.

- If you are unable to find the information for which you are searching within these hyperlinked sites, you can revise your keywords and submit a new request.

So how does a search engine find all of those Web sites? To answer the question requires an overview of the search engine's three main parts:

- The search engine program or software itself is the main component. This program searches through the millions of records stored in its database.

- The second part is a *spider*, or crawler. The spider is a search engine robot that searches the Internet for the keywords. It feeds the pages it finds to the search engine. It is called a spider because it crawls the Web continually, examining Web sites and finding and looking for links. Every month or so, it may return to a previous Web site to look for changes.

- The third part of the search engine is the index or indexer. When the spider finds a page, it submits it to the index. Once a Web page is indexed, it then becomes available to anyone using that search engine.

Some search engines claim to index all words, even the articles "a," "an," and "the." Other search engines index all words except articles and stop words such as "www," "but," "or," "nor," "for," "so," or "yet." Some of the search engines index all words without reference to capitalization. Other engines differentiate uppercase from lowercase.

In some searches, you might receive thousands of hits. Trying to find information in such a large list can be a bit overwhelming. Some search engines may include a relevance rating percentage assigned to each hit, beginning with 100%, but currently most search engines simply list the hits in order of relevance, so the first few hits will probably have more relevant content than those farther down the list. Figure 26-1 shows the results of a search for video games. As you move down the list of hits, the hits are rated as less relevant; that is, these sites do not contain all of the search words or contain only one or two instances of the keywords. At this point, you have several options:

- You can click on any of the links and review the information at that site.
- You can redefine your keywords.
- You can use another search engine.

FIGURE 26-1
Hits for a search of video games using AltaVista

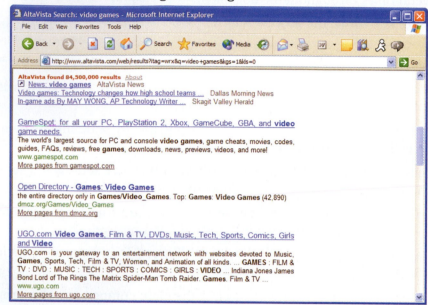

Using another search engine might be your best choice. It is impossible for any one search engine to index every page on the Web. Also, each search engine has its own personal algorithm that it uses to index Web sites. An algorithm is a formula or set of steps for solving a particular problem. Therefore, using a different engine may provide a totally different list of hits. There are many popular search engine sites, and you may need to try several before you find the information you are seeking. Table 26-1 lists some popular search engines.

TABLE 26-1
Search engines

SEARCH ENGINE	URL
Lycos	www.lycos.com
Yahoo!	www.yahoo.com
AltaVista	www.altavista.com
Google	www.google.com
Ask Jeeves	www.ask.com
Excite	www.excite.com
WebCrawler	www.webcrawler.com
AlltheWeb	www.alltheweb.com

STEP-BY-STEP 26.1

1. Launch your browser and go to **www.lycos.com**.

2. In the search box, enter the keywords **cookie recipes** and click the **Search** button or press **Enter**.

3. The page that opens should give you an indication of the number of hits the search engine found; there may be thousands or hundreds of thousands of hits, but only about 10 hyperlinks and descriptions will be listed on the first page of the search results. Browse through the page. Click links if you would like to find more information on cookie recipes.

4. Use your browser's navigation tools to return to the Lycos search page and leave the browser open for the next Step-by-Step.

Technology Timeline

SEARCH ENGINE OPTIMIZATION

Research in the days before the Internet was a bit more hit and miss. If you were interested in finding out more about an academic subject, you might go to a library and riffle through the card catalog, looking for a general subject heading that might have some books on the subject. Then you would find the books, consult the table of contents or index, and try to find more specific information. If you wanted more general information, such as the ratings of consumer organizations for a specific make of car, you would probably have to find some recent issues of a magazine published by a consumer group and then page through each magazine to find details about the particular make of automobile.

When you look for information on the World Wide Web, however, much of the searching and sorting is now automated. When Web site developers register their sites with search engines, they normally provide a list of keywords that will help get their site on a user's search results list. Web sites can often improve their rankings (or where they appear in the list) by employing cutting-edge Web marketing technology. For example, there are a number of organizations that offer search engine optimization services to Web site operators. These services might include an in-depth analysis of keywords that people will use in search engines, design of banner ads and buttons to be placed on the Web site of a search engine, etc.

In addition, for a fee, you might use a service (such as Wordtracker) to find out all the keywords that people use to find products or services similar to yours, then make sure those keywords appear in your Web page.

There are also a number of "pay-per-click" search engines operating online. With this type of search engine, Web site owners bid on keywords. When a person uses the keywords in a search, the links in the search results list appear in order from highest to lowest bid on the keywords. The owner of the Web site pays the search engine the per-click fee only when someone clicks the link to the site.

Specialty Search Engines

Specialty search engines, sometimes called category-oriented search tools, generally focus on a particular topic. If you know you are looking for information in a particular format, your best bet is to search a site that specializes in indexing and retrieving that information. Here are some examples:

- You're looking up a former classmate or a long-lost cousin; try the Switchboard Web site at *www.switchboard.com* or Yahoo's people search at *people.yahoo.com*.

- You want to download a shareware game called Renegade Racers; try the Shareware Web site at *www.shareware.com*.

- You wrote down the telephone number of a computer consultant you met at a conference, but you can't remember the name of her company; use *www.anywho.com* to do a reverse lookup and find out the name of the company with that telephone number.

- You want to do a little online jewelry shopping; try Catalog City at *www.catalogcity.com* or Bottom Dollar at *www.bottomdollar.com*.

- Are you thinking about your future and what careers options you may have? Try CareerBuilder at *www.careerbuilder.com* to find a database of over 250,000 jobs.

These are just a few examples of the many hundreds of specialty Web sites. If you are looking for a particular information source, but are not sure where to look, try the Beaucoup Web site at *www.beaucoup.com* (Figure 26-2). This site contains links to more than 3,000 specialty search engines. For a super search, you can also enter keywords at this site and search 10 different search engines at one time. Some specialty search engines are listed in Table 26-2.

FIGURE 26-2
Beaucoup Web site

TABLE 26-2
Specialty search engines

MAPS AND TRAVEL INFORMATION	PEOPLE AND COMPANIES	COMPANIES AND CAREERS	WORLD DATA
Microsoft's www.expedia.com	PeopleSite at www.peoplesite.com	Arthur's Job Base at www.ajb.com	World Health Organization at www.who.int
MapQuest at www.mapquest.com	Yellow Pages at www.yellow.com	Monster Job Bank at www.monster.com	CIA World Factbook at www.odci.gov/cia/publications/factbook
Hotel Lodging Rooms at www.irsus.com/rooms.htm		Career Resource Center at www.careers.org	World Bank at www.worldbank.org
Great Outdoors at www.gorp.com			

Multimedia Search Engines

Are you interested in finding graphics, video clips, animation, and even MP3 music files? Then a multimedia search engine is probably the best way to go. For music and MP3, you might want to try the Lycos search engine at *mp3.lycos.com/* or use *www.audiofind.com*.

Corbis at *www.corbis.com/* boasts that it is the world's largest collection of fine art and photography. Google's search engine at *www.google.com* has an images tab, and AltaVista at *www.altavista.com* has a special tab for images, audio, and video. Or try Ditto, the visual search engine at *www.ditto.com*, to search for pictures, photographs, and artwork.

> **Computer Concepts**
>
> MP3 is a file format that allows audio compression at near-CD quality. Audio file sharing is an area that is changing rapidly on the Internet; free download sites that were prevalent a few years ago have been replaced by more regulated sites where you can download high-quality audio files for a small fee.

3-3.3.2
3-3.3.3
3-3.3.4

Techniques for Searching

As the Internet continues to expand and more and more pages are added, effective searching requires new approaches and strategies. Remember that the more specific your search, the more likely you will find what you want. Tell the search engine precisely what it is you're searching for. To find relevant information, you must use a variety of tools and techniques.

Phrase Searching

If you want to search for words that must appear next to each other, than phrase searching is your best choice. A phrase is entered using double quotation marks and only matches those words that appear adjacent to each other and in the order in which you specify. For example, if you were searching for baseball cards, enter the phrase "baseball cards" in double quotation marks. The results will contain Web sites with the words "baseball cards" adjacent to each other. Without the quotation marks, the search engine would find Web pages that contain the words *baseball* and *cards* anywhere within each page.

If you are searching for more than one phrase, you can separate multiple phrases or proper names with a comma. To find Mickey Mantle baseball cards, you would enter "baseball cards," "Mickey Mantle." It is always a good idea to capitalize proper nouns because some search engines distinguish between upper- and lowercase letters. On the other hand, if you capitalize a common noun such as *Bread*, you will get fewer returns than if you typed in *bread*.

Search Engine Math

You can use **math symbols** to enter a formula to filter out unwanted listings. For example:

- Put a plus sign (+) before words that must appear (also called an inclusion operator).

- Put a minus sign (-) before words that you do not want to appear (also called an exclusion operator).

- Words without qualifiers need not appear, but are still involved in sorting your search.

You're making cookies for a party and would like to try some new recipes. Your search words are +cookie+recipes. Only pages that contained both words would appear in your results. Now let's suppose that you want recipes for chocolate cookies. Your search words are +cookie+recipe+chocolate. This would display pages with all three words.

To take this a step further, you don't like coconut. So you don't want any recipes that contain the word *coconut*. You will find that the minus (-) symbol is helpful for reducing the number of unrelated results. You would write your search phrase as +cookie+recipe+chocolate-coconut. This tells the search engine to find pages that contain cookie, recipe, and chocolate and then to remove any pages that contain the word coconut. To extend this idea and to get chocolate cookie recipes without coconut and honey, your search phrase would be +cookie+recipe+chocolate-coconut-honey. Simply begin subtracting terms you know are not of interest, and you should get better results. You will find that almost all of the major search engines support search engine math. You can also use math symbols with most directories.

Boolean Searching

Recall that when you search for a topic on the Internet, you are not going from server to server and viewing documents on that server. Instead you are searching databases. **Boolean logic** is another way that you can search databases. This works on a similar principle as search engine math, but has a little more power. Boolean logic consists of three logical operators:

- AND

- NOT

- OR

Returning to our cookie example, you are interested in a relationship between cookies and recipes. So you may search for "cookies AND recipes." The more terms you combine with AND, the fewer returns you will receive. Or you want chocolate cookie recipes without coconut. You would search for "cookies AND recipes AND chocolate NOT coconut."

OR logic is most commonly used to search for similar terms or concepts. For example, you search for "cookies AND recipes OR chocolate" to retrieve results containing one term or the other or both. The more terms you combine in a search with OR logic, the more results you will receive from your search.

Some search engines assist you with your logical search through the use of forms. For example, look for a hyperlink that says *Advanced Search* or *Advanced Options* on a search engine's main page to open an advanced search form. Using this form, you can specify the language, words, and phrases to include and to omit, and even specify a time period, as you can see in Figure 26-3. Some search engines do not support Boolean logic, but most do provide a form that allows searching to be refined with filters or specific criteria.

FIGURE 26-3
Ask Jeeves's advanced search form

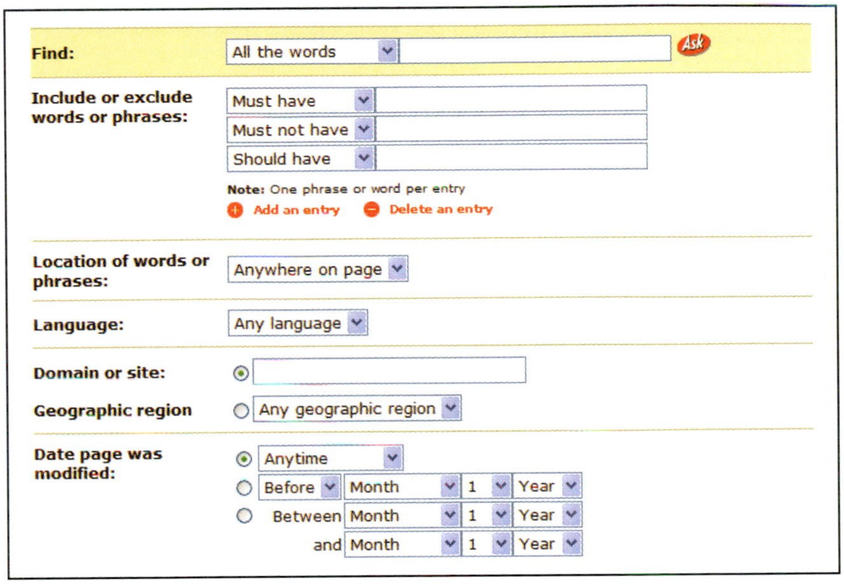

Find:	All the words ▾			Ask
Include or exclude words or phrases:	Must have ▾			
	Must not have ▾			
	Should have ▾			
	Note: One phrase or word per entry			
	➕ Add an entry ➖ Delete an entry			
Location of words or phrases:	Anywhere on page ▾			
Language:	Any language ▾			
Domain or site:	◉ [ ]			
Geographic region	○ Any geographic region ▾			
Date page was modified:	◉ Anytime ▾			
	○ Before ▾ Month ▾ 1 ▾ Year ▾			
	○ Between Month ▾ 1 ▾ Year ▾			
	and Month ▾ 1 ▾ Year ▾			

STEP-BY-STEP 26.2

1. Go to one of the search engines listed in Table 26-1, such as Yahoo.

2. In the search box, enter **cookies AND recipes AND chocolate**, and then click the **Search** or **Go** button, or simply press **Enter**.

3. Note the number of hits the search engine finds. Go back to the home page of the search engine.

4. In the search box, enter **cookies AND recipes AND chocolate NOT coconut**, and press **Enter**.

5. Again, note the number of hits; it is probably fewer than in the first search.

6. Click one or more of the hyperlinks to review the information provided by some of the Web sites.

7. When you are done, leave your browser open for the next Step-by-Step.

Wildcard Searching

The * symbol, or asterisk, is considered a *wildcard character*. If you don't know the spelling of a word or you want to search plurals or variations of a word, use the wildcard character. For example, you want to search for "baseball cards and Ichiro Suzuki," but you're not sure how to spell Ichiro. You can construct you search using a wildcard—"baseball cards" and "I* Suzuki."

Some search engines only permit the * at the end of the word; with others you can put the * at the end or beginning. Some search engines do not support wildcard searches.

Title Searching

When a Web page author creates a Web page, the Web page generally contains an HTML (hypertext markup language) title. The title is entered between title tags, such as

<Title>Internet Tutorials</Title>

When you go to a Web site, the title is what appears on the title bar at the top of the Web page. In Figure 26-4, the title bar indicates the subject of the Web site.

FIGURE 26-4
University Libraries—Title bar example

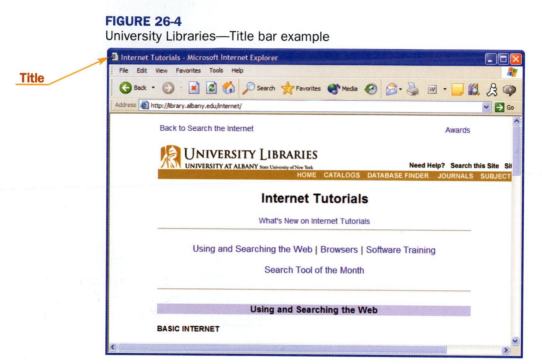

Many of the major search engines allow you to search within the HTML document for the title of a Web page. If you did a title search for "Internet Tutorials," then most likely one of your results or hits would be the page shown in Figure 26-4. Not all search engines support title searches.

Other Search Features

Another feature provided by several search engines is a ***related search***. These are preprogrammed queries or questions suggested by the search engine that often lead to other Web pages containing similar information. A related search can dramatically improve your odds of finding the information you are seeking. Several search engines offer this feature, although they may use different terminology. You may see terms such as "similar pages," "related pages," or "more pages like this." Google uses the phrase *Similar pages*, as shown in Figure 26-5, to provide a hyperlink to pages that are related to the selected search result. All of these terms basically mean the same thing.

FIGURE 26-5
Google search result with "Similar pages" hyperlinks

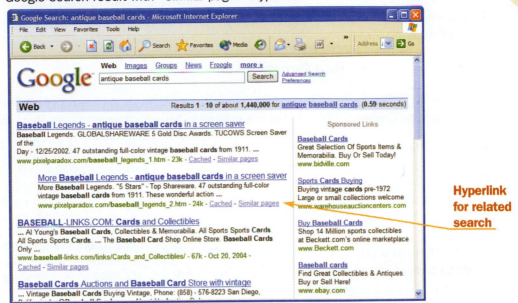

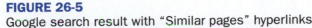 *Saving, Copying, and Printing Information from Web Sites*

3-3.2.7
3-3.2.8
3-3.2.9

As you view pages on the Web, you'll find a lot of things you'd like to save to a computer disk so that you can refer to them later without having to connect to the Internet. Browsers have features that enable you to save a complete Web page or any part of a Web page. This includes text, images, or hyperlinks.

Saving Data from a Web Page

You can save the contents of an entire Web site to disk. With the site open in your browser, you simply use the browser's Save As command. Most browsers give you options for saving, such as saving the entire Web site, including graphics, links, and text; or saving it in HTM/HTML only format, in which you will see "placeholders" for graphic links; or saving it as a text file in which only the text is saved.

Once you've saved the site, you can open it from a disk. The application in which you open it depends on the save options you chose. For example, if you chose to save it as a text file, you can open it in your word-processing program. If you chose to save it in HTM/HTML only format, you can open it in your word-processing program, in an HTML editing program, or in your browser. Note that you don't have to be connected to the Internet in order to open the site file in your browser.

In the next exercise, you will practice saving a Web page and then opening the saved file. Check with your instructor to make sure you have permission to save a Web page to the computer you are using.

STEP-BY-STEP 26.3

1. Use the **History** button on the browser toolbar to return to a search engine you used in a previous exercise in this lesson.

2. In the search box, key **Hope Diamond** and then press Enter.

3. One of the Web sites listed in the search results should be for the Encyclopedia Smithsonian's entry for the Hope Diamond. Click on that link to jump to a page with information about this famous gem.

4. On the **File** menu, select **Save As**.

5. In the Save As dialog box, select the location on disk where you save your assignments to save the Web page.

Note
You can check to make sure the page you want to save is not too large; the search results listing should include the approximate size of each Web page in the information about the page under its hyperlink. In Figure 26-5, the first site in the list is 23K in size.

6. Save the Web page using different options. Click the **down arrow** next to the Save as type text box to see what options are available. Be sure to use different filenames that identify each save option; for example, *Hope Diamond HTML Only*, *Hope Diamond Text*, and so forth.

7. Open Word and experiment with opening the different versions of the Web site.

8. Close the files you opened in Word and then close Word.

9. Use your browser to open an HTML version of the file offline:

   a. Select **Open** from the **File** menu and then click the **Browse** button in the Open dialog box to navigate to the location where you saved the Hope Diamond Web page files.

   b. Rest the mouse pointer on the filename if necessary to view a ScreenTip that indicates if the file type is HTML Document. (If you are using Internet Explorer, you may see lowercase "e" icon next to the HTML file.)

   c. Select the file and click **Open**, and then click **OK** in the Open dialog box to open the file in your browser.

   d. Use the scroll bar to scroll through the Web page file.

10. Leave the browser open for the next Step-by-Step.

Copying and Printing Information from a Web Page

You can also copy and save specific elements of a Web page to disk and use them in a new document or file. For example, you might want to save a photographic image to disk, or copy a paragraph of text you want to quote in a report. You can then open these in other applications or paste them into new files, such as a word-processing document, where you can edit and manipulate them as desired.

Or maybe you just want to print a copy of a Web page. You can do that directly from your browser. Most browsers provide previewing and page setup options that enable you to control how the Web page prints. Make sure your instructor has given you permission to print a Web page before completing the following exercise.

S TEP-BY-STEP 26.4

1. The Hope Diamond Web page you accessed in Step-by-Step 26.3 should still be displayed in your browser. Click the **Refresh** button to reload the page from the Web, or use the **History** button to open the History pane and find recently used links if the page is no longer open.

2. Highlight a paragraph of text, and then select the **Copy** command on your browser's Edit menu.

3. Open Word and paste the text in a new blank document.

4. Save the file with a name of your choice in the location where you save your assignments.

5. Go back to the Web page in your browser. Right-click a graphic image of the Hope Diamond and choose the Save Picture As command from the shortcut menu. Select a format for the image and the location to which you want to save it.

6. Open a new document in PowerPoint or Word and use the **Insert Picture** command to insert the image file you saved from the Web page.

7. Return to your browser and find another graphic image. Right-click the image and then select **Copy** from the shortcut menu.

8. Switch back to the open PowerPoint or Word document and use the **Paste** command to insert the image file you copied from the Web page.

9. Save the document file to the location where you save assignments, using a filename of your choice. Then close the file and the application and return to your browser.

10. Select **Print Preview** on the **File** menu to preview the Web page in your browser.

11. Print the Web page:
    a. Click the **Page Setup** button on the Print Preview toolbar to open the dialog box containing page setup options. Notice that there are options to change the orientation or margins of the Web page, or even change the default header or footer.
    b. Change the top margin to 1.5" and then click **OK** to close the Page Setup dialog box.
    c. Click the **Print** button on the Print Preview toolbar to open the Print dialog box.
    d. Make sure the **All** option is selected in the Page Range section, and then click **Print**.

12. The screen should return to the browser window with the Hope Diamond page. Leave the browser open for the next Step-by-Step.

Bookmarking and Downloading Web Sites

3-3.2.6
3-3.2.10

Favorites and Bookmarks

The Web has so much to offer that it is very likely you are going to find some sites you really like and want to return to often. It is easy to keep these sites just a mouse click away by bookmarking them, or adding them to your Favorites or Bookmark list. Internet Explorer, the browser for Windows XP, uses Favorites to refer to saved Web site locations.

To add a site to your list of sites using the Internet Explorer browser:

■ Go to the site you want to add.

■ On the Favorites menu, click Add to Favorites.

■ To revisit any of your Favorites, just click the Favorites button and then select the shortcut to the site.

As your list begins to grow, you can organize it by creating folders. You can organize by topics in much the same way you organize files in folders in other applications or in a file drawer.

STEP-BY-STEP 26.5

1. Use your browser's navigation tools to return to one of the search engines you used in this lesson. With the search engine's home page open in your browser, add the site to your Favorites.

   a. Make sure the page displayed is the search engine's home page, not the search results page for your last search.

   b. Select **Add to Favorites** from the **Favorites** menu and then click **OK** in the Add Favorites box.

2. Open the **Favorites** menu again. You should see the name of the search engine in the list at the bottom of the menu.

3. To create a folder named *Search Engines* in your Favorites list, select **Organize Favorites** and then click **Create Folder** in the Organize Favorites dialog box.

4. Name the new folder **Search Engines** and then click the name of the search engine in the list of favorite sites in the text box at the right of the dialog box.

5. Click the **Move to Folder** button in the dialog box and then select the **Search Engines** folder in the Browse for Folder dialog box and click **OK** to move the search engine bookmark to the Search Engines folder.

6. Click the **Close** button to close the Organize Favorites dialog box.

7. Click the **Home** button on the browser's toolbar to return to your home page.

8. Select your **Search Engines** folder from the **Favorites** menu, and then click the link for the search engine Web page you saved. Remain in this screen for the next Step-by-Step.

>
> **Note** ☑
>
> Downloaded files can introduce a virus or install spyware on your computer, so be careful about downloading "free" files that provide screen savers, cursors, and other accessories for your computer. To protect your computer system and data, only download files from sources you can trust.

Downloading a File from a Web Site

There are a number of circumstances in which you may find you want to download a file from a Web page. Note that you should only download files from reliable sources, but there are many of these on the Web, including shareware and freeware sites offer useful computer programs and games that you can download for a small cost or at no cost. You may need to download a patch or an update from the software manufacturer for an application program installed on your computer, or you may want to download clip art, a file of information, or an audio or video file available on a Web site. Most sites that have files to download provide an interface that makes the process of downloading simple. A series of steps or dialog boxes provides instructions about how to successfully download a file.

STEP-BY-STEP 26.6

1. In the search box in the search engine Web page displayed in your browser, key **Microsoft Clip Art**.

2. One of the links in the search results list (probably the first one) is the Microsoft Office Clip Art and Media Home Page. Click the link to open the page, which should be similar to the screen shown in Figure 26-6.

FIGURE 26-6
Microsoft Office Clip Art and Media Home Page

3. In the Search text box at the top of the page, select **Clip art** from the drop down list.

4. Key **computer** in the text box to the right of the Search text box and then click the **Go** button.

5. Select one of the clip art images of a computer or computer-related item by clicking in the small box under the picture. You should see a check mark in the box after you select it.

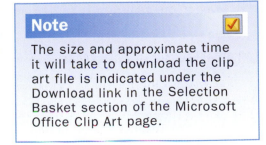

Note   ☑

The size and approximate time it will take to download the clip art file is indicated under the Download link in the Selection Basket section of the Microsoft Office Clip Art page.

STEP-BY-STEP 26.6 Continued

6. Click the **Download 1 item** link at the bottom of the Selection Basket section in the pane at the left of the Web page. Notice that the information in the window that opens indicates that the clip art will be stored in the My Pictures\Microsoft Clip Organizer folder.

7. Follow the Download Instructions in the window: Click the **Download Now** button in the window, and if prompted, click the **Open** option.

8. When the file has been downloaded, the graphic will display in the Microsoft Clip Organizer window. Click the window's **Close** button to close it.

9. Open a blank document in Word.

10. Select **Picture** from the **Insert** menu and then select **Clip Art** from the submenu to open the Clip Art pane.

11. Key **computer** in the Search for text box and make sure that **All collections** is the option displayed in the Search in text box, then click **Go**.

12. Find the computer clip art you downloaded and insert it in the Word document, and then save the document to your assignments folder using a filename of your choice.

13. Close the document and close Word.

14. Follow your instructor's directions about disconnecting from the Internet, if necessary, and then close your browser. Turn off your computer if your instructor tells you to do so.

> **Note**
>
> If you are asked to download any other file or control and your instructor prefers that you not download any program files, you may be able to select the option that allows you to continue without downloading a control or file and then complete the steps in this exercise.

> **Note**
>
> If this is the first time clip art has been downloaded from Microsoft Office Online, the Add Clips to Organizer dialog box may appear after you download the graphic. Click the **Later** button to close the dialog box and access your clip art in the Microsoft Clip Organizer window.

SUMMARY

In this lesson you learned:

■ Search engines are used to find specific information on the Internet.

■ A search engine is a software program that creates an automated index of Web sites.

■ Concept-based searching occurs when the search engine returns hits that relate to keywords.

■ Stemming relates to the search engine finding variations of the word.

■ Keywords describe the information you are trying to locate and most search engines support keyword searches.

■ Meta tags are special tags embedded in a Web page; many search engines use the tags to create their index.

- A search engine has three main parts: the search engine software, a robot or spider that searches for keywords, and an index.

- Specialty search engines focus on a particular topic.

- Multimedia search engines focus on video, animation, graphics, and music.

- Use double quotation marks around a set of words for phrase searching.

- Use the plus and minus sign for inclusion and exclusion of words within a search.

- Boolean searches use the three logical operators OR, AND, and NOT.

- Many search engines offer advanced search options that let you filter search results with specific criteria.

- The * symbol is used for wildcard searching.

- Some search engines support title searching.

- A related search is a preprogrammed question suggested by the search engine.

- You can save, copy, and print text, images, and links from Web pages as well as entire Web pages.

- For sites you will return to often, you can bookmark the Web address and add it to your Favorites folder.

- When you download a file from a Web site, make sure the provider of the file is a reliable source. Most sites that provide files to download include a simple form or dialog boxes to help you through the process of downloading.

VOCABULARY *Review*

Define the following terms:

Boolean logic	Math symbols	Spider
Hits	Related search	Wildcard character
Keywords	Search engine	

REVIEW Questions

TRUE/FALSE

Circle T if the statement is true or F if the statement is false.

T   F   **1.** It is not possible to save a Web page on a disk as a text file.

T   F   **2.** Keywords describe the information you are trying to locate.

T   F   **3.** The higher the relevance rating percentage, the more likely your search terms are included.

T   F   **4.** If you bookmark a Web site or save it as a favorite, the Web site address will be listed on your browser's File menu.

T   F   **5.** Boolean searches and math symbol searches are identical.

MULTIPLE CHOICE

Circle the best response for each of the following statements.

1. _____ occurs when the search engine includes other variations of the keyword.
   A. Concepts
   B. Stemming
   C. Meta tags
   D. Natural language

2. The _____ is a search engine robot that roams the Internet looking for keywords.
   A. index
   B. searcher
   C. spider
   D. wart hog

3. An asterisk is a symbol for a _____ character in a search.
   A. wildcard
   B. Boolean
   C. math
   D. meta

4. A Web page author uses _____ tags to specify keywords within a Web page document.
   A. math
   B. spider
   C. Boolean
   D. meta

5. If you were looking for video and music resources, you might use a _____ search engine.
   A. multimedia
   B. sports
   C. phrase
   D. spider

PROJECTS

PROJECT 26-1

1. Use search engine math symbols to conduct searches for the following:
   A. Carnivals and circuses in Canada, but not in Vancouver.
   B. Skateboards and roller blades in Florida.

2. Conduct searches for the same topics using Boolean logic.

3. Prepare a short report that describes the differences in search results using these two search methods.

PROJECT 26-2

1. Use the advanced search option on your favorite search engine to search for information about your favorite band or musical group.

2. Check the size of some of the Web pages listed in your search results and save a small site (less than 50K) as a text file in your assignments folder if your instructor gives you permission to do so.

3. Link to some of the other sites in your search results list and use the information you find to create a one-page report that includes at least one example of a graphic or excerpted text that you have saved or copied from a Web page.

4. Also include within the report what search engine you used and why, how many sites you found, and how you were able to narrow the search.

TEAMWORK PROJECT

You have been assigned to work as a group on a science project. The project involves selecting a type of insect and providing information about the life and habits of the insect. Working in a group with two other students, decide what insect you would be interested in researching and then create a "Search Strategy" form that you can use to search the Internet. Within the form, list possible search tools and ways in which to search. Include the URLs for any suggested search engines or directory Web sites. Make a copy of the form for each student in your group, and then individually use the form to find information about the insect. Then, meet as a group again and compare the information you found. Did you all find similar information, exactly the same information, or very different information when you did your searches?

CRITICAL *Thinking*

ACTIVITY 26-1

Select a topic of your choice to research on the Web. Try to be as specific as possible in the topic you choose; for example, "Olympic gold medalists" or "national parks in the Eastern United States." Search for information using three different search engines. Refer to Table 26-1 for a list of some popular search engines. Be sure to use exactly the same search techniques (such as keywords, Boolean operators, or related searches) for each search. Create a table with a separate column for each search engine. Then under the column headings, list the top 10 sites that the search engine locates. Determine which engine provided you with the highest-quality results.

EVALUATING ONLINE INFORMATION

<table>
<tr>
<td valign="top">

OBJECTIVES

Upon completion of this lesson, you should be able to:

- Identify types of Internet resources.
- Identify criteria for evaluating electronic information.
- Use assessment tools to evaluate electronic information.
- Understand the rules of copyright.
- Cite Internet resources appropriately.

Estimated Time: 1 hour

</td>
<td valign="top">

VOCABULARY

Copyright

Currency

Navigation

Plagiarism

Public domain

</td>
</tr>
</table>

Information is only as good as the source. Anyone, anywhere, can put anything on the Internet. It may be true; it may not be true. How can you determine if the information is legitimate? Developing the ability to evaluate information critically on the Internet is a very important skill today because so many people depend on electronic resources in so many areas of their lives. For example, you may have used information you found on the Internet to research a paper for a science class, and of course you want to ensure that the data you use is accurate. But consider some other types of information you might depend on, such as consumer reports on the safety of a certain make of automobile, unbiased news about candidates running for office in your city or state, guidelines for training your pet, or information about your health. You don't want to be steered wrong in any of these areas, and you must carefully assess the wealth of information available.

Types of Internet Resources

3-4.1.1

The types of electronic resources include the following:

- journals and journal articles
- magazines and magazine articles
- newspapers and newspaper articles
- e-mail
- mailing lists
- commercial sites

- organizational sites
- subject-based sites

Some of these are presented in complete form; others are only portions of the document. Regardless of the type, the site should give information about

- the publisher's identity
- article reviewer information
- special hardware requirements
- availability of older copies of the article, newspaper, or journal
- the currency of the site

Search Engines

You learned that search engines are programs written to query and retrieve information stored in a database. They differ from database to database and depend on the information stored in the database itself. Examples of search engines are AltaVista, Excite, Yahoo, and Google. If you used one of the many search engines available to locate information on the Internet, you need to know

- how the search engine decides the order in which it returns information requested. The top spaces (the first sites listed) are often sold to advertisers by the search engines. Therefore, the first sites listed are not always the best sites or the most accurate and reliable. Figure 27-1 shows an example of "sponsored sites" in search results.

- how the search engine searches for information and how often the information is updated.

You may be surprised to find that even the most academic subjects result in sponsored sites in your search results. Sponsored sites are unlikely to provide balanced and impartial information and you should consider the intent of the sites when judging the reliability of information provided on them. In addition, if information in a search result appears to be out of date or irrelevant, consider trying the search again with a different search engine and compare the results when assessing the information.

FIGURE 27-1
Sponsored sites in a Yahoo search result for "photosynthesis"

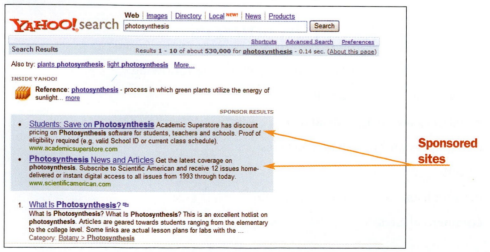

Subject Directories

Most subject directories are organized by subject categories, with a collection of links to Internet resources. These resources are arranged by subject and then displayed in a series of menus. Subject directory searches often provide a more guided approach than entering keywords into a search engine. When you use subject directories and the information they provide, look for the following qualities to determine if the directory is reliable and useful:

- They are easy to use.

- The Web sites have been handpicked and evaluated.

- Most links include some type of description.

- They produce better quality hits on searches for common items.

Some popular subject directories include the Librarian's Index at *www.lii.org*, Encyclopedia Britannica at *www.britannica.com*, and Galaxy at *www.galaxy.com*.

Mailing Lists

When you subscribe to a mailing list, you will receive information regularly from other members of the list. Sometimes the postings are so numerous they are overwhelming, and you may find it difficult to sort through the information to find useful material. However, if the mailing list is maintained by a reputable organization (an educational or research institute, or a professional organization, for example), the postings may provide you with new insights and specific data you could not easily find elsewhere. You must apply the same types of criteria you use to assess other electronic information to determine the usefulness, validity, and relevance of the information you receive.

3-3.3.6
3-4.3.1

Criteria for Evaluating Electronic Resources

The Internet provides opportunities for students, teachers, scholars, and anyone needing information to find it from all over the world. It is fairly easy to locate information and to publish it electronically. However, because anyone can put information on the Internet, it is not always accurate or reliable. Anyone using information obtained from the Internet needs to develop skills to evaluate what they find.

Computer Concepts

The Internet epitomizes the concept of *caveat lector:* Let the reader beware.

The pages on the Web have so many different looks. Some pages are full of pictures, sounds, animations, links, and information. Some are very exciting; others may be just plain. Sometimes the appearance of the page alone may draw you to a site and, after reading it, you realize it is not the site you need.

Following are some questions you may want to ask when you open a Web page:

- Did the page take a long time to load?

- Are the graphics on the page related to the site?

- Are the sections on the page labeled?

- Who wrote the information on this page?

- How can you communicate with the author?
- When was the page last updated?
- Are there appropriate links to other Web pages?
- Is it easy to follow links?
- Can you tell what the page is about from its title?
- Is the information useful to you?
- How old is the information?
- Does any of the information contradict information you found someplace else?
- Did the author use words like *always, never, best, worst*?
- Do you think the author knows the information he or she is sharing?

These questions represent just the beginning of the process involved in evaluating electronic information.

Assessing Information on Web Sites

3-3.3.5

Determining Authorship

A well-developed resource identifies its author and/or publisher. You should be able to find enough information to determine whether the originator is a reliable source. What expertise or authority does the author have that qualifies him or her to distribute this information? Figure 27-2 shows a banner at the bottom of a Web site that offers links to contact someone about the site, find

---

 Ethics in Technology

RESTRICTING INTERNET ACCESS

In various situations, people might want to block access to specific Internet sites or to sites that contain certain content. For instance, parents often want to prevent their children from visiting sites with adult-oriented material. Or companies might want to deny their employees access to online shopping and entertainment sites that are not business related.

There are several tools to restrict site access. A low-tech solution is to simply have someone oversee computer users and what is on their monitors. At the other end of the spectrum, there are software programs that can be installed on a computer or network that will automatically block access to user-specified sites or to sites with specified content. Your browser or Internet service provider may offer settings you can use to control access to certain types of sites, and search engines such as Google provide controls that can be used to filter inappropriate sites from search result listings.

answers to frequently asked questions (FAQ), copyright information, and the privacy policy of the site's sponsor. Click the Contact or About Us link on a Web site's home page to look for a name and e-mail address of the person who created or maintains the information. You can always contact him or her for information regarding credentials and expertise.

FIGURE 27-2
Links to more information about the creators and policies of a Web site

If you can find the author's name but contact information for the author is not visible, a search by the author's name using a search engine may provide more details about the author. It may also lead to other information by the same author. If an e-mail address is visible on the Web site, use it to request information regarding the author.

The domain extension of the URL will also give you information concerning the appropriateness of the site for your area of study. Examples:

- .edu for educational or research information
- .gov for government resources
- .com for commercial products or commercially sponsored sites
- .org for nonprofit organizations
- .mil for military branches

Relevance and Reliability

Does the information on the site meet the needs of my research? Is the purpose of this Web site stated? Is the information accurate? Is the information in-depth enough? Has the information been reviewed? Does the information come from a source that can be trusted? Don't take any information presented on the Internet at face value. The source of the information should be clearly stated, whether it is original or borrowed from somewhere else.

Computer Concepts

The U.S. Centers for Disease Control and Prevention maintain a Web site at *www.cdc.gov/hoax_rumors.htm* that provides information specifically about health-related hoaxes perpetrated on the Internet.

The overall layout of the page is also important. The page should be free of spelling and grammatical errors. Even if the page appears to contain valuable information, misspelled words and incorrect grammar can be warning signs that the information itself may not be completely reliable.

Validity and Bias

Make sure you understand the agenda of the site's owner. Is it trying to sell a product or service? Is it trying to influence public opinion? As you read through the information, pay close attention to determine whether the content covers a specific time period or an aspect of a topic or whether it is more broad. To determine the validity of the information, check other resources, such as books or journals at the local library, that contain similar information.

The style of writing and the language used can reveal information about the quality of the site. If the style is objective, the chances are the information is worthy of your attention.

However, if it is opinionated and subjective, you may want to give second thought to using it. Ideas and opinions supported by references are additional signs of the value of the site.

Dating Your Data

An important consideration when assessing the information on a Web site is its *currency*, which refers to the age of the information, how long it has been posted, and how often it is updated. Some sites need to be updated more often than others to reflect changes in the kind of information. Medical or technological information needs to be updated more often than historical information. Out-of-date information may not give you the results you need. Does the site contain dead links—links that are no longer active? Dead links are a clue that the information on the Web site may not be up to date.

Computer Concepts

The Internet changes daily, and Web sites often move to new locations. Reputable sites provide a link to their new URL address from the old address for a certain period of time to make it easy for users to locate the new site. Sometimes the old URL address will be programmed to automatically redirect you to the new site.

Navigating the Site

Navigation is the ability to move through a site. Being able to move quickly through the links on a Web site is an important element of an effective site. Having the information laid out in a logical design so you can locate what you need easily adds to the efficiency of the site. The consistency of the layout from page to page adds to the ability to navigate easily. The first page of a Web site should indicate how the site is organized and the options available. There may also be a link to a site map that can give you a good idea of the overall organization of the site.

Moving through a site is done by clicking on the links on the page. Some pages consist of many links; others may only contain a few. Regardless, the links should be

- Easy to identify
- Grouped logically
- Pertinent to the subject of the original page

There should be a link on each page that will take you back to the home page and one that will allow you to e-mail the author. Most sites on the Internet have numerous links that will take you to additional sites of similar information. Sometimes, however, it is not information you can use. Decide whether the site you plan to use has useful information or whether it is just a site that links you to more and more sites. Also, determine whether the links go only to other pages within the site. This will help you assess the objectivity of the information on the site.

Assessment Tools

You can find information about almost anything on the Internet. So it may not be a surprise to find that there is an online tutorial that will guide you in assessing the quality of the information you locate on the Internet. It gives specific information regarding evaluating electronic resources. Visit *www.sosig.ac.uk/desire/internet-detective.html* and surf though the pages of this site for some tips. Your instructor may give you additional directions for using this site.

You also can use the information in this lesson to construct a survey to assess the electronic resources you find. Figure 27-3 shows a sample survey form.

FIGURE 27-3
Survey form

CRITERIA FOR EVALUATING ELECTRONIC RESOURCES

1. Can you identify the author of the page?   Yes _____   No _____

2. Is an e-mail address listed?   Yes _____   No _____

3. Can you access the site in a reasonable time?   Yes _____   No _____

4. Is the text on the screen legible?   Yes _____   No _____

5. Are the commands and directions easy to follow?   Yes _____   No _____

6. Is the information current?   Yes _____   No _____

7. When you perform a search, do you get what you expect?   Yes _____   No _____

8. Are instructions clearly visible?   Yes _____   No _____

9. Is the information updated regularly?   Yes _____   No _____

10. Make any comment here you would like concerning the site.

_____

_____

Identify a site on the Internet and use the survey to evaluate it. You may select a site such as a magazine article of interest to you, the White House or Smithsonian sites you used in the previous lessons, or any topic on which you may want to gather information.

Remember, anyone can put information on the Internet. Evaluate any resources that you choose to use carefully to ensure you have a high-quality resource that could really be of value to you.

Computer Concepts

You can find out more about Internet or e-mail hoaxes, such as the sick child who wants to get in the Guinness Book of World Records for most e-mails received or the third word that ends in -gry, at *www.snopes.com*.

3-4.3.2

Web Sites and Copyright Rules

For the most part, information displayed on an Internet site is easy to copy. Often you can select whatever text or graphics that you want to copy, use the browser's Copy command, and then paste it onto another document. Or you can print out an entire page displayed on your monitor. The ease with which information can be copied, however, does not mean that users have a legal right to do so. Internet publications can claim the same legal protection as books, newspapers, CDs, movies, and other forms that are protected by copyright rules.

Most sites have copyright information. *Copyright* is the exclusive right, granted by law for a certain number of years, to make and use literary, musical, or artistic work. Even if the copyright notice isn't displayed prominently on the page, someone wrote or is responsible for the creation of whatever appears on a page. This means that you cannot use the information as your own. You must give credit to the person who created the work.

If Internet content, such as music files, is copyrighted, it cannot be copied without the copyright holder's permission. To do so is a violation of copyright laws. It can lead to criminal charges for theft as well as civil lawsuits for monetary damages.

> ### Computer Concepts
>
> The Internet is an open and volatile arena where information can be posted easily and quickly. Some people abuse the ease with which information can be disseminated and use a Web site or e-mail to spread untrue stories or rumors. *Libel* is the deliberate communication of misinformation or false information intended to harm a person or organization, and it is illegal.

A company's logo or other graphic information may be protected as a trademark, which means much the same thing as copyright but relates specifically to visual or commercial images rather than text or intellectual property. In addition, processes and business methods may be protected by patents, which guarantee the inventor exclusive rights to the process or method for a certain period of time.

Copyright and patent law does provide certain exceptions to the general prohibition against copying. If copyright or patent protection has lapsed on certain material, then it is deemed to be in the *public domain* and is available for anyone to copy or use. Also, the law allows for the fair use of properly identified copyrighted material that is merely a small part of a larger research project, for instance, or cited as part of a critique or review.

Citing Internet Resources

Internet resources used in reports must be cited. In an academic setting, claiming someone else's words as your own is *plagiarism*. You must give proper credit to any information you include in a report that is not your original thought. This will also provide the reader of the document with choices for additional research. It will also allow the information to be retrieved again.

> ### Note ☑
>
> For information concerning using MLA style for citing sources, visit *www.mla.org*.

You can find general guidelines for citing electronic sources in the *MLA Handbook for Writers of Research Papers*, published by the Modern Language Association. *The Chicago Manual of Style* is another source for this information.

Here are some samples of citing Internet resources as suggested in the *MLA Handbook for Writers of Research Papers*:

■ *Online journal article:* Author's last name, first initial. (date of publication or "NO DATE" if unavailable). Title of article or section used [Number of paragraphs]. Title of complete work. [Form, such as HTTP, CD-ROM, E-MAIL]. Available: complete URL [date of access].

- *Online magazine article:* Author's last name, first initial. (date of publication). Title of article. [Number of paragraphs]. Title of work. [Form] Available: complete URL [date of access].
- *Web sites:* Name of site [date]. Title of document [Form] Available: complete URL [date of access]
- *E-mail:* Author's last name, first name (author's e-mail address) (date). Subject. Receiver of e-mail (receiver's e-mail address).

SUMMARY

In this lesson, you learned:

- There are various types of Internet resources including electronic journals, magazines, newspapers, Web sites, and e-mail messages.
- Search engines, subject directories, and mailing list postings each present different requirements for evaluation, but information from any electronic source should be assessed before depending on its validity and reliability.
- The criteria for evaluating Internet resources include authorship, content, appearance, ease of use, date, copyright information, objectivity, and quality control.
- Internet publications and Web site content can claim the same legal protection as books, newspapers, CDs, movies, and other forms that are protected by copyright law.
- It is important to cite any information that you use from the Internet. The MLA style is widely used for citing electronic resources.

VOCABULARY *Review*

Define the following terms:		
Copyright	Navigation	Public domain
Currency	Plagiarism	

REVIEW *Questions*

TRUE/FALSE

Circle T if the statement is true or F if the statement is false.

T F 1. It can be assumed that all information found on the Internet is accurate.

T F 2. The age of an article will affect its usefulness to a user.

T F 3. Everyone who puts information on the Internet is an authority on the particular subject.

T F 4. Spelling and grammatical errors on a Web page should not affect a user's opinion of a site.

T F 5. All sites should have an e-mail address for the author so the user can make contact.

MULTIPLE CHOICE

Circle the best response for each of the following statements.

1. All of the following are types of Internet resources *except* _____.
   A. journal articles
   B. commercial sites
   C. CD-ROMs
   D. e-mail

2. Some information on the Internet is classified as _____, which means it can be used without citation or permission.
   A. patented
   B. public domain
   C. copyrighted
   D. precited

3. Search engines often sell _____ in search result lists, which are spaces sold to advertisers by the search engine company.
   A. sponsored sites
   B. subject-based sites
   C. databases
   D. bookmarked sites

4. Postings on a reputable _____ can provide you with specific data and unique points of view on a subject of common interest.
   A. subject directory
   B. organizational site
   C. sponsored site
   D. mailing list

5. All of the following are criteria for evaluating information on a Web site *except* _____.
   A. authorship
   B. listing in search engine results
   C. age of information
   D. ease of navigation

PROJECTS

PROJECT 27-1

Search the Internet for Web sites containing information on Olympic gold medalists. In the results list, pick at least two sites that you think might contain useful information. Using the survey form shown in Figure 27-3, evaluate each site. Write a one-page report on your evaluation of the sites. Be sure to include the URL of the site and elaborate on what you found in answer to each of the survey questions.

PROJECT 27-2

Choose a topic to research on the Internet. Print the first two sites that you find. Using the information you studied in this lesson, evaluate the navigations system of each site and critique the two sites. Report your findings by comparing and contrasting the reliability and validity of the two sites in a short report.

 ## TEAMWORK PROJECT

Your supervisor has informed you that she has contracted the services of a Web designer to create a Web page for your video/multimedia store. However, she would like to be able to talk intelligently with the Web designer when telling him or her exactly what she wants on the Web page. She has asked you and the other part-time employee at the store to work together to provide her with samples of Web pages for five video/multimedia stores. She also wants you to provide her with a critique of each page. Work with your teammate to collect and evaluate the information your supervisor has requested.

CRITICAL *Thinking*

ACTIVITY 27-1

You want to design a Web site on a topic of your choice. Sketch out a design for the home page of the Web site. Review the evaluation criteria discussed in this lesson and make sure your Web site follows the criteria of a reputable site with accurate information.

TECHNOLOGY AND SOCIETY

As the age of innovation blazes its way into the world of technology, dramatic changes are taking place in every aspect of life—from home to school to the workplace. And the changes are swift and dramatic. Just as soon as we settle in and become comfortable with a new technological change, along comes something more innovative and different. As things look now, the world is in for a lot more of this type of change.

3-4.1.2
3-4.1.3
3-4.3.4

E-Commerce

You have probably read about the Industrial Revolution and how it affected our world. The Internet economy is being compared to the Industrial Revolution. *Electronic commerce*, or e-commerce, which means having an online business, is changing the way our world does business.

Within this electronic business, one can buy and sell products through the Internet. We find e-commerce in every corner of the modern business world. Over a billion people will be connected to the Internet by the year 2005 if predictions prove correct. Internet speed will increase as more people add cable modems or other high-speed connection options. All of this activity and increased speed indicate more online businesses. Some analysts predict that, within the next 10 years, the value of Internet-based business will account for up to 10% of the world's consumer sales. The Center for Research in Electronic Commerce at the University of Texas indicates that over two thirds of the thousands of online companies are not the big Fortune 500 companies—they are smaller companies.

When it comes to buying online, many people hesitate because they fear someone will steal their credit card number. However, *digital cash* is a new technology that may ease some of those fears. The digital cash system allows someone to pay by transmitting a number from one computer to another. The digital cash numbers are issued by a bank and represent a specified sum of real money; each number is unique. When someone uses digital cash, there is no way to obtain information about the user.

Computer Concepts

Want to find out more about the Internet and electronic commerce? The Library of Congress provides a Web site located at *www.loc.gov/ rr/business/ecommerce/ inet-business.html* with links to other sites that explain how to do business online.

As you read about electronic commerce, you may wonder about what effects it will have on you personally. You or someone in your family may have already made a purchase online. You can quickly compare product features and prices to help you make an informed decision about any purchase, large or small. Or maybe you are a shopper who is always looking for a bargain; in that case, the online auction houses such as e-Bay are probably for you. Buying online will become much more common in the future, and you may find it becomes a way of life.

Almost everyone with a bank account now takes advantage of the convenience of ATMs to deposit or withdraw money. These automated banking machines are seen everywhere; they are located at most banks but also in supermarkets, convenience stores, restaurants, even at the ballpark or museum. They allow people to do their banking almost anywhere, anytime. "Banker's hours" are definitely a thing of the past.

You may not even need to get cash from an ATM for your shopping, however. Electronic checks and debit cards are making cash more obsolete every day. If you swipe your ATM card or debit card through the little machine at the cashier's station at your local store and then enter your personal identification number or "PIN," information about your account is automatically transferred to the store's computers and the amount of your purchase is deducted from your balance.

Rarely a day goes by that you or someone in your family doesn't receive junk mail delivered by your local postal worker, and much of it is advertising goods and services for you to buy. But now that junk mail has begun to increase electronically, augmented by spam, which, as you learned in Lesson 24, is commercial junk mail sent to your e-mail address. Several states are already looking at ways to legislate spam.

Computer Concepts

A *dot com* business is one that exists almost entirely in the virtual world of the Internet. The company may have real offices and "live" employees, but it makes contact with its customers electronically rather than at a mall or corner store. The Web sites of these businesses usually use the domain extension *.com*, which is said "dot com."

Other aspects of our changing economy that you might consider are the new categories of jobs being generated by electronic commerce. These might be something you want to consider as you look toward a future career. Some examples include Web masters, programmers, network managers, graphic designers, Web developers, and so forth. You may also think about going into an online or "dot com" business for yourself. Individuals with imagination and ambition will discover that the greatest source of wealth is their ideas.

Whatever career you choose to pursue, you may find that computers are used to provide online training for your work and Internet job searches help you create your resume, post it, and find the perfect position. Or when you start that Internet business yourself, you may take advantage of those computer postings to find the perfect employees to make your company a success.

Technology and Education

There are many similarities between today's schools and those of 40 or 50 years ago. In many classrooms, the students still sit in rows and the teacher stands at the front of the class, lecturing and using a chalkboard. However, in other classrooms, a technological revolution is taking place. Schools are being wired for high-speed Internet access—or even wireless connections—every year, and students as young as preschoolers may have the opportunity to learn to use computers at school. Even students who attend schools without access to computers have the chance to use electronic resources at local libraries and public Internet centers.

Many people predict that technology will change the entire structure of education. Others believe the way in which most students receive education today—students and teacher in a traditional classroom—will remain for many years. Regardless of who is right, one thing is certain: Technology is having a tremendous impact on education in general and in more and more classrooms around the world.

Internet

The Internet and the World Wide Web are the biggest factors affecting education today. For instance, not so long ago, if a science teacher gave the class a project to find out how a television works, the students would go to the library and do the research. In many of today's classrooms, the students most likely go to the Internet, and maybe to the How Stuff Works Web site shown in

Ethics in Technology

SPAM, SPAM, SPAM, SPAM

If you use the Internet often and have an e-mail account, you have most likely encountered spam. Internet spam has several definitions. It is defined as electronic junk mail or junk newsgroup postings, or even unsolicited e-mail. This unsolicited e-mail is most likely some type of advertising or get-rich scheme, similar to the junk mail you receive almost every day. With traditional junk mail, however, the people who send the mail pay a fee to distribute their materials.

Spam, in contrast, is similar to receiving a postage-due letter. Even though you don't pay the postage as it arrives in your electronic mailbox, you are still paying for it indirectly. The charges are in the form of disk space, connection time, or even long-distance Internet connections.

Be aware that if you sign Web site guest books, post to newsgroups, or request information from a Web site, you are leaving information about yourself. This information can be collected by various software programs and your e-mail address may be added to a list that can be sold over and over again. You can limit spam in a number of ways. Several services exist to which you can submit a complaint or report about a spam provider. There are also many spam-blocking and filtering services, as well as services and programs that hide your e-mail address from potential spammers. Visit *spam.abuse.net* to learn more.

Figure 28-1, to find this information. Using the Internet, it is fast and easy to find the information you need, but remember that it is always important to evaluate the information you find online for reliability, relevance, validity, and objectivity.

FIGURE 28-1
How Stuff Works Web site

Many textbooks published today have an associated Web site where students can access Web-based projects, find study aides to accompany the text, and do homework. It is even possible for students using a particular textbook to open an online version of the textbook with a password provided by their instructor. This can considerably lighten the load in a student's backpack as he or she travels back and forth to school! Publishers may provide a Web site for a series of textbooks or for each individual book. Look in the front pages of a textbook that has been published recently to see if there is a Web site that accompanies it.

Computer Concepts

According to the National Center for Education Statistics, 93% of public schools are connected to the Internet, and the number of connected schools increases every day.

Distance Learning

For years many people have been receiving their education via distance-learning methods. These methods include television and correspondence courses that are completed through the mail. In the last few years, however, the Internet has become a way to deliver distance learning. At the elementary and secondary school levels, the Department of Education supports an initiative called the Star Schools Program. This program provides distance education learning to more than millions of learners annually. Imagine being able to complete high school from home—this is possible in some states.

Computer Concepts

Project Gutenberg was one of the earliest educational uses of the Internet—it began as a text-based project by Michael Hart in 1971, before the World Wide Web even existed. More than 13,000 books, mostly older works of literature that are in the public domain in the United States, are available to download at *www.gutenberg.org*.

New types of programs are on the market to help teachers develop online courses. These programs are an integrated set of Web-based teaching tools that provide guidance and testing for the student. Two of the most popular of these are Blackboard and WebCT.

Computer-Based Learning

Everyone learns in different ways and at different rates. Likewise, information can be presented in many formats and at different levels. This could be presented through lecture, homework, group projects, movies, and so forth. The more ways in which information can be presented, the more opportunities everyone has to use their own learning style so they can master the particular topic.

You may have heard the terms *computer-based learning* or computer-assisted instruction (CAI). These are examples of ways you and your instructor can use the computer for instruction. It is basically using a computer as a tutor. For many students, this is one of the most effective ways for them to learn. For example, you may have difficulty understanding a specific mathematics concept, such as how to calculate percentages. Your instructor may suggest a special computer program to help reinforce that difficult concept. Using such a program provides you with the opportunity to master the idea by reviewing the concept as many times as necessary. Figure 28-2 shows students using terminals in a computer lab to help them learn subject matter.

FIGURE 28-2
Students at work in a computer lab

Simulations

Learning doesn't have to be dull, boring work. Learning can actually be fun especially if it is done through computer simulation. *Simulations* are models of real-world activities.

They are designed to allow you to experiment and explore environments that may be dangerous or unavailable. Using simulations, you can explore other worlds and settings without leaving your classroom. With this type of model, you learn by doing.

You can find simulations on the Internet or on a CD-ROM disk that you would run from a local computer.

Some examples of simulations are as follows:

- Many of you have probably heard about fortunes being made and lost in the stock market. If you would like to see how good your investing skills are, you might want to try the Stock Market Game located at *www.smgww.org*. This simulation is for students of all ages—from middle school to adults. By playing this game, you learn about finance and the American economic system. To participate in this game (shown in Figure 28-3), you invest a hypothetical $100,000 in the stock market and follow your investments over a 10-week time period.

FIGURE 28-3
Stock Market simulation game

- Maybe you are interested in outer space and would like to explore Mars. You can do this through simulation. Use a search engine and the keywords *Mars exploration simulation* to find relevant Web sites such as *www.exploremarsnow.org*.

- One of the earliest and still most popular simulations is SimCity. Go to *www.simcity.com* to find out more about the program and view some sample screens. Several versions of this program have been released. It is used extensively in schools throughout the world. This problem-solving software program allows the user to create a city, including highways, buildings, homes, and so forth. You can govern the city as mayor to learn more about political science or micromanage the Sim family's affairs for a hands-on lesson in sociology. Figure 28-4 shows a typical SimCity simulation screen.

FIGURE 28-4
City simulation

Science and Technological Innovation

3-4.1.1
3-4.1.2
3-4.1.4

Our world is changing at an ever-increasing pace. Currently, people around the world are able to communicate with each other almost instantaneously. Advances in technology affect how we are treated for illnesses and injuries, how our cars are manufactured and how they work, even how the meter reader calculates our water bill.

Computers are working behind the scenes in almost every area of human life today. Computer programs make it possible to predict dangerous weather and warn people in time to prepare for storms. Electronic devices help disabled people communicate, become more mobile, and participate in many more activities. For example, TDD (Telecommunications Device for the Deaf) technology allows hearing-impaired people to use a telephone, "smart" buses can lower steps to allow disabled people to board the bus or may have a lift for a wheelchair, and personal computers offer a myriad of accessibility options that permit people with many types of disabilities to work and communicate more easily.

The amount of available information to any person with access to electronic devices, from radios and televisions to computers and cell phones, is increasing every day. In fact, it is continuing to increase faster than we can process it. On the positive side, the information and discoveries are contributing to a better lifestyle for many people. Predictions are that we will learn to cure illnesses and to continue to increase our life span.

But there's another aspect to all of this. Within all of this change, other predictions are that an antitechnology backlash is possible. Many people feel technology is creating a world out of control. Moral and cultural dilemmas are becoming more and more common, and many people want to return to a simpler, slower way of life.

Whether society could and would return to something simpler is highly debatable. Even today, there are very few places in the world one can live that are not being affected by technology. And many scientists say we're "only at the Model-T stage" of what's to come. Let's take a brief look at some of the predicted and possible scientific changes on the horizon.

Artificial Intelligence

Some of you who enjoy science fiction may have read the book or seen the movie *2001: A Space Odyssey*. In this movie, originally released in the late 1960s and re-released in 2000, a computer referred to as HAL controls a spaceship on its way to Mars. This computer has a type of artificial intelligence, so it never makes a mistake. No computer such as HAL yet exists, but the concept of artificial intelligence is still a branch of computer science. Computer scientists have made major advancements in this area.

Computer Concepts

The term *artificial intelligence* was coined in 1956 by John McCarthy at the Massachusetts Institute of Technology.

The concept of *artificial intelligence* (AI) has been around for many years. The goal for this kind of software is to process information on its own without human intervention. There are many ways in which artificial intelligence applications are being developed and used today. Some examples are as follows:

- *Game playing:* An area where the most advances have been made.

- *Natural language:* Offers the greatest potential rewards by allowing people to interact easily with computers by talking to them.

- *Expert systems:* Computer programs that help us make decisions. For instance, an expert system may help someone determine the best type of insurance for his or her particular needs, or decide the features they want in a "custom" designed house.

- *Robotics:* When we think of robotics, we may think of humanoid robots like those in *Star Wars*. In real life, however, robotic design did not originally take this path. Robots have been used mostly in assembly plants, often doing dangerous or repetitive tasks. More recently, some specialized robots have been developed that do have a humanoid appearance, and robot devices such as NASA's Mars Rover Spirit and Jason, the robotic submarine operated by Woods Hole Oceanographic Institute, allow exploration of hostile environments unsafe for humans. One of the newest types of robots is called a *bot*, and it does its work in cyberspace; bots are robotic software programs commonly used by search engines to sort information.

Computer Concepts

Honda Motor Company has created a humanoid robot called Asimo that can walk, recognize and respond to verbal commands, and manipulate objects. Go to *http://world. honda.com/ ASIMO/technology/operation.html* to see Asimo and learn more about Honda's robotics program.

Genetic Engineering

The human life span has almost tripled in the last 200 years. We can now expect to live more than 80 years. Some scientists think that the average life span in the twenty-first century will continue to increase, possibly dramatically. One of the major factors contributing to this increase is genetic engineering, which refers to changing the DNA in a living organism. There are groups of people who argue against this technology. The supporters, however, point out the many benefits. Here are some examples:

- Increasing crop plants' resistance to disease and drought

- Causing a fish used for food to grow to full size in half the usual time

- Enabling a fruit to ripen without getting too soft

Virtual Reality

The term *virtual reality* (VR) means different things to different people. A general definition is an artificial environment that feels like a real environment. This environment is created with computer hardware and software. Virtual reality and simulation share some common characteristics. Simulation is sometimes referred to as desktop VR. However, with virtual reality, there is more of a feeling of being in the actual environment—of using all or almost all of the five senses. The user is completely immersed inside the virtual world, generally through a specially wired helmet. The helmet contains the virtual and auditory displays.

Virtual reality is used in many different ways and areas. Some examples are as follows:

- *Education:* The creation of virtual environments can help students understand a subject, such as a particular period in history, for instance. Imagine experiencing World War II as though you were really there. Or maybe you would like to experience what it would be like to live during the age of dinosaurs. With a virtual world, you feel as though you are really there.

Historically Speaking

CYBER CAMPAIGNING

The Bill of Rights says that "Congress shall make no law . . . abridging the freedom of speech . . . or the right of the people peaceably to assemble," in part to ensure the freedom to support the candidate of your choice with your words and actions. Campaigning for office in the early days of the country depended on partisan newspapers that were the first means of spreading the word about candidates. Later, presidential hopefuls, such as Benjamin Harrison, embarked on "whistle-stop" train trips, using new technology to contact more potential voters. Franklin D. Roosevelt reached his constituents with "fireside chats" on the radio that connected voter and president in a way that anticipated television, an innovation that allowed almost every voter to see and hear the candidates' campaign. Most recently, people now use the Internet to find news "on demand" at any time of the day or night.

John McCain was the first presidential candidate to use the Internet to secure an advantage in his primary campaign in 2000. McCain's campaign raised $1 million online in 48 hours after his victory in the New Hampshire primary. But in 2004, Howard Dean recognized the full potential of the Internet during his primary run. In addition to raising funds quickly online, Dean's Director of Internet Outreach, Zephyr Teachout, used an application called MeetUp to make it easy for supporters to contact each other, post messages, and get involved in the campaign at a grassroots level.

The success of the McCain and Dean Web sites proved that the Internet could be a powerful tool in a campaign, and every candidate had a Web presence in the 2004 election, where they signed up volunteers, forwarded messages from the candidates, solicited donations, and even previewed media ads for their supporters. The Bush organization employed an E-Campaign Director, Michael Turk, to supervise the online effort, and the Kerry campaign had a Cyber Organizer, Luis Miranda. Candidate Web sites will continue to play an important role in future elections as more and more people turn to the Internet for news and information.

■ *Training:* You may have had an opportunity to play Doom or Turok: Dinosaur Hunter or some of the other virtual games. If so, you may have felt you were part of the action. You can control much of the environment and make choices about what your next move will be. A variation of this type of virtual reality is being used to train pilots, navigators, and even astronauts. These individuals are put into virtual life-and-death situations where they must make decisions. This helps prepare them in the event that a similar situation occurs in real life.

■ *Medicine:* One example of a medical VR application is the "Anatomic VisualizeR," being developed at the University of California, San Diego. This project is a virtual reality–based learning environment that will enable medical students to actively learn human anatomy. At a university in Germany, a VR system allows student surgeons to practice operations.

■ *Miniaturized chips:* Researchers at Texas Instruments have developed an advanced semiconductor manufacturing technology. The transistors are so small that more than 400 million of them will fit onto a single chip the size of a fingernail. And we can expect that this type of technological advance will continue.

Computer Concepts

The holodeck on *Star Trek: Next Generation* illustrates how far virtual reality technology may advance in the next few decades. Do you think such a realistic "virtual environment" may be a form of entertainment in the future?

These are just a few examples of activities taking place today. As in the past, it is fairly certain that scientific discovery and technological innovation will greatly affect our economic and military developments in the future. Predictions are that science and technology will continue to advance and become more widely available and utilized around the world. Some people forecast, however, that the benefits derived from these advancements would not be evenly distributed.

The Wired Workplace

3-4.1.1

How will technology affect us as individuals in our work and social life? Although no one knows what the future will bring, predictions are many. Many people predict that, with high-skilled work more in demand, semi-skilled work will start to disappear. We've already discussed some of the changes taking place in education and how genetic engineering is helping increase life expectancy. As a result of these advances, what types of changes can we expect in the economy and in our personal lives?

One thing is certain about the technological revolution: knowledge is the greatest asset. However, knowledge will be limited by time—it can be incredibly valuable one moment and worthless the next. The spread and sharing of knowledge, the development of new technologies, and an increased recognition of common world problems present unlimited opportunities for economic growth.

Consider banking, finance, and commerce. Electronic technology is having a dramatic effect on these industries. Think about money. Will it become obsolete? Already, huge amounts of money zip around the globe at the speed of light. Technology is affecting the way information and money is transmitted (Figure 28-5).

Will our personal life become almost like *Star Trek*? Many people predict it will. Technology is affecting our work environment and almost every aspect of our personal lives.

FIGURE 28-5
Transmitting data

In the twentieth century, society witnessed all types of changes in the places people lived. They moved from the farms to the cities and then to the suburbs. The twenty-first century will also witness changes as the home becomes the center for work, entertainment, learning, and possibly even health care. More and more people will telecommute or run a business from their home. As a result, they will have to manage their lives in a world of uncertainty. This will be a great change for many people. They will have to make decisions about how to separate their business and personal lives.

Computer Concepts

The economy created by the Internet is generating enormous environmental benefits by reducing the amount of energy and materials consumed by businesses. It is predicted that the Internet will revolutionize the relationship between economic growth and the environment.

Some examples of potential technological advances that can affect our personal lives are as follows:

- *Clothes that fight odor and bacteria:* Some clothing companies are manufacturing clothes that keep you comfortable and smelling good. For example, when the temperature drops, jackets grow warmer and sweat socks resist bacteria and odors. Your clothing may even be able to kill mosquitoes on contact!

- *The flying car:* This has long been a fantasy of the American public, but the question is how long will it be before we all have flying cars? It will probably be a few more years before we're flying around like the Jetsons, but there are possibilities on the horizon. Moller International has developed a personal vertical takeoff and landing vehicle (VTOL). The Skycar is able to operate in a much less restrictive area than a helicopter or airplane and is less expensive and safer. These factors allow this type of future transportation to be addressed and investigated for the first time.

- *Voice recognition:* Some people forecast that, within the next few years, written language will be dead and writing may become an ancient art form. Instead, we will talk to computers or computer-like devices that utilize *voice recognition* technology, and they will reply. Voice recognition devices are also being used to adapt environments to make life easier for people with disabilities. Imagine being able to control kitchen appliances or other household equipment with voice commands. This technology already exists and is being incorporated into more devices all the time.

■ *Nonlethal weapons:* A company in San Diego is working on a nonlethal weapon that uses two ultraviolet laser beams. These two beams of UV radiation ionize paths in the air to create "wires" in the atmosphere. This device is harmless, but it can immobilize people and animals at a distance.

■ *Space travel:* Would you like to take a trip around the world—that is, by low-earth orbit? You may be able to do so in the near future. Scaled Composites, Inc., and founder Burt Rutan and his partners won the $10 million Ansari X Prize in October 2004 when their private rocket plane SpaceShipOne reached the lower limits of space for the second time. The company is now working with Richard Branson's recently formed Virgin Galactic company to develop a fleet of commercial vehicles to provide the public the opportunity to visit space in the near future.

Computer Concepts

Electronic ink will have a far-reaching impact on our society. The ink itself is a liquid that can be printed onto nearly any surface. You can learn about electronic ink at *www.eink.com*.

FIGURE 28-6
Scaled Composites Web site—SpaceShipOne

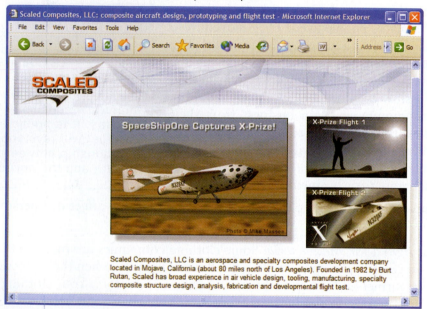

■ *Smart shoes and smart seats:* When we think of technology, not too many of us consider our shoes. No matter how expensive our shoes are, they can still become uncomfortable after wearing them for long hours. A technology called expansive polymer gel uses a micro voltage to expand or contract the gel. Weight can be evenly distributed and heat dissipated. This technology is also being applied to car seats.

Computer Concepts

You can find out more about SpaceShipOne at *www.scaled.com*.

■ *Smart houses:* The smart house uses computers to help the family live a healthy, happy, and safe life. A smart house, among other things, keeps the temperature at a comfortable level while monitoring the amount of electricity being used, helps the family plan and prepare healthy meals, monitors devices within the home and schedules maintenance, and provides accommodations for individuals with disabilities.

So what does the future hold? No one really knows. You can be assured, however, that it will be exciting and ever changing. Don't get left behind as technology moves us all forward. You can stay informed about changes and advancements in many fields by reading specialized periodicals and reviewing online updates, asking questions of professionals including your doctor, elected representatives, and instructors. Simply by paying attention when you read the daily newspaper (online or the old-fashioned paper version) or watch the news, you may learn about a new technology that will soon change your life forever!

SUMMARY

In this lesson, you learned:

- Electronic commerce is the buying and selling of goods and services using the Internet and is predicted to grow at an ever-increasing rate.

- Digital cash allows someone to pay online by transmitting a number from one computer to another.

- Technology is having a tremendous impact on how students learn; many people predict that it may change the entire structure of education.

- The Internet is the biggest factor affecting education today.

- Online courses through the Internet are becoming very popular.

- Many schools use computer-based learning to reinforce concepts.

- Simulations are models of real-world activities.

- Information is continuing to increase faster than we can process it.

- Some people predict an antitechnology backlash.

- Artificial intelligence is software that can process information on its own without human intervention.

- Genetic engineering refers to changing the DNA in a living organism.

- Virtual reality is an artificial environment that feels like a real environment and is used in education, training, medicine, research, and other areas.

- In the new global economy, knowledge is the greatest asset.

- New jobs and new job categories are being developed because of the Internet and electronic commerce.

- In the twenty-first century, many more people will probably work from their homes.

- Some technological advances are clothes that fight odors, flying cars, voice recognition, nonlethal weapons, space travel, smart shoes, smart seats, and smart houses.

- It is important to stay informed about advances in technology that will affect many aspects of your life.

VOCABULARY *Review*

Define the following terms:

Artificial intelligence	Digital cash	Virtual reality
Bot	Electronic commerce	Voice recognition
Computer-based learning	Simulations	

REVIEW *Questions*

TRUE/FALSE

Circle T if the statement is true or F if the statement is false.

T   F   **1.** With digital cash, you can pay someone by transmitting a number from one computer to another.

T   F   **2.** Virtual intelligence is software that processes information without human intervention.

T   F   **3.** It is a real possibility that, within the few decades, individuals will be able to purchase a ticket to orbit the earth.

T   F   **4.** There are only a few applications for virtual reality.

T   F   **5.** Simulations are models of real-world activities.

MULTIPLE CHOICE

Circle the best response for each of the following statements.

1. The buying and selling of goods on the Internet is called _____.
   A. economic commerce
   B. electronic commerce
   C. on-hand business
   D. local commerce

2. New technology is causing _____ changes in our society.
   A. some
   B. no
   C. major
   D. a few

3. The biggest factor affecting education today is the _____.
   A. government
   B. school board
   C. Internet
   D. other students

4. _____ is the delivery of education over the Internet.
   A. Simulation
   B. Distance learning
   C. Virtual reality
   D. None of the above

5. A(n) _____ is a software program that is commonly used by search engines to sort information.
   A. bot
   B. HAL
   C. simulation
   D. artificial spider

PROJECTS

PROJECT 28-1

Visit the U.S. Geological Survey's Water Science for Schools Web site located at *ga.water.usgs.gov/edu/*. Review the Web site and then go to the Activity Center. Complete the Surveys and Challenge Questions.

PROJECT 28-2

The year is 2070. You were born in 2055. Write a letter to someone who lived 50 years ago and tell him or her about your life and your community.

 TEAMWORK PROJECT

Working with a partner, research some recent technological advances that sound like something out of a science fiction story. First make a list of ideas, such as flying cars, video phones, or bacteria genetically altered to produce insulin for diabetics. You may want to visit a Web site such as *www.creativitypool.com* to find some up-to-the minute ideas and future inventions. Divide the inventions you have listed between you and your partner and individually research and consider how these new ideas and products may impact our lives. Compare your research and create a short presentation about what you and your partner predict will be the two most society-altering advances of this decade.

CRITICAL *Thinking*

ACTIVITY 28-1

It is predicted that, in the next few years, the home and business will merge for many people; more and more people will work from home. Would you consider working from home? Why or why not? What advantages and disadvantages do you see?

SECURITY, PRIVACY, AND ETHICS ONLINE

As the use of computers has grown in volume and importance, protecting computer systems and the information they hold has become increasingly important. This lesson explores the many issues regarding the risks of computing and the measures you can take to minimize those risks. In addition, the phenomenon of computer crime is examined in detail, along with actions that can reduce its impact. Computer users also have certain responsibilities that govern their use of technology, including following guidelines and policies for use as well as protecting their own privacy, exercising ethical conduct online, and maintaining a safe work environment.

3-4.2.3
3-4.2.4

Safeguarding Software and Data

One ever-present threat to a computer system is an electrical power failure. Electricity not only provides the power to operate a computer, but it also is the medium by which data is stored. An unexpected power outage, for example, can wipe out any data that has not been properly saved.

To safeguard computer systems against power outages, electric cords should be secured so that they cannot be accidentally disconnected. Another option is to install an uninterruptible power source, usually a battery that kicks in if the normal current is interrupted. Surge suppressors, which plug into electric outlets, can protect against power spikes, which can damage computer hardware and software. They wear out over time, however, and need to be monitored and replaced as necessary. To safeguard data as it is being entered, active files should be saved frequently. Some programs do this automatically; others require users to do it manually.

Computer Concepts

Data backup systems include disk and tape devices that make archive copies of important files and folders. You should back up data to storage media that can be removed and stored in a separate location from your computer.

Even saved data can be lost or corrupted by equipment failure, software viruses or hackers, fire or flood, or power irregularities. So it is essential to back up important files regularly. Backing up files entails saving them to removable disks or some other independent storage device that can be used to restore data in the event that the primary system becomes inaccessible. A hard-disk crash can result in a catastrophic loss of data if it occurs on a critical system and the files have not been properly backed up.

Backup procedures should place a priority on files that would be difficult or impossible to replace or reconstruct if they were ever lost, such as users' data files. Secure backup procedures used by large organizations include a regular schedule for backing up designated files, and a means of storing backup files off site so that they will survive intact if the main system is destroyed either by natural disaster or by criminal acts.

Computer Crime

3-4.2.4
3-4.3.1
3-4.3.4

A well-planned data backup system can help ward off or minimize the risks of computer crimes affecting you. But what is a *computer crime*? It is a criminal act committed through the use of a computer. For example, accessing someone else's system and changing information, creating a computer virus and causing it to damage information on others' computers, and using a computer program to improperly obtain private information about an individual or organization are all computer crimes. It can also involve the theft of a computer and any equipment associated with the computer.

Computer crime is a bigger problem than most people realize. Billions of dollars every year are lost to corporations because of this often undetected, and therefore unpunished, crime. Computer crimes have increased since data communications and computer networks have become popular. Many computer crimes consist of stealing and damaging information and stealing actual computer equipment. Other types of computer crimes can include the following:

- unauthorized use of a computer
- infection of a computer by a malicious program (a virus)
- harassment and stalking on the computer
- theft of computer equipment
- copyright violations of software
- copyright violations of information found on the Internet

Computer Concepts

The FBI's National Crime Information Center has a division for computer crimes.

Computer Fraud

Computer fraud is conduct that involves the manipulation of a computer or computer data in order to obtain money, property, or value dishonestly or to cause loss. Examples of computer fraud include stealing money from bank accounts and stealing information from other people's computers for gain.

Managers and supervisors in companies should be aware of certain signs that may be indicators of computer fraud:

- Low staff morale: Unhappy staff members may decide the company owes them.
- Unusual work patterns.
- Staff members who appear to be living beyond their income.

> **Computer Concepts**
>
> The first known computer crime, electronic embezzlement, was committed in 1958.

Computer Hacking

Computer *hacking* involves invading someone else's computer, usually for personal gain or just the satisfaction of invading someone else's computer. Hackers are usually computer experts who enjoy having the power to invade someone else's privacy. They can steal money, or change or damage data stored on a computer.

It is estimated that hacking causes millions of dollars of damage each year. There have been several high-profile cases of hacking in the United States.

Computer Viruses

A *virus* is a program that has been written, usually by a hacker, to cause corruption of data on a computer. The virus is attached to an executable file (like a program file) and spreads from one file to another once the program is executed. Figure 29-1 illustrates how a virus spreads.

FIGURE 29-1
How a virus can spread

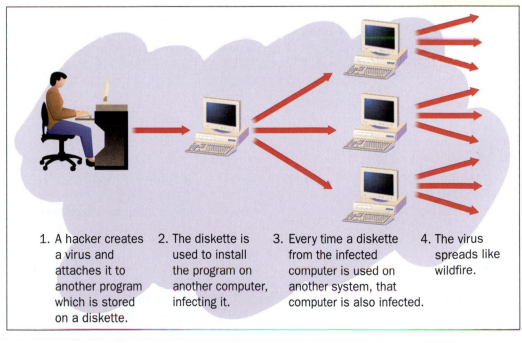

1. A hacker creates a virus and attaches it to another program which is stored on a diskette.

2. The diskette is used to install the program on another computer, infecting it.

3. Every time a diskette from the infected computer is used on another system, that computer is also infected.

4. The virus spreads like wildfire.

A virus can cause major damage to a computer's data or it can do something as minor as display messages on your screen. There are different variations of viruses.

- A *worm* makes many copies of itself, resulting in the consumption of system resources that slows down or actually halts tasks. Worms don't have to attach themselves to other files.

- A *time bomb* is a virus that does not cause its damage until a certain date or until the system has been booted a certain number of times.

- A *logic bomb* is a virus triggered by the appearance or disappearance of specified data.

- A *trojan horse* is a virus that does something different from what it is expected to do. It may look like it is doing one thing while in actuality it is doing something quite opposite (usually something disastrous).

>
> **Note**
>
> Web sites that offer updates and bulletins about new viruses and other computer threats can keep you informed about these threats. Check out *www.virusbtn.com* for information about many kinds of computer security issues.

In order to protect your computer against virus damage:

- Use antivirus software. This software should always run on your computer and should be updated regularly.

- Be careful in opening e-mail attachments. It is a good idea to save them to disk before reading them so you can scan them.

- Don't access files copied from floppy disks or downloaded from the Internet without scanning them first.

You can prevent a virus from infecting your computer and spreading to other computers by diligently scanning files that you did not create yourself to make sure they are clean. Many programs have a built-in virus scan feature that activates when a new file is opened; in other cases, you can use an antivirus program to scan a file before opening it.

Software Piracy

The illegal copying or use of computer programs is called *software piracy*, and it is a widespread problem. Many people don't think there is anything wrong with copying someone else's software to avoid paying the price to buy it. Companies are taking the initiative to stem the problem, however. Now many software programs come with a license number or key that must be used to install the program correctly or to register it with the company online before you can use the program. In some cases, the registration number must be "unregistered" before the program can be installed on another computer to prevent the unauthorized use of software.

Some programs are offered on the Internet at no cost—this software is called *freeware*. Other programs are distributed on the Internet as *shareware*. Shareware is available to a user at no cost to use for a trial period, but then the developer expects to be paid a fee for the software, which may have taken many hours of programming to develop. Many people, even many businesses, however, use shareware (such as programs to compress files or maintain a schedule) with no intention of paying for it.

Other Computer Crimes

Theft of computer time is also a crime committed regularly on the job. This crime is committed when an employee uses a company's computer for personal use such as running a small side business, keeping records of an outside organization, or keeping personal records. While you are working on these types of tasks, you are not being as productive as you could be for your employer.

Using the information you see on someone else's screen or printout to profit unfairly is theft of output. In addition, changing data before it is entered into the computer or after it has been entered into the computer is called *data diddling*. Anyone who is involved with creating, recording, encoding, and checking data can change data.

 ## *Security Issues*

3-1.1.6
3-3.1.5
3-4.3.1
3-4.3.4
Computer security is necessary in order to keep hardware, software, and data safe from harm or destruction. Some risks to computers are natural causes, some are accidents, and some are intentional. It is not always evident that some type of computer crime or intrusion has occurred. Therefore, it is necessary that safeguards for each type of risk be put into place. It is the responsibility of a company or an individual to protect their data.

The best way to protect data is to effectively control the access to it. If unauthorized persons gain access to data, they may obtain valuable information or trade secrets. Perhaps worse, they might change data so that it provides misleading information or destroy data outright so that no one can use it.

The most common form of restricting access to data is the use of passwords, as shown in Figure 29-2. Users may need a password in order to log on to a computer system or to specific parts of it. Companies often establish password-protected locations on hard drives and networks so that certain people have access to certain areas but not to others. In order to maintain secure passwords, they should be changed frequently so that people who no longer need access are locked out again. Tips for creating secure passwords include using a mixture of upper- and lowercase letters, using numbers as well as letters, and adding punctuation keys such as & or % to the password. The challenge is to create passwords that are easy for you to remember but difficult for anyone else to decipher, because you should never write down a password or share it with anyone else. More password protection is broken by people who gain access through a shared password or lost "cheat sheet" than by anyone guessing your "secret code."

FIGURE 29-2
Passwords are used to protect data against unauthorized use

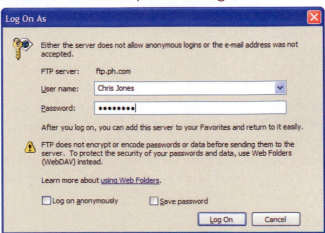

It's important for all users to maintain password security in order to keep out unauthorized users, hackers, and other computer criminals. Never reveal a password to anyone without authorization. Inform the appropriate people if you discover that someone knows passwords he or she shouldn't know. And avoid using the same or similar passwords for other applications or Internet accounts.

> **Note**
>
> You can create secure passwords that you *can* remember. String together the first letter of a line from a song or poem, for example, to create a password such as IlmhiSF!—all you have to remember is "I left my heart in San Francisco," then add that punctuation mark. A password like this is nearly impossible for someone to guess.

Other security measures include the following:

- Electronic identification cards to gain access to certain areas within a building or department.

- Firewalls, which consist of special hardware and software, protect individual companies' networks from external networks. A firewall would allow users inside the organization the ability to access computers outside of their organization but keep outside users from accessing their computers.

- Antivirus software to protect data on your computer.

Companies and organizations must plan for security before it is needed rather than handling breaches in security as they occur. For example, any company that handles sensitive information or needs to protect its data should take the following kinds of precautions:

- Institute a very selective hiring process that includes careful screening of potential employees. Do not keep employees on staff who refuse to follow security rules. This measure will prevent internal theft or sabotage.

- Regularly back up data and store it offsite.

- Employ *biometric security measures*, which examine a fingerprint, a voice pattern, or the iris or retina of the eye, as shown in Figure 29-3. These must match the entry that was originally stored in the system for an employee for that employee to gain access to a secure area. This method of security is usually used when high-level security is required.

Internet Security

The security and privacy of personal information on the Internet is improving all the time. It is still necessary, however, to take precautions to protect both personal and business-related information. Many Web sites and online accounts require the use of passwords. Typically, users choose their own passwords for their accounts, and they tend to use passwords that are easy to remember. Problems can arise, however, if passwords become known to unauthorized persons. The same strategies for keeping passwords secure noted in the previous section apply to Internet passwords as well.

It is important to use different passwords for Internet sites than you use for access to your computer at work. There have been instances of corporate spies having devised online scams using e-mail contests to elicit passwords from employees of target companies. Once the spies know those passwords, they then use them to break into companies' internal computer networks, because they know that a large number of employees are lazy and will have used their internal security passwords for Internet site passwords as well.

FIGURE 29-3
Biometric security measures

Another common security concern on the Internet is credit card information. Because the Internet makes transactions so quick and easy, credit card numbers that fall into the wrong hands can cause lots of headaches for cardholders very quickly. Although there are effective encryption technologies to keep credit card numbers secure, you can make yours even more secure by following simple precautions. Only purchase from Internet sites that you know are reputable and trustworthy. Read and understand online companies' privacy and consumer-protection policies before you buy. Be sure that any credit card information is transmitted in a secured, encrypted mode.

> **Note**
>
> Several e-mail scams have been uncovered that appear to be from legitimate companies but ask you to provide a Social Security number to verify your account. Most companies assure customers they would never ask for sensitive information in an e-mail, so it is best to be suspicious of any solicitation for private information via e-mail.

Of course, credit card information isn't the only personal information that you may want to protect. The same precautions ought to be taken whenever you are asked to disclose anything about yourself that you don't want made known generally or given to market research companies; for example, avoid providing your telephone number on Web forms. It is usually not a required field even for online purchases. Keep in mind that any information you give out can quickly end up in places you never dreamed of. Disclose only what you think is legitimately necessary for the intended purpose. Don't give out personal information to unknown parties. Use code names when appropriate to protect your identity and personal security.

Preserving Privacy

3-4.3.1
3-4.3.3
3-4.3.5

The amount of personal information available on each of us is astonishing. You would probably be very upset to know the extent to which this information is available and to whom it is available. There are many companies who gather information to create databases and sell or trade this information to others.

Any time you submit information on the Internet, it is possible for this information to be gathered by many persons and used for various situations. Information can also be gathered from online data regarding school, banking, hospitals, insurance, and any other information supplied for such everyday activities.

Much of the information gathered and sold results in your name being added to mailing lists. These lists are used by companies for marketing purposes. Junk e-mails are used for the same purpose. Information regarding one's credit history is also available to be sold.

Cookies and Spyware

You might be surprised at how much information about your computer use is tracked by cookies and spyware. You learned a little about both of these technological troublemakers in Lesson 25. Cookies, as you may remember, are small files that are created when you visit a Web site and are stored on your computer, then accessed again the next time you visit the same site. They may make it easier for you to use the Web site when you return, but they may also provide the Web site owner with information about you and your computer, and they often take up disk storage space that you might want to use for other data. It's a good idea to "clean up" the unnecessary cookies on your computer frequently with a utility program designed for that purpose.

Spyware doesn't have any redeeming qualities. It is a program installed on your computer without your knowledge, usually when you download a file. Spyware not only tracks your Web habits, it can even take over control of your computer and direct you to Web sites you have not chosen to visit. Spyware can be harmful as well as annoying; firewalls consisting of hardware and software features can protect your computer from unauthorized spyware programs.

Private Property—But Not Yours

If you work for a company that provides you with e-mail, you should know that the information you send is available to the company; it is the company's property. It can be accessed from backup copies made by the system.

Since any information gathered from (or documents created on) a company's computer system is company property and not an individual worker's personal property, they normally have no right to personal privacy regarding those things. The company has a right to access any data on their computers and use it for its legitimate purposes. If the company monitors its Internet logs, for instance, and discovers that an employee has been spending a lot of time visiting Web sites that bear no relation to work-related duties, it can discipline the employee. Likewise, if an employee uses a company computer in a way that harms the company—contracting a computer virus through unauthorized activities, for example, or allowing hackers into the company's system—he or she can be disciplined or fired.

Other Legal and Ethical Issues

3-4.3.6

The ease of obtaining information from the Internet and of publishing information on it can contribute to other legal problems as well. Just because information is obtained from an Internet site does not mean that someone can copy it and claim it as their own, even noncopyrighted information. That's plagiarism. The Internet does not relieve an author of responsibility for acknowledging and identifying the source of borrowed material.

Likewise, the Internet does not relieve anyone of the burden of ensuring that information they publish is true. If someone publishes information about another person or organization and it is not true, they can be sued for libel and forced to pay compensation for any damage they caused. The Internet makes widespread publication of information easy. It also creates the potential for huge damages if the information turns out to be false.

> **Computer Concepts**
>
> Don't pass on chain e-mails or communications that reference rumors or private information. There is no legitimate reason for forwarding such e-mails, and it may get you in trouble for not following guidelines or even for breaking a law.

Identity Theft

The free flow of information via the Internet also creates opportunities for criminals to gather personal information, acquire credit, and conduct transactions using false identities. *Identity theft*, as it is called, is a growing problem that can cause big headaches for unsuspecting victims. Identity theft is often used for fraudulent purchases or other economic crimes. Credit card numbers, Social Security numbers, and even telephone card numbers are routinely used, in the wrong hands, in crimes that are costly to companies and individuals.

Using someone's personal data to defraud them or to deceive someone else is a serious crime. Other significant criminal problems that the Internet has been feeding include making sexual advances to minors, posting anonymous threats, and circulating rumors to manipulate stock prices. All are made easier by the Internet, but they are just as illegal and just as wrong.

Unethical Computer Behavior

Not all improper activities that make use of the Internet are necessarily illegal, however. Pranks, hoaxes, and making unfair use of free-trial "shareware" software may not be against the law, but they can still cause harm to innocent people—often more harm than their perpetrators might realize. The Internet is a powerful tool, for good and ill, which needs to be handled with care.

Legal Protection for Technology Issues

A computer crime is a violation of federal law if it involves a breach of national defense, theft of atomic energy, or prohibited use of other restricted information. A crime may also break a federal law if it involves a bank or almost any financial institution, interstate communications, or used a computer or data on a computer owned by the U.S. government.

With the rise of computer crimes and other technology issues, many federal and state laws have been passed in an effort to assist those injured by these offenses. However, many of the offenses are difficult to prove and the laws are not easy to enforce. Following is a list of some of the laws that protect users:

- The Copyright Act of 1976: Protects the developers of software.

- Software Piracy and Counterfeiting Amendment of 1983.

- Electronic Communication Privacy Act, 1986: Prohibits the interception of data communications.

- Computer Fraud and Abuse Act, 1986: Prohibits individuals without authorization from knowingly accessing a company computer to obtain records from financial communications.

- Computer Matching & Privacy Protection Act, 1988: Regulates how federal data can be used to determine whether an individual is entitled to federal benefits.

- Many states also have laws governing computer crimes in their states.

 Ethics in Technology

THE GOLDEN RULE OF COMPUTER ETHICS

You probably heard the Golden Rule when you were in elementary school—"Do unto others as you would have them do unto you." The Golden Rule applies to computer ethics, too. Would you appreciate it if someone used their computer to cause you financial harm or to ruin your reputation? Of course not, and you should extend the same courtesy to other people. Don't give in to the urge to snoop around in other people's files or interfere with their work by accessing and changing data in files. You wouldn't want someone to mess with your hard work or private files, would you? And if you had spent a few months creating a great computer game, how would you feel if all your friends started passing copies of the game around to all their friends, without even giving you credit for the program, not to mention cheating you out of any potential profit for your work?

If you do write computer programs, think about the social consequences of the programs you write. Don't copy software illegally, and don't take other people's intellectual property and use it as your own. Just because something is posted on the Web does not mean it is "free" for anyone to use. Use your computer in ways that show consideration of and respect for other people, their property, and their resources. In short, think of the Golden Rule and follow it whenever you face an ethical dilemma at your computer.

Responsibilities of Technology Users

3-4.3.7
3-4.3.8

If you are using your own computer at home, you are responsible for your own ethical conduct. However, if you use computers and access the Internet at school or at work, then you must be aware of the policies or guidelines that the institution has in place. Computer users have an obligation to understand and follow these policies. If you do not know the policies of your school or employer, you may be able to find a copy of the guidelines online, or contact the system administration for information about how you can review the policies.

It is also a computer user's responsibility to stay informed about changes and advancements in computer technology, product upgrades, and virus threats. If you have a computer, it is important to keep your antivirus protection up to date. You can find out how to do this at the Web site of your antivirus program provider; you can also find updates and bulletins about software and hardware at company Web sites.

As a responsible computer user, keep in mind that you can lead by example when you recycle products such as used computer paper and ink cartridges. In addition, old computer hardware such as monitors can create an environmental hazard if disposed of improperly. Consider asking your school or business to donate unneeded computer hardware to charitable organizations that refurbish it and provide it to individuals and organizations who would otherwise be unable to take advantage of computer technology. In addition, your knowledge and experience using computers is also a commodity you can share generously. Community centers, schools, and other organizations welcome knowledgeable volunteers to serve as tutors to help other people learn how to use computers effectively.

Maintaining a Safe Working Environment

3-4.2.1
3-4.2.2

A safe working environment is important for the people who work with computers as well as for the computers themselves. As with any type of electrical equipment, computer systems pose various potential hazards. Wires need to be out of the way so people don't trip over them and so they do not impede movement in the event of an emergency. Power cords must be properly installed and insulated so they do not pose a fire hazard, and the power supply and distribution must be adequate to avoid overloads. Equipment also has to be ventilated and cooled to prevent excessive heat buildup.

Computer operators need to take precautions to avoid chronic physical maladies such as repetitive motion injuries, eyestrain, and back problems that can arise over time. A well-designed work area, use of ergonomic furniture, good posture, and taking the time to change positions periodically throughout the day are all effective ways to minimize these types of injuries. Eyestrain can be avoided or minimized by using a high-resolution monitor, adequate and properly positioned lighting, and taking regular breaks to allow eye muscles to relax.

> **Note**
>
> Repetitive stress injuries are now common in young people who use computers or play video games frequently. When the same motion is repeated, it puts stress on a joint and the tendons and muscles around it, and the constant stress irritates the joint and surrounding tissue. Take frequent breaks, stretch, and remain relaxed rather than tense while you work to help prevent these kinds of injuries.

SUMMARY

In this lesson, you learned:

- Back up data frequently and consistently to avoid losing important information due to a power outage, hardware failure, natural disaster, or computer crime.

- Computer crime has become a major problem, costing companies billions of dollars annually.

- Computer fraud is conduct that involves the manipulation of a computer or computer data for dishonest profit.

- Computer hacking involves invading someone else's computer for personal gain. Sometimes it is done for financial gain and sometimes just as a prank.

- A computer virus is a program that has been written to cause corruption of data on a computer. There are different variations of viruses. These include worms, time bombs, logic bombs, and trojan horses.

- Other computer crimes include theft of computer time, data diddling, and using information from another person's screen or printouts.

- To protect yourself against viruses, install and keep an antivirus program running on your computer. Be sure to update it regularly.

- E-mail attachments can contain viruses. It is a good idea to save any message to disk if you are not familiar with the sender. After saving it to a disk, you can scan it for viruses.

- Computer security is necessary in order to keep hardware, software, and data safe from harm or destruction.

- The best way to protect data is to control access to the data. The most common way to control access to data is to use passwords.

- Companies purchase personal information obtained on the Internet to sell to various companies for marketing purposes.

- Identity theft is a computer crime that involves using another person's identification data to defraud or deceive.

- Laws have been passed in an effort to assist those who have been harmed by computer crimes and offenses, but they are difficult to enforce.

- It is important to know and follow the policies of the organization or company whose computers you use.

- Users of technology are obligated to act responsibly when using computers, disposing of computer parts and materials, and sharing their knowledge.

- Maintaining a safe working environment when using computer equipment involves setting up the equipment properly and taking appropriate precautions to avoid physical injuries caused by computer use.

VOCABULARY*Review*

Define the following terms:

Biometric security measures	Hacking	Time bomb
Computer crime	Identity theft	Trojan horse
Computer fraud	Logic bomb	Virus
Data diddling	Software piracy	Worm

REVIEW*Questions*

TRUE/FALSE

Circle T if the statement is true or F if the statement is false.

T   F   1. Biometric security measures involve examining a fingerprint, a voice pattern, or the iris or retina of the eye.

T   F   2. A computer crime may involve the theft of a computer and any equipment associated with the computer.

T   F   3. Hackers only invade other people's computers for fun.

T   F   4. Laws to police computer use are among the easiest kinds of laws to enforce.

T   F   5. Worms, time bombs, logic bombs, and trojan horses are variations of viruses.

MULTIPLE CHOICE

Circle the best response for each of the following statements.

1. _____ is a criminal act that is committed through the use of a computer.
   A. Hacking
   B. Privacy
   C. Copyright
   D. Biometrics

2. _____ software should always be running on a computer in order to protect data and programs from corruption or destruction.
   A. Biometrics
   B. Fraud
   C. Copyright
   D. Antivirus

3. A(n) _____ is a program that has been written to cause corruption of data on a computer.
   A. shareware
   B. antivirus program
   C. virus
   D. biometric

4. _____ control access to computer data.
 A. Passwords
 B. Hackers
 C. Trojan horses
 D. Worms

5. A virus that does not cause its damage until a certain date is called a(n) _____.
 A. worm
 B. time bomb
 C. antivirus software
 D. logic bomb

PROJECTS

PROJECT 29-1

Many colleges and universities have formal statements regarding the ethical use of their computer systems. Use the Internet or contact a local college or university to obtain a copy of such a statement. After reading it carefully, rewrite it to include any additional rules you believe should be included.

PROJECT 29-2

Computer crimes have been responsible for the loss of millions of dollars. Some crimes result in more loss than others. Use the Internet and other resources to locate information on lost revenue due to the top five computer crimes. If you have access to spreadsheet software, prepare this information in a spreadsheet and perform formulas that will not only add the totals, but also display the percentage of each crime's portion. Some keywords that may be helpful are *computer crimes*, *computer crime costs*, *hackers*, *viruses*, and *software piracy*. Use various search engines to research each term.

 ### TEAMWORK PROJECT

Working with a partner, research some programs in your community that represent a responsible approach toward technology use. You may find information about schools or office supply stores that recycle printer cartridges, a charitable organization that collects old computer hardware for reuse, or volunteer programs at a library or community center that help young people or senior citizens become computer savvy. Make a list of the programs you find and then select one and create a presentation to persuade people to participate in the program. If possible, share your team's presentation with your class.

CRITICAL *Thinking*

ACTIVITY 29-1

Use the Internet and other resources to identify early security measures that were used to protect computers and computer data. Describe how these measures counteracted the intrusions made. Then, visit the Web sites of some companies that make computer security devices such as *www.pcguardian.com*. Write a report of your findings.

LIVING ONLINE

REVIEW *Questions*

TRUE/FALSE

Circle T if the statement is true or F if the statement is false.

T   F   **1.** A LAN is generally confined to a limited geographical area.

T   F   **2.** The Internet is an example of a LAN.

T   F   **3.** Satellites and microwave signals are examples of physical transmission media.

T   F   **4.** ARPANET was the name of the first Web browser.

T   F   **5.** Computers on the Internet communicate with each other using TCP/IP protocols.

T   F   **6.** Government agencies typically use the *.irs* domain name extension.

T   F   **7.** A newsgroup is an Internet-supported discussion forum.

T   F   **8.** The home page is the first Web page displayed when you launch your browser.

T   F   **9.** You can save only text on a Web page to disk.

T   F   **10.** Google, Lycos, and Ask Jeeves are examples of search engines.

MATCHING

Match the description in Column 2 to the correct term in Column 1.

Column 1	Column 2
___ 1. Keywords	A. A computer program written to cause corruption of data on a computer.
___ 2. Shareware	B. A computer program that makes copies of itself, resulting in the corruption of system resources that slows down or actually halts tasks.
___ 3. Hits	C. Process of invading someone else's computer, usually for personal gain or just for the fun of it.
___ 4. Hacking	D. Changing data entered into a computer.
___ 5. Virus	E. The exclusive right, granted by law for a certain number of years, to make and dispose of creative work.
___ 6. Spider	F. Material that is available for anyone to copy because its copyright protection has lapsed or does not exist.
___ 7. Worm	G. Software that can be used for a trial period without charge.
___ 8. Public domain	H. Words on a Web page that are specified in searches.
___ 9. Copyright	I. Search engine robot that searches the Internet for information on a specific topic.
___ 10. Data diddling	J. The number of returns you get when searching the Web using a search engine.

PROJECTS

PROJECT 1

1. Start your Web browser and create a Favorites folder. Give the folder a name of your choice, such as *Project 1 Sites*.

2. Use a search engine of your choice to find information on the following topics:
   A. Popular Web browsers
   B. Shareware games
   C. Domain names
   D. Free e-mail providers

3. Save the most informative Web sites to your Favorites folder.

4. Copy pertinent information on each topic to a word-processing document.

5. Save the documents with filenames of your choice, and then print the documents. Close all open files.

PROJECT 2

1. Start Outlook or the program you use to send and receive e-mail on your computer.

2. Use Word or your word processor to format one of the documents you saved in Project 1 (or format a new document that includes information copied from a Web site if you didn't complete Project 1), and then save and close the document.

3. Send an e-mail to yourself and attach the document.

4. Create a folder in your e-mail program to contain the e-mail message you sent in step 3.

5. When you receive the e-mail message, move it to the new folder.

6. Open the attached file and print a copy. Then, close all open programs.

PROJECT 3

1. Go to one of the Web sites you found in Project 1.

2. Evaluate the Web site using the form in Figure 27-3 in Lesson 27.

3. Prepare a one-page report on the design and quality of content you found at this site. Be sure to touch on all the criteria listed in Figure 27-3.

SIMULATION

JOB 1

The human resource manager at your company has asked you to help her create a training presentation for employees about responsible computer use. The presentation should cover topics such as computer security, Internet use, and proper disposal of printouts and storage media that are no longer needed. She wants you to provide information on the following:

- Backing up data

- Using passwords to access company computers

- The company's policy on employee use of the Internet

- Appropriate ways to safely dispose of discarded paper, used CDs, and other computer waste

You might search the Web for examples of employee handbooks to see how other companies address these issues. Or, interview the human resource managers of some local companies and ask them about their policies on these issues. Then create a slide presentation that explains your company's policies, how the policies can be followed effectively by employees, and any consequences that can result from failing to follow the policies.

IC³ - Module 1: Computing Fundamentals 2005 Standard

Standardized Coding Number		Objectives & Abbreviated Skill Sets	Page
Objective 1.1		**Identify types of computers, how they process information and how individual computers interact with other computing systems and devices**	
IC³-1	1.1.1	Categorize types of computers based on their size, power and purpose	P4, P7
IC³-1	1.1.2	Identify types of microcomputers	P7
IC³-1	1.1.3	Identify other types of computing devices	P5
IC³-1	1.1.4	Identify the role of the central processing unit	P19
IC³-1	1.1.5	Identify how the speed of the microprocessor is measured	P19
IC³-1	1.1.6	Identify the role of types of memory and storage and the purpose of each, including RAM, ROM and CD ROMs	P23
IC³-1	1.1.7	Identify concepts related to how memory is measured, including bits, bytes and megabytes	P23
IC³-1	1.1.8	Identify the flow of information between storage devices (such as floppy or hard disks) to the microprocessor and RAM in relation to everyday computer operations	P10, P25, P64, P74, P75, P79, P83
IC³-1	1.1.9	Identify the differences between large systems and desktop computers and appropriate uses for large vs. small systems	P5, P10
IC³-1	1.1.10	Identify that computers integrate into larger systems in a variety of ways	P12
IC³-1	1.1.11	Identify how computers share data, files, hardware and software	P12
Objective 1.2		**Identify the function of computer hardware components**	
IC³-1	1.2.1	Identify the types and purposes of external computer components, including standard input and output devices	P25
IC³-1	1.2.2	Identify the types and purposes of internal computer components	P10, P19, P44
IC³-1	1.2.3	Identify the types and purposes of specialized input devices (e.g. digital cameras and touch screens)	P25
IC³-1	1.2.4	Identify the types and purposes of specialized output devices (e.g. projectors)	P32
IC³-1	1.2.5	Identify the types and purposes of storage media (e.g. DVDs and network drives)	P35
IC³-1	1.2.6	Identify ports used to connect input and output devices to a computer (e.g. USB ports and Ethernet ports)	P46
IC³-1	1.2.7	Identify how hardware devices are installed on a computer system	P46
Objective 1.3		**Identify the factors that go into an individual or organizational decision on how to purchase computer equipment**	
IC³-1	1.3.1	Identify criteria for selecting a personal computer	P44
IC³-1	1.3.2	Identify factors that affect computer performance	P19, P44
IC³-1	1.3.3	Identify hardware and software considerations when purchasing a computer	P44
IC³-1	1.3.4	Identify other factors that go into decisions to purchase a computer including warranties and support agreements	P44
Objective 1.4		**1.4 Identify how to maintain computer equipment and solve common problems relating to computer hardware**	
IC³-1	1.4.1	Identify how to protect computer hardware from theft or damage	P51
IC³-1	1.4.2	Identify factors that can cause damage to computer hardware or media (e.g. heat and humidity)	P35, P51, P75
IC³-1	1.4.3	Identify how to protect computer hardware from fluctuations in the power supply, power outages and other electrical issues	P51
IC³-1	1.4.4	Identify common problems associated with computer hardware such as inoperable hardware devices	P50

IC³-1	1.4.5	Identify common problems that can occur if hardware is not maintained properly	P49
IC³-1	1.4.6	Identify maintenance that can be performed routinely by users such as cleaning and defragmenting hard drives	P49
IC³-1	1.4.7	Identify maintenance that should ONLY be performed by experienced professionals	P49
IC³-1	1.4.8	Identify the steps required to solve computer-related problems	P50
Objective 2.1		**Identify how software and hardware work together to perform computing tasks and how software is developed and upgraded**	
IC³-1	2.1.1	Identify how hardware and software interact	P4, P25, P32, P58, P95
IC³-1	2.1.2	Identify simple terms and concepts related to the software development process	P60
IC³-1	2.1.3	Identify issues relating to software upgrades such as pros and cons and methods to upgrade	P86, P110
Objective 2.2		**Identify different types of software, general concepts relating to software categories, and the tasks to which each type of software is most suited or not suited**	
IC³-1	2.2.1	Identify fundamental concepts relating to word processing and common uses for word-processing applications	P60, P96
IC³-1	2.2.2	Identify fundamental concepts relating to spreadsheets and common uses for spreadsheet applications	P60, P96
IC³-1	2.2.3	Identify fundamental concepts relating to presentation software and common uses for presentation applications	P60, P96
IC³-1	2.2.4	Identify fundamental concepts relating to databases and common uses for database applications	P60
IC³-1	2.2.5	Identify fundamental concepts relating to graphic and multimedia programs and common uses for graphic or multimedia software	P60
IC³-1	2.2.6	Identify the types and purposes of different utility programs	P60
IC³-1	2.2.7	Identify other types of software	P60
IC³-1	2.2.8	Identify how to select the appropriate application(s) for a particular purpose, and problems that can arise if the wrong software product is used for a particular purpose	P60, P93
Objective 3.1		**Identify what an operating system is and how it works, and solve common problems related to operating systems**	
IC³-1	3.1.1	Identify the purpose of an operating system and the difference between operating system and application software	P64, P110
IC³-1	3.1.2	Identify different operating systems including DOS, Windows and Macintosh	P64
IC³-1	3.1.3	Identify the difference between interacting with character-based and graphical operating systems	P66, P110
IC³-1	3.1.4	Identify the capabilities and limitations imposed by the operating system	P64
IC³-1	3.1.5	Identify and solve common problems related to operating systems	P44, P111
Objective 3.2		**Manipulate and control the Windows desktop, files and disks**	
IC³-1	3.2.1	Identify elements of the Windows desktop	P118
IC³-1	3.2.2	Manipulate windows such as minimizing windows	P76, P125
IC³-1	3.2.3	Shut down, logoff and restart the computer	P111, P130
IC³-1	3.2.4	Use the Windows Start menu and Taskbar	P83, P111, P115, P118, P128, P148
IC³-1	3.2.5	Manipulate desktop folders and icons	P142
IC³-1	3.2.6	Manage files using the Windows Explorer/File Manager	P158, P162, P166, P167, P169, P177, P179, P183, P184

IC³-1	3.2.7	Identify precautions one should take when manipulating files including using standardized naming conventions	P179, P184, P188
IC³-1	3.2.8	Solve common problems associated with working with files	P188
Objective 3.3		**Identify how to change system settings, install and remove software**	
IC³-1	3.3.1	Display control panels	P137
IC³-1	3.3.2	Identify different control panel settings	P137
IC³-1	3.3.3	Change simple control panel settings such as date and time settings	P140
IC³-1	3.3.4	Display and update a list of installed printers	P137
IC³-1	3.3.5	Identify precautions regarding changing system settings	P137, P140
IC³-1	3.3.6	Install software including installing updates from online sources	P86
IC³-1	3.3.7	Identify common problems associated with installing and running applications	P86

IC³ - Module 2: Key Applications 2005 Standard

Standardized Coding Number		Objectives & Abbreviated Skill Sets	Page
Objective 1.1		**Be able to start and exit a Windows application and utilize sources of online help**	
IC³-2	1.1.1	Start a Windows application	P204, P205, P231
IC³-2	1.1.2	Exit a Windows application	P216
IC³-2	1.1.3	Identify and prioritize help resources, including online help within software and contacting a help desk	P216
IC³-2	1.1.4	Use various forms of automated help	P216
Objective 1.2		**Identify common on-screen elements of Windows applications, change application settings and manage files within an application**	
IC³-2	1.2.1	Identify on-screen elements common to Windows applications (e.g. menus, toolbars and document windows)	P205, P207, P319, P390
IC³-2	1.2.2	Display or hide toolbars	P209
IC³-2	1.2.3	Switch between open documents	P205, P391
IC³-2	1.2.4	Change views	P205, P232
IC³-2	1.2.5	Change magnification level	P209
IC³-2	1.2.6	Create files	P216, P225, P308
IC³-2	1.2.7	Open files within an application and from the Windows desktop, identify file extensions including .xls or .doc	P209, P210, P389
IC³-2	1.2.8	Save files in specified locations/formats	P209, P210, P389
IC³-2	1.2.9	Close files	P216
IC³-2	1.2.10	Identify and solve common problems relating to working with files (e.g. product or version incompatibility)	P205, P216
Objective 1.3		**Perform common editing and formatting functions**	
IC³-2	1.3.1	Navigate around open files using scroll bars, keyboard shortcuts, etc.	P205, P244, P391
IC³-2	1.3.2	Insert text and numbers in a file	P227
IC³-2	1.3.3	Perform simple editing (e.g. cut, copy and move information)	P242, P244
IC³-2	1.3.4	Use the Undo, Redo and Repeat commands	P243, P334
IC³-2	1.3.5	Find information	P249
IC³-2	1.3.6	Replace information	P249
IC³-2	1.3.7	Check spelling	P259
IC³-2	1.3.8	Perform simple text formatting	P250
IC³-2	1.3.9	Insert pictures into a file	P298
IC³-2	1.3.10	Modify pictures in a file	P298
IC³-2	1.3.11	Add drawn objects into a file, including creating and modifying objects	P305
Objective 1.4		**Perform common printing functions**	
IC³-2	1.4.1	Format a document for printing	P261, P349
IC³-2	1.4.2	Preview a file before printing	P261
IC³-2	1.4.3	Print files, specifying common print options	P261, P349
IC³-2	1.4.4	Manage printing and print jobs	P261, P349
IC³-2	1.4.5	Identify and solve common problems associated with printing	P261
Objective 2.1		**Be able to format text and documents including the ability to use automatic formatting tools**	
IC³-2	2.1.1	Identify on-screen formatting information, including breaks, paragraph markers etc.	P250
IC³-2	2.1.2	Select word, line, paragraph, document	P230

IC³-2	2.1.3	Change line and paragraph spacing	P250
IC³-2	2.1.4	Indent text	P250
IC³-2	2.1.5	Create and modify bulleted and numbered lists	P250
IC³-2	2.1.6	Use outline structure to format a document	P250
IC³-2	2.1.7	Insert symbols/special characters	P247
IC³-2	2.1.8	Insert date and time	P247
IC³-2	2.1.9	Insert, view and print document comments	P233
IC³-2	2.1.10	Display the ruler	P232, P250
IC³-2	2.1.11	Use tabs	P250
IC³-2	2.1.12	Insert and delete a page break or section break	P250
IC³-2	2.1.13	Insert, modify and format page numbers	P295
IC³-2	2.1.14	Create, modify and format headers and footers	P295
IC³-2	2.1.15	Create, modify and format footnotes and endnotes	P296
IC³-2	2.1.16	Apply borders and shading to text paragraphs	P292
IC³-2	2.1.17	Create, modify and apply styles	P308
IC³-2	2.1.18	Copy formatting (Format Painter)	P258
IC³-2	2.1.19	Use language tools	P259, P311
IC³-2	2.1.20	Use track changes in a document	P233
IC³-2	2.1.21	Display document statistics	P259
Objective 2.2		**Be able to insert, edit and format tables in a document**	
IC³-2	2.2.1	Create a table	P271, P284
IC³-2	2.2.2	Insert and edit data in a table	P278
IC³-2	2.2.3	Modify table structure	P272, P281
IC³-2	2.2.4	Format tables	P274
IC³-2	2.2.5	Sort data in a table	P282
Objective 3.1		**Be able to modify worksheet data and structure and format data in a worksheet**	
IC³-2	3.1.1	Identify how a table of data is organized in a spreadsheet	P321
IC³-2	3.1.2	Select information with the keyboard and mouse including selecting rows, columns and worksheets	P321
IC³-2	3.1.3	Insert and modify data	P328, P343
IC³-2	3.1.4	Modify table structure	P325, P327, P346
IC³-2	3.1.5	Identify and change number formats, including currency, date and time and percentage formats	P331
IC³-2	3.1.6	Apply borders and shading to cells	P331
IC³-2	3.1.7	Specify cell alignment (e.g. wrapping text within a cell)	P331, P341
IC³-2	3.1.8	Apply table AutoFormats	P345
Objective 3.2		**Be able to sort data, manipulate data using formulas and functions and add and modify charts in a worksheet.**	
IC³-2	3.2.1	Sort worksheet data	P347
IC³-2	3.2.2	Demonstrate an understanding of absolute vs. relative cell addresses	P369
IC³-2	3.2.3	Insert arithmetic formulas into worksheet cells	P363, P371
IC³-2	3.2.4	Demonstrate how to use common worksheet functions (e.g. SUM, AVERAGE and COUNT)	P363, P369
IC³-2	3.2.5	Insert formulas that include worksheet functions into cells	P363
IC³-2	3.2.6	Modify formulas and functions	P363
IC³-2	3.2.7	Use AutoSum	P370
IC³-2	3.2.8	Identify common errors made when using formulas and functions	P363

IC³-2	3.2.9	Draw simple conclusions based on tabular data in a worksheet	P382
IC³-2	3.2.10	Insert and modify charts in a worksheet	P376, P379, P380
IC³-2	3.2.11	Be able to identify if a presented chart accurately represents worksheet data shown in a table	P382
IC³-2	3.2.12	Identify appropriate chart types for presenting different types of information	P376
Objective 4.1		**Be able to create and format simple presentations**	
IC³-2	4.1.1	Identify effective design principles for simple presentations	P394
IC³-2	4.1.2	Manage slides (e.g. delete a slide)	P398
IC³-2	4.1.3	Add information to a slide	P395, P409, P411, P413
IC³-2	4.1.4	Change slide view	P393
IC³-2	4.1.5	Change slide layout	P416
IC³-2	4.1.6	Modify a slide background	P395
IC³-2	4.1.7	Assign transitions to slides	P419
IC³-2	4.1.8	Change the order of slides in a presentation	P421
IC³-2	4.1.9	Create different output elements (speaker's notes, handouts, etc.)	P422
IC³-2	4.1.10	Preview the slide show presentation	P402
IC³-2	4.1.11	Navigate an on-screen slide show	P391

IC³ - Module 3: Living Online 2005 Standard

Standardized Coding Number		Objectives & Abbreviated Skill Sets	Page
Objective 1.1		**Identify network fundamentals and the benefits and risks of network computing**	
IC³-3	1.1.1	Identify terminology relating to telecommunications, networks and the Internet	P487, P489, P530
IC³-3	1.1.2	Identify types of networks	P496
IC³-3	1.1.3	Identify how networks work	P493
IC³-3	1.1.4	Identify benefits of networked computing	P487
IC³-3	1.1.5	Identify the risks of networked computing	P496
IC³-3	1.1.6	Identify fundamental principles of security on a network	P601
Objective 1.2		**Identify the relationship between computer networks, other communications networks (like the telephone network) and the Internet**	
IC³-3	1.2.1	Identify the different ways the telephone system is used to transmit information	P489
IC³-3	1.2.2	Identify that telecommunication devices such as modems convert information from analog to digital and digital to analog formats	P493
IC³-3	1.2.3	Identify the units used to measure data transmission rates	P489, P493
IC³-3	1.2.4	Identify the Internet as a "super network" of smaller computer networks and that computers connect to the Internet via the "onramp" of a smaller computer network	P487
IC³-3	1.2.5	Identify the hardware and software required to connect to the Internet	P493, P498
IC³-3	1.2.6	Identify different types of Internet connections and the advantages and disadvantages of each connection type	P493, P530
IC³-3	1.2.7	Identify the roles and responsibilities of an Internet Service Provider (ISP)	P530
Objective 2.1		**Identify how electronic mail works**	
IC³-3	2.1.1	Identify how electronic mail works on a network and on the Internet	P503, P507
IC³-3	2.1.2	Identify the components of an electronic mail message	P507
IC³-3	2.1.3	Identify the components of an electronic mail address	P507
IC³-3	2.1.4	Identify when to use different electronic mail options	P516
IC³-3	2.1.5	Identify different ways electronic mail is accessed	P507, P520
IC³-3	2.1.6	Identify the difference between standard electronic mail and other forms of messaging, such as paging or Instant Messaging	P520
Objective 2.2		**Identify how to use an electronic mail application**	
IC³-3	2.2.1	Read and send electronic mail messages	P507, P510
IC³-3	2.2.2	Identify ways to supplement a mail message with additional information	P507
IC³-3	2.2.3	Manage attachments	P510, P516
IC³-3	2.2.4	Manage mail	P510
IC³-3	2.2.5	Manage addresses	P517
IC³-3	2.2.6	Identify the purpose of frequently used mail-configuration options	P516
Objective 2.3		**Identify the appropriate use of e-mail and e-mail related "netiquette"**	
IC³-3	2.3.1	Identify the advantages of electronic mail	P503
IC³-3	2.3.2	Identify common problems associated with electronic mail	P503, P507, P510, P515
IC³-3	2.3.3	Identify the elements of professional and effective e-mail messages	P515
IC³-3	2.3.4	Identify when other forms of correspondence are more appropriate than e-mail	P515
IC³-3	2.3.5	Identify when to include information from an original e-mail message in a response as a method of tracking the "history" of e-mail communication	P510, P515
IC³-3	2.3.6	Identify appropriate use of e-mail attachments and other supplementary information	P507, P516
IC³-3	2.3.7	Identify issues regarding unsolicited e-mail ("spam") and how to minimize or control unsolicited mail	P503, P510, P515, P516
IC³-3	2.3.8	Identify effective procedures for ensuring the safe and effective use of electronic mail	P507, P510, P515

Objective 3.1		Identify different types of information sources on the Internet	
IC³-3	3.1.1	Identify terminology related to the Internet	P528, P531
IC³-3	3.1.2	Identify the purpose of a browser in accessing information on the World Wide Web	P531
IC³-3	3.1.3	Identify different elements of a Web site	P542
IC³-3	3.1.4	Identify different types of Web sites by their extensions, and the purposes of different types of sites	P542
IC³-3	3.1.5	Identify the difference between secure and unsecure Web sites (such as password-protected sites or sites secure for online transactions) and how to tell if a Web site is secure	P601
IC³-3	3.1.6	Identify different ways of communicating and corresponding via the Internet	P538
Objective 3.2		Be able to use a Web browsing application	
IC³-3	3.2.1	Identify the make-up of a Web address/Uniform Resource Locator (URL)	P542
IC³-3	3.2.2	Navigate the Web using a browser	P528, P530, P531
IC³-3	3.2.3	Reload/Refresh the view of a Web page	P531
IC³-3	3.2.4	Show a history of recently visited Web sites and delete the list of recently visited Web sites	P531, P542
IC³-3	3.2.5	Find specific information on a Web site	P549
IC³-3	3.2.6	Manage Bookmarked sites/Favorite sites	P561
IC³-3	3.2.7	Save the content of a Web site for offline browsing	P559
IC³-3	3.2.8	Copy elements of a Web site including copying text or media to another application	P559
IC³-3	3.2.9	Print all or specified parts of a Web site	P559
IC³-3	3.2.10	Download a file from a Web site to a specified location	P561
IC³-3	3.2.11	Identify settings that can be modified in a Web browser application	P535
IC³-3	3.2.12	Identify problems associated with using a Web browser	P535
Objective 3.3		Be able to search the Internet for information	
IC³-3	3.3.1	Identify the ways a search engine classifies and looks for Web sites	P550
IC³-3	3.3.2	Identify other ways of searching for information on the Web	P555
IC³-3	3.3.3	Use a search engine to search for information based on specified keywords	P555
IC³-3	3.3.4	Search effectively	P555
IC³-3	3.3.5	Identify issues regarding the quality of information found on the Internet	P572
IC³-3	3.3.6	Identify how to evaluate the quality of information found on the Web	P571
Objective 4.1		Identify how computers are used in different areas of work, school and home	
IC³-3	4.1.1	Identify how computers and the Internet are used to collect, organize, and evaluate information and promote learning	P569, P587, P590
IC³-3	4.1.2	Identify the technology and processes involved with computers operating "behind the scenes" in everyday activities	P581, P587
IC³-3	4.1.3	Identify the impact of electronic commerce (e-commerce) on business, individuals and governments	P581
IC³-3	4.1.4	Identify technologies that support or provide opportunities to the disabled and disadvantaged such as voice recognition	P583, P587
Objective 4.2		Identify the risks of using computer hardware and software	
IC³-3	4.2.1	Identify how to maintain a safe working environment that comply with legal health and safety rules	P607
IC³-3	4.2.2	Identify injuries that can result from the use of computers for long periods of time	P607
IC³-3	4.2.3	Identify risks to personal and organizational data	P597
IC³-3	4.2.4	Identify software threats, including viruses and WORMS	P507, P597, P598

Objective 4.3		Identify how to use computers and the Internet safely, legally, ethically and responsibly	
IC³-3	4.3.1	Identify reasons for restricting access to files, storage devices, computers, networks, and certain Internet sites	P571, P598, P601, P604
IC³-3	4.3.2	Identify concepts related to intellectual property laws including copyrights, trademarks and plagiarism	P575
IC³-3	4.3.3	Identify the principles regarding when information can or cannot be considered personal, including the difference between computer systems owned by schools or businesses that may have rules and guidelines as to who owns data stored on the system, and computers owned by individuals	P604
IC³-3	4.3.4	Identify how to avoid hazards regarding electronic commerce, including giving credit card information only on secure sites	P542, P581 P598, P601
IC³-3	4.3.5	Identify how to protect privacy and personal security online, including understanding how Web sites track your activity online using "cookies" and other "behind-the-scenes" systems	P604
IC³-3	4.3.6	Identify how to find information about rules regarding the use of computers and the Internet, including laws, use policies at school, and company guidelines at places of employment	P605
IC³-3	4.3.7	Identify how to stay informed about changes and advancements in technology	P607
IC³-3	4.3.8	Identify how to be a responsible user of computers and the Internet	P607

GLOSSARY

8.3 alias Windows will assign a short filename, called an "alias," to each file with a long name so these files can be used with programs that don't support long filenames. The short filename can have a maximum of eight characters and a three-character extension.

A

Absolute cell reference A cell reference that does not change when the formula is copied or moved to a new location.

Active cell In Excel, a selected cell.

Active window The window currently in use. The title bar of the active window is always darker (or displayed in a different color) to distinguish it from other open windows that may be visible in a tiled or cascaded screen.

Address Bar The space in some application windows that displays the name of the open folder or object.

Address book Part of most e-mail programs; used to keep a list of contacts and their e-mail addresses.

Algorithm A set of clearly defined, logical steps that solve a problem.

Alignment Describes how text is positioned between the left and right margins on a page: left, center, right, or justified.

American Standard Code for Information Interchange (ASCII) Coding system that computers of all types and brands can translate.

Application file icons Icons that start an application, such as a word processor or spreadsheet program.

Applications software Also called productivity software; helps you perform a specific task such as word processing, spreadsheets, and so forth.

Archive To save or transfer data to a storage device or folder for the purpose of saving space or organizing the data.

Argument A value, cell reference, range, or text that acts as an operand in a function formula.

Artificial intelligence Type of software that can process information on its own without human intervention.

Ascending order Sorts alphabetically from A to Z and numerically from the lowest to the highest number.

Attributes Style characteristics applied to text such as bold, italic, and underline.

B

Background A pattern or picture that can be used on the desktop.

Banner A full-width headline that spans across multiple newsletter-style columns, such as the title for a newsletter or report.

Biometric security measures Examine a fingerprint, voice pattern, or the iris or retina of the eye.

Bit In binary, a bit represents a zero or one.

Boolean logic Way to search databases; consists of three logical operators—AND, NOT, OR.

Boot The process of starting a computer.

Bot Type of robot used by search engines on the Internet.

Bridge A special computer that connects one local area network to another.

Browser Software program used to retrieve documents from the World Wide Web (WWW or Web) and to display them in a readable format.

Byte A byte is another word for character; generally represented by eight bits.

C

Cache A storage location on a computer's hard disk used to temporarily store Internet files.

CD-ROM Disk that can store up to 680 MB of data; data can only be read from it.

Cell The intersection of a single row and a single column.

Cell reference Identifies the column letter and row number (e.g., A1 or B4).

Central processing unit (CPU) Also known as the microprocessor; the brains of the computer.

Channel Media, such as telephone wire, coaxial cable, microwave signal, or fiber-optic cable, that carry or transport data communication messages.

Chart A graphical representation of worksheet or table data.

Clicking Pressing and releasing the left (primary) mouse button.

Client A computer that uses the services of another program.

Client/server network Computer configuration in which one or more computers on the network acts as a server.

Clip art Prepared pictures and other artwork you can insert into a document.

Clip Organizer A wide variety of pictures, photographs, sounds, and video clips that you can insert in your document.

Clipboard A temporary storage area for text and/or graphics that are to be cut or copied and then pasted to another location.

Command buttons Rectangular buttons in a dialog box that execute an instruction. An ellipsis following a command button name (i.e., Browse...) indicates that another dialog box will appear if this command is chosen.

Commands Instructions to perform an operation or execute a program. In Windows, commands can be issued by making menu selections, clicking on a toolbar button, or clicking on a command button in a dialog box.

Comment An electronic note that is not part of the text of a document but appears in a balloon viewable in the document's margin.

Communications channel Link from one computer to another through which data can be transmitted.

Computer Electronic device that receives, processes, and stores data and produces a result.

Computer-based learning Using the computer for learning and instruction.

Computer crime Criminal act committed through the use of a computer, such as getting into someone else's system and changing information or creating a computer virus and causing damage to others' information.

Computer fraud Manipulation of a computer or computer data to obtain money, property, or value dishonestly or to cause loss.

Computer system Hardware, software, and data working together.

Contacts Persons with whom you communicate.

Contents pane Provides a more detailed view of a portion of the tree pane by displaying all the folders and files contained in the drive or folder currently selected in the tree pane. It is on the right side in the Windows Explorer window.

Control Panel A program accessed from the Start menu that provides specialized features used to change the way Windows looks and behaves.

Controller Device that controls the transfer of data from the computer to a peripheral device and vice versa.

Cookies Small text files created by some Web pages when you visit the site that may include information about your preferences for the Web page; cookie files are stored on your computer.

Copy To duplicate a selection, file, folder, and so forth so that you can place it in another position or location.

Copyright The exclusive right, granted by law for a certain number of years, to make and dispose of literary, musical, or artistic work.

Crop To trim a graphic.

Currency On a Web page, this refers to the age of the information, how long it has been posted, and how often it is updated

D

Data Information entered into the computer to be processed that consists of text, numbers, sounds, and images.

Data communications Transmission of text, numeric, voice, or video data from one machine to another.

Data diddling Act of changing data before it is entered in the computer or after it has been entered.

Database A collection of related information organized for rapid search and retrieval.

Database software Software that makes it possible to create and maintain large collections of data.

Datasheet A database table in Access.

Datasheet view A view in Access that displays the table data in columns and rows.

Default (1) A setting that is automatically used unless another option is chosen. (2) In any given set of choices, the choice that is preselected, the selection that is in effect when you open a program, or the settings established during the installation process.

Descending order Sorts alphabetically from Z to A and numerically from the highest to the lowest number.

Design view A view in Access that displays the field names and what kind of values you can enter in each field. Use this view to define or modify the field formats.

Desktop The first screen you see when the operating system is up and fully running. It is called the desktop because the icons are intended to represent real objects on a real desktop.

Desktop publishing The process of using a computer to combine text and graphics to create an attractive document.

Desktop shortcuts Icons you can create and place on the desktop to represent an application, folder, or file. When you click the shortcut icon, the application, folder, or file opens immediately.

Desktop theme A set of predefined elements, such as icons, fonts, colors, and sounds, that determine the look of your desktop.

Destination When copying or moving a file, the location (disk and/or folder) where the copied or moved file will reside.

Dialog box An information-exchange window in which the user selects options, sets defaults, chooses items from lists, or otherwise provides information Windows needs before it can execute a command.

Digital cash Allows someone to pay by transmitting a number from one computer to another.

Disk Cleanup A program that enables you to clear your disk of unnecessary files.

Disk Defragmenter Rearranges disk files, storing each file in contiguous blocks.

Distance learning Schooling concept in which students in remote locations receive instruction via telecommunications technology.

Document A data file in a software application.

Document file icons Icons that share the same distinctive feature, a piece of paper with a superimposed graphic, that help create a link between a document and an application.

Domain name Identifies a site on the Internet.

Double-click To point to an object and then quickly press and release the primary mouse button twice.

Drag-and-drop Drag the mouse to move or copy selected text to a new location.

Dragging Placing the mouse pointer on an object and then pressing and holding down the primary mouse button while moving the object on the desktop.

Drawing canvas An area upon which you can draw, arrange, and resize multiple shapes.

Drawing objects Artwork that you create using drawing tools.

DVD Also called Digital Versatile Disk; video output, including full-length movies, can be stored on this medium.

E

Electronic commerce Business conducted over the Internet; also called e-commerce.

Electronic mail Transmission of electronic messages over networks.

Embedded chart A chart created on the same worksheet as the data.

Emoticons Keyboard symbols used in e-mail and other electronic communication to show emotion, such as :-o to show surprise.

Endnote A note that appears at the end of a document and provides the source of borrowed material or explanatory information about specific text.

Entry Data entered into a cell.

Execution cycle (E-cycle) The amount of time it takes the central processing unit to execute an instruction and store the results in RAM.

Exit effect Controls the animation effects at the end of the animation sequence on a PowerPoint slide.

Extension The part of a filename that comes after the period, called a "dot;" it usually has two or three characters in older operating systems and up to four characters in Windows 95 and following; typically identifies the type of file.

Extranet A network configuration that allows selected outside organizations to access internal information systems.

F

Field A single piece of information in a database.

Field name A label to identify a field in a database.

Field properties Specifications that allow you to customize an Access field beyond choosing a data type.

Field selector A small box or bar that you click to select a column in a table in Datasheet view.

File compatibility The ability of a file to be opened or used in an application without a problem or format conflict.

File transfer protocol (FTP) Internet standard that allows users to download and upload files with other computers on the Internet.

Filename A name assigned to a file for identification.

Fill handle A small square in the bottom right corner of an active cell in a worksheet.

Filling A method of copying data in a worksheet.

Firewall A combination of hardware and software that creates a buffer between an internal network and the Internet to prevent unauthorized access.

First line indent Only the first line of the paragraph is indented.

Folder A way to organize files into manageable groups.

Folder bar Provides a hierarchical display of all objects on the desktop. It is also called the tree pane and is on the left side in the Windows Explorer window.

Font The general shape and style of a set of characters.

Footer Text and/or graphics appearing at the bottom of each page of a document.

Footnote A note that appears at the bottom of a page and provides the source of borrowed material or explanatory information about specific text on that page.

Format The shape, size, color, and other characteristics of text and other elements of a document.

Format Painter A Microsoft Office feature used to copy and apply font and size formatting as well as basic graphic formatting, such as borders, fills, and shading, from one part of a document to another.

Formulas Equations used to calculate values in a spreadsheet cell.

Fragmented files Files that are not stored in contiguous clusters, but rather are divided into subparts that are stored in different disk location. It takes longer for a disk drive to access fragmented files than unfragmented files.

Function formula A special formula that names a function instead of using operators to calculate a result.

G

Gateway A combination of software and hardware that links two different types of networks that use different protocols or rules to exchange messages.

Graphical user interfaces (GUIs) An operating system with graphical symbols representing files, programs, and documents.

Graphics Items other than text including photos, clip art, and drawing objects.

Graphics software Application used to create artwork with a computer.

Gridlines Nonprinting lines that display on the screen to show the boundary lines of a table.

H

Hackers Expert computer users who invade someone else's computer either for personal gain or simply for the satisfaction of being able to do it.

Hacking Invading someone else's computer, usually for personal gain or simply for the satisfaction of invading someone else's computer.

Hanging indent In a paragraph, all lines but the first "hang" (are indented) to the right of the first line.

Hard column break A manual column break.

Hard disk drive A data storage unit inside a computer that can store a large quantity of data (60GB or more), but cannot easily be removed from the computer.

Hard page break A manual page break.

Hardware The tangible, physical equipment that can be seen and touched.

Header Text and/or graphics appearing at the top of each page in a document.

Header row Labels at the top of columns in a worksheet.

Hits Any time a piece of data matches search words you specify.

Home page First page that is displayed when a browser is launched.

Hub A junction where information arrives from connected computers or peripheral devices and is then forwarded in one or more directions to other computers and devices.

Hyperlink Text or graphic in a Web page or other document that a user clicks to jump to another location in the file, another file, or another Web page.

Hypertext markup language (HTML) Protocol that controls how Web pages are formatted and displayed.

Hypertext transfer protocol (HTTP) Protocol that defines how messages are formatted and transmitted over the World Wide Web.

I

I-beam The shape the mouse pointer takes when it is positioned on text in a document.

Icons Graphic images or symbols that represent applications (programs), files, disk drives, documents, embedded objects, or linked objects.

Identity theft The crime of obtaining someone else's personal data and using it for financial gain or to defraud or deceive.

Impact printers Type of printer that uses a mechanism that actually strikes the paper to form characters.

Input devices Enable the user to input data and commands into the computer.

Insert mode In this default mode, new text is inserted between existing characters.

Instant messaging A form of electronic communication that allows you to send and receive text messages in "real time" from friends and colleagues who are currently online.

Instruction cycle (I-cycle) The amount of time it takes the central processing unit to retrieve an instruction and complete the command.

Internet The largest network used as a communication tool.

Internet Explorer A Web browser used for communication on the Internet.

Intranet A network designed for the exclusive use of computer users within an organization that cannot be accessed by users outside the organization.

K

Keyboard Common input device for entering numeric and alphabetic data into a computer.

Keywords Words that describe the information the user is trying to locate.

L

Landscape orientation The document prints with the long edge of the page at the top.

Language translators Systems software that converts code written in a programming language into machine language that the computer can understand.

Linking Feature that allows data to be transferred among programs and updated automatically.

Local area network A series of connected personal computers, workstations, and other devices, such as printers or scanners, within a confined space, such as an office building.

Log off To exit the account you are using, but keep the computer on for you or another user to log on at a later time.

Log on To access a computer system by identifying yourself and, if prompted, entering a password.

Logic bomb Computer virus triggered by the appearance or disappearance of specified data.

M

Main memory Also called random access memory, or RAM, it is like short-term memory. It stores data while the computer is running. When the computer is turned off or if there is a loss of power, any data in the main memory disappears. The computer can read from and write to this type of memory.

Mainframe computers Large, powerful computers that are used for centralized storage, processing, and management of very large amounts of data.

Math symbols Use the plus and minus signs to filter out unwanted hits.

Mathematical functions Perform calculations that you could do using a scientific calculator.

Maximize To enlarge a window on the computer to fill the computer screen.

Memory   Where data is stored on the computer's motherboard.

Menu   A list of commands or options grouped under specific headings or titles (e.g., File, Edit) on a window's menu bar.

Merge   In Excel, to combine multiple cells into a single cell, usually done to create a title or informational text for the worksheet.

Merging cells   Converting two or more cells into a single cell.

Microcomputer   Sometimes called a personal computer; used at home or the office by one person; can fit on top of or under a desk.

Microprocessors   An integrated circuit silicon chip that contains the processing unit for a computer or a computerized appliance.

Minicomputers   Type of computer that is designed to serve multiple users and process significant amounts of data; larger than a microcomputer, but smaller than a mainframe.

Minimize   To reduce a window on the screen to a button on the taskbar.

Mixed cell reference   A cell reference that contains both relative and absolute cell references.

Modem   Communications hardware device that facilitates the transmission of data.

Motherboard   A circuit board that contains all of the computer system's main components.

Mouse   A pointing device that serves as a faster, more effective alternative to the keyboard in communicating instructions to the computer.

Mouse buttons   Special buttons placed on the mouse that, when pressed, perform various tasks, such as starting applications and moving elements around the screen.

Move   To cut or remove a selection, file, folder, and so forth from one position or location and place (paste) it in another position or location.

MS-DOS   Microsoft's Disk Operating System; originally introduced with the IBM PC in 1981.

Multimedia software   Application used to create output that integrates several different types of media such as text, images, audio, video, and animation.

Multitasking   Running two or more distinct computer operations simultaneously: one in the foreground, the other(s) in the background.

My Computer   A feature that displays the contents of your computer, provides information about different system resources, and allows you to perform tasks, such as formatting disks and running applications.

My Documents   A personal folder for storing files you create and use.

My Network Places   If connected to a network, it is used to display all connected computers and servers and to browse networked files.

N

Navigation   Ability to move through a Web page.

Network   Connects one computer to other computers and peripheral devices.

Network drive   A disk drive located on another computer or server that provides space you can use for data storage.

Network interface cards (NICs)   An add-on card for a computer in a network that enables and controls the sending and receiving of data in a network.

Network operating system   An operating system that runs on a network server.

Newsgroup   Discussion forum or a type of bulletin board.

Nonimpact printers   Type of printer in which characters are formed without anything striking the paper.

Normal view   The display of a document in a simple layout.

Normal view (in PowerPoint)   A view of a presentation that shows the outline pane, the slide pane, and the notes pane.

Notebook computer   Similar to a microcomputer; however, it is smaller and portable.

O

Office Assistant   An animated Help character that offers tips and messages in Microsoft Office applications.

Operand   A number or cell reference in a spreadsheet formula.

Operating systems   Systems software that provides an interface between the user or application program and the computer hardware.

Operator   A symbol that tells Excel what mathematical operation to perform in a worksheet formula.

Optical storage devices Devices that enable the computer to give the user the results of the processed data.

Option buttons Allow you to choose one option from a group of options; also called radio buttons.

Order of evaluation The sequence used to calculate the value of a complex formula.

Orientation Determines whether your document will be printed lengthwise or crosswise on the sheet of paper. The default page orientation in all Office applications is portrait (taller than wide), but you can change it to landscape (wider than tall).

Output devices Enable the computer to give you the results of the processed data.

Overtype mode In this mode, new text replaces existing characters.

P

Packets Units of data sent across a network. When a large block of information is sent, it is broken up into smaller data packets that are sent separately and then reassembled in their original order at the other end.

Parallel ports Computer ports that can transmit data eight bits at a time; usually used by a printer.

Parent folder A folder containing one or more subfolders.

Path Identifies the disk and any folders relative to the location of the document.

Peer-to-peer network Computer architecture in which all of the computers on a network are equal and there is no computer designated as the server.

People Users of the computers who enter data and use the output.

Personal information management software (PIMS) Software designed to organize and manage personal tasks, appointments, and contacts.

Placeholders Provide placement guides for adding text, pictures, tables, or charts.

Plagiarism Claiming someone else's words as your own.

Plotter An output device used to produce charts, engineering plans, and other large-size printed material with lines drawn by pens that move on rails.

Plug and play Technology that allows a hardware component to be attached to a computer so that it is automatically configured by the operating system, without user intervention.

Pointer On-screen object (whose shape changes depending on the function) that can be moved and controlled by the mouse.

Pointing device Device, such as a mouse or trackball, that allows the user to select objects on the screen.

Points A unit of measure for fonts. (One inch equals approximately 72 points.)

Portrait orientation The document prints with the short edge of the page at the top.

Presentation software Software that is used to create and edit information to present in an electronic slide show format.

Presentations Slide shows created using special graphics application software that can be displayed on screen or projected using a projector attached to a computer.

Primary key Uniquely identifies each record in an Access table.

Print Layout view The display of a document that shows the document as it will look when it is printed.

Problem solving A systematic approach of going from an initial situation to a desired situation.

Protocol Standard format for transferring data between two devices. TCP/IP is the agreed-upon international standard for transmitting data.

Public domain Information or content to which copyright protection does not apply and that is available for anyone to copy.

Q

Query Enables you to locate multiple records matching a specified criteria in a single action.

R

Radio buttons Allow you to choose one option from a group of options; also called option buttons.

Random access memory (RAM) Where instructions and data are stored on a temporary basis. This memory is volatile.

Range A selected group of cells.

Read-only memory (ROM) Permanent storage; instructions are burned onto chips by the manufacturer.

Receiver   Computer that receives a data transmission.

Record   A group of fields in a database.

Record selector   A small box or bar that you click to select a row in a table in Datasheet view.

Related search   Preprogrammed queries or questions suggested by the search engine.

Relational database   A collection of interconnected database tables that can be searched without knowing how the tables are organized.

Relative cell reference   A cell reference that is adjusted when the formula is copied or moved to a new location.

Report   A database object that allows you to organize, summarize, and print all or a portion of the data in a database.

Restore   To return a maximized or minimized window to its previous size.

Right-click   To quickly press and release the shortcut menu button (usually the right button).

Router   A device that directs traffic on a network by dividing data into smaller packets that travel by different routes and then are reassembled at their destination.

S

Save   To store a document file on a disk or other storage medium.

Scanner   An input device that can change images into codes for input to the computer.

Scroll   To move (using scroll boxes or scroll arrows) through a list, a block of text, a document, or any display larger than the current window or screen.

Scroll bar   Bar on the right side or bottom of a window that you click to bring different parts of a document into view.

Search   To examine the contents of a computer file, folder, disk, database, or network to find particular information.

Search engines   Tools that allow you to enter a keyword to find sites on the Internet that contain information you need.

Select (highlight)   To point to an object and then press and release the primary mouse button.

Sender   Computer that sends a data transmission.

Serial ports   Computer ports that can transmit data one bit at a time; often used by a modem or a mouse.

Server   A computer that handles requests for data, e-mail, file transfers, and other network services from other computers (clients).

Shortcut   A pointer to an application or document file; double-clicking the shortcut icon opens the actual item to which the shortcut is pointing.

Shortcut keys   A combination of two or more keystrokes that, when pressed, carries out a specific action or function.

Shortcut menu   A list of the command options most commonly performed from the current window display.

Shortcut menu button   The secondary mouse button, usually the right button.

Simulations   Models of real-world activities.

Sizing handles   Small squares or circles surrounding a graphic or object indicating that it is selected.

Slide design   Specifies a color scheme, text format, background, bullet style, and graphics for all the slides in a PowerPoint presentation.

Slide Finder   A PowerPoint feature that enables you to find and copy slides from one presentation to another.

Slide layout   The way text and objects are arranged on a PowerPoint slide.

Slide Master   A template used to make uniform changes to slide characteristics such as background color, repeated graphics, or text, font, and text color.

Slide Show view   Allows you to view a PowerPoint slide in full view.

Slide Sorter view   Displays PowerPoint slides as thumbnails.

Soft page break   Page breaks that Word automatically formats as needed when text reaches the bottom margin.

Software   Intangible set of instructions that tells the computer what to do.

Software development   The multistep process of designing, writing, and testing computer programs.

Software piracy   The illegal copying or use of computer programs.

Sorting   The process of creating a list organized on a specific criterion.

Source When copying a file, the file that is being copied.

Spam Unsolicited commercial e-mail that is sent to many people at the same time to promote products or services; also called "junk" e-mail.

Spider Program that searches the Web; called a spider because it crawls all over the Web.

Splitting cells Converting a single cell into two or more cells.

Spreadsheet An organized table of financial or other numerical information.

Spreadsheet software Used to store, manipulate, and analyze numeric data.

Standard desktop The screen you see immediately after logging on to Windows 2003.

Standard toolbar The bar, usually located near the top of a window, that contains buttons that instantly execute commands or access various functions.

Start button A button on the taskbar that, when clicked, opens the Start menu.

Statistical functions Describe large quantities of data.

Status bar A message or information area, usually located at the bottom of a window, that displays specific details about the currently selected object or the task being performed.

Strikethrough A type attribute that makes text appear as if it is crossed out.

Style Set of formatting characteristics that you can apply to text, tables, and lists in your document.

Subfolder A folder within another folder.

Submenu A menu within another menu. A submenu is indicated when there is a right-pointing arrow next to a menu option.

Supercomputers Largest and fastest computers, capable of storing and processing tremendous volumes of data.

Superscript A letter or numeral set above the text base line in a document.

Surge protectors Devices that protect electronic equipment from variations in electric current.

System clock An electronic pulse that is used to synchronize processing; it controls the speed of the central processing unit.

Systems software A group of programs that coordinate and control the resources and operations of a computer system.

T

Taskbar The horizontal bar at the bottom of the desktop that includes the Start button, minimized window buttons, and a row of icons usually related to input and output devices.

Technology The application of scientific discoveries to the production of goods and services that improve the human environment.

Telecommunications Electronic transfer of data.

Teleconferencing Telecommunications service in which parties in remote locations can participate via telephone in a group meeting.

Template A file that contains formatting and text that you can customize to create a new document similar to, but slightly different from, the original.

Thesaurus A feature in Word that allows you to quickly find alternative words or synonyms for a word in your document.

Thumbnails Miniature pictures of clip art and photos.

Time bomb Computer virus that does not cause its damage until a certain date or until the system has been booted a certain number of times.

Title bar The horizontal band in a window that displays the name of the program, data file, or another type of window.

Toggle Use the same procedure to turn an option on or off.

Toolbar A bar near the top of a window that has groups of icons or buttons that will execute certain commands when clicked.

Transitions Determine the changes in the display that occur as you move from one PowerPoint slide to another in Slide Show view.

Transmission media Media used to transmit data from one device to another; may be wireless or physical.

Tree pane Provides a hierarchical display of all objects on the desktop. It is also called the Folder bar and is on the left side in the Windows Explorer window.

Trojan horse Computer virus that does something different from what it is expected to do.

Troubleshooting Analyzing problems to correct faults in the system.

U

Uniform Resource Locator (URL) Address that tells the browser where to locate the page. It is keyed into the address bar.

Uninterruptible power source (UPS) A battery power source that provides electric current during a power outage.

Universal serial bus (USB) Standard for computer ports that support data transfer rates of up to 12 million bits per second.

Unix Operating system developed by AT&T. It is considered portable, meaning it can run on just about any hardware platform.

User interface Part of the computer's operating system that users interact with.

Utility software Systems software that performs tasks related to managing the computer's resources, file management, diagnostics, and other specialized chores.

V

Virtual reality An artificial environment used in education, medicine, training, research, and other fields.

Virus A computer program that is written to cause corruption of data.

Voice recognition Input devices that are used to issue spoken or voice commands to the computer.

W

Web Layout view Document view that allows you to see text and graphics as they would appear in a Web browser.

Web server Computer that houses and delivers Web pages.

Wide-area networks Computer networks that cover a large geographical area. Most WANs are made up of several connected LANs.

Wildcard characters The asterisk (*) and question mark (?) characters used to represent unknown characters in a search for filenames, words, or phrases.

Window Rectangular area of the screen used to display a program, data, or other information.

Windows Explorer A program that lets you browse through, open, and manage your computer's disk drives, folders, and files (that is, move, copy, rename, and delete files).

Wizard A Windows program that simplifies a task by guiding you through a series of prompts and questions.

Word wrap Text automatically moves to the next line when it reaches the right margin.

Word-processing software Software you use to prepare text documents such as letters, reports, flyers, brochures, and books.

Workbook A collection of related worksheets.

Worksheet A grid of rows and columns containing numbers, text, and formulas.

Worm Computer virus that makes many copies of itself, resulting in the consumption of system resources that slows down or actually halts tasks.

INDEX

A

Absolute cell reference, 369–370
Access, 100, 203
    essentials of, 431–453
    extension *mdb*, 210
    manage and report database
    information, 455–477
Access 2000, 434
Access 2003, 434
Accessibility Options, 138
Access indicator, 533
Access screen, parts of, 431–435
Active Server Pages, 540
Active task, in Outlook window, 504
Active window, 126–127
Add Clips to Organizer dialog box, 564
Add Exit Effect dialog box, 421
Addition, 364
Add or Remove Programs, 138
Address bar, 118–119, 166, 533
Address book, manage, 517–520
Administrative Assistant, 115
Adobe Photoshop, 102
Adobe Studio, 102, 540
Advanced Research Projects Agency
    (ARPA), 528
Advanced toolbar, in Outlook
    window, 504
AI. *See* Artificial intelligence (AI)
AIX, 8, 66
Algorithm, 58–60, 552
Alignment, 253–254, 352–353
All Programs, 114
AlltheWeb, 552
AltaVista, 570
    as e-mail service, 504
    as multimedia search engine, 555
    as search engine, 552
    for translating search results, 550
ALU. *See* Arithmetic/Logic
    Unit (ALU)
American Standard Code for
    Information Interchange (ASCII), 22
America Online, 504
America Online Instant Messenger
    screen, 521
Analysis Report dialog box, 192
AND logical operator, 556
Andreessen, Marc, 528

Ansari X Prize, 592
Answer Wizard, 276
Antivirus software, 508, 602
Antivirus utility, 63
Appearance and Themes, 138, 142–143
Apple Computer, 8, 44, 64
    graphical user interface (GUI), 67
    history of, 64
    Motorola chip, 44
Apple Macintosh II, 21
Apple Power Macintosh, 64
AppleWorks, 104
Application
    close, 216
    navigate windows screens, 205–207
    start, 204–205
Application file icon, 178–179
Applications software, 46, 60–61
Application window, 207–208
Architecture, 495
Archive, 510
Area chart, 376
Argument, 370, 373
Arithmetic/Logic Unit (ALU), 21
ARPA. *See* Advanced Research
    Projects Agency (ARPA)
Arrow keys, 26, 321
Arrows, 438
Arthur's Job Base Web site, 555
Artificial intelligence (AI), 588
Ascending order sort
    in Access, 460–461
    in Excel, 347
    in Word table, 282
ASCII. *See* American Standard Code
    for Information Interchange (ASCII)
Asimo, 588
Ask Jeeves, 103, 552, 557
Ask Jeeves Web site, 17
Assessment tools, 574–575
ATM, 582
AT&T, 66
Attributes. *See* Font attributes
Audio-video interleaved (.AVI),
    102–103
Authorship, 572–573
AutoComplete, 312–313, 324
AutoCorrect, 324
    in Excel, 367
    in PowerPoint, 417, 444

AutoFill, 329
    to copy formula to range of
    cells, 369
    enter data with, 343–345
AutoFit, 282, 332
AutoFit Selection, 327
AutoFormat, 345–346
AutoFormat dialog box, 345
AutoRecover, 312
AutoShape, 308, 409–411
AutoSum, 370
AutoText, 312–313
AVERAGE function, 372, 382
.AVI. *See* Audio-video interleaved (.AVI)

B

Babbage, Charles, 7
Background design, 144–145
Backup utility, 63
Banner, 292
Bar chart, 376
Bar code scanner, 28
BASIC, 22
Basic controllers, 22
BCC. *See* British Broadcasting
    Corporation (BBC)
Bcc (blind copy), 508, 515–516
Beaucoup Web site, 554
Berners-Lee, Tim, 528
Bias, validity and, 573–574
Biometric security measure, 602–603
Bit, 22, 494
Bitmapped (.BMP), 102
Blackboard, 585
Block senders, 517
.BMP. *See* bitmapped (.BMP)
Bookmarks, 561–562
Boole, George, 169
Boolean logic, 169, 556
Boolean search, 556–557
Borders, 118, 292–294
Borders and Shading dialog box, 277
Bot, 588
Bottom Dollar Web site, 554
Branson, Richard, 592
Break dialog box, 256
Bridge, 495
British Broadcasting Corporation
    (BBC), 541